THE REAL GUIDE

SPAIN

REAL GUIDE CREDITS

U.S. Series Editor: Edie Jarolim
U.S. Assistant Editor: Marc S. Dubin

Series Editor: Mark Ellingham
Editorial: Martin Dunford, John Fisher, Jack Holland
Production: Susanne Hillen
Typesetting: Greg Ward
Design: Andrew Oliver

Special **thanks** to Nicola Baxter, Jules Brown, Jonathan Buckley, and Greg Ward for editing; to Rosie Ayliffe, Susanne Hillen, and Greg (again!), on the production front; and to Pilar Vazquez and Esteban Pujals for boundless knowledge and hospitality over the years.

The Publishers and authors have done their best to ensure the accuracy and currency of all information in the *Real Guide Spain*; however, they can accept no responsibility for any loss, injury, or inconvenience sustained by any traveler as a result of information or advice contained in the guide.

Published in the United States and Canada by Prentice Hall Trade Division.
A division of Simon and Schuster, Inc., One Gulf + Western Plaza, New York, NY 10023.

Typeset in Linotron Univers and Century Old Style.
Printed in the United States by Bookcrafters.

Library of Congress Cataloging-in-Publication Data

Ellingham, Mark
Spain, Real Guide / written and researched by Mark Ellingham and John Fisher : with additional contributions by Graham Kenyon, Nicola Baxter, Greg Ward, Jules Brown, Sarah Ozanne, Chris Stewart, Fergus Ferguson, Gordon McLachlan, Marc Dubin, Damien Rea, Teresa Farino, and Manuel Dominguez.

630p
Rev. ed. of: The rough guide to Spain 1987
Includes Index.

ISBN 0-13-783820-4 : $12.95
1. Spain– Description and travel – 1981 – Guide-books.
I. Fisher, John, 1958- . II. Kenyon, Graham. III. Ellingham, Mark. Rough Guide to Spain. V. Title.
DP14.E58   1989
914.6'0483–dc19

88-27165
CIP

THE REAL GUIDE

SPAIN

WRITTEN AND RESEARCHED BY

MARK ELLINGHAM AND JOHN FISHER

With Additional Accounts By
Graham Kenyon, Nicola Baxter, Greg Ward,
Jules Brown, Sarah Ozanne, Chris Stewart,
Fergus Ferguson, Gordon McLachlan,
Marc Dubin, Damien Rea, Teresa Farino,
and Manuel Dominguez.

PRENTICE HALL ■ NEW YORK

CONTENTS

Introduction viii

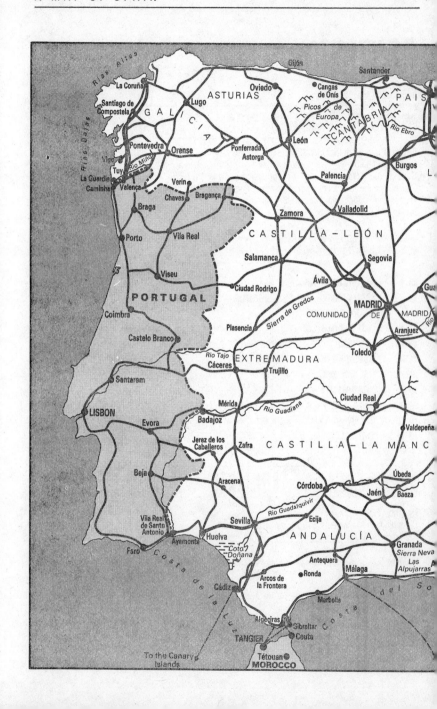

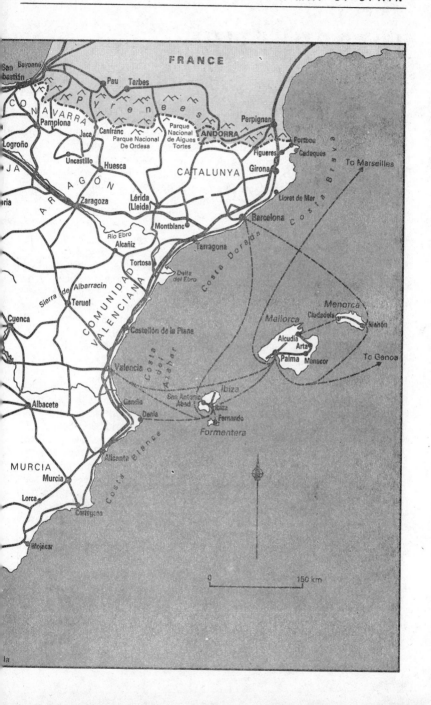

INTRODUCTION

S pain carries with it an unrivaled burden of preconceptions — crowded, sunny beaches, magnificent Moorish palaces, castles (and rain) in Spain — all of which are to some extent true. But travel for any length of time and such notions are dramatically taken apart. It's a huge country which in the north can look like Ireland, in the south like Africa, and which boasts a cultural diversity to match. The tourist hype inevitably concentrates on the beaches and on a magnificent monumental history which takes in Romans, Moors, and the "Golden Age" of Renaissance imperialism. Yet while monuments certainly survive, modern Spain is breaking out in numberless — and often surprising — ways. The sheer pace of change, barreling into the twentieth century in the wake of the thirty year dictatorship of Generalissimo Franco, is astonishing.

As it enters the 90s, Spain is enjoying the fastest economic growth in Europe, and a vitality — reveling in the nation's new-found self-confidence and rediscovered democracy — which is almost palpable. For the first time in centuries, there is a feeling of political stability, and for the first time Spanish culture has been allowed off the leash. Already in the past fifteen years, virtually every aspect of life has been radically transformed; there is a belief here that northern Europe has had its day, and that in future the south will lead the way. 1992, Spaniards believe, will be the year which restores them to their rightful place among Europe's leading nations. In that year Barcelona will host the Olympics, Sevilla the World Fair, and Madrid will be the official "Cultural Capital of Europe." The fact that it will also be the 500th anniversary of Columbus's "discovery" of America is seen as just one final portent of a new era. Vast works are underway to ensure that the world takes notice.

All of this makes Spain a tremendously exciting place to visit, with an infectious enthusiasm which it is hard not to catch. In the **cities** there is a tremendous amount going on — in clubs, on the streets, in fashion, in politics — and even in the most out of the way places there's nightlife, music, and entertainment, not to mention the more traditional fiestas, which as often as not you'll walk into quite unawares, to be carried away on a tide of exuberant celebration. There's considerable sophistication too, and some great modern architecture among the more usual concrete blocks.

Having said all this, when you get out into the **countryside** you can still find villages which have been decaying steadily since Columbus set sail. With new prosperity the rural areas are more and more depopulated as the young head for the greater promise of the cities. Another of the most extraordinary features of Spanish travel is an enormous regional and local diversity which can take you in a few hours (sometimes in a few minutes) to scenes of total contrast.

In this sense, and certainly in physical terms, it's almost impossible to summarize Spain as a single country. Basques, Catalans, Gallegos, and

Castilians display radical differences in almost every aspect of their lives. Catalunya is vibrant and go-ahead; Galicia rural and underdeveloped; the Basque country suffering post-industrial depression; Castile and the south still, somehow, quintessentially "Spanish." But they all have tremendous characters of their own.

To a degree these variations are determined by climate and by **topography.** Spain is, again unexpectedly, as mountainous a nation as any in Europe and the *sierras* have always formed formidable barriers to centralization or unification. The deserted *rías* of the northwest — green and damp — could hardly be more different to the endless windswept plains of Castile, to the great Moorish cities of the south, the developed wastelands of the concrete costas, or the eerie desert landscapes of Almería.

Another triumph of the new Spain is that the regions have at last been allowed to explore these identities, through varying degrees of political control over their own affairs. So if you travel in Catalunya you'll find the Catalan language replacing Castilian everywhere, or in the Basque country you'll come across the autonomous Basque police force, marked out by their red berets. This was the very diversity which Franco set out to crush, and the fact that it is flourishing now says much for the political maturity which Spain has finally achieved.

WHERE AND WHEN TO GO

The identity and appeal of each region is more fully explored in their respective chapter introductions — and there's much to be said for limiting yourself to one or two and really getting a feel for their individuality and character. If you want a broader sweep, though, there are definite **highlights** to Spanish travel: the three great cities of Barcelona, Madrid, and Sevilla; the Moorish monuments of Andalucía and the Christian ones of Old Castile; beach-life in Ibiza or on the more deserted sands around Cádiz and in the north; and, for some of the best hiking in Europe, the Pyrenees and the Asturian Picos de Europa. To get the most of Spain, though, you should escape the throng for at least some of your visit — and it is towards these possibilities, well off the standard tourist trails, that much of this *Real Guide* is directed.

In terms of **climate**, late spring and early autumn are ideal, especially spring before all the colour has been sapped out of the countryside. But the weather varies enormously from region to region. The high plains of the center suffer from fierce extremes, stiflingly hot in summer, bitterly cold and swept by freezing winds in winter: what rain there is comes in spring and fall. The Atlantic coast, in contrast, has a temperate pattern with depressions rolling in off the ocean, a permanent tendency to damp and mist, and a relatively brief, humid summer. The Mediterranean south is warm virtually all year round, and in Almería positively sub-tropical, attracting off-season package trippers even in December.

In high summer the other factor worth considering is **tourism** itself. Spain plays host to some thirty million tourists a year — one for every resident — and all the better known resorts are packed from June to September, when the major sights like Toledo become little more than processing plants for endless coach tours. August, Spain's own holiday month, sees the coast at its most crowded; Madrid on the other hand is virtually empty, with many of its bars and restaurants — even museums — closed for the duration. Whatever time of year, though, smaller, inland towns see few visitors, and contrary to popular legend there are beaches beyond the major costas. There's no need to feel trapped.

Average Maximum Temperatures °C (°F)						
	Jan	March	May	July	Sept	Nov
Madrid	9	15	21	31	25	13
Castile	(49)	(59)	(70)	(88)	(77)	(56)
Malaga	17	19	23	29	29	20
Costa del Sol	(63)	(67)	(74)	(84)	(84)	(68)
Sevilla	15	21	26	35	32	20
Inland Andalucia	(59)	(69)	(79)	(95)	(90)	(68)
Cadiz	15	18	23	29	29	20
Costa de la Luz	(59)	(65)	(74)	(84)	(84)	(68)
Pontevedra	14	16	20	25	24	16
Galicia	(58)	(61)	(68)	(77)	(75)	(61)
Santander	12	15	17	22	21	15
Cantabrian coast	(54)	(59)	(63)	(72)	(70)	(59)
Barcelona	13	16	21	28	25	16
Catalonia	(56)	(61)	(70)	(83)	(77)	(61)
Cap Bagur	14	16	20	27	25	16
Costa Brava	(57)	(61)	(68)	(80)	(77)	(62)
Valencia	15	18	23	29	27	19
Costa del Azahar	(59)	(65)	(74)	(84)	(81)	(66)
Alicante	16	20	26	32	30	21
Costa Blanca	(61)	(68)	(78)	(90)	(86)	(70)
Mallorca	14	17	22	29	27	18
Balearic Islands	(58)	(63)	(72)	(84)	(81)	(65)

Note that these are all *midday temperatures* — and whilst Sevilla, generally reckoned the hottest city in Spain, can soar into the 90sF in midsummer it is a fairly comfortable 75-80F (23-27C) through much of the morning and late afternoon. Equally, bear in mind that temperatures in the north, in Galicia for example, can drop down to 38-40F (3-5C) at night in *winter*, whilst in the most mountainous regions it can get extremely cold at any time of year.

PART ONE

THE

BASICS

GETTING THERE

The last few years have seen a big increase in the volume of North American travelers to Spain, and as a result there is now a fair variety of direct charters and scheduled services from most parts of the U.S. to Madrid, and sometimes to Barcelona. On the whole, these represent the best value, as well as the most convenient, approaches. Coming from Canada, however, you may want to consider flying via Britain, from where there are very cheap charters to a number of Spanish destinations.

DIRECT FROM THE USA

Most scheduled services hub through New York, although there are a couple of non-stop flights out of California. Fares, whether published as through or calculated as add-ons to "gateway" cities, are within the realm of possibility from most larger cities in the country. The discount outlets advertising in the Sunday travel sections have the most competitive fares, as often on major carriers as with charter companies like *Spantax*, the student/youth agencies have relatively little to offer.

EAST COAST

Seat consolidator prices start at around $190 one-way, $390 round-trip on the **New York–Madrid** route; the most likely agent is *Access International*, 250 W. 57th St., Suite 511, New York, NY 10107, ☎212/333-7280 or ☎800/825-3633. There are a handful of other operators whose prices vary from the above figures up to $260 one-way, $450 return. **Washington, D.C.–Madrid** tickets can be found for $230–260 one-way, $420–500 round-trip, depending on the season: the agent, again, is *Access International*.

In the **student/youth** agency category the reliable *Nouvelles Frontières* is probably the most flexible — welcoming non-student/youth travel

---

Branches of *CIEE* in the Eastern and Central United States

Head Office: 205 E. 42nd St., New York, NY 10017; ☎800/223-7401

GEORGIA
12 Park Place South, Atlanta, GA 30303; ☎404/577-1678

ILLINOIS
29 E. Delaware Place, Chicago, IL 60611; ☎312/951-0585

MASSACHUSETTS
79 South Pleasant St., 2nd Floor, Amherst, MA 01002; ☎413/256-1261
729 Boylston St., Suite 201, Boston, MA 02116; ☎617/266-1926
1384 Massachusetts Ave., Suite 206, Cambridge, MA 02138; ☎617/497-1497

MINNESOTA
1501 University Ave. SE, Room 300, Minneapolis, MN 55414; ☎612/379-2323

NEW YORK
35 W. 8th St., New York, NY 10011; ☎212/254-2525
Student Center, 356 West 34th St., New York, NY 10001; ☎212/661-1450

RHODE ISLAND
171 Angell St., Suite 212, Providence, RI 02906; ☎401/331-5810

TEXAS
1904 Guadalupe St., Suite 6, Austin, TX 78705; ☎512/472-4931
The Executive Tower, 3300 W. Mockingbird, Suite 101, Dallas,TX 75235; ☎214/350-6166

Branches of STN in the Eastern and Central United States

AUSTIN
2002 A Guadalupe St., Austin, TX 78705; ☎512/474-1512

BOSTON
273 Newbury St., Boston, MA 02116; ☎617/266-6014

CHICAGO
3249 N. Broadway, Chicago, IL 60657; ☎312/525-9227

DALLAS
6609 Hillcrest Ave., Dallas, TX 75205; ☎214/360-0097

NEW YORK
17 E. 45th St., Suite 805, New York, NY 10017; ☎212/986-9470

ers as well — if not the cheapest at $200–260 one-way New York–Madrid, $410–450 return (depending on the time of week/year); STN offerings are similar but they're leerier about booking those over 32. CIEE has very attractive round-trips at $340-500, one-ways roughly half that price, but reserves them strictly for students. Many of these tickets are on Pan Am.

Flying scheduled airlines at **full fare**, your most obvious options are Pan Am, the Spanish national carrier Iberia (565 Fifth Ave., New York, NY, ☎800/221-9741) and KLM (☎800/ 556-7777). Their 14-day advance purchase, 7-to-180 day APEX **New York–Madrid** tickets are priced identically at $467–518 low season, $594–664 shoulder period, and $652–722 high season (the higher figure applies to weekend travel), though Iberia make their flights more tempting by including one **free internal add-on** to either Málaga, Las Palmas, Tenerife, or Santiago.

Iberia also has relatively expensive APEX fares in the $600–750 range out of **Miami**; here

there are only two seasons and weekend premiums are in effect. KLM flights are all routed through Amsterdam and continue to Valencia, Málaga, Alicante, Barcelona, and Mallorca as well as Madrid; for their through fare to the capital out of **Atlanta** add roughly $130 to the New York figures, and note that tickets to the outlying Spanish cities will be substantially more expensive. An advantage of flying Pan Am, besides their greater frequency, is that you can fly **"open-jaw"** to/from their many destinations in Europe — e.g. into Madrid, out of Athens — and pay just half the APEX price for each city's leg as long as you reserve both legs of the trip from the States and observe the time restrictions.

WEST COAST
From **San Francisco** or **Los Angeles**, there are numerous offers of $500–600 round-trip fares advertised by **seat consolidators** in the San Francisco Examiner/Chronicle and Los Angeles Times Sunday travel sections; one-ways will set

Branches of CIEE in the Western United States

CALIFORNIA
2511 Channing Way, Berkeley, CA 94704; ☎415/848-8604
UCSD Student Center, B-023, La Jolla, CA 92093; ☎619/452-0630
5500 Atherton St., Suite 212, Long Beach, CA 90815; ☎213/598-3338
1039 Broxton Ave., Los Angeles, CA 90024; ☎213/208-3551
4429 Cass St., San Diego, CA 92109; ☎619/270-6401

312 Sutter St., San Francisco, CA 94108; ☎415/421-3473
919 Irving St., San Francisco, CA 94122; ☎415/566-6222
14515 Ventura Blvd., Suite 250, Sherman Oaks, CA 91403; ☎818/905-5777

OREGON
715SW Morrison, Suite 1020, Portland, OR 97205; ☎503/228-1900

WASHINGTON
1314Northeast 43rd St., Suite 210, Seattle, WA 98105; ☎206/632-2448

Branches of *STN* in the Western United States

HONOLULU
1831 S. King St., Suite 202, Honolulu, HI 96826;
☎808/942-7755

LOS ANGELES
920 Westwood Blvd., Los Angeles, CA 90024;
☎213/824-1574
7204 Melrose Ave., Los Angeles, CA 90046;
☎213/934-8722

2500 Wilshire Blvd., Los Angeles, CA 90057;
☎213/380-2184

SAN DIEGO
6447 El Cajon Blvd., San Diego, CA 92115;
☎619/286-1322

SAN FRANCISCO
166 Geary St., Suite 702, San Francisco, CA
94108; ☎415/391-8407

you back $300–350, depending on the agent and the season, and are slightly more difficult to find. The most consistent outlet is *Airkit*, 16 California St., San Francisco, CA 94111 (☎415/362-1106), or 1125 W. 6th St., Los Angeles, CA 90017 (☎213/482-8778).

Among the **student/youth** agencies, *CIEE* has the most advantageous prices at $560–700 round-trip between any Pacific city and Madrid, but reserves these fares for students. Otherwise try *Nouvelles Frontières* or *STN* with their offerings in the $640–800 range (depending on season — these are simply add-ons to their basic services out of New York). In most cases one-ways will be roughly half the round-trip price.

The only non-stop, **full-fare** scheduled airline service to **Madrid** from **Los Angeles** is offered by *Iberia* (☎800/772-4642). This runs two to four days a week. Shoulder-season, 7-to-180-day APEX fares are $777–837 (higher on weekends), with a Spanish internal flight again thrown in. Low season prices run $651–711, high season ones $835–895, and the connecting flight to Los Angeles from anywhere on the West Coast is included ("common-rated" in the airlines' lingo).

Pan Am's prices out of **San Francisco**, **Los Angeles**, or **Seattle** to **Madrid** are almost identical, although they hub through New York; while they don't offer any deals on onward flights

within Spain, again they are more useful for constructing "open-jaw" itineraries within Europe. *KLM* also links Los Angeles twice weekly with the Spanish cities noted above, via Amsterdam, but is markedly more expensive out of California than the other two companies.

CENTRAL U.S.

The **Chicago–Madrid** route is comparatively well served by the **seat consolidators**, with *TFI* (☎800/223-6363) offering round-trip fares from $460 and up. *Access International* 55 E. Washington St., Suite 220, Chicago, IL 60602 (☎312/977-4800 or 800/825-3633) is not far behind at about $480, with one-ways starting at $260.

If convenience is more important than money, *Pan Am* does have through APEX tickets from **Dallas** to **Madrid** (price structure virtually identical to the Pacific Coast fares) and from **Chicago** to **Madrid** ($596–646 low season, $722–792 shoulder, $780–850 high, with weekends surcharged and 180-day maximum stay) but again all these flights hub through New York. *Iberia's* flights out of Chicago to Madrid are marginally cheaper and have the further advantage of one internal Spanish freebie. *KLM* flies out of Chicago and **Houston** to Madrid via Amsterdam for the same price as *Pan Am*.

Branches of *Nouvelles Frontières*:

In the United States
NEW YORK 19 W. 44th St., Suite 1702, New York, NY 10036; ☎212/764-6494
LOS ANGELES 6363 Wilshire Blvd., Suite 200, Los Angeles, CA 90048; ☎213/658-8955
SAN FRANCISCO 209 Post St., Suite 1121, San Francisco, CA 94108; ☎415/781-4480

In Canada
MONTREAL 1130 ouest, bd. de Maisonneuve, Montréal, P.Q. H3A 1M8; ☎514/842-1450
QUEBEC 176 Grande Allée Ouest, Québec, P.Q. G1R 2G9; ☎418/525-5255

DIRECT FROM CANADA

The news is mostly bad. On "direct flights" to Spain, even *Travel Cuts* can only offer non-student charters **Toronto/Montreal–Madrid** *starting* at CDN$750 round-trip, CDN$450 one-way (students less 5–10%). This usually makes a stop in London. You might also contact *Iberia* in Montreal (1224 Peel St., 2nd Floor, ☎514/861-7211) just on the off-chance that they have a current special offer.

Budget alternatives are to fly via the U.S., or, generaly cheaper, via London. Count on a minimum of CDN$380–480 round-trip, CDN$300 one-way from Toronto, the same out of Montreal, and CDN $598–689 return, $389 one-way out of Vancouver.

VIA GREAT BRITAIN

FLIGHTS

There are **charter flights from Britain** to Spain throughout the year; out of season, or if you're prepared to buy at the last minute, these can be absurdly cheap. Charters are usually block-reserved by package-vacation firms, but even in the middle of August they're rarely completely full and spare seats are always being sold off at discounts. Times were when the only outlets for these were semi-legitimate "bucket shops," but you can now often pick up excellent deals at the big downtown London travel agents as well, or at any specialist budget or student/youth travel company. The widest selection of ads for London departures is invariably found in the classified

---

Offices of *Travel CUTS* in Canada (Known as *Voyages CUTS* in Quebec)

Head Office: 187 College St., Toronto, Ontario M5T 1P7; ☎416/979-2406

BRITISH COLUMBIA
Room 326, T.C., Student Rotunda, Simon Fraser University, Burnaby, British Columbia V5A 1S6; ☎604/291-1204
1516 Duranleau St., Granville Island, Vancouver V6H 3S4; ☎604/689-2887
Student Union Building, University of British Columbia, Vancouver V6T 1W5; ☎604/228-6890
Student Union Building, University of Victoria, Victoria V8W 2Y2; ☎604/721-8352

ALBERTA
1708 12th St. NW, Calgary T2M 3M7; ☎403/282-7687
10424A 118th Ave., Edmonton T6G 0P7; ☎403/471-8054

SASKATCHEWAN
PlaceRiel Campus Centre, University of Saskatchewan,Saskatoon S7N 0W0; ☎306/343-1601

MANITOBA
University Centre, University of Manitoba, Winnipeg R3T 2N2; ☎204/269-9530

ONTARIO
University Centre, University of Guelph, Guelph N1G 2W1; ☎519/763-1660
Fourth Level Unicentre, Carleton University, Ottawa, K1S5B6; ☎613/238-5493
60 Laurier Ave. E., Ottawa K1N 6N4; ☎613/238-8222
Student Street, Room G27, Laurentian University, Sudbury P3E 2C6; ☎705/673-1401
96 Gerrard St. E., Toronto M5B 1G7; ☎ (416) 977-0441
University Shops Plaza, 170 University Ave. W., Waterloo N2L 3E9; ☎519/886-0400

QUÉBEC
Université McGill, 3480 rue McTavish, Montréal H3A 1X9; ☎514/398-0647
1613 rue St. Denis, Montréal H2X 3K3; ☎514/843-8511
Université Concordia, Edifice Hall, Suite 643, S.G.W. Campus, 1455 Blvd. de Maisonneuve Ouest, Montréal H3G 1M8; ☎514/288-1130
19 rue Ste. Ursule, Québec G1R 4E1; ☎418/692-3971

NOVA SCOTIA
Student Union Building, Dalhousie University, Halifax B3H 4J2; ☎902/424-2054
6139 South St., Halifax B3H 4J2; ☎902/424-7027

pages of the London listings magazine *Time Out*. Check also the local evening papers (such as the *Standard*) and *The Sunday Times* and *The Observer*.

For flights to **northern Spain** — Santiago, Vigo, or La Coruña — try *Pilgrim-Air* (227 Shepherds Bush Rd., London W6 7AS; ☎01/748-1333 or 748-4999). Another **specialist agency** worth trying in London is *Springways Travel* (71 Oxford St., London W1, ☎01/734-0393), though since many Spaniards living in the UK use their services to shuttle back and forth fairly cheaply, you'll face stiff competition for seats. From November to March (except around Christmas) you should be aiming at around £70 round-trip to Málaga, Alicante, or Mallorca (generally the three cheapest destinations); by mid-June (and through until mid-September) the going rate will rise to a little over £100.

Students — and anyone **under 26** — can also take advantage of a range of special discount flights, most frequently to Madrid and Barcelona. The best firms for these in London are **STA Travel** (at 86 Old Brompton Rd., SW7, ☎01/581-8233, and other addresses), and **USIT** (52 Grosvenor Gdns., SW1, ☎01/730-6525, and many student campuses). These agencies can usually get you to Madrid for about £50–60 one-way, £100–110 round-trip; to Barcelona for about £59 outbound or a much more advantageous £65 round-trip; and to Malaga for approximately £80 both ways. These companies can be worth calling for charters as well, whether you're a student/youth or not.

Spain's national airline, *Iberia*, has the widest range of **scheduled flight** destinations, including regular direct services to Santiago, Bilbao, and Sevilla, as well as all the standard ports of entry. They are rarely the cheapest option going but they do reduce prices out of season and, in the face of considerable recent losses, are beginning to offer attractive and competitive possibilities. Contact their London office (169 Regent St., W1, ☎01/437-5622) or any of their agents (like *Mundi Color*, 276 Vauxhall Bridge Rd., SW1, ☎01/834-3492).

TRAINS

From London to **San Sebastián** or **Barcelona** takes just under 24 hours by train, setting out from Victoria station at around 9am, changing trains (and crossing stations, from Nord to Austerlitz) in Paris around 6–8pm, and again at

the Spanish border (at Hendaye/Irún or Cerbère/Port Bou) around dawn. It's an efficient approach, and can be an interesting one if you stop off en route.

If you're **under 26** there are three methods of discounted rail travel available to you. The best known — and possibly the best value — is buying an **InterRail pass** (currently £139 from British Rail or any travel agent). This gives you a month's unlimited travel on all European (and Moroccan) railways, and 50% discounts in Britain, on the Channel ferries, and on ferries from Spain to the Balearics or Morocco. Since Spain itself has an extensive rail network this is basically a bargain — though be prepared (see "Getting Around" below) to pay various and unpredictable supplements on some of the Spanish services. Apart from age (**Senior Citizen InterRail** passes are also available for anyone over 65) the only restriction is that you must have been resident in Europe for at least six months. (Some agents, though, are not too strict on this). **EurRail**, the North American rail pass, is nowhere near as good a deal, unless you're planning to virtually live on Spanish (and other European) trains for the month or two of its validity.

The alternative to these — again for those under 26 only, but with no other restrictions — is a discounted rail ticket sold by **Eurotrain** (through *USIT*: 52 Grosvenor Gdns., London SW1, ☎01/730-6525) or **Transalpino** (71/75 Buckingham Palace Rd., London SW1, ☎01/834-9656). These can be written out for journeys from any station in Britain to any major station in Europe or Morocco; they remain valid for two months and allow as many stopovers as you want along a prespecified route (which can be different going out and coming back). The cheapest of these tickets to Spain — to San Sebastián or Barcelona — works out at just under £60 one-way (£115 both ways); travel right down to the south, to Málaga, and you can expect to pay over £70 one-way (£140 round-trip). As with an InterRail pass, the Spanish conductors may charge supplements on certain trains.

If you need to buy a **ticket out of Spain**, *Transalpino* has an office in Madrid at Plaza de España 9. *Eurotrain* tickets (essentially identical) are available at *TIVE*, the Madrid student agency, c/Fernando el Católico 88 (☎91/4019011).

If you're **over 26** you'll have to buy a **standard rail ticket**, reservable through any travel agent or at London's Victoria station (European information line ☎01/834-2345). Prices are approximately one-third higher than the youth fares quoted above.

The two standard **routes down** — and the cheapest — are to San Sebastián (for Madrid, Old Castile and the northwest) and to Barcelona (convenient for the Pyrenees and the Balearics). There are, however, two minor alternative routes which cross the central Pyrenees to enter Aragón at Canfranc or Catalunya at Puigcerda. On the first of these British Rail will only write you a ticket as far as Oloron (in France), from where you must take a bus to Canfranc on the Spanish side. The French, in a fit of Gallic pique, have recently shut the international line between the two points to keep people from using the much cheaper ski slopes at Cadanchú in Spain. Similarly on the Catalan route, British Rail fares are only sold through to French Bourg-Madame, just over the frontier from Puigcerda, where you must change trains and buy another ticket.

BUSES

There are two regular **bus routes** from Britain to Spain:

● **London–Algeciras** (48 hr.), via Paris, Bordeaux, San Sebastián (26 hr.), Vitoria, Burgos, Madrid (33 hr.), Córdoba, Málaga, and the Costa del Sol.

● **London–Alicante** (35 hr.), via Figueras (24 hr.), Gerona, Barcelona (26½ hr.), and Valencia (32 hrs.)

Both routes are operated by **Eurolines** (☎01/ 730-0202) in London and by **Iberbus/Linebus** (☎91/4672565) in Madrid. **Miracle Bus** (408 Strand, London WC2, ☎01/379-6055) is one of the better agencies for long-distance bus tickets, and sometimes undercuts *Eurolines* prices. Departures, from April to October, occur around four times weekly to Algeciras, daily to Barcelona (continuing 3 times weekly to Alicante). Out of season the service drops to twice a week to Algeciras, three to Barcelona (where they finish). In both Britain and Spain tickets are reservable through most major travel agents; *Eurolines* tickets are available at any *National Express* bus terminal. One-way fares are around £50 to San Sebastián, £60 to Madrid, £55 to Barcelona, £70 to Alicante; round-trip tickets cost just under double these figures unless you're under 26, in which case there's a special £99 round-trip to most destinations in Spain.

To San Sebastián or Barcelona the journey is long but quite bearable — just make sure you take along enough to eat, drink and read, and a small amount of French and Spanish currency for coffee, etc.. There are stops for around twenty minutes every four or five hours and the routine is also broken by the Dover-Calais/Boulogne ferry (which is included in the cost of a ticket).

An alternative strategy is to use the **combination plane/bus** round-trip scheme offered by *Pegasus Holidays* (☎01/773-2323 but reservable through many agents). For £62 to £90, depending on the season, you fly out to Madrid, are put up for a night in a hotel, and then go back to Britain by bus on specified days.

DRIVING OR HITCHING

The bus routes above are along the most direct road routes from London to Spain; if you plan to **drive** them yourself you'll want to roughly double the times given, unless you're into non-stop marathons. Alternatively, for a little more expense, you can take the easy way out and use the **car/passenger ferry** from **Plymouth to Santander**. This is operated by *Brittany Ferries* (☎0705/827701), takes 24 hours, and runs twice weekly for most of the year. Ticket prices vary according to the season, but they're never cheap, ranging from £57 to £84 for a car plus £48 to £55 per person. They are best purchased in advance, again through any major travel agent.

The usual **ferry links** between Britain and France — Dover–Calais and Folkestone– Boulogne — will be your best options if you're making for Barcelona. For San Sebastián (and Madrid/the north west) you might want to consider one of the ferries to Le Havre (from Portsmouth), Cherbourg (from Portsmouth and Weymouth), St-Malo (from Portsmouth), or even Roscoff (from Plymouth). Any of these cuts out the trek around or through Paris, and allows some interesting detours in Britanny and along the French Atlantic coast.

If you're **hitching**, it's worth getting hold of the RAC (Royal Automobile Club) road maps, since these detail the main service stations on the expressways down through France. Hitching on major French routes — and Spanish ones too — can be frustrating, and stopping people to ask directly for rides in the cafes is about the only technique that works. In any case don't try to hitch from the Channel ports to Paris (a real no-no: arrange a ride while you're still on the ferry), nor, still worse, out of Paris itself. If you can afford it, perhaps the best approach is to buy a *Transalpino*, *Eurotrain*, or *Eurolines* ticket to somewhere south of Paris and set out from there. Lille or Orléans are reasonably well poised for Barcelona, Tours or Chartres for San Sebastián. If you plan to spend some time **in Paris** on your way, one possible ploy is to join *Allostop*, the French ride-sharing association. For the princely sum of 35F (ca. $6) they will enroll you for a single journey and put you in touch with a driver going your way (to whom you contribute gas costs). The Paris *Allostop* office is at 84 Passage Brady (☎42 46 00 66; open Mon.–Fri. 9am–7:30pm, Sat. 9am–1pm and 2–6pm).

RED TAPE AND VISAS

U.S. and Canadian citizens need only a passport to enter Spain; the former get to stay 180 days, the latter three months.

If you want to **stay longer** you'll either need to get a special visa at the nearest Spanish consulate before departure, or a *permanencia* (residence permit). These are issued by the *Jefatura de Policia* in small towns, or by the *Servicio de Extranjeros* in bigger cities. It's advisable to apply for this a couple of weeks before your time runs out, and to have proof that you're going to be able to support yourself without working (easiest done by keeping bank exchange forms every time you change money). Many people get around this law by simply leaving the country for a few days when their time runs out and getting a new date stamp upon re-entry, but the legality of this is somewhat dubious. If you cross over into Portugal or France for this purpose make sure that your passport gets stamped (this isn't done routinely) and come back into Spain at least a couple days later by a different border post.

COSTS, MONEY, AND BANKS

Despite domestic inflation, and despite rising international prices which have affected the tourist industry, Spain remains one of the less expensive countries in western Europe — certainly cheaper for travelers than Germany, France, Italy or the UK. Prices are no longer absurdly low, as they were in the tourist boom years of the 1960s and 1970s, but there are few places where you'll get a better deal on the cost of rooms, simple meals, and drink. If you're prepared to cut corners — to buy some of your own food, hitch occasionally, and so on — **you could get by quite easily on as little as $20 a day. If you can spend $30–40 you'd really be living quite well.**

Rooms can usually be found for 600–1200ptas ($5.50–10.50) single, 900–1500ptas ($8–13.50) double, while campgrounds start at around 350ptas (just over $3) a night per person. The cost of **eating** can vary wildly, but in most towns there'll be restaurants offering a basic three-course meal for somewhere between 500 and 800ptas ($4.50–7). As often as not, though, you'll end up wandering from one bar to the next sampling *tapas* without getting round to a real sit-down meal — this is certainly tastier though rarely any cheaper, (see *Eating and Drinking* section). **Drink**, and wine in particular, costs ridiculously little; $4 will see you through a night's very substantial intake of the local vintage. Long-distance **transportation**, if used extensively, may prove a major expense. Although prices compare well with the rest of Europe, Spain is a very large country. Madrid to Sevilla for example, a journey of over 500 kilometers, costs around 2800ptas ($25.50) by bus or train. Urban transit almost always operates on a flat fare of 50–60ptas (roughly 50 cents).

All of the above, inevitably, is affected by **where you are and when**. The big cities and tourist resorts are invariably more expensive than remoter areas, and certain regions tend also to have higher prices — notably the industrialized north, Euskadi and Aragón, and the Balearic Islands. Prices are jacked up too to take advantage of special events. Despite official controls you'd be lucky to find a room in Sevilla during its April Feria, or in Pamplona for the running of the bulls, at less than double the usual rate. As always, if you're **traveling alone** you'll end up spending much more than you would in a group of two or more — sharing rooms and food saves greatly. An ISIC **student card** is worth having — it'll get you free or reduced entry to many museums and sites as well as occasional other discounts — or a FIYTO **youth card** (available to anyone under 26) is almost as good.

One thing to look out for on prices generally is the addition of **IVA**, the Spanish value-added tax (national sales tax), which may come as an unexpected extra when you pay the bill — especially in more expensive establishments.

MONEY

The exchange rate for the Spanish **peseta** seems to be relatively stable at around 110 to the U.S. dollar. Coins come in denominations of 1, 5, 10, 25, 50, 100, and 200 pesetas; notes as 100 (rare), 200 (ditto), 500, 1000, 2000, 5000, and 10,000 pesetas. You can take in as much money as you want (in any form), but you're only allowed to take 100,000 pesetas out unless you can prove that you brought more with you in the first place (not that this is likely to prove a major worry).

Probably the safest and easiest way to carry your funds is in **travelers' checks**, which can be exchanged in banks or (in major resorts) *casas de cambio*. Most **credit cards** are recognized too, and useful for emergencies or for such extra expenses as car rental, as well as for cash advances at banks. *Visa*, which has an arrangement with the *Banco de Bilbao*, is the most useful; *Mastercard* is less widely accepted.

BANKS (AND ALTERNATIVES)

Spanish **banks** and *cajas de ahorro* (equivalent of a savings and loan) have branches in all but the smallest towns, and most of them should be prepared to change travelers' checks (albeit occasionally with reluctance for certain brands, and almost always with hefty commissions — at $2–4 *minimum* per transaction, some of the highest in Europe). The *Banco Central*, the *Banco de Bilbao*, and the *Banco Hispano-Americano* are three of the best and most widespread; all will change most brands of travelers' checks efficiently and give cash advances on credit cards; commissions at the *Banco Central* are generally the lowest in the country. Elsewhere you may have to line up at two or three windows, a twenty-to-thirty-minute process.

Banking hours are Mon.–Fri. 9am–2pm, Sat. 9am–1pm (except in summer when no banks open on Sat.). Outside these times it's usually possible to change cash at larger hotels (often with lower or no commission) or, in the cities and big resorts, with travel agents, who may initially grumble but will eventually give a rate with the commission built in — useful for small sums in a hurry. Many branches of *El Corte Ingles*, a major department store, and *American Express* (particularly in Madrid and Barcelona) also have efficient exchange facilities which offer competitive rates and charge a flat 1% commission on cash, 2% on travelers' checks — with no minimum commission, and again useful for smaller sums.

HEALTH AND INSURANCE

No inoculations are required for Spain, though if you plan on continuing to North Africa, typhoid and polio boosters are highly recommended.

For minor complaints you go to a *farmacía*, which you'll find in almost any village; in larger towns there's usually one where they speak English. Pharmacists are highly trained, willing to give advice, and able to dispense many drugs which would be available by prescription only in the USA or Canada.

In more serious cases you can get the address of an English-speaking physician from the local police or *Turismo*. In **major emergencies** dial

091 for the *Servicios de Urgencia*, or look up the *Cruz Roja Española* (Red Cross) which runs a national ambulance service.

INSURANCE

You can run up a large bill at the doctor's or even at the most basic of state hospitals, so it would be wise to look into medical coverage beforehand. Before you purchase special **travel insurance**, whether for medical or property mishaps, check that you won't duplicate any **existing plans** which you may have. For example, **Canadians** are usually covered for medical expenses by their provincial health plans (but may only be reimbursed after the fact). Holders of **ISIC** cards are entitled to $2000 worth of accident coverage and sixty days ($100 per diem) of hospital in-patient benefits for the period during which the card is valid. **Students** will often find that their student health coverage extends for one term beyond the date of last enrollment. Bank and charge **accounts** (particularly American Express) often have certain levels of medical or other insurance included. **Homeowners' or renters'** insurance often covers theft or loss of documents, money, and valuables while overseas, though exact conditions and maximum amounts vary from company to company.

Only after exhausting the possibilities above might you want to contact a specialist travel insurance company; your travel agent can usually recommend one. Travel insurance offerings are quite comprehensive, anticipating everything from charter companies going bankrupt to delayed or lost baggage, by way of sundry illnesses and accidents. **Premiums** vary widely, from the very reasonable ones offered primarily through student/youth agencies (though available to anyone), to those so expensive that the cost for anything more than two months of coverage will probably equal the cost of the worst possible combination of disasters. Note also that very few insurers will arrange on-the-spot payments in the event of a major expense or loss; you will usually be reimbursed only after going home.

A most important thing to keep in mind — and a source of major disappointment to would-be claimants — is that *none* of the policies insure against **theft** of *anything* while overseas. (Americans have been easy pickings for foreign thieves — a combination of naivete on the part of the former, an all-Americans-are-rich attitude among the latter — and companies were going broke paying robbery/burglary claims.) North American travel policies apply only to items **lost** from, or **damaged** in, the custody of an identifiable, responsible third party, i.e. hotel porter, airline, luggage consignment, etc.. Even in these cases you will still have to contact the local police to have a complete report made out so that your insurer can process the claim. If you are planning to stay some time in Spain, and travelling via London, it can be a good idea to investigate taking out a **British policy**, which should allow cover for theft.

INFORMATION (THE SNTO) AND MAPS

The **Spanish National Tourist Office (SNTO) produces and gives away an impressive amount of maps, pamphlets, and special interest leaflets, many of them useful supplements to this guide. Perhaps most helpful are their large, glossy pamphlets on the principal Spanish towns. There are well over fifty of these, covering every major resort and provincial capital, and although their text isn't always to be relied upon, they do usually contain excellent town plans and an enticing range of color photos. It's a good idea to collect as many as possible, along the routes and in the regions that you plan to cover, before leaving; in the towns and cities themselves they often run out of supplies.**

In addition you may want to pick up the SNTO's *Mapa de Campings* (marking every official campground), their lists of youth hostels, paradores, or (province by province) hostales, and particularly if you're going to be traveling by train, their *Mapa de Communicaciones*.

In Spain itself you'll find SNTO offices in virtually every major town (addresses are detailed in the guide) and from these you can usually get more specific local information, especially the invaluable *Datos Informativos* leaflets which include a town map and lists of everything from local business hours and hotels to automobile mechanics and laundromats. SNTO offices are often supplemented by separately administered provincial or municipal **Turismo** bureaus. These vary enormously in quality — the Basque and Catalan ones are superb — but they are often more useful for strictly regional information, and cannot be relied on to know anything about what goes on outside their jurisdiction. Spanish tourist offices usually function Mon.–Fri. 9am–1pm and 3:30–6pm, Sat. 9am–1pm.

In addition to the various free leaflets, the one extra you'll probably want is a reasonable **road map**. This is best bought in Spain, where you'll find a good selection in most bookshops (*librerías*) and at street kiosks or gas stations. Among the best are those published by *Editorial Almax*, which also produces good indexed streetplans of the main cities. A good second choice, especially if you're shopping before arrival, is the 1:800,000 map put out by *RV* (*Reise- und Verkehrsverlag*, Stuttgart) and packaged in Spain by *Plaza & Janes*.

Hikers can get more detailed maps from *La Tienda Verde* at Maudes 38, Madrid, and *Llibreria Quera* at Petritxol 2, Barcelona. Both of these stores — and many other bookstores in Spain, for that matter — stock the full line of topographical maps issued by two government agencies: the *IGN* (*Instituto Geográfico Nacional*), and the *SGE* (*Servicio Geográfico del Ejército*). Quads are available at scales of 1:200,000, 1:100,000, 1:50,000, and even occasionally 1:25,000. The various SGE series are considered to be more current and accurate by those in the know. A Catalunya-based company, *Editorial Alpina*, produces 1:25,000 map-booklets for most of the mountain and foothill areas of interest, and these are also on sale at the two stores cited as well as in many tourist shops in the areas covered by the booklets. In the **USA** some of these maps can be obtained from *Map Link*, 529 State St., Santa Barbara, CA 93101 (☎805/963-4438). If you're stopping in **England** on the way to Spain, *Stanford's*, 12–14 Long Acre, London WC2E 9LP (☎01/836-1321) has an even more complete stock.

If you can read Spanish at all, the Spanish **travel magazine** *Viajar* regularly features articles on some of the more obscure corners of the country — well informed and good reading. The Spanish edition of *GEO* also occasionally has reports on domestic destinations.

GETTING AROUND

Most of Spain is well covered by both bus and rail networks and for journeys between major towns there's often little to choose between them in cost or speed. On shorter or less obvious routes buses tend to be quicker and will also normally take you closer to your destination; some railway stations are several miles from the town or village they serve and you've no guarantee of a connecting bus. Approximate journey times and frequencies can be found in the "Travel Details" at the end of each chapter, and local peculiarities are also pointed out in the text of the guide. Car rental is also worth considering costs among the lowest in Europe.

BUSES

Unless you're traveling on a rail pass, **buses** will probably meet the majority of your transportation needs; many smaller villages are accessible only by bus, almost always leaving from the capital of their province. Service varies in quality, but on the whole the buses are reliable and comfortable enough, with prices pretty standard at around 550ptas per 100 kilometres. The only real problem involved is that many towns still have no main bus station, and buses may leave from a variety of places (even if they're heading in the same direction, since some destinations are served by more than one company). Where a new terminal has been built, it is often on the outer fringes of town. As far as possible departure points are detailed in the text or the "Travel Details."

One important point to remember is that all public transportation, and the bus service especially, is drastically reduced on **Sundays and holidays** — it's best to not consider traveling to out-of-the-way places on these days. The words to look out for on timetables are *diario* (daily), *laborables* (workdays, including Saturday), and *domingos y festivos* (Sundays and holidays).

TRAINS

RENFE, the Spanish rail company, operates a horrendously complicated variety of **trains**. Half of the time their own employees don't seem to know about all of the special tickets and reductions available. An ordinary train, much the same speed and cost as the bus, will normally be described as an *expreso* or *rapido. Semi-directos* and *tranvias* (mostly short-haul electrified trolleys) are somewhat slower, while anything described as a *correo* (mail train) will be excruciatingly slow, stopping at every hamlet along the way. Expresses, in ascending order of speed and luxury, are known as *Electrotren, TER, Talgo,* or *Pendular.* The latter two categories, complete with muzak and air-conditioning, are the most expensive, costing as much as 60–70% more than a standard second-class ticket; the other two cost 40–50% more.

InterRail and EurRail **passes** are valid on all of these, but there's a supplement for traveling on any of the expresses, and sometimes on *expresos* and *rapidos* too. The apparently random nature of these surcharges — which seem to depend on the individual train guard — can be a source of considerable irritation, not to mention expense. One way around the problem, or at least a method of knowing what you're letting yourself in for, is to reserve a ticket in advance. For a small fee (ca. 100ptas) this will get you a large, computer-printed ticket which will satisfy the most unreasonable of guards. International rail passes will almost certainly *not* be valid on Spain's surviving private rail lines: along the north coast from Bilbao to El Ferrol, in the east from Alicante to Denia (both run by *FEVE*), and the Nuria line in the Catalan Pyrenees. The **FEVE** company has in the past offered a three-month summer pass for travel on its north-coast line to those under 26 and may do so again; for 5000ptas or so you get a souvenir tote bag, a compass, a route map, and a guidebook (in easy Spanish) thrown in.

SPAIN: TRAINS

In recent years many bona fide train services have been phased out in favor of **rail buses** operated jointly by RENFE and a private bus company. This is particularly true when the connection is either indirect or the daily trains (sometimes train) leave(s) at inconvenient times. On some routes the rail buses outnumber the conventional departures by a ratio of four to one. The buses are bearable — though heavily air conditioned — and prices per kilometer are the same as on "real" trains. These services *usually* leave and arrive from the bus stations/stops of the towns concerned. As with the private rail lines detailed above, rail passes are not valid.

TICKETS AND DISCOUNTS

RENFE offers a whole range of discount fares on its *días azules* ("blue days" — which cover most of the year, with the exception of peak holiday weekends). If you're over 65, traveling with children under fourteen, or in a group of ten or more, or planning a round-trip to be done on the same or separate "Blue Day," you can get up to fifty percent oFf. A *Chequetren* pass gives a 15 percent discount; it costs a minimum of 25,000ptas (for travel worth up to 29,500ptas), but this can be shared between six (named) people.

Tickets can be bought at the stations between sixty days and two hours before the train leaves from the *venta anticipada* window, or in the final two hours from the *venta inmediata* window. Don't leave it for the last minute, however, as lines are often considerable. Often there is a further subdivision into *largo recorrido* (long-distance) trains and *cercanías* (locals). Larger towns almost all have a much more convenient RENFE office in the center as well. They sell tickets in advance and dish out schedule pamphlets; you can also buy the *Guia RENFE* **timetable** here (and at major stations) — useful if you plan to travel extensively by train.

You can **change** the departure date of an electronically issued, reserved-seat *largo recorrido* ticket without penalty up to a few hours before your originally scheduled departure. An actual cancellation and a **refund** of the same sort of ticket entails losing 10 percent of purchase price, but this can be done up to thirty minutes before the departure of your train.

CARS

While getting around on public transportation is cheap and easy enough, you'll obviously have a great deal more freedom if you have your **own car**. Major roads are generally good, especially in the north, and traffic, while a little hectic in the cities, is generally well behaved. But there are a couple of drawbacks. First, you'll be spending more (even with a full car); gasoline prices are almost double what they are in North America, and in the big cities at least you'll probably want to pay extra for a hotel with parking (or be forced to stay on the outskirts). Second, the rate at which tourists' cars are **broken into** is alarming — never leave anything visible in the car.

Before you go, it's best to get an **International Driver's Licence** (available from AAA or its local equivalent), though in practice North American licenses will be honored. A bail bond or extra coverage for legal costs is also worth having, since if you do have an accident it'll be your fault, as a foreigner, regardless of the circumstances. Away from main roads you yield to vehicles approaching from the right, but rules are not too strictly observed anywhere. Speed limits are posted and (on the main highways at least) speed traps are common. If you're pulled over for any violation, the Spanish police can and usually will levy a stiff on-the-spot **fine** before letting you go on your way, especially since as a foreigner you're unlikely to want, or be able, to appear in court.

Spanish auto mechanics are perfectly competent; you shouldn't have too much trouble having your car repaired if it **breaks down** unless you insist on driving a large or rare model. Locals mostly drive small French Renaults or Peugeots, or Spanish-made Seats (basically a Fiat), but Seat dealers double as VW and Audi supply points, and Ford franchises are almost as common. You might, however, have some problems getting parts for Japanese cars, with the exception of Nissan Patrols and vans, or Suzuki jeeps.

Renting a car lets you out of many of the hassles, and it's not too expensive. You'll find a choice of companies in any major town, with the biggest ones — *Hertz, Avis, Europcar*, etc. well represented at the airports as well as in town centers. These all charge about the same, upwards of $190 a week, but you can usually get a deal from local operators (*Atesa* is the main

Spanish company) for around $110–130. Tourist offices will provide a list of addresses, but the car, and the contract, should always be checked carefully before setting out. If you are traveling via Britain, and buying a flight from there to Spain, it is worth enquiring about car rental on offer; many British agents have excellent offers, and you can of course pick the car up on arrival at the airport.

Mopeds and motorcycles are often rented out with insurance that doesn't include theft. You will generally be asked to produce a driver's license as a deposit for mopeds or motorcycles, and if you plan to rent one (on the Balearics for instance) it's certainly worth bringing one. If the bike breaks down and you have to leave it — or if it's stolen — then at least you won't be trapped without a passport. Crash helmets, incidentally, have been obligatory since 1982; as yet, however, the law is not widely observed.

Taxis in city areas are incredibly cheap and are certainly the safest way to travel late at night. Make full use of them, particularly in Madrid and Barcelona.

HITCHING

On the whole **hitching** in Spain, at least as a serious means of long-distance travel, is pretty poor. The road down the east coast (Barcelona–Valencia–Murcia) is notoriously difficult, and trying to get out of either Madrid or Barcelona can prove to be a nightmare. On the other hand, thumbing on back roads can be surprisingly productive; as always seems to be the case, the fewer cars there are, the more likely they are to stop. Regionally there's considerable variation as well; the Basque country, and the north in general, often prove quite easy, whereas Andalucía involves long, hot waits. Always carry some water with you and some kind of hat or cap — lifts too often dry up at some shadeless junction in the middle of nowhere.

PLANES

Both *Iberia* and the smaller, slightly cheaper *Aviaco* operate an extensive network of **internal flights**. These are not much cheaper than local airlines in North America and are only really worth considering if you're in an extraordinary hurry and need to cross the entire peninsula. The main exception is getting to, and between, the **Balearic Islands** where flights are only marginally more expensive than the ferries. In peak season you may well have to reserve long in advance for these (see the *Balearics* chapter for more details).

SLEEPING

ROOMS

Spain must have some of the cheapest **rooms** in Europe — in almost any town you'll be able to get a double for around 900–1500ptas ($8–14), a single for 600–1200ptas ($5.50–10.50). Only in major resorts and a handful of "tourist cities" (like Toledo or Sevilla) need you pay more. We've detailed where to find cheap places to stay in most of the destinations listed in the guide, but as a general rule all you have to do is head for the cathedral or main square of any town, invariably surrounded by an old quarter full of accommodation possibilities. In Spain, unlike most countries, you don't seem to pay any more for a central location (this goes for bars and cafes, too), though you do tend to get a comparatively bad deal if you're traveling on your own as there are relatively few single rooms; out of season it's always worth bargaining over the price of a double — you may get it for half-price.

The one thing all travelers need to master is the elaborate variety of types and places to stay. Cheapest of all are **fondas** (identifiable by a square blue sign with a white **F** on it, and often positioned above a bar), closely followed by **casas de huespedes** (**CH** on a similar sign), **pensiones** (**P**) and, less commonly, **hospedajes**. Distinctions between all of these are somewhat blurred, but in general you'll find food served at both *fondas* and *pensiones* (some of which may offer rooms only on a meals-inclusive basis). *Casas de huespedes* — literally "guest houses" — are traditionally for longer stays and to some extent, particularly in the older family seaside resorts, they still are.

Slightly more expensive (starting from around 1200ptas double) are **hostales** (marked **Hs**) and **hostal-residencias** (**HsR**). These are categorized from one star (cheap) to three stars (much less so), though even so prices vary enormously according to location — in general the more remote, the less expensive. Most *hostales* offer good functional rooms, usually with private shower, and, for doubles at least, they can be excellent value. The *residencia* designation means that no meals other than breakfast are served.

Moving up the scale you finally reach **hoteles** (**H**), again star-graded by the authorities (from 1☆ to 5☆). One-star hotels cost no more than three-star *hostales* — sometimes they're actually cheaper — but at three stars you pay a lot more, at four or five you're in the luxury class with prices to match. Near the top end of this scale there are also state-run **paradores**: beautiful places, often converted from castles, monasteries, and other "minor" Spanish monuments. If you can afford them these are pretty amazing value for what you get. Even if you can't afford to stay, the buildings are often worth a look in themselves, the bars worth a visit for a classy drink.

Outside all of these categories you will sometimes see **camas** (beds) and **habitaciones** (rooms) advertised in private houses or above bars, often with the phrase "*camas y comidas*" (beds and meals). These can be the cheapest of all options, particularly if you're offered one at a bus station and the owner is prepared to bargain.

Youth hostels (*Albergues Juveniles*), on the other hand, are rarely very practical, except in northern Spain (especially the Pyrenees) where it can be difficult for solo, short-term travelers to find any other bed in summer. Only about twenty Spanish hostels stay open all year — the rest operating just for the summer (or spring and summer) in temporary premises — and in towns they tend to be inconveniently located. The most useful are detailed in the guide, or you can get a complete list (with opening times and phone numbers) from the YHA or *Turismo*. However, be warned that they tend to have curfews, are often block-reserved by school groups, and demand production of a YHA card (though this is generally available on the spot if you haven't already bought one from your national organization). At 350–450ptas a person, too, you can quite easily pay more than for a cheap double room in a *fonda* or *casa de huespedes*.

In isolated mountain areas the *Federacion Español de Montañismo* (c/Alberto Aguiler 3, Madrid 15; ☎91/4451382 or Apodaca 16, Madrid 4) and three Catalunya-based clubs (the FEEC, the CEC, and the UEC) run a number of **refugios**: simple, cheap dormitory-huts for climbers and hikers, generally unequipped beyond bunks and a very basic kitchen. Also, and again off the beaten track, it is sometimes possible to stay at Spanish **monasteries**. Often severely depopulated, these may rent empty cells for a small charge (around 250ptas or so a person). You can just turn up and ask — many will take visitors regardless of sex — but if you want to be sure of a reception it's best to approach the local *Turismo* first, and phone ahead. There are some particularly wonderful monastic locations in Galicia, Catalunya, and, oddly enough, Mallorca.

Monasteries and youth hostels aside, if you have any **problems** with Spanish rooms — overcharging, most obviously — you can usually produce an immediate resolution by asking for the *libra de reclamaciones* (complaints book). By law all establishments must keep this and bring it out for regular inspection by the police. Nothing is ever written in them . . ..

CAMPING

There are some 350 authorized **campgrounds** in Spain, predominantly on the coast. They usually work out at about 300ptas (just under $3) per person a night (but more for lone travelers — you're charged per person *and* per tent). Again we've detailed the most useful in the text, but if you plan to camp extensively then pick up the free *Mapa de Campings* from the National Tourist Board, which marks and names virtually all of them. A complete *Guía de Campings*, listing full prices, facilities, and exact locations, is available at most Spanish bookshops for 325ptas.

Camping outside campgrounds is legal — but with certain restrictions. You're not allowed to camp "in urban areas, areas prohibited for military or touristic reasons, or within 1km of an official campground." What this means in practice is that you can't camp on tourist beaches (though you can, discreetly, nearby) but with a little sensitivity you can set up a tent for a short period almost anywhere in the countryside. Whenever possible ask locally first.

EATING AND DRINKING

There are two ways to eat in Spain: you can go to a *restaurante* or *comedor* (dining room) and have a full meal, or you can have a succession of *tapas* (small snacks) or *raciones* (larger ones) at a bar or bars. At the bottom line a *comedor* — where you'll get a basic, filling, three-course meal with a drink — is usually the cheapest option, but they're often tricky to find, and drab places when you do. Bars, where you can do the rounds sampling local (often house) specialties, tend to be a lot more interesting.

BARS, TAPAS, AND SNACKS

One of the advantages of eating in **bars** is that you are able to experiment. Many places have food laid out on the counter, so you can see what's available and order by pointing without necessarily knowing the names; others have blackboards (see the lists below). **Tapas** are small portions, three or four small chunks of fish or meat, or a dollop of salad, which traditionally used to be served up free with a drink. These days you have to pay for anything more than a few olives, though a single helping rarely costs more than 50–150ptas unless you're somewhere very flashy. **Raciones** are simply bigger plates of the same, and can be enough in themselves for a light meal; *pinchos* (small kebabs) are often also available. (Make sure you always make it clear whether you want a *racion* or just a *tapa*). The more people you're with, of course, the better; half a dozen *tapas* or *pinchos* and three *raciones* can make a varied and quite filling meal for three or four people. If you're pushed for money, or just hungry, you can also order most *tapa/racion* fare as **bocadillos** (sandwiches in French rolls); some bars specialize in these, and you can often get them prepared (or get the materials to do so) at grocery shops.

Tascas, bodegas, cervecerías and **tabernas** are all types of bars where you'll find *tapas* and *raciones*. Most of them have different sets of prices depending on whether you stand at the bar to eat (the basic charge) or sit at tables (up to 50% more expensive — and even more if you sit out on a terrace). **Pubs**, incidentally, are ritzy modern bars where there is usually music and sometimes members-only admission; they rarely serve food.

The most usual **fillings for bocadillos** are *lomo* (loin of pork), *tortilla* and *calamares* (all of which may be served hot), *jamón* (York or, much better, *serrano*), *chorizo*, *salchichon* (and various other regional sausages — like the small, spicy Catalan *butifarras*), *queso* (cheese), and *atún* (probably canned).

Standard tapas and raciones might include:

Aceitunas	Olives
Albondigas	Meatballs
Anchoas	Anchovies
Berberechos	Cockles (a shellfish)
Boquerones	Mild anchovies
Calamares	Squid
Callos	Tripe
Caracoles	Snails
Carne en salsa	Meat in tomato sauce
Champiñones	Mushrooms
Chorizo	Sausage
Cocido	Stew

Empanadilla	Fish/meat turnover
Ensaladilla	Russian salad
Escalibada	Eggplant salad
Gambas	Shrimp
Habas	Beans
Habas con jamón	Beans with ham
Hígado	Liver
Huevo cocido	Hard-boiled egg
Jamón serrano	Cured ham
Jamón York	Fresh ham
Mejillones	Mussels
Navajas	Razor clams
Patatas Alli Olli	Potatoes in mayonaise
Patatas Bravas	Spicy potatoes
Pimientos	Peppers
Pincho moruno	Kebab
Pulpo	Octopus
Riñones al Jerez	Kidneys in sherry
Salchichon	Salami
Sepia	Cuttlefish
Tortilla Española	Potato omelet
Tortilla Francesa	Plain omelet

For **breakfast** you're probably better off in a bar or cafe too, though some *hostales* and *fondas* will serve the "Continental" basics. Traditionally, it's *churros con chocolate* — long tubular doughnuts (not for the weak of stomach) with thick drinking chocolate. But most places also serve *tostadas* (toasted rolls) with oil (*con aceite*) or butter (*con mantequilla: y mermelada*, and jam), or more substantial egg dishes (*huevos fritos* are fried eggs). Cold *tortilla* also makes an excellent breakfast.

Coffee and pastries (*pastas*) or doughnuts are available at most cafes too, though for a wider selection of cakes you should head for one of the many excellent *pastelerías* or *confiterías*. In larger towns, especially in Catalunya, there will often be a *panadería*, *croissantería*, or *pizzería* serving quite an array of appetizing (and healthier) baked goods besides the obvious bread, croissants, and pizza. For ordering coffee see *Drinks* following.

MEALS AND RESTAURANTS

Once again, there's a multitude of distinctions. You can sit down and have a full meal in a *comedor*, a *cafetería*, a *restaurante*, or a *marisquería* — all in addition to the more food-oriented bars.

Comedores are the places to seek out if your main criteria are price and quantity. Sometimes you will see them attached to a bar (often in a room behind), or as the dining room of a *pensión* or *fonda*, but as often as not they're virtually unmarked and spottable only if you pass an open door. Since they're essentially workers' cafes they tend to serve more substantial meals at lunchtime than in the evenings (when they may be closed altogether). When you can find them — the tradition, with its family-run business and marginal wages, is on the way out — you'll probably pay around 350–600ptas for a *cubierto*, or complete meal.

Replacing *comedores* to some extent, are **cafeterías**, which the local authorities now grade from one to three cups. These can be good value, too, especially the self-service places, but their emphasis is more northern European and the light snack-meals served tend to be a little dull. Food here often comes in the form of a *plato combinado* — literally a combined plate — which will be something like eggs and french fries or *calamares* and salad (or occasionally a weird combination like steak and a piece of fish), often with bread and a drink included. This, again, will generally cost in the region of 200–450ptas. *Cafeterías* often serve some kind of *menú del día* (see below) as well. You may prefer to get your *plato combinado* at a bar, and in small towns with no *comedores* or *menús del día* that will be the only place, and way, to eat inexpensively.

Moving up the scale there are **restaurantes** (designated by one to five forks) and **marisquerías**, the latter serving exclusively fish and seafood. Cheaper *restaurantes* are often not much different in price to *comedores*, and will also generally have *platos combinados* available. A fixed-price *cubierto*, *menú del día* or *menú de la casa* (all of which mean the same), is often better value, though: two or three courses plus wine and bread for 400–800ptas. In the less

expensive places ordering a la carte will bump the bill up not much more than 20% over the price of a *menú*. Move above two forks, however, or find yourself in one of the more fancy *marisquerías* (as opposed to a basic seafront fish-fry cafe), and prices can escalate rapidly. In addition, in all but the most rock-bottom establishments it is customary to leave a small tip; the amount is up to you, though 10percent of the tab is quite sufficient.

You'll find numerous recommendations, most geared towards the cheaper possibilities, in the main body of the guide. Spaniards generally eat very late, so most of these places serve food from around 1 until 4pm and from 8pm to midnight.

As with *tapas* and *raciones*, **restaurant dishes** vary enormously from region to region. The list below is no more than a selection, with the main Spanish dishes and a handful of local specialties. Wherever possible you'll do best by going for the latter; some are mentioned in the regional chapters that follow, others you'll simply see people eating. *Querría un tal plato* (I'd like a dish of that sort) can be an amazingly useful phrase . . .

BASICS

Pan	Bread
Mantequilla	Butter
Huevos	Eggs
Aceite	Oil
Pimienta	Pepper
Sal	Salt
Azucar	Sugar
Vinagre	Vinegar
Miel	Honey
Botella	Bottle
Vaso	Glass
Tenedor	Fork
Cuchillo	Knife
Cuchara	Spoon
Mesa	Table
La Cuenta	Bill

SOUPS (*SOPAS*)

Sopa de ajo	Garlic soup
Caldo	Broth
Sopa de mariscos	Seafood soup
Caldo de gallina	Chicken soup
Sopa de pescado	Fish soup
Caldo verde or gallego	Thick cabbage-based broth
Sopa de pasta (fideos)	Noodle soup
Sopa de cocido	Meat soup
Gazpacho	Cold tomato and cucumber soup
Caldillo	Clear fish soup

FISH (*PESCADOS*)

Anguila	Eel
Angulas	Elvers (baby eel)
Atún	Tuna
Bacalao	Cod (often salt)
Bonito	Bonito
Boquerones	Anchovies (mild)
Chanquetes	Whitebait
Congrio	Shark
Gallo	Rex sole
Jurelas	Like *boquerones*
Lenguado	Sole (sand dab)
Merluza	Hake
Mero	Perch
Pez espada	Swordfish
Rape	Monkfish
Raya	Ray, skate
Salmonete	Mullet
Sardinas	Sardines
Trucha	Trout

SEAFOOD (*MARISCOS*)

Almejas	Clams
Calamares	Squid
Centolla	Spider-crab
Cigalas	King prawns
Conchas finas	Large scallops
Gambas	Shrimp
Langosta	Lobster
Langostinos	Giant king prawns
Mejillones	Mussels
Necora	Sea-crab
Percebes	Goose-barnacles
Pulpo	Octopus
Sepia	Cuttlefish
Vieiras	Scallops
Merluza/Calamares a la Romana	Cod/squid (or just about anything else) fried in batter.
Calamares en su tinta	Squid in ink.
Paella	Classic Valencian dish with saffron rice, chicken, seafood etc.
Arroz a la banda	Similar to paella but with no chicken.
Zarzuela de mariscos	Seafood casserole.

MEAT (*CARNE*) AND POULTRY (*AVES*)

Callos	Tripe
Carne de vaca	Beef
Cerdo	Pork
Chuletas	Chops
Cochinillo	Suckling pig
Conejo	Rabbit
Codorniz	Quail
Cordero	Lamb
Criadillas	Testicles
Escalope/Milanesa	Breaded schnitzel
Hígado	Liver
Lengua	Tongue
Lomo	Loin (of pork)
Perdiz	Partridge
Pollo	Chicken
Pato	Duck
Pavo	Turkey
Riñones	Kidneys
Ternera	Veal
Habas con jamón	Ham and beans
Lazón con grelos	Pig's feet with turnips

Fabada Asturiana	Hot pot with butter beans, blood pudding, etc.
Fabes a la Catalana	Catalan version of the above

VEGETABLES (*VERDURAS y LEGUMBRES*)

Acelga	Chard
Alcachofas	Artichokes
Arroz	Rice
Berenjenas	Eggplant
Champiñones/Setas	Mushrooms
Coliflor	Cauliflower
Cebollas	Onions
Espinacas	Spinach
Garbanzos	Garbanzos
Grelos	Turnips
Habas	Broad beans
Judías blancas	Haricot beans
Judías verdes, rojas, negras	Green, red, black beans
Lechuga	Lettuce
Lentejas	Lentils
Patatas (fritas)	Potatoes (French fries)
Pepino	Cucumber
Pimientos	Peppers
Puerros	Leeks
Repollo	Cabbage
Tomate	Tomatoes
Zanahoria	Carrots
Arroz a la Cubana	Rice with banana and egg
Pimientos rellenos	Stuffed peppers
Ensalada (mixta/verde)	(Mixed/green) salad
Menestra/Panache de verduras	Vegetable medley
Pisto manchego	Ratatouille
Verduras con patatas	Boiled potatoes with greens

FRUIT (*FRUTAS*) AND SWEETS (*POSTRES*)

Albericoques	Apricots
Chirimoyas	Cherimoyas
Cerezas	Cherries
Ciruelas	Plums, prunes
Datiles	Dates
Fresas	Strawberries
Higos	Figs

Limón	Lemon
Manzanas	Apples
Melocotónes	Peaches
Melón	Melon
Naranjas	Oranges
Nectarinas	Nectarines
Peras	Pears
Piña	Pineapple
Plátanos	Bananas
Sandía	Watermelon
Toronja	Grapefruit
Uvas	Grapes
Arroz con leche	Rice pudding
Crema catalana	Catalan custard
Cuajada	Cream-based dessert served with honey
Flan	Creme caramel
Helados	Ice cream
Melocotón en almíbar	Peaches in syrup
Membrillo	Quince paste
Nata	Whipped cream (topping)
Natillas	Custard
Yogur	Yogurt

CHEESE

Cheeses (quesos) are on the whole local, though you'll get the hard, salty Queso manchego everywhere. Mild sheep's cheese (queso de oveja) from the province of León is widely distributed and also worth asking for.

SOME COMMON TERMS

al ajillo	in garlic
asado	roast
a la Navarra	stuffed with ham
a la parilla/plancha	grilled
a la Romana/rebozado	fried in egg batter
al horno	baked
alli olli	with mayonnaise
cazuela, cocido	stew
en salsa	in (usually tomato) sauce
frito	fried
guisado	casserole
rehogado	baked.
Soy vegeteriano. hay algo sin carne?	I'm a vegetarian. Is there anything without meat?

DRINKS

Vino (wine), either *tinto* (red), *blanco* (white), or *rosado/clarete* (rosé) is the invariable accompaniment to every meal and is, as a rule, extremely cheap. The most common bottled variety is *Valdepeñas*, a good standard wine from the central plains of New Castile; *Rioja*, from the area round Logroño, is better but a lot more expensive. Both are found all over the country. There are also scores of local wines — some of the best in Catalunya (*Bach, Sangre de Toro* and the champagne-like *Cava*) and Galicia (*Ribeiro* or *Fefiñanes*) — but you'll rarely be given any choice unless you're at a good restaurant. Otherwise it's whatever comes out of the barrel, or the house bottled special (ask for *caserío* or *de la casa*). This can be great, it can be lousy, but at least it will be distinctively local. In a bar a small glass of wine will generally cost around 30–50ptas: in a restaurant, if wine is not included in the menú, prices start at around 150ptas a bottle. If it is included you'll usually get a whole bottle for two people, a *media botella* (a third to a half of a liter) for one.

The classic Andalucian wine is **sherry** — *Vino de Jerez*. This is served chilled or at *bodega* temperature — a perfect drink to wash down *tapas* — and, as everything Spanish, comes in a perplexing variety of forms. The main distinctions are between *fino* or *Jerez seco* (dry sherry), *amontillado* (medium), and *oloroso* or *Jerez dulce* (sweet), and these are the terms you should use to order. Similar — though not identical — are *montilla* and *manzanilla*, dry sherry-like wines from the provinces of Córdoba and Huelva. These too are excellent and widely available.

Cerveza, lager-type beer, is generally pretty good, though more expensive than wine. It comes in 300-ml bottles (*botellines*) or, for about the same price, on tap — a *caña* of draft beer is a small glass, a *caña doble* larger. Many bartenders will assume you want a *doble*, so if you don't, say so. Equally refreshing, though often deceptively strong, is **sangría**, a wine-and-fruit punch which you'll come across at fiestas and in tourist bars.

In mid-afternoon — or even at breakfast — many Spaniards take a *copa* of **liqueur** with their coffee (for that matter many Spaniards drink wine and beer at breakfast, too). The best are *anis* (like Pernod) or *coñac*, excellent local brandy with a distinct vanilla flavor (try *Soberano*). Most **spirits** are ordered by brand name, since there are generally cheaper Spanish equivalents for standard imports. *Larios Gin* from Malaga, for instance, is about half the price (and at least two-thirds the strength) of a *Gin Gordons*. Almost any mixed drink seems to be collectively known as a *Cuba Libre*. Juice is *zumo*; orange, *naranja*; lemon, *limon*; tonic is *tónico*.

Soft drinks are much the same as anywhere in the world, but try in particular *granizado* (an iced fruit-squash) or *horchata* (a milky drink made from tiger nuts) from one of the street stalls which spring up everywhere in summer. You can also get these drinks from **horchaterías** and from **heladerías** (ice cream — *helados* — parlors), or in Catalunya from the wonderful milk bars known as *granjas*. Although you can drink the **water** almost everywhere it usually tastes better out of the bottle — inexpensive *agua mineral* comes either sparkling (*con gas*) or still (*sin gas*).

Coffee — served in cafes, *heladerías* and bars — is invariably espresso, slightly bitter and, unless you specify otherwise, served black (*cafe solo*). If you want it white ask for *café cortado* (small cup with a drop of milk) or *café con leche* (with considerably more). For a large cup ask for a *doble* or *grande*. Coffee is also frequently mixed with brandy, cognac, or whiskey, all such concoctions being called *carajillo*.

COMMUNICATIONS: MAIL, PHONES, AND MEDIA

POSTE RESTANTE AND MAIL

You can have letters sent **poste-restante** to any Spanish post office: they should be addressed (preferably with the surname underlined and in capitals) to *Lista de Correos* followed by the name of the town and province. To collect, take along your passport and, if you're expecting mail, ask the clerk to check under all of your names — letters are often to be found filed under Christian names.

American Express in Madrid and Barcelona will hold mail for a month for customers, and have special windows for mail pickup.

Post Offices (*Correos*) are generally found near the center of towns and are open from 8–12am and again from 5–7:30pm, though the branches in large cities have much more extended hours.

Outbound mail is reasonably reliable, with letters or cards taking around a week to ten days to get to North America.

PHONES

Spanish **phones** work well and you can make international calls direct from almost any cabin (marked *teléfono internacional*) or from *Telefónica* offices (where you pay afterwards). Rates are slighly cheaper after 10pm. Dial 07, wait for the International tone, then continue with the country code (1 for USA/Canada), the area code, and finally the local number. Cabins take 5-, 25-, or 100-peseta pieces — rest them in the groove at the top and they'll drop when someone answers. For international calls, make sure you have a good stock of 100-peseta pieces. Spanish provincial (and some overseas) dialing codes are displayed in the cabins; the standard Spanish response is *digáme* (speak to me).

MEDIA

British **newspapers** and the *International Herald Tribune* are on sale in most large cities and resorts. There's also a weekly Madrid English-language newspaper — the *Iberian Sun* — and several magazines produced by and for the expatriate communities on the *costas*, all are of limited interest though occasionally they carry details of local events and entertainment.

Of the **Spanish papers** the best is *El Pais* — liberal, supportive of the current government, and the only one with much serious analysis or foreign news coverage. The rest are mostly well out to the right. Most notorious is *El Alcázar* — openly aligned with *Fuerza Nueva* and the army extremists, it was deeply implicated in the 1981 Tejero coup, printing coded messages and, the day before, a photo of the Cortes captioned "Everything ready for Monday's action." Also on the right are *ABC*, solidly elitist with a hard moral line against divorce and abortion, and the Catholic *Ya*. *Diario 16* is fairly centrist. The regional press is generally run by local magnates and again right-wing, though often supporting local autonomy movements. Nationalist press includes *Avui* in Catalunya, printed largely in Catalan, and the Basque papers *Eja* and *Egin*, the latter a supporter of ETA, and mostly in Euskara.

If you have a **radio** which picks up short-wave you can tune in to the BBC World Service, broadcasting in English for most of the day on frequencies between 12MHz (24m) and 4MHz (75m).

BUSINESS HOURS AND HOLIDAYS

Almost everything in Spain — shops, museums, churches, tourist offices — closes for a siesta of at least two hours in the hottest part of the day. There's a lot of variation (and the siesta tends to be longer in the south) but basic summer working hours are 9:30am–1:30pm and 4:30–7:30pm. Certain shops do now stay open all day, and there is a move towards "normal" working hours. Nevertheless, you'll get far less aggravated if you accept that the early afternoon is best spent asleep, or in a bar, or both.

Museums, with very few exceptions, follow the rule above, with a break between 1 and 4 in the afternoon. Their summer schedules are listed in the guide; watch out for Sundays (most open mornings only) and Mondays (most close all day). Admission charges vary a lot but there's usually a big reduction or free entrance if you show an *ISIC* or *FIYTO* card.

Getting into **churches** can present more of a problem. The really important ones, including most cathedrals, operate in much the same way as museums and almost always have some entry charge to see their most valued treasures and paintings, or their cloisters. Other churches, though, are usually kept locked, opening only for worship in the early morning and/or the evening (between around 6–9pm). So you'll either have to try at these times, or find someone with a key.

This is time-consuming but rarely difficult, since a sacristan or custodian almost always lives nearby and most people will know where to direct you. You're expected to give a small tip, or donation. For all churches "decorous" dress is required, i.e. no shorts, bare shoulders, etc.

One other factor — **official holidays** and **local festivals** — can disrupt your plans. There are fourteen national holidays and scores of local ones (different in every town and village, usually marking the local saint's day); any of them will mean that everything except bars (and *hostales*, etc.) locks its doors. The nationwide legal holidays are: January 1, January 6 (Epiphany), Good Friday, Easter Sunday, Easter Monday, May 1, Corpus Christi (early or mid-June), June 24 (King's Name-Saint Day), July 25 (Feast of Santiago), August 15 (Assumption of the Virgin), October 12 (National Day), November 1 (All Saints), December 6 (Constitution Day), December 8 (Immaculate Conception), and Christmas Day.

In addition to all of these, **August** is Spain's designated vacation month, when the big cities — especially Madrid — are semi-deserted, and many of the shops and restaurants, even museums, close. In contrast it can prove nearly impossible to find a free bed in the more popular coastal and mountain resort at these times; similarly, seats on planes, trains, and buses should be booked well in advance .

FIESTAS, THE BULLFIGHT, AND SOCCER

It's hard to beat the experience of arriving in some small Spanish village, expecting nothing more than a bed for the night, to discover the streets decked out with flags and streamers, a band playing in the plaza and the entire population out celebrating the local fiesta. Everywhere in the country, from the tiniest hamlet to the great cities, will take at least one day off a year to devote to partying. Usually it's the local saint's day, but there are celebrations too of harvests, of deliverance from the Moors, of safe return from the sea — any excuse will do.

Each festival is different. In the Basque country there will often be bulls running through the streets, and the ancient Basque sports which resemble nothing so much as Scottish Highland games; in Andalucía horses, *flamenco* and the guitar are an essential part of any celebration; in Valencia you'll see stylized battles between Christians and Moors, huge bonfires, and stunning fireworks; but there is always music, dancing, traditional costumes, and an immense spirit of enjoyment. The main event of most fiestas is a parade, either behind a revered holy image, or a more celebratory affair with fancy costumes and *gigantones*, grotesque giant carnival figures which run down the streets terrorizing children!

Although these take place throughout the year — and it is often the obscure and unexpected event which proves to be most fun — there are certain occasions which stand out. **Easter Week** (*Semana Santa*) and **Corpus Christi** (in early June) are celebrated all over the country with magnificent religious processions. Easter, particularly, is worth trying to coincide with — head for Sevilla, Málaga, Granada, or Córdoba, where huge *pasos*, floats of wildly theatrical religious scenes, are carried down the streets, accompanied by weirdly hooded penitents atoning for the year's misdeeds. Among the biggest and best known of the other **popular festivals** are: the Cádiz *carnavales* (first to third week of February); The *Fallas de San José* in Valencia (12–19 March); Sevilla's enormous *April Feria* (last ten days of the month); Jerez's *Horse Fair* (early May); the *Romería del Rocío*, an extraordinary pilgrimage to El Rocío near Huelva (arriving there on Whitsunday); Pamplona's riotous *Fiesta de San Fermín*, most famous of the bull-runnings (6-14 July); the *Feast of St. James* at Santiago de Compostela (25 July); and the mock battles between *Christians and Moors* in Elche (10–15 August), ending with a centuries-old mystery play.

The list is potentially endless, and although you'll find the major events detailed at the end of each chapter we can't pretend that this is an exhaustive list. Local tourist offices should have more information about what's going on in their area at any given time. Outsiders are always welcome at Spanish festivals, the one problem being that during any of the most popular you'll find it difficult and expensive to find a bed. The usual solution is to live it up all night and sleep it off in a park by day.

> **Note** that saints' day festivals — indeed all Spanish celebrations — can **vary in date**, often being observed over the weekend closest to the dates given in our "Fiestas" listings at the ends of chapters.

THE BULLFIGHT

Bullfights are an integral part of many Spanish festivals. In the south, especially, any village that can afford it will put on a **corrida** for an afternoon; in big cities like Madrid or Sevilla, the main festival times are accompanied by a week-long (or more) season of prestige fights.

In recent years bullfights, which were anathema to many younger Spaniards during their years of patronage under Franco, have staged something of a comeback, with the elaborate language of the *corrida* becoming quite a cult. Though bullfights are quite obviously cruel and often squalid, few people are as horrified by the event as they expect to be. You're as likely to be bored and confused by your first bullfight as sickened. If you go to a few it's easy to become hooked — easy, too, to forget that what you're witnessing is the ritual slaughter of six animals. If you do decide to go, here's a brief guide.

There are basically three stages to **the fight** itself: the *suerte de picar* in which a mounted *picador* drives his short-pointed lance into the bull's neck and gets it to try to toss his padded, blindfolded horse, thus tiring the bull's powerful neck and back muscles; the *suerte de banderillas* in which three *banderilleros* dodge the bull's charge and plant their barbed darts in his back; and the *suerte de matar* when the *matador* exhibits his fancy skills on the exhausted animal before getting it into a position where he can drive a sword between its shoulders and straight through to the heart for an instant kill. In practice you're unlikely to see a single bull killed cleanly in an entire afternoon.

A normal bullfight will work through six bulls in this way, have three matadors, each with his own team of assistants, and can last for as long as three hours. For a really good kill the matador is awarded the bull's ears or tail — the better the display, the more pieces he gets. If he is playing a bull particularly well the band will strike up and accompany the action.

Seats are all expensive (1000ptas and up); the cheapest are *gradas*, the highest rows at the back, from where you can see everything that happens without too much of the gory detail. Front row *barreras* are only for the really bloodthirsty. Seats are also divided into *sol* (sun), *sombra* (shade), and *sol y sombra* (which becomes shaded after a while).

SOCCER

To foreigners, the bullfight is easily the most celebrated of Spain's spectacles. In terms of popular support in modern Spain, however, it ranks far below soccer. If you want the excitement of a genuinely Spanish afternoon out, a stadium will have infinitely more atmosphere than anything you'll find in the Plaza de Toros. Soccer matches are pretty easy to get to — just follow the crowds to the game. We've given details of stadiums for the big teams in Madrid and Barcelona, *Real Madrid, Atletico Madrid,* and *FC Barcelona*, which continue to dominate domestic soccer as they have for much of the past forty years. Other good league teams to catch on your travels around the country could include *Atletico Bilbao, Sporting Gijon, Real Sociedad* (San Sebastian), and *Real Betis* (Sevilla).

MUSIC AND MOVIES

MUSIC

An account of Spain's diverse musics appears in the *Contexts* section of this guide. Enough to say, here, that you should catch all that is going. Traditional **flamenco** — the country's most famous sound — is best witnessed in its native Andalucía, and particularly at one of the major fiestas. There are also some specifically *flamenco* festivals in the summer, most notably at Cartagena and around Granada. Clubs and bars which feature *flamenco* performers tend on the whole to be expensive and tourist-oriented, while the traditional *peñas* (clubs) are often members-only affairs. However it is possible to find accessible places which cater for aficionados, and in Andalucía itself almost any flamenco guitarist you come across is likely to be extremely good. Just watch the cost of the drinks.

If you're anywhere in Spain between about December 18 and January 3, watch for performances in local churches of **villancicos.** These are Christmas carols in local style — they can be *flamenco*, waltz, or polyphonic — and are sung by fairly large *coral/rondalla* groups of instrumentalists and vocalists of both sexes. When they're good they're extremely beautiful, and it's obviously a non-boozy, family-oriented spectacle.

Rock music in Spain may tend to follow British and American trends, but the scene is considerably livelier — and less slavishly derivative — than in almost any other west European country, at its best drawing from a broad range of influences in which traditional Spanish and Latin American rhythms play a major part. There are some excellent home-grown bands and regular gigs in most of the big cities, especially in the north. At present Madrid seems to have the most original bands, and you'll find the more promising clubs and venues listed in the following chapter. Both Madrid and Barcelona attract major international concerts from time to time, usually staged in their giant football stadiums. Wherever you are, keep an eye out for posters or check the entertainments sections in the local press — you'll find local bands airing their talents at just about any fiesta.

Because of relatively large expatriate populations, Madrid and Barcelona are also good places to hear **Latin American and African** music — again, keep your eye out for wall posters and check the club and dance-hall listings in the local papers.

Jazz also has a considerable following, and there are several excellent jazz festivals through the summer: notably in San Sebastián in the middle of July, and in Barcelona, Santander, and Sitges. Worth checking out too is the International **Festival of Guitar** in Córdoba (early July), where most of the great classical guitarists put in an appearance along with exponents of Latin American and *flamenco* styles. Among its more adventurous practitioners, *flamenco* (to the outrage of purists) touches on modern jazz — look out especially for the brilliant Paco de Lucia.

MOVIES

Movie-going remains a remarkably cheap and popular entertainment, with crowded theaters in every town. The majority of what's screened is the usual Hollywood fare poorly dubbed into Spanish, but in the cities you will find more exciting options and some films in their original language with subtitles. Look for *voz* or *version original* (*subtitulada*), abbreviated 'v.o.', in the listings; 'v.e.' means *version Español*.

Spanish film has itself been flourishing as never before since the end of censorship, though its most famous figure still seems to be the late **Luis Buñuel**, most of whose work was completed in exile in France and Mexico. His pre-World War II collaborations with Salvador Dali, *El Perro Andaluz* (*Un Chien Andalou*) and *L'Age d'Or* are surrealist masterpieces. After these came a succession of great, relatively conventional films, of which *The Discreet Charm of the Bourgeoisie* (1972) and *That Obscure Object of Desire* (1977) are perhaps the best known. Of currently active directors, **Carlos Saura** must be the best known; his recent films *Blood Wedding* and *Carmen* are extraordinary amalgams of film, *flamenco* and (in the latter case) opera. **Victor Erice** is a name to look out for too, in the wake of his obsessive, slow-paced dramas like *The Spirit of the Beehive* and *The South*. Regional film is perhaps best represented by the *Diamond Square*, a 1982 production by Catalunya's Francesco Betriu, in which the life of a Catalan woman is traced from the 1920s through the grim post-civil-war years. Hottest contemporary director of all is **Pedro Almodovar** (*Law of Desire; Woman on the Edge of a Nervous Breakdown*), dubbed "the Spanish John Walters" for his bizarre backdrops of transexuality, homoeroticism, and traditional Spanish life.

TROUBLE, THE POLICE, AND SEXUAL HARASSMENT

While you're unlikely to encounter any trouble during the course of a normal visit, it's worth remembering that the Spanish police, polite enough in the usual course of events, can be extremely unpleasant if you get on the wrong side of them. There are three basic types: the Guardia Civil, the Policía Municipal, and the Policía Nacional, all of them armed.

The **Guardia Civil**, in green uniforms and ridiculous patent-leather hats, are the most officious and the ones to avoid. Though their role has been cut back since the days when they operated as Franco's right hand, they remain a reactionary force (it was a *Guardia Civil* colonel, Tejero, who held the Cortes hostage in the failed coup of February 1981). If you do need the police — and above all if you're reporting a serious crime such as rape — you should always go instead to the more sympathetic **Policía Municipal**. In the countryside there may be only the *Guardia*; though they're usually helpful, they are inclined to resent the suggestion that any crime exists on their turf and you may end up feeling as if you are the one who stands accused. The **Policía Nacional** are mainly seen in cities, armed with submachine guns and guarding key installations such as embassies, stations, post offices, and their own barracks. They are also the force used to control crowds and demonstrations. In Euskadi there exists an additional autonomous Basque police force, distinguished by their red *boinas* or berets.

Nude bathing or **unauthorized camping** are the activities most likely to bring you into contact with officialdom, though a warning to cover up or move on is more likely than any real confrontation. **Topless** tanning is commonplace at all the trendier resorts — above all in the Balearics — but in country areas, where attitudes are still very prudish, you should take care not to upset local sensibilities.

In theory you're supposed to carry **identification** at all times, and the police can stop you in the streets and demand it. In practice they're rarely bothered if you're clearly a foreigner.

A more common source of trouble for travelers is **petty theft**, which has risen to almost epidemic proportions in cities like Sevilla and Barcelona — home, sadly, to widespread heroin use. In general, if you take normal precautions, and aren't be too sloppy with waving money around, you've little to worry about. If you should be attacked hand over the money and start contacting your lost credit-card hotline, travelers' check representative, etc. if necessary.

Drivers face greater problems, most notoriously from break-ins. Vehicles are rarely stolen, but luggage and valuables left in cars do make a tempting target and rental cars are easy to spot. Adequate insurance is the only sure answer, but never leave anything of value in the car even so. If you have an **accident** while driving, try not to make a statement to anyone who doesn't speak English. The SNTO in your home country can provide a list of the most important rules on the road in Spain.

Spanish **drug laws** are in a somewhat bizarre state at present. After the socialists came to power in 1983, cannabis use (possession of up to 8gm of what the Spanish call *chocolate*) was made a decriminalised offence. Subsequent pressures, and an influx of harder drugs, have changed that policy and — in theory at least — any drug use is now forbidden. However, the police are in practice little worried about personal use. Larger quantities (and any other drugs) are a very different matter. If you visit Morocco, don't even think of bringing back the local specialties.

Should you be **arrested** on any charge you have the right to contact your **consulate** (see the *Directory*), and although they're notoriously reluctant to get involved they are required to assist you to some degree if you have your passport stolen or lose all your money.

SEXUAL HARASSMENT

There are so many oppressive limitations imposed on women's freedom to travel that any 'warnings' seem merely to reinforce the situation. That said, almost everyone agrees that sexual harassment is a more constant, and at times more threatening, problem than in most of the rest of western Europe. You get commented on almost as a matter of course, and without very clear understanding of Spanish it's hard to know the different levels this can take. Consequently, it can be hard to deal with situations that you'd cope with quite routinely at home.

All these problems are at their worst on the **Mediterranean coast**, where loads of macho Spaniards converge in search of "easy" tourists. On the north coast, where tourism remains predominantly Spanish, it's not on the whole so bad. Most women experience the most constant and direct harassment in Andalucía, where the classic images of male machismo are very much a part of life.

It takes a lot of confidence for women to **hitch** in Spain, especially on the coast. Cars do, however, stop quite frequently so it's possible to pick your rides (always ask where they are going before volunteering information yourself). The same applies for **camping outside authorized campgrounds**. In villages it's usually best to ask people if and where you can camp, thus making yourself known and accepted rather than just "some foreigner in the field"; you may even be offered a free room or yardspace.

WORK

Unless you've some particular skill and have applied for a job advertised in your home country, the only real chance of long-term work in Spain is in language schools or with a family as an au pair. There is a positive mania for learning English in Spain, and any college-educated, native speaker, Spanish-speaking or not, should, with persistence, be able to get a job teaching it. If you have a TEFL (Teaching of English as a Foreign Language) or ESL (English as a Second Language) certificate, you could end up with a position in 48 hours or less.

Finding a teaching job is mainly a question of pacing the streets, stopping in at every language school around and asking about vacancies. You may be employed on a semiofficial level, but problems are rare; in the big cities there's almost always a shortage of teachers. For the addresses of schools look in the Yellow Pages under *Idiomas* or *Escuelas Idiomas*. You could also try advertising **private lessons** (better paid at 1200-1800ptas an hour) on the *Philologia* noticeboards of university faculties. When working for an academy, never accept an hourly rate of less than 800ptas.

Another very good possibility, so long as you've got reasonable Spanish, is **translation work**, most of which will be business correspondence — look in the Yellow Pages under *Traductores*. Your best chances for both types of work will be in Madrid, Barcelona, Salamanca, or Granada — the latter especially for translating.

Work as an **au pair** can be arranged through various agencies, while individuals advertise in the national paper *El Pais* and in the Madrid Catholic paper *Ya* (look under *Trabajo*). One of the most reliable agenices is the *International Cultural Relations Agency* (c/Miguel Angel 13 3°, Madrid 10; ☎91/4193216). No work permit is needed for au pair work .

TEMPORARY WORK

If you're looking for **temporary work** while you're in Spain the best chances are in the **bars and restaurants** of the big Mediterranean resorts. This may help you have a good time but it's unlikely to bring in very much money; pay (often from British bar owners) will reflect your lack of official status or work permit. If you turn up in spring and are willing to stay through the season you might get a better deal — also true if you're offering some special skill like windsurfing (there are "schools" sprouting up all along the coast).

Quite often there are jobs at **yacht marinas**, too, scrubbing down and repainting the boats of the rich. The SET publishes a map-list of yacht clubs and marinas, richest of which is Puerto Bañus near Marbella; just turn up and ask around, especially from March until June.

As a foreigner you've no hope at all of work on **harvests** — France is much more viable. **Students**, however, can get various types of community work through the *Viajesu* agency in Madrid (c/Fernandes de los Rios; near Moncloa metro). Much of this is very low-paid, often food and bed only, but it can be an interesting way to spend the summer and learn Spanish.

DIRECTORY

ADDRESSES are written as: c/Picasso 2, 4°
izda. — which means Picasso street (*calle*) no. 2,
4th floor, left- (*izquierda*) hand apartment or
office; dcha. (*derecha*) is right; cto. (*centro*)
center. Other confusions in Spanish addresses
result from the different spellings, and sometimes words, used in Catalan, Basque, and
Gallego — all of which are to some extent
replacing their Castilian counterparts — and
from the gradual removal of Franco and other
fascist heroes from the main *avenidas* and
plazas. On this latter front, Avenidas del Generalissimo are on the way out all over the country
(often changing to "Libertad" or "España"); so too
are José Antonios, General Molas, Falanges, and
Caudillos. Note that a lot of maps — including
the official SET ones (and even, on occasion,
ours) — haven't yet caught up; nor have a handful of right-wing-controlled towns. In some towns
dual numbering systems are in effect, and looking at the plates it's difficult to tell which is the old
and which the new scheme.

AIRPORT TAX You can happily spend your last
pesetas — there's no departure tax.

BAGGAGE If you are camping, or traveling long-
term, you may need a backpack, but for shorter
visits you're better off with something smaller
and lighter. A nylon duffel bag is big enough to
hold a sleeping bag and adequate clothes, and
much easier to load on buses, trains, and planes.

BRING . . . Film and tampons are expensive in
Spain; an alarm clock is useful for early-morning
rural buses (often the only one of the day); a

flashlight is good for campgrounds and caves;
concentrated liquid travel-wash saves money,
space and spills; and a universal plug makes it
easier to use.

CONSULATES U.S. citizens will find themselves
represented in Madrid, Barcelona, Sevilla, and
Valencia. Canadians have only their embassy in
Madrid. See under "Listings" in these cities.

CONTRACEPTIVES Condoms no longer need to
be smuggled into Spain — as during the Franco
years. Along with the pill (prescription only),
they're available from most *farmacías* and
increasingly from vending machines in the trendier bars — AIDS (*SIDA*) has very definitely
reached Spain.

CUSTOMS The usual import regulations (2
bottles of liquor, 4 of wine, 200 cigarettes, 50
cigars, etc.) apply if you're coming directly from
North America, half those levels if coming from
Europe. Additionally, you can only take 100,000
ptas out of the country unless you can prove you
brought more in in the first place. Don't attempt
to smuggle drugs in, especially from Morocco.

ELECTRICITY Current in most of Spain is 220
volts AC (just occasionally it's still 110V). North
Americans will need to bring both a 220-to-110-
volt step-down transformer *and* a plug adaptor
with a round, two-pin end. as long as you have an
adaptor for European-style two-pin plugs.

FEMINISM The Spanish women's movement,
despite having to deal with incredibly basic
issues (like trying to get contraception available
on social security), is radical, vibrant, and growing fast. Few groups, however, have permanent
offices and if you want to make contact it's best
to do so through the network of feminist bookshops in the major cities. Some of the more
established are: **Madrid** — *Libreria de Mujeres*,
c/San Cristóbal 17 (near Plaza Mayor);
Barcelona — *Libreria de les Dones*, c/Llado 10;
Valencia — Libreria Dona, c/Gravador Esteve
34; **Sevilla** Libreria Feminista, c/Zaragoza 36;
Granada — *Libreria Mujer*, c/Carnicería 1.

FISHING Fortnightly permits are easily and
cheaply obtained from any *ICONA* office —
there's one in every big town (addresses from the
local *Turismo*).

GAY LIFE Ibiza is now Europe's major gay resort,
surpassing even Greek Mykonos, and attitudes

there, and in the major cities and resorts, are fairly relaxed. Madrid, Barcelona, and Cádiz in particular have large gay communities and a thriving scene. The age of consent is 18.

HOSPITAL EMERGENCIES Dial 091.

KIDS/BABIES don't pose great travel problems. *Hostales, pensiones,* and *restaurantes* generally welcome them and offer reductions; *RENFE* allows children under three to travel free on trains, with half price for those under seven; and some cities and resorts — Barcelona is particularly good — have long lists or special pamphlets on kids' attractions. As far as babies go, food seems to work out quite well (*hostales* often prepare food specially — or will let you use the kitchen to do so) though you might want to bring powdered milk — babies, like most Spaniards, are pretty contemptuous of the UHT (ultra heat-treated) stuff generally available. If you're traveling in the north, or out of season, however, bear in mind that most *hostales* (as opposed to more expensive hotels) don't have any heating systems — and it can get cold. Disposable diapers are very widely available; sterilizing tablets, etc. shouldn't really be necessary. Many *hostales* will be prepared to baby-sit, or at least to listen out for trouble. This is obviously more likely if you're staying in an old-fashioned family-run place than in the fancier hotels.

LANGUAGE COURSES are offered at most Spanish universities, and in a growing number of special language schools for foreigners. For details overseas and a complete list write to a branch of the *Spanish Institute* — addresses from the nearest SET.

LAUNDRIES You'll find a few self-service laundromats (*lavanderías automáticas*) in the major cities but they're rare — you normally have to leave your clothes for the full (and somewhat expensive) works. Note that you're not allowed by law to leave laundry hanging out of windows over a street. A dry cleaner is a *tintorería*.

LUGGAGE CONSIGNMENT After a long period of absence following terrorist actions in the late 1970s, self-service *consignas* are back at most important Spanish railway stations. You'll find lockers large enough to hold most backpacks, plus a smaller bag to boot, which cost about 125ptas a day. (Put the coin in to free the key). These are not a viable alternative for long-term storage however, as they're periodically emptied out by station staff. Bus terminals have manned *consignas* where you present a claim stub to get your gear back; cost is about the same.

SKIING There are resorts in the Pyrenees, Sierra Nevada, and outside Madrid and Santander, all detailed in the relevant chapters. The SNTO's "Skiing in Spain" pamphlet is also useful. If you want to arrange a weekend or more while you're in Spain, *Viajes Ecuador* (the biggest travel firm in the country, with branches in most cities) are good for arranging cheap all-inclusive trips.

SWIMMING POOLS Most Spanish towns — even quite small places — have a *piscina,* a life-saver in the summer and yet another reason not to keep exclusively to the coast.

TAMPONS *Tampónes* are available from *farmacías* — but at nearly twice the North American cost.

TIME Spain is six hours ahead of eastern standard time, nine hours ahead of pacific standard time, etc. Daylight saving is observed from the last week in March until the last week in September, so for most of October knock an hour off of the differences cited above.

TOILETS Public ones are averagely clean but very rarely have any paper (best to carry your own). They're often squat-style. The most common euphemisms are *baños* (literally "bathrooms"), *servicios, retretes,* or *sanitarios. Damas* (Ladies) and *Caballeros* (Gentlemen) are the usual gender signs, though you may also see the confusing *Señoras* (Women) and *Señores* (Men).

Metric Weights and Measures

1 ounce = 28.3 grams	1 inch = 2.54 centimeters (cm)
1 pound = 454 grams	1 foot = 0.3 meters (m)
2.2 pounds = 1 kilogram	1 yard = 0.91 meters
1 pint = 0.47 liters	1.09 yards = 1m
1 quart = 0.94 liters	1 mile = 1.61 kilometers (km)
1 gallon = 3.78 liters	0.62 miles = 1km

PART TWO

THE

GUIDE

CHAPTER ONE

MADRID AND AROUND

Madrid lies almost at the exact center of Spain, capital more by geographical accident then as a result of any intrinsic virtues. When Felipe II moved the seat of government here in 1561 he raised the town from relative obscurity, not only because its climate was good for his gout, but to create a symbol of the unification and centralization of the country. With few natural advantages — Madrid is

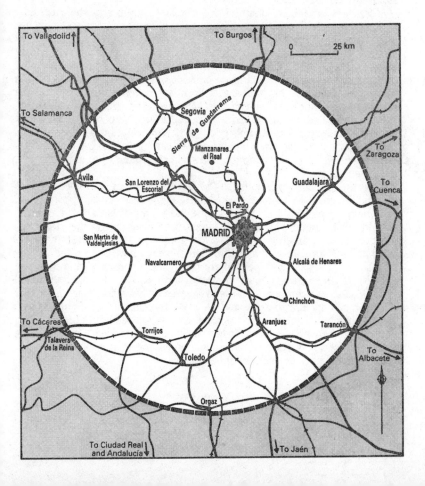

300km from the sea on a 650-meter-high plateau, freezing in winter, burning in summer, and with no river to speak of — it has been only the determination of successive rulers to maintain and promote a strong, central capital that has produced the vast modern city of today, with a population of some five million.

For all their efforts, Madrid has never compared in terms of historic or architectural interest with the "Great Cities" of Spain: Sevilla, Toledo, Granada. Its single obvious lure is the **Prado**, which with its unrivaled collections of Bosch, Goya, and Velázquez (and, since 1981, Picasso's *Guernica*) ranks among the finest art galleries in the world. While "sights" may be thin on the ground, Madrid is a fascinating, complex city in its own right, and a place that grows in stature as you get to know it. For what the city lacks in monuments is more than made up for by its inhabitants. At night, when the streets come alive with a thousand **bars**, clubs, discos, and *tascas*, there's an amazingly dynamic (and diverse) scene.

Madrileños, as the residents of the city are known, are wholeheartedly determined to have a good time. They need little prompting — any excuse will do — to go out for a drink, a meal, a dance or just to *pasear* (stroll around). Perhaps life inside a cramped Madrid apartment encourages people to take to the streets, though every observer of the past century has noted this trait. Whatever, there are more bars in some streets in Madrid than in the whole of Norway; clubs that stay open way beyond breakfast time; and restaurants where two of you can stuff yourselves and still have change from a 2000-peseta note to take a taxi home. You'll find the best of Spain's rock bands in the capital (and some good jazz, too) while on a different level there's the **Rastro**, the city's famous and sprawling flea-market, and a traditional **street life** based around the cafes and *chocolaterías*, or in summer on the open *terrazas*.

Even the lack of monuments isn't in fact too much of a loss, for within a remarkably small radius of the capital are some of the country's greatest. **Toledo**, above all, is a storehouse of the most magnificent art and architecture in Spain. Immortalized by El Greco, who lived and worked there for most of his later career, the town is a living museum to the many cultures — Visigothic, Islamic, Jewish, and Christian — which have shaped the destiny of Spain. **Segovia** and **El Escorial** are hardly less impressive. And there are smaller places too, less known to foreign tourists, like the beautiful walled city of **Ávila**, or **Aranjuez**, an oasis in the parched Castilian plain, famed for its asparagus, its strawberries, and its lavish baroque palace. None of these are much more than an hour from the capital. On the natural level, when you've had enough of the oven-like heat and consequent smog of mid-summer Madrid, two minor mountain ranges, the sierras of **Gredos** and **Guadarrama**, provide a convenient escape.

MADRID

Coming into modern **MADRID** can be a depressing experience, for in recent years it has come to be surrounded by some of the world's ugliest suburbs, acres of high-rise concrete seemingly dumped without thought onto the dustiest parts of the plain. Don't get too depressed, though, as the middle of town is nothing like this. In its newer parts, the Spanish capital has followed the usual pattern of international urban development, with wide boulevards, high-rises, and a grid street system. The great spread to suburbia was encouraged under Franco, who also extended the city northwards along the spinal route of the Paseo de la Castellana, to accommodate his ministers and minions during development orgies of the 1950s and 1960s. Large, impressive, and unbelievably sterile, these constructions leave little to the imagination.

The city's development from its inorganic beginnings owes much to the French tastes of the Bourbon dynasty in the eighteenth century, when for the first time Madrid began to develop a style and flavor of its own. The Royal Palace, Tapestry Factory and Library were all built at this time. The early nineteenth century brought invasion and turmoil to Spain as Napoleon established his brother, Joseph, on the throne. Madrid, however, continued to flourish, gaining some very attractive buildings and squares. With the onset of the twentieth century, the capital became the hotbed of the political and intellectual discussion which divided the country; *tertulias* (political/philosophical discussion circles) sprang up in cafes across the city (some of them are still going) as the country entered into the turbulent years of the end of the monarchy and the foundation of the Second Republic. The civil war, of course, led to forty years of isolation, and for a modern capital city, Madrid can still seem surprisingly provincial. It is not yet used to, nor does it cater to, foreigners or visitors in the manner of London or Paris. But attitudes are changing rapidly, especially since entry into the European Community, seen by many as a sign of Spain's acceptance into the European mainstream.

Since Franco, Madrid has set itself a new course for cultural expansion and entered the 1980s as arguably the most progressive city in Europe. Its late mayor actively urged young people to use the city as an inspiration and, with official encouragement and subsidy, music, film, art, and design all flourished tremendously. The results of this *"Movida Madrileña"* are now seen on an international level. Equally importantly, since the return to democracy, the natural predilection of the *Madrileño* for going out and having a good time has blossomed into an art form; when the excuses run dry, an impending fiesta will conveniently provide a new one.

Orientation

The layout of Madrid is pretty straightforward. At the heart of the city — indeed at the very heart of Spain since all distances in the country are measured from here — is the **Puerta del Sol**. Around it lie the oldest parts of Madrid, neatly bounded to the west by the river (though the Manzanares barely deserves the name, drying to the merest trickle in summer), and on

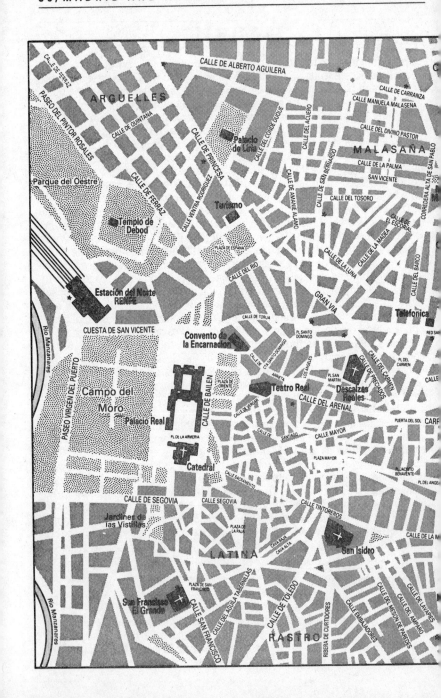

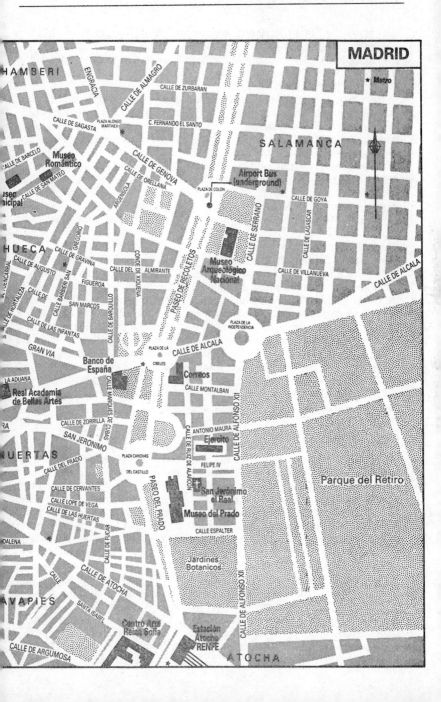

the east by the **Retiro Park** and, beyond that, the M30 expressway. Modern Madrid heads north, its axis a long boulevard (the Paseo de la Castellana) stretching from the center to the northern train station of Chamartín. Outer suburbs and satellite *urbanizaciones* surround the main hub of the city, but hold no great allure for visitors.

The city's historical development is equally easy to follow; south of the Puerta del Sol lie what remain of the sixteenth-century developments of the Habsburg kings, the **Plaza Mayor,** and the cramped streets around it leading down to the Rastro. North as far as the Gran Vía (still marked on some maps as the Avenida de José Antonio) extends the area opened up by the Bourbons in the eighteenth century, along with the **Royal Palace** and the **Prado,** equidistant to the west and east respectively from the Puerta del Sol. In architectural terms, the farther from the center you venture, the less interesting the city becomes; but in terms of appreciating Madrid, you'll find the bars and the vitality of some of the outlying areas make them well worth visiting.

Points of Arrival

If this is your first stop in Spain, you are likely to arrive some way from downtown. The **airport** is 16km out of town but regularly connected by bus; it takes about half an hour and the terminal is the underground parking lot in the Plaza Colón, with pedestrian entrance from the c/de Goya. **Trains** from France arrive at the *Estación de Chamartín,* the second newest of Madrid's stations but rather isolated in the north of the city. A metro line connects it with the center, plus there are regular connections by *tranvía* with the *Estación de Atocha* (for travel to Andalucía or Portugal). Take any *tranvía* headed in that direction. **Bus terminals** are scattered through the city, but the largest — used by all international services — is the *Estación Sur de Autobuses* (c/Canarias 17; Metro *Palos de la Frontera*), five blocks south of Atocha down the Paseo de las Delicias.

Getting Around

By far the easiest way of getting around within Madrid is by **Metro,** and the system serves most places you're likely to want to get to. It runs from 6am until nearly 2am with a flat fare (currently) of 60 pesetas. You can get a free color map of the system (*Plano del Metro*) at any station, rather clearer than our black-and-white illustration. The urban **bus network** is more comprehensive but also more complicated and slightly more costly (smaller microbuses charge marginally more again). Where there's no metro stop we've indicated which bus to take, otherwise you'll simply have to ask; there's an information kiosk in the Plaza de Cibeles, whose advice you should trust before that of any obsolete handout, since the lines were all reorganized in late 1988. Like the metro, buses run until almost 2am but there are also several all-night lines around the central area. At night, though, it's very much safer to take a **taxi** — there are thousands of them and they're surprisingly cheap.

If you're using public transportation extensively there are a few useful ways of saving money. You can buy "*Bonobus*" **passes** from various outlets around

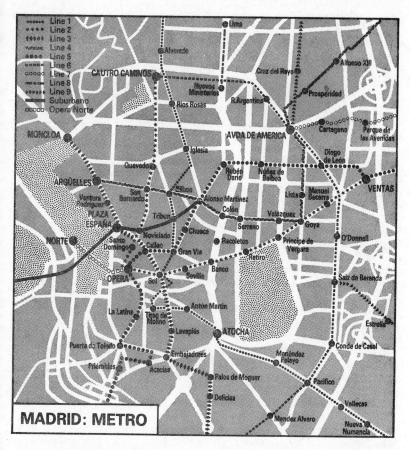

town which give you ten journeys for 450ptas. Any metro station sells a strip card, good for ten underground journeys and valid until used for 410ptas. Alternatively there are monthly passes if you're planning to stay a while, but these must be ordered before the month in question, and put into service before the tenth of the month. The three- and five-day *Metrotour* passes were abolished in the 1988 public transit shuffle but it's worth asking if they've been reinstated.

Turismo offices giving free maps and info can be found at the Airport (Barajas) in International Arrivals (☎91/5221165; Mon.–Sat. 8am–8pm, Sun. 12:30–5pm), in the Torre de Madrid in the Plaza de España (c/Princesa 1; ☎91/2412325; Mon.–Fri. 9am–7pm, Sat. 9:30am–1:30pm), at c/Duque de Medinaceli 2 (☎91/4294630; Mon.–Fri. 9am–3pm), and in the Chamartín station. There's also a municipal tourist office at Plaza Mayor 3(☎91/2665477; Mon.–Fri. 10am–1:30pm and 4–7pm, Sat. 10am–1:30pm). You can buy indexed street **maps** from kiosks throughout the city center.

Accommodation

The various *Turismo* offices can also help you find **somewhere to stay**, but their lists are far from complete and in any case it's a service which you shouldn't really need; once you start to look there's an astonishing amount of cheap accommodation available in the old town. Many buildings in the more popular areas house two or three separate *hostales* or *fondas*, each on a separate floor or floors. If you're staying slightly longer term, you'll find that there is a great deal of temporary accommodation, usually reasonably priced, available to rent.

Pensiones and *Hostales*

Probably the cheapest accommodation of all is to be found in the area immediately **around the Estación de Atocha**, though many of the places closest to the station are rather grim dives, crowded with migrants from the south looking for work, and at night the area can feel threatening. Better to head up Calle Atocha towards the center, where you'll find better pickings above all in the streets surrounding the **Plaza Santa Ana**.

The *Pensión Mollo* (c/Atocha 104; ☎91/2287176), close to the station on the way up, or the *Hostal Buelta* (in c/Drumen, first to the left as you walk up; ☎91/2399807) aren't bad if you're heavily laden, but c/León, c/del Principe, and c/de Echegaray all offer several more attractive options, while c/Cruz and c/Espoz y Mina, just beyond the Plaza Santa Ana, are literally packed with possibilities. Many of these are largely occupied by long-term guests, but on the whole they put out signs when full, saving fruitless searches up many flights of stairs. There's little point picking out individual places when there are so many (and so small in terms of bed capacity) but ones we have enjoyed include: *CH Marcelino* (c/Cruz 27), *Hostal Regional* (c/del Principe 18; ☎91/2223373), *Pensión Marrón* (c/León 32; ☎91/2394650), *Hostal Alonso* (c/Espoz y Mina 17; ☎91/2915679), and *Hostal Escadas* (c/Echegaray 5; ☎91/4296381).

If you're prepared to pay slightly more you could try along the **Carrera de San Jerónimo** — where nos. 3, 11, 18, and 32 house various *hostales* — or even the **Paseo del Prado** itself, very close to Madrid's most expensive hotels, where the *Hostal Sud-Americana* (Paseo del Prado 12; ☎91/4292564) is surprisingly reasonable.

Again more expensive, but with one of the higher concentration of possibilities in Madrid, is the **Gran Vía**. The huge old buildings here hide an array of choices at every price, often with a delightfully decayed elegance, though frequently also extremely noisy from outside traffic. Among the cheapest are — starting from the east — no.12, especially the *Hostal Delfina* (4th floor; ☎91/2226423); nos. 44 and 50, each with several; and no.61, near the Plaza de España, where the *Alcázar Regis* (☎91/2479317) is rightly extremely popular, and often full.

North of the Gran Vía, especially up c/**Fuencarral** and in the streets leading off it to either side, you'll find another fertile area. Though this seems rather out-of-the-way it actually has a lot going for it: considerably quieter than places south of Gran Vía, with a small-town atmosphere and a staggering number of reasonably priced restaurants, and handily placed between the main sights and the Malasaña area where some of the livelier nightlife is. Possibilites on Fuencarral itself include the *Hostal Zamoran* (no.18; ☎91/2322060), *Hostal Ribadavia* (no.25; ☎91/2311058), the *CH Corrales* (no. 41), and *Hostales Sil* (☎91/4488972) and *Serrano* (☎91/4488987 — both at No.95). Fuencarral, however, can be almost as noisy as the Gran Vía, especially if you have a room facing the street, and it's well worth considering a spot on one of the side streets. Just west are two streets running parallel, Valverde and Barco; near their Gran Vía ends they're expensive and a bit sleazy, but up toward the Plaza de San Ildefonso there are some okay *pensiones* and *casas de huéspedes*; *Hostal Lopez* at Barco 25 (☎91/2210432) and *Pensión Alfayate* at Valverde 44 (☎91/2329170) are about as far down these streeets as you'd want to go. About halfway up Fuencarral, c/Santa Bárbara 2 has the *Hostal Comercio* (☎2310091), or there's the *Hostal Residencia Dominguez* (c/de Santa Brígida 1; ☎91/2321547) on the opposite side of Fuencarral. A bit farther up still, in the streets leading west from Metro *Tribunal*, c/Palma is a good hunting ground, with the *Palma* and the *Fernandez* at no. 17 (☎91/4475488 and 4478015 respectively) and at least three establishments at no. 61, including *Los Perales* (☎91/2227191). Try also *Gallardo* at Espíritu Santo 18, two blocks south (☎91/2319530).

Still north of the Gran Vía, but a ways distant from Fuencarral, are two more nuclei of reasonable accommodation. The junction of c/Barbieri and c/San Marcos in the heart of **Chueca** has a cluster of places in all price ranges; try, for example, *Elorriaga* (San Marcos 18; ☎91/2212212), or *Estrella* (Barbieri 1, ☎91/2228492). You'll find a similar concentration well west of Fuencarral on **c/de la Luna** towards Metro *San Bernardo*, and on the side streets leading north such as c/Pizarro (the *Guadiana*, for example at no. 3; ☎91/2327101) and c/de las Minas. On c/Luna itself try no.6, with the *Gracia* (☎91/2226368), *del Mar* (☎91/2317215), and *Luna* (☎91/2324585), or the *Julia* (☎91/2224176) and *Nueva Montaña* ☎91/2216085 at no.34. Note that we've paid most attention to mid-range *hostales*, with bathless doubles for approximately 1400–1900ptas; as with the Atocha district, on virtually any of the blocks listed there will be numerous, less expensive *pensiones* and more luxurious two-star *hostales*, often in the same building.

Youth Hostels

There are two **youth hostels** in Madrid, one central, one some way out. The first is at c/Santa Cruz de Marcenado 28 (☎91/2474532), north of the Plaza de España near the Palacio Liria; it's often full but when it is they'll help you find somewhere else nearby. The *Hostel Richard Schirmann* is in the Casa de Campo (Metro *Lago*, or bus #33; ☎91/4635699) — not very convenient but at least you get fresh air. For general YHA information, dial ☎91/4450800.

Campgrounds

There are half a dozen campgrounds within 30km of Madrid, but only two which are significantly closer. *Osuna*, out near the airport along the Avenida de Logroño (☎91/7410510) is friendly, with good facilities and reasonable prices, but the ground is rock-hard and, with planes landing and taking off overhead, it's extremely noisy. *Madrid* (☎91/2022835) is a second-class site about 7km north of the center off the road to Burgos, slightly cheaper and with fewer facilities but preferable in most other ways. Both of these are open all year round, and neither is easily accessible by public transport: for *Osuna* take the metro to *Canillejas*, then bus #105; for *Madrid* it's Metro *Plaza de Castilla* followed by bus #129.

The City

The Puerta del Sol marks the very middle of Madrid and therefore the heart of Spain. So it is here that our discussion of the city begins. Take heed of our earlier comments, however, and above all the fact that it is not Madrid's monuments which are its most exciting aspect, but the life and character of its individual quarters or *barrios*. So although this chapter is arranged in a spiral outwards from the Puerta del Sol (handily following the historical growth of the city), it doesn't necessarily imply that the earlier parts are the more interesting.

Sol and Plaza Mayor

The **Puerta del Sol** (Gate of the Sun) is the hub of the capital in more than merely a metaphorical sense. From here begin six of Spain's National (road) Routes and, beneath the streets, three of the city's twelve metro lines converge. To mark the fact that this is also the center of the nation, a stone slab in the pavement outside the main building on the south side (the one with the clock) shows **Kilometer Zero**. This focal building has traditionally been, and currently still is, the *Dirección General de Seguridad* of the National Police, but in keeping with the new mood in Spain it's earmarked to become the offices of the Community of Madrid in the near future. Across the road from the zero-kilometer marker, at the end of the c/del Carmen, is a statue of a bear pawing a bush; this is both the emblem of the city and a favorite meeting place.

Sol is also the natural place for *Madrileños* to gather, whether to celebrate or to demonstrate. On New Year's Eve (*Nochevieja*), the whole square is packed with people awaiting the clock to chime midnight and on every stroke marking the end of the old year, they swallow a grape (by this time, most have enjoyed a good few grapes in liquid form as well). To make it more of a place to meet, and to make life more pleasant for pedestrians, the Puerta (which when all is said and done amounts to little more than a big traffic junction) has recently been redesigned to allow for easier bus entry; private cars are not allowed through during working hours.

North of Sol, c/de Preciados and c/del Carmen head towards the Gran Vía; both have been pedestrianized and constitute the most popular **shopping mall** in Madrid. Giant branches of the department stores *El Corte Ingles* and *Galeriás* are to be found in c/de Preciados.

West, c/del Arenal leads towards the Opera and Royal Palace. About halfway along the ancient church of **San Gines**, Mozarbic in origin with a picture of the money-changers chased from the temple by El Greco hanging within (but open only during services), stands in uneasy juxtaposition with a cult temple of the twentieth century: *Joy Eslava*, one of Madrid's biggest discotheques. Behind the disco is the *Chocolatería San Ginés* which at one time catered for the early rising workman but has since been bought by the disco owners, retiled and restyled, and now churns out *churros* and hot chocolate for the late-to-bedders. It opens in the evening from 7 to 10pm to offer solace to late-night shoppers and then again from midnight through until after the club closes. For snacks throughout the working day, *Ferpal* nearby is a more regular sandwich bar.

Calle Mayor, which runs **southwest** from Sol, also to end close to the Royal Palace, is one of Madrid's oldest and most important thoroughfares, taking you through the heart of the medieval city. About two-thirds of the way along is the **Plaza de la Villa**, a living example of Spanish architectural development through three centuries. The oldest survivor is the restored *Torre de los Lujanes*, a fifteenth-century building in Mudejar style, where Francis I of France is said to have been imprisoned in 1525 after being captured at the battle of Pavia (in Italy). Next in age is the *Casa de Cisneros*, built by a nephew of Cardinal Cisneros in sixteenth-century Plateresque style, and to complete the picture the *Ayuntamiento* (or *Casa de la Villa*) was begun in the seventeenth century, but remodeled in a baroque mode. Baroque is taken even further around the corner in c/San Justo, where the parish church of San Miguel shows the fully unreined imagination of the eighteenth-century Italian architects who designed it.

Walking straight from the Puerta del Sol to the Plaza de la Villa, you could easily and obliviously walk straight past the most important landmark in Madrid, certainly in architectural and possibly also in historical terms. This is the **Plaza Mayor**. Set back from c/Mayor, and quite unexpected given its surroundings, it's an almost perfectly preserved, and extremely beautiful, seventeenth-century arcaded square. Planned by Felipe II and Juan Herrera (architect of El Escorial) as the public meeting place of the new capital, it was not finished until 1619 (thirty years later), during the reign of Felipe III, who sits astrides the stallion in the central statue.

In its time the square has witnessed some of the great moments of Madrid's history: the Inquisition held its *autos-da-fé* here (and the public executions which followed); kings were crowned; festivals and demonstrations passed through; bulls were fought; and gossip was spread. The more important of the events would be watched by royalty from the *Casa Panadería*, named after the bakery which it replaced. Nowadays it's mostly tourists who wander around the statue and pack out the (expensive) cafes, but an air of grandeur still clings to the place, and even today the plaza performs several public functions. In the summer months it becomes an outdoor theater and music stage, in the autumn there is a book fair, and in the winter, just before Christmas, it becomes a bazaar for festive decorations and religious regalia, with everything you'd ever want to make your own home nativity scene. Every Sunday, too, stamp sellers and collectors convene to talk philately together while their numismatic counterparts rummage through rare coins in an open-air market.

Around and below the square are some of the city's liveliest *mesones*. In c/ Cuchilleros, as you chomp your way through your *bocadillo* and knock back *sangría*, you're likely to be serenaded by passing *tunas* — musical gangs dressed in knickerbockers and waistcoats who wander around town playing and passing the hat (as often as not they're university students attempting to supplement their grant).

Santa Ana and Huertas

This area forms a rough triangle bordered to the east by the Paseo del Prado, on the north by c/Alcalá, and along the south by c/Atocha, with the Puerta del Sol at the western tip. Here Madrid next spread after extending beyond the immediate area of the Royal Palace and the Plaza Mayor. Most of the houses date from the nineteenth century and are well connected with a great literary history: there are streets named after Cervantes and Lope de Vega (where one lived and the other died), the *Atheneum* club is here, as is the *Círculo de las Bellas Artes* (Fine Arts Institute) and the *Teatro Nacional*. It is in this *barrio*, too, that the *Cortes* (Spain's parliament) sits. For most visitors, though, a more immediate attraction than all these is the fact that this district, especially between the Puerta del Sol and the Plaza Santa Ana, is crowded with excellent bars and *tascas*.

Huertas is the slightly more pompous area. Heading up c/Alcalá from the Puerta del Sol you reach the **Bellas Artes** building just before the junction with the Gran Vía. Here you'll find almost every aspect of the arts under one roof, not quite the Rockefeller Center but lively all the same. There is a theater, music hall, exhibition gallery, movie-house (the *Filmoteca Nacional*), and, equally important, a very pleasant bar. Reputedly the haunt of film directors and the like, its marble and leather decor (with a nude — statue — reclining in the middle of the floor) attracts a fairly posey clientele, but it's not in the least exclusive, nor especially expensive.

Farther east, where Alcalá meets the Paseo del Prado at the **Plaza de la Cibeles**, the imposing structure with the golden ball houses the offices of the *Banco de España*. The wedding-cake edifice on the opposite side of the plaza is the **Palacio de Comunicaciones**, Madrid's main post and telegraph office, from where you can mail, cable, and collect just about any sort of written item. Awash in a sea of traffic between the two stands the fountain and statue of the goddess Cibeles, which survived the bombardments of the civil war by being swaddled from helmet to hoof in sandbags. It was designed, as were the two other fountains gushing magnificently along the Paseo del Prado, by Ventura Rodríguez, who is honored in modern Madrid by having a metro station and a street named after him. The **Prado** itself (covered in its own section later) lies a few hundred meters to the south, and indeed the whole area between the Paseo del Prado and the Parque del Retiro is liberally scattered with museums and galleries (again, see "Museums and Galleries" below).

Immediately north of the Prado sits the *Hotel Ritz*, one of Madrid's most elegant. Opposite, the Carrera San Jerónimo leads back toward the Puerta del Sol past **Las Cortes** — the Parliament — a well-guarded building on the

Plaza de las Cortes. Facing it is another of the city's fanciest hotels, the *Palace*. The bullet holes from Tejero's attempted coup of 1981 are still evident in the ceiling of the parliament chamber. Not far from here on c/Jovellanos, the **Teatro de la Zarzuela** should be on your list to visit if you're a fan of operetta. The leather-bound literary atmosphere of the **Ateneo** (the Atheneum, c/Prado 21 in the other direction from the Cortes) is rather different. Many of its members take part in the surviving *tertulias* at some of the city's more ancient and polished cafes. **Listings** for what is going on in these establishments, as well as in the **Teatro Nacional** in the Plaza Santa Ana, can be found in Madrid's daily papers or the weekly *Guía del Ocio*.

South of c/San Jerónimo, two streets named after perhaps the greatest figures of Spain's seventeenth-century literary golden age, Cervantes and Lope de Vega, run parallel to each other. Bitter rivals in life, both are probably spinning in their graves now, since Cervantes is interred in the **Convento de las Trinitarias** on the street named after Lope de Vega, while the latter's house (**Casa de Lope de Vega**) finds itself on c/de Cervantes. This house is well worth visiting for its reconstruction of life in seventeenth-century Madrid (Tues.–Sun. 10am–5pm, closed from mid-July to mid-Aug.).

The next street south of c/Lope de Vega is the Calle de las Huertas, along which you could, if you so wished, barhop your way back towards the Plaza Santa Ana and still richer hunting grounds for eating and drinking. Bars are liberally spread along both sides of the street. See the "Restaurants, Cafes, and Bars" section for more details.

Opera and the Palacio Real

West of Sol, c/del Arenal ends in the Plaza Isabel II opposite the **Teatro Real** or Opera House, which gives the area its name. Not a particularly large hall, it is nonetheless the city's most prestigious, and the only venue for opera in Madrid (though *zarzuelas*, operettas, are performed at the theater in c/Jovellanos). Built in the mid-nineteenth century, it almost sank in the early twentieth as a result of subsidence of underground canals. But it reopened in the mid-1960s and has been the most popular haunt for fur coats and diamanté ever since. Saturday morning rehearsals are open to the public — often a good way of getting to see shows which are otherwise sold out.

Around the back, the opera house is separated from the palace by the **Plaza de Oriente**. There are a couple of tacky souvenir shops here, and a ritzy cafe, but otherwise it's a surprisingly underused square. Even the statues are rejects: 44 of them, depicting Spanish kings and queens, were designed originally to go on the palace facade but found to be too heavy (some say too ugly) for the roof to support. In the center of the square is one superb statue of Felipe IV on horseback. This was based on designs by Velázquez, and Galileo is said to have helped with the calculations to make it balance.

The chief attraction of this otherwise rather barren area, however, is the **Palacio Real** (Royal Palace). It is a building which above all scores high on statistics: it claims more rooms than any other European palace; a **library** with one of the biggest collections of books, manuscripts, maps, and musical scores in the world; an **armory** with an unrivaled collection of weapons dating back to the fifteenth century; and an original **pharmacy**, a curious mixture of alchemist's den and early laboratory, its walls lined with jars labeled for various remedies.

The palace and gardens are of Italian conception and the layout of the facade is based on drawings made by Bernini for the Louvre. Built after the previous palace burned down on Christmas Day 1734, this was the principal royal residence from then until Alfonso XIII went into exile in 1931; both Joseph Bonaparte and the Duke of Wellington also lived here briefly.

The present royal family inhabits a more modest residence on the western outskirts of the city, using the Palacio Real only on state occasions, at which times it is closed to the public (opening hours otherwise are Mon.–Sat. 10am–1:30pm and 4–6:15pm, Sun. 10am–1:30pm in summer; Mon.–Sat. 10am–12:45pm and 3:30–5:15pm, Sun. 10am–12:45pm in winter). Times for guided tours (in English, Spanish, German, and French), which are compulsory for the main apartments, are posted. This grand tour is pretty long, but rarely allows you time to contemplate the extraordinary opulence: acres of Flemish and Spanish tapestries, endless rococo decoration, bejeweled clocks, and pompous portraits of the monarchs.

In the **Sala del Trono** (Throne Room), Juan Carlos's and Sofia's thrones are new additions, and you should also take time, if you can, to look at the three rooms with ceilings by Tiepolo, which are of far higher quality artistically than most of the rest of the decoration. The best one is in the Throne Room, a giant fresco representing the glory of Spain and an extraordinary achievement for an artist by then in his 70s.

The same ticket admits you to all the outbuildings and annexes of the Palace, and need not necessarily be used all at once (you can spread your visits over several days if you want). The **Armería Real** is much as you'd expect, a huge room full of guns, swords, and armor, with such curiosities as El Cid's sword and the suit of armor which you can see being worn by Carlos V in his equestrian portrait in the Prado. Especially fascinating are the complete sets of armor, with all the spare parts and gadgets for making adjustments that originally came with them.

The **Biblioteca Real** (Royal Library) is also full of valuable manuscripts, including a first edition of Don Quixote, though the guides seem more interested in the quantity of books than their quality. Immediately north of the palace the **Jardines Sabatini**, the royal gardens, are also open to the public, while around to the rear is the larger park of the **Campo del Moro** (access only from the far, west side off the Paseo de la Virgen del Puerto. Here you'll find the **Museo de Carruajes** (entrance again covered by palace ticket), a collection of state coaches and the like from the sixteenth century to the present day.

The semi-derelict building to the south of the Palace is the former *Iglesia Mayor de Santa María de la Almudena*, still awaiting reconstruction and reinstatement as the **Cathedral of Madrid** since its bombing during the civil war. In the meantime, the capital is without a cathedral. Beyond, c/Bailen crosses c/Segovia on a high viaduct which was constructed as a royal route from the palace to the church of San Francisco el Grande, avoiding the rabble and river which both flowed below. It was also a prime choice for suicide leaps until the Torre de Madrid was built.

Plaza de España and Gran Vía

North of the Palace, c/Bailen runs into the **Plaza de España**, home to a couple of the most imposing buildings in the city and little else. The **Torre de Madrid**, which houses the main tourist office, is the tallest skyscraper in the capital, and the Edificio de España the second highest. They look over an elaborate monument to Cervantes in the middle of the square, which in turn towers over the bewildered bronze figures of Don Quixote and Sancho Panza. There always seem to be people hanging out around the statues, which indeed is about the most interesting thing to do here, although there is a bar atop the Torre from which you get a wonderful view and tremendous vertigo. In c/Martín de los Heros, which runs out of the square to the northwest, the *Alphaville* complex houses some of the most adventurous movie screens in Madrid. Behind them is the *Princesa* complex with shops, clubs, bars, and a branch of the ubiquitous *VIPS* fast-food chain.

Emerging from the other side of this complex, the **Palacio de Liria** is almost opposite at c/Princesa 22. This is the residence of the Duke and Duchess of Alba; the Duchess is an old school friend of England's Queen Elizabeth and is probably (with some 180 honors of one sort or another) the most titled person in the world. It is possible to visit the palace and its stunning art collection, but only by written appointment.

The main virtue of the Plaza de España, however, is as starting point of the **Gran Vía**, which heads southeast towards the Plaza Callao, and from there east to the Plaza de la Cibeles, effectively dividing the old city to the south from the newer parts northwards. Permanently jammed with traffic and crowded with shoppers and sightseers, it's appropriately named, although its brash commerciality is perhaps not the image Madrid would like to convey. One of the delights of braving the crowds and walking along it are the movie palaces, many of which still advertise with vast hand-painted billboards (and all of which have very reasonably priced seats). There's little of particular note to look out for other than these. The Plaza Callao is a major bus terminus and a place to buy a pass; the **Telefónica** building, as well as being the easiest place to make long-distance, international, or collect calls, was for much of the defense of Madrid during the civil war the chief observation post for the Republican artillery (when the Nationalist front line stretched across the Casa de Campo). Consequently it was itself much bombarded. Opposite, c/Montera leads down to the Puerta del Sol, reverberating with the sounds of pinball machines; just about every doorway takes you into an amusement arcade.

On an entirely different plane, one of the hidden treasures of Madrid, the **Convento de las Descalzas Reales**, also lies just to the south of the Gran Vía on the Plaza de las Descalzas. The convent was founded by Juana de Austria, daughter of Carlos V, sister of Felipe II and, at 19, already the widow of Prince Don Juan of Portugal. In her wake came a succession of titled ladies (the name means the Convent of the Barefooted Royals) who brought fame and, above all, fortune; the place is unbelievably rich. You're taken (on another of those whistle-stop guided tours) through the cloisters and up a ridiculously fancy stairway to a series of rooms packed with treasures of every kind. Outstanding are the rooms in which the nuns — except the Empress Maria of Germany who had luxurious private quarters — used to sleep. They're hung now with a series of Flemish tapestries based on designs by Rubens and a striking portrait of St. Francis by Zurbarán. The nuns kept no records so that the *Joyería* (Treasury) is piled high with jewels and relics of uncertain provenance. No one is quite sure what many of the things are, nor which bones came from which saint, but it's an exceptional hoard. The convent is still in use, but it's open to the public Saturday and Tuesday through Thursday from 10:30am to 12:30pm and from 4 to 5:15pm, and on Friday and Sunday from 10:30am to 12:30pm.

By contrast the **Convento de la Encarnación**, back towards the Palacio Real and covered by the same ticket (same hours), can only be an anticlimax. Although more spacious and better laid out, its decoration is nowhere near as impressive, and of the hundreds of paintings the place contains, only the frescoed chapel ceiling (by Bayeu) is of much interest.

Retiro

When you tire of sightseeing, Madrid's many parks make a great place to escape for a few hours. The most central and most popular of them is the **Parque del Buen Retiro**, a delightful mix of formal gardens and wider open spaces. Originally the grounds of a royal retreat (*retiro* in Spanish), it's been public property for more than a hundred years; the palace itself burned down in the eighteenth century. In its 330 acres you can jog, boat, picnic (though not on the grass), have your fortunes told, and above all promenade. A number of small kiosks and cafes sell drinks and *bocadillos*. Busiest day is Sunday when half of Madrid, its spouse, in-laws, and the kids turn out for the *paseo*. Dressed to show off their best, the families stroll around the various activities, nodding at neighbors, and building up an appetite for a long Sunday lunch.

Strolling aside, there's almost always something going on in the park, from boating or feeding the carp in the pond (*el estanque*) to concerts and *ferias* organized by the city council; in the summer months films are shown in the evenings, free, in the area known as La Chopera. Around the pond you'll find (on Sunday) puppet shows for children, fortune tellers, and *pipa* (sunflower seed) stalls. Traveling exhibitions of one artistic kind or another are frequently housed in the beautiful **Palacio de Velázquez** (no relation to Diego) and the nearby **Palacio de Cristal** (normal hours for both are Tues.-Sat. 10am–2pm and 5–7pm, Sun. 10am–2pm). Look out, too, for "The Fallen Angel," claimed to be the world's only statue to the devil, in the south of the park. And if you still have energy to burn, there's a council-sponsored exercise track (others in Madrid are in the Casa de Campo and the Complutense University campus).

Leaving the park, the northwestern exit takes you to the Plaza de la Independencia, in the center of which is one of only two remaining gates from the old city walls. Built in the late eighteenth century, it was the biggest in Europe at that time. Like the bear-and-bush, the **Puerta de Alcalá** has become one of the monumental emblems of Madrid. Southwest of the park are the **Jardines Botanicos** (Botanical Gardens), whose entrance faces the southern end of the Prado. Opened in 1781 by Carlos III (known as *El Alcalde* — "the mayor" — for his urban improvement programs), the gardens once contained over 30,000 plants. Renovated after years of neglect, they are really delightful to walk through, and the worldwide collection of flora is fascinating for any amateur botanist. Under an edict issued when the gardens were opened, *Madrileños* are still theoretically entitled to help themselves to cuttings of any plant or medicinal herb.

Between these two, and immediately behind the Prado, the church of **San Jerónimo el Real** is *the* society church of Madrid. It is here that heirs to the Spanish throne have always been crowned and here that Juan Carlos ascended the throne in 1975. Opposite is the *Real Academia Española de la Lengua* (the Royal Language Academy). Their job is to make sure that the Spanish language is not corrupted by foreign or otherwise unsuitable words; the results are entrusted to the official dictionary that they sporadically publish. Judging by the most recent edition you have to wonder in which century the sixty current members have been living, since it bears virtually no relation to the Spanish you'll hear spoken on the streets.

On the other side of the botanical gardens slopes c/Claudio Moyano, lined with the stalls of a small **book market**. You can buy anything here, new or old, from second-hand copies of Captain Marvel in Spanish to Cervantes or Jackie Collins. There's always something of interest, often quite a selection of dog-eared paperbacks in English, and usually one or two surprises. You'd be lucky to find anything valuable, but prices are low and it's a pleasant stroll. Though at its busiest on Sundays, some of the stalls are open every day of the week.

Latina to Lavapies: the Rastro

The area south of the Plaza Mayor and of c/Atocha has traditionally been working class, Madrid's Brooklyn as it were. In many places the old houses survive, huddled together around narrow streets, but the character of **Latina** and **Lavapies** is beginning to change as their inhabitants, and the districts themselves, become younger and more fashionable. Typical, perhaps, is *La Corrala*, originally a tenement block built in 1872 (on c/Sombrerete near Metro *Lavapies*) which has been completely renovated and is now distinctly chic, with small apartments opening onto baclonies that surround a central patio. In summer, the residents use this open space for theatrical performances.

Part of the reason for this rise in status must be **the Rastro**, which is as much part of Madrid's weekend ritual as a church service or a *paseo*. It is a gargantuan, thriving, thieving shambles of a street market which sprawls south from Metro *Latina* to the Ronda de Toledo, especially along Ribera de Curtidores. Through it, crowds flood between 10am and 3pm every Sunday, and increasingly on Fridays and Saturdays too. You can get second-hand clothes, military surplus items, budgies and canaries, sunshades, razor blades, fine antiques or Taiwanese transistors, cutlery and coke spoons — in fact just about anything, plausible or unimaginable. Some of it (broken telephone dials, plastic shampoo bottles half full of something which may or may not be the original contents . . .) is such junk that it's inconceivable that anyone could want it. Other things may be quite valuable, but don't expect to find real bargains, or the hidden Old Masters of popular myth; the serious antique trade has mostly moved off the streets and into the shops around it. On the pavement, though, there's a lively drug trade, right under the noses of the police (who mostly seem to turn a blind eye); the shop called *Marijuana*, in Plaza Cascorro at the head of the Rastro, doesn't actually sell the stuff, but it will supply most of the accoutrements. One warning if you visit: keep a tight grip on your bags, pockets, cameras, and jewelry.

On a rather different tack, if you continue right to the bottom of the Rastro, you'll see a large arch, the **Puerta de Toledo**, at one end of the Ronda de Toledo. The only surviving relation to that of Alcalá in the Plaza Independencia, this was built originally as an *arc de triomphe* to honor the conquering Napoleon. After his defeat in the Peninsular Wars, it became a symbol of the city's freedom.

Latina is also home for two of the largest churches in Madrid. **San Isidro**, dedicated to the patron saint of Madrid (and containing his remains as well as those of the city's patroness, Santa María de la Cabeza), is on c/de Toledo near the top of the Rastro. In the absence of a real cathedral in the capital, this acts as one, although its chief attribute is its size; it's as bleak as it is big. Next door is the paroquial school, which has been in existence considerably longer than the church and counts among its former pupils such Spanish literary notables as Calderón de la Barca, Lope de Vega, Quevedo and the more modern Jacinto Benavente. The last-named has a plaza named after him nearby which houses some truly seedy movie theaters.

A far grander, richer and more elaborate church is that of **San Francisco el Grande**, west of here in the namesake plaza at the end of Carrera San Francisco. Built towards the end of the eighteenth century as part of Carlos III's renovations of the city, it has a dome larger even than that of St. Paul's in London. Inside (Tues.–Sat., 11am–1pm and 4–7pm) are paintings by, among others, Goya and Zurbaran, and frescoes by Bayeu.

Chueca, Malasaña, and the North

The chief reason to venture north of the Gran Vía is for eating and **nightlife**. Although the late-late-nightclubs and discos are scattered around about the city, some even a few kilometers from the center (see "Music, Nightlife, and Culture"), it is in Chueca and Malasaña that you'll find by far the heaviest concentration of bars and clubs downtown. Chueca has also been dubbed (and daubed) **Zona Gay**, and most of the city's many gay places are located here.

The heart, in all senses, of **Malasaña** is the Plaza Dos de Mayo, named for the insurrection against Napoleanic forces on May 2, 1808; the rebellion and its aftermath are depicted in a series of Goyas at the Prado. The surrounding district bears the name of one of of the martyrs of the uprising, fifteen-year-old Manuela Malasaña, who is also commemorated in a street (as are several other heros of the time). Every year on May 1–2 all of Madrid shuts down to honor them, but more excitingly the plaza is the scene of festivities lasting well into the night.

More recently, the neighborhood was the original nursery of the "*movida Madrileña*," the "happening scene" of the late 1970s and early 1980s. As the country relaxed after the death of Franco and the city developed into a thoroughly modern capital under the leadership of the late Mayor Tierno, Malasaña became the mecca and stomping ground of the young. Bars appeared behind every doorway, drugs were sold quite brazenly in the streets, and there was an extraordinary atmosphere of new-found freedom. But times have changed; with a substantial rise in petty street crimes, of which over ninety percent are drug-related, the police (and the residents) are no longer so tolerant of the "*chocolate*" sellers. At the same time the young and trendy are growing older and more respectable and Malasaña is too much in a time warp to have kept up with today's increasingly yuppified crowd. Life goes on, nightlife especially, but the *movida* has, for the most part, moved on.

From Chueca east to the Paseo Recoletos (the beginning of the long Paseo de la Castellana) are some of the city's most enticing streets. Offbeat restaurants, small private art galleries, and odd corner shops are to be found here in abundance, and the c/Almirante has some of the city's more fashionable clothes stores too. The Ministry of Culture fronts the Plaza del Rey, which is also worth a look for the other odd buildings surrounding it, especially the one with seven chimneys which is supposedly haunted by a mistress of Felipe II who disappeared in mysterious circumstances. Don't be surprised by the number of blind people around here; the headquarters of *ONCE* (the organization for the blind which runs a lottery to raise money for them and to provide employment as ticket sellers) are on c/Prim, and many of the sellers come here to collect their allocation of tickets. There are a number of more or less radical theaters in this area, too, including Madrid's *Centro Cultural* beneath the Plaza Colón to the north. At street level here is a statue of Columbus (Cristóbal Colón) and some huge stone blocks arranged as a megalithic monument to the discovery of the Americas.

To the north spreads the new city of Franco. The buildings are modern all the way up the Paseo Castellana to the Plaza Castilla, but the mentality of the people around here is probably the most old-fashioned in Madrid. Nor is even the best of the new architecture very exciting. As far as sightseeing goes, forget it; probably the most exciting attraction would be the Estación de Chamartín, a functional, modern rail palace complete with bowling alley, disco, and nearby shopping center. Around c/Orense, the young *pijos* (snobby offspring of well-to-do families) frequent the many night-dives of the Azca *urbanización*. Easily the most famous sight up north, however, is the Santiago Bernabeu football stadium, home of *Real Madrid* and setting of the 1982 World Cup finals.

The West: Parque del Oeste, Moncloa, and the Casa de Campo

Northwest of the Plaza de España Madrid becomes largely academic and residential. The **Ciudad Universitaria** houses the University Complutense (one of two universities in Madrid), which spreads itself around a vast campus beyond Metro *Moncloa*. Each faculty occupies a huge individual block, separated from the next one by vast open spaces: supposedly this was Franco's way of guaranteeing that the students would be unable to block the streets in the fashion of Paris in 1968. (The original university, founded in 1927, was almost completely destroyed by bombardment during the civil war). Unless you want to visit the **Contemporary Art Museum**, there's little else to entertain you, and even the contents of that are supposed to soon be moved to the new *Centro de Arte Reina Sofía* by Atocha station.

If you are up here, the student haunts — the Cuatro Caminos and Arguelles *barrios* above all — are good for bars and basic restaurants (though not worth any special trip) and also promising territory for apartments if you plan to stay longer.

The **Parque del Oeste** also lies northwest of the Plaza de España, stretching from the railroad tracks of the Estación del Norte up to Moncloa. At the southeastern end is the **Templo de Debod**, a fourth-century B.C. Egyptian temple that was given to Spain in recognition of the work done by Spanish engineers on the Aswan High Dam (which inundated its original site). Reconstructed here stone by stone, it seems almost comically incongruous, though perhaps less so when used as the venue for frequent concerts. The Paseo del Pintor Rosales limits the park at its northeastern edge, and is lined with expensive high-rise apartments commanding views all the way across to the Guadarrama mountains over 60 kms away to the northwest. Walking through the park in this direction, you'll come to a large rose garden, and next to it a *teleférico*, which takes you high over the river to the middle of the Casa de Campo.

If you want to jog, play tennis, swim, picnic, go on wild rides, or see pandas, then the **Casa de Campo** is the place to head. This enormous (4300-acre) expanse of heath and scrub is in parts surprisingly wild for a place so easily accessible from the city; other sections have been tamed for more conventional pleasures. Far larger and more natural than the city parks, the Casa de Campo can be reached by metro (*Batan* or *El Lago* stops), various buses, or the aforementioned cable car. The walk from the Estación del Norte station via the Puente del Rey isn't too strenuous either. Throughout the park there are picnic tables and cafe/bars; a jogging circuit has been set up, with exercise posts along its route; there is a municipal, open-air swimming pool (summer only); tennis courts; and rowboats to hire on the lake. The Zoo (10am–8pm daily) is perenially popular and there's a large, but rather dull, **Parque de Atracciones** (amusement park). By the lakeside, the *Rockodromo* quite often stages free summertime concerts.

If you take the *teleférico* (whose small cabins are a haven for amorous couples) you'll see below you the rail lines to Galicia and other parts of the north. These terminate at the **Estación del Norte**, a quietly spectacular construction of white enamel, steel, and glass which enjoyed a starring role in the film *Reds*. About 300m from the station along the Paseo de la Florida (c/ Valladolid on some maps) is the **Ermita de San Antonio de la Florida** (daily except Wed. 10am–1pm and 4–7pm). The #46 bus runs past, or it's ten minutes' walk from Metro *Norte*. This little church on a Greek cross plan was built by an Italian, Felipe Fontana, between 1792 and 1798, and decorated by Goya, whose frescoes are the main reason to visit. In the dome is a depiction of a miracle performed by St. Anthony of Padua, while around it (in a reversal of convention) are heavenly bodies of angels and cherubs holding back curtains to reveal the main scene. This shows the saint resurrecting a dead man to give evidence in favor of a prisoner falsely accused of murder (the saint's father). Beyond this central group, Goya created a gallery of characters reacting with wonder, interest, or indifference — all in all, an astonishingly modern work for its day. A lesser fresco of the angels adoring the Trinity adorns the apse. Aside from Goya's work, the *ermita* also houses the artist's mausoleum (a second chapel was built alongside to allow parish services to continue), making it something of a place of pilgrimage. Two more good reasons for coming this way are the *Casa Mingo* restaurant (see "Eating") and *El Lido*, another of the city's **open-air pools**, north along the Paseo by the Puente (Bridge) de los Franceses.

The Prado

No one should visit Madrid without seeing **the Prado**, one of the oldest and greatest collections of art in the world. Originally opened to the public in 1819, it houses all the finest works collected by Spanish royalty — for the most part avid, discerning, and wealthy buyers — as well as many of the best items from other Spanish sources: over 3000 paintings in all. With one outstanding exception, twentieth-century paintings are not included. The exception, however, is probably the most famous and emotive picture of all modern Spanish art: Picasso's *Guernica*. Secretly brought from New York in October 1981, it is exhibited in a separate section which draws long lines to view it through a bulletproof protective screen. It was Picasso's own wish that the painting should come to the Prado once democracy was restored in Spain.

Situated on the Paseo del Prado, the gallery's **opening hours** are Tuesday to Saturday from 9am to 7pm, Sundays and holidays from 9am to 2pm; the nearest metro stations are *Banco* or *Atocha*, or there are any number of bus routes going past. Entry is free with a student card, 400ptas otherwise.

The museum's **highlights** are the Flemish collection — including almost all of Bosch's best work — and of course its incomparable display of Spanish art, particularly Velázquez and Goya but including all the great names, El Greco, Zurbarán, Murillo, and Ribera among them. There's also a huge section of Italian works collected by Carlos V and Felipe II, both great patrons of the Renaissance, and a strong showing of later Flemish pictures collected by Felipe IV. Even in a full day you couldn't really hope to do justice to everything in the Prado, and it's much more enjoyable to make short visits with a clear idea of what you want to see. If you are tempted to get full value out of the long opening hours, however, there's a good cafeteria and bar.

Major reorganization for the installation of air-conditioning and much-needed better lighting has been going on for years now, so you may find displays moved or temporarily closed. What follows is only a partial guide, slanted by our own tastes; catalogues describing every painting individually are on sale in the museum, along with reproductions of the most popular works. For more information on Spanish artists, see the *Contexts* section of this book.

Flemish Masters

Perhaps the best approach to the museum is through the side entrance on c/ Felipe IV. Immediately to your right on the ground floor the early Flemish masters are currently displayed. The great triptychs of **Hieronymus Bosch** (1450–1516, known in Spain as *El Bosco*) — the early *Hay Wain*, the middle-period *Garden of Earthly Delights* and the late *Adoration of the Magi* — are familiar from countless reproductions but infinitely more chilling in the original. His hallucinatory genius for the macabre is at its most extreme in these, but reflected here in many more of his works, including three versions of *The Temptations of St. Anthony* (though only the smallest of these is definitely an original). See also the amazing table-top of *The Seven Deadly Sins*, displayed without a label in the center of the room.

Bosch's visions were refined and developed by Pieter Breughel the Elder, whose *Triumph of Death* must be one of the most frightening canvases ever painted. Another elusive painter, Joachim Patinir, is represented by four of his finest works. From an earlier generation, Rogier van der Weyden's *Deposition* is outstanding; its monumental forms make a fascinating contrast with the miniature-like *Pieta* by the same artist. There are also important works by Memling, Bouts, Gerard David, and Massys. The few **German paintings** are dominated by the four Dürers; the magnificent *Adam* and *Eve* was only saved from destruction at the hands of the prudish Carlos III by the intervention of his court painter, Mengs.

The Rest of the Ground Floor

In the rooms opposite the Flemish collection are currently shown the newly-cleaned **El Grecos** from Illescas, along with the reunited upper and lower parts of a *St. Sebastián*. Here, too, is temporarily displayed a selection of the rich Prado holdings of **José Ribera** (*Lo Spagnoletto*), above all his masterpiece *The Martyrdom of St. Bartholomew*.

The long, central downstairs gallery houses the **early Spanish collection**. See in particular the the huge *retablo* by Nicolas Frances; the anonymous *Virgin of the Catholic Kings*; Bermejo's *Santo Domingo de Silos*; and Pedro Berruguete's *Auto da Fe*. In the following gallery are displayed a series of eighteen canvases on mythological subjects designed for Felipe IV's hunting lodge in El Pardo, a project supervised by **Rubens**, though he executed only a few of them himself. The smaller rooms beyond this house an endless series of original works by Rubens, and a notable collection of Van Dycks. Their contemporaries — including Jan Bruegel (his *Five Senses* has figures by Rubens) and David Teniers, whose scenes of lowlife get a whole room to themselves — are also well represented. On the other hand, for political reasons, Spanish monarchs collected very few works painted in seventeenth-century Protestant Holland; the only important exception is an early Rembrandt, *Artemesia*.

The Golden Age
Upstairs, to the left of the entrance, are paintings of the early **Italian School** including a series of panels (three of the original four) by **Botticelli** illustrating a story from the *Decameron — Nastagio degli Onesti*. Here too, in a series of about fifteen rooms, are the superb **Titian** (*Tiziano*) portraits of Carlos V and Felipe II as well as works by Tintoretto, Bassano, Caravaggio, and Veronese. The armor worn by Carlos V in his equestrian portrait can still be seen in the armory at the Royal Palace.

Continuing through the first floor you come to the great **Spanish painters**. Outstanding here is **Velázquez** (1599–1660), court painter of Felipe IV, whose family is represented in many of the works. His masterpiece *Las Meninas* has a room to itself; of it Manet said "After this I don't know why the rest of us paint," and the French poet Theophile Gautier asked, "But where is the picture?" because it seemed to him a continuation of the room. *Las Hilanderias*, showing the royal tapestry factory at work, is also magnificent, while *Los Borrachos* (The Drunkards) and *The Surrender of Breda* are barely less impressive. In fact almost all of the fifty works on display (around half of the artist's surviving output) repay close attention. In the adjacent rooms are many examples of **Zurbarán**, **Murillo** and **Alonso Cano**, mostly on religious themes.

The works of **El Greco** are shown in the central gallery. You have to go to Toledo to fully appreciate his extraordinary genius, but the large upright religious works, ranging from the Italianate *Trinity* to the visionary late *Adoration of the Shepherds* succeed in giving some indication of it. Off this gallery, opposite the elevators, is a bizarre *Feast of Herod*, an enormous depiction of a seventeenth-century banquet crowded with identifiable portraits. This is attributed to an obscure Polish artist, Bartolómaeus Strobl.

Goya
In the gallery beyond are various seventeenth-century works, including examples of Caravaggio, Poussin, and Claude. The far end of the building, though, is devoted almost entirely to **Francisco de Goya** (1746–1828), an artist whom many see as the inspiration and forerunner of Impressionism and modern art. His many portraits of his patron, Carlos IV, are remarkable for their lack of any attempt at flattery while those of Queen Maria Luisa, whom he despised, are downright ugly. He was an enormously versatile artist; contrast the voluptuous *Maja Vestida* and *Maja Desnuda* (The Clothed and Naked Belles) with the horrors depicted in *Dos de Mayo* and *Tres de Mayo* (on-the-spot portrayals of the rebellion against Napoleon in the streets of Madrid and the subsequent reprisals). Then again there are the series of "Cartoons" — designs for tapestries — and, downstairs, the extraordinary *Black Paintings*, a series of murals painted on the walls of his home by the

deaf and embittered painter in his old age. The most recent Goya acquisition, *The Marquesa de Santa Cruz*, hit the headlines when it was smuggled out of Spain and ended up on the London art market. It was withdrawn from sale at the last moment after furious protests from the Spanish government, but they still had to fork out $7.5 million to bring it home.

Extensions to the Prado

The Prado's original extension, the **Casón del Buen Retiro** (again entered off c/Felipe IV; same hours and ticket), houses **nineteenth-century Spanish art**. Considering the riches which have gone before, this is of remarkably little interest; skip it unless you've time to kill. But the same building also houses perhaps the most exciting single work in the entire collection, **Picasso's** *Guernica*. It's reached through a separate entrance at the back, where you have to pass through a rigorous security check. Even fifty years after its execution the picture, a rendering of the German bombing of the Basque town of Guernica, can still excite fierce political passions. There is a long gallery displaying fascinating preliminary sketches and explanatory detail before the work itself, superbly displayed in a large room of its own, which has a huge allegorical ceiling fresco by Luca Giordano.

A second extension has recently been opened in the **Palacio de Villahermosa**, diagonally opposite the main gallery at the end of the Carrera de San Jerónimo. This briefly housed a changing series of exhibitions, often drawn from the museum's own holdings, but at the time of writing is being converted to house the Old Masters section of the **Thyssen-Bornemisza** collection. By far the most spectacular private art collection in the world, this was built up over just two generations by the current Baron Heinrich Thyssen-Bornemisza and especially by his father, a German industrialist who sank his profits into art at a time between the world wars when paintings were relatively cheap. The news that the collection had outgrown the baron's Swiss home and that he was looking for a home for it caused a furious bidding competition, with the Swiss, German, and British governments eventually losing out to the Spanish; the final decision was swayed by the baron's fifth wife (a Spaniard) and the promise of a title putting him immediately in the upper echelons of the Spanish nobility. The initial loan is for ten years, starting from late 1989; the rumor mill has it that whether it stays thereafter may depend on the nationality of the baron's wife in 1999. Other parts of the collection are going to Barcelona, while the modern art will stay in Lugano (Switzerland), but this is the most important fraction.

Highlights include a superb selection of **Renaissance portraits**, among which is Holbein's celebrated *Henry VIII*, the only one of the many variants in existence which is definitely genuine. A *Spanish Infanta* by Juan de Flandes may represent the first of the king's wives, Catharine of Aragón. Among the **Italians**, Ghirlandaio and Sebastiano del Piombo stand out, along with a *Young Knight* by Carpaccio which is one of the earliest known full-length portraits. **Flemish** works include a Memling with an exquisite still life on the reverse, and devotional panels by Van Eyck, Van der Weyden, Christus, and the exceptionally rare Jacques Daret, only three other of whose works have survived. From a similar period there is also work by **Dürer** and Lucas van

Leyden. The two **El Grecos**, one early, one late, make an interesting comparison with each other and with those in the main Prado collection. Finally **Caravaggio**'s monumental *St. Catherine of Alexandria* is the centerpiece of an important display of works by followers of this innovator of chiaroscuro.

Madrid's Other Museums and Galleries

The Prado aside, Madrid can still hold its head up as an international center of museums and galleries. While not as rich as London or Paris, perhaps, there are still plenty of fascinating smaller collections and private galleries. Most of these are closed on Monday.

Museo Lazaro Galdiano (c/Serrano 122; bus #19 or #51 from Plaza de la Cibeles, or walk twenty blocks; Metro *Ruben Dario* not far; Tues.–Sun. 10am–2pm; closed Aug.). Easily the pick of the smaller museums, this private collection was given to the state by José Galdiano in 1948. Spread over the four floors of his former home, the vast jumble of artwork contains some really exquisite pieces and almost nothing which is not of great value (although some of the attributions are dubious). Among the paintings are two by Bosch (one, *St. John the Evangelist on Patmos*, is an important work, the other may not be genuine) and works by Gerard David, Dürer (another doubtful attribution), and Rembrandt in addition to the many Spaniards: Berruguete, Murillo, Zurbarán, and Velázquez among them. El Greco — whose *Adoration of the Magi* was painted long before he arrived in Spain — and Goya are also particularly well represented. *The Savior*, hidden away in a room of Renaissance sculpture on the ground floor, is a beautiful little picture which the museum claims as a Leonardo da Vinci; sadly, no one else seems to agree. Of the other exhibits a collection of clocks and watches (many of them once owned by Carlos V) and some superb early Limoges enamels stand out.

Real Academia de Bellas Artes de San Fernando (c/Alcalá 13; Metro *Sol*; Tues.–Sat. 9am–7pm, Sun. 9am–2pm). Art buffs who have some appetite left after the Prado will find the Real Academia next on their list. You have to plow through a fair number of dull academic canvases, but there are hidden gems, particularly in the second and third rooms. They include some small Goyas, especially *The Burial of the Sardine*, five portraits of the monks of the Merced order by Zurbarán, and many other Spanish artists; a curious *Family of El Greco* may be by the great man or his son. Two other rooms are devoted to foreign artists, especially Rubens. Upstairs, the paintings are less interesting although there is a series of engravings by Picasso. Also, scattered throughout the museum, is a dismembered *Massacre of the Innocents* by sculptor José Gines. A separate gallery houses temporary exhibitions (Tues.–Sat. 10am–2pm and 4–8pm).

Museo Arqueológico (c/Serrano 13; Metro *Serrano*; Tues.–Sun. 9:15am–1:45pm). A well set-out display includes the celebrated Celto-Iberian bust known as *La Dama de Elche* (probably 4th-3rd c. B.C.), the slightly later *Dama de Baza*, and a wonderfully rich hoard of Visigothic treasures found at Toledo. In the gardens you can visit a replica of the Altamira Caves complete with convincing copies of their prehistoric wall paintings — the only way you'll get to "see" them now that the real thing is closed to the public.

Centro de Arte Reina Sofia (c/Santa Isabel 52; Metro *Atocha*; Wed.–Mon. 10am–9pm). The new one. Once a hospital, now a huge exhibition center, this for the moment houses Spain's most prestigious temporary art exhibitions, sometimes several at once. There's talk of installing modern art here permanently. Movie theater (mostly art films), shop, excellent bookshop, library, restaurant, and cafe on the premises too.

Museo Español de Arte Contemporaneo (Avda. Juan de Herrera 2; Metro *Moncloa*; Tues.–Sat. 10am–6pm, Sun. 10am–3pm). A relatively poor and rather dated museum of contemporary art. Picasso is represented by a series of *The Painter and the Model*, there are a couple of early Dalís and some reasonable work by Miró, but you'll find much better modern art in Cuenca (for abstracts) and in Catalunya. The sculpture garden is enjoyable, though, and the temporary exhibitions are often good. Some of the museum's works may be moved to the *Centro de Arte Reina Sofiá*.

Museo de America (Avda. Puerta de Hierro in Ciudad Universitaria; Metro *Moncloa*; Tues.–Sat. 10am–7pm, Sun. 10am–2pm, but erratic). Traces the Spanish conquest of the Americas, with numerous Inca and Aztec artifacts.

Museo de Artes Decorativas (c/Montalbán 12; Metro *Banco de España* or *Retiro*; Tues.–Fri. 10am–3pm, Sat. and Sun. 10am–2pm). Period furniture and decorations in a beautiful mansion. The many *azulejos* are particularly fine.

Museo Cerralbo (c/Ventura Rodríguez 17; Metro *Ventura Rodriguez*; Tues.–Sun. 10am–2pm and 4–7pm; closed Aug.). The private collection of the Marqués de Cerralbo; paintings, furniture, armor, and artifacts provide insights into the (comparatively recent) lifestyle of the Spanish aristocracy.

Museo del Ejército (c/Mendez Nuñez 1; Metro *Retiro*; Tues.–Sun. 10am–2:30pm) As well as military history, the Army Museum has a large collection of arms and armor, including a sword of El Cid's, and some bizarre trophies like the *boina* (beret) of the Basque guerilla general Zumalcarregui.

Museo Municipal (c/Fuencarral 78; Metro *Tribunal*; Tues.–Sat. 10am–2pm, Sun. 10am–3pm). Better known for its superb Churrigueresque facade than its contents, this eighteenth-century building houses exhibits tracing the development of Madrid from prehistoric times. There are some fascinating scale models of the city as it used to be.

Museo Sorolla (General Martínez Campos 37; Metro *Ruben Dario*; Tues.–Sat. 10am–6pm, Sun. 10am–2pm; closed Aug.). The paintings of Joaquín Sorolla (1863–1923) displayed in his home. The best are striking, others just obsessively preoccupied with beaches, naked bodies, and their reflections and refractions in the water.

Real Fabrica de Tapices (c/Fuenterrabia 2; Metro *Menéndez Pelayo*; Mon.–Fri. 9:30am–12:30pm; closed Aug.). The Royal Tapestry Factory still turns out hand-made tapestries (very expensive), many of them based on the Goya "cartoons" in the Prado. You can watch the actual manufacturing process.

Circulo de Bellas Artes (c/Alcalá 42; Metro *Sevilla* or *Banco*; Tues.–Sat. 9am–7pm, Mon. and Sun. 9am–2pm). Fashionable venue for traveling exhibitions.

Museo Taurino (Plaza de Toros las Ventas; Metro *Ventas*; Tues.–Sun. 10am–1pm and 6–6:30pm, but erratic). The bullfight museum is full of matadors' costumes, as grand as medieval ecclesiastical vestments, and the heads of slaughtered bulls. Also an extraordinary collection of old posters, including a Nazi one complete with swastika.

Others There are many other museums, which the *Turismo* will be happy to give you full details of. They include more **military museums** (Air and Naval), several **specialist** collections (Geology, Railroad, and Mineral, for example) and other oddities such as the Wax Museum and the newly opened planetarium.

The Facts

In the following sections, restaurants, cafes, and bars are covered under headings which correspond to the areas used to divide the city in the body of the text, so finding somewhere nearby to eat or drink should prove a simple task.

As far as **food** goes, downtown Madrid has been overrun by burger joints and fast food in general; you'll find both *McDonald's* and *Burger King* within littering distance of the Puerta del Sol. Fortunately these emporiums of formica and the potted plastic fern have not encroached too greatly on Spanish eating habits, and it's still easy to find a tastier, cheaper, and more ecologically sound meal in virtually any corner of the city (with a surprising number of good-value places right in the center).

Restaurants, Cafes, and Bars

Sol and Plaza Mayor

The downtown area is the most varied in Madrid in terms of price and choice of food. Indeed there can be few places in the world which rival the area **south of the Puerta del Sol** (and into Huertas) in terms of sheer number of places to eat and drink. C/Espoz y Mina, south off the Carrera San Jerónimo, is a good place to start. Here *Las Bravas*, for example, is a straightforward bar which serves some very tasty *tortillas* and *patatas bravas*. There is a similar dive along Alvarez Gato, a passageway nearby. In either of these you'll stand up to eat. At Alvarez Gato 5, the *Mesón Asturias* serves up a very decent home made *menú* for 500ptas — at that price (or, elsewhere, slightly below) shopping and cooking for yourself are a waste of time and money. Spectacular seafood displays in many of the bars are very good value too. Pasaje Matheu, between Espoz y Mina and c/Victoria, offers the rare Madrid pleasure of eating outside on a pedestrian street without being assaulted by cars; competing outfits here offer *menús* for 600–800ptas, and if necessary there are even cheaper meals on Victoria itself. Right on the Puerta del Sol itself, at the corner of c/Mayor, the cafe *La Menorquina* is good for breakfast or snacks — try one of their *napolitanas* (custard/cream croissants, approximately).

Around the **Plaza Mayor** are a number of more stylish, and expensive, restaurants. *El Botín*, for example, (c/Cuchilleros 17; ☎91/2664217) is a favorite haunt of tourists who come to follow the footsteps and drinking habits of Hemingway and to eat various creatures slaughtered in their infancy. The dishes most in demand are roasted baby pigs (*cochinillo*) and lambs (*lechal*). These cost about $13 a head: specialties like *angulas* (baby eels) cost even more. But surprisingly, the streets off the Plaza Mayor also house a number of basic restaurants with reasonable prices. The stand-up seafood *tapas* bar *Casa Rua*, c/Ciudad Rodrigo 3, is popular and family/shopper-oriented, and a good hundred pesetas cheaper than anywhere else nearby.

To the east, fans of *jamón serrano* should definitely visit the *Museo de Jamones*, on **Carrera San Jerónimo** near the Paseo del Prado (with a more expensive branch on the Gran Vía). Here hundreds of hams hang from the ceilings, and you can sample the different (expensive) varieties over a glass or two. Closer to the center on the same street, *L'Hardy* is a pricy restaurant known for its nineteenth-century dining room.

Santa Ana and Huertas

This area is not only one of the best to find cheap accommodation, it's also an excellent choice to feed well and inexpensively, and there are plenty of good bars too. Restaurants which specialize in *menús del día* for the many local workers and inhabitants alternate with *hostales* and *pensiones* along streets like c/Echegaray and Ventura de la Vega, while c/de las Huertas and the Plaza Santa Ana are great for bar hopping.

Calle Echegaray is packed with **eating places** (even a Japanese restaurant), one of the best of which — also more expensive than most — is *Garrabatou*. *Casa Parra* at no.16 is a quiet, arty sort of cafeteria. Prices tend to be slightly lower in **Ventura de la Vega**, where you'll find good food and value at *Hylogui*, *Ballesteros*, *Casa Ramon*, and *Luarques*. Around the corner in the narrow c/Manuel Fernández y González you'll come across *La Chuleta*, for excellent *tapas*, and the somewhat spiffier *La Trucha*. Ask for *un plato de verbena* and you'll get a plateful of varied canapes with smoked salmon and caviar. Farther east towards the Paseo del Prado, the *Edelweiss* (c/Jovellanos 7; ☎91/2210326) is a fairly posh place (linen napkins and tablecloths) whose cuisine leans heavily towards the Germanic, with portions to match. There's a good **vegetarian** restaurant, *Biotika*, at Amor de Dios 3 just off c/Huertas, and nearby (at c/Santa María 15) an exceptionally cheap place to eat identified simply as *Comidas Económicas*.

As for **bars**, if you want to "mellow out", this is your part of town. There is still a whiff of patchouli floating about c/**Huertas** of a summer's evening, when there are customers in droves and more than enough bars to content them all. You can either follow the hippie trail into dens of intense discussion or stagger around in Hemingway's footsteps in search of total alcoholic oblivion. Among the best are: *Yesterday's* at no.10, a "romantic" bar with soft music and Irish coffees; the classically pretty *Fontaneria* (no.38) and more earthy

Distrito (no.53), both of them popular with *modernos*; and the grande dame of the whole scene, *La Fídula* (no.57). Here you can sip on *fino* to the accompaniment of classical tunes performed from the tiny stage.

Two of the most spectacular **tiled bars** in Madrid are to be found in this part of town too. The most extravagant example is *Los Gabrieles* (c/ Echegaray 17), but *Viva Madrid* (c/Manuel Gonzales, next door to *La Trucha*) is almost as good. The *Cervecería Alemana* in **Plaza Santa Ana** was one of Hemingway's favorite haunts and consequently full of Americans: *Dick Tracy*, nearby in c/Principe, is a modern, fashionable contrast. Elsewhere, try *La Luna* in c/León, a perenially popular dive, or the *Filmo* and *Café Central* in Plaza Matute, though the latter sometimes has a cover charge during the busy hours. One of the trendiest hangouts during the day is the lounge bar of the *Círculo de Bellas Artes* in c/Alcalá, corner c/Marqués de Casa Riera. Very neo-neo, with marble floors and low-slung sofas, it's an extremely popular meeting place.

Opera

The area in front of the Palacio Real is not one you'd visit on purpose for something to eat or drink, but if you're here during the day there are plenty of places to keep you going.

As far as **restaurants** go, it's a pretty four-star and exclusive selection, typified by *Clara's* in the Plaza Isabel II facing the Teatro Real. The *Café Oriente*, too, in the Plaza de Oriente, is a *pijo* (rich kids) place to feed, but it does have a small *terraza* outside which gives a good view of the tour buses always parked in the square. *Mi Pueblo* (Costanilla de Santiago 20; ☎91/2476930) is a place many Madrileños take friends on special occasions. Though the same cooking can be had elsewhere and cheaper, this place does have table cloths and two types of wine glasses. Less expensive places can be found up towards the Plaza Santo Domingo and the Gran Vía.

With **bars** you'll have a bit more luck. *El Anciano Rey de los Vinos*, on c/ Bailen more or less opposite the ruined cathedral, serves wine and sherry in the traditional manner straight from the barrel. The area also boasts one of the oldest established **flamenco** clubs in Madrid, the *Café de Chinitas*, (c/ Torija 7, ☎91/2485135). It is not cheap, but then again, not totally tacky.

Plaza de España and Gran Vía

The **Gran Vía** is the heart of the **fast food** area, and for once there's little which seems authentically Spanish. The one outstanding exception is *Plata*, at c/Jardines 11, two blocks south of the Gran Vía of c/Montera. Always mobbed (so get there early whether for lunch or dinner), it dishes up some of the best and cheapest (500ptas *menú*) food in the city, which makes the surly service worth enduring. Otherwise, *VIPS* in the Princesa shopping complex is open till 3am which can be handy, but you probably wouldn't choose to eat there any other time. There is a very popular pizza place, *Goffredo's*, at c/Martín de los Heros 4, opposite which is the *Elba,* serving all manner of food from far off places, though mainly from around the Mediterranean. Two Mexican restaurants offer *tacos* and *frijoles* behind the Edificio España: *El Charro* (c/San Leonardo 3) and *A Todo México* (c/San

Bernardino 4). *La Llama*, next door to the latter, serves even more exotic Peruvian fare.

For **bars**, head north from the Plaza de España, where the back streets towards Argüelles are popular haunts of students venturing down from the university area to the northwest.

Retiro

Although there are plenty of kiosks serving food in the park, and a good value cafe/bar in the Prado, this is not an area known for cheap restaurants. There are plenty of **expensive** ones though. Both the hotels *Ritz* and *Palace*, facing each other across the Neptune fountain in the Plaza Canovas del Castillo, have fine restaurants, with the Ritz possibly having a slight edge in class. Better than either is *Horcher* (c/Alfonso XII 6; ☎91/2391922), one of the city's glitziest restaurants at about $60 a head.

Two excellent **traditional cafes** near the Plaza de la Cibeles offer a more modest alternative. The *Café León* on c/Alcalá, and the *Café Gijón* on the Paseo de Recoletos, preserve much of their nineteenth-century atmosphere of gossip and intrigue. The latter serves a lunchtime *menú* and has a summer terrace. The aforementioned *Museo de Jamón*, on Carrera San Jeronimo, lies also within easy walking distance of the Prado, or to the south you'll get a simple, inexpensive meal at the *Bar Gil*, on the Paseo del Prado as you approach Atocha.

Latina, Lavapies, and the Rastro

Continuing south from Sol and Huertas, this is another area with great places to eat and some marvelous old bars, still serving wines from the cask and sherries from the barrel. For **tapas** the Latina area is particularly good, especially along c/Cava Alta and c/Cava Baja. For a good Spanish lunch, stop in at *Latina*, Cava Alta 3; *Casa Lucio* (c/Cava Baja 35; ☎91/2653252) claims to have served the king, is priced accordingly, and was founded by defectors from *Schotis* (11 Cava Baja 11; ☎91/2653230), in the same category. The *Posada de la Villa* (9 Cava Baja 9; ☎2661860) is somewhat cheaper, but a carnivore haven like the above two. Both specialize in huge hunks of roast meat. If you can't face that, **macrobiotic** fare can be found at *El Granero de Lavapies*, c/Argumosa 10, near Metro *Lavapies* (weekdays 1–4pm only).

The **bars** are even livelier: low on style, but high on noise and atmosphere. Heavy metal, punk, post-punk, and rock mount decibel barrages from one bar to the next. Follow the Vespas and the bass-line. On a Sunday morning, before, after, or during a visit to the Rastro, *La Bobia* in c/San Millan is the place where a vertible rogue's gallery meets.

Much more civilized, the little park of **Las Vistillas**, on the south side of the viaduct on c/Bailen, has a number of *terrazas* in which to eat or drink outside. It's named for the "little vistas" to be enjoyed in the direction of the Guadarrama mountains to the northwest.

Malasaña, Chueca, and Points North

If you just want a good square meal with no trendy posturing, then you'll think you've died and gone to heaven if you stumble on the lode of eateries here. The bars, too, form an important counterweight to the action south of the Gran Vía.

For cheap **meals, Chueca** is certainly the best value and often rock-bottom priced. The area bounded by c/San Marcos on the south, c/Pelayo on the west, c/Libertad on the east, and c/Gravina on the north is the most densely packed with establishments. Working away from the Gran Vía, we have enjoyed: *La Vascongada*, c/San Bartolome 10, for game and *menús*; *El Bierzo*, c/Barbieri 10, one of the cheapest in Madrid; and *El Tigre*, c/San Marcos 23, doling out huge portions on a 500-peseta *menú*. Calle Pelayo is particularly rich — *Castillo* at no. 8 (not to be confused with a mediocre namesake on c/Augusto Figueroa) serves good food a la carte at *menú* prices; *Miami* at no. 19 is as un-Floridian as can be imagined, with bow-tie service, huge portions, and insanely low prices; and *La Union* at no. 26 is similar. All of these places conveniently close on different days of the week, so there's always one open; it's difficult to comprehend how they can stay in business as such prices — they probably get by on the loyal patronage of their "regulars."

For less home-style and more adventurous fare, *El Comunista* (*Tienda de Vinos*) on c/Augusto Figueroa is a long-established tradition around here, or you can scarf Peruvian food at *El Inca* (c/Gravina 23; ☎91/2327745). Slightly northeast of the delineated quad, eat decent pizzas at *Casa Gades* (c/Conde de Xiquena 4; ☎2323051), or, for those without shame in Spain, *Hollywood* (c/Tamayo y Baus) serves some of the best hamburgers in the capital and is open until 1am.

If you're absolutely down to your last peseta, cross Fuencarral to **Malasaña**, where *Restaurante Fernandez* (Palma 6) will feed you, simply but fillingly, for about 400ptas; it's always packed with locals and adventurous budget travelers. *Dos Santos*, on the atmospheric Plaza de San Ildefonso, is even plainer, but good for a cheap, quiet lunch. *Bar Fer-Mar*, on c/Santa Barbara leading off the square, has a lunchtime *menú* for 450ptas. **Breakfast** is also close at hand; the *Croissantería* on the corner of c/Corredera Alta de San Pablo and San Ildefonso has some of the best stuffed croissants in the city, plus ice cream and coffee; for slightly more traditional fare (fruit juice, *tortilla*, plain croissant) crowd the bar at *Rocablanca* at Fuencarral 69. Slightly more expensive or exotic options include *Casa de China*, on c/Corredera Alta around the corner from the *Fernandez*; *Gonzalo* at c/Barco 39; *Altamar*, slightly out of the way at c/Luna 28/32, for good seafood *menús*; *Cabada*, Espiritu Santo 12; a very fancy *Restaurante Vegetariano* at c/Marqués de Santa Ana 34; and on the Plaza Dos de Mayo itself, *Maragato* and the adjacent Frenchified *Pepe Botella*. For **dessert**, besides the *croissantería* noted, there's a *heladería* at Fuencarral 60, one of the oldest ice cream and *horchata* bars in Madrid, but closing perversely early (ca. 9:30pm); *Creperie Ma Bretagne* on c/San Vicente Ferrer will be open until after midnight.

Bars run into the hundreds. In **Chueca** one of the nicest places for an aperitif is the *Bodega Ángel Sierra* (Plaza Chueca), or for a vermouth straight from the barrel take yourself to the marvelously tacky *Los Pepinillos* (c/Hortaleza 59). Excellent straightforward *tapas* are served up at the *Bar Santander*, c/Pelayo 15. For **cocktails**, there is the old established *Chicote* on the Gran Vía or, much more chic, *Cock* (c/Reina 16, just behind). The traditional *Café Gijon* (Paseo de Recoletos 21) has already been mentioned: the *Café Comercial* on the Glorieta de Bilbao (c/Fuencarral, Metro *Bilbao*) is a younger version.

In **Malasaña**, again, you don't need to look hard to find a bar. Among the more pleasant are *Casa Camacho* (San Andrés 2) and *El Maño* (Jesús del Valle 1), both *bodegas* serving wine from the barrel; the *Ardosa* (Colón 13), an odd mix of locals after wine and young trendies inhaling imported beer; and the positively bizarre *Diplodocus* (c/ Manuela Malasaña, near the corner of c/Monteleón), where drinks with dinosaurian names are complemented by a Flintstones decor.

Up at the **northern end of Chueca**, around Plaza Alonso Martínez and adjoining Plaza Santa Bárbara, is a younger area full of disco bars. Head-ing up c/Barquillo you'll start to see them — *Cliche* and *Cariatide* for example — but the thickest concentration is in c/Campoamor, with places like *Impacto* (no. 5), *Chatarra* (no. 12), and *Rebote* (no. 15). Nearby, at c/Santa Teresa 12, the *Café Paris* is a dimly-lit cafe-bar with a good restaurant at the back.

Still **farther north**, the area around the **Plaza Olavide** (due north of Bilbao) is both a cheap place to eat and an up-and-coming area for nightlife. *La Tarterie*, for example, on the corner of c/Cardenal Cisneros and c/Albuquerque, specializes in inexpensive quality quiche, and *Rajaja*, corner of c/Trafalgar and c/Albuquerque, is a good nearby bar. To the **northeast**, the area around Metro *Prosperidad* is one of the few places in Madrid where you still seem to get free *tapas* with your drinks. *Cervecería Victoria* in c/Viñaroz and *Mejilloneria La Toja* are both good bets for this.

The length of the **Paseo Castellana** is crowded with much more upscale *terrazas* (sidewalk cafe-bars) throughout the summer months. One of the most popular is *El Teide* (up from *Café Gijón*). Most of these are open till 2 or 3am — they're at least as popular as any disco.

The West

Picnicking in the Casa de Campo aside, the west doesn't hold much in the way of culinary interest. However one excellent **restaurant** deserves recom-mendation: *Casa Mingo*, an Asturian place on the Paseo de la Florida next to the chapel of San Antonio de la Florida. Here you eat roast chicken (which is basically all they serve) washed down with cider and followed up by *yemas* (candied egg-yolk) or aged roquefort-like cheese (*cabrales*). It's good value and great fun.

Music, Nightlife, and Culture

The bars of Chueca and Malasaña, or down south in Huertas, could easily fill every night of your stay, and many of them have good music too, but they are by no means the end of life after dark in Madrid. For a start, the music scene in Madrid sets the pattern for the rest of the country, and the best **rock bands** either come from Madrid or make their name here. You won't find anything radically new or different, but there are some surprisingly good Spanish bands. For names to look out for, check the "Music" section in *Contexts*.

Venues change constantly, and clubs and discos fall in and out of fashion, but even where a place has closed down a new alternative usually opens up in the same place (thanks to the licensing laws). For live bands many of the venues are in Salamanca, northeast of the center — *Sala Universal* (Dr. Esquerdo 2) or *Jacara* (Príncipe de Vergara 90), for example. *Astoria* (Puente de Segovia, behind the Palacio Real) and the *Rock Club* are also likely settings. Bigger concerts are usually held in one of the soccer stadiums; for all of them, keep an eye out for the posters.

Discos and disco bars can be found all over the city. Of the big ones, *Pacha* (c/Barcelo 11) seems to be the eternal survivor. Once a theater and still very theatrical, *Pacha* is exceptionally cool through the week, less so at the weekend when the out-of-townies take over. *Boccacio* (c/Marqués de la Ensenada 16) flows in and out of fashion with more frequency than shoulder pads. *Aire* (Carrera Bermudez 8 in Argüelles) is hypermodern; *Ya'sta* is thoroughly way out, punky, and arty (and open very late); *Kitsch* (c/Galileo 26) is similar, raving until around 5am. *Amnesia* (Paseo de la Castellana 93) outdoes them all by closing at 8am, a rather yuppie place where you go for the last drink of the night. But the most *in* place of all at the moment, and a positive battlefield at the door, is *Archy* (c/Marqués de Riscal 11).

Chueca is not just the home of some of the liveliest bars in the city, but also of Madrid's **gay scene**. All around the Plaza Chueca, graffiti-plastered walls proclaim the existence of a *Zona Gay*, and in the surrounding streets, especially c/Pelayo, you'll find at least a dozen gay bars or clubs. They include *LL's*, *Leather* and *Cuero* (all in c/Pelayo — the last two are supposedly leather-oriented but not many people in Madrid seem to like dressing à la Village People). *Cruising* (c/Perez Galdos 5) does live up to is name though, *Ras* (c/Barbieri 7) is good, and the several bars in c/Infantas which constantly change names (current identities include *Phalos* and *Bachelor*) are busy places. There is an all-night sauna in c/Pelayo.

Over in **Malasaña**, there's a more radical feel to the clubs and bars, and the music is often a few decibels higher. If you like it loud, then head for *Pentagrama* (c/Palma), *Eligeme*, or *King Creole* (both in c/San Vicente Ferrer). For a thoughtful and folksy atmosphere, make for *Café Manuela* or *Estar* (c/San Vicente Ferrer), and to find out what life must have been like for those who remember Country Joe and the Fish, go to the *Tetería de la Abuela* (Granny's Teapot) in c/Espiritu Santo 19. To see where it all began, the very essence of the *movida*, then the *Via Lactea* (c/Velarde 18) is the place to go. Still with its original early 1980s decor, it was here that Spain's more fashionable designers, directors, pop stars and painters used to hang out. Sweet young things come here nowadays in pale imitation.

Other musical tastes are reasonably well catered for as well. **Jazz** clubs include *Clamores* (c/Albuquerque, near metro Bilbao), *Colegio Mayor San Juan Evangelista* (at the university), *El Sol de Jardines* (c/Jardines, south of the Gran Via near metro Gran Via) and the *Café Central* in the Plaza del Angel in Santa Ana. **South American** music can also be good here — try one of the *Barrio Latinos* at c/Segovia 19 or Tetuan 27, and look out for publicity for summer festivals, at which *salsa* is always popular. **Flamenco** is not native to Castile, and most of the places you can see it are strictly for the tourists. If you're prepared to pay, though, you can get the real thing: try the *Café de Silverio* (Manuela Malasaña 20, Thurs.–Sun. late) or *Café de Chinitas*, (c/ Torija 7, in Opera).

Movie theaters can be found all over the downtown area, but most of the films are of course in Spanish. A couple of places which regularly show foreign films in the original language are *La Filmoteca* in the Torre de Madrid (Plaza de España) and *Alphaville*, nearby off c/Princesa. Check, for example, the *Versión original (subtitulada)* listings for foreign movies in the back pages of *El País*. The *Sala Olimpia* in the Plaza de Lavapies has open-air screenings in summer and is the venue for all sorts of alternative events; there are also free films at *La Chopera* (The Poplar Grove) in the Parque del Retiro on summer nights.

Classical Spanish theater performances can be seen regularly at the *Teatro Español* (Plaza Santa Ana) and more modern works in the *Centro Cultural de la Villa* (Plaza de Colón) and in the beautiful *Círculo de Bellas Artes* (Marqués de Casa Riera 2) as well as at many commercial theaters. Classical music and opera is staged at the *Teatro Real* (Plaza Isabel II) and operetta at the *Teatro de la Zarzuela* (c/Jovellanos 4). Cultural events in English are held from time to time at the British Institute (c/ Almagro 5, Metro *Alonso Martinez*), which can also be a useful point for contacts.

Listings for all the above can be found in the rather staid weekly *Guía del Ocio*, which also has extensive lists of restaurants. The national newspapers also cover most of the events going on in Madrid, with full details of film and theater; *El País* is the most thorough and easiest to use. *La Villa de Madrid* is a biweekly newspaper issued free by the municipality, mostly covering current events and issues, but with minimal listings. There's also *En Madrid*, a free tourist office publication, with monthly details in English of the major events, festivals and exhibitions.

At all times, look out for festivals — which may involve the whole of Madrid or an individual *barrio* — and for special events organized by the municipality. The more important dates are included in our listings. Some of the best events are part of the city-council-sponsored *Veranos de la Villa*: free summer concerts put on in the parks, which could range from classical to African music.

Listings

Airlines Almost all have their offices along the Gran Vía or on c/de la Princesa, its continuation beyond the Plaza de España. Exceptions are *Iberia* (Plaza Canovas de Castillo 4; ☎91/4112545) and *British Airways* (c/Serrano 60 5°; ☎900/(toll-free)177777). The *Iberojet* counter at the airport sells discounted seats on scheduled flights if you're prepared to line up and take the risk of not getting on.

Airport Madrid-Barajas, 16km out — regular buses to/from the underground terminal in the Plaza de Colón, starting at about 5am. 24-hour money exchange.

Baggage storage If you want to leave your bags there's a *consigna* at the *Estación Sur de Autobuses* (c/Canarias 17), at the *Auto-res* and *Continental Auto* station, at the airport bus terminal beneath Plaza Colón, and lockers at Atocha and Chamartín stations; for these last your luggage may have to pass through an X-ray check. Many of the bars around the stations will also lock them up for you, but be sure to establish the price, and beware of rip-offs.

Banks Main branches along the c/Alcalá and Gran Vía. *American Express* at Plaza de las Cortes 2 (entrance on Marqués de Cuba; open Mon.–Fri. 9am–5:30pm, 9am–noon Sat., mail desk same hours).

Books In English from *Booksellers S.A.* (c/José Abascal 48; Metro *Iglesias* or *Ríos Rosas*) or *Turners* on C/Genova (Metro *Alonso Martínez*). *Años Luz Libros* (Francisco de Ricci 8; Metro *San Bernardo* or *Argüelles*) has an excellent selection of guide books — including this one. For second-hand volumes try the market on c/Claudio Moyano.

Bullrings Madrid has two, *Carabanchel* (Avda. Matilde Hernández; Metro *Vista Alegre*) and the monumental *Las Ventas* (c/Alcalá 237; Metro *Ventas*). Both have *corridas* throughout the summer.

Buses The main bus depot is the *Estación Sur de Autobuses* (c/ Canarias 17; Metro *Palos de la Frontera*) but by no means all companies use it, though all international lines do. Others are *Auto-Res* (Fernández Shaw 1, Metro *Conde Casal*; services to Castile, Valencia and Extremadura); *Continental Auto* (Alenza 20, Metro *Ríos Rosas*; for Cantabria, Euskadi, and Burgos); *La Sepuldevana* (Paseo de la Florida 11, Metro *Norte*; for Segovia and other points in Old Castile, plus Talavera); and *Herranz* (c/Isaac Peral 10, Metro *Moncloa*; for El Escorial). Always check with the tourist office first — companies tend to move around.

Car rental *Atesa* (Princesa 25; ☎91/2415004); *Avis* (Gran Vía 60, ☎91/2472048); *Europcar* (García de Paredes 12; ☎91/4488706); *Hertz* (Gran Vía 88; ☎91/2421000); and many more. All of these have branches at the airport.

Condoms They're sold at every *farmacía*, but Madrid also boasts a specialist condom shop: *La Discreta* at c/Jardines 19 (Metro *Gran Vía*).

Crime Tourists in Madrid, as anywhere, are prime targets for pickpockets and petty thieves. The main shopping areas, and anywhere with crowds, are their favorite haunts; burger places and the Rastro Sunday market seem especially popular. The simple answer is never to carry more than necessary, and take care of anything valuable. The police are usually sympathetic; you may not get anything back, but they will give you a report form which is necessary for insurance claims. There is even a mobile police van parked outside the station (main building) in the Puerta del Sol.

Embassies Australia (Paseo de la Castellana 143; ☎91/2798501); New Zealand (Fernando el Santo 16; ☎91/4190200); Canada (Nuñez de Balboa 35; ☎91/4314300); USA (Serrano 75; ☎91/2763600).

Environment *Green Party* Pilar de Zaragoza, 83, 28028 Madrid. *Greenpeace* : c/Barquillo 38, 28004 Madrid (☎91/4195254). *Comisión Anti-OTAN de Madrid* (anti-NATO): Campomanes 13; meetings Weds. at 7:30pm.

Farmacías Distinguished by a green cross. There is always one open in every district — the "night shift" is published in the papers, or a notice on the door of any pharmacy will tell you where the nearest open one is.

Feminism Center for contacts: *Asemblea de Mujeres de Madrid* (c/Barquillo 44, 2° izqda). Bookshop: *Librería de Mujeres* (c/San Cristóbal 17).

Festivals The main fiesta is for San Isidro Labrador, Madrid's patron saint, for several days on either side of **May 15**. Others include **May 2**, in Malasaña; **June 13**, around the Ermita de San Antonio de la Florida; bonfires for San Juan in the Retiro from **June 17–24**; **July 9–16** in Chamberí and elsewhere; **August 15** in Latina; **September 24–29** autumn festival in Chamartín; **October 12** in Salamanca; and many others. The tourist offices have fuller details.

Hospitals Central ones include the *Anglo-Americano* (c/Juan XXIII 1, in the University City, Metro *Moncloa*) and *Ciudad Sanitaria La Paz* (c/Dr. Esquerdo 52). For an ambulance, dial ☎91/7344794 or 2523264.

Hiking maps *La Tienda Verde*, Maudes 38, 28003 Madrid (Metro *Ríos Rosas*; ☎91/2336454).

Laundromats Calle Barco 26 (a bit north of Gran Vía; c/Marcenado 15 (Metro *Prosperidad*); c/Donoso Cortés 17 (Metro *Quevedo*); c/Hermosilla 121 (Metro *Goya*); c/Palma 2 (Metro *Tribunal*).

Monday Most museums close. Exceptions are the Palacio Real, San Antonio de la Florida, and the Real Academia (am only).

Police Head office: Puerta del Sol 7. In emergencies dial 092.

Post office Main post office is the *Palacio de Comunicaciones* in the Plaza de la Cibeles (Mon.–Sat. 9am–10pm, Sun. 10am-1pm for stamps and telegrams; 9am–8am for *Lista de Correos* — poste restante — and certified/registered delivery). Branch offices, for example on c/Cruz Verde on the edge of Malasaña, are only open from 9am to 2pm.

Ride sharing An organization called *Asociación para el Auto-Stop Compartido* arranges shared journeys in private cars for a semiannual, yearly or one-shot membership fee (total cost around 4000ptas to Paris, 1000ptas to Alicante). Call them at ☎91/2656565 or stop in at c/Estudios 9.

Soccer *Real Madrid* plays at the *Estadio Bernabeu* in the north of the city (bus #5 or #M12 from the centre), *Atletico Madrid* at the *Estadio Vicente Calderón* in the southwest (bus #34, #35, or #23 from downtown). Check the papers for matches.

Summer For all intents and purposes, Madrid shuts down from about July 20 until September 1 — this means museums, restaurants, and businesses small or large — and it can be very difficult to get anything done. A good two-thirds of the 5 million *Madrileños* are off touring the countryside . . .

Swimming pools The most central among many are the *Aluche* municipal pool (General Fanjul 14, Metro *Latina*); *El Lago* (Av. Valladolid 83, popular with gays; Bus #46); *El Lido*, an open-air pool on the Paseo de la Florida by the Puente de los Franceses; and the open-air pool in the Casa de Campo (Metro *El Lago*).

Telephones International calls can be made from any phone booth or, preferably, from the main *Telefónica* (Gran Vía 28; open 24 hr.). This branch, however, can be traffic-noisy, and from 9am–2pm you're better off at a substation (e.g. c/Virgen de los Peligros 10, south of the Gran Vía). *Telefónica* also handles telexes and faxes (about $8 per page overseas).

Trains The stations are *Chamartín* (for the north, northeast, and France; ☎91/2273160), *Atocha* (for the south, southeast, west and Portugal) and *Norte* (or *Príncipe Pío*; for the northwest; ☎91/3141000). Each has a metro station of the same name. Tickets can also be bought at *RENFE* head office, Alcalá 44 (Mon.–Fri. 8am–2:30pm and 4–7pm, Sat. 8am–1:30pm but there are long lines here and at the stations. Atocha and Chamartín are connected by *tranvía*, with a stop at Recoletos in halfway between. At Atocha a new terminal has largely supplanted the old one; don't wander into the obsolete building by mistake.

Travel agents The Spanish economy has begun to generate a large middle class of avid travelers, and the increased passenger volume has lowered air fares; in late summer, for example, you can expect to pay 11,000ptas one-way, 15,000 round-trip for a charter to London; 22,000 ptas for a one-way charter to Athens; and perhaps 27,000ptas for a scheduled economy flight to New York ... not too bad. The main student travel agency is *TIVE* (Fernando el Católico 88; Metro *Quevedo*; ☎4019011). Non-students could try the following competent budget travel agencies: *Universal/Unijoven* (c/San Bernardo 98; Metro *San Bernardo*), and *Mundojoven* (Hortaleza 8; Metro *Gran Vía*). In a class of its own is *Años Luz* (c/Rodríguez de San Pedro 2, suite 1202; Metro *San Bernardo*; ☎91/4455962), which offers flights and trips to just about any known destination (Iceland, Western Sahara, Brittany, Mozambique . . .), runs a travel bookshop (see bookshops, above), and coordinates a hitchhikers/drivers service for arranging lifts throughout Spain.

Turismo Offices are at the airport (Barajas) in International Arrivals (☎91/5221165; Mon.–Sat. 8am–8pm, Sun. 12:30–5pm); in the Torre de Madrid in the Plaza de España (c/Princesa 1; ☎91/2412325; Mon.–Fri. 9am–7pm, Sat. 9:30am–1:30pm); at c/Duque de Medinaceli 2 (☎91/4294630; Mon.–Fri. 9am–3pm) and in the Estación de Chamartín. There's also a municipal tourist office at Plaza Mayor 3 (☎91/2665477; Mon.–Fri. 10am–1:30pm and 4–7pm, Sat. 10am–1:30pm).

What's on The most comprehensive listings of what's going on and where are found in the weekly *Guía del Ocio*, available at every kiosk (90ptas). The daily paper *El País* also has good coverage of what's happening in the capital and the municipality produces a paper, *Villa de Madrid*, available from various culture centers. The free *Turismo* handout *En Madrid* is also more useful than you might expect.

AROUND MADRID

In a ring around the capital are some of Spain's most fascinating cities. All the destinations below can be treated easily as a day trip from Madrid, but they also lie on the main routes out. **Aranjuez** sits directly astride the road into central Andalucía, and from **Toledo** you can continue in this direction or strike eastwards towards Extremadura. To the northwest the roads lead past **El Escorial**, through the dramatic scenery of the **Sierra de Guadarrama**, with Madrid's weekend ski resorts, to Ávila and Segovia. From Ávila it's just a short step on to Salamanca, or there are beautiful routes down through the **Sierra de Gredos** into Extremadura. From **Segovia** the routes to the north to Valladolid, Burgos, and beyond — await. To the east there's less of interest, but **Alcalá de Henares** and **Guadalajara** can both offer a worthwhile break in the journey into Aragón and Catalunya.

Wherever you're going it's a good idea to pick up **leaflets and maps** from the *Turismo* in Madrid first; you'll save considerable time and irritation later.

Toledo

By anyone's reckoning **TOLEDO** is one of the greatest cities in Spain, and for sheer concentration of attractions it ranks with anywhere in Europe. It's not a big place — the harsh craggy surroundings allow no room for expansion — but at every twist of the tangled streets there's a new source of fascination. Capital of medieval Spain until 1560, it remains the seat of the Catholic Primate and a city redolent of past glories.

The **setting** has much to do with it: in a landscape of abrasive desolation, Toledo sits on a rocky mound isolated on three sides by a looping gorge of the Río Tajo (Tagus). Every available inch of this outcrop has been built on; houses, synagogues, churches, and mosques are heaped upon one another in a haphazard spiral which the cobbled lanes infiltrate as best they can. You're bound to get lost but that's part of the charm; Toledo, above all other towns in Spain, is a place to wander and absorb. It *is* a veritable museum of art and architecture and you shouldn't leave without seeing at least the El Grecos, the cathedral, synagogues and Alcázar, but give it all time . . . stumble upon things. Enter any inviting doorway and you may well find stunning patios, rooms, chapels, and ceilings, often of Mudejar workmanship, which can be as rewarding as the great sights. Despite encroaching modernity — the Tajo, for example, is very polluted, its waters depleted by industry and agriculture — and despite the quite extraordinary number of bus tours which pour through, Toledo should prove to be one of the most extravagant of Spanish experiences. The packaged hordes are in any case easy enough to avoid; simply slip into the back streets or stay the night, since by 6pm the buses will have all packed up and gone home.

Toledo was known to the Romans, who captured it in 193 B.C., as Toletum, a small but well-defended town. Taken by the Visigoths, who made it their capital, it was already an important cultural and trading center by the time the Moors arrived in 712. The period which followed, with Mozarabic (Arabized)

Christians, Jews, and Moors living together in relative equality, was one of rapid growth and prosperity, which saw Toledo become the most important northern outpost of the Muslim emirates. Though there are few physical remains of this period, save the miniature mosque of *El Cristo de la Luz*, the long domination has left a clear stamp on the atmosphere and shape of the whole city.

When Alfonso VI and El Cid retook the town in 1085, Moorish influence scarcely weakened. Although Toledo became capital of Castile and the base for campaigns against the Moors in the south, the city itself was a haven of cultural tolerance. Not only was there a school of translators revealing the scientific and philosophical achievements of the East, but Arab craftsmen and techniques were responsible for many of the finest buildings of the period: look, for example, at the churches of **San Roman** or **Santiago del Arrabal** or at any of the old **city gates**. At the same time Jewish culture remained powerful. There were at one time at least seven **synagogues** — of which two, **Santa María la Blanca** and **El Transito**, survive — and Jews occupied many of the positions of power. The most famous was Samuel Levi, treasurer and right-hand man of Pedro the Cruel until the king lived up to his name by murdering him and stealing his wealth. From this period, too, dates the most important purely Christian monument, Toledo's awesome **cathedral**.

The golden age was ended abruptly in the sixteenth century by the transfer of the capital to Madrid, following hard on the heels of the Inquisition's mass expulsions of Jews and Moors. The city played little part in subsequent Spanish history until the civil war (see the **Alcázar**) and it remains, despite the droves of tourists, essentially the medieval city so often painted by El Greco.

The Cathedral

In a country so overflowing with massive religious institutions, the chief **Cathedral** just has to be something special, and it is. A robust Gothic construction which took over 200 years (1227–1493) to complete, it has a richness of internal decoration in almost every conceivable style, with masterpieces of the Gothic, Renaissance, and baroque periods. The exterior is best appreciated from outside the city, where the 100-meter spire and the weighty buttressing can be seen to advantage. From the street it's less impressive, so hemmed in by surrounding houses that you can't really sense the scale or grandeur of the whole.

There are eight doorways, but the main entrance is through the **Puerta de Mollete** beside the main tower, which leads into the **cloister**. Here tickets are sold for the various chapels, chapter houses, and treasuries which require them. (The main body of the cathedral is closed from 1pm–3:30pm; the parts which need tickets can be visited from 10:30am–1pm and 3:30pm–7pm, 3:30–6pm in winter. On Sun. am the *coro* cannot be visited, and on Mon. the New Museums are closed.) Inside, the central nave is divided from four aisles by a series of clustered pillars supporting the vaults, 88 in all, the aisles continuing around behind the main altar to form an apse. There is magnificent **stained glass** throughout, mostly dating from the fifteenth and sixteenth centuries, and particularly in two rose windows above the north and

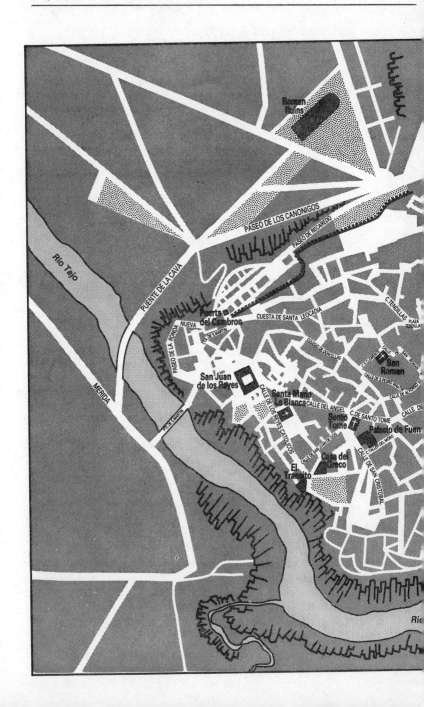

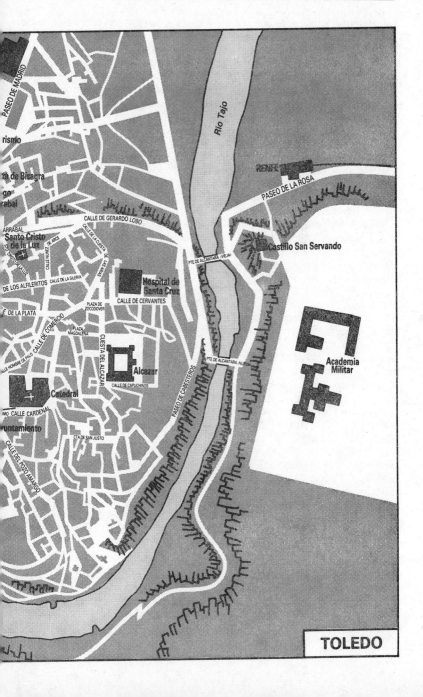

Rio Tajo

PASEO DE MADRID

rismo

ta de Bisagra

go
rabal

RENFE

PASEO DE LA ROSA

CALLE DE GERARDO LOBO

ARRABAL
**Santo Cristo
de la Luz**

Castillo San Servando

CALLE DE LA CUESTA DE LA SARRA

CALLE NUÑEZ DE ARCE

DE LOS ALFILERITOS   CALLE DE LA SILERIA

PTE. DE ALCANTARA (VIEJA)

F. DE LA PLATA

Mospital de
Santa Cruz

CALLE DE CERVANTES

PLAZA DE
ZOCODOVER

CALLE DE COMERCIO

PLAZA
MAGDALENA

CALLE HOMBRE DE PALO

CUESTA DEL ALCAZAR

Alcazar

PTE. DE ALCANTARA (NUEVA)

**Academia
Militar**

CALLE DE CAPUCHINOS

PASEO DE CABESTEROS

Catedral

MO CALLE CARDENAL

untamiento

CTA DE SAN JUSTO

CALLE DEL POZO AMARGO

TOLEDO

south doors. Beside the south door (*Puerta de los Leones*) is a huge, ancient **fresco of Saint Christopher**.

At the physical heart of the church, blocking the nave, is the **Coro** (Choir), itself almost a museum of sculpture. The carved wooden stalls are in two tiers. The lower level, by Rodrigo Aleman, depicts the conquest of Granada, with each seat showing a different village being taken by the Christians. The portraits of Old Testament characters on the stalls above were done in the following century, on the north side by Philippe Vigarni and on the south by Alonso Berruguete, whose superior technique clearly shows. He also carved the large **Transfiguration** here from a single block of alabaster. The *reja* (grille) which encloses the *coro* is said to be plated with gold, but it was covered in iron to disguise its value from Napoleon's troops and they have never managed to clean it off again.

The **Capilla Mayor** stands directly opposite. Its gargantuan altarpiece, stretching clear to the roof, is one of the triumphs of Gothic art, overflowing with intricate detail and fanciful embellishments. It contains a synopsis of the entire New Testament, culminating in a Calvary at the very summit. To either side are the tombs of the mighty, including (on the left) those of kings Alfonso VII and Sancho III and (on the right) those of Sancho II and the powerful Cardinal Mendoza.

Directly behind the main altar is perhaps the most extraordinary piece of fantasy in the cathedral, the **Transparente**. Baroque and wildly extravagant with its marble cherubs sitting on fluffy marble clouds, it's wonderful all the same, especially when the sun reaches through the hole punched in the roof specifically for that purpose. You'll notice a cardinal's hat hanging from the vaulting just in front of this. Spanish primates are buried where they choose, with the epitaph they choose, and with their hat hanging above them, where it stays until it rots. One of them chose to be buried here, and there are other pieces of headgear dotted around the cathedral.

There are well over twenty **chapels** around the walls, all of which are of some interest. There are fine tombs, particularly in the Capilla de Santiago, the octagonal Capilla de San Idelfonso and the gilded Capilla de los Reyes. In the **Capilla Mozarabe** mass is still celebrated daily according to the ancient Visigothic rites. When the church tried to ban the old ritual in 1086 the people of Toledo were outraged. The dispute was put to a combat, which the Mozarabe champion won, but the church demanded further proof: trial by fire. The Roman prayer book was blown to safety, while the Mozarabe version remained, unburnt, in the flames. Both sides claimed victory, and in the end the two rituals were allowed to coexist. If you want to look inside, get there at 9:30am, when the mass is celebrated; otherwise it's locked.

The Capilla de San Juan houses the riches of the cathedral **Treasury**, above all a solid silver *custodia* (repository for eucharist wafers) 3m high and weighing over 200 kilos. It was made by German-born silversmith Enrique de Arfe in the sixteenth century, and gilded seventy years later. The **Sacristia** contains a still more impressive accumulation of wealth, this time artistic; a *Disrobing of Christ* and portraits of the Apostles by El Greco, Cardinal Borja portrayed by Velázquez, and Goya's *Christ Taken by the Soldiers* are just some of the highlights. In the adjoining rooms, the so-called New Museums have recently been laid out. These contain works of art that were previously locked away or poorly displayed. Among them are more El Grecos and paintings by Caravaggio, Gerard David, and Morales. Most interesting is El Greco's most important piece of sculpture (only a few pieces survive), a polychromed wooden group of San Ildefonso and the Virgin. The **Sala Capitular** (Chapter House) has a magnificent sixteenth-century *artesonado* ceiling and portraits of all Spain's archbishops to the present day. Lastly, the cathedral's **tower** (entrance in c/Hombre de Palo) doesn't have regular visiting hours, but the views from it are superb — it's worth asking about access.

El Greco — and a Tour of Toledo

Even if you've never seen Toledo — and even if you've no idea what to expect — there's an uncanny familiarity about one's first view of it, with the Alcázar and the cathedral spire towering above the tawny mass of the town. This is due to **El Greco**, whose constant depiction of the city (as background, even, for the Crucifixion) seems to have stuck, albeit unwittingly, somewhere in everyone's consciousness. Domenico Theotocopoulos, "the Greek," was born on Crete in 1541 and settled in Toledo in about 1577 after failing to get work on the decoration of the Escorial. His paintings — the most individual, most intensely spiritual visions of all Spanish art — are extraordinary; however often he repeats the same subject, they always offer some new surprise or fresh insight. And Toledo is full of them.

His masterpiece, *The Burial of the Count of Orgaz*, is arguably the city's outstanding attraction, outshining even the multifarious delights of the cathedral. It's housed, alone, in an annex to the church of **Santo Tomé** (10am–1:45pm and 3:30–6:45pm, 3:30–5:45pm in winter) and depicts the count's funeral, at which St. Stephen and St. Augustine appeared to lower him into the tomb. It combines his genius for the mystic, exemplified in the upper half of the picture where the count's soul is being received into heaven, with his great powers as a portrait painter and master of color. The figures watching the burial are portraits of contemporaries, including (it is said) Lope de Vega, Cervantes, and El Greco himself. Felipe II, though still alive when it was painted, is among the heavenly onlookers. Jan Morris wrote of this picture that "it epitomizes the alliance between God and the Spanish ruling classes . . . (who) expect miracles as a matter of policy, and are watching the saints at work rather as they might watch . . . any foreign expert sent to do a job."

From Santo Tomé the c/de los Amarillos leads down to the old *Judería* (Jewish quarter) and to the **Casa del Greco** (Tues.–Sat. 10am–2pm and 4–6pm; Sun. 10am–2pm), part of the house where the artist lived for much of his time in Toledo. The apartments themselves have been restored in a completely bogus, folksy style, but there are some interesting pictures, including sketches by Velázquez and, in the room which was supposedly El Greco's studio, a study of his own hand. The **museum** which the house contains is very much more worthwhile, displaying many fine El Grecos, among them his famous *View of Toledo* and another complete series of the Twelve Apostles, done later and subtly different from the set in the cathedral. Incidentally, for thrilling, uncluttered **views** of Toledo, walk along the

Carretera de Circunvalación which runs along the opposite bank of the Tajo from the city, from one of the medieval fortified bridges to the other. This takes a well-spent hour, which will show to advantage the skyline so familiar from various El Grecos (though several other bridges have disappeared in the intervening centuries). For the panorama most resembling *Storm Over Toledo*, you have to climb the hill above the westerly bridge of San Martín.

The Taller del Moro, the Synagogues, and San Juan de los Reyes

Between Santo Tomé and the Casa del Greco you pass the entrance to the **Palace of the Counts of Fuensalida**, a beautiful fifteenth-century mansion where Carlos V's Portuguese wife Isabel died. You used to be able to visit her treasures but it is now closed to the public. A garden separates it from the **Taller del Moro**, three fourteenth-century rooms of a Mudejar palace which was later used by masons working on the cathedral, with magnificent Mudejar decoration and doorways intact. It is approached through its own entrance in the c/Taller de Moro (Tues.–Sat. 10am–2pm and 4–7pm; Sun. 10am–2pm).

Almost next door to the Greco house, on c/Reyes Católicos, is the synagogue of **El Transito**, built along Moorish lines by Samuel Levi in 1366. It became a church after the expulsion of the Jews, but is being restored to its original form. The interior is a simple galleried hall, brilliantly decorated with polychromed stucco-work and superb filigree windows. Hebrew inscriptions praising God, King Pedro, and Samuel Levi surround the walls. Nowadays it houses a small **Sephardic Museum** (Tues.–Sat. 10am–2pm and 4–5:45pm; Sun. 10am–2pm), tracing the distinct traditions and development of Jewish culture in Spain. During restoration there are restrictions on the number of visitors allowed in at any one time, though admission is free until works are completed. The only other surviving synagogue — **Santa María la Blanca** (10am–7pm, 10am–6pm in winter) is a short way down the same street. Like El Transito, which it predates by over a century, it has been both church and synagogue, though it looks more like a mosque. Four rows of octagonal pillars each support seven horseshoe arches, all of them with elaborate and individual designs molded in plaster, while it has preserved from its time as a church a fine sixteenth-century *retablo*. The whole effect is quite stunning, accentuated by a deep red floor tiled with decorative *azulejos*.

Continuing down c/Reyes Católicos, you come to the superb church of **San Juan de los Reyes** (10am–2pm and 3:30–7pm, 3:30–6pm in winter), its exterior bizarrely festooned with the chains worn by Christian prisoners from Granada released on the reconquest of their city. It was originally a Franciscan convent founded by the "Catholic Kings," Fernando and Isabella, to celebrate their victory at the Battle of Toro and in which, until the fall of Granada, they had planned to be buried. Designed by Juan Gras in the decorative late Gothic style known as Isabelline (after the queen), its double-storied cloister is quite outstanding; the upper floor has an elaborate Mudejar ceiling, and the crests of Castile and Aragón, seven arrows and a yoke, are carved everywhere in assertion of the new unity brought by the royal marriage. This theme is continued in the airy church where imperious eagles support the royal shields.

From the Puerta de Cambrón to Santo Cristo de la Luz

If you leave the city here by the *Puerta de Cambrón* you can follow the Paseo de Recaredo, which runs alongside a stretch of Moorish walls to the Hospital de Tavera (10:30am–1:30pm and 3:30-6pm). This, a Renaissance palace with beautiful twin patios, houses the private collection of the Duchess of Lerma. The gloomy interior is a reconstruction of a sixteenth-century mansion scattered with fine paintings, including a *Day of Judgement* by Bassano; the portrait of Carlos V by Titian is a copy of the original in the Prado. The hospital's archives are kept here too: thousands of densely hand-written pages chronicling the illnesses treated. The museum contains several works by El Greco and Ribera's gruesome portrait of a freak "bearded woman." Also here is the death mask of Cardinal Tavera, the hospital's founder, and his ornate marble tomb (the last work of Alonso Berruguete).

Toledo's main gate, the **Nueva Puerta de Bisagra**, has become marooned in a constant swirl of traffic, but it still seems a formidable obstacle for any invader to overcome. Its patterned tile roofs bear the coat of arms of Carlos V. Alongside is the gateway that it replaced, the ninth-century Moorish gate through which Alfonso VI and El Cid led their triumphant armies in 1085. The main road bears to the left, but on foot you can climb towards the center of town by a series of stepped alleyways, after a glance at the intriguing exterior of the Mudejar church of **Santiago del Arrabal**.

The Cuesta del Cristo de la Luz leads up here past the tiny mosque of **Santo Cristo de la Luz**. Built by Musa Ibn Ali in the tenth century on the foundations of a Visigothic church, it's one of the oldest Moorish monuments surviving anywhere in Spain. Only the nave however, with its nine different cupolas, is the original Arab construction; the apse was added when the building was converted into a church, and is claimed to be the first product of the Mudejar style. The head of a Visigoth peering out from one of the capitals is proof, if any were needed, of Moorish tolerance. According to legend as King Alfonso rode into the town in triumph, his horse stopped and knelt before the mosque. Excavations revealed a figure of Christ, still illuminated by a lamp which had burned throughout three and a half centuries of Muslim domination — hence the name *Cristo de la Luz*. The mosque itself, set in a small park and open on all sides to the elements, is so small that it seems more like a miniature summer pavilion, but with an elegant simplicity of design that few of the great monuments can match. It has recently been fenced in and there are no set hours for visiting, but the caretaker lives across the street and will normally appear to let visitors in. He'll also show you through the garden where you can climb to the battlements of the **Puerta del Sol**, a great fourteenth-century Mudejar gateway.

The Alcázar

At the heart of modern life in Toledo is the **Plaza de Zocodover** (its name derived from the Arabic word *souk*), where everyone converges for an after-noon *copa*. Dominating it, as it does the whole of Toledo, is the bluff, impos-ing **Alcázar** (9:30am–7pm, closes 6pm in winter; entrance at the back). There has probably always been a fortress on this commanding position, but the present building is basically the one put up by Carlos V, though it has been burned and bombarded so often that almost nothing is original. The most recent destruction was in 1936 during one of the most symbolic and extraordinary episodes of the civil war, involving a two-month siege of the Nationalist-occupied Alcázar by the Republican town.

On July 20 Colonel Moscardó and a group of Nationalist rebels under his command were driven into the Alcázar, and barricaded themselves in with a large group that included 600 women and children and up to 100 left-wing hostages (the latter were never seen again). After many phone calls from Madrid to persuade them to surrender, a Toledo attorney phoned Moscardó with an ultimatum: within ten minutes the Republicans would shoot his son, just captured that morning. Moscardó declared that he would never surrender and told his son "If it be true, commend your soul to God, shout *Viva España*, and die like a hero." (His son was actually shot with others a month later in reprisal for an air raid.) Inside, though not short of ammunition, the defenders had so little food that they had to eat their horses.

The number of Republican attackers varied from 1000 to 5000, with people coming from Madrid to take potshots from below. Two of the three mines they planted under the towers exploded but nothing could disturb the solid rock foundations. The besiegers tried spraying gasoline all over the walls then setting fire to it, but with no effect. Finally, Franco decided to relieve Moscardó and diverted an army that was heading for Madrid. On September 27 Varela commanded the successful attack on the town, which was followed by the usual bloodbath — not one prisoner was taken.

Franco's regime completely rebuilt the fortress as a monument to the glorification of its defenders (the fascist newspaper *El Alcázar* also commemorates the siege) and their propaganda models and photos are still displayed. But objectionable exercise though this is, it's a fascinating story, and the Alcázar also offers the best views of the town, its upper windows level with the top of the cathedral spire (though in recent years access has been restricted — part of the building is still occupied by the military). Across the river the ancient **Castillo de San Servando** stands next to a modern military academy.

Museums

The **Hospital de Santa Cruz** (Tues.-Sat. 10am-7pm, closes 6pm in winter, Sun. 10am-2pm), a superlative Renaissaice building in itself, houses some of the finest El Grecos in Toledo, including *The Assumption*, a daringly unorthodox work of feverish spiritual intensity, and a *Crucifixion* with the town as backdrop. As well as outstanding works by Goya and Ribera, the collection also contains a mass of ancient carpets and faded tapestries (including a magnificent fifteenth-century Flemish tapestry called *The Astrolabe*), a military display (note the flags borne by Don Juan of Austria at the Battle of Lepanto), sculpture, and a small archaeological collection. Don't miss the patio with its ornate staircase — the entrance is beside the ticket booth.

The **Museo de Arte Visigotico** (10am-2pm and 4-6:30pm; closed Sun pm. and all Mon.) is housed in a very different, though equally impressive building, the church of **San Román**. Here Moorish and Christian elements — horseshoe arches, early murals, and a splendid Renaissance dome —

combine to make it the most interesting church in Toledo. Its twelfth-century Mudejar tower originally stood apart from the main body of the church, in the manner of Muslim minarets. Visigothic jewelry (though the best is in the *Museo Arqueológico* in Madrid), documents, and archaeological fragments make up the bulk of the collection.

A few new museums have opened in Toledo recently. Not far from the Visigothic museum, in the **Convento de Santo Domingo el Antiguo**, the nuns display their art treasures in the old choir (11am–1:30pm and 4–7pm). More interesting is the high altarpiece of the church, El Greco's first major commission in Toledo. Unfortunately, most of the canvases have gone to museums and are here replaced by copies, leaving only two *St. John*s and a *Resurrection* in situ. The **Posada de la Hermandad**, near the market square at the back of the cathedral, is a recently restored building now the home of temporary exhibitions. Other exhibitions are staged at the **Museo de Arte Contemporaneo**, in a refurbished sixteenth-century house near Santo Tomé.

Practicalities

You'll need to stay in Toledo. A day can't possibly do justice and even in two you'd be hard pressed to see everything. In the evening, with the crowds gone and the skyline picked out by floodlights, it's a different city entirely. Unfortunately on a weekend, or during the summer, or with a combination of the two, overnighting can be difficult to arrange, and you may have to steel yourself for the possibility of having to make two day trips out of Madrid, moving on, or crashing in one of the campgrounds (see below).

Toledo's **Turismo**, outside the city walls between the Puerta de Bisagra and the Hospital de Tavera (Mon.–Sat. 9am–2pm and 4–6pm; closed Sat. pm and all day Sun.) has full lists of places to stay, maps, and a useful information board outside for when it's closed. But it's awkward to get to on arrival, so if your priority concern is **accommodation**, head directly for the old town. Among the more central cheap establishments are *Pensión Lumbreras* (Juan Labrador 7, ☎925/221571); *Fonda Segovia* (Recoletos 2/4, 300m northwest of the Zocodover); a *CH* on Calle de la Merced 2, corner Buzones, *María Soledad* (Soledad 1); *Pension Descalzos* (Descalzos 30 ☎925/222888); and *Fonda la Perala* (Perala 29, ☎925/221831). There are also *fondas* in Cuesta del Can and c/Nuncio Viejo, all still central, though mostly unmarked. Moving up a notch, there is the *Hostal la Armas* at the corner of Plaza Zocodover itself, on c/de Armas, the *Hostal Lino* (Santa Justa 9, ☎925, ☎925/223350), the *Hostal Labrador* (J. Labrador 16, ☎925/222620), and (as a last resort) the *Hostal Santa Bárbara*, just opposite the railroad station (☎925/220298). At slow times of the year guides hover in the Zocodover, pouncing on those arriving with baggage and finding a room for a small fee. Since the places listed are scattered all over town, and the guides will know which have space, this can save time and shoe leather.

The **youth hostel** (with a nice, free swimming pool) is on the outskirts of town in a wing of the castle of San Servando (☎925/224554) and is quite good; so is the food, which can be taken half or full board (worth at least one meal a day). A YHA card is generally required, but if they're not full (unusual) you might be able to talk your way in without one. Of the two **campgrounds**, *Circo Romano* (at c/Circo Romano 21) is on the opposite side of town from the hostel, an easy ten-minute walk from the Puerta de Bisagra, though slightly more (with a hill to climb) from the bus station and almost a half hour from *RENFE*. Although the grounds are well amenitied, with a *bar/restaurante* and a swimming pool (hefty charge), it's dusty and stony, most of the patrons are car campers, and it's not much good for tents. The other campground, *El Greco*, is 1½km out of town on the road to Madrid. Sometimes there are also rooms available in the **university dorms** — ask at the *Oficina de Información Juvenil* in c/Trinidad, by the cathedral.

Eating is relatively expensive in Toledo, though there are a few bright spots. Two of the most inexpensive restaurants in town, *La Bisagra* (c/Arrabal 14) and *Arrabal*, face each other from opposite sides of the road, just uphill from the Puerta Bisagra. *Mesón* (sic) on c/Real 15, just below the Plaza Merced, does *menús* for 500–600ptas; in the same neighborhood you can get cheap *comidas* (lunch only) at *Casa Pedro*, just inside the Puerto del Cambrón. The *Bar la Taurina* (Cordonerías 2, north of the cathedral) also has a reasonable lunchtime menu. The *Mesón la Hiedra*, at Nuncio Viejo 23, is not so cheap as the foregoing but is a rather original food bistro. The *Café Alex* on the adjacent square makes a quiet outdoor retreat, since cars can't get in or by — a rarity here. Several outdoor cafes on c/Santa Fe, behind the Zocodover, to the northwest, are popular with young people in the evenings. On the opposite side of the Zocodover, a few not overly inflated restaurants can be found in the Plaza de la Magdalena and in the small surrounding alleys; try *El Nido*. In c/Barrio Rey, in the same area, some establishments offer local game specialities (partridge, pheasant, quail) quite cheaply. Another local (and expensive) speciality is marzipan; the *Casa Telesfon* on the Zocodover sells several varieties.

There are ten direct (plus one changing) trains a day **from Madrid** to Toledo (6am–10pm, from Atocha) and 28 buses (half-hourly, 6am–10pm); either takes a little under ninety minutes. Toledo's **train station**, a marvelous mock Mudejar creation, is some way out on the Paseo de la Rosa, a beautiful twenty-minute walk or a bus ride (#1, #3 or #5) to the heart of town. The new **bus station** is on Avenida de Castilla la Mancha in the modern, lower part of the city; buses run frequently to Zocodover, though if you take shortcuts through the barrio just below the walls it a mere ten minutes to the Bisagra gate.

Heading **onward** (or back) from Toledo there are several places where you might consider breaking the journey. ILLESCAS, toward Madrid, used to be worth going to for five more works by El Greco in the **Hospital de la Caridad**, but they are currently "on loan" to the Prado. Check before you go since it is otherwise an undistinguished, scruffy town. Heading south towards CIUDAD REAL you pass through ORGAZ, where the Count came from, now a quiet village with a beautiful plaza and small castle. Also to the south, GUADAMUR has an outstanding castle, and is served by three buses a day from Toledo. The rail routes east offer a yet more worthwhile stop: in ARANJUEZ.

Aranjuez and Chinchón

The beauty of **ARANJUEZ** is its greenery — it's easy to forget just how dry and dusty most of central Spain is until you come upon this little oasis at its heart. It was once the spring and autumn retreat of the Spanish royal family, and their palaces and luxuriant gardens remain the principal attraction. But Aranjuez is famed, too, for the succulence of its fruit and vegetables, particularly (in summer) giant strawberries and fresh asparagus. There are stalls all along the main road dishing out strawberries and cream (*fresas con nata*) and several excellent restaurants on the banks of the Tajo. *La Rana Verde* (the Green Frog) is the most famous of these, but it's very expensive; you can eat much more cheaply in the middle of town, if in rather less elegant surroundings. Or buy your own food from the *Mercado de San Antonio* near the Jardines Isabel II, always overflowing with local produce.

The **Palace and Gardens** were an attempt by the Spanish Bourbon monarchs to create a Versailles in Spain; Aranjuez clearly isn't in the same league but it's a pleasant place to while away a few hours. The gardens are open all day, the buildings (covered by one joint ticket) daily except Tuesday from 10am to 1pm and 3:30 to 6:30pm between May and September. The eighteenth-century **Palacio Real** is more remarkable for the ornamental fantasies inside than for any virtues of architecture. There are hundreds of rooms, all exotically furnished, most amazingly so in the **Porcelain Room**, entirely covered in decorative ware from the factory which used to stand in Madrid's Retiro park. The Smoking Room is a copy of one of the finest halls of the Alhambra in Granada, though executed with rather less subtlety. Most of the palace dates from the reign of the nymphomaniac Queen Isabel II, and many of the scandals and intrigues which led to her eventual abdication were played out here.

Outside, on a small island, are the fountains of the **Jardín de la Isla**. The **Jardín del Principe**, on the other side of the main road, is more attractive with shaded walks along the river and any number of spots for a siesta. At its far end is the **Casa del Labrador** (Peasant's House) which is anything but what the name implies. Richard Ford described it well over a century ago as "another plaything of that silly Charles IV, a foolish toy for the spoiled children of fortune, in which great expense and little taste are combined to produce a thing which is perfectly useless." Great expense, certainly, for the house contains more silk, marble, crystal, and gold than would seem possible to fit into so small a place, as well as a huge collection of fancy clocks. The guided tour goes into great detail about the weight and value of every item. Also in the gardens, by the river, is a small **boating museum** with the brightly colored launches in which royalty would take to the river. A bus service occasionally connects the various sites, but all are within easy walking distance of each other, and it's a very pleasant place to stroll.

If you'd like a **swim** after your exertions there's a pool in the attractive **campground** *Camping Soto del Castillo* (open May–Sept.; ☎91/2941395) on the far side of the riverbank, easiest reached by the footbridge near the museum. There are also a few **hostales** dotted around the town (the *Rusiñol*, c/san Antonio 26, is good; ☎91/8910155), but you probably won't want to stay; Aranjuez functions principally as a respite from the heat and dust of Madrid, or to break your journey back from Toledo or en route to the south. Which is not to say that it isn't a relaxing place to enjoy Spanish provincial life. The **Turismo** is on Plaza Santiago Rusiñol. Aranjuez is a major **rail** junction (with trains to Madrid's Atocha station every 15 min. throughout the day) and in summer an old wooden steam train called the *Tren de la Fresa* (Strawberry Train) does excursions to Madrid(reserve through a travel agent), and train enthusiasts won't begrudge the extra cost. The town is also on the main **road** to Andalucía, and thus a good point to try **hitching** and infinitely preferable to standing in the suburbs of Madrid. If heading south on the train, make sure that you have a ticket with a seat reserved for each leg of the journey, since many of the trains to Sevilla are full.

Another brief excursion from Madrid is to the picturesque village of **CHINCHÓN**, home of the **anís** (anisette) drunk all over Spain. You can visit some of the factories where it's made (some in the fifteenth-century castle) or simply sit in the elegant Plaza Mayor and sample it. On the high altar of the **Iglesia de la Asunción** (1537–1626), in the plaza, stands Goya's *The Assumption of the Virgin*. Occasional bullfights and theatrical productions are put on here. For cheap eating try the *Mesón del Duende* or *Mesón del Comendador*. Buses run sporadically from Aranjuez and regularly back to Madrid.

El Escorial

Northwest of Madrid extends the line of mountains formed by the Sierra de Guadarrama and the Sierra de Gredos, snowcapped and forbidding even in summer. Beyond them lie Ávila and Segovia, but on this side, in the foothills of the Guadarrama, is San Lorenzo del Escorial and the bleak **Real Monasterio del Escorial**, part convent, part palace, part mausoleum.

It's an enormous building, rectangular, overbearing, and severe, which from the outside looks more like a prison than a palace. It was designed and built between 1563 and 1584, Juan Bautista de Toledo being the original architect, but his one-time assistant, Juan de Herrera, is normally given all the credit. Planned by Felipe II as a monastery and mausoleum where he himself would live the life of a monk, it was a place from which he could, as he boasted "rule the world with two inches of paper." Later monarchs had less ascetic lifestyles, enlarging and richly decorating the palace quarters, but Felipe's simple rooms, with the chair that supported his gouty leg and the deathbed from which he could look down into the church where mass was constantly celebrated, remain the most fascinating. The whole place, in the words of nineteenth-century traveler Augustus Hare, is "a stone image of the mind of its founder." About 7km away is "Felipe's Seat," a chair carved into a rocky outcrop with a view out towards the palace. His Majesty is supposed to have sat here to watch the construction going on. If you have your own car, it still offers a great view; take the Ávila road and turn off after 3km.

The complex is run by the *Patrimonio Nacional*, which means that through parts of it (the Pantheons and the Palace) you have no choice but to be shepherded by officious guides in groups of up to a hundred at a time. You can

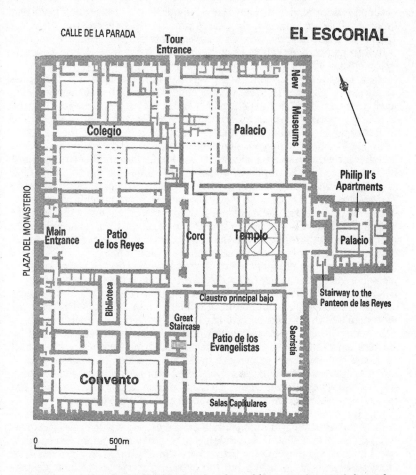

CALLE DE LA PARADA

Tour Entrance

EL ESCORIAL

New Museums

Colegio

Palacio

Philip II's Apartments

PLAZA DEL MONASTERIO

Main Entrance

Patio de los Reyes

Coro

Templo

Palacio

Stairway to the Panteon de las Reyes

Biblioteca

Claustro principal bajo

Great Staircase

Patio de los Evangelistas

Sacristia

Convento

Salas Capitulares

0 _____ 500m

avoid the worst by coming just before lunch, and by not going straight to the royal apartments, where everyone heads when the bus or train arrives.

Go instead to the west gateway, facing the mountains, and through the traditional main entrance. Above the doorway is a gargantuan statue of St. Lawrence holding a gridiron, the emblem of his martyrdom. It leads into the **Patio de los Reyes**, named after the six statues of the kings of Israel on the facade of the church straight ahead. To the left is a school, to the right the monastery, both of them still in use. In the **church**, notice above all the flat vault of the *coro* above your head as you enter, apparently entirely without support, and the white marble Christ carved by Benvenuto Cellini (carried on men's shoulders from Barcelona). It's one of the few things permanently illuminated in the cold, dark interior, but put some money in the slot to light up the main altarpiece and the whole aspect of the church is brightened. The east end is decorated by Italian artists: the *retablo* is by Pelegrino Tibaldi and Federigo Zuccaro, and the sculptures are by the father-and-son team of Leone and Pompeo Leoni, who also carved the two facing groups of Carlos V with his family and Felipe II with three of his wives (Mary Tudor is excluded).

Back outside and around to the left are the **Sacristia** and the **Salas Capitulares** (Chapter Houses) which contain many of the monastery's religious treasures, including paintings by Titian, Velázquez, and Jose Ribera. Beside the sacristy a staircase leads down to the **Panteón de los Reyes**, the final resting place of all Spanish monarchs since Carlos V, with the exception of Felipe V and Fernando VI. Alfonso XIII, who died in exile in Rome, was recently brought to join his ancestors. The whole operation is strictly ritualized; the deceased lie in gilded, black-and-brown marble tombs, kings (and Isabel II) on one side, their spouses on the other. Just above the entry is the *Pudrería*, a separate room in which the bodies rot for twenty years or so before the cleaned-up skeletons are moved here. Their many children are laid in the **Panteón de los Infantes**; the tomb of Don Juan, Felipe II's bastard half-brother, is grander than any of the kings', while the wedding-cake babies' tomb with room for sixty infants is almost full.

The **Library** has probably the most valuable collection of books in Spain, including the tenth-century *Codex Albeldensis*, Saint Teresa's personal diary, a Bible entirely in gold lettering, and some gorgeously executed Arabic manuscripts. A wooden planetarium, made in Florence in 1572, demonstrates the movements of the planets according to the Ptolemaic and Copernican plans. The library is also a splendid hall in itself; the shelves were designed by Herrera to harmonize with the architecture, and the frescoes on the barrel vault and between the windows are by Tibaldi and his assistants, and show the seven Liberal Arts. What remains of the Escorial's art collection — works by Bosch, Gerard David, Dürer, Titian, Zurbaran, and many others — are housed in the elegant suite or rooms known as the **New Museums**.

Finally, there's the **Palace** itself — endless apartments stuffed with treasures — for which you have to join the official convoys. Don't miss the quarters inhabited by Felipe II, but unless you're profoundly interested in inlaid wood it's not worth paying the extra to see the **Maderas Finas** rooms. The craftsmanship is magnificent, but the entrance charge exorbitant (deliberately so, since too many visitors would damage the delicate decoration). You can wander at will in some of the courtyards (most notable is the **Main Cloister**, with frescoes of the life of the Virgin by Tibaldi) and in the **Jardín de los Frailes** on the south side (open only during lunch). There's more to see than you can cram into a single day without total exhaustion, and you're liable to wind up agreeing with Hare that while the Escorial "is so profoundly curious that it must of necessity be visited, it is so utterly dreary and so hopelessly fatiguing a sight that it requires the utmost patience to endure it." It's open Tuesday through Sunday from 10am to 1:30pm and 3:30 to 6:30pm; restoration work may entail the temporary closure of some rooms.

One ticket covers all the above as well as the **Casita del Príncipe** and the **Casita del Arriba**. These two eighteenth-century royal lodges, both stuffed with decorative riches, lie within easy walking distance of the main complex.

They were built by Juan de Villanueva, Spain's best neoclassical architect, and are thus worth seeing in themselves, as well as for their formal gardens. The Casita del Arriba, which served as present King Juan Carlos' student digs, is a short way up into the hills and affords a good view of the Escorial complex; follow the road to the left from the main entrance and then stick to the contours of the mountain around to the right — it's well signposted. The Casita del Principe is larger and perhaps more worthwhile, with an important collection of Giordano paintings and four pictures made from rice paste; it's in the Jardines del Principe below the monastery, a small park which also provides a handy and pleasant shortcut if you're walking back down to the train station (about 20 min. this way).

Practicalities

There are well over twenty trains a day **from Madrid** (7am-11pm; Atocha or Chamartín stations) and ten buses (eight on Sun.). The bus is faster, slightly cheaper, and takes you right to the monastery. If you arrive by train get immediately on the local bus which shuttles up to the center of town — they leave promptly and it's a long uphill walk. You could stay in El Escorial (there are several *hostales*, the cheapest being *Malagon*, San Francisco 2, ☎91/8901576 or *Parilla Principe*, c/Floridablanca 6, ☎8901611; and a campground 2km out on the road to Ávila) but it's preferable to arrive early, spend the day here, and continue in the evening to ÁVILA (fifteen trains daily, last at 10pm) or head back to Madrid. **Eating** is expensive everywhere, but try the bar just inside the gate. Farther up the hill on c/Reina Victoria, near the bus and train arrival point from Madrid, there are a few not overly-inflated restaurants. Also, *Restaurante Cubero* on c/Don Juan Delegraz has cheap menus. Alternatively, grab a *bocadillo* from a drink stall on c/Floridablanca and save your appetite for somewhere else. **Turismo** (Mon.–Sat. 10am–1:30pm; closed Sun.) is at c/Floridablanca 10.

The Valle de los Caídos

Nine kilometers north of El Escorial lies the entry to the **VALLE DE LOS CAÍDOS** (Valley of the Fallen); from here a road (along which you are not allowed to stop) runs 6km to a huge underground basilica crowned by a vast cross; reputedly the largest in the world, it can be seen for miles around, especially from the road to Segovia. Ostensibly a monument to the civil war dead of both sides, the debased and grandiose architectural forms employed, the constant inscriptions "Fallen for God and for Spain", and the proximity to El Escorial clue you in to its true function as a memorial to General Franco and his regime. The dictator himself lies buried behind the high altar, while the only other named tomb, marked simply 'Jose Antonio', is that of his guru, Jose Antonio Primo de Rivera, nephew of the 1920s dictator and the Falangist leader shot dead by Republicans at the beginning of the war.

The church is a real shocker, its nave (hollowed out of the rock by political prisoners) resembling nothing so much as a railroad tunnel. A funicular ascends to the base of the cross, from where the one compensation in a visit to this place is realized in the form of a superlative view over the Sierra de Guadarrama, and the valley now irredeemably marred by this monstrosity.

To add to the general sense of tastelessness, the site is shamelessly exploited as a tourist trap, and continually inundated with excursion buses. Other than riding one of these, the only way to reach the "shrine" by public transportation is by taking the 3:15pm service run by *Herranz* from El Escorial (tickets from *Bar Bolero* opposite the post office); it returns at 5:30pm (6:15pm July to mid-Sept.). The site is open from 10am to 7pm and the funicular up to the cross operates from 10:30am to 2pm and 4 to 7:30pm. Come if you want to be outraged, but don't attempt to see it as well as El Escorial in a single day; your time is much better devoted to the latter.

Ávila

Two things distinguish ÁVILA: its medieval walls — over two perfectly preserved kilometers of them surround the old town — and Santa Teresa, who was born here and whose spirit still dominates the city, set on a high plain with the peaks of the Sierra de Gredos looming in the background. It's the walls which first impress, especially if you time it right and approach the city with the evening sun highlighting their golden tone and the details of the 88 towers around the ramparts. At closer quarters they're more of a hollow facade — the old city within is more or less in ruins, and modern life takes place almost exclusively in the new developments outside the fortifications.

The legacy of **Santa Teresa** is no less concrete, expressed in the many convents and churches with which she was associated. There are an extraordinary number of them in Ávila, all claiming some connection with the saint, and a wealth of really beautiful Romanesque churches. Teresa was born to a noble family in Ávila in 1515, and by the age of seven she was already deeply religious, running away with her brother to be martyred by the Moors. The spot where they were recaptured and brought back, **Las Cuatro Postes**, is a fine vantage point from which to admire the walls. Eventually she became a nun at the convent of **La Encarnación**, going on to reform the controlling Carmelite order, found many convents of her own, and become one of the most important figures of the Counter-Reformation.

Perhaps the most interesting of the monuments associated with the saint is the **Convento de las Madres** (or San José), the first one she founded. Its museum contains relics and memorabilia including the coffin in which she once slept, and assorted personal possessions. The tomb of her brother Lorenzo is in the larger of the two churches. The **Convento de Santa Teresa** is built over the saint's birthplace. Most of it can't be visited, but you can go into the rather dull baroque church and see, in a chapel, the very spot where she was born. There are pictures of the saint demonstrating her powers of levitation to various august bodies and a stained glass panel of her meeting with the infant Jesus. In the reliquary (beside the gift shop) are memorials of Teresa's life, including not only her rosary beads, but one of the fingers she used to count them with.

The third major point of pilgrimage is the **Convento de la Encarnación** (9:30am–1pm and 4–6pm), in which she spent 27 years as a nun. The rooms are labeled with the various things the saint did in each of them, and everything she touched or looked at or could have used is on display. In a small museum a map shows the convents she founded and nearby appears a selection of her sayings — pithiest, and endorsable by most at this stage of their travels, is: "Life is a night in a bad hotel." Frankly the place is pretty dull, though reasonably good value as a museum, but this and the preceding establishments are major focuses of pilgrimage, especially with Spanish schoolgirls brought in by the busload to experience firsthand the life of the woman they are supposed to emulate.

The most beautiful churches in Ávila, the cathedral, San Vicente, and the convent of Santo Tomás, are less directly associated with its most famous resident. The **Cathedral** (8am–1pm and 3–7pm, 3–5pm in winter) was started in the twelfth century but has never been finished, as evidenced by the missing tower above the main entrance. The earliest parts were as much fortress as church, and the apse actually forms an integral part of the city walls. Inside, the succeeding changes of style are immediately apparent; the old parts are Romanesque in design and made of a strange red-and-white, mottled stone, but then there's an abrupt break and the rest of the main structure is pure white and Gothic. Although the proportions are exactly the same, this newer half of the cathedral seems infinitely more spacious. The *coro*, whose elaborate carved back you see as you come in, and two chapels in the left aisle, are Renaissance additions. Visit the carved stalls in the *coro* (by Cornelius, a Dutchman), the museum with its monstrous silver *custodia* and ancient religious images, and the tomb of a fifteenth-century bishop known as *El Tostado* (the Toasted One).

The basilica of **San Vicente**, like the cathedral, is something of a mixture of architectural styles. Its twelfth-century doorways, and the portico which protects them, are magnificent examples of Romanesque art, while the church itself shows the influence of later trends. San Vicente was martyred on this site, and his tomb depicts a series of particularly gruesome deaths; in the crypt you can see the slab on which he and his sisters were executed by the Romans. The church shares with nearby **San Pedro** a warm pink glow in the sandstone from which it's constructed — a characteristic aspect of Ávila but seen nowhere so clearly as here.

El Real Monasterio de Santo Tomás (daily 10am–1pm and 4–7pm, 4–6pm Sun.) was founded as a Dominican monastery (which it still is) in 1482, but greatly expanded over the following decade by Fernando and Isabella, whose summer palace it became. Inside are three exceptional cloisters, the largest of which houses an **oriental collection**, a strangely incongruous display built up by the monks over centuries of missionary work in the Orient. On every available surface is carved the yoke-and-arrows motif of the *Reyes Católicos* surrounded by pomegranates, symbol of the newly-conquered kingdom of Granada (*granada* means "pomegranate" in Spanish). In the **church** is the elaborate tomb of Prince Juan, Fernando and Isabella's only son, whose early death opened the way for Carlos V's succession and caused his parents so much grief that they abandoned their newly completed home here. It was damaged by Napoleon's troops, who stabled their horses in the church. Notice also the tomb of the prince's tutors, almost as elaborate as his own, and the thrones occupied by the king and queen during services. The notorious inquisitor Torquemada is buried in the sacristy. Santo Tomás is quite a walk downhill from the south of the town — you can get back up by the #1 bus, whose circular route takes in much of the old city.

One final point: if you want to take a **walk around the top of the walls**, there's only one place to climb up — through the gardens of the *parador*.

Practicalities

There are fifteen **trains** a day from Madrid via El Escorial to Ávila, with onward connections to Salamanca (five a day) and on the main northern line to Valladolid, where you can change for almost anywhere in the north: Burgos and San Sebastián, León, Santander, even Galicia. The **railroad station** is at the bottom of Avda. José Antonio, to the east below the new part of town; head straight up this broad avenue to its end by the large church of Santa Ana, cut around the church and bear left up c/del Duque de Alba. You'll arrive at the Plaza Santa Teresa, just outside the walls by a gate known as the *Puerta del Alcázar* and very close to the cathedral. **Buses** to and from Madrid (two daily) and Segovia (four) use a terminal on the Avenida de Madrid; from here you can walk past a small park to the church of Santa Ana and follow the route outlined above, or go straight up Avda. de Madrid to San Vicente, again just outside the walls. The **Turismo** (Mon.–Fri. 8am–3pm and 5–7pm, Sat. 9am–2pm) is in the Plaza de la Catedral, directly opposite the cathedral entrance.

Cheap **rooms** are easy enough to come by, though many of them are around the railroad station or at the bottom of Avda. José Antonio, which is neither the most central nor the most pleasant place to be based. Try instead around the Plaza Santa Teresa (*Fonda la Abulense*, ☎918/211495 and *Casa de Huespedes la Española*, ☎918/211823, both in c/de Estrada). Within the walls places are likely to be more expensive, but the *Hostal Continental* (Plaza de la Catedral 6, ☎918/211502), *Hostal Casa Felipe* (Plaza de la Victoria 12, ☎918/213924), and *Hostal el Rastro* (Plaza del Rastro 1, ☎918/211218) are all pleasant and not too exorbitant. For cheap **meals** you're best off in the very heart of the old town around the strange unfinished Plaza de la Victoria or, again, down by the railroad station. Two places off the said plaza are *Vinos y Comidas*, c/Carramolino 14 (closed Sun.) for very cheap *menús*, and the *Bar el Rincon*, Plaza Zurraquin 6, for a more expensive but generous 3-course *menú*. Local specialities include *cordero asado* (roast lamb) and *ternera* (veal), as well as various sickly-sweet *yemas* (candied egg yolk) and other cakes and confections — you'll get them in the touristy restaurants near the cathedral.

Onwards

Leaving Ávila, Salamanca is just a couple of hours on by bus or train. Just over halfway you pass through PEÑARANDA DE BRACAMONTE, a crumbling old town with a couple of large plazas and ancient churches. From here, if you have your own vehicle, you can continue to Salamanca on the slightly longer route through **ALBA DE TORMES**. Here Santa Teresa died, and the Carmelite convent which contains the remains of her body (not much of it to judge by the number of relics scattered around Spain) is another major target of pilgrimage. There are the remains of a castle too, and several other interesting churches. Heading north towards Valladolid, road and rail both pass through Medina del Campo with its beautiful castle. To the east, Segovia (see below) is less than two hours away by bus.

The Sierra de Gredos: Hiking

Simply as a route, though, the road heading southeast through the **SIERRA DE GREDOS** towards Extremadura is by far your most attractive option. **MOMBELTRÁN**, on a minor road about halfway between Ávila and Jarandilla makes a good stopover point, especially if you have your own car; though there are only two expensive *hostales*, there is also a summer-only campground some 4km below the village, or with permission you can always camp on local farmland. The fourteenth-century castle of the dukes of Albuquerque is set against a stunning mountain backdrop, and there's also a fine Gothic church.

ARENAS DE SAN PEDRO, 65km farther on (difficult hitching), is a rather large town with numerous *hostales* and restaurants. Here too there's a somewhat prettified castle, and from here you can either continue to Jarandilla and Plasencia, or with more difficulty (one daily bus, hitching impossible) cut south to Talavera for the main route into central Extremadura.

However the main reason to halt in Arenas is to make one's way up to the villages of El Hornillo and El Arenal, 6km and 9km away respectively. They're appealing settlements, though from a walker's point of view perversely amenitied; **EL ARENAL** has the *fondas* but **EL HORNILLO** is the trailhead for one of two recognized trekking routes over the Gredos watershed. This will take you most of a day to accomplish, exchanging the pine and granite of the steep south slopes for the *matorral* (scrub thickets), cow pastures, and big horizons on the northern, Ávila side. You'll emerge on the twelve-kilometer asphalt road linking HOYOS DEL ESPINO, a village in the Tormes valley, and the so-called Plataforma, jump-off point to the highest peaks of the Gredos, almost exactly halfway between the two. Call it a day just above the Plataforma, where there's lots of camping space in the high Pozas meadows, and proceed the next morning up to the **Circo de Laguna Grande**.

This, two hours beyond Pozas on a well-defined trail, is the centerpiece of the Gredos range, with its highest point Almanzor (2593m) looming above, surrounded by hoodoo pinnacles sculpted into utterly improbably shapes. The valley with its huge lake is popular with hordes of day-trippers and weekenders from all of the central Castilian cities, and the *refugio* will be full in late summer, especially on weekends; camping, even better than at Pozas, is an accepted alternative.

The path, actually Alfonso XIII's old hunting route, continues west for a couple of hours before ending abruptly at the edge of the sharp, scree-laden descent into the **Circo de las Cinco Lagunas**. The drop is amply rewarded by virtual solitude, even in mid-August, and the sure sighting of *Capra pyrenaica gloriae*, the graceful (and almost tame) Gredos mountain goat.

Protected by law since the 1920s, they now number in the several thousands and frequent the north slopes of Gredos in the warmer months. The owners of the very rare tents here, by the shores of the three larger lakes, enjoy the most secluded campsite in central Spain and most certainly haul them up the trail from Navalperal village, west of Hoyos in the Tormes valley.

If you're coming to the Gredos alpine zone directly from Ávila, know that there's regular bus service only along the main road to BARCO DE ÁVILA, and from there very uncertain connections along the secondary road looping through the Tormes valley, past Navalperal and Hoyos; you may have to hitch much of this. No matter how you arrive, it's best to leave the Laguna Grande/Pozas area via the well-defined trail which heads due south over a broad pass to Candeleda; this will involve another day-long walk but it's all downhill. Crossing a Roman bridge over the Santa María River tips you off that your destination isn't too far. Try to get to CANDELEDA by late afternoon, for a choice of buses to Talavera or (later) Jarandilla. The town itself is no great shakes, though amazingly popular with Spanish summer vacationers; the three *hostales* (best is *La Pastora*) are reserved weeks in advance, with the overflow camping next to the river west of town. The nearest official campground is at MADRIGAL DE LA VERA, 12km west and somewhat more attractive as a village. If you haven't yet had enough of the Gredos, there is yet another transalpine route from Madrigal to Bohoyo, a hamlet near Navalperal on the north side of the range.

Segovia and La Granja

Heading northwest from the capital, both road and rails strike through the heart of the **Sierra de Guadarrama** — a beautiful journey. The road is occasionally marred by suburban development (especially around NAVACERRADA, Madrid's main ski resort) but from the train it's almost entirely unspoiled. If you want to base yourself in the mountains for a while you'd do best to head for **CERCEDILLA** (ninety minutes by train on the Madrid–Segovia line but off the main road), an Alpine-looking village that's an excellent base for summer walking. Cercedilla is not exactly in the backwoods — *Madrileños* pour in at weekends — but it does offer several places to stay (try the *Hostal Longinos* on the main street; ☎91/8520557) and a clutch of good restaurants. From here you can embark on a wonderful short train ride to the **Puerto de Navacerrada**, the most important pass in the mountains and the heart of the ski area. There's a mountain-lodge-type **youth hostel** (☎91/8521423) on the hill behind the station.

Segovia

For so small a city, **SEGOVIA** has a quite remarkable number of outstanding architectural monuments. Most celebrated are the Roman aqueduct, the cathedral, and the fairy-tale Alcázar, but the less obvious attractions — the crowd of ancient churches and the many mansions scattered through the lanes of the old town — are what really makes it worth visiting.

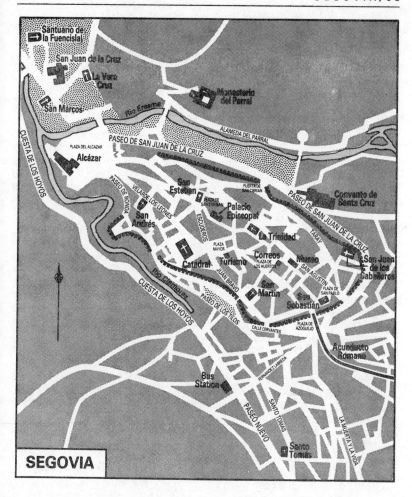

SEGOVIA

You can get here by **train** from Madrid (12 daily from Atocha station) or
bus (4; *La Sepuldevana*, Paseo de la Florida 11; Metro *Norte*) and there are
onward connections by bus to Ávila (four daily) and Valladolid (three a day)
or train to Valladolid (three again). The railroad station is some way out of
town; take bus #3 to the central Plaza Franco. Surprisingly, this main square,
right by the cathedral and surrounded by pricey cafes, is the place to start
looking for somewhere to stay. There are two cheap **fondas** (*Cubo* and
Aragon, ☎911/433527) on different floors of the same building at Plaza Mayor
4, their ideal position making up for a certain lack of luxury. Several others
can be found in the surrounding streets; the small *Casa de Húespedes Velarde*
in Plaza Guevara is about the cheapest. The **youth hostel**, on Paseo Conde
de Sepulveda (☎911/420027) near the train station, has no curfew, is open

throughout the day, and is very spacious. **Turismo** is also in the plaza (Mon.–Fri. 9am–2pm and 4–6pm, Sat. 9am–2pm; closed Sun.); most significant facts are displayed in the window if it's closed. They'll give you a list of *hostales* but otherwise you're on your own. There's also a **campground**, *Camping Acueducto* (open July–Sept.), a couple of kilometers out on the road to La Granja.

The Calle de la Infanta Isabella, which opens off the plaza beside the *Turismo*, is packed with noisy **bars** and cheap **places to eat**. (Isabella la Catolica was proclaimed queen here, in the otherwise unremarkable church of San Miguel). Segovia's culinary speciality is roast suckling pig (*cochinillo asado*) and you'll see the pink little piglets hanging in the windows of many restaurants. But it's very expensive unless you're in a large group, and to many tastes overrated. Don't eat in the plaza itself or in any of the restaurants near the aqueduct — they're strictly for those with money to burn.

The City

The **Cathedral** (daily in summer 9am–7pm, winter Mon.–Fri. 9am–1pm and 3–6pm, Sat.–Sun. 9am–6pm) was the last major Gothic building in Spain, probably the last anywhere. Accordingly it takes that style to its logical (or illogical) extreme, with pinnacles and flying buttresses tacked on at every conceivable point. Though impressive for its size alone, the interior is surprisingly bare for so florid a construction and spoiled by a great green marble *coro* at its very center. The treasures are almost all confined to the museum which opens off the cloisters (entrance 75ptas).

Down beside the cathedral the c/de los Leones leads past a line of souvenir shops to the church of San Andrés and on to a small park in front of the **Alcázar** (10am–7pm in summer, 10am–6pm in winter; entrance 120ptas). It's an extraordinary fantasy of a castle which looks, with its narrow towers and many turrets, like something out of Disneyland. And indeed it is something of a sham — originally built in the fourteenth and fifteenth centuries but almost completely destroyed by a fire in 1862, it was rebuilt as a deliberately hyperbolic parody of the original. Still, it should be visited, if only for the magnificent panoramas from the tower.

Keep left on the way back into the center and you'll come to the **Plaza San Esteban**. Even if restoration work on the square and church is still going on, it's worth seeing for its superb, five-storied, twelfth-century tower. A little farther on, the church of **La Trinidad** preserves perhaps the purest Romanesque style in Segovia. Each span of its double-arched apse has intricately carved capitals, every one of them unique. One other Romanesque church in the typical Segovian style, with tower and open porticoes, is **San Millan**, which lies between the aqueduct and the bus station. The interior has been restored to its original form.

The best of the ancient churches, though, is undoubtedly **Vera Cruz** (Tues.–Sun. 10:30am–1:30pm and 3:30–7pm, closes 6pm in winter), a remarkable twelve-sided building outside town in the valley facing the Alcázar. It was built by the Knights Templar in the early thirteenth century on the pattern of the church of the Holy Sepulcher in Jerusalem, and once housed part of the True Cross (hence its name; the sliver of wood itself is now in the nearby village church at Zamarramala). Inside, the nave is circular, and its heart is occupied by a strange two-storied chamber — again twelve-sided — in which the knights, as part of their initiation, stood vigil over the cross. Climb the tower for a highly photogenic vista of the city. While you're over here you could also visit the prodigiously walled monastery of **San Juan de la Cruz** (10am–1:30pm and 4–6pm), with the gaudy mausoleum of its founder-saint.

One of the lesser-known sights of Segovia is the **Synagogue**, which now serves as the convent church of **Corpus Cristi**, in a little courtyard at the end of c/Juan Bravo and very near the east end of the cathedral. You can see part of its exterior from the Paseo del Salón, near which are the streets of the old *Judería*. It is very similar in style to Santa María la Blanca in Toledo, though less refined. During the last century it was badly damaged by fire, so what you see now is a reconstruction, but historic synagogues are so rare in Spain that this is still of interest. Opening times are unpredictable.

The **Aqueduct**, over 800m long and at its highest point towering some 30m above the Plaza de Azoguejo, stands up without a drop of mortar or cement. No one knows exactly when it was built, but probably around the end of the first century A.D. under the Emperor Trajan. Supposedly it's still in use, bringing water from the Río Frio to the city, but there was certainly no water in it when we looked, and in recent years traffic vibration and pollution have been threatening to undermine the entire structure. If you climb the stairs beside the aqueduct you can get a view looking down over it from a surviving fragment of the city walls.

Back towards the center is the **Plaza Juan Bravo**, surrounded by fine buildings including the **Torre de Lozoya** (open evenings and Sunday lunchtimes for exhibitions) and the church of **San Martín** which demonstrates all the local stylistic peculiarities, though the best of none of them. It has the characteristic covered portico, a fine arched tower and a typically Romanesque aspect; also, like most of Segovia's churches, it can only be visited when it's open for business, during early morning or evening services. In the middle of the plaza is a statue of Juan Bravo, a local folk hero who led the *comuneros* rebellion against Carlos V's attempts to take away their traditional rights. Notice the facades of the buildings, many of them displaying the local taste for plaster decoration (*esgrafado*) which is as common on new structures as it is on old.

Segovia is an excellent city for walking. A good route is to follow the signposted bypass road outside the city, particularly to the south, where there are ever-changing views of the cathedral and Alcázar from across the valley. The road then doubles back along the other side of the Alcázar, passing near San Juan de la Cruz and La Vera Cruz. From there you can continue to the **Monasterio del Parral**; better still, follow the track which circles behind La Vera Cruz. El Parral is a sizeable and partly ruined complex occupied by Hieronymites, an order found only in Spain. If you ring the bell for admission (Mon.–Fri. 9am–1pm and 3–6:30pm) you will be shown the cloister and church; the latter is a late Gothic building with rich sculpture at the east end. Perhaps the best view of Segovia is found by taking the main road north towards CUELLAR or TUREGANO; a panorama of the whole city, including the aqueduct, gradually unfolds. It is also enjoyable to walk through any of the historic quarters of the city, often located well away from the center; each has a village atmosphere of its own.

La Granja

Just twenty-plus minutes by bus (nine daily) from Segovia is the beautiful summer palace of **SAN ILDEFONSO DE LA GRANJA**, or simply La Granja. The palace was built by the first Bourbon king of Spain, Felipe V, no doubt homesick for the luxuries of Versailles. Its glories are the mountain setting and the extravagant wooded grounds, but it's worth casting a quick eye over the palace (10am–1:30pm and 3–4:30pm). Though destroyed in parts and damaged throughout by a fire in 1918, much has been well restored. The most striking thing about the long series of rooms is their perfect symmetry which gives you the uncanny feeling, as you stand looking through the open doorways, of gazing into a mirror endlessly reflecting the same room. Everything is furnished in plush French imperial style but it's almost all of Spanish origin — the huge chandeliers, for example, were made in the crystal factory (which still exists) in San Ildefonso itself.

The **gardens** are open all day until 8pm. On Thursday, Saturday and Sunday afternoons in summer you have to pay to get in and the fountains are switched on after 6pm. They're really fantastic, especially the last — *La Fama* — which has a central jet nearly 50m high. In the town are several bars and restaurants where you can while away any spare time. There is one bus direct to Madrid, which leaves at 8pm when the gardens close; otherwise connect via Segovia (last bus at 9:30pm).

Onwards

La Granja is back towards Madrid, but heading on northwards from Segovia you're faced with a couple of fairly straightforward choices. The most obvious next step is to Valladolid. If you take the train you'll pass through both Coca and Medina del Campo (see *Old Castile*) with their magnificent castles; the road, more direct, is of less interest, although en route there's another impressive ancient castle at **CUELLAR**. Even more impressive is the one at **TUREGANO**, a village lying about halfway along the road to Aranda de Duero; it's essentially a fifteenth-century structure enclosing an early thirteenth-century church, and you have to track down the sacristan of the parish church to get inside. Northeast of Cuellar, a beautiful drive skirts the Sierra de Guadarrama towards either Burgos or Soria (both in *Old Castile*), while westwards you could strike directly towards Galicia on the rail line through Zamora (again see *Old Castile*) and Orense (covered in *Galicia*).

North of Madrid — El Pardo and Manzanares el Real

The shortest and easiest excursion from Madrid is to **EL PARDO** just 9km north; local buses leave every ten to fifteen minutes from c/Martín de los Heros (Metro *Moncloa*). Originally the favorite hunting grounds of the royal family, the palace was greatly modified in the eighteenth-century under the Bourbons, and a town laid out. It was Franco's chosen residence, and his spirit lives on in the form of a heavily-guarded garrison. The **palace** (guided tours workdays 10am–12:30pm and 3–5:30pm, Sun. 10am–1pm; closed Tues.) isn't wildly exciting, but the interior is pleasant enough. Among its attractions are a chapel and a theater, along with a portrait of Isabella la Catolica by her court painter Juan de Flandes, and an excellent collection of tapestries, many after the Goya cartoons in the Prado. Unfortunately you have to endure a tiresome detailing of the uses Franco found for the rooms and what he did in them. To visit the **Casita del Principe**, which cannot be entered from the gardens, you must return to the main road. Like the two at El Escorial, this was built by Juan de Villanueva; its highly ornate and frivolous interior is open the same times as the palace. Climb up the hill to the well-signposted Capuchin convent (closed at lunchtime) with various interesting works of art, including a *St. Onofre* by Ribera, and a *Dead Christ* by Gregorio Fernández, commissioned by Felipe II on the birth of his son and heir.

Some 50km north of Madrid, on the shores of the Embalse de Santillana, lies **MANZANARES EL REAL**, a town which in former times was disputed between the capital and Segovia. Nowadays it is a rather tacky resort, almost exclusively geared to the throngs from Madrid who pour in at the weekend; their villas dot the landscape for miles. The ruggedly beautiful **La Pedriza**, a nearby spur of the Sierra de Guadarrama, has been declared a national park. Much of it is technical climber's country — the ascent to the jagged Peña del Diezmo is popular — although hikes are also a possibility.

In Manzanares itself, the one attraction is the **castle**, which despite its eccentric appearance is a perfectly genuine fifteenth-century construction, built around an earlier chapel. It was soon modified into a palace by the architect Juan Guas, to which end he built an elegant gallery on the south side, false machilocations on the other, and studded the tower with stones resembling cannon balls. The interior (10am–2pm and 3–6pm; free) has been heavily restored. There are a couple of *hostales* in town and a campground outside. **Buses** to Manzanares are run by *Hermanos de Julia Colmenarejo* (c/Mateo Inurria 11; Metro *Plaza de Castilla*); three services daily each way, five on Sundays. The train station is 6km out of town.

East of Madrid: Alcalá de Henares, Nuevo Baztán, and Guadalajara

Leaving the capital to the east there's considerably less to detain you. **ALCALÁ DE HENARES**, little over 30km away, is an ancient university town and the birthplace of Cervantes; there are some superb old university buildings — endowed by Cardinal Cisneros (also known as Cardinal Jimenez) at the beginning of the sixteenth century — and two houses in which Cervantes is supposed to have been born. In the sixteenth century the students numbered 1200 and the university was a rival to Salamanca's, but in 1836 it moved to Madrid and the town went into decline. Almost all the artistic heritage was lost in the civil war. Nowadays it's virtually a suburb of Madrid, with trains (Chamartín or Atocha) and buses (from Avda. América 18; Metro *America*) every few minutes throughout the day, and while it makes a very easy afternoon trip or short stopover on the way out, it's not somewhere you'd want to stay for too long.

You should, however, see the **University**, with a fabulous Plateresque facade and a Great Hall (the *Paraninfo*, entered through the *Hosteria del Estudiante*, an expensive restaurant at the back) with a gloriously decorated Mudejar *artesonado* ceiling (11am–2pm and 6–8pm Sun./hol. and daily in Aug.). Next door, the **Capilla de San Ildefonso** has another superb ceiling, intricately stuccoed walls, and the Italian marble tomb of Cardinal Cisneros. Of Cervantes' two birthplaces the one on c/Mayor (10am–2pm) is the more worthwhile: though the house itself is hardly thirty years old it's authentic in style, furnished with genuine sixteenth-century objects, and contains a small museum with a few early editions and other curiosities related to the author. **Turismo** (Mon.–Fri. 11am–2pm, weekends 11am–2pm and 4–6pm) is just off the central Plaza de Cervantes; they have maps and further information, and from here nothing of interest is more than a short walk. You'll find no shortage of places to eat downtown and, if you want to stay, several *pensiones* on the Plaza de Cervantes itself.

Twenty kilometers southeast of Alcalá, or 45km from Madrid, lies **NUEVO BAZTÁN**, a place of rather specialized attraction, which should appeal to anyone interested in architecture, planning, or the unusual. It is a planned town, designed and built in 1709–13 by Jose de Churriguera in response to a commission from the royal treasurer who aimed to develop a local decorative arts industry. It is now semideserted, though brash modern villas are being built on lots nearby for well-heeled commuters to the capital. As a focus, Churriguera built a palace and church as one architectural unit. The latter has a massive twin-towered facade and a central dome, but the inside is nothing more than a chapel, with *retablos* by the architect. Behind, now fenced off, is the Plaza de Fiestas with great balconies for watching celebrations. The houses of the workers comprise the rest of the settlement. *Empresa Izquierdo*, c/Goya 80 (Metro *Goya*) run two buses daily from Madrid but only on Sunday does the timetable conspire to give you any time there, which is handy since that's the only day the church is guaranteed to be open, and it's as good an example of a baroque church as you'll find in Spain.

GUADALAJARA, beyond Alcalá, is not terribly exciting despite its famous name. Severely battered during the civil war, it's now a small industrial city, provincial and rather dirty. There are, however, one or two worthwhile buildings which survived bombardment, notably the **Palacio del Infantado**. This, the former home of the Duke of Mendoza, boasts a wonderful decorative facade and cloister-like patio, and now houses a fairly average local art museum.

The main road and railroad to Zaragoza and Barcelona both pass through Alcalá and Guadalajara, and continue more or less parallel throughout their journeys. Sigüenza (described in *New Castile and Extremadura*) and Medinaceli (see *Old Castile*) each make excellent resting points on your way. From Guadalajara you can also cut down to Cuenca, and from there continue towards Valencia and the coast. This is a very beautiful drive, past the great dams of the Embalse de Entrepeñas and Embalse de Buendia, but an easier route to Cuenca is to take the Valencia road via Alcalá de Henares as far as Tarancón then veer left. The train from Madrid to Cuenca and Valencia goes via Aranjuez.

fiestas

February
Second weekend Santa Agueda women's festival in SEGOVIA, when women take over the city administration and parade and celebrate in traditional costume. Occurs to an extent throughout the province, especially in ZAMARRAMALA just outside the city.
Carnival (the week before Lent) is the excuse for lively fiestas all over the place.

March/April
Holy Week *Semana Santa* is celebrated everywhere, but with great formality and processions in TOLEDO, passion plays (especially on the Saturday) in CHINCHÓN.

May
15 The *Fiestas de San Isidro* in MADRID — which spread for a week either side of this date — are among the country's biggest. Music, parades, and loads of free entertainment.
Corpus Christi (variable — the Thursday after Trinity, therefore sometimes falls in June) sees a very solemn, costumed religious procession in TOLEDO.

June
24 San Juan y San Pablo. A lively procession, with floats and music, in SEGOVIA.
30 In HITA (Guadalajara) the fiesta has a medieval theme, with performances of old theater,

feasts, dances, and sporting events including falconry and bull-lancing.

July
Both Segovia and Ávila have big festivals around the **middle of the month**: in SEGOVIA a weeklong festival of chamber music, in ÁVILA a more normal, rowdy affair with bullfights, music, and dances.

August
15 Celebrations for the *Virgen de la Asunción* in CHINCHÓN include an *encierro*, with bulls running through the street.
25 Good fiestas in LA GRANJA (near Segovia) and ORGAZ (Toledo).
Third week of the month marks the August fiestas in TOLEDO, in honor of the *Virgen del Sagrario*; amazing fireworks on the final weekend.
28 Bull running in CUELLAR (Segovia).

September
ARANJUEZ holds a fiesta **early in the month**, with concerts in the palace gardens and more usual celebration.

October
Second week ÁVILA goes wild for the *Feria de Santa Teresa*. Organ recitals in the churches too.

travel details

Buses
From Madrid
Leaving from *Estación Sur de Autobuses* (c/ Canarias 17; Metro *Palos de la Frontera*) to Albacete/Alicante (3 daily; 4/6 hr.), Ciudad Real (4; 4 hr.); Córdoba (1; 8 hr.), Gijón (3; 7 hr.), Granada (1; 8 hr.), Jaén (3; 6 hr.), León (2; 5½ hr.), Málaga (1; 8 hr.); Sevilla (1; 10hr); Teruel (4; 5½ hr.), Toledo (24; 1½ hr.), Zaragoza/Barcelona (4;

5/10 hr.), and international services to France and Portugal
Auto-Res (Fernandez Shaw 1; Metro *Conde Casal*) to Badajoz (7 daily; 6 hr.), Cáceres (7; 4–5 hr.), Trujillo (7; 4–5 hr.), Mérida 7; 5 hr.), Ávila (2; 1½ hr.), Salamanca (12; 2½-3½ hr.), Zamora (5; 4 hr.), Valladolid/Palencia (2; ¾ hr.), Valencia (14; 5–6 hr.), and Cuenca (6; 3 hr.)
Continental Auto (c/Alenza 20; Metro *Ríos Rosas*)

to Burgos (4; 4 hr.), San Sebastián (3; 8 hr.), Santander (2; 7 hr.), El Burgo de Osma (2; 4 hr.), Soria (6; 3–4 hr.), Pamplona (2; 6 hr.), Bilbao (4; 7 hr.), Logroño (2; 5½ hr.), Aranda (5; 3 hr.), and Guadalajara (3; 1½ hr.).

From Toledo to Ciudad Real (for the south; 1 a day; 3 hr.), and Talavera de la Reina (for Extremadura; 4; 2 hr.)

From Ávila to Segovia (4; 2 hr.) and Salamanca (5; 1½ hr.)

From Segovia to Valladolid (3; 2½ hr.)

Trains from Madrid

From Atocha Station (Metro _Atocha_) to Lisbon/Porto (5 daily; 11/13 hr.), Badajoz via Ciudad Real (3; 7–10 hr), Cáceres (5; 4–6 hr.), Segovia via Chamartín (9; 2–3 hr.), Almería (2; 8–11 hr.), Algeciras (1; 11 hr.), Córdoba (6; 5–7 hr.), Granada (2; 7–10 hr.), Jaén (3; 6 hr.), Málaga (2; 7–9 hr.), Sevilla (6; 6–9 hr.), Cádiz (3; 8–11 hr.), and most destinations in the south and west.

From Chamartín (Metro _Chamartín_) to Paris (8 daily; 14 hr.), Alicante (4; 9 hr.), Córdoba (5; 5–7 hr.), Algeciras (1; 11 hr.), Málaga (5; 7–10 hr.), Cáceres (1; 5 hr.), Barcelona via Tarragona (4; 10–12 hr.), Bilbao (3; 7–8 hr.), Burgos/San Sebastián (14; 4/8 hr.), Pamplona (1; 6 hr.), Santander (3; 8–10 hr.), Zaragoza (4; 5–7 hr.), Valencia via Atocha and Cuenca(8; 5–8hr) and all other trains to the east and northeast.

From Principe Pío (Metro _Norte_) to León (5; 4–6 hr.), Oviedo (3; 7–9 hr.), Salamanca via Ávila (4; 3½–4 hr.), Astorga/Lugo/El Ferrol via Ávila (2; 5½/10/12 hr.), Zamora/Orense via Ávila (4; 6–8 hr.), Santiago/La Coruña (2; 9/11 hr.), Pontevedra (2; 9–11 hr.), Vigo (2; 8–10 hr.), and all other points in the northwest.

CHAPTER TWO

NEW CASTILE AND EXTREMADURA

T he vast area covered by this chapter is some of the most traveled, yet least visited country in Spain. From Madrid the tourist hordes thunder non-stop across the plains of New Castile to Valencia and Andalucía, or follow the great rivers through Extremadura into Portugal. And at first sight it is understandable. **New Castile** in particular is Spain at its least welcoming: a vast bare plain, burning hot in summer, chillingly exposed in winter. But the first impression is not an entirely fair one — away from the main highways the villages of the plain are as welcoming as any in the country, and in the northeast, where the mountains start, is the extraordinary cliff-hanging city of **Cuenca** and the historic cathedral town of **Sigüenza**. New Castile is also the agricultural and wine-growing heartland of Spain and the country through which Don Quixote cut his despairing swath. **Toledo**, one of the most history-packed cities in Spain, is also part of the province but is included in the Madrid chapter, as it makes a logical excursion from the capital.

It is in **Extremadura**, though, that there is most to be missed. This harsh environment was above all the cradle of the *conquistadores*, the home of the men who opened up a new world for the Spanish empire. Remote before and forgotten since, it enjoyed a brief golden age when the heroes returned with their gold to live in a flourish of splendor. **Trujillo**, the birthplace of Pizarro, and **Cáceres** both preserve entire towns built with their wealth, the streets crowded with the ornate mansions of home-coming empire builders. Then there is **Mérida**, the most completely preserved Roman city in Spain, and the monasteries of **Guadalupe** and **Yuste**, the one fabulously wealthy, the other rich in imperial memories. For little-visited, wild scenery, northern Extremadura has several areas of outstanding natural beauty to choose from. The most forbidding is the mountain region of **Las Hurdes** and the most important in terms of fauna is the **Parque Natural de Monfragüe**.

NEW CASTILE

The region that was for so long called New Castile is now officially known as Castilla-La Mancha, and has recently had Madrid taken out of its domain. Although the heavily cultivated plains that cover much of the terrain are a less bleak landscape than they once were — the name La Mancha comes from the Arab *manxa*, meaning steppe — the various provinces of the region

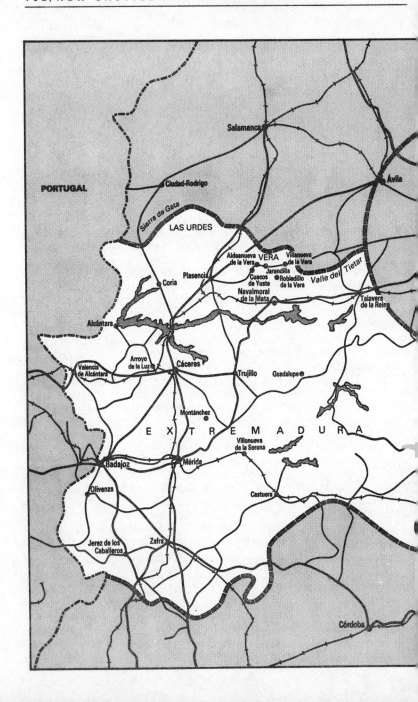

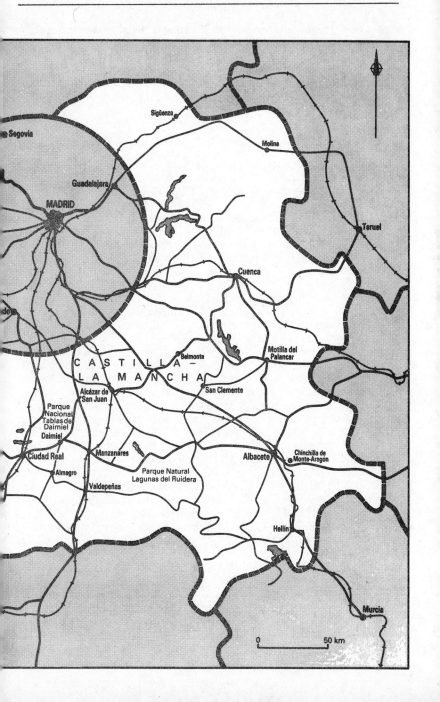

do not differ greatly from each other in character, and the interesting places are widely spaced on an arc drawn from Madrid, with little in between that calls for exploration. The most enticing town is Cuenca, southeast of Madrid; Sigüenza lies a long way north, virtually on the border of Old Castile. About the same distance from Madrid, but due south, is Ciudad Real, less attractive but at least not so impoverished in terms of surrounding places to visit.

East of Madrid: Cuenca and Sigüenza

The mountainous country of the northeastern corner of New Castile, as dramatic as any in Spain, is a complete contrast to the majority of the drab province, and in the romantic city of CUENCA, surrounded by a startling craggy landscape, it has a fitting center. The river Huecar, and the Júcar into which it runs, enclose the old city on three sides, and it is their deep gorges which lend the place its extraordinary character. Cross one of the many bridges and you start to climb steeply (most of the streets are stepped) towards the Plaza Mayor, a part of town almost impossible to avoid. Entered through the arches of the baroque **Ayuntamiento,** this is the heart of the medieval quarter.

Ahead of you is the ugly unfinished facade of the **Cathedral** (daily 10am–1pm and 4-6pm), someone's misguided attempt to beautify a simple Gothic building. The interior is much more attractive, though also much subjected to "improvements" — most noticeably the *coro* blocking the nave. Outstanding features are the carved Plateresque arch at the end of the north aisle and the chapel next to it with distinctly unchristian carvings around its entrance, a badly damaged barrel-vault ceiling, and some fine tombs. The east chapel, directly behind the high altar, has a superb *artesonado* ceiling, but normally it can barely be glimpsed through the locked door. Next to it is the cathedral **museum** whose highlights are in the treasury — a Byzantine diptych unique in Spain, and an amazing pair of embroidered green shoes, part of some particularly vain bishop's gear. In the corridor outside the treasury are two canvases by El Greco and an excellent *Crucifixion* by Gerard David.

The artistic highlight of Cuenca, however, is the **Museo de Arte Abstracto,** (Mon.–Fri. 11am–2pm and 4-6pm, Sat. 11am–2pm and 4-8pm open until 8pm; closed Sun. pm) housed in the finest of the city's hanging houses, the *Casas Colgadas*. This wonderful museum is privately run by a group of leading artists of Spain's "abstract generation" and displays work by (among many others) Jose Guerrero, Lucio Muñoz, Antonio Saura, and Fernando Zobel. The houses themselves, with their cantilevered balconies, are almost as absorbing as the exhibition.

There are other sights in Cuenca, but the chief attraction is the place itself. Have a drink in one of the bars opposite the cathedral in the Plaza Mayor and you can appreciate what it must feel like to live in one of the houses hanging off the cliff edge, and walk along the gorge of the Huecar to look up at the **Casas Colgadas** and the other less secure-looking buildings above the river. At night the effect is magical.

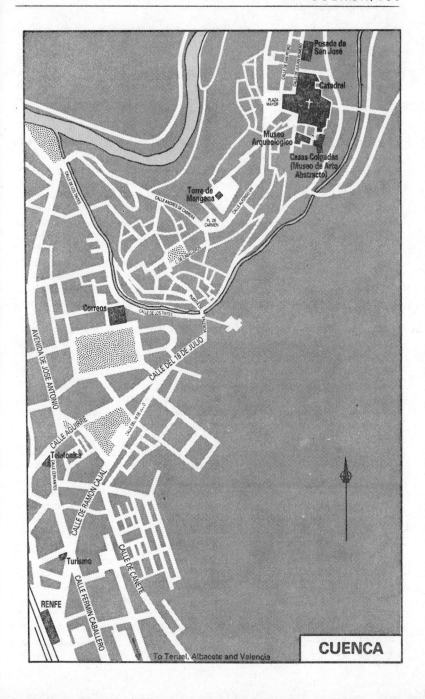

CUENCA

Whether you arrive by **train** (unbearably slow) or **bus** you'll be at the bottom of the modern part of town. There are **hostales** and **fondas** in the side streets to either side of c/Ramón y Cajal and c/18 de Julio, which lead up towards the old town, but very few in the old town itself. The *Hosteria Central* (c/Alonso Chirino, ☎966/231511) and *Camas Lopez* (Sánchez Vela 11, ☎966/223839) are both reasonable, or if you're prepared to pay considerably more for a room with a view in the old town you could try the *Posada San Jose* (c/Julián Romeso 4, ☎966/211300) near the cathedral. Cuenca's **Turismo** (open Mon.-Fri. 9am–2pm and 4–6pm, Sat. 9:30am–1:30pm) is on c/Calderón de la Barca, at the foot of the hill by the fancy hotels.

Sigüenza

SIGÜENZA, in the extreme north of the province, off the road towards Zaragoza and France and on the main rail line to Barcelona, is a charming little town with a quite extraordinarily beautiful cathedral. A sleepy place, it seems quite untouched by the twentieth century. But appearances are deceptive: taken by Franco's troops in 1936, it was on the Nationalist front line for most of the Civil War. The cathedral has been restored, the Plaza Mayor recobbled, and the bishop's castle (now a *parador*) rebuilt virtually from rubble, so that the only evidence today is in the facades of some of the unrestored buildings, pockmarked by bullets and shrapnel.

From the station (surrounded by a small clutch of *hostales* and *fondas*), streets lead up towards the **Cathedral**, built in the pinkish stone which characterizes the town. Started in 1150 by its first bishop, Bernardo of Toledo, it is essentially Gothic, with three rose windows, but has been much altered over the years. Facing you when you step inside is a huge marble *coro* with an altar to a thirteenth-century figure of the Virgin — put a coin in the slot and it lights up like a fairground stall. This is one of those buildings where every door is locked and you have to pay for the privilege of seeing inside; for once, it is well worth it. The most famous treasure is the alabaster tomb of Martin Vasquez de Arce, known as *El Doncel*; a favorite of Isabella la Catolica, he was killed fighting the Moors in Granada. On the other side of the building is an extraordinary doorway in three styles: Plateresque at the bottom, Mudejar in the middle, and Gothic at the top. The whole thing was built in the sixteenth century, and it's a fascinating experiment, if not entirely successful. The sacristy has a superb Renaissance ceiling carved by Covarrubias with 304 heads, each different and each supposedly a portrait of a local dignitary. In a chapel opening off this (with an unusual cupola, best seen in the mirror provided) is an El Greco *Annunciation*. And don't bypass the cloister, with more of the cathedral's treasures, including a collection of seventeenth-century Brussels tapestries.

Opposite the cathedral is a small **art museum** with a surprisingly large collection of mediocre religious works. Its star exhibit is a particularly saccharine Zurbarán of Mary as a child. From the Plaza Mayor, overseen by the cathedral's pencil-thin bell tower, you can walk up to the castle via **San Vicente**. A church of much the same age as the cathedral, it's interesting mainly as a chance to see just how many layers of remodeling had to be peeled off by the restorers; a very ancient figure of Christ above the altar is the only thing to detain you inside. The **castle** itself started life as a Roman fortress, was adapted by the Visigoths and further improved by the Moors for their *Alcazaba*. Reconquered in 1124, it became the official residence of the warlike Bishop Bernardo and his successors, who almost completely remodeled it. The *parador* is a copy, rebuilt from ruins in the 1960s, of that period, but at least the scenic views from the walls are entirely genuine.

Heading on north, MEDINACELI is just over the border in Old Castile — a couple of stops on the train.

La Mancha

There is a huge hole in the middle of the tourist map of Spain between Toledo and the borders of Andalucía, and from Extremadura almost to the east coast. This is the great bulk of New Castile. The tourist authorities try hard to push their *Route of Don Quixote* but unless you're completely enamored of the book it's not of great interest — when you've seen one windmill you've seen them all. Nevertheless, while it's largely true that the monotonous plain is best crossed quickly if at all, there are a few places, even in the heart of the dreary plateau of La Mancha, which merit a visit if you've got time to spare or want to break your journey.

CIUDAD REAL, capital of the province at the heart of this flat country, makes a good base for excursions. It's not the most exciting of places, but neither is it entirely without interest, and it has connections by bus with most villages in the area. The fourteenth-century church of **San Pedro** is a cool, airy Gothic edifice, refreshingly uncluttered. It contains the alabaster tomb of its founder and a good Baroque altarpiece. Don't bother with the ugly cathedral, but the nearby **Provincial Museum** is worth a visit — excellently displayed in a modern building, there are two floors of local archeology and a third devoted to artists of the region. The **Puerta de Toledo**, an elegant Mudejar gate and the only surviving fragment of the medieval walls, is at the northern edge of the city on the Toledo road. The **Turismo** is on the Avda. Martires near the **railroad station**, and the **bus station** on c/Inmaculada Concepción. There are several **hostales** around the Plaza Mayor on c/Cruz and c/Vasquéz.

Not far east of Ciudad Real is **ALMAGRO**, a village whose main claim to fame is the *Corral de las Comedias* (9am–1pm and 4:30–8pm), a perfectly preserved sixteenth-century theater. Plays from the sixteenth and seventeenth centuries — the "Golden Age" of Spanish theater — are regularly produced here and there's a theater festival in the spring. The auditorium is tiny, but wonderfully atmospheric, and you can wander around backstage and through the galleries. Although it boasts a *parador* in the former Franciscan convent, Almagro is a little-spoiled, very quiet, elegant village. Admire also the Plaza Mayor, unusual in the design of the surrounding glassed-in upper stories, a northern influence brought by members of the Fugger family

(Carlos V's bankers) who settled here. There's a small **fonda** built around a flower-decked patio on the road leading from the plaza to the Convent of the Knights of Calatrava.

Buses from Ciudad Real continue from here to **VALDEPEÑAS**, center of the most prolific wine region in Spain. The wine is more attractive than the place, and testing it is the town's major pleasure — most of the big **bodegas** are outside Valdepeñas along the main Madrid–Cádiz road, but there are a few downtown, one of them almost opposite the bus and rail stations. A windmill on the Madrid road at the north edge of town is supposedly the biggest in Spain; it houses a museum of the works of local artist Gregorio Prieto. More enticing is the public swimming pool behind it; the grass strip outside this is a good place to hitch out from.

Heading south beyond Valdepeñas you enter Andalucía through the narrow mountain **gorge of Despeñaperros** (literally, "throwing over of the dogs"), once a notorious spot for banditry and still a dramatic natural gateway which signals a change in both climate and vegetation, or as Richard Ford put it, "exchanges an Eden for a desert." The first towns of interest, and really more tempting places to break your journey than anywhere in La Mancha, are ÚBEDA and BAEZA . These are both connected by bus with the railroad station of LINARES-BAEZA, which is also where you'll want to change trains if you're heading for CÓRDOBA. JAÉN, the first city on the main bus and train routes, is comparatively dull.

The Parque Nacional de las Tablas de Daimiel

If you're **heading to Madrid** by train from Játiva, Alicante, or Murcia, you'll pass through Albacete, part of La Mancha. Nearby **CHINCHILLA DE MONTE ARAGÓN** is a gaunt hilltop fortress worth stopping at if you've got your own vehicle, but otherwise don't go out of your way. **ALBACETE** itself is almost entirely modern and though there are plenty of places to stay downtown there's not much reason to do so. It's famous for its daggers and switchblades but, in Richard Ford's words, "the object of a Spanish knife is to 'chip bread and kill a man" and our readers are advised to have as little to do with them as may be."

Despite the arid monotony of most of the New Castile landscape, bird lovers have a treat in the "oasis" of **La Mancha Húmeda** (Wet La Mancha). This is an area of lagoons and marshes (both brackish and fresh) along the high basin of the Río Guadiana . Needless to say, the wet areas only exist for part of the year (generally from October/December, depending on when the rains come, until May). During that period you'll find one of the largest congregations of wintering ducks and breeding birds in the peninsula. The best area is that which in 1973 was designated the **Parque Nacional de las Tablas de Daimiel**, to the northeast of Ciudad Real; there is a reception center from where two walking tracks leave, which allow good observation of the birds. The **Parque Natural de las Lagunas de Ruidera,** northeast of Valdepeñas, has water all year round, although there will obviously be fewer birds in summer.

EXTREMADURA

From Madrid the main road and railroad towards Extremadura and Portugal run west, more or less parallel, through Talavera de la Reina and Navalmoral de la Mata. Neither town is particularly attractive, but they are both places where the bus stops and from where there are important connections to other parts of the province. **TALAVERA** has always been one of the most important centers of ceramic manufacture in Spain, and nowadays the town is covered in the dust from a score of porcelain factories. While there, it is worth taking time out from hanging around the bus station to look in the many shops down the main street displaying the local products. Much is the usual mass-produced tourist trash, but there are still a few real craftsmen working here. **NAVALMORAL** has even less to offer but again it's a major meeting place for bus routes to more engrossing places: north off the main road to the **Monastery of Yuste** and **Plasencia** or, again, south to **Guadalupe** — the only place in Cáceres province which can really be said to be exploited touristically, albeit on a small scale.

A gastronomic note: Extremadura, to many Spaniards, means **ham**. Along with the Sierra Morena in Andalucia, the Extremaduran sierra is the only place in the country which supports the pure-bred Iberian pig, from which comes the best *jamón serrano*. For its ham to be as highly flavored as possible, the pig, a subspecies of the European wild boar exclusive to the Iberian peninsula, is allowed to roam wild and eat acorns for several months of the year. The undisputed kings of hams in this area, praised at length by Richard Ford in his *Handbook for Travellers*, are those that come from **MONTÁNCHEZ**, in the south of the region. The village is midway between **Cáceres** and **Mérida**, so if you're in the area try some in a bar, washed down with local red wine — but be warned that the authentic product is extremely expensive, a few thin-cut slices costing the price of a whole meal.

Guadalupe

The small town of **GUADALUPE**, dominated in every way by its massive monastery and the miraculous image of the Virgin which it houses, lies in the heart of the Sierra de Guadalupe. The steep forested slopes which surround the place are cut by innumerable small streams, and while they make getting there laboriously slow it's worth it just for the extraordinary contrast with the arid plain from which you've come. The town itself is a fitting complement to the countryside, a shambles of narrow cobbled streets and overhanging houses around an arcaded plaza, the whole overshadowed by the monastery's bluff ramparts. There is a timeless feel only slightly marred by modern development on the outskirts, and a brisk trade in plastic copies of the finest religious treasures.

Pleasant as the town is, it is only the presence of the **Monasterio de Nuestra Señora de Guadalupe** which has brought fame and tourism to the area. The ancient image of the Virgin, said to have been carved by St. Luke, was discovered by a shepherd some time in the thirteenth century, but it wasn't until the Reconquest that the first monastery could be built to house it in 1340. Nothing of that original shrine survives, but what there is is a fantastically rich mixture of styles crammed one on top of the other and an insight into the incredible wealth which the Spanish church has amassed. (Franciscans, supposedly wedded to poverty, now occupy what was once the richest monastery in Spain). Tasteful is not the word, but it's certainly impressive.

Start with the old **church** (open all day) whose weighty bronze doors open in the middle of the main facade on to the Plaza Mayor. The gloom of the Gothic interior is, like the rest of this rambling edifice, packed with treasures from generations of wealthy patrons. Note especially the many fancy *rejas* (grilles) and, in the lower central part of the altar, the image of the Virgin.

The entrance to the monastery proper is to the left of the church, and visiting hours are from 9:30am to 1pm and 3:30 to 6:15pm. You have to take a guided tour and, as always, the object is to get you through the place as quickly as possible; try not to be rushed. This said, they often allow you to join another tour without paying again, if so you desire. I can do no more than mention the highlights here, beginning with the unusual Mudejar cloister — two brick stories of horseshoe arches with a strange pavilion or tabernacle in the middle. The **museum** holds an apparently endless collection of rich vestments, early illuminated manuscripts, and other religious paraphernalia, along with some fine artworks including a triptych by Isenbrandt and a small Goya. The **Sacristia**, though, is the finest room of all — unaltered since it was built in the seventeenth century, it contains eight paintings by Zurbarán. Apart from their intrinsic value, it is almost unique to see such works in their original context — the frames match the window frames and the pictures themselves are a planned part of the decoration of the room. From here, and climbing higher into the heart of the monastery, you pass through various rooms filled with jewels and relics, before the final ascent to the Holy of Holies. From a tiny room high above the main altar you can look down over the church while a panel is spun away to reveal the climax of the tour, the cossetted image itself, bejeweled, richly dressed, and blackened by centuries of candle smoke.

On the way out visit the *hostal*, converted from an unused section of the monastery. The bar in its Gothic cloister is one of the world's more unusual places to enjoy a quiet beer or a *Cuba Libre*. This and the *parador* — which has immaculately kept gardens for an evening stroll — are where the wealthier pilgrims stay; in the narrow streets leading down from the Plaza Mayor there are several perfectly adequate **fondas**. *Fonda Sanchez* is spotlessly clean and very cheap; two bars in the square itself, *Meson Tipico Isabel* and *Meson Extremeño,* have rooms. Buses stop at the town entrance, beside the *Bar-Restaurante Taruta*, which also has cheap rooms.

Good **views** of Guadalupe are easy to obtain — there is a modern *mirador* almost immediately below the monastery, and going along the road to Talavera affords another vantage point. A truly superb view of the town set in its surrounding hills can also be enjoyed from the road north to Navalmoral. Five kilometers beyond, the Chapel of El Humilladero marks the spot where pilgrims to the shrine caught their first glimpse of the monastery. The surrounding **sierra** is a very wild and beautiful region, with steep rocky crags abutting on the valley sides. It's worth exploring in itself, though you really need your own transportation to do so. At CABAÑAS DEL CASTILLO a mere handful of houses, most empty as only twelve inhabitants remain, nestle against a massive crag which is a favorite target for the few climbers that know it. Unlike most dying villages, all is orderly and emanates peace and tranquillity.

Conquistador Towns — Trujillo and Cáceres

To continue from Guadalupe to Trujillo you can either take a bus through ZORITA or the longer but more frequent connection via NAVALMORAL. This main road has to recommend it a view from the **Puerto de Miravete** which is fabulous even from a speeding vehicle. An elegant bridge takes the road across the gorge of the Tagus before it starts to switchback its way steeply up to the pass. Behind you is spread all the country you have covered, almost as far as Madrid. In the foreground the brilliant white twin domes of a nuclear power plant at ALMARAZ look deceptively tranquil; on the other side further vistas open up with TRUJILLO itself on a slight rise in the far distance. At its heart is a walled town virtually untouched since the sixteenth century, redolent above all of the exploits of the conquerors of the Americas; Pizarro was born here, as were many of the tiny band who defeated the Incas with him.

From the bus station work your way uphill through the narrow streets to the huge **Plaza Mayor** where a statue of the town's most famous son bars the way to the monuments on the hill behind. Also in the plaza, if you can dodge the traffic, is the **Turismo** and a couple of **fondas**. If these are full, and they probably will be unless you arrive early, check with the *Turismo* people for details of any private rooms available; otherwise you'll have to go back down to the Madrid road, where there are several *hostales* opposite c/Sola and c/de Pardos. Another, rather grim, is built over the bus station. The best place to eat, handily in the square, is called *La Trolla* — you'll probably find a huge salad and omelette on your plate before they've even asked you what you want to order for first course, and thereafter helpings are automatically replenished, should you somehow have room for them.

It is around the Plaza Mayor that life revolves for the visitor. In the southwest corner is the **Palacio de la Conquista**, perhaps the grandest of Trujillo's mansions, its roof surrounded by statues representing the twelve months. Just one of the many built by the Pizarro clan, it was originally inhabited by Francisco's uncle Hernando and his Inca bride. Diagonally opposite is the bulky church of **San Martín** with the tomb, among others, of the Orellana family; Francisco de Orellana was the first explorer of the Amazon. From here you can begin to climb into the walled town and towards the Moorish castle at its highest point. The c/de Ballesteros leads up to the walls, past the domed **Torre Del Alfiler** with its coats of arms and storks' nests, and through the gateway known as the Arco de Santiago — here, to the left, is **Santa María Mayor**, the most interesting of the town's many churches. The building is basically Gothic, but it's built on the site of a mosque and contains a beautiful raised Renaissance choir noted for the technical mastery of its almost flat vaults. There is a fine Hispano-Flemish reredos of 25 panels by Fernando Gallego, and tombs including those of the Pizarros and Diego García de Paredes, known as the "Estremeño Samson." Among other exploits, this giant of a man is said to have defended a bridge against an entire French army armed only with his gargantuan sword and to have picked up the font (now underneath the *coro*) to carry holy water to his mother. Francisco de Pizarro was baptized here too. Thanks to its advanced state of disrepair the church is now rarely used for services, so if you find it locked ask around — someone nearby will have the key.

The **castle** is now virtually in open countryside; for the last hundred meters of the climb you see nothing but the occasional broken-down remnant of a wall clambered over by sheep and the local dogs. The fortress itself, though, has been restored, its original Moorish towers much added-to by later defenders. From an alcove above the main gateway a huge statue of the Virgin watches over the town, and a flight of stairs leads up to a chapel immediately behind it. Much of the rest is fenced off for further restoration, and the main attraction is the panoramic view of the town and its environs from the battlements. Looking out over the barren heath which rings the town, the extent to which the old quarter has fallen into disrepair is abundantly evident, as is the castle's superb defensive position,

Of the many remaining mansions, or *solares*, the most interesting is the **Palacio de Orellana-Pizarro**, which nowadays houses the local school. Go in through the superb Renaissance arched doorway to admire the courtyard: an elegant patio decorated with the alternating coats of arms of the Pizarros — two bears with a pine tree — and the Orellanas.

Cáceres

CÁCERES is in many ways remarkably like Trujillo: its center is an almost perfectly preserved medieval town adorned with mansions built on the proceeds of American exploration, and (even more than in Trujillo) every available tower and spire is crowned by a clutch of storks' nests. But Cáceres is a much larger and livelier place, a rapidly growing provincial capital which is also home to the University of Extremadura. To most visitors it's the more attractive of the two (along with Toledo and Cuenca, it was declared a World Heritage site by UNESCO in 1986), especially if you come while the students are around to enliven the nightlife. The places to head for are the bars and *bodegas* in the main plaza and the streets leading northward off it; when school is in session there's often live music.

As ever the heart of things is the Plaza Mayor; the cheap **places to stay** are all in its immediate vicinity — the *Hotel Goya* in the plaza itself, with extremely amicable proprietors, and a couple more in the streets beyond that. The #1 bus goes to the plaza from the main road between the **railroad station** and the new **bus station** over the way. Even with a map you'll proba-

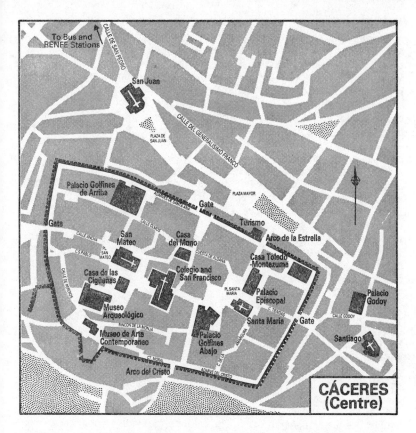

CÁCERES
(Centre)

bly get lost among the winding alleys of the old town, so as a preliminary orientation stand in the Plaza Mayor opposite the **Turismo** (Mon.–Fri. 10am–1:30pm and 5–8pm). To your left is the **Torre del Bujaco** (whose foundations, at least, date back to Roman times) with a chapel next to it and steps leading up to the low **Arco de la Estrella**, a new entrance built by Manuel Churriguera in the eighteenth century. To the right is the Moorish **Torre del Horno**, made of adobe and one of the best-preserved Moorish mud-brick structures surviving in Spain. A staircase leads up to another gateway, and beyond this is the most intact stretch of the ancient walls with several more of the original towers. Though basically Moorish in construction, the walls have been added to, altered, and built against ever since. Around the other side of the old town one Roman gateway, the **Arco del Cristo**, can still be seen.

Once through the Estrella gate, the **Casa de Toledo-Montezuma** with its domed tower is immediately to the left. To this house a follower of Cortés brought back one of the New World's more exotic prizes — a daughter of the

Aztec emperor as his bride. Of all the crumbling buildings, this is the one in most imminent danger of collapse and one of the very few not currently in use. Elsewhere most of the mansions are at least partly inhabited or have been restored as government offices or museums. Directly ahead is the **Plaza Santa María** with an impressive group of buildings around a refreshingly uncluttered Gothic church, far the best of the churches in Cáceres. It is well worth putting your money in the slot to see the fine sixteenth-century, carved wood *retablo* lit up, while in the surrounding gloom are the tombs of many of the town's great families. Outside, beneath the storks at the foot of the tower, is a modern statue of San Pedro de Alcántara, its toes already polished bright by the lips of the faithful.

The church of **San Mateo**, on the site of the ancient mosque at the town's highest point, is another Gothic structure with several attractive chapels, including one where 5ptas will buy you a picture of San Martín de Porres and three hundred days' indulgence. For 25ptas you get a plastic model. Next to the church is the **Casa de las Cigüeñas** (House of the Storks) whose narrow tower was the only one allowed to preserve its original battlements when the rest were shorn by royal decree. It is now some kind of military installation and although the tower features on the cover of the Tourist Board's leaflet as well as on half the postcards in Cáceres, soldiers discourage the taking of further snapshots.

In the same square, the Plaza San Mateo, is the **Museo Arqueológico** (9am–1pm and 4–7pm), housed in the *Casa Veletas*. It's worth visiting not so much for its collection — though the relics of local history and folk art are better displayed than usual — as for the building itself. Typical of the local style, its beautifully proportioned rooms are arrayed around a small patio and preserve the cistern (*aljibe*) of the original Moorish Alcázar with five rows of excellent horseshoe arches. It also has an extraordinary balustrade of Talavera ceramic jugs. The museum ticket admits you to the **Fine Arts** section in the *Casa del Mono* (House of the Monkey), a mansion adorned with grotesque simian gargoyles. The exhibits start with some graceful early relgious sculpture and attempt to trace the history of Spanish art to the present day. It's a strange mix, including a second-rate El Greco, but again well displayed in a beautiful old building. Finally there is a **Contemporary Art Museum** in the *Casa de los Pereros* in the street of that name. It has no permanent display, but they put on some surprisingly enterprising shows.

Something could be said about almost every building within the old walls, but notice above all the **family crests** — in particular on the *Casa del Sol* — and the magnificent facade of the **Palacio de los Golfines de Abajo**. Outside the walls the church of **Santiago** in the plaza of the same name is the most rewarding sight, along with the **Palacio Godoy** opposite it. The former is only open for masses, but has a fine altarpiece by Alonso Berruguete. Try also to take a walk through the ancient streets after dark. When the tourists have gone and the traffic is silent, it feels an unnervingly long way from the twentieth century.

North From Cáceres

If Extremadura is little known, northern Extremadura is still less so. Yet it is some of the most attractive country in this part of Spain, and what it lacks in great monuments it makes up in natural grandeur. As far as Plasencia the country is pretty flat, but the journey is broken by the vast **Embalse de Alcántara**. One of a series of new reservoirs harnessing the power of the Tajo (Tagus) and boosting local agriculture, it has swallowed a huge tract of land. The old road and railroad disappear into its depths to reemerge at intervals on higher ground, while the new versions run parallel to each other around the shore, crossing the many inlets on double-decker bridges. At one point the tower of a castle breaks surface while at the northern end are the remains of a Roman bridge, high and dry where everything else has been flooded.

Arroyo de la Luz and Alcántara

A regular bus service runs between Cáceres and **ARROYO DE LA LUZ** (Stream of Light). Despite its romantic name, this is one of the least memorable of the Extremaduran towns, and only those interested in its one "sight" should bother going. The gaunt, virtually windowless, late Gothic church of **La Asunción** houses a huge *retablo* with twenty panels by the local artist Luis Morales "El Divino" — by far the most important collection of his work. His heart-on-sleeve style has always appealed to the people of Spain, although it has found less favor with art historians. There can be no doubt that it is much more impressive when seen as a group in situ than in a museum. To see it, you have to ask for the keys from the local police at the side door of the *Ayuntamiento* which faces the south side of the church. There's only one place to stay — a two-star **hostal** named after the painter, at the edge of town where the buses stop.

Two buses a day continue to the isolated but much more interesting town of **ALCÁNTARA**, passing through landscape that becomes ever bleaker. The name of the town comes from the Arabic for 'bridge', and it's the beautiful six-arched **Roman bridge**, finished in A.D. 105, which is still the outstanding sight. Held together without mortar, this is reputed to the loftiest bridge ever built by the Romans; there's a triumphal arch dedicated to Trajan in the center, a tiny Classical temple at one end, and a medieval fortress at the other. In total contrast is the massive hydroelectric dam nearby; completed in 1970, it confines the long, narrow *Embalse de Alcántara*. Workers from France and elsewhere invade the town from time to time to work on the dam; no doubt they earn a good deal more than the local farmers who have to scratch a living from the unpromising land.

The town itself is built high above the river. The dominating landmark is the recently restored **Convento San Benito**, headquarters of the Knights of Alcántara, one of the great orders of the Church Militant. For all its enormous bulk, it's only a fragment; the nave of the church was never built. Outside, the main feature is the double-arcaded Renaissance, gallery at the back; it now serves as the backdrop for a season of classical plays which moves here from Mérida in August. To see the interior (regularly 10am–2pm Wed., Thur., and Fri.; possible access at other times) you have to knock at the entrance to the side of the walled-up front of the church. You are shown the cloister and the Plateresque east end — a picture of fallen glory, with the organ reduced to a wooden cage and the elaborate wall tombs now empty shells.

The town also contains the scanty remains of a castle, numerous mansions, and street after street of humbler whitewashed houses. The place is marvelous for scenic walks, whether in Alcántara itself, along the banks of the Tajo, or — best of all — in the hills on the opposite bank. The **Turismo** (free maps available) is at the entrance to the town on the road to Cáceres; opposite is the *Restaurante Antonio* which does cheap, tasty meals. There's only one official **place to stay**, the *Hostal Cruz de Alcántara* on the main street, c/ General Franco. However, the influx of foreign workers prompts bars, shops, and private homes to rent rooms (an example of the last is no. 12 on the same street). If you have difficulty, ask in the bars, at the tourist office, or even the local police — the people are very hospitable. The **buses**, which only go to and from Cáceres, stop at a little square ringed by cafes at the entrance to the historic part of the town. Try the *Bar Sevilla* (actually under the name *Centenario Terry*).

Northeast is the **Convento del Palancar**, a monastery founded by San Pedro de Alcántara in the sixteenth century and said to be the smallest in the world at only seventy square meters. It's hard to imagine how a community of about ten monks could have lived in these cubbyholes — San Pedro used to sleep sitting upright in his cubicle of a bedroom! There is now a small monastic community in the more modern monastery alongside; ring the bell and a monk will come and show you around. To get there head for the Puerto de los Castaños on the main Cáceres–Plasencia road, and take the Torrejoncillo road. After 4km you should take the marked left fork to reach the village of PEDROSO DE ACIM.

The Parque Natural de Monfragüe

To the east, between Plasencia and Trujillo, lies the **Parque Natural de Monfragüe**, the only protected natural area in Extremadura and a very important refuge for flora and fauna. The reserve basically consists of a rugged valley 30km by 6km, through which the dammed-up Tajo runs — a generally rocky landscape, but with a diversity of rivers, woods, scrubland, and pasture that makes it amenable to wildlife.

Before it was given special status in 1979, the area was in a bad way . Industrial pollution of the Tajo was a major problem, and the completion of two dams in the late 1960s further disrupted the environment by submerging trees and slowing the flow of water. The rapid, indiscriminate planting of eucalyptus by the rapidly expanding paper industry, and its destruction of bushes and trees which were traditional sites for nesting and shelter, made things even worse; by 1977 almost 10,000 acres had been destroyed. After a public campaign, protection was eventually given. Ten years later, funding is slim, local industry hostile, and most people remain unaware of the park's existence.

There are over 200 species in the park. It is certain that Spanish lynx still prowl here since their footprints have been spotted, but the warden hasn't seen one in the five years he's been working there. Most important is the bird population, especially **birds of prey** such as the black crane (only breeding population in Europe), the black vulture (not averse to eating tortoises), the griffon vulture (partial to carrion intestine), the Egyptian vulture (not above eating human excrement), the Spanish imperial eagle (identifiable by its very obvious white shoulder patches), the golden eagle (loads of them), and the eagle owl (largest owl in Europe).

Ornithologists should visit in May and June, botanists in March and April — and everbody should avoid the period from mid-summer to September, when the heat is stifling.

Getting Around the Park

The problem with visiting the park is its relative inaccessibility and the limited information or guidance for visitors, which means you can easily wander unawares onto private estates. One road runs through it, the C524 from Trujillo to Plasencia, and there's a rudimentary **bus** service between these two towns (a bus leaves Plasencia at 2:45pm Mon.–Sat., and one leaves Trujillo in the morning). It's not a good hitching route — once beyond PALAZUELO (10km from Plasencia) traffic is very infrequent. The bus from Plasencia stops at the main village, **VILLAREAL DE SAN CARLOS** — a weird place, dead except for a fairly basic **information center** and cafe, both frequented by earnest zoologists. Bookshops in town sell a useful guide on the park by José Luis Rodríguez for about $9, presently only in Spanish. **Paths** lead from here into the park, but since it's not easy to figure out where you are permitted to wander, keep to the tracks. There's no accommodation in Monfragüe and no **camping**, except for the designated area in Villareal.

A specific place to aim for in the park, near Villareal, is the **Sanctuario de Monfragüe**, a castle built high up on a rock, with a chapel next to it. The bus driver will let you off here, if asked, and it's a short walk up to the observation point, from where on a clear day you can see the villages of La Vera, many kilometers to the north. You can also approach the castle from a marked path up from Puente Cardenal; if coming from Villareal, there's a fountain on the opposite side of the bridge on the left, known as the *Fuente del Frances* after a young Frenchman who died there trying to save an eagle — the path starts from there. On the other side of the park, just before Trujillo, you'll pass through the *dehesas*, strange Africa-like plains which are among the oldest woodlands in Europe. The economy of the *dehesas* is based on grazing, and the casualties among these domestic animals are what enable the eagles and vultures of Monfragüe to thrive.

Plasencia and Above the Río Tajo

In the shadow of the Sierra de Gredos, surrounded on three sides by the Río Jerte (from the Greek *Xerte*, meaning "joyful"), PLASENCIA looks more impressive from afar than it actually is. Once you get up into the old city the walls are virtually impossible to find — for the most part they're propping up the back of someone's house — and the cathedral is barely half built. There are however some interesting details worth seeking out.

The **Cathedral** is in fact two churches — old and new — built back to back. Work began on the second at the beginning of the sixteenth century and continued under two architects for almost forty years, but when neither managed to finish it, the open end was simply bricked up. The fact that the completed building would have been a particularly lofty Gothic construction only adds to the foreshortened feel of the interior. It does have some redeeming features, most notably the Renaissance choir stalls intricately carved by Rodrigo Aleman and described with some justice by the National Tourist Board as "the most Rabelaisian in Christendom." Opposite the cathedral is the **Casa del Deán**, (Dean's House) with an interesting balcony like the prow of a ship. Continuing away from the cathedral along c/Blanca you come out at the Plaza de San Nicolas, where, according to local tradition, the church was built to prevent two local families from shooting arrows at each other from adjacent houses. Although there are a large number of mansions in the old part of town, it's no rival for Cáceres — but it does have the plus of a range of lively bars and shops.

Finding good **places to eat** is difficult here, but try the area between the cathedral and the Plaza Mayor. Easily the best in town is *La Muralla*, just inside the Arco de Barrozana: take the c/de los Quesos from the Plaza (opposite c/Talavera) and turn left at the Palacio Grijalva at the bottom — *La Muralla* is just down on the right. It's a small, friendly *pensión* that offers **rooms** too, with hotel standards at hostal prices. Two other **places to stay** are both near to the main square: *La Humilde Cabaña*, just off c/Talavera, on the right as you head down it from the square, and the clean and unpretentious *Pensión Santamaria* on c/Trujillo, the street that leads down off the Plaza to the Cáceres road. There is a **Turismo** in the same street. Tuesday is a good day to be here, when the **market**, held in the Plaza Mayor since the twelfth century, happens — great characters from the villages all about.

The arcaded Plaza Mayor is ringed with banks and cafes, all of them much frequented by farmers in town for a day's business. **Bars** are thick on the ground in Plasencia, with over fifty in the old part alone! It's certainly worth sampling some, because this is the land of the *pincho*, a little titbit of food provided free with your beer or wine. Ask to try the local *pitarra*, slightly more expensive than other wines, and made for non-commercial distribution. The number-one street for bars is c/Patalón, where there are eleven in a short interval; go down c/Talavera from the main square and it's the second turning on the left. The bars *Madrid*, *Nuevo Pino* and *La Herradura* are good for *pinchos* and *pitarra* and the *Asador el Refugio* for its fish, squid, and octopus *pinchos*.

The **valley of the Jerte** continues for 50km to the pass of Puerto de Tornavacas, the boundary with Ávila province. Although the overdeveloped villages aren't particularly interesting (save CABEZUELA and JERTE itself), the countryside is pleasant enough — but you need a car to explore it. The valley is renowned for its cherry trees, which for a ten-day period in spring cover the slopes with white blossom. If you're anywhere in the area at this time, it's worth the effort to see it.

A line of hills border the valley on each side. On the **northern side** there are two roads which cross over the main Plasencia–Salamanca road — the route through the villages of EL TORNO and CABEZABELLOSA (from where there's a great view over the plain), and the more interesting Puerto de Honduras route between Cabezuela in El Valle and HERVÁS (where there's a fascinating former Jewish quarter). The latter is the highest road in Extremadura, rising to 1430m, but it's in bad condition. On the **southern side** the main point of interest is the pass of Piornal, just behind the village of the same name. The best approach is via the villages of CASA DEL CASTAÑAR and CABRERO. Once at the pass you can continue over to La Vera and the beautiful village of Garganta la Olla.

La Vera and the Yuste Monastery

La Vera is the area between the River Tietar to the south and the high sierras of Ávila to the north, especially characterized by the streams or *gargantas* which descend from the mountains and give the region its green vegetation. To see the most picturesque of the region's villages take the Jarandilla road from Plasencia.

CUACOS, one of the most appealing places along this road, is famed for its monastery, which is probably the most important excursion from Plasencia (20km to the west). From the village the **Monasterio de Yuste**, to which Carlos V retired after renouncing the cares of his empire, is a two-kilometer uphill walk, but a very pleasant one through the woods. There is nothing especially dramatic about the place, just a simple beauty and the rather gloomy accoutrements of the emperor's last years. His apartments are still draped throughout in black, and you are shown the little sedan chair in which he was brought here, and another designed to support the old man's gouty legs. If you believe the guide, the bed and even the sheets are the very ones in which Carlos died — since the place was sacked during the Peninsular War and deserted for years after the suppression of the monasteries it seems unlikely, but you never know. A door by the bed opens out over the church and altar so that even in his final illness Carlos never missed a service.

The **village** itself is much more interesting than it at first appears. If you arrive by bus from Plasencia you're going to have to spend a good part of the day here, since in each direction there is just one connection early in the morning and another in the afternoon. Fortunately you couldn't hope to find a more attractive village, nor one so little touched by tourism. Just off the main road is the tiny Plaza de Don Juan de Austria with the house (its upper floor reconstructed) where Carlos's illegitimate son Don Juan lived when visiting his father. Locals claim that the surrounding houses, their overhanging upper floors supported on gnarled wooden pillars, are sixteenth-century originals; they certainly look it. From the beams under the overhang, tobacco is hung out to dry after the harvest. There's nothing in particular to see, but spend some time wandering through the flower-decked streets down to the dusty Plaza de España or to the fourteenth-century church, a lovely building in a parlous state of disrepair. Back on the main road you can while away the hours in one of several bars.

At the moment there's just one small **fonda** in Cuacos, but the area's tourist potential has been more fully realized in the nearby villages of **ALDEANUEVA DE LA VERA** and **JARANDILLA**, each of which has a **campground** and a choice of **hostales**. You could easily hitch this far; getting lifts is rarely a problem around here — the trouble is that no one seems to be going further than the next village. Given the choice, Jarandilla is the more interesting, with two comfortable *hostales* opposite a castle converted into a **parador**.

At the mountain village of **EL GUIJO DE SANTA BARBARA**, 4½km above Jarandilla, the road gives out, leaving the ascent of the rocky valley to walkers. An hour's hike away is the pool known as *El Trabuquete* and a high meadow with shepherds' huts; another hour along disused and elusive tracks brings you to PIMESAILLO. The really adventurous can take the steep, pathless valley on the left, beyond Pimesaillo; on the other side is the fabulous *Garganta de Infierno* (Stream of Hell) and the natural swimming pools known as *Los Pilones*. You eventually come out on the El Valle road between Cabezuela and Jerte. If you start from the El Valle side look for the track marked *Campamento de Carlos Quinto* near a roadside bar/restaurant. Going in either direction, budget two walking days to enjoy it properly.

Beyond Jarandilla lies **VILLANUEVA DE LA VERA**, in recent years the subject of national and international controversy over its *Pero Palo* fiesta in which donkeys are alleged to be severely maltreated.

In the other direction from Cuacos, off the main road, is **GARGANTA DE LA OLLA**. Here there are a couple of specific things to look out for; the **Museum of the Inquisition** (if you speak Spanish, the guide is a mine of information) and the **Casa de la Piedra** (House of Stone), a house whose balcony is secured by a three-pronged wooden support resting on a rock. The latter is hard to find; begin by taking the left-hand street up from the square and then start asking.

Las Hurdes

Las Hurdes, the abrupt rocky lands which rise to meet the Batuecas area of Salamanca province, have always been apart from their surroundings and have always been a rich source of mysterious tales. According to legend Las Hurdes were unkown to the outside world until the time of Columbus, when two lovers fleeing from the Court of the Duke of Alba chanced upon them. The people who welcomed them were unaware of the existence of other people or other lands. Shields and other remnants belonging to the Goth Rodirigo and his court of seven centuries earlier were discovered by the couple, giving rise to the saying that the Hurdanos are descendants of kings. Fifty years ago the inhabitants of the remoter areas were still so unused to outsiders that they hid in their houses if anyone appeared. Luis Buñuel filmed an unflatteringly grotesque documentary, *Land Without Bread*, here in the 1930s, in which it was hard to discern any royal descent in his subjects. Modernity has crept up on the region now, but the locals, perhaps doubly wary after Buñuel's enterprise, may be suspicious and unfriendly if you start taking photographs. Tact is essential.

Las Hurdes can be reached from Béjar, 70km south of Salamanca, by taking the C515 secondary road towards SOTOSERRANO. Beyond this village the first place in Las Hurdes is RIOMALO DE ABAJO. From Plasencia take the C204 via Montehermoso and Villanueva de la Sierra; the first Las Hurdes village by this route is PINOFRANQUEADO, called *El Pino* by locals. The Michelin map no. 447 is seriously deficient for Las Hurdes — if necessary, look in a branch of the *Caja de Ahorros* bank for a really detailed map of the province. NUÑOMORAL is a good base for excursions, with an excellent inexpensive *hostal* next to the *Banco Central*. If you're camping you may want to take advantage of their good suppers. In this rocky area, tiny terraces have been constructed on the river bed as the only way of getting the stubborn land to produce anything.

To the north, the tiny village of **LA HUETRE** is worth a visit; take a right fork just before the village of CASARES. The typical slate-roofed houses are for once in good condition and it has an impressive situation, surrounded by steep rocky hills. To the south, LA BATUEQUILLA and LA HORCAJADA are two minute settlements populated by a handful of families; both can be reached from RUBIACO on the road between Nuñomoral and Vegas de Coria. **EL GASCO** is known for a huge waterfall beneath the Miacera Gorge, but the cascade is very difficult to reach (don't mistake it for a smaller one nearer the village), and the settlement itself is smelly and squalid. AVELLANAR and HORCAJO have traditional houses.

The Sierra de Gata

The **Sierra de Gata**, northwest of Las Hurdes, is a series of wooded hills with some outcrops of higher ground, rising slowly to the province of Salamanca. Isolated and as yet little visited, it's most easily approached from Plasencia — take the C204, the Montehermoso road, and as you leave town the turnoff is on the right after the bridge over the Jerte, on the road to Cáceres. Follow it for 38km, and 1km after Pozuelo de Zarzón there's another fork on the left, marked Villasbuenas de Gata. When you've reached the Cadalso turnoff you're in the Sierra de Gata.

ROBLEDILLO DE GATA is a fascinating village of old houses packed tightly together. Unfortunately a large part of this beautiful and formerly wooded valley was burned by forest fires in recent summers — most of them, as with similar fires in Las Hurdes, were deliberately started to claim insurance money. In the hilltop village of **SANTÍBAÑEZ EL ALTO** the oldest houses are built entirely of stone, without windows, and most of the streets are too narrow for traffic. At the top of town, look out for a tiny bull-ring, castle remains, and the old cemetery — there's a wonderful view over the Borbollón reservoir from here.

ACEBO has a massive church and is surrounded by orange trees; it also has a bar on the edge of the village, *Casa Maura*, which serves excellent white *pitarra* wine. GATA itself is very picturesque, and you might want to ascend to the Torre de Almenara, between Gata and the village of Torre de Don Miguel. A track leads there from a pass between the two villages; paths are not maintained in these areas, so some bush-whacking will be necessary. The hamlet of TREVEJO and its rough cobbled streets are from another age; someone will probably offer to take you up to its castle. SAN MARTÍN DE TREVEJO is one of the nicest of the many picturesque villages around; if you're here at mealtime make for the *Bar Avenida del 82*, also referred to as the *casa de la Julia* after the lady who runs it — very cheap and good village fare in great abundance. Here, and in ELIJAS and VALVERDE DEL FRESNO, you may hear the curious *maniago* dialect, a mix of Castilian Spanish and Portuguese that the locals speak among themselves in prefer-ence to Castilian.

Mérida

One-time capital of the Roman province of Lusitania, **MÉRIDA** (the name is a corruption of *Augusta Emerita*) contains more **Roman remains** than any other city in Spain; indeed it has one of the most remarkable assemblages of monuments from that epoch to be found anywhere. For anyone at all inter-ested in antiquities it is a must, but it won't please everyone. Many visitors enticed here by National Tourist Board photographs of the Roman theater leave feeling short-changed, as the various excavated sites are scattered between patches of ugly later development, thus making it impossible to get any idea of the scale or layout of the Roman city. So anyone prone to be bored by archaeology should give Mérida a wide berth.

The Roman Sites
Built on the site of a Celto-Iberian settlement, Mérida was the tenth city of the Roman empire and was also the final stop on the *Vía de la Plata*, the Roman road which began in Astorga. It was bound by the rivers Guadiana and Albarregas, and extended as far as the modern bullring and Roman circus, covering a little less than the triangular area occupied by the modern town. Start your tour by the magnificent **Puente Romano** (Roman Bridge) over the islet-strewn Guadiana — sixty arches long and still strong enough to take modern traffic. It is defended by an enormous, plain **Alcazaba**, built by the Moors to replace a Roman construction. The interior consists mostly of a rather barren archeological site, although in the middle there's an *aljibe* (cistern) to which you can descend by either of a pair of staircases. (Mon.-Sat. 8am–1pm and 4–7pm in summer; 9am–1pm and 3–6pm in winter; Sun. 9am–2pm throughout the year). Part of the fortress has been restored for use as government offices, a concert hall, and an information point.

Nearby is the sixteenth-century Plaza de España, the heart of the modern town. On a street just off it is the so-called *Templo de Diana*, currently the object of an overzealous restoration project. Behind the other side of the plaza is a convent which now houses the **Museo Visigotico** (Mon.–Fri. 9am–2pm and 4–6pm), with about a hundred lapidary items; just behind this is the **Arco Trajano**, an unadorned triumphal arch 15m high and 9m across.

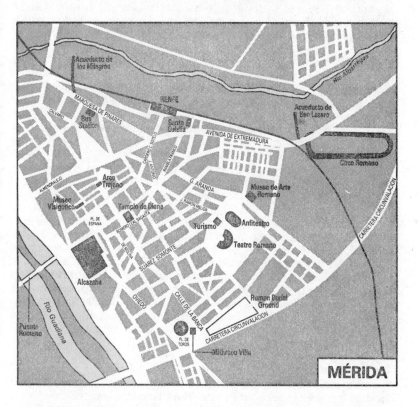

By far the most important single site, though, is that containing the **Teatro Romano** and **Anfiteatro** (8am–9pm in summer; 8am–6pm in winter). The theater, one of the best preserved anywhere, and one of the most beautiful monuments of the entire Roman world, dates from about 15 B.C., a present to the city from Agrippa. The two-tier colonnaded stage is in a particularly good state of repair. Many of the lower seats have been rebuilt entirely, while the upper ones offer rather less than the last word in comfort to the audiences of the annual July season of classical plays. Behind the stage you can see excavations of various rooms. The adjacent amphitheater is a slightly later and much plainer construction. As many as 15,000 people — almost half the current population of Mérida — could be seated around the oval stadium to watch gladiatorial combats and fights with wild animals. At the gates is the new **Turismo**, which has free maps of Mérida and other towns in the region.

Just across from these buildings is the vast, red-brick bulk of the new **Museo Nacional de Arte Romano** (Tues.–Sat. 10am–2pm and 5–7pm; Sun. 10am–2pm). The building itself is constructed around the excavations of a Roman wall, and is a free modern interpretation of classical motifs. The exhibits, superbly displayed on three tiers in a vast hall, include statues from the theater, the Mithraeo villa (see below), and the vanished forum, plus a number of mosaics — the largest being hung on the walls so that they can be examined at each of the three levels.

There are the remains of two **Roman villas** in Mérida as well. The first, immediately below the museum, is notable for its mosaics, especially a vigorous depiction of grape-treading (open Mon.–Sat. 9am–1pm and 4–7pm in summer; 9am–1pm and 3–6pm in winter; Sun. 9am–2pm). The other, the **Mithraeo** (same hours), is situated in the shadow of the Plaza de Toros; it has a magnificent but damaged mosaic, now under cover, showing river gods. A short walk away is a Roman burial ground, with two family sepulchers.

The remaining monuments are in the vicinity of the railroad. A feat of imagination is required to recreate the **circus** in one's mind, as almost nothing of the masonry is left. Where once horses and chariots raced, joggers now complete the circuit. The most impressive of the two remaining aqueducts is the **Acueducto de los Milagros**, of which a satisfying portion survives in the midst of vegetable gardens. Its tall arches of granite with brick courses brought water to the city in its earliest days from the reservoir at PROSERPINA, 5km away (a good place to swim — and it has a May–Oct. **campground**). The best view of the aqueduct is from yet another Roman bridge, that over the Albarregas, which is so low and inconspicuous that it's easy to miss; it was over this span that the *Vía de la Plata* entered the city. Between the aqueducts is the Transitional church of **Santa Eulalia** which in the seventeenth century acquired a porch made from fragments of the former Temple of Mars.

Practicalities

Whatever one's opinion of the worth of the sights of Mérida, there's no question that it is a lively place for its size. The whole area between the railroad station and the Pl. de España is full of **bars and cheap restaurants**. Those who want to indulge themselves at a modest cost will find four-course menus available at the *Restaurante Naya*, very close to the station, and the *Restaurante Aragon* on c/Cervantes. Budget **accommodation**, on the other hand, is not plentiful — there's a noticeable lack of *fondas*. The places to try are mostly close to the **bus station** on c/Marquesa de Pinares. Just across the road, on Avda. de Extremadura, is *Hostal Nueva España*; in the opposite direction is *Hostal Salúd*, on c/Vespasian. Going towards Pl. de España on c/Delgado Valencia (from the station go up c/Cardero and continue into the next street) is *Hostal La Mezquita*, while on Pl. Sta. Clara behind the main square is *Hostal Guadiana*.

Badajoz

The valley of the Guadiana, followed by road and railroad, waters rich farmland between Mérida and **BADAJOZ**. The main reason for visiting Badajoz,
the scene of innumerable sieges and traditional gateway to Portugal, is still to
get across the border. It's not somewhere you would want to stay long. Crude
modern development has largely overrun what must once have been an
attractive city center, and few of the monuments have survived.

At the very heart of town lies the Plaza de España and a squat thirteenth-
century **Cathedral** (daily 11am–1pm), whose nave and tower have a fortress-
like aspect — it was prettified a little in the Renaissance period by adding a
portal and embellishing the tower. The **Turismo** is just off the square in the
c/de San Juan. For a more favorable overall impression climb to what
remains of the Alcazaba; it's largely ruined, but it does have restored
Moorish entrance gates and fragments of a Renaissance palace inside. Follow
c/de San Juan, or any of the streets leading in the same general direction,
and you will come to its fort. Defending the townward side is the octagonal
Moorish *Torre Espantaperros* (it means "dog-scarer," the dogs in question
being Christians) which houses the **Museo Arqueológico**, closed for restoration at the moment. Along the base of the fortifications to the left is the
Plaza Alta, once an elegant arcaded concourse, now seedy. From here a path
leads up through the walls to a small park inside the Alcazaba. There's a fine
view from the ramparts.

The Guadiana is the city's only other distinguished feature, and especially
a graceful bridge over it, the **Puente de Palmas**. Designed by Herrera
(architect of the Escorial) as a fitting first impression of Spain, it leads into
the city through the **Puerta de Palmas**, once a gate in the walls, now standing alone as a sort of triumphal arch.

From the plaza behind this arch lead two streets — c/Melchor de Evora
and c/Coronel Yague — where you'll find the cheapest **places to stay**. A
quieter alternative is c/Primo de Rivera on the south side of the cathedral;
halfway along it there is a whole clutch of pensions. There are some rather
more luxurious *hostales* (but still extremely cheap) in c/Muñoz Torero which
leads down from the Plaza de España towards the river; this area, a couple of
blocks below the plaza, is also the place to look for reasonably-priced **food
and lively bars**. On c/Muñoz Torero itself, the *Bar-Restaurante El Tronco*
has excellent, fiery regional food — but it's not all that cheap, so you'll save
money by eating at the bar. There's a **youth hostel** at 10A Avda. de Jose
Antonio, the broad street which follows the line of the city walls, or you could
join the gypsies **camping** among the trees along the river bank. A new **bus
station** has been built but it is in an awkward location in wasteland beyond
the ring road at the southern edge of the city. It's a fair way from downtown
and a long way from the railroad station, but buses #3 and #4 connect with
the former, and buses #1 and #2 with the latter. The **railroad station** is on
the far side of the river, straight up the road which crosses the Puente de
Palmas. Any bus crossing the bridge will take you there.

Olivenza and Southwards

Twenty-five kilometers southwest of Badajoz lies **OLIVENZA**, a good destination for a morning excursion. This whitewashed town seems to have landed up in the wrong country; long disputed between Spain and Portugal, it has been Spanish since 1801. Yet not only is the character of the town and its buildings clearly Portuguese, the Castilian tongue still has some years to wait to gain its final triumph. The oldest inhabitants still cling to Portuguese — you may overhear them talking in their preferred language as they relax in the main square where the buses stop.

Olivenza has long been strongly fortified, and traces of the walls and gates can still be seen, even though houses were later built up against them. Three towers of the castle survive. This complex is normally kept locked, although a museum inside is supposed to be open on Saturday afternoon and Sunday morning — typically, these are about the only times there are no buses to and from Badajoz. More accessible are the two churches of **Santa María del Castillo**, right beside the castle, and **Santa María Magdalena**, just around the corner. Both have sturdy bell towers and light, airy interiors (adorned with *azulejos* tiles and ornate Baroque altars) which are in total contrast to what one normally finds in Spain. The latter is in the distinctive Portuguese Manueline style, with arcades of twisted columns; the former is a more sober Renaissance affair with three aisles of equal height, and a notable work of art in the huge "Tree of Jesse" *retablo*. The churches are normally open all morning and again in the evening. Just across the street from Santa María Magdalena is a former palace, now the public library, with a spectacular Manueline doorway. And continuing down this street, then taking the first turning on the left, you come to the early sixteenth-century **Hospital**, which still serves its original purpose; the walls of its chapel are covered with more *azulejos*.

Should you want to stay, there's a one-star **hotel** on the fringes of the town, and a restaurant directly facing it.

Heading South

The route south toward Andalucía crosses territory that for the most part is harsh and unrewarding, fit only for sheep and the occasional cork or olive tree. The road from Badajoz to Jerez de los Caballeros is typical of the region, striking across a forbidding, parched landscape, passing through villages where the main form of nourishment seems to be dust. Some of these hamlets, low huts and a whitewashed church strung out along the road, look as if they have been dumped from some low-budget western set of a Mexican frontier town. It's cruel country which bred cruel people, if we are to believe the names of places like VALLE DE MATAMOROS (valley of the Moor-slayers), and one can easily understand the attraction which the New World and the promise of the lush Indies must have held for its inhabitants.

Jerez de los Caballeros

Not surprising then, that **JEREZ DE LOS CABALLEROS** is one of those towns which produced a whole crop of *conquistadores*. The two most celebrated are Vasco Nuñez de Balboa, discoverer of the Pacific, and Hernando de Soto, who in exploring the Mississippi became one of the first Europeans to set foot in North America. You're not allowed to forget it — the bus station is in the Plaza de Vasco Nuñez de Balboa, complete with a statue of Vasco in the very act of discovery, and from it the Calle Hernando de Soto (also known as the Hero of Florida) leads up into the middle of town.

It's a quiet, friendly place, passed through by many tourists but stayed in by few. Grass grows up through most of the cobbled streets and there's no hurry about anything — though when I was there the place was consumed by a heated controversy over who had won the annual fishing competition. There's just one **pensión**, and that's hard to find: ask in the Plaza de España for the *Bar Cancelas*, where they have some basic, but clean and cheap rooms.

Jerez is famous for its **church towers**, and from a distance they dominate the walled old town. A passion for building spires gripped the place in the eighteenth century, when three churches erected new ones. The silhouette of each is clearly based on that of the Giralda at Sevilla, but they are all distinctively decorated: the first is on San Miguel, in the Plaza de España at the very heart of the town, and is made of carved brick; the second is the unmistakable red-, blue-, and ocher-glazed tower of San Bartolomé, on the hill above it; and the third, rather dilapidated, belongs to Santa Catalina, outside the walls. Above the central square the streets climb up to the recently restored remains of a **castle** of the Knights Templar (this was once an embattled frontier town), mostly fourteenth-century but with obvious Moorish influences. Adjoining the castle, and predating it by over a century (as do the town walls), is the church of **Santa María**. Built on a Visigothic site, it's more interesting seen from the battlements above than it is from the inside. The clock tower is a further embellishment to the skyline, and keeps remarkably good time as well. In the small park below the castle walls a cafe commands fine views of the surrounding countryside, but above all of the magnificent sunsets.

Zafra and the Sierra Morena

If you plan to stick to the main routes or are heading south from Mérida, **ZAFRA** is rather less of a detour, though it's also much more afflicted by tourists. It's famed mainly for its **Castle** — now converted into a *parador* but still worth a look for the white marble Renaissance patio designed by Juan de Herrera. Two beautiful arcaded plazas, the Plaza Grande and the Plaza Chica, adjoin each other in the town center. The most attractive of several interesting churches is **Nuestra Señora de la Candelaria**, with nine panels by Zurbarán in the *retablo* and a chapel by Churriguera; and you shouldn't miss the tombs of the Figueroa family (original inhabitants of the castle) in the Convent of Santa Clara. The **Turismo**, as well as a **hostal** and a **fonda**, is in the Plaza de España, close by the *parador*; there are more cheap rooms to be found in the road leading down to the station.

Beyond Zafra the main road and the railroad head straight down through the **Sierra Morena** towards SEVILLA. By **road** it's more interesting — though bus services are less frequent — to head down through FREGENAL

DE LA SIERRA (where the road from Jerez de los Caballeros joins up) into the very heart of the Sierra close to ARACENA . On the **train** you can reach another interesting part of the Sierra by getting off at the station of CAZALLA-CONSTANTINA; if you're heading for CÓRDOBA and eastern Andalucía, change at LOS ROSALES before reaching SEVILLA.

fiestas

February
First weekend *La Endiablada* at ALMONACID DEL MARQUESADO (near Cuenca), a very old festival which sees all the boys dressing up as devils and parading through the streets.
Carnival (the week before Lent) again celebrated everywhere.

March/April
Holy Week (*Semana Santa*) celebrated with considerable ritual (floats, penitents, etc.) in CUENCA.
Pascua (**Passion of the Resurrection**) launches a major fiesta in TRUJILLO.

May
Early/mid-May fair at CÁCERES. Also — again with no fixed date — *Cabalata*, muleteer races, at ATIENZA (on the road between Sigüenza and Aranda de Duero).

June
23–27 *San Juan*. Particularly manic festival in the picturesque town of CORIA (55km west of Plasencia) with a bull let loose in the town for two or three hours a day, everyone dancing and drinking in the streets, and running for their lives when it appears.
Ancient Drama Festival in the Roman theater at MÉRIDA.

September
First week *Vendimia* — grape harvest — celebrations at VALDEPEÑAS; major fair at TRUJILLO also early in the month.
Spanish Classical Drama Festival at ALMAGRO (Ciudad Real).

October
1 *San Miguel*. Fiesta of some kind at any town or church named after the saint — particularly at BADAJOZ.

travel details

Buses
From Cuenca to Valencia (2 daily; 4 hr.) and Madrid (4 daily; 3 hr.)
From Ciudad Real to Toledo (1 daily; 3 hr.), Madrid (4 daily; 4 hr.), Almagro (5 daily; 1 hr.), Valdepeñas (3 daily; 2 hr.), and Jaén (2 daily; 4 hr.)
From Talavera to Toledo (5 daily; 1¾ hr.), Madrid (frequently; 3 hr.), and Guadalupe (2 daily; 2½ hr., originating in Madrid, from where journey takes 4½ hr.)
From Navalmoral to Guadalupe (2 daily; 3 hr.) and Plasencia (via Jarandilla — 2 daily; 2–4 hr.)
From Trujillo to Guadalupe (1 daily; 3 hr.), Cáceres (5 daily; 1½ hr.), and Mérida (4 daily; 2 hr.)
From Cáceres to Guadalupe (1 daily; 4 hr.), Madrid (7 daily; 4–5 hr.), Trujillo (7 daily; 1 hr.), Arroyo de la Luz (6 daily; ½ hr.), Alcántara (2 daily; 1½ hr.), Valencia de Alcántara (2 daily; 2¼ hr.), Plasencia (5 daily; 1½ hr.), Badajoz (2 daily; 2 hr.), Mérida (3 daily; 1½ hr.), Salamanca (3 daily; 3½ hr.), Caminomorisco, (1 daily; 2½ hr.), Sevilla (3 daily; 5 hr.), and Coria (4 daily; 1½ hr.)
From Plasencia to Jarandilla (2 daily; 2 hr.) and Salamanca (6 daily; 2 hr.)
From Badajoz to Mérida (5 daily; 1½ hr.), Sevilla (5 daily; 4 hr.), Zafra (5 daily; 2 hr.), Córdoba/Málaga (1 daily; 5/7½ hr.), Lisbon (at least 1 each day; 7 hr.), Madrid (7 daily; 6 hr.), Cáceres (2 daily; 2 hr.), Olivenza (7 daily; ½ hr.), Caya (Portuguese frontier — 4 daily; ½ hr.), and Valencia de Alcántara (3 daily; 1½ hr.)
From Mérida to Madrid (7 daily; 5 hr.), Cáceres (1 daily; 1½ hr.), Trujillo (1 daily; 1½ hr.), Zafra (2 daily; 1½ hr.), Sevilla (10 daily; 3½ hr., some stopping in Zafra), and Jerez de los Caballeros (1 daily; 2 hr.)

Trains

Madrid–Cuenca 5 daily in about 3 hr., via Aranjuez (1 hr.)

Cuenca–Valencia 4 daily (3–4 hr.)

Madrid–Sigüenza 10 daily (1½–2½ hr.)

Sigüenza–Barcelona 3 daily (at least 8 hr.), via Zaragoza (3–4 hr.)

Madrid–Cáceres 4 daily in 5–7 hr. via Talavera (2 hr.) and Navalmoral (3 hr.)

Cáceres–Lisbon 2 daily (4½ hr.)

Cáceres–Sevilla 1 daily (6 hr.) via Mérida (2 hr.) and Zafra (3½ hr.)

Cáceres–Madrid 5 daily (4½–6 hr.)

Cáceres–Plasencia 1 daily (2 hr.)

Cáceres–Valencia de Alcántara 2 daily (2½ hr.)

Madrid–Badajoz 4 daily in 7–9 hr. via Ciudad Real (3 hr.); 1 via Cáceres (7 hr.)

Badajoz–Sevilla 3 daily in 5–7 hr. via Mérida (1 hr.) and Zafra (2–3 hr.)

Badajoz–Mérida 7 daily (1 hr.)

Badajoz–Plasencia 1 daily (4 hr.)

Badajoz–Lisbon 3 daily (3½ hr.)

Badajoz–Cáceres 1 daily (2 hr.)

Mérida–Madrid 6 daily (6 hr.)

Mérida–Plasencia 1 daily (3 hr.)

Mérida–Cáceres 4 daily (1 hr.)

Mérida–Sevilla 1 daily (5 hr.)

CHAPTER THREE

ANDALUCIA

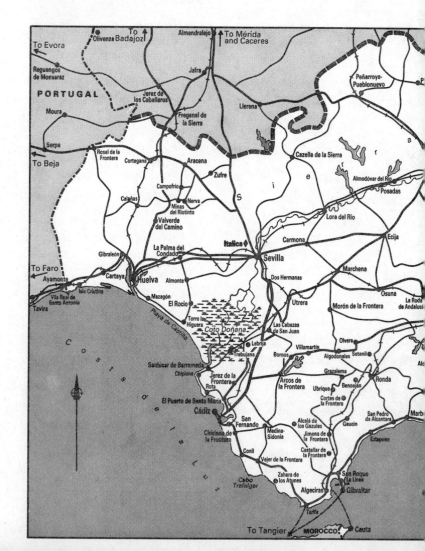

A bove all else — and there is plenty — it is the great **Moorish monuments** that compete for your attention in Andalucía. The Moors, a mixed race of Berbers and Arabs who crossed into Spain from Morocco and North Africa, occupied *al-Andalus* for over seven centuries. Their first forces landed at Tarifa in A.D. 710 and within four years they had conquered virtually the entire country; their last kingdom, Granada, fell to the Christian Reconquest in 1492. Between these dates they developed the most sophisticated civilization of the Middle Ages, centered in

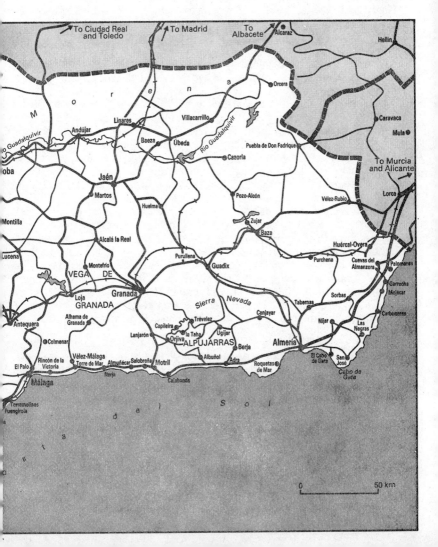

turn on the three major cities of **Córdoba, Sevilla,** and **Granada.** Each one preserves extraordinary brilliant and beautiful monuments, of which the most perfect is Granada's **Alhambra palace,** arguably the most exciting building in all of Europe. Try and see Sevilla first, since its charm and interest is less dramatic, and its (superb) Christian cathedral almost too obtrusive when you've become accustomed to the sensuality and human scale of Moorish architecture.

These three cities have, of course, become major tourist destinations, but the smaller **inland towns** of Andalucía are often totally ignored and unspoiled. These offer amazing potential; Renaissance towns like **Úbeda, Baeza** and **Osuna, Guadix** with its cave suburb, Moorish **Carmona,** the stark white hill towns around **Ronda,** are all easily accessible by local buses. Traveling for some time here you'll get a feel for the landscape of Andalucía: occasionally spectacularly beautiful but more often impressive on a huge, unyielding scale, distinguished by a patchwork of colors and the interaction of land and buildings, or the gradual appearance of villages grouped beneath their castle and church.

The province also, of course, takes in **mountains** — including the **Sierra Nevada,** Spain's highest range. You can ski here in February, and then drive down to the coast to swim the same day. Perhaps more compelling, though, are the opportunities forwalking in the lower slopes, **Las Alpujarras.** Alternatively, there's good hiking to be had in the gentler (and much less-known) slopes of the **Sierra Morena,** north of Sevilla.

On the coast it's easy to despair. Extending to either side of **Málaga** is the **Costa del Sol,** Europe's most developed resort area, with its beaches hidden behind a remorseless density of concrete hotels and apartment complexes. However, the province takes in two alternatives, very much less developed and with some of the best beaches in all Spain. These are the villages **between Tarifa and Cádiz** on the Atlantic, and those **around Almería** on the southeast corner of the Mediterranean. The Almerian beaches allow warm swimming through all but the winter months; those near Cádiz, more easily accessible, are fine from around June to September. Near Cádiz, too, is the Coto Doñana, Spain's largest and most important nature reserve, whose remarkable bird- and wildlife can be visited on short prearranged tours.

Realities and Festivals

Unemployment, or underemployment, in Andalucía is the highest in Spain — well over 20 percent — and an even larger proportion of the population is still engaged in agriculture. Rural life is bleak; you soon begin to notice the appalling **economic structure,** at its most extreme in this part of Spain, of vast absentee-landlord estates and landless peasants. The Andaluz villages, bastions of anarchist and socialist groups before and during the civil war, saw little economic aid or change over the Franco years — or indeed since, even though the Socialist Party has its principal power base in Andalucía. The day laborers, *jornaleros,* earn a precarious living from seasonal work, and in 1986 the regional government launched an unusual land reform in an effort to head off a peasants' revolt. Numerous instances of land occupation have often resulted in violent clashes between laborers and the Civil Guard, and, ironically, it seems that Spain's entry into the European Community will do little to better their plight. Over the next four years there's going to be a lot of building going on in preparation for the *Expo 92* show in Sevilla, with road and rail projects underway for faster connections within the region and with Madrid and Barcelona.

For all its poverty, Andalucía is also Spain at its most exuberant: the home of flamenco and the bullfight, and those wild and extravagant clichés of the Great Spanish Dream. These really do exist and are best absorbed at one of the hundreds of annual **ferias** and **romerías**. The best of them include the giant April Fair in Sevilla, the ageless pilgrimage to El Rocío near Huelva in late May, or the Easter celebrations at Málaga and Sevilla. For local events see the lists at the end of this chapter.

THE COSTA DEL SOL

Perhaps the outstanding feature of the **Costa del Sol** is its ease of access. Hundreds of charter flights arrive here every week, and it's often possible to get an absurdly cheap ticket from London (see *Basics*). **Málaga airport** is positioned midway between Málaga, main city on the coast, and Torremolinos, its most grotesque resort. You can get to either town, cheaply and easily, by taking the electric railroad, which runs every half hour (6:30am–11:30pm daily) along the coast between Málaga and Fuengirola. Granada, Córdoba, and Sevilla are all within easy reach of Málaga; so too, and covered in this section, are Ronda and the "White Towns" to the west, and a handful of relatively restrained coastal resorts to the east. **Beaches** along this stretch are generally grit-grey rather than golden and the sea is none too clean; it has earned in certain circles the nickname of *Costa de la Mierda* (Coast of Shit). However, a new integrated sanitation system is nearing completion which will prevent raw sewage from being discharged into the sea.

Economically, the coastal hinterland is undergoing a gradual resurgence, in contrast to the general decline in the rest of Andalucía. In recent years the cultivation of subtropical fruits such as mangoes, papayas, guavas, lichees, and avocados has replaced the traditional orange, lemon, and almond trees. Most farm laborers, however, can't afford coastal land; those who buy are often former migrants to France and Germany who have been forced to return because of the (un)employment situation there.

The Carretera Nacional N340

A special note of warning has to be made about the Costa del Sol's main high-way, which is one of the most dangerous roads in Europe. Nominally a National Highway, it's really a hundred-kilometer-long city street, passing through the middle of towns and *urbanizaciones*. Drivers treat it like a motor-way, yet pedestrians have to get across, and cars are constantly turning off or into the road — hence the terrifying number of accidents, with over a hundred fatalities a year on average. A large number of these involve inebri-ated British package-holiday tourists who are further handicapped by lack of familiarity with left-hand-drive vehicles and traffic patterns. The first few kilometers between the airport with its various rent-a-car booths and Torremolinos are among the most treacherous of the entire N340. *The* worst stretch is heading west from Marbella: around thirty accidents a year occur on each kilometer between Marbella and San Pedro.

Plans have been approved for a new motorway which will link the Costa del Sol with Madrid and Sevilla, and so reduce traffic on the N340. In the meantime, don't make dangerous (and illegal) left turns from the fast lane; be particularly careful after a heavy rain, when the hot, oily road surface sends you easily into a skid; and pedestrians should cross at traffic lights, a bridge, or an underpass if possible.

Málaga and Inland

MÁLAGA seems at first just a rather large and ugly town. It's the second city of the south (after Sevilla) and also one of the poorest: *official* unemployment figures for the area estimate the jobless at one in four of the workforce. Yet though many people get no farther than the rail or bus stations, and though the clusters of high rises look pretty grim as you approach, it can be a surprisingly attractive place. Around the old fishing villages of El Palo and Pedregalejo, now absorbed into the suburbs, are a series of small beaches and a *paseo* lined with some of the best fish and seafood cafes in the province. And downtown, overlooking the town and port, are the Moorish citadels of the Alcazaba and Gibralfaro — excellent introductions to the architecture before pressing on to the main sites at Córdoba and Granada.

The Alcazaba and the Town

The Alcazaba, certainly, is the place to make for if you're killing time between connections. Open Monday through Saturday from 10am to 1pm and from 4 to 7pm (Sun. 10am–2pm), it is visible and prominent from most points downtown, and just fifteen minutes' walk from the train or bus stations. At its entrance stands an unfortunate-looking Roman theater, accidentally unearthed and partially built over. The citadel too, is Roman in origin, and interspersed among the Moorish brick of the double- and triple-arched gateways are blocks and columns of marble. The main structures were begun by the Moors in the eighth century, probably soon after their conquest since Málaga was an important port, but the palace, higher up the hill, dates from the early decades of the eleventh century. It was the residence of the Arab Emirs of Málaga, who carved out an independent kingdom for themselves upon the breakup of the Western Caliphate. Their independence lasted a mere thirty years, but for a while the kingdom grew to include Granada, Carmona, and Jaén. The palace, restored as an archaeological museum, has some fine stucco work, 1920s Moorish-style ceilings (a big vogue during Art Nouveau and Art Deco in Spain), and good collections of pottery, for which Málaga was renowned during the thirteenth and fourteenth centuries.

Above the Alcazaba, and connected to it by a long double wall, is the Gibralfaro castle (free access). Take the road to the right of the Alcazaba,

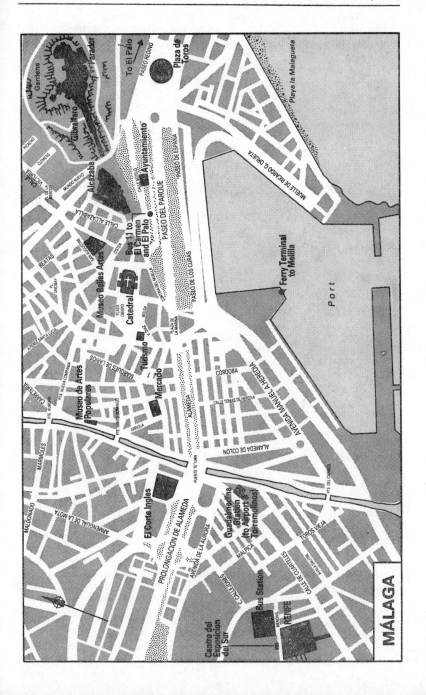

MÁLAGA

then a path up through gardens), a ramble of towers, bougainvillea-draped ramparts and sentry-box-shaped Moorish wells. Last used in 1936 during the civil war, it affords terrific views over the city and the complex fortifications of the Alcazaba. A parador, with pleasant terrace cafe, is nearby.

Most conspicuous from the heights is Málaga's peculiar and unfinished **Cathedral** (daily 10am–1pm and 4–5:30pm; closed Mon.), strangely lacking a tower on the west front, the result of a radical Malagueño bishop having donated the earmarked money to the American War of Independence against the British. Unfortunately it also lacks any real inspiration, distinguished only by an intricately carved and ultrarealistic seventeenth-century *sillería* (choir stall).

More interesting is the **Museo de Bellas Artes**, just around the corner on c/San Augustín, which retains a few childhood drawings by Picasso, the city's most famous native. He was born a hundred yards away in the Plaza de la Merced, and it was in Málaga that his prodigious talent for drawing was first noticed: "When I was a child I could draw like Raphael," he later wrote; "it took me all my life to learn to draw like a child." It was here too that young Picasso saw the first solid shape that he wanted to draw: *churros*, those oil-steeped fritters that Spaniards never tire of dipping into their breakfast chocolate.*

Fish and Other Pursuits

Málaga's greatest claim to fame is undoubtedly its **fried fish**, acknowledged as the best in Spain. It's served everywhere, but if you want an exceptional fish bar that's cheap and very popular, try *Los Culitos* in c/Circo, just above Plaza Victoria at the end of c/Victoria (the street which extends beyond the Alcazaba). It's closed on Thursdays.

Alternatively, take bus # 11 (from the Paseo del Parque) out to **Pedregalejo**, where the seafront **paseo** begins. Almost any of the cafes and restaurants here will serve you up terrific fish, though a few, most notably *El Cabra*, are beginning to get very overpriced. Farther on, after the paseo disappears, you find yourself amid fishing shacks and smaller, sometimes quite ramshackle cafes. This is **El Palo**, an earthier sort of area for the most part, and an even better place to eat. Right at its far end, just before the *Club Nautico*, is the locally famed *El Tintero II* (stay on bus #11 and ask for 'Tintero Dos'), a huge beach restaurant where the waiters charge around with plates of fish (all costing the same for a plate) and you shout for, or grab, anything you like. The fish to go for are, above all, *mero* (a kind of gastronomically evolved cod) and *rosada* (equally indefinable), along with Andalucian

---

* The *Plaza de la Merced* is also the square in which Málaga's political demonstrations are held. One of the strangest took place in 1982, following the imprisonment of the local flamenco singer El Cabrero for uttering the blasphemous but very common oath *Me cago en Dios!* (I shit on God!). The demonstration, organized by the Anarchist union CNT, involved the erection of a stage onto which, uttering the phrase in turn, trooped some 200 blasphemers ...

The oath, incidentally, remains an offense under Spanish law, and shouldn't be used. Spaniards normally euphemize it to the similar-sounding *Me cago en diez* (I shit on ten).

standards like *boquerones* (mild anchovies — approximately), *gambas* (shrimp), and *calamares*, *chopos*, *sepia* and *jibia* (different kinds of squid).

Back in town, if you're not after seafood, the *Bar Los Pueblos* does good, inexpensive food all day (their bean soups and *estofados* are their speciality; *gazpacho* is served in half-pint glasses); it's in c/ Ataranzas just along and in the same street as the commercial market. A good Arab restaurant is *Al-Yamal*, c/Blasco de Garay 3; it's not cheap, but is authentic, serving up meat in spicy sauces, couscous and other typical Arab food.

At night the streets just back from the **Pedregalejo** seafront host most of the action. Along and off the main drag, Juan Sebastián Elcano, there are dozens of discos and smaller bars. Look out for *Bobby Logan*, a disco in a beautiful building but with lousy music; *S.A. Company*, a small, lively bar; *Duna* a big, overdecorated and pricey place with dancing; and the pseudo-Moroccan *Safi*. In the streets parallel, closer to the seafront, more nightspots can be found on the Carretera del Palo and on c/Bolivia (try *Whizz* and the trendy *Zona Málaga*). Recently, all-night bars have opened on the beach itself: *La Chancla* bursts forth at midnight and continues until 3am or later.

The **center** of Málaga is comparatively quiet in the evenings, though there's an interesting place to drink, *Terral* on c/ Cister, which has good *tapas* and occasional exhibitions. A lively bar, with great food in the evenings, is the *Antigua Reja* on Pl. de Uncibay off c/de Mendez Nuñez. For something really cheap, try the *Cafe Los Pueblos*, opposite the *mercado* (see below).

A number of traditional bars serve the sweet **Málaga wine** (Falstaff's "sack"), made from muscatel grapes and dispensed from huge barrels; try it with shellfish at a great old bar, the *Antigua Casa*, at the corner of c/Pastora, on the Alameda. The new wine, *Pedriot*, is incredibly sweet; much more palatable is *Seco Anejo*, which has matured for a year.

Arriving, Rooms, and Practicalities

Arriving in Málaga from the airport the **electric train** provides the easiest approach (every 20–30 mins; in the evening they're very full). From the arrivals lounge, follow the *Ferrocarril* signs through the parking lot, cross via the pedestrian underpass, and stay on the train right to the end of the line, the *Centro/Almameda* stop. The stop before this is the *RENFE*, the main **railroad station**, a slightly longer walk into the heart of town. Going **out to the airport**, trains leave the *Centro/Alameda* station on the hour and half hour (daily from 6:30am to 11pm); remember that there are two airport stops: first *Nacional*, for domestic flights, then *Internacional* for international departures. The line is very cheap, and if you want to **hitch** west from Málaga it's worth buying a ticket to Fuengirola, the western-most stop, where you can easily join the highway.

The **bus station** is just behind the RENFE station, a bit to the right as you face the RENFE logo from the esplanade. Unusually, all buses (run by a number of different companies) operate from this same terminal. There's a useful machine in the station which saves lining up at the (usually helpful) information desk: indicate your destination and it details the connections and departure time of the next bus. In midsummer it's best to arrive an hour or so early for the bus to Granada, since tickets occasionally sell out.

Málaga also has the remnants of a **passenger ferry** port, though these days there is a service only to the Spanish enclave of Melilla in **Morocco**. If you're heading for Fes and eastern Morocco, or for **Algeria**, this is quite a useful connection — particularly so for taking a car over — though most people go for the quicker services at Algeciras and Tarifa, to the west. Sailings are daily except Friday, generally leaving around 8:30pm; the crossing takes ten hours. Tickets from *Compañía Aucona* at c/Juan Díaz 1.

To stock up on food for any of these trips, search out the excellent indoor **mercado** just north of the Alameda (about half way along) in a wrought-iron, Mudejar-style building.

Málaga boasts dozens of *fondas*, so reasonably **cheap rooms** are rarely hard to come by. You may well get offers at the train (or possibly the bus) station, and so long as they're fairly central these will probably be as good as any (*casas de huespedes* between the train station and the *Centro/Alameda* station, on c/de Cuarteles, are cheap but extremely dingy). C/Cordoba is another popular area for *fondas*, but a noisy street. Numerous possibilities are to be found in the grid of streets just north of the Alameda. Among these you might try c/Martinez (*Hostal Palma*, run by a friendly elderly couple, is one of the best), c/Bolsa (*Cordoba* at no.9), c/San Augustín (by the cathedral — *La Macarena* at no.9) or the traditional c/Camas ("Beds' Street"), full of real dives and something of a red-light district. Below the Alameda, c/Trinidad Grund (*Montecarlo* and *Trianon*, both at no.23) and c/Casas de Campos (*Bolivia* at no.10, *Remedios* at no.15) are also possibilities. For something quiet, the *Hostal El Cenachero* in c/Barroso (left off the seafront end of c/Cordoba) is very clean, reasonably priced, and has friendly owners.

The closest **campground** is the *Balneario del Carmen*, a rather gritty affair amid the decaying and elegant remains of an old "bathing station"; it's 3km out of town towards El Palo on the Avda. Juan Sebastián Elcano, but well-positioned for the Pedregalejo *paseo* — get there on bus #11.

If you have difficulties the **Turismo** (c/Marqués de Larios 5; open Mon.–Fri. 9:30am–1:30pm and 4–6pm; Sat. 9:30am–1pm) can provide full lists and a larger, more detailed map of the city than the one printed here

Inland — El Chorro Gorge and Antequera

Some 50km north of Málaga, **El Chorro Gorge** is an amazing place. It's impressive in itself — an immense rent in a vast limestone massif — but the real attraction is a concrete catwalk, *El Camino del Rey*, which threads the length of the gorge hanging precipitously halfway up its side. Built in the 1920s as part of a burgeoning hydroelectric scheme, it used to figure in all the guidebooks as one of the wonders of Spain; today it's largely fallen into disrepair, and will probably collapse completely unless (unlikely) renovation takes place. But at present, despite a few distinctly wobbly — and decidedly dangerous — sections, with the random hole in the concrete through which you can see the gorge hundreds of feet below, it's still possible to walk much of its length. You will, however, need a very good head for heights, and at least a full day starting from Málaga. If you've neither, it's possible to get a glimpse of both gorge and *camino* from any of the trains going north from Málaga — the line, slipping in and out of tunnels, follows the river for quite a distance along the gorge, before plunging into a last long tunnel just before its head.

To explore the gorge (*La Garganta*), and walk the *camino*, the best approach is to take the train (or drive/hitch) to EL CHORRO station. From here it's around 12km to the trailhead and the beginning of the gorge, and to some magnificent lakes and reservoirs for swimming, such as the *Embalse del Guadalhorce*. You can camp along the rocky shore; alternatively the tiny village of ARDALES, 4km beyond the lake, has shops, bars, a lone *fonda* on the main square, and two daily buses to/from Ronda. The walk is a beautiful one, but hitching is also quite feasible with one of the vehicles associated with the utility company.

From the railroad station take the road below you signposted *Pantano De Guadalhorce*, crossing over the dam and turning right, and following the road towards the hydroelectric plant. After 10km you'll come upon the bar-restaurant *El Mirador*, poised above the various lakes and reservoirs of the Guadalhorce scheme. From the bar a dirt track on its right (just manageable by car) leads in 2km to an abandoned power plant at the mouth of the gorge. The footpath to the left of this will take you into the chasm and to the beginning of El Camino. Although it is marked 'No Entry' you'll probably come upon quite a number of young Spaniards exploring the catwalk. The first section, at least, seems reasonably safe — despite places where it is only a meter wide and where parts of the handrail are missing — and this is in fact the most dramatic part of the canyon. Towards the end, where the passageway gets really dangerous, the gorge widens and it's possible to climb down and follow along the riverbank or have a swim.

Leaving El Chorro you'll basically have to return the way you came — though with good chances of getting a ride. The nearest towns are Alora and Antequera, but joining the railroad you don't need to confine yourself to these options.

ANTEQUERA, however, on the main rail line to Granada, is a place you might want to stop for a while. In itself it's an ordinary, modern town but it does have peripheral attractions in an outrageous baroque church, **El Carmen**, and a group of three prehistoric **dolmen caves**. The most impressive and famous of these is the *Cueva de Menga*, its roof formed by an immense 180-ton monolith. To reach this, and the nearby *Cueva de Viera*, take the Málaga road out of town — the turning, rather insignificantly signposted, is about a kilometer along this on the left. Both caves are open daily except Tuesday, Thursday and Friday from 10am to 1pm and from 4 to 7pm. A third cave, *El Romeral*, is rather different (and later) in its structure with a domed ceiling of flat stones; it is again to the left of the Málaga road, 2km farther on, past a sugar factory (where the management has the key). If you want or need to stay in Antequera there's a good cheap **pensión** opposite the bus station on the main Alameda.

With your own vehicle you could go to **BOBASTRO**, the remains of a Mozarabic (Arabised Christian) settlement on top of a mountain. The castle was said to be the most impregnable of all Andalucía, but only a church, carved into an enormous boulder, remains of the once-great fortress. It's located a few kilometers beyond El Chorro, with a further detour of several more kilometers off the main road. Descend the road from the summit to where a blackened sign points towards the pine trees; from here it's a 400-meter walk.

EL TORCAL, 13km south of Antequera, is possibly the most geologically arresting of Spain's national parks. A massive high plateau of glaciated limestone tempered by a lush growth of hawthorn, ivy, wildrose, and fauna, it's painlessly explored using the **walking routes** that radiate from the center of the park. Perhaps the best designed and most exciting is the yellow-blazed route, (marked by arrows; 3km) which ends with suitable drama on a cliff edge and magnificent views over a valley. This is also the most popular walk, and in the summer you may find yourself competing with gangs of schoolkids who arrive en masse on vaguely educational trips. More peaceful is the red-blazed route (5km; allow 5 hr.), great for strolling and taking in the looming limestone formations, eroded into vast surreal sculptures.

Though **no buses** link El Torcal to Antequera, it's an easy enough walk (take the 3310 road to Villaneuva de la Concepción and head down the first turning on the right to El Torcal) with good chances of hitching a ride, especially on weekends, when it's also possible to persuade one of the school buses to give you a lift back. Failing this, five daily buses run workdays from Málaga (one on Sundays) or it's quite acceptable to **camp** in the park — but take plenty of provisions.

East from Málaga: The Coast to Almería

The eastern stretch of the **Costa del Sol**, from Málaga to Almería, is generally not too inspiring. It is far less developed than the wall-to-wall concrete from Torremolinos to Marbella in the west, but still not exactly unspoiled. If you're looking for a village and a beach and not much else, then you'll probably want to keep going at least to Almería.

There's certainly little to tempt anyone before Nerja. **RINCÓN DE LA VICTORIA**, a no-nonsense, scruffy sort of place, is a local resort for Malagueño families. It's a functional spot to swim if you've a day to fill before catching a plane home, but nothing more. **TORRE DEL MAR**, 32km farther on, is a place to actively avoid — a Torremolinos of concrete high rises and a gray, gritty beach without the money or fun.

NERJA at least was a village before it was a resort, so it has some character, and development (more villas, fewer high rises) has been shaped around it. The beaches are reasonably attractive, too, with a series of coves within walking distance if you want to escape the main mass of crowds. The main drawback, and a thorny problem through most of the summer, is scarce accommodation. There are a dozen or so **hostales**, but many are reserved well in advance, and you could find yourself in for a morning's trooping round the streets asking for a space in a private house. The **Turismo** at Puerta del Mar 4 (closed Sun.) will supply lists and, as much as they can, help. In c/ Granada *The Book Center* buys and sells secondhand books, mainly paperbacks, and also rents **bikes** (by the day or week) if you want a little more freedom about where you go off to swim. This opens up the possibility, for instance, of **MARO**, a tiny village 6km east along the coast (a single *hostal* there) with its cove-beach down below a headland. Also close to Maro, and the standard trip from Nerja, are the **CUEVAS DE NERJA** (open all day), a heavily commercialized series of caverns, impressive in size though otherwise not tremendously interesting. They contain a number of prehistoric paintings, but these are not presently on public view.

Beyond Nerja the road climbs inland, running high above the coast until it surfaces at **LA HERRADURA**, a fishing village/resort suburb of Almuñecar, and for anyone with their own wheels a good place to stop off and swim. **ALMUÑECAR** itself is marred by a number of towering vacation apartments, though if you've been unable to find a room in Nerja you might want to hole up here for a night. The rocky beaches are rather dirty, and eating out can be a rip-off, but the old town is attractive. Half a dozen good value **fondas** and **hostales** ring the central Plaza de la Rosa in the old part of town; two of the best, *Pension Casa Ruiz* (☎958/631152) and *Fonda Heredia* are in c/San José. There's a **Turismo** on the beach at the Paseo del Altillo, shut between 1pm and 5pm in the week, and open Saturday morning.

SALOBREÑA, however, on towards Motril and the road to Granada and Las Alpujarras, is infinitely preferable. A white hilltop town gathered beneath the shell of its Moorish castle, it is set back 2km from the sea, and so comparatively little developed. On its beach — a fair sandy strip, only partially flanked by hotels — is a good year-round **campground**, *El Peñon*. Along and off the c/de Hortensia, the main avenue that winds down from the town to the beach, are a few **pensiones** and **hostales**, cheapest the *Pension Arneda* on c/Nueva. The house above the *farmacia* also has a reasonably-priced room.

MOTRIL is inland and mildly industrial. The best thing to do here is to have a *cerveza* and jump straight on to another bus, either to Granada (a great route, skirting the Sierra Nevada) or to Almería. If you want a smallish place to stop off at before Almería try **CASTELL DE FERRO**, much the best of an anonymous sprawl of resorts. It's quite sheltered, has a good, wide beach (with a **campground** on the edge), a **youth hostel**, *Albergue Juvenil Reyes Catolicos*, off the main road (open July and August only), and even preserves remnants of its former existence as a small fishing village.

West: the Worst of the Costa del Sol

West of Málaga — or more correctly west of Málaga airport the real **Costa del Sol** gets going, and if you've never seen this level of touristic development it's quite a shock. These are certainly not the kind of resorts you could envisage in Greece or even Portugal, though most Americans will be reminded of Miami Beach. In recent years, there has also been a second wave of property development, this time homes and leisure complexes, with massive international investment. It's estimated that 300,000 foreigners live on the Costa del Sol, the majority of them retired and British. Today the

Costa del Sol is the richest, fastest-growing, and most fashionable resort area in the Mediterranean, with marina developments like Puerto Banús attracting Arab as well as European and North American money.

Approached in the right kind of spirit it is quite possible to have fun in **Torremolinos**, and at a price in **Marbella**. But if you've come to Spain to be in Spain, or even just to forget what an inner-city housing project looks like, put on the shades and stay on the coach at least until you reach **Estepona**. You are not going to make any new discoveries. It is all far too late . . .

Torremolinos and Fuengirola

Approaching Torremolinos — easiest done on the electric railroad — is a rather depressing business. There are half a dozen beaches and stops, but it's a drab, soulless landscape of kitchenette apartments and half-finished developments. **TORREMOLINOS**, to its enduring credit, is certainly different: a vast, grotesque parody of a seaside resort which in its own kitschy way is fascinating. This bizarre place, lined with sweeping (but crowded) beaches and infinite shopping arcades, crammed with (genuine) Irish pubs and (probably less genuine) real estate agents, has a large permanent expatriate population of British, Germans, and Scandinavians. It's a weird mix, which, in addition to thousands of retired people, has attracted — due to a previous lack of extradition arrangements between Britain and Spain — an extraordinary concentration of British crooks, one of the train robbers among them. And Torremolinos's own social scene is strange in itself, including, among the middle-of-the-road family discos, a thriving, pram-pushing gay transvestite scene. All in all an intriguing blend of the smart and the squalid, bargains and rip-offs.

If any of these possibilities attracts you — or you're simply curious about the awfulness of the place — it's easy enough to stay. There are a few *hostales*, but you can walk into almost any travel agent and, for remarkably little, get them to book you into one of the concrete monsters. The more elegant part (where there are good fish restaurants along the seafront) verges on the second of the beaches, **La Carihuela**. About 2km farther on, to the left of the road at "El Rocio," there's also a **youth hostel**; to get there take any of the buses towards Fuengirola and ask for "Benalmadena Costa." Be wary, however, of accepting free accommodation from the Torremolinos evangelists (who often invite hitchhikers to their villa), as it's not always so easy to leave their community after a week or two of heavy, "religious" mindgames.

The sheer competition between Torremolinos's restaurants, clubs, and bars is so intense that if you're prepared to walk around and check a few prices you can have a pretty good night on remarkably little. And, if you're looking to replenish your stock of reading material, *George's Secondhand Bookshop*, on the first floor at no.26 c/San Miguel — the main shopping street in the middle of town, close to the train station — is an excellent and cheap source of used paperbacks.

Fuengirola

FUENGIROLA, half an hour along the train line from Torremolinos, is very slightly less developed and infinitely more staid. It's not so conspicuously ugly, but it is distinctly middle-aged and family-oriented. The huge, long beach has been divided up into a series of restaurant-beach strips, each renting lounge chairs and pedal-boats; at the far end is a windsurfing school.

Marbella and Beyond

MARBELLA stands in considerable contrast, after another dull sequence of apartment-villa *urbanizaciones*, to most of what's come before. It is undisputedly the "quality resort" of the Costa del Sol. Everything costs considerably more, the restaurants and bars are more stylish, and phones are handily installed on the beach. It has the highest per capita income in Europe and more Rolls Royces than any European city apart from London (although many of the classy cars here are rumored to have been stolen elsewhere and reregistered in Spain). In an ironic twist of history, there's been a massive return of Arabs to the area, especially since King Fahd of Saudi Arabia built a White House look-alike, complete with adjacent mosque, on the town's outskirts.

To be fair, it's all decidely tasteful and the town has been spared the worst excesses of concrete architecture which the last years of the Franco regime inflicted upon Torremolinos. Marbella also retains the greater part of its **old village** — set back a little from the sea and the new development. Slowly, this original quarter is being bought up and turned into "quaint" clothes boutiques and restaurants but oddly enough this process isn't that far advanced. You can still sit in an ordinary bar in a small, old square and look up beyond the whitewashed alleyways to the mountains of Ronda.

It's in the old town, too, that you'll find Marbella's only budget **pensiones** — of which the cheapest is *Pensión Luisa* (they have roofspace, often the only possibility in this hugely popular resort) in c/San Francisco, near the church of the same name. Farther up the road is the *Africa Youth Hostel*, while at no. 18 there's a friendly (though small) family-run place. The old village, still partially walled, is hidden from the main road and easy to miss; to get there turn left out of the bus station, walk straight for about 500m, and then turn left again.

If you need help in finding a room it is probably worth calling in at the **Turismo**, if only for their townplan/guide and list of addresses; they're at Avda. Miguel Cano 1, by the Alameda park, and open Monday through Friday, 9:50am to 1pm and 5 to 7:30pm, Saturday from 10am to 1pm.

The truly rich don't, however, stay in Marbella itself. They lie around on phenomenally large and luxurious yachts at the marina and casino complex of **PUERTO BANÚS**, 6km out of town towards San Pedro. This fact is worth noting simply because it's sometimes possible to find work scrubbing and repairing said yachts — and the pay can be very reasonable. All you need is charm and arrogance.

West to Estepona

The coast continues to be upscale (or "money-raddled" as Laurie Lee put it) until you reach Estepona, thirty or so kilometers west. About the only place on this strip which isn't purely a holiday *urbanización* is the small town of **SAN PEDRO DE ALCÁNTARA**, an uninspiring resort striving to go the way of Marbella but hindered by the fact that it's set back from the sea. It has a Thursday-morning flea market — trashy in all senses of the word — and that's about it. Not a place for a vacation.

If you feel an irresistible urge to stop along this part of the Mediterranean coast **ESTEPONA** is about the only good bet, a more or less Spanish resort (insomuch as that's possible around here). Overall, it's got a drab appearance and lacks the enclosed hills that give Marbella character, but it is at least humanly developed; the hotel and apartment blocks which sprawl along the front are restrained in size, and there's space to breathe. The long dark-pebbly beach has been enlivened a little by a promenade studded with flowers and palms, and, away from the seafront, the old town is very pretty, with cobbled alleyways and two delightful plazas.

Estepona has a **campground** and a number of **hostales**. The *Hostal de los Pinos* is behind the eastern esplanade, below the old town; it's reasonably priced, very clean, and cheap meals are available. Most of the **restaurants** in town, especially in the Puerto Deportivo, are expensive and international-style. There's an excellent *churrería* towards the southern end of c/Mayor (one block back from and parrallel to the promenade) — get there before 11am as they sell out early. Another good place for buying food is the covered market in the mornings.

If you're sufficiently motivated, you can eat out of town. Head south along the coast until you pass the new Puerto de la Duquesa marina; just under a kilometer farther on is the tiny fishing village of **LA DUQUESA**, which has two excellent restaurants (*Antonio's Fish Bar* being the cheaper of the two). A little closer to Estepona, **SAN LUIS LAS SABINILLAS** is an unlikely and unpretty little resort, but if you're passing through, stop off at the *Restaurante La Tinaja*, a cozy establishment run by a young English/Gibraltarian couple and offering an unusual and good value menu of home-cooked dishes.

Estepona has the biggest fishing fleet west of Málaga. The daily dawn market in the port, where the returning fleets auction off the fish they've just caught, is worth getting up early for — be there at 6am, since by 7am it's all over. From May onward, the bullfighting season gets underway in a modern bullring reminiscent of a Henry Moore sculpture. At the beginning of July, the *Fiesta y Feria* week transforms the place, bringing out whole families in flamenco-style garb.

There are also a couple of excursions you can make from here, best perhaps is the trip to **CASARES**, one of the "white villages" (see Ronda). In keeping with the genre, it clings tenaciously to a steep hillside, below a castle, and has attracted its fair share of arty types and expatriates. But it remains comparatively little-known; bus connections are feasible for a daytrip. To the west of Estepona, inland from the village of **MANILVA**, are the remarkably well-preserved **Roman sulphur baths**. If you want to partake of these health-giving waters you'll have to put up with the overpowering stench of sulphur, which clings to your swimwear for weeks, and be prepared to dive into a subterranean cavern.

Beyond Estepona are more grayish beaches (a trademark of the Costa del Sol that always seems surprising — you have to round the corner at TARIFA before you meet yellow sand) and more grayish, sporadic developments before the road turns inland towards San Roque and Gibraltar.

San Roque and La Línea

SAN ROQUE was founded by the people of Gibraltar fleeing in 1704 from the British, who had captured the Rock and looted their homes and churches. They expected to return within months, since the British had taken the garrison in the name of the Archduke Carlos of Austria whose rights they had been promoting in the War of the Spanish Succession. But it was the British flag that was raised on the conquered territory — and so it has remained.

The **"Spanish-British frontier"** lies 8km away at **LA LÍNEA**, obscured by San Roque's huge oil refinery. After sixteen years of (Spanish-imposed) isolation, the gates were finally reopened in February 1985, and crossing is now a routine affair of passport stamping. Be warned that, if you're planning on a stay in Gibraltar, accommodation there is very expensive and in summer you probably won't strike lucky at one of the few cheap places available; La Línea is therefore a better bet. Starting from the border, head towards the Plaza de Constitución, a large modern square. The **Turismo** is on the right, just before the square (they have town maps with *hostales* indicated), the **bus station** on the left. Calle Real (a pedestrianized shopping street) leads off to the left from the far end of the square, and at the end of this street the Plaza de la Iglesia opens out; here you'll find the best-value **hostales**. *La Giralda* is cheap and has a friendly owner; showers are hot and free, and there's a hot plate in the kitchen for preparing simple meals. Almost directly opposite is the *Hostal Sevilla*, with three or four others in the area; the slightly more expensive *Hostal Bahia* is more modern and clean.

For **food**, there's a **market** north of c/Real and on the same street the *Bar Jerez* has cheap and varied *tapas*. The same is true of *Blanco y Negro*, a couple of streets north near Pl. de Iglesia, opposite which is *El Economica*, an inconspicuous *comedor* with a cheap *menú del día*. There are also a couple of pubs, a burger bar, a pizzeria, and countless other bars and cafes. There are no sights as such; it's just a fishing village which has exploded in size due to the jobs in Gibraltar and Algeciras.

Local **buses** from La Línea to Algeciras take forty minutes, with departures every half hour. The closest mainline railroad station is San Roque-La Línea (not a walkable distance), from where you can pick up a train to Ronda and beyond. Buses link La Línea with Sevilla, the journey taking four hours, and others go as far as Ayamonte on the Portuguese border, a seven-hour trip.

Gibraltar

GIBRALTAR's interest is essentially that of a novelty: a genuine one in the strange, looming physical presence of its rock, and an increasingly dubious one in its preservation as one of Britain's last remaining colonies. **Sovereignty** of the Rock (a land area smaller than the city of Algeciras across the water) will beyond doubt eventually return to Spain, but at present, neither side is in much of a hurry. For Britain it's a question of precedent — Gibraltar is too similar a situation to the Falklands/Malvinas, whose 1983 war pushed the Spanish into postponing an initial frontier-opening date. For Spain too, there are unsettling parallels with the *presidios* (Spanish enclaves) on the Moroccan coast at Ceuta and Melilla — both at present officially part of Andalucía. And, still more diplomatically pertinent, there is the thorny issue of Spain's recent entry into the European Community. The British presence is in fact waning and the British Crown clearly wants to steer Gibraltar towards a new, harmonious relationship with Spain. To this end they seem to be running down the significance of the military base on the rock, reducing the number of British troops by a half in 1990.

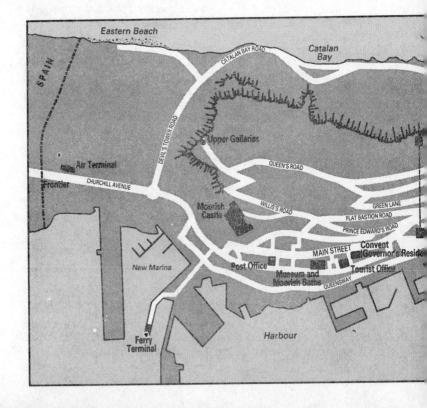

The Gibraltarians see all these issues as irrevelant in the light of their firmly stated opposition to a return to Spanish control of the Rock, and they have the evidence at hand. In 1967, just before Franco closed the border in the hope of forcing a quick agreement, the colony voted on the issue — rejecting it by 12,138 votes to 44. Most people would probably sympathize with that vote — against a Spain that was then still a dictatorship — but more than twenty years have gone by, Spanish democracy is now secure, and the arguments are becoming increasingly tenuous. Despite its impressive claims to law and order, Gibraltar is no model society either; its dirty jobs, for instance, are nearly all done by Moroccans on one-year contracts, who are housed in old army barracks. March 1988 saw a change in the trend of internal politics when the first-ever Socialist government was elected, but the leader, Joe Bassano, continues to oppose back-room deals between Britain and Spain on the future of the colony. A wily ex-trade union leader, he is attempting to make the rock more self-reliant, encouraging its status as an "offshore" base — a kind of "Hong Kong of the Mediterranean". Already, some 24,000 companies, many somewhat dubious, are registered in Gibraltar.

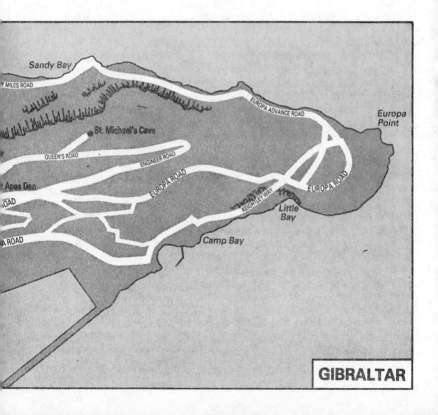

GIBRALTAR

What most outsiders don't realize about the political situation is that the Gibraltarians feel very vulnerable, caught between the interests of two big states; they are well aware that the British government's concern is purely strategic and not the "wishes of the people" as it claims. Resentment of their colonial masters is keenly felt in a practical way as well; space is at a premium and the biggest social problem is housing, but the British Government will give no money for new homes. Many locals live in cramped and often unhealthy conditions, while no expense appears to be spared to build homes for families of the servicepeople stationed here. Until very recently Brits were imported over from the UK to fill all the top civil service and Ministry of Defense jobs, a practice which, to a lesser degree, still continues. Large parts of the Rock are no-go areas for "natives"; the South District in particular is taken up by facilities for the armed services. Local people also protest about the British nuclear-powered submarines which dock regularly at the naval base, and secrecy surrounds the issue of whether nuclear warheads and/or chemical and biological weapons are stored in the arsenal, probably deep inside the Rock itself.

Yet Gibraltarians still cling to British status — perhaps simply because they have known nothing other than British rule since the former population was displaced — and all their institutions are modeled on English lines. Contrary to popular belief, they are of neither mainly Spanish nor British blood, but an ethnic mix descended from Genoese, Portuguese, Spanish, Minorcan, Jewish, Maltese, and British forebears. English is the official language, but more commonly spoken is what sounds to an outsider like perfect Andalucian Spanish. It is in fact *yanito*, an Andalucian dialect with borrowed words which reflect their diverse origins — only a Spaniard from the South can tell apart a Gibraltarian and an Andalucian. Yet schoolchildren are taught to look to the UK, learning little of Spanish culture and language.

Gibraltar remains a curious place to visit, not least for witnessing the bizarre process of its opening to mass tourism from the Costa del Sol. Ironically, this threatens to both destroy Gibraltar's highly individual society and at the same time to make it much more British — after the fashion of the expatriate communities and huge resorts of the Costa. The frontier opening has benefitted most people: the locals can buy cheaper goods in Spain and stretch their legs, and the boom the Rock is witnessing (after a long recession) should benefit the whole surrounding Campo area. The Royal Naval Dockyard has now been replaced with *Gibrepair*, a commercial ship repair yard which, in the long term, will lead to diversification of the Gibraltar economy and reduce dependence on Britain. But, unsurprisingly, the less well-off are not receiving the benefits, since land that does become available is given over to luxury hotels, and offices to feed the mushrooming finance center.

"Justifiable Homicide"

March 1988 witnessed a chain of events that thrust Gibraltar back into the public eye. On the afternoon of March 6 a group of plainclothes British troops from the SAS (commando-style battalion) shot dead Mairead Farrell, Sean Savage, and Danny McCann, all members of an IRA active service unit, who it was later claimed had planted a bomb in the colony. It quickly became clear that no bomb had been planted (though one did exist, hidden in a car in Spain); that Farrell, Savage, and McCann were unarmed; and that the SAS, rather than firing to avert a "terrorist act," had deliberately shot to kill. Witnesses saw Savage shot again while on the ground, and it was obvious to the SAS men that none of the IRA unit had weapons.

The British parliament's support of the shootings, prompted by disinformation given out by the Foreign Minister Geoffrey Howe; the intimidation of Gibraltarian witnesses (in particular one Carmen Proetta, who claimed to see two of the unit raise their hands in surrender, and was branded as "The Tart of Gib" by the tabloid *Sun* newspaper), and a stage-managed inquest months later, all clouded the true picture of what happened.

The results of the murders were not so indistinct. At the funerals of Farrell, Savage, and McCann a week later a lone Ulster Unionist gunman tossed grenades and shot indiscriminately into the crowd. Three people were killed, and at the subsequent funeral of one of them, Kevin Brady, two British troops out of uniform and apparently sightseeing were dragged from their car, stripped, and shot dead. As much as anything, it was the deaths of the soldiers, graphically reported in the media, that reinforced popular British opinion in support of the SAS action — and which probably helped to persuade a Gibraltar jury to bring in a verdict of "justifiable homicide" on the original SAS shootings.

Arriving, Orientation, and Practicalities

The town and rock have a neccessarily simple layout. **Main Street** (La Calle Real) runs for most of the town's length a couple of blocks back from the port; from the frontier it's a short bus ride or about a fifteen-minute walk. In and around Main Street are most of the shops (cheap duty-free whisky is a major attraction), including *The Gibraltar Bookshop* at no. 300 which sells good paperbacks. This is also where most of the pubs (British-style) and hotels are. For general **information**, go to the John Mackintosh Hall at the south end of Main Street — it's the cultural center, with exhibitions, a library, and so on. The main paper is the daily *Gibraltar Chronicle*, which claims to be unbiased but is in fact controlled by the military.

Accommodation

Shortage of space means that there's only one remotely cheap **place to stay:** the *Toc H Hostel* on Lime Wall Road, a bit of a doss house and likely to be full (parallel towards the sea; ☎350/73431; about £1.70 a person). There's a bed-and-breakfast place in Irish Town, charging about £8 a night — for information, go to the **tourist office** at the Piazza, John Mackintosh Square, halfway along Main Street. Otherwise, you're going to have to pay normal British hotel prices (the *Queen's Hostel*, ☎350/74000, on Boyd Street, the next cheapest option, charges £14 for a single, £24.50 for a double). You're actually much better off walking back across the border and staying in La Línea or getting the bus to Algeciras (buses on the hour and half-hour, journey time 30 min.).

It's therefore particularly unfortunate that **no camping** is allowed; there's no official campground and if you are found "in the act," or inhabiting abandoned bunkers, you will more than likely be arrested and fined. This law is enforced by Gibraltar and Ministry of Defense police, and raids of the beaches are regular.

Food

Eating is less problematic, though by Spanish standards still relatively expensive. Pub snacks or fish and chips are usual standbys, *Smiths Fish and Chip Shop* in Irish Town being a good place, although its curries are less than authentic. For pub food, *Royal Calpe* (Main Street) and the *Calpe Hounds* (Cornwalls Lane) are among the best, both fixing substantial, cheapish meals. The *Chuck Wagon* (Engineers Lane) serves breakfast, take-out burgers, pizzas, etc., and other similar joints abound. If you're really short on cash, the cheapest option is to pop into the canteen of the Moroccan workers' hostel in *The Casemates* at the bottom of Main Street — a nice change from British food, though unfortunately, this is only an option for men.

Pubs all tend to mimic traditional English styles (and prices), the difference being that they are open all day and often into the wee hours. The *Royal Calpe* has a beer garden, *The Horseshoe* has tables outside and shows videos, and the *Gibraltar Arms* also has outdoor seating. All three are grouped together in Main Street. For something slightly alternative and without frills, the *Cantina* (Engineers Lane) is best.

Onward Travel

Two decidedly functional attractions of Gibraltar are its opportunities for reasonably cheap **flights to Britain** (standby one-way fares are about £70; *GB Airways* ☎350/79200), and its role as a **hydrofoil port for Morocco**. *Transtour* hydrofoils to Tangier leave at least daily in summer, but much less frequently out of season. The timetable is subject to weather conditions, however, and the trip is very rough even at the best of times. The hydrofoil takes just one hour, making day trips a possibility; get tickets from *Gibline*, 98 Georges Lane (£18 same-day round trip, £12 one way, £20 ordinary round trip, Thurs.–Sun). There's also a **catamaran service** on days when the hydrofoil's not crossing, which is about the same time and price. By **plane** Tangier is twenty minutes away, (£35 single).

In season only, the hydrofoil also goes to **Mdiq**, near Tetouan on Morocco's Mediterranean coast, which gives a gentler introduction to the country. The journey takes approximately the same time as to Tangier.

If you're looking for really exotic destinations, at the end of summer the yacht marina fills up with boats heading for the **Canaries**, **Madeira**, and the **West Indies** — many take on crew to work in exchange for passage.

For travelling on through Spain, **RENFE** tickets can be bought from *Pegasus Travel* (☎350/72252).

Other Things

Gibraltar is a good place to change **money**, since the exchange rate is slightly higher than in Spain and there's no commission charged. The currency used here is the Gibraltar pound; if you pay in pesetas, you generally fork over about five percent more. If you're staying around a while, it's not a bad place to look for work, although competition abounds, so be persistent. For men, there are some laboring jobs (on the docks), for women the best possibilities are bar jobs. Gibraltar Radio broadcasts vacancies on Tuesday around noon, but door-to-door (or site-to-site) footslogging is vital. Another possibility is crewing work on a yacht — look at the noticeboard in the chandler's store on Marina Bay, or put an ad there yourself.

And lastly, a warning about **dope** — it's abundant but not decriminalized in Gibraltar, and you'll be fined by the police if caught.

Around the Rock

From near the end of Main Street you can hop on a **cable car** (9:30am–7:15pm Mon.–Sat., last trip down 7:45pm; £3 round trip) which will carry you up to the summit — **The Top of the Rock** as it's logically known — via **Apes' Den** half way up, a fairly reliable viewing point to see the tailless monkeys and hear the guides explain their legend. From The Top you can look over to the Atlas Mountains and down to the town, its elaborate water catchment system cut into the side of the rock, and ponder over whether it's worth heading for one of the beaches. From the Apes' Den it's an easy walk south along Queens Road to **St. Michael's Cave**, an immense natural cavern which led ancient people to believe the rock was hollow and gave rise to its old name of *Mons Calpe* (Hollow Mountain). It was used during the last world war as a bomb-proof military hospital and nowadays for occasional concerts. If you're adventurous you can arrange at the tourist office for a guided visit to **Lower St. Michael's Cave**, a series of chambers going deeper down and ending in an underground lake.

Although you can be lazy and take the cable car both ways, you might instead walk up via Williss Road to visit the **Tower of Homage**. Dating from the fourteenth century, this is the most visible remains of the old **Moorish Castle**. Farther up you'll find the **Upper Galleries**, blasted out of the rock during the Great Siege of 1779–82, in order to be able to point guns down at the Spanish lines. To walk down, take the **Mediterranean Steps** — they're not very well signposted and you have to climb over O'Hara's Battery, a very steep descent most of the way down the east side, turning the southern corner of the Rock. You'll pass through the Jews' Gate and into Engineer Road. From here, return to town through the Alameda Gardens and the **Trafalgar Cemetery**, overgrown and evocative, with a good line in epitaphs. The grand tour of the Rock takes a half to a full day, and all sites on it are open from 10am to 7pm in summer, 10am to 5:30pm in winter; if you visit all the attractions, buy a reduced-price ticket which includes the Cave as well.

Back in town, incorporated into the **Gibraltar Museum** (open 10am–6pm Mon.–Sat.), are two well-preserved and beautiful fourteenth-century **Moorish Baths**. This, along with the **casino**, and the **miniature golf**, is about the extent of it all. Gibraltar has plans to reclaim an area equivalent to that of the present town from the sea, and is currently doing feasibility surveys on pumping up sand from the seabed. But at present there is just the one tiny fishing village at **Catalan Bay** which is where you'll find the **beach** with most character. The inhabitants of the village like to think of themselves as very distinct from the town people on the other side of the Rock. About thirty miles of recent tunnels, or **galleries**, have been bored through the Rock for military purposes, but they are now being adapted to help solve the territory's traffic-flow crisis brought on by the extraordinary surplus of cars.

Algeciras

ALGECIRAS sprawls around the far side of the bay to Gibraltar, spewing out smoke and pollution in its direction. The last town of the Spanish Mediterranean, it must once have been an elegant resort; today it's simply and unabashedly a port and industrial center, its suburbs still extending on all sides, and almost all construction of modern vintage. When Franco closed the border with Gibraltar at La Línea it was Algeciras that he decided to develop to absorb the Spanish workers formerly employed in the British naval dockyards, thus breaking the area's dependence on the Rock.

Most travelers are scathing about the city's seedy ugliness, and unless you're waiting for a bus or train, or heading for Morocco, there's admittedly little reason to stop. Yet some touch of color is added by the groups of Moroccans in transit,* dressed in flowing *djelabas* and yellow slippers, and lugging around unbelievable amounts of possessions. Algeciras has a real port atmosphere, and even passing through it's hard to resist the urge to get on a boat south, if only for a couple of days in Tangier.

And this is easily done: there are three or four **crossings to Tangier** each day (a 2½-hr. trip), and six or seven to the Spanish *presidios* of **Ceuta** (1½hr.), the latter little more than a Spanish Gibraltar doing brisk business in duty-free goods. Alternatively you can go by **hydrofoil** — either from here (daily, 1 hr.), or from Tarifa, half an hour by bus down the coast. Tickets are available at scores of travel agents all along the waterfront and on most approach roads; there's no difference in price between them, though some may give you a better rate of exchange than others if you want to pay in foreign currency. Wait till Tangier — or if you're going via Ceuta, Tetouan — before buying any Moroccan currency; rates in the embarkation building kiosks are very poor. Beware also those ticket sellers who congregate around the dock entrance wearing official Ceuta/Tangier badges: they add a whopping "commission" to the normal price of a ticket. InterRail/EurRail card holders should note that they're entitled to a 20 percent discount on the standard ferry price: if you have trouble getting this go to the official sales desk in the embarkation building.

---

*It's easy to take a rather romantic view of this exotic hustle and bustle, but there's a miserable story behind some of it. Algeciras is the main port for Moroccan migrant workers, who drive home every year during their holidays from the factories, farms, and mines of France, Germany, and the Low Countries. Half a million cross Spain in the six weeks from the end of June to the beginning of August. When transitting Spain they are often the victims of all levels of racial discrimination (and are still referred to as *los moros*), from being ripped off to being violently attacked and robbed.

At Algeciras the **railroad** begins again, heading north to Ronda, Córdoba, and Madrid. The route to Ronda — one of the best journeys in Andalucía — is detailed below; there are six departures a day. For Madrid (and Paris) there's a night express, currently leaving at 11pm, and also cheapish *Linebus/ Iberbus* buses to Paris and London. For Málaga hourly **buses** leave from a bar on the main seafront avenue, just back from the port; from here too, less frequently, are direct connections to Granada. Buses to Barcelona leave from in front of the harbor offices, but the journey is appallingly slow and takes 21 hours (versus a theoretical 20 on the train), with a change in Málaga. For Tarifa, Cádiz, Sevilla, and most other destinations you'll need the **main bus station**, in c/San Bernardo, 250m or so behind the port, beside the *Hotel Octavio* and just short of the **train station**: to get there follow the railroad tracks. The bus to La Línea also goes every half hour from here.

Staying in Algeciras

If you're waiting for any of these possibilities, Algeciras has plenty of cheapish **hostales** and **pensiones** in the grid of streets between the port and the railroad station. There are several in c/Duque de Almódovar, c/Santacana and c/Rafael de Muro; if you have trouble finding space, pick up a plan and check out the list in the **Turismo** (on the main seafront *avenida*, towards the river and railroad line). Prices tend to go up dramatically in mid-season, but lots of simple *casas de huespedes* cluster around the market.

The port/harbor area also has the best **places to eat** — among them, down by the tourist office and invariably crowded, the very good value *Casa Alfonso*. The **markets** are useful places to buy food, as well as vibrant and fascinating places to look around; the main one is held on Plaza Palma, down by the port.

Ronda and the White Towns

Andalucía is dotted with small, brilliantly whitewashed settlements — the **Pueblos Blancos** or "White Towns" — most often straggling up hillsides towards a castle or towered church. All of them look great from a distance, though many are rather less interesting on arrival. Perhaps the best lie in a roughly triangular area between Málaga, Algeciras, and Sevilla; at its center, in a region of wild mountainous beauty, is the spectacular town of **Ronda**.

To Ronda from the Coast

Of several possible approaches to Ronda from the coast, the route up from Algeciras is by far the most rewarding — and worth going out of your way to experience. From Málaga most of the buses to Ronda follow the coastal highway to San Pedro before turning into the mountains: dramatic enough, but rather a bleak route, with no villages and only limited views of the dark rock face of the Serrania. The train ride up from Málaga is better, with three connecting services daily, including a convenient 6pm departure after the last bus leaves.

The **Algeciras route** — via Gaucín — is possible by either bus or train, or, if you've time and energy, can be walked in four or five days. En route, you're always within reach of a river and there's a series of hill towns, each one visible from the next, to provide targets for the day (CASARES is almost on the route, but more easily reached from Estepona).

The first "White Town" on the route proper is **CASTELLAR DE LA FRONTERA**, a bizarre village within a castle, whose population, in accord with some grandiose scheme, was moved downriver in 1971 to the "new" town of La Almoraima. The relocation was subsequently dropped and a few villagers moved back to their old houses, but most of them have been taken over by retired German hippies (affluent ones with Mercedes). The result is sad: suspicion from the Spanish locals and hostile 'exclusivity from the Germans. Best to move on after a brief look around this peculiar setup; there are some bars but no one will rent you a room for the night.

JIMENA DE LA FRONTERA lacks any such traumas; again, it's a hill town but it's far larger and more open, rising to a grand Moorish castle with a triple-gateway entrance. In town are several bars and a beautiful old **fonda** (which isn't easy to find — you'll need to ask); there's also a **hostal** at the railroad station, a little way out.

Beyond Jimena it's quite a climb through woods and olive groves to reach **GAUCÍN**, though there's a bar halfway at the hamlet of San Pablo. Gaucín, almost a mountain village, commands tremendous views (to Gibraltar and the Moroccan coast on a very clear day) and makes a great place to stop over; it has a **fonda**. You can reach the village by bus, but far more rewarding is the (manageable) 8km walk from its railroad station of EL COLMENAR.

Between Gaucín and Ronda are a handful of tiny villages but the most interesting course is to take the train to the station of BENAOJÁN-MONTEJAQUE: from here it's an hour's hike to the prehistoric **Cuevas de la Pileta** (see below). From Benaoján, Ronda is just three stops (and half an hour) down the line.

Ronda

Rising amid a ring of dark, angular mountains, you only appreciate the full natural drama of **RONDA** as you enter the town. Built on an isolated ridge of the sierra, it's split in half by a gaping river gorge (the *Tajo*) that drops sheer for 130m (400 ft.) on three sides. Still more spectacularly, the gorge is spanned by a stupendous eighteenth-century arched bridge, while tall whitewashed houses lean from its precipitous edges.

Much of the attraction of Ronda lies in this extraordinary view, or in walking down by the river, following one of the donkey tracks that stud its rich green valley. (Bird-watchers should look out for the lesser kestrels, rare in northern Europe, nesting in and launching themselves from the cliffs beneath the Alameda park. Lower down you can spot crag martins). But the town itself is of equal interest and, surprisingly, has sacrificed little of its character to the flow of day-trippers from the Costa del Sol.

The Town

Ronda divides into three parts: on the near (northwest) side of the gorge, where you'll arrive, is the largely modern **Mercadillo** quarter. Across the bridge is the old Moorish town, the **Ciudad**, and its **San Francisco** suburb.

The **Ciudad** retains intact its Moorish plan and a great many of its houses, interspersed with a number of fine Renaissance mansions. It is so intricate a maze that you can do little else but wander at random. However, at some stage, make your way across the bridge and along the c/Marqués de Parada, which winds round to the left. At no.17 in the street is the somewhat arbitrarily-named **Casa del Rey Moro**, an early eighteenth-century mansion built on Moorish foundations. From its garden a remarkable underground stairway (the *Mina*) descends to the river; these 365 steps, guaranteeing a water supply in times of siege, were cut by Christian slaves in the fourteenth-century.

Farther down the same street is the **Palacio del Marqués de Salvatierra**, a splendid Renaissance mansion with an oddly primitive, half-grotesque frieze of Adam and Eve on its portal; the house is still used by the family but can usually be visited (mildly interesting guided tour for 100ptas; 11am–2pm and 4–6pm, Sun. 11am–2pm; closed Thurs.). Just down the hill you reach the two old town bridges — the **Puente Viejo** of 1616 and the single-span Moorish **Puente de San Miguel** — and nearby, on the southeast bank of the river, are the distinctive hump-shaped cupolas and bizarre glass roof-windows of the old **Baños Arabes**. A sign in front of them announces that the local authorities are restoring the cultural monument but there's usually an unofficial caretaker loitering about who will let you take a look for a small tip. Dark and musty, they seem a provincial version of the baths in Granada's Alhambra.

At the centre of the Ciudad quarter stands the cathedral church of **Santa María Mayor**, originally the Arab town's Friday mosque. Externally it's a graceful combination of Moorish, Gothic, and Renaissance styles with the the belfry built on top of the old minaret. Inside (by the ticket desk — 100ptas charge) you can see an arch covered with Arabic calligraphy, and just in front of the current street-door a part of the old Arab *mihrab*, or prayer niche, has been exposed. Across the square — perhaps the finest in Ronda — is the **Casa de Mondragón**, probably the real palace of the Moorish kings. It's been closed for years for restoration but it's worth asking around to see if you can get in; three of the patios preserve original stucco work and there's a magnificent carved ceiling.

Near the end of the Ciudad are the ruins of the **Alcázar**, destroyed by the French in 1809 ("from sheer love of destruction" according to Richard Ford) and now partially occupied by a school. Once it was virtually impregnable — as indeed was this whole fortress capital, which ruled an independent and isolated Moorish kingdom until 1485, just seven years before the fall of Granada. The principal gate of the town, through which passed the Christian conquerors (led personally by Fernando), stands to the southeast of the Alcázar at the entrance to the suburb of San Francisco.

The **Mercadillo** quarter, which grew up in the wake of the Christian conquest, is of comparatively little interest, with just a couple of buildings worth a quick look. The first is a remarkably preserved inn, the sixteenth-century **Posada de las Ánimas** in c/Cecilia, the oldest building in the quarter and slept in by no less than Miguel Cervantes. The other is the **bullring**, close by the Plaza de España and the beautiful clifftop *paseo* from which you get good views of the old and new bridges. Ronda played a leading part in the development of bullfighting and was birthplace of the modern *corrida* (tournaments). The ring, built in 1781, is one of the earliest in Spain; at its May feria *corridas* take place in eighteenth-century costume. You can visit the bullring to wander round the arena, and there's a museum inside.

Around Ronda: the Cueva de la Pileta

Walks around Ronda are pretty limitless. One of the best, and a good way to get a sense of the town as a rural market center set among farmland, is to take the path down to the gorge from the Mondragón palace terrace. In the

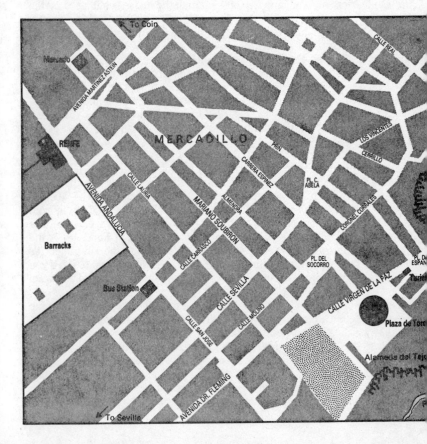

fields below there's a good network of paths and some stupendous views, although unfortunately there are also several fairly ferocious dogs. A couple of hours' walk will bring you to the main road to the northwest where you can hitch or walk back the 4-5km into the Mercadillo; half a day's walking would presumably take you all the way round the town — it certainly looks feasible. Another excursion is to an old, unused **aqueduct** set in rocky pasture — from the market square just outside the Ciudad in the San Francisco area, take the straight residential street which leads up and out of town. After about an hour it ends in olive groves, by a stream and a large water trough. A path through the groves leads to the aqueduct.

Farther afield, if you're mobile or energetic, are the ruins of a **Roman theater** at a site known as **Ronda la Vieja**, 12km from the town and reached by turning right 4km down the main road to Arcos/Sevilla. From here a track leads off towards the strange "cave village" of Setenil (see p.159).

The most interesting trip out from Ronda, though, is to the prehistoric **Cueva de la Pileta**, a fabulous series of caverns with some remarkable

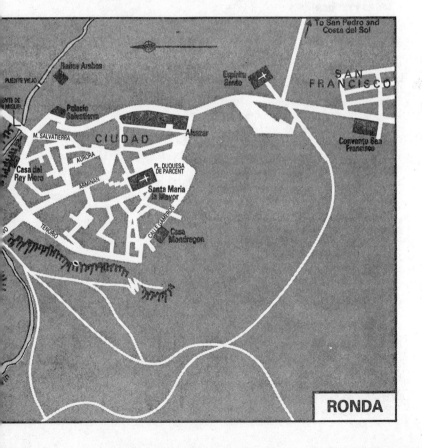

paintings of animals (mainly bison), fish, and what are apparently magic symbols. These etchings and the occupation of the cave date from around 25,000 B.C. — hence predating the famous caves at Altamira — to the end of the Bronze Age. To reach the caves take an Algeciras-bound local train (4 daily) to the Estación Benaoján-Montejaque (35 min.; departures times vary with season); or a bus, which drops you a little closer. At the train station, there's a bar here should you want to stock up on drink before the hour-long hike to the caves. Follow the farm track from the right bank of the river until you reach the farm house (approximately 30 min.). From here a donkey track will bring you onto the main road just before the signposted turnoff for the caves. If you're driving, follow the road to Benaoján, and keep going for 4 to 5km beyond. The caves are officially open from 9am to 2pm and 4 to 7pm daily; go up to the shelter at the cave entrance and wait (ignore the sign in the small car park that says 'Call'). The tour (200ptas) lasts one hour on average, but can be longer, and is in Spanish only.

Ronda Practicalities

All the **places to stay** are to be found in the Mercadillo quarter, though two of the cheapest are very close to the bridge around the Plaza de España: one, an unnamed *casa de huespedes*, is in the square itself (on the right facing the bridge), the other, *Huespedes La Española* is in the alleyway (c/José Aparicio) behind the seldom open **Turismo** and has some rooms with amazing views. Another cheap bet is the *Hostal Ronda Sol* (☎952/874497) on c/ Cristo, near the intersection with c/Sevilla. If these are all full try one of the places in c/Lorenzo B. Gomez, or on c/Sevilla, such as the *Hostal Morales* (☎952/871538), or if you're feeling extravagant the *Hotel Polo* (☎952/ 872447), which though not cheap is unusually luxurious for its price. Less classy but less expensive is the *Hotel Royal* (☎952/871141) opposite the Alameda.

As for **eating**, most of the bargain options are grouped around the far end of the Plaza del Socorro. As you leave it on c/Almendra, the *Restaurante Faroles* is very popular, as is the adjacent *Las Cañas*; there's a lively (but expensive) *tapas* bar, *La Cancela*, in a modern arcade just behind and another, *La Rosalejo* on the street running off the square towards c/Sevilla. Also on the square, next to the arcade, is *Doña Pepa*, a family-oriented bar with good *menús* and breakfasts including freshly squeezed orange juice. In the arcade itself, next to the **correos** and a health-food shop, a vegetarian restaurant, *Todo Natural* (closed Sun.) has recently been opened up by two English women and an Australian. The *Polo*'s restaurant is expensive but very good.

Generally less promising is the Plaza de España, whose establishments are the domain of bused-in day-trippers. However, you get an amazing view over the gorge from the bar in the middle of the bridge — reached by a stairway in the plaza, and operating only seasonally (there is another, always open, on the northwest edge of the chasm). The bridge bar was originally the town prison and last saw use during the civil war. Ronda was the site of some of the south's most vicious massacres, as prisoners were thrown alive down into the gorge — events which Hemingway included in *For Whom the Bell Tolls*. These days, Ronda remains a major military garrison post and houses much of the Spanish Africa Legion, Franco's old crack regiment. Wandering around town in their tropical green coats and tasseled fezes, they have a mean reputation.

Towards Cádiz and Sevilla

Buses for many destinations depart from Ronda (see *Travel Details*), but don't desert the area yet. Almost any route north or west of Ronda is reward-ing, taking you past a whole series of white towns, many of them fortified since the days of the Reconquest from the Moors — hence the mass of 'de la Frontera' suffixes.

Ubrique and Medina Sidonia
Perhaps the best of all the routes, though slightly tricky and time-consuming without your own transport, is **to Cádiz** via Ubrique, Alcalá de los Gazules and Medina Sidonia. This skirts the nature reserve of **Cortes de la Frontera** (which you can drive through by following the road beyond Benaoján) and, towards Alcalá, runs through forests of cork oaks.

UBRIQUE itself is an interesting place — a natural mountain fortress which was one of the last Republican strongholds in the civil war. According to Nicholas Luard's book, *Andalucia*,

> *It proved so difficult for the besieging nationalists to take they eventually called up a plane from Sevilla to fly over the town and drop leaflets carry-ing the message: 'Ubrique, if in five minutes from now all your arms are not piled in front of the Guardia Civil post and the roofs and terraces of your houses are not covered in white sheets, the town will be devastated by the bombs in this plane'. The threat was effective, although not quite in the way the nationalists had intended. Without spreading a single white sheet or leaving a gun behind them Ubrique's citizens promptly aban-doned the town and took to the hills behind.*

This is a civil war story typical of these parts. More unusual, however, is that the town today is relatively prosperous, surviving very largely on its medieval guild craft of leather-making.

Farther west, **MEDINA SIDONIA** is the old ducal seat of the Guzman family, one of Spain's most famous. Depopulated and now somewhat ramshackle, it nevertheless offers glimpses of sixteenth-century grandeur.

Setenil, Olvera, and Teba
Much closer to Ronda, and feasible as a day trip from the town or as a circuitous route towards Sevilla, are Setenil and Olvera. **SETENIL**, on a very minor road — and the bus route — to Olvera (or a possible hike on from Ronda La Vieja), is the strangest of all the white villages, its cave-like streets formed from the overhanging ledge of a gorge. The cottages — sometimes two or three stories high — have natural roofs in the rock. There are a couple

of bars but as yet no place to overnight. **OLVERA**, 15km beyond, and dominated by a fine Moorish castle, has a couple of *pensiones* if you want to stay and explore the region, with its river, olive groves, and stark backdrop of the Sierra de Lijar.

Visiting either Setenil or Olvera, don't be fooled into taking the train from Ronda to Setenil station: it's a good 8km from the village itself. Best to take the afternoon bus and walk or hitch the 11km back to Ronda via **ARRIATE**; rides are pretty easy to get. Alternatively, walk or hitch to Setenil in the morning and take the afternoon bus on to Olvera and spend the night.

A bit farther northwest of Setenil lies **CAÑETE LA REAL** (the Almargen-bound bus from Ronda at 2pm passes through), with a medieval castle and a baroque church. There doesn't appear to be anywhere to stay however, so this might be better as a stopover for those with cars. Again for those with a vehicle, **TEBA** is nearby, a small community situated in the mountains five or six kilometers south of the N342 between Campillos and Olvera, or straight up on the C341 from Ronda. It's easily seen from the N342 and is approached by way of a single, clearly marked road which winds its way up to the town. The lower square you come upon has all the places to stay: three clean, friendly, and relatively cheap **fondas**. Progressing up the hill to the heart of the town you are left in no doubt as to Teba's political persuasions — there's an enormous hammer and sickle painted on the tarmac in the middle of the crossroads. Higher up are the remains of a Moorish castle, constructed on Roman ruins, which has a superb keep; as you'd imagine, the views from here over the surrounding countryside are spectacular. Aside from this and the parish church, which has frescoes and Flemish paintings, Teba has a calm and prosperous air, and the feeling of being well cared for.

Zahara and Arcos

Heading directly to Sevilla from Ronda you pass below **ZAHARA DE LA SIERRA** (or *de los Membrillos* — "of the Quinces"), perhaps the most perfect example of these fortified-hill *pueblos*. Set in beautiful country, a landmark for miles around, its red-tiled houses huddle around a church and castle on a stark outcrop of rock. Once an imortant Moorish town, its capture by the Christians in 1483 opened the way for the conquest of Ronda — and ultimately Granada. Again there are a couple of **places to stay** — a *fonda* and a *casa de huespedes*.

Of more substantial interest, and a better place to break the journey from Ronda to Jerez/Cádiz (or as a detour en route to Sevilla), is **ARCOS DE LA FRONTERA**. This was taken from the Moors in 1264, over two centuries before Zahara fell — an impressive feat, for it stands high above the river Guadalete on a double crag and must have been a wretchedly impregnable fortress. This dramatic location, enhanced by low, white houses and fine sandstone churches, gives the town a similar feel and appearance to Ronda — only Arcos is poorer and, quite unjustifiably, far less visited. The streets of the town, despite particularly manic packs of local bikers, are if anything more interesting, with their mix of Moorish and Renaissance buildings. At the heart is the Plaza de España, easily reached by following the signs for the *parador*, which occupies one side of it. Flanking another two sides are the castle walls and the large Gothic-Mudejar church of **Santa María de la Asunción**; the last side is left open, offering plunging views to the river valley.

The only **accommodation** in the old town is at the *parador*, perched on a rock pedestal. Even if you've no intention of staying, it's a good location for a drink. In the new town are a couple of places on either side of the main street, c/Corredera; *Fonda Comercio* and *Pension Galvin* (☎956/700511). Alternatively, try the cheaper *Fonda Escribano* at Alta 1 (☎956/701654); or, more upscale, the *Hostal Voy-Voy*, Ponce de León 9 (☎956/701320).

A road to the left of town, towards Ronda, leads down to a couple of sandy **beaches** on the riverbank (buses every half hour), a rather swanky two-star hostal, and a tiny **campground**. If you swim in the Bornos reservoir, or farther along toward the namesake village, take care — there are said to be whirlpools in some parts.

SEVILLA, CÓRDOBA, AND THE WEST

With the major exception of **Sevilla** — and to an extent **Córdoba** — the west and center of Andalucía are not greatly visited. The coast here, certainly the Atlantic **Costa de la Luz**, is a world apart from the Mediterranean resorts, with the entire stretch between Algeciras and Tarifa designated a "potential military zone." This probably sounds grim — and in parts, marked off by *Paso Prohibido* signs, it is — but the ruling has also had happier effects, preventing foreigners from buying up land and placing strict controls even on Spanish developments. So, for a hundred or more kilometers you pass little more than a couple of dozen hotels and campgrounds — small, easy-going, and low-key even at the one growing resort of **Conil**. On the coast, too, there is the attraction of **Cádiz**, one of the oldest and, though it's now in decline, most elegant ports in Europe.

Inland rewards include the smaller towns between Sevilla and Córdoba, Moorish **Carmona** particularly. But the most beautiful, and neglected, parts of this region are the dark, ilex-covered hills and poor rural villages of the **Sierra Morena** north of Sevilla. Perfect hiking country with its network of streams and reservoirs between modest peaks, this is also a botanist's dream, brilliant with a mass of spring flowers. On a more organized level, though equally compelling if you're into bird-watching or wildlife, is the huge nature reserve of the **Coto Doñana**, spreading back from Huelva in vast expanses of *marismas* — sand dunes, salt flats and marshes. The most serious of the Spanish reserves, Doñana is vital to scores of migratory birds and to endangered mammals like the Iberian lynx. It can be visited by Land Rover tour from the new beach-resort complex of **Matascalanas/Torre de Higuera**, accessible from Huelva or Sevilla.

Sevilla

"Seville," wrote Byron, "is a pleasant city, famous for oranges and women." And for its heat, he might perhaps have added, since SEVILLA's summers are intense and start early, in April. But the spirit, for all its nineteenth-century chauvinism, is about right. Sevilla has three important monuments and an illustrious history, but what it's essentially famous for is its own living self — the greatest city of the Spanish south, of Carmen, Don Juan, and Figaro, and the archetype of Andalucian promise. This reputation, for gaiety and brilliance, for theatricality and intensity of life, does seem deserved. It is expressed above all and on a phenomenally grand scale at the city's two great festivals — the **Semana Santa** (during the week before Easter) and the **April Feria** (which lasts five days at the end of the month). Either are worth considerable effort to get to. Sevilla is also Spain's most important center for **bullfighting**, after Madrid.

Modern Realities

Despite its considerable elegance and charm, the social reality of the city has been bleak in recent years. Sevilla has definite modern wealth, having cornered the Spanish arms industry, and its lucrative export trade to Latin America. But it also lies at the centre of a depressed agricultural area and has an unemployment rate of nearly 40 percent — the highest in Spain, with Malaga. Petty crime is a big problem, and the motive for stealing is usually cash for heroin. Bag-snatching is common (often Italian-style, from passing *motos*) as is breaking into cars. There's even a special breed called *semaforazos* who break the windows of cars stopped at traffic lights and grab what they can. Western-style amateur bank robberies also seem to be in fashion. Be careful, but don't be put off. As one of the consuls in Sevilla put it: "This is not a dangerous city. No one gets mugged. I know of no town where the streets are safer at night." For violence against persons, at least, this is probably true.

Sevilla's most famous present-day native son is Prime Minister **Felipe Gonzalez**; his deputy Alfonso Guerra also hails from the city. Another, more bizarre Sevillano is one **Gregorio XVII**, who calls himself the true Pope — in defiance of his excommunication by the Vatican, "Pope Greg" is leader of a large ultra-reactionary order which has made the dead Franco a saint, and which gives out free beer and churros to all who call at their headquarters. He himself conspicuously enjoys the good life and stalks the city's bars, dressed in full silken regalia, along with his papal entourage.

On a more international note, Sevilla will share the world stage with Barcelona in 1992, when it hosts a fair to celebrate the 500th anniversary of Columbus's discovery of the New World. The equivalent of $2 billion is going into **Expo 92** to make it the "event of the century", and over 40 countries have already agreed to participate. The exhibition ground is at La Isla de la Cartuja, where Columbus' remains are said to have rested before finally being moved to the Dominican Republic. What all this means for visitors to the city between now and then is a flurry of 'closed for repairs' signs.

Orientation and Rooms

Split in two by the Río Guadalquivir, Sevilla is fairly easy to find your way around (though hell if you're driving). The **old city** — where you'll want to spend most of your time — sprawls along the west bank. At its heart, side by side, stand the three great monuments: the **Giralda tower**, the **Cathedral**, and the **Alcázar**, with the cramped alleyways of the **Barrio Santa Cruz**, the medieval Jewish quarter and now the heart of tourist life, extending north of them. Off to the left (on our plan) is the main shopping and commercial district, its most obvious landmarks the **Plaza Nueva** and **Campaña**, and the smart pedestrianized c/**Sierpes** which runs between them. Across the river — where the great April fair takes place — are the very much earthier, traditionally working-class districts of **Los Remedios** and **Triana**.

Points of arrival, too, are straightforward and central though there's a slight confusion in the city's two distinct **railroad stations**: **San Bernardo**, a few minute's walk northeast of the Barrio Santa Cruz, and **Plaza de Armas**, down by the river. Trains from Málaga, Granada and Cádiz arrive at San Bernardo; most of the others, including the majority of trains from Madrid, at Plaza de Armas. The **main bus station** is at the Plaza de San Sebastián, a couple of blocks from San Bernardo, and serves most companies and destinations. Exceptions include buses from/to **Badajoz** and **Extremadura** (*La Estrella* terminal in c/Arenal, by the bullring), **Carmona** (corner of c/Cruz Conde and c/Orleans, behind the old tobacco factory) and the province of **Huelva** (*Empresa Damas*, c/Segura, near Plaza de Armas).

The most attractive **area to stay** is undoubtedly **Barrio Santa Cruz**, though the *pensiones* and *hostales* here know this and reflect it in their prices. In mid-season, especially, you can find yourself paying ridiculous amounts for what is little more than a cell. None the less there are a dozen or so places in the quarter itself, other rather cheaper options on its periphery, and they're at least worth a try before heading elsewhere. Individual addresses don't seem worth giving here — you just have to wander about and see which have space — but as a general guide, here are the best streets to look in, starting at the top (north) of the **Barrio** and moving down towards the Cathedral:

c/**Cruces**,one block in from c/Santa María la Blanca: two *casas de husespedes*.

c/**Farnesio**: off c/S.M. La Blanca: a *CH* and a *hostal*.

c/**Ximenez de Enciso**, towards the cathedral: *camas* at no.11.

c/**Abades**, left off c/Mateus Gago: *CH*.

c/**Mateus Gago**: *pensiones*.

And **on the periphery**, heading out towards Pilate's House:

c/**Archeros**, off c/S.M. La Blanca: a *CH* and a *hostal*.

Pl. **Curtidores**, at end of c/Archeros: a *CH* at no.6, also a pricey *hostal*.

c/**Tintes**, another block on: two cheapish *hostales*.

c/**Vidrio**, parallel to Tintes: good *fonda* at no.9, *pensión* at no.19.

c/**San Esteban**, at end of Tintes and Vidrio: a *CH* at no.8, two *hostales*.

Elsewhere in Sevilla much the most promising area is the triangle of streets **below Plaza Nueva** — bordered (on the right) by c/Zaragoza and (on the left) c/San Eloy, c/Canalejas and c/Gravina. Calle San Eloy itself has probably the highest concentration of *hostales* and *fondas* of any street in the city — cheapest is the *Fonda Ramos* at no. 45 (☎954/226938).

The nearest **campground** is some 12km out along the Carmona road; it's in the middle of nowhere but there's a bus from the city every half hour, leaving from the corner of c/Cruz Conde and c/Orleans in a kind of parking lot in the grid of streets above the tobacco factory. An alternative (and not much more remote) is the site at Dos Hermanas, on the road to Cádiz — frequent buses run between there and Sevilla.

The Giralda and Cathedral

Open Mon.–Sat. 10:30am–1pm and 4:30–6:30pm; Sun 10:30am–1pm.

Sevilla was one of the earliest **Moorish conquests** (in 712) and, as part of the Caliphate of Córdoba, became the second city of *al-Andalus*. When the Caliphate broke up in the early eleventh century it was by far the most powerful of the independent states (or *taifas*) to emerge, extending its power over the Algarve and eventually over Jaén, Murcia and Córdoba itself. This period, under a series of three Arabic rulers from the Abbadid dynasty (1023–91), was something of a golden age. The city's court was unrivaled in wealth and luxury and was sophisticated too, developing a strong chivalric element and a flair for poetry — one of the most skilled exponents being the last ruler, al Mu'tamid, the "poet-king." But with sophistication came decadence and in 1091 Abbadid rule was usurped by a new force, the **Almoravides**, a tribe of fanatical Berber Muslims from North Africa, to whom the Andalusians had appealed for help against the rising threat from the northern Christian kingdoms.

The Almoravides, after initial military successes, failed to consolidate their gains in al-Andalus and attempted to rule, through military governors, from Marrakesh. In the middle of the twelfth century they were in turn supplanted by a new Berber incursion, the **Almohads**, who by around 1170 had recaptured virtually the entire former territories. Sevilla had accepted Almohad rule in 1147 and became the capital of this last real empire of the Moors in Spain. Almohad power was sustained until their disastrous defeat in 1212 by the combined Christian armies of the north, at Las Navas de Tolosa. In this brief and precarious period Sevilla underwent a renaissance of public building, characterized by a new vigor and fluidity of style. The Almohads rebuilt the Alcázar, enlarged the principal **mosque**, and erected a new and brilliant minaret, a tower over 100m (330 ft.) tall, topped with four copper spheres that could be seen from miles around.

The Giralda

The Sevilla minaret — the **Giralda** — was the culmination of Almohad architecture and served as a model for those at their imperial capitals of Rabat and Marrakesh. It was used by the Moors both for calling the faithful to prayer (the traditional function of a minaret) and as an observatory, and was so venerated that they wanted to destroy it before the Christian conquest of the city. This they were prevented from doing by the threat of Alfonso (later King Alfonso X) that "if they removed a single stone, they would all be put to the sword." Instead the Giralda (named after the sixteenth-century *giraldillo* or weather vane on its summit) became the bell tower of the Christian cathedral.

Beyond doubt the most beautiful building in Sevilla, it continues to dominate the skyline. You can ascend to the bell-chamber for a remarkable view of the city — and, equally remarkable, a glimpse of the Gothic details of the cathedral's buttresses and statuary. But perhaps most impressive of all is the tower's inner construction, a series of 35 gently inclined ramps wide enough to allow two mounted guards to pass.

The Moorish structure took twelve years to build (1184–96) and derives its firm, simple beauty from the shadows formed by blocks of brick trellis-work, different on each side, and relieved by a succession of arched niches and windows. The harmony has been spoiled by the Renaissance-era addition of balconies and, to a still greater extent, by the four diminishing stories of the belfry — added, along with the Italian-sculpted bronze figure of "Faith" which surmounts them, in 1560–68, following the demolition by an earthquake of the original copper spheres. Notwithstanding, it remains in its perfect synthesis of form and decoration one of the most important and beautiful monuments of the Islamic world.

The Cathedral

After the reconquest of Sevilla by Ferdinand III (1248) the Almohad mosque was consecrated to the Virgin Mary, as was the practice with all Spanish mosques taken from Islam, and retained in use as the Christian cathedral. Thus it survived until 1402, when the cathedral chapter dreamt up plans for a new and unrivaled monument to Christian glory: "a building on so magnificent a scale that posterity will believe we were mad." To this end the mosque was demolished, while the canons, inspired by their vision of future repute, renounced all but a subsistence level of their incomes to further the building. From the old structure only the Giralda and the Moorish entrance court, the **Patio de los Naranjos**, were spared. The patio is entered to the north of the Giralda, from c/Alemanes, through the **Puerta del Perdón** — the original main gateway, sadly greatly marred by Renaissance embellishments. In the center of the patio remains a Moorish fountain, used for the ritual ablutions before entering the mosque.

The **Cathedral** was completed in just over a century (1402–1506), an extraordinary achievement for, in accord with the plans of the chapter, it is the largest Gothic church in the world. As Norman Lewis says, "it expresses conquest and domination in architectural terms of sheer mass." Though built upon the huge rectangular base-plan of the old mosque, the Christian architects (probably under the direction of the French master architect of Rouen Cathedral) added the extra dimension of height. Its central nave rises to 42 meters, and even the side chapels seem tall enough to contain an ordinary church. The total area covers 11,520 square meters — half as much again as St. Paul's in London and exceeded only by St. Peter's in Rome.

Sheer size and grandeur are, inevitably, the chief characteristics of the cathedral. But as you grow accustomed to the gloom two other qualities stand out with equal force: the rhythmic balance and interplay between the parts, and an impressive overall simplicity and a general restraint in decoration. All successive ages have left monuments of their own wealth and style, but these have been limited to the two rows of side chapels. In the main body of the cathedral only the great box-like structure of the *coro* (the choir) stands out, blocking off the central portion of the nave and providing, as Jan Morris wrote, "an intellectual focus for the whole building . . . where all the thought and reason of the cathedral seems to be concentrated."

The coro extends and opens on to the Capilla Mayor, dominated by a vast Gothic **retablo** composed of 45 carved scenes from the life of Christ. The lifetime's work of a single craftsman, Pierre Dancart, this is the supreme masterpiece of the cathedral — the largest and richest altarpiece in the world and one of the finest examples of Gothic wood-carving. Stand around for a while and the guides will provide staggering statistics on the amount of gold involved.

Behind the Capilla Mayor (and directly to your left on entering the cathedral) you pass the domed Renaissance **Capilla Real**, built on the site of the original royal burial chapel and containing the body of Ferdinand III (*El Santo*) in a suitably rich silver shrine before the altar. The large tombs on either side of the chapel are those of Ferdinand's wife, Beatrice of Swabia, and his son, Alfonso the Wise. At the end of this first aisle are a series of rooms designed in the rich Plateresque style in 1530 by Diego de Riano, one of the foremost exponents of this predominantly decorative architecture of the late Spanish Renaissance. Through a small antechamber here you enter the curious oval-shaped **Sala Capitular** (Chapter House), whose elaborate domed ceiling is mirrored in the marble decoration of the floor. It contains a number of paintings by Murillo — the finest of which, a flowing *Conception* full of motion, is executed high above the bishop's throne. Alongside this room is the grandiose **Sacristía Mayor** which houses the treasury. Amid a confused collection of silver reliquaries and monstrances — dull and prodigious wealth — are displayed the keys presented to Ferdinand by the Jewish and Moorish communities on the surrender of the city; sculpted into the latter in stylized Arabic script are the words "May Allah render eternal the dominion of Islam in this city."

Just beyond the entrance to the sacristy is an enormous nineteenth-century **Monument to Christopher Columbus** (*Cristóbal Colón* in Spanish), erected originally in the cathedral of Havana. By a wry stroke of irony, however, Cuban independence was declared seven years later and it had to be shipped to Sevilla. The mariner's coffin is held aloft by four huge allegorical figures, representing the kingdoms of León, Castile, Aragon and Navarre; note how the lance of Castile is piercing a pomegranate, symbol of Granada, the last Moorish kingdom to be reconquered.

If the monument inspires you, or you have a fervent interest in Columbus' travels, the **Lonja**, opposite the cathedral, is worth a visit. This, the city's old stock exchange building, now houses the remarkable **Archives of the Indies** (open Mon.–Sat. 10am–3pm). Among the selection of documents on display are Columbus's log and a changing exhibition of ancient maps and curiosities.

The Alcázar

Open daily 9am–12:45pm and 3–5:30pm ; Sun. 9am–12.45pm only.

Rulers of Sevilla have occupied the site of the **Alcázar** from the time of the Romans. Here was built the great court of the Abbadids, which reached a peak of sophistication and exaggerated sensuality under the cruel and ruthless al-Mu'tadid — a ruler who enlarged the palace in order to house a harem of 800 women, and who decorated the terraces with flowers planted in the skulls of his decapitated enemies. Later, under the **Almohads**, the complex was turned into a citadel, forming the heart of the town's fortifications. Its extent was enormous, stretching to the Torre del Oro on the bank of the Guadalquivir.

Parts of the Almohad walls survive, but the present structure of the palace dates almost entirely from the Christian period. Sevilla was a favored residence of the Spanish kings for some four centuries after the reconquest — most particularly of **Pedro the Cruel** (1350–69) who, with his mistress Maria de Padilla, lived in and ruled from the Alcázar. Pedro embarked upon a complete rebuilding of the palace, employing workmen from Granada and utilizing fragments of earlier Moorish buildings in Sevilla, Córdoba and

ALCÁZAR

Valencia. This formed the nucleus of the Alcázar as it is today and despite numerous restorations necessitated by fires and earth tremors it offers some of the best surviving examples of **Mudejar architecture** — the style developed by Moors working under Christian rule. It's not entirely satisfactory, however, for later monarchs have left all too many traces and additions. Isabella built a new wing in which to organize expeditions to the Americas and control the new territories; Carlos V married a Portuguese princess in the palace, adding huge apartments for the occasion; and under Felipe IV (ca. 1624) extensive renovations were carried out to the existing rooms. On a more mundane level, kitchens were installed to provide for General Franco, who stayed in the royal apartments whenever he visited Sevilla.

The Alcázar is entered from the Plaza del Triunfo, adjacent to the cathedral. The gateway, flanked by original Almohad walls, opens on to a courtyard where Pedro (who was known as "the Just" as well as "the Cruel" depending on one's fortunes) used to give judgement; to the left is his **Sala de Justicia.** The main facade of the palace stands at the end of an inner court, the **Patio de la Montería** (Court of the Royal Bodyguard); on either side are galleried buildings erected by Isabella. This principal facade is pure fourteenth-century Mudejar and, with its delicate, marble-columned windows, stalactite frieze, and overhanging roof, is one of the finest things in the whole Alcázar. But it's probably better to look around the **Casa del Oceano** (or *de las Americas*), the sixteenth-century building on the right, before entering the main palace. Founded by Isabella in 1503, this gives you a standard against which to assess the Moorish forms. Here most of the rooms seem too heavy, their decoration ceasing to be an integral part of the design. The only notable exception and success is the chapel with its magnificent *artesonado* ceiling inlaid with golden stars; within is a fine altarpiece depicting Columbus (in a red cloak) and Carlos V (in gold) sheltering beneath the Virgin.

Entering the **Main Palace** the "domestic" nature of Moorish and Mudejar architecture is immediately striking. This involves no loss of grandeur but simply a shift in scale: the apartments are remarkably small, shaped to human needs, and take their beauty from the exuberance of the decoration and the imaginative use of space and light. There is, too, a deliberate disorientation in the layout of the rooms which makes the palace seem infinitely larger and more open than it really is. From the entrance court a narrow passage leads straight into the central courtyard, the **Patio de las Doncellas** (Patio of the Maidens), its name recalling the Christians' tribute of one hundred virgins presented annually to the Moorish kings. The court's stucco work, *azulejos* (tiles), and doors are all of the finest Granada craftsmanship. Interestingly, it's also the one room where Renaissance restorations are successfully fused — the double columns and upper story were built by Carlos V, whose *Plus Ultra* (None Greater) motto recurs in the decorations here and elsewhere.

Past the **Salon de Carlos V**, distinguished by a superb ceiling, are three rooms from the original fourteenth-century design built for Maria de Padilla (who was popularly thought to use magic in order to maintain her hold over Pedro — and perhaps over other gallants at court, too, who used to drink her bath water). These open on to the **Salon de Embajadores** (Salon of the

Ambassadors), the most brilliant room of the Alcázar, with a stupendous *media naranja* (half-orange) wooden dome of red, green, and gold cells, and horseshoe arcades inspired by the great palace of Medina Azahara outside Córdoba. Although restored, for the worse, by Carlos V — who added balconies and an incongruous frieze of royal portraits to commemorate his marriage to Isabel of Portugal here — the room stands comparison with the great rooms of Granada's Alhambra. Adjoining are a long dining hall (*comedor*) and small apartment installed in the late sixteenth century for Felipe II.

Beyond is the last great room of the palace — the **Patio de las Muñecas** (Patio of the Dolls), which takes its curious name from two tiny faces decorating the inner side of one of the smaller arches. It's thought to be the site of the harem in the original palace. In this room Pedro is reputed to have murdered his brother Don Fadrique in 1358; another of his royal guests, Abu Said of Granada, was murdered here for the sake of his jewels (one of which, an immense ruby which King Pedro later gave to Edward, the "Black Prince", now figures in the Crown of England). The upper story of the court is a much later, nineteenth-century restoration. On the other sides of the patio are the **bedrooms** of Isabella and of her son Don Juan, and the arbitrarily named *Dormitorio del los Reyes Moros* (Bedroom of the Moorish Kings).

To the left of the main palace loom the large and soulless apartments of the **Palacio de Carlos V**. Something of an endurance test, with endless tapestries and pink-orange or yellow paintwork, their classical style asserts a different and inferior mood. Best to hurry through to the beautiful and rambling **Alcázar gardens**, the confused but enticing product of several eras. Here are the vaulted baths in which Maria de Padilla bathed, and the tank specially built for Felipe V (1733), who whiled away two solitary years at the Alcázar fishing in it and preparing himself for death through religious flagellation. Also here — though it's currently in the throes of drastic emergency resuscitation — is an unusual maze of myrtle bushes.

The Plaza de España and Maria Luisa Park

Laid out in 1929 for an abortive "Fair of the Americas," the Plaza de España and adjoining Maria Luisa park are among the most pleasant — and impressive — public spaces in Spain. They are an ideal place to spend the middle part of the day, just ten minutes or so walk to the east of the cathedral and center.

En route you pass by the **Fabrica de Tabacos**, the city's old tobacco factory and the setting for Bizet's *Carmen*. Now part of the university, this is a massive structure, built in the 1750s and for a time the largest building in Spain after El Escorial. At its peak in the following century it was also the country's largest single employer, with a labor force of some 4000 women *cigarreras* — "a class in themselves" according to Richard Ford, and forced to undergo "an ingeniously minute search on leaving their work, for they sometimes carry off the filthy weed in a manner her most Catholic majesty never dreamt of."

The **Plaza de España**, beyond, was Sevilla's last attempt at monumentality, a vast semicircular complex designed as the centerpiece of the Spanish-

Americas Fair. With its fountains, monumental stairways, and mass of tile-work, it would seem strange in most Spanish cities but here it looks entirely natural, carrying on the tradition of civic display. At the Fair the Plaza was used for the Spanish exhibit of industry and crafts, and around the crescent are *azulejo* scenes and maps of each of the provinces — an interesting record of the country at the tail end of a moneyed era.

Spaniards and tourists alike come out to the plaza to potter about in the little boats hired out on its tiny strip of canal, or to hide from the sun and crowds amid the ornamental pools and walkways of the **Parque de Maria Luisa**. The park is pretty self-explanatory in its attraction, designed like the plaza in a mix of 1920s art deco and mock Mudejar. Scattered about, and around its edge, are more buildings from the Fair, some of them amazingly opulent, built in the last months before the Wall Street crash undercut the scheme's impetus — look out, in particular, for the stylish **Guatemala building**, off the Paseo de la Palmera.

Toward the end of the park, the grandest mansions from the Fair have been adapted as **museums**. The furthest houses the city's **Archeology** collections (daily except Mon. 10am–2pm); worth wandering in if you find yourself here when it's open. The main exhibits are Roman mosaics and arti-facts from nearby Italica, along with a unique Phoenician statuette of Astarte-Tanit, the virgin-goddess once worshipped throughout the Mediterranean. Opposite is the fabulous-looking **Popular Arts Museum** (same hours), generally besieged by schoolkids but with interesting displays relating to the April Feria.

Santa Cruz, Triana, the River, and Churches

After the Maria Luisa, perhaps the two best areas of Sevilla in which to drink and wander are the Barrio Santa Cruz and the banks of the Guadalquivir.

Santa Cruz is very much in character with the city's romantic image, its streets narrow and tortuous to keep out the sun, the houses brilliantly white-washed and barricaded with *rejas* (iron grilles) behind which girls once kept chaste evening rendezvous with their *novios*. Almost all of the houses have patios, often surprisingly large, and these in summer become the principal family living-room. One of the most beautiful is within the baroque **Hospicio de los Venerables Sacerdotes**, near the center in a plaza of the same name — one of the few buildings in the *barrio* to actively seek out.

Down by the **Guadlaquivir** are more pedal-boats for idling away the after-noons, and at night a surprising density of local couples. The main riverside landmark here is the twelve-sided **Torre del Oro**, built by the Almohads in 1220 as part of the Alcázar fortifications. It was connected to another small fort across the river by a chain which had to be broken by the Castilian fleet before their conquest of the city in 1248. The tower later saw use as a reposi-tory for the gold — hence its name — brought back to Sevilla from the Americas. It now houses a small **naval museum** (open Tues.–Sat. 10am–2pm, Sun. 10am–1pm; closed Mon.).

One block away is the **Hospital de la Caridad** (10am–1pm and 3:30–7pm) founded by Don Miguel de Manara, the inspiration for Byron's Don

Juan, in 1676. According to the testimony of one of Don Miguel's friends, "there was no folly which he did not commit, no youthful indulgence into which he did not plunge . . . (until) what occurred to him in the street of the coffin." What occurred was that Don Miguel, returning from a reckless orgy, had a vision in which he was confronted by a funeral procession carrying his own corpse. He repented his past life, joined the Brotherhood of Charity (whose task was to bury the bodies of tramps and criminals), and later set up this hospital for the relief of the dying and destitute, for which purpose it is still used. Don Miguel commissioned a series of twelve paintings by Murillo for the chapel, seven of which remain. Alongside them hang two *Triumph of Death* pictures by Valdes Leal. One, depicting a decomposing bishop being eaten by worms (beneath the scales of justice labeled *Ni mas, Ni menos* — "No More, No Less"), is so powerfully repulsive that Murillo declared that "you have to hold your nose to look at it."

Farther along, past the Plaza de Armas station, lies the **Museo de Bellas Artes** (Pl. del Museo, open daily except Mon. 10am–2pm). Housed in recently modernized galleries in a beautiful former convent, this is certainly worth a visit; outstanding are the paintings by Zurbarán of Carthusian monks at supper and El Greco's portrait of his son.

Modern art, incidentally, is often exhibited in the **Museo del Arte Contemporaneo** (c/S. Tomás 5, by the tourist office; open Tues.–Sat. 9am–2pm, Sun. noon–2pm) and at the privately run **Galería Juana de Aizpara** (c/Canalejos 10, Santo Cruz). Also in the Barrio, at the far end of the Jardínes de Murillo, is the **Museo de Murillo** (c/Sta. Teresa 8; Sun., Tues.–Fri. 10am–2pm and 4–7pm; Sat. 10am–2pm, closed Mon.). The artist's former home, it is furnished with contemporaneous artworks, craftsmanship and furniture.

Triana

Over the river is the **Triana** barrio, scruffy and lively, and not at all touristy. This was once the heart of the city's gypsy community and, more specifically, home of the great flamenco dynasties of Sevilla, who were kicked out by developers earlier this century and are now scattered throughout the city. The gypsies lived in extended families in tiny, immaculate communal houses called *corrales* around courtyards glutted with flowers; today only one remains intact. The *barrio* is still, however, the starting point for the annual pilgrimage to El Rocío (at the end of May), when a myriad of painted wagons leave town, drawn by elephantine oxen. It houses, too, the city's oldest working ceramics factory, the *Santa Ana*, where the tiles, many still in the traditional geometric Arabic designs, are painted by hand. Otherwise, specific "sights" are scant, but the quarter is a good place for an evening's drinking.

Churches — and Pilate's House

Sevilla's **churches** display a fascinating variety of architectural styles. Several are converted mosques with bell chambers built over their minarets, others range through Mudejar and Gothic (sometimes in combination), Renaissance and Baroque. Most are kept locked except early in the morning, or in the evenings from around 7 until 10pm — a promising time for a church crawl, especially as they're regularly interspersed with bars.

For a good circuit head first towards Gothic **San Pedro**, where a marble tablet records Velazquez's baptism, and **San Marco**, with a fine minaret-tower. Nearby, in this old cobbled part of town, is the fifteenth-century **Convento de Santa Paula**, its church decorated with a vivid ceramic facade and superb *azulejos*. Further on you meet the last remaining stretch of Moorish **city walls** — remains of the Almoravid fortifications which once spanned twelve gates and 166 towers. Now there's only one gate, the **Puerta Macarena**; beside it a basilica houses the city's cult image and patroness of matadors, *La Esperanza Macarena*, a tearful Virgin seated in the midst of amazingly gaudy magnificence.

Looping down towards the river from here you reach the **Convento de Santa Clara** (entered from c/Sta Clara no. 40) — once part of the palace of Don Fadrique, brother of Alfonso X, and with a Romanesque-Gothic tower dating from 1252. A couple of blocks away are the distinctive columns (two at the far end are Roman) of the **Alameda de Hercules**. This leads back towards downtown, with two more churches worth a look on the way: the Renaissance chapel of the **Old University** and baroque **San Salvador**, the latter built on the site of Sevilla's first Friday mosque (part of whose minaret is incorporated in its tower).

Of numerous mansions, by far the finest is the so-called **Casa de Pilatos** (daily 10am–1pm and 3–8:30pm), built by the Marques de Tarifa on his return from a pilgrimage to Jerusalem in 1519 and popularly thought to have been in imitation of the house of Pontius Pilate. In fact it's an interesting and harmonious mixture of Mudejar, Gothic, and Renaissance styles, featuring brilliant *azulejos*, a tremendous sixteenth-century stairway, and the best domestic patios in the city.

Outside the City: Roman Italica

Open daily, except Mon., 9am–7:30pm.

The Roman ruins and remarkable mosaics of **ITALICA** lie some 9km to the north of Sevilla, an excellent respite from the city, just outside the village of SANTIPONCE. They're easily reached by bus; departures, about every half hour, are from the junction of c/Marqués de Paradas and c/Luis de Vargas by the Plaza de Armas railroad station.

Italica was the birthplace of three emperors (Trajan, Hadrian, and Theodosius) and one of the earliest Roman settlements in Spain, founded in 206 B.C. by Scipio Africanus as a home for his veterans. It rose to considerable military importance in the second and third centuries A.D., was richly endowed during the reign of Hadrian (117–138), and declined as an urban center only under the Visigoths, who preferred Sevilla, then known as Hispalis. Eventually the city was deserted by the Moors after the river changed its course, disrupting the surrounding terrain.

Throughout the Middle Ages the ruins were used as a source of stone for Sevilla, but somehow the shell of its enormous **amphitheater** — the third largest in the Roman world — has survived. Today it's crumbling perilously, but you can clearly detect the rows of seats, the corridors, and the dens for wild beasts. Beyond, within a rambling and unkempt grid of streets and

villas, around twenty **mosaics** have been uncovered. Most are complete, including excellent colored floors with birds, Neptune and the Seasons, and several fine black-and-white geometric patterns.

There's also a well-preserved **Roman theater** in Santiponce itself, signposted from the main road.

Practicalities : Eating, Drinking, and Nightlife

Food

Sevilla can be an expensive city, and if you want to **eat** well you'll generally have to steer clear of the sights and of the **Barrio Santa Cruz**. A couple of exceptions are the *Bodegon Pez Espada* (c/Hernando Colón, near the cathedral) and the *Buffet Libre* restaurant on c/Mateus Gago, about 100m into the Barrio. The *Pez Espada* is excellent for cheap fried seafood; the buffet, which seems to make its money from the drink it sells, has seafood and *paella* and allows you to refill your plate as many times as you like. Also reasonably priced is the *Bar-Pizzeria El Artesano*, Mateus Gago 11, popular with young locals. There's another self-service restaurant on c/Sta. María Blanca, and other good bars and cafes nearby. *Las Teresas* is a "ham gallery" with cured hams lining the walls — enticing, though not cheap.

These recommendations apart, the two most promising central areas are down **towards the bullring** and around the Plaza de Armas station. For the first follow c/García de Vinuesa below the cathedral; at its end is a confused grid of streets with a good *frituría* (fried fish shop), some very reasonable *bocadillo* (sandwich) bars, and a selection of grocery/delicatessen shops if you want to make up your own lunch.

The **Plaza de Armas** area is slightly seedier but has the cheapest *comidas* (full set meals) this side of the river. Wander down c/Marqués de Paradas, and up c/Canalejas and c/San Eloy, and check out what's available. On San Eloy the *Bodeguita San Eloy* has a certain local fame for its *pringa bocadillos* — tasty, if best unspecified, grilled meats. Farther out — and easiest reached by following Sierpes to its end — there's a good student-oriented *bodega* in c/ Tarifa, others in nearby c/ Feria.

Still further, off Plaza Encarnación, you'll find a rare and very reasonable **vegetarian restaurant** in c/Jerónimo Hernández, off c/Regina. Another *Buffet Libre* is on Avda. de la Constitución 10. Near the Museo de Bellas Artes, in c/Pedro del Toro, the *Restaurante Salva* is good and cheap. There's a reasonably inexpensive menu at the *Meson del Rociero*, around the side of the *Corte Ingles* department store — it's small and fills quickly, notably with Latin American researchers from the Archivo de Indias.

Bars

For straight drinking and occasional *tapas* you can be much less selective. There are bars all over the town — a high concentration of them with barreled sherries from nearby Jerez and Sanlucar (the locals drink the cold, dry *fino* with their *tapas*, especially shrimp); a *tinto de verano* is wine with lemonade, a summer drink.

One of the liveliest places in **Santa Cruz**, and with fairly ordinary prices, is *La Gitanilla* in c/Ximenez de Enciso, though perhaps the best *tapas* bar in the city, with just about every imaginable snack, is *Bar Modestro* (up at the north corner of the quarter by Avda. Menendez Pelayo — ask for it by name, it's well known). *La Moneda* is a lively student bar off the Avda. de la Constitución and off that street in c/García de Vinuesa is a very good traditional bar with barreled wine. Plaza Sta. Teresa also has a couple of bars worth searching out.

Try too some of the places across the river in **Triana** — particularly in c/Castilla and c/Betis, off to the left as you cross over Puente Isabel II — and in and around c/Salado in **Los Remedios**.

Music and Discos

Flamenco — or more accurately *Sevillana* — music and dance are offered at dozens of places around the city, some of them extremely tacky and expensive. Unless you've heard otherwise avoid the fixed "shows" (*tablaos*) and stick to bars — again c/Salados in Los Remedios can be rewarding — or the street. The best music I've heard in Sevilla was in c/Alvarez Quintero, only a stone's throw from the cathedral, where a totally manic duo, an accordionist and a one-eyed drummer and singer, took over the night and most of the bars around.

An excellent **bar** which often has spontaneous *flamenco* is *La Carboneria* off the Pl. del Salvador. It used to be the coal merchant's building (hence the name) and is a large, simple, and welcoming place. *La Garrocha* has an interior like a combination youth hostel/milk bar, and a horrendous amplification system, but good *flamenco* when all is said and done.

For **rock music** the bars in c/Tarifa (at the end of Sierpes) can again be worth a look. So too can c/Trastamara, near Plaza de Armas, though the main places here (*Trastamara 24* at no. 24, *DOK* at no. 22) are essentially **gay clubs**. In c/Marqués de Paradas near the Puente Isabel II is the **disco-pub** *Poseidon*: free entrance, drinks not too expensive, open till 3am.

Major **concerts**, whether touring British bands or big Spanish acts like Paco de Lucia or Miguel Rios, usually take place in one or other of the football stadiums. Check the local press, or when school is in session the university noticeboard, for possibilities. Through the summer there are occasional **free concerts**, held in the Plaza San Francisco (by Plaza Nueva) and other squares.

Directory

Airport Mainly internal flights run by *Iberia* (c/Almirante Lobo); connecting buses leave from the bar opposite their office.

Banks Numerous places on the Avda. de la Constitución. *American Express* is represented by *Viajes Alhambra* (c/Coronel Segui 3, off Pl. Nueva).

Books/newspapers Reasonable selection of English books — mainly on Spain — at *Libreria Pascuallazaro* (Sierpes 4), and in the *El Corte Ingles* department store on the Campaña. Good newspaper stand at the Campaña

HOLY WEEK AND THE APRIL FERIA

Sevilla boasts two of the largest festival celebrations in Spain. The first, **Semana Santa** (Holy Week), always spectacular in Andalucía, is here at its peak with extraordinary processions of masked penitents and carnival-style floats. The second, the **April Feria**, is unique to the city: a one-time market festival, long converted to a week-long party of drink, food, and *flamenco*. The Feria follows hard on the heels of Semana Santa. If you have the energy, experience both.

Semana Santa

Semana Santa is obviously a religious festival, but for most of the week solemnity isn't the key note — there's lots of carousing and general frivolity, and bars are full day and night. In essence, it involves the marching in procession of brotherhoods of the church (*cofradías*) and penitents, followed by *pasos*, elaborate platforms or floats on which sit seventeenth-century images of the Virgin or Jesus. For weeks beforehand the *cofradías* painstakingly adorn the hundred or so *pasos*, spending as much as $200,000 on costumes and precious stones. The bearers (*costaleros*) walk in rhythm to *saetas*, short, fervent, *flamenco*-style hymns about the Passion and the Virgin's sorrows.

The official **route** goes from Plaza de la Campaña along c/Sierpes through the cathedral, and around the Giralda and the baroque Bishop's Palace. *Pasos* leave churches all over town at different times of the day, from early afternoon onward, snaking through the city and back to their resting place hours later. **Good Friday** morning is the climax, when the *pasos* leave the churches at midnight and move through the town for much of the night. The highlight is the viewing in the cathedral of *La Macarena*, an image of the patroness of bull fighters, and by extension, of Sevilla itself.

The pattern of events changes every day; a loose **timetable** is issued with local papers and is essential if you want to know which events are where — the ultra-Catholic *ABC* paper has best listings. On Maunday Thursday women dress in black and it's considered respectful for tourists not to dress in shorts or t-shirts. Triana is a good location on this day, and there's always a crush of spectators outside the cathedral and c/Sierpes, the most awe-inspiring venue. Plaza de San Francisco, behind the *ayuntamimento*, is a good viewing point.

The April Feria

The *Feria de Abril* lasts for ten days and nights near the end of the month. For its duration a vast area on the far bank of the river, the *Real de la Feria*, is totally covered in rows of *casetas*, canvas pavilions or tents of varying sizes. Some of these belong to eminent Sevillana families, some to groups of friends, others to clubs, trade associations, or political parties. In each one — from around 9 at night until perhaps 6 or 7 the following morning — there is *flamenco* singing and dancing. Many of the men and virtually all the women wear traditional costume, the latter in an astonishing array of brilliantly colored flounced gypsy dresses.

The sheer size of this spectacle is extraordinary, and the dancing, with its intense and knowing sexuality, a revelation. But most infectious of all is the universal spontaneity of enjoyment; after wandering around staring with the crowds you wind up a part of it, drinking and dancing in one of the "open" *casetas* which have commercial bars. Among these you'll usually find lively *casetas* erected by the anarchist trade union *CNT* and various leftist groups.

Earlier in the day, from around noon until 3pm, Sevillana society **parades** around the fairground in carriages or on horseback. An incredible extravaganza of display and voyeurism, this has subtle but distinct gradations of dress and style; catch it at least once. Each day, too, there are **bullfights** (at around 5:30pm: tickets in advance from the ring), generally reckoned the best of the season.

end of c/Sierpes. British newspapers and the *International Herald Tribune* are also sold in the international bookshop on c/Reyes Católicos.

Bullfights Details and tickets from the Plaza de Toros or (with commission) from the kiosks in c/Sierpes. Bar *La Bolera* at the end of c/Feria is virtually a bullfight museum — a traditional pre- or post- *corrida* haunt.

Buses/trains See "Arrival" for details and addresses of the various terminals. For train tickets/info go to the *RENFE* office, off the Plaza Nueva at c/Zaragoza 29. Several of the travel agents around the cathedral and on Avda. de la Constitución sell bus tickets direct to the Algarve (daily in summer and good value).

Car rental Most agents are along the Avda. de la Constitución. One of the cheapest operators, represented in the foyer of the *Hotel Alfonso XIII* (by the tobacco factory), is *Atesa*.

Consulate U.S., Paseo de las Delicias 7 (☎954/231885).

Coto Doñana Details on the procedures for visiting this nature reserve are given under the section on the park (see Huelva). If you want to do anything out of the ordinary the office responsible for its administration is the *Estacion Biological de Doñana* (c/Paraguay 1). To book jeep tours contact *Centro de Recepcion del Acebuche*, Avda. de la Constitución 21 (☎954/221440).

Feminism Best contact is the *Libreria Feminista* at c/Zaragoza 36.

Flea market A *rastro* takes place on Thursday mornings along the c/Feria past the Plaza Encarnación, and a bigger one on Sunday at the Alameda de Hercules.

Food market A cheap and cheerful one takes place daily in Triana — immediately on the right as you cross Puente Isabel II.

Hiking maps 1:50,000, 1:100,000 and 1:200,000 military maps from the *Servicio Geografico del Ejercito* (Plaza de España building, Sector Norte).

Hospital English-speaking doctors available at the *Hospital Universidad* (Avda. Dr. Fedriani; ☎378400). Dial 091 for emergency treatment.

Police Bag-snatching is big business. If you lose something get the theft documented at the Pl. de la Gavidia station (☎954/228840).

Post Office Avda. de la Constitución, by the cathedral; *Lista de Correos* (poste restante) stays open Mon.–Fri. 9am–8pm, Sat. 9am–1pm.

Rock concerts Official agents for many concerts, in Sevilla and elsewhere in Spain, are *Viajes Melia*, Avda. de la Constitución 30, opposite the cathedral.

Soccer Sevilla has two major-league teams — *Sevilla CF* (currently the better one, which plays at the Sánchez Pizjuan stadium) and *Real Betis* (Estadio Benito Villamarin). Match schedules from local or national press.

Telephone office Pl. Nueva 3 (Mon.–Sat. 9am–1pm and 5:30–9pm).

Turismo Avda. de la Constitución 21 (☎954/221404); open 9am–7pm Mon.–Sat., 9:30am–1:30pm Sun.

The Sierra Morena

The longest of Spain's mountain ranges, the **SIERRA MORENA** extends almost the whole way across Andalucía — from Rosal on the Portuguese frontier to the dramatic pass of Despeñaperros, north of Linares. Its hill towns marked the northern boundary of the old Moorish Caliphate of Córdoba and in many ways the region still signals a break, with a shift from the climate and mentality of the south to the bleak plains-villages of Extremadura and New Castile. The range is not greatly known — with its highest point a mere 1110m, it is not a dramatic *sierra*, and even Andalusians can have trouble placing it. All of which, of course, is to your advantage.

Practicalities

The Morena's climate is mild — sunny in spring, hot but fresh in summer — but it can be very cold in the evenings and mornings. Tracks are still more common than roads, and tourism, which the government of Andalucía is keen to encourage, has so far meant little more than a handful of new signs indicating areas of special interest.

A good time to visit is between March and June, when the flowers, perhaps the most varied in the country, are at their best. You may get caught in the odd thunderstorm but it is usually bright and hot enough to swim in the reservoirs or splash about in the clear springs and streams, all of which are good to drink. If your way takes you along a river, you will be entertained by armies of frogs and turtles plopping into the water as you approach, by lizards, dragonflies, bees, hares, and foxes peering discreetly from their holes — and most often no humans present for miles around.

The locals maintain that, while the last bears disappeared only a short time ago, there are still a few wolves around in remoter parts. Of more concern to anyone hiking in the Sierra, however, are the **toros bravos** (fighting bulls), since you are quite likely to come across them. The black ones are the only dangerous ones; the red ones, although equipped with some daunting headgear, are not aggressive. Apparently, too, a group of bulls is less to be feared than a single one, and a single one only if he directly bars your way and looks mean. The thing to do, according to expert advice, is to stay calm, and without attracting the bull's attention, stroll around. If you even get a whiff of a fighting bull, though, it might well be best to adopt the time-honored technique — drop everything and run.

East–west **transportation** in the Sierra is very limited. Most of the bus services are radial and north–south, with Sevilla as the hub, and this leads to ridiculous situations where, for instance, to travel from Santa Olalla to Cazalla, a distance of some 53km, you must take a bus to Sevilla, 70km away, and then another up to Cazalla — a full day's journey of nearly 150km just to get from one town to the next. The obvious solution if you want to spend any amount of time in Morena is to organize your routes around **hikes** and to supplement this by hitching. Hitching can be very difficult in Spain, but in areas like this, where cars are few and bound to be making for the same destination as you, drivers usually seem willing to give rides. A bicycle too could be good, though your own car much less so — this is not Michelin car-window-view territory. If you have a **bike**, you'll need a ten-speed touring or mountain model, especially for the road between El Real de la Jara and El Pintado (Sta. Olalla–Cazalla). The roads around Almonaster, and between Cazalla and Constantina, are very bad for cycling.

Buses from Sevilla to the Sierra leave from the *San Sebastian* terminal by the bullring. If you just want to make a quick foray into the hills, ARACENA is probably the best target (and the most regularly served town). If you're planning on some hiking it's also a good starting poin;: before you go, however, be sure to get yourself a good **map** from the military *Servicio Geografico* in the Plaza de España — these are well-produced and cheap, and though crammed with misleading information they do point you in the right direction to get lost somewhere interesting.

Aracena — and its Sierra

The highest town in the Sierra Morena — guarded to its south by a small offshoot of the range — ARACENA has a sharp, clear air, all the more noticeable after Sevilla. It is a substantial town, capital of the western end of the Sierra and with 10,000 inhabitants. There are a couple of *hostales*, a hotel, and two **fondas** — the most enticing of which (at the bottom end of the scale) is the *Carmen*, a homey sort of place with a good cheap restaurant. There's also a **campground**, about 5km out on the Sevilla road, or twelve kilometers away at the bridge end of the nearby *embalse*, it's possible to camp for free near a bar called the *Primitivo* (which it is). The camping area is on private land but the locals don't seem to mind. Aracena being at the heart of a prestigious *jamón*-producing area, you should eat anything with ham in it, and, when they're available, the delicious wild asparagus and local snails — rooted out from the roadside and in the fields in spring and summer respectively.

The town itself is undistinguished but pretty, rambling up the side of a hill topped by the **Iglesia del Castillo** — a Gothic-Mudejar church built by the Knights Templar around the remains of a Moorish castle (one of dozens in the Sierra). This is certainly worth the climb, but Aracena's principal attraction is the **Gruta de las Maravillas**, the largest and arguably the most impressive cave in Spain. Discovered, so they say, by a local boy in search of a lost pig, the cave is now illuminated and open daily from 10am–7pm. A guide takes you around in groups as soon as a dozen or so people have assembled; on Sunday there is a constant procession, but usually plenty of time to gaze and wonder. The cave is astonishingly beautiful, and quite a laugh too — the last chamber of the tour is known simply as the *Sala de los Culos* (Room of Buttocks), its walls and ceiling an outrageous naturally sculpted exhibition, tinged in a pinkish-orange light. Close by the cave's entrance are a couple of restaurants, slightly extravagant but excellent.

Villages Around Aracena

Surrounding Aracena you'll find a scattering of attractive but economically depressed villages, most of them dependent on the **jamón industry** and its curing factory at Jabugo. *Jamón serrano* (mountain ham) is a *bocadillo* standard throughout Spain and some of the best, *jamón de bellotas* (acorn-fed ham), comes from the Morena. Herds of sleek grey pigs grazing beneath the trees are a constant feature here: in October the acorns drop and the pigs, waiting patiently below, gorge themselves, become fat and are promptly whisked off to the factory to be slaughtered and then cured in the dry mountain air.

The **villages** — Jabugo, Aguafria, Almonaster La Real — all make rewarding destinations for walks, though all are equally ill-served by public transport and you may well find yourself in for a hike both ways. The most interesting, and with several *hostales* in spite of its tiny size, is **ALMONASTER**. As at Aracena the castle here was originally Moorish before undergoing graceful fifteenth-century conversion into a church.

Closer at hand, a fine eleven-kilometer walk from Aracena takes you past chestnut orchards and great clumps of oregano to the **Peña de Arias Montano**, an isolated church or *ermita* peering over a cliff above the village of ALAJAR. The Sierra Morena is liberally dotted with these buildings, almost always in isolated spots and dedicated to the Virgin. This one, like most, is distinguished more by the beauty of its setting than for any intrinsic architectural qualities.

Zufre and Across to Cazalla

From Aracena a single daily **bus** — currently at 6:45am — covers the 25km southeast to Zufre (For those going farther afield, there's a direct bus to Lisbon). If you miss it, you'll have to walk, which takes the best part of a day but can be good in itself. Three hours out of Aracena you come upon the **Embalse de Aracena**, one of the huge reservoirs that supply Sevilla, dammed by a massive construction across the southern end of the valley. From here a lovely but highly circuitous route will take you down towards Zufre along the **Rivera de Huelva**.

Zufre

ZUFRE itself must be one of the most spectacular villages in Spain, hanging like a miniature Ronda on a high palisade at the edge of a ridge. Below the crumbling Moorish walls the cliff falls away hundreds of feet, terraced into deep green gardens of orange trees and vegetables. Within the town the **Ayuntamiento** and **church** are both interesting examples of Mudejar, the latter built in the sixteenth century on foundations of a mosque. In the basement of the Ayuntamiento, too, are a gloomy line of stone seats, said to have been used by the Inquisition. The focus of the town, however, is the **Paseo**, a little park with rose gardens, a balcony, a bar at one end, and a *casino* (barclub) at the other. Here the villagers gather for much of the day: there is little work either in Zufre or its surrounding countryside, and even the local bullring has been relegated to twice-annual use: once at the beginning of the season in March, the other at the town's September *feria*. Tourist development, so far at least, is limited to the ironically-named **Bar Moderno**, Zufre's combination restaurant-hotel. The facilities are a little limited — you eat with the family and sleep upstairs in one of three interjoining rooms — but it's a friendly place and good value.

Santa Olalla

SANTA OLALLA DEL CALA, the next village to the east, has no bus link with Zufre though every morning several locals drive the sixteen kilometers there for work or school, so it's not hard to arrange a lift. If you walk it's again memorable — a flattish route through open country with fields of wheat, barley, and pigs, and then a sudden view of the Moorish **castillo** above the town. There have actually been several half-hearted attempts at the reconstruction of this but they haven't been helped by its adaptation in the last century as the local cemetery — the holes for coffins in the walls rather spoil the effect. Below its walls, once again, is the parish church, fifteenth-century with a fine Renaissance interior.

Coming from Zufre it's a surprise to find **hostales** in Santa Olalla, but the town is actually on the main Sevilla-Badajoz road and sees a fair amount of traffic — and regular buses to both cities. These stop outside the *Bar Primitivo*, an admirable place to sleep, eat, or just drink, all for a very reasonable price; its name is that of the owner, and no judgement.

East to Real de Jara

Again there are no buses east or west so to continue along the Morena you'll have to walk or try to hitch the eight kilometers to Real de Jara. Halfway, after winding through stone-walled olive groves, the road flattens out into a grassy little valley above the river Calla — a spot where the villages of Real and Olalla hold their joint *romería* at the end of April. These country *romerías* are always good to stumble upon, and if you happen on one in the Sierra you should be well looked after. Proceedings start with a formal parade to the local *ermita* but they're very soon given over to feasting and dancing, the young men wobbling about on donkeys and mules in a wonderful parody of the grand *hidalgo* doings of Jerez and Sevilla, children shrieking and splashing in the river, and everyone dancing *Sevillanas* to scratchy cassettes.

REAL DE LA JARA is in much the same mold as Santa Olalla: two Moorish castillos (both in ruins), a *casa de huespedes* (at Real 6), a very welcome public swimming pool, and again no buses. To continue east from here requires persistence and, unless you've a lot of energy, a run back and forth from Sevilla. CAZALLA DE LA SIERRA, the next village, is some 45km along a mountainous route which sees few cars. The one relief, 30km on, is the **Embalse del Pintado**, another huge reservoir — at present alarmingly low after a decade of scant rains.

Cazalla and the Central Sierra

Another "regional" Sierra capital, CAZALLA DE LA SIERRA, seems quite a metropolis if you've arrived on foot. Not only does it have four **fondas** (the best in Plaza Iglesia, the rest in the main street, c/Llana) but there are numerous bars and even a pub — pronounced 'pa' in Andaluz — where the locals go to drink cocktails and listen to jazz and rock music. If this is all too much of a shock, a more traditional bar and restaurant, still lively, is the *Boleras* in Plaza Manuel Nosea — right next to the *Guardia Civil*, who are themselves ensconced in a beautiful former nunnery.

The main sight is the church of **Nuestra Señora de la Consolación** at the southern end of town, an outstanding example of Andalucian architecture begun in the fourteenth century, continued with some nice Renaissance touches, and finally completed in the eighteenth century. The place to make for, however, is **La Plazuela**, where you'll find the local *casino*. This is essentially a place to drink and relax — quieter and more comfortable than most of the bars — and serves as a kind of club, with locals paying a nominal monthly membership charge. Most towns of Cazalla's size have one, and tourists and visitors are always welcome to use the facilities free of charge — worth doing since the membership rule means everybody drinks at reduced prices.

Within easy wandering distance of Cazalla are some fine spots and a walk of just four kilometers will take you east to the **Ermita del Monte**, a little eighteenth-century church on a wooded hill above the Rivera de Huensa.

Farther afield you can actually take a **bus** (at 6:45am or 1pm) as far as the ESTACIÓN DE CAZALLA Y CONSTANTINA, a twenty-minute ride to the east. Here three or four trains a day run northwest to ZAFRA (*not* Zufre) and Extremadura, and a similar number follow the river down towards El Pedroso and ultimately Sevilla. The daily buses connect Cazalla with Sevilla, too. If you're headed for El Pedroso, though, you might as well walk from the station — a lovely route, with great river swimming and a fabulous variety of valley flora and fauna; it takes about five hours.

El Pedroso and Constantina

When you reach **EL PEDROSO**, a pretty little town with a notable Mudejar church, ask the woman who runs the station *cantina* for a **room** — which she'll supply. Across the road is an excellent **tapas bar**, the *Serrania*, which serves up local specialities such as venison, hare, pheasant, and partridge. El Pedroso is somewhat less depressed than most towns in the sierra due to the local factory, the *fabrica*, one stop up on the train line, which employs most of the locals making a nebulous, undefined product.

Eighteen kilometers farther to the east — and perhaps as good a place as any to cut back to Sevilla if you're not counting on hiking the whole length of the range — you reach **CONSTANTINA**, an important mountain town with a population of almost 15,000. There are two **fondas** in the main walking-street and one *comidas y camas* place in the Alameda; try the *fondas*. High above the town is the **Castillo de la Armada**, particularly impressive and surrounded by shady gardens descending in terraces to the old quarters. At the base is the parish **church**, once again with a Mudejar tower, Moorish influence having died hard in these parts. The town itself is lively and beautiful, and set in lovely countryside. Returning from Constantina to Sevilla, there are two buses a day (at 6:45am and 3pm).

The Costa de la Luz

Stumbling on the villages along the **Costa de la Luz**, between Algeciras and Cádiz — is like entering a new land after the dreadfulness of the Costa del Sol. The journey west from Algeciras seems in itself a relief, the road climbing almost immediately into rolling green hills, offering fantastic views down to Gibraltar and across the straits to the just-discernible white houses and tapering mosques of Moroccan villages. Beyond, the Rif Mountains hover mysteriously in the background and on a clear day, as you approach Tarifa, you can distinguish Tangier on the edge of its crescent-shaped bay.

Tarifa

TARIFA, spreading out beyond its Moorish walls, was until the mid-1980s a quiet village, known in Spain, if at all, for its abnormally high suicide rate — a result of the unremitting winds that blow across the town and its environs. Today it's a prosperous, popular, and at times very crowded, resort, following its discovery as Europe's prime **windsurfing** locale. There are equipment rental shops throughout the length of the main street, and in peak season crowds of windsurfers pack out every available bar and *hostal*. Even in winter, there are windsurfers to be seen — drawn by regular competitions held year-round.

If windsurfing is not your motive, there can still be an appeal in wandering the crumbling ramparts, gazing out to sea or down into the network of lanes that surround the fifteenth-century (but baroque-fronted) church of San Mateo. The **castle** was site of many a struggle for this strategic foothold into Spain: it took the name of Guzman el Bueno ("the Good"), Tarifa's infamous commander during the Moorish siege of 1292, who earned his surname for a superlative piece of tragic drama. Guzman's nine-year-old son had been taken hostage by a Spanish traitor and surrender of the garrison was demanded as the price of the boy's life. Choosing "honor without a son, to a son with dishonor," Guzman threw down his own dagger for the execution.

Accommodation and Practicalities

Tarifa has a half-dozen places to stay, though finding a bed in summer can be a struggle. The *Hostal Tarik* in the western part of town, overlooking the coast from c/San Sebastián 32/36 (☎956/685240), is very clean and has helpful owners. In the same area there are two more *hostales*. Built into the west wall of the old quarter is an excellent *fonda-restaurante* called the *Villanueva*, a newly remodeled but noisy *Hostal La Calzada* by San Mateo church, and two reasonable *casas de huespedes*: one close by the *Villanueva*, another (*Facundo*) 200m out on the main road to Cádiz.

Also on the main Cádiz-Algeciras road you'll find the **bus station**, a supermarket, a **laundromat**, and adjacent fried-fish and *churro* stalls. Just off the highway on Amador de los Ríos, *Hostal las Fuserias* is better than it looks, with a laundry area and a shady courtyard, and far preferable to the overpriced *Hosteria Tarifa* on the same street.

For eating, the *Chan*, *Villanueva*, and *Agobio*, all within a few hundred meters of each other just outside the western wall, have cheap *menús*; most pleasant for lunch is the *Bar Alameda* on the Alameda, which does reasonable *platos combinados*. Of the dozen other bars, pubs, and discos, the German-run *Point* is a windsurfers' hangout and a good place for finding long-term accommodation as well as secondhand windsurfing gear.

The town also offers the tempting opportunity of a quick approach **to Morocco**, with Tangier feasible as a daytrip on the once-daily seasonal hydrofoil. Currently this goes at 9:30am, returning at 4:30 or 6:30pm (Spanish time — which is 2 hr. ahead of Moroccan, beware confusions). The trip takes just half an hour; tickets are available from the embarkation office on the quay or in advance from travel agents. If you're planning to do a day-trip you'd be wise to book a few days ahead of time — or you may find that a tour company has block-reserved more or less the whole boat. This crossing is a lot more expensive (1000ptas) than going from Algeciras but might be a better bet if the latter is chock-full in summer or when Moroccans are returning home for the two major Islamic festivals (in April and June during the early 1990s).

Tarifa Beach

Heading northwest from Tarifa, you find what are perhaps the best **beaches** along the whole Costa de la Luz — wide stretches of yellow or silvery-white sand, washed by some magical combers. The same winds — the eastern *Levantera* and western *Poniente* — that have created such perfect conditions for windsurfing can, however, be a problem for more casual enjoyment, sand-blasting those attempting to relax on towels or mats and whipping the water into whitecaps.

The **beaches** beckon immediately west of the town. They get better as you move past the tidal flats and the mosquito-ridden estuary — until the dunes start, and the first camper vans lurk among the bushes. At **"TARIFA BEACH,"** a little bay 9km out from town, there are restaurants, campgrounds, and a *hostal* at the base of a tree-tufted bluff. Germans have started a windsurfing school here, which acts as the center for the sport. For more seclusion head to one or other of the **beach-campgrounds** on either side, signposted from the main road or accessible by walking along the coast. Each of these — RÍO JARA, TORRE DE LA PEÑA and PALOMA — are well-equipped and inexpensive.

Bolonia and Barbate

Around the coast from Paloma are extensive ruins of the Roman town of **BOLONIA**, or *Belo Claudia*, where you can make out the remains of three temples and a theater, as well as numerous houses (guided tours at 10am, 11am, 12am, 1:15pm, 4pm, 5pm, 6:15pm). The site lies sheltered by the cape known as PUNTA CAMARINAL and can be reached down a small side road which turns off the main Cádiz road 15km after Tarifa. There's also a fine beach here with bars and eating places. Alternatively it's a good walk along the coast from either Paloma or, from the west, Zahara de los Atunes (about 3½ hr. with a couple of natural obstacles en route).

ZAHARA, a small fishing village beginning to show signs of development, has a fabulous eight-kilometer-long beach There's a smallish ritzy hotel and three *hostales*, none of them very cheap and usually full until at least the end of September; *Nicolas* by the lagoon is probably the cheapest. Camping is also feasible, but don't forget the insect-repellent.

BARBATE DE FRANCO, next along the coast and linked by daily bus (except Sundays), is not such a good bet: an ugly little town dominated by its harbor and canning industry. The catch of the bluefin tuna, the largest of the tuna family weighing in at around 200 kilos each, is a ritual which has gone on here for a thousand years, still using almost the same methods. The season lasts from April to June as they migrate south towards the Mediterranean, and from early July to mid-August when they return, to be herded and caught by huge nets. The biggest market is Japan, where it is eaten raw as sushi. Tuna numbers are declining and the season getting shorter — probably the result of overfishing — much to the concern of the people of Barbate, nearby Conil de la Frontera, and Zahara de los Atunes, since the catch represents an important source of income.

LOS CAÑOS DE MECA, a very small village connected to Barbate by a tiny road that loops around by the sea, has a long, beautiful beach, and encroaching development. Just west, however, towards CAPE TRAFALGAR, is a **campground**.

Vejer de la Frontera

Not to be missed, if you find yourself on the Costa de laLuz, is **VEJER DE LA FRONTERA**, a classically white and Moorish-looking hill town set in a cleft between great protective hills that rear high above the road from Tarifa to Cádiz. If you arrive by bus, it's likely to drop you at two *hostal/restaurantes* way below the town (incidentally the only places to eat, and an option for accommodation). The road winds up for another 4km but just by one of the bus-stop cafes there's a donkey path that takes only about twenty minutes. This is a perfect approach — for the drama of Vejer is in its isolation and its position, which gradually unfolds before you.

Until the last decade the women of Vejer wore a long dark cloak that veiled their faces like nuns; this custom seems now to be virtually extinct, but the town does have a remoteness and Moorish feel as explicit as anywhere in Spain. There's a castle and a church of curiously mixed styles (mainly Gothic and Mudejar) but the main fascination lies in exploring the brilliant white and labyrinthine alleyways, wandering past iron-grilled windows, balconies and patios, and slipping into a succession of bars. At one of these, *Pena Flamenca Aguilar de Vejer*, you can sample *manzanilla* from the barrel and take in weekend flamenco performances. Try, too, the *Bar Chirino* on Plaza Franco, which contains a photographic history of the town. The only **accommodation** is the slightly pricey but excellent *Hostal la Jonda* — ask for directions.

Conil

Back on the coast, a dozen or so kilometers on, is **CONIL** — an increasingly popular resort and threatening to become a little too much so for its own good. Outside July and August, though, it is still a good place to rest up, and in mid-season the only real drawback is trying to find a room. Accommodation needs are served by various **rooms** to rent (ask about), plus a couple of *hostales*. If you **camp** you've less to worry about; there are two campgrounds, the central *camping municipal* and, much better, a new setup at the tiny resort of FUENTE DEL GALLO (3-km walk — despite all signs to the contrary; open from March to October).

Conil town is at present in a rather indeterminate state, midway between its old existence as a poor fishing village and its new one as resort. At least the majority of the tourists are Spanish (with a lesser number of Germans) and if you are here in mid-season, there are plenty of fairs and loads of good bars — including a church-like place which often hosts bands.

The **beach**, Conil's *raison d'être*, is a wide bay of brilliant yellow stretching for miles to either side of town and lapped by an amazingly, not to say disarmingly, gentle Atlantic — you have to walk halfway to Panama before it reaches waist height. Walking along the coast to the east — back towards Barbate — the beach is virtually unbroken until it reaches the cape, the perhaps familiar-sounding **Trafalgar**, off which Lord Nelson achieved victory and death on October 21, 1805.

Moving on from Conil, most **buses** leave from the junction on the main road — 2km from the town — and seats must be booked in advance at the *Transportes Comes* office in the Plaza de España; the ticket includes a ride on the local bus to the junction.

Towards Cádiz

One last seaside possibility before Cádiz is the picturesque little village of **SANCTI PETRI**, its beach sheltered by a castle-capped island. This is accessible from **CHICLANA DE LA FRONTERA**, in itself unmemorable though a useful road junction with sporadic buses to MEDINA SIDONIA (see the "White Towns").

Beyond Chiclana you emerge into a weird landscape of marshes, dotted with drying salt pyramids, in the midst of which lies the town of **SAN FERNANDO** — once an elegant place (and still so downtown) but quickly being swallowed up by industrial suburbs. These extend until you reach the long causeway that leads to Cádiz, an unromantic approach to what is one of the most extraordinarily sited and moody towns of the south.

Cádiz

CÁDIZ is the oldest settlement in Spain, founded around 1100 B.C. by the Phoenicians and one of the country's principal ports ever since. Its greatest period, however, and the era from which the central part of town takes most of its present appearance, was the eighteenth century. Then, with the silting up of the river to Sevilla, the port enjoyed a virtual monopoly on the Spanish-American trade in gold and silver, and on its proceeds were built the cathedral — itself golden-domed (in color at least) and almost oriental when seen from the sea — the public halls and offices, and the smaller churches.

Inner Cádiz, built on a peninsula-island, remains much as it must have looked in those days, with its grand open squares, sailors' alleyways, and high, turreted houses. Literally crumbling from the effect of the sea air on its soft limestone, it has a tremendous general feel — slightly seedy, definitely having seen better days, but still full of mystique. Unlike most other ports of its size, it seems immediately relaxed, easy-going, and not at all threatening, even at night. Perhaps this is due to its reassuring shape and compactness, the presence of the sea making it impossible to get lost for more than a few blocks. But it probably owes this tone as much to the town's tradition of liberalism and tolerance — one maintained all through the years of Franco's dictatorship, even though this was one of the first towns to fall to his forces, and was the port through which the Nationalist armies launched their invasion. In particular Cádiz has always accepted its substantial gay community, and even today "coming from Cádiz" has its connotations.

Practicalities

Arriving by **train** you'll find yourself on the periphery of the old town, close by the Plaza de San Juan de Dios, busiest of the many squares. By **bus** you'll be a few blocks farther north, along the water — either at the *Los Amarillos* terminal (which serves Rota, Chipiona, and the resorts west of Cádiz) or, just beyond in the Plaza de Independencia at the *Estación de Comes* (used by buses from Sevilla, Tarifa and most other destinations toward Algeciras). *Los*

Amarillos also runs a twice-daily service through Arcos to Ubrique, with a connection there to Ronda — by far the best route.

The **Plaza Juan de Dios**, protruding across the neck of the peninsula from the port and the first long stretch of Cádiz's naval dockyards, has several cafes and cheap **restaurants**. *La Caleta*, whose interior is built like the bow of a ship, serves wonderful *champiñones al Jerez* (mushrooms in sherry) and other hearty *raciones*. In the square's top right-hand corner, *El 9*, *Pasaje Andaluz*, and *La Economica* are good. Also around the square are a dense network of alleyways crammed with **hostales, fondas**, and straightforward flophouses or brothels. *El Sardinero*, actually on the square at the junction of c/Fernando, is a good place to stay; so is *La Aurora* at c/Sopranis 8. In general, though, the more salubrious *pensiones* and *hostales* are to be found a couple of blocks away, towards the cathedral or **Plaza de Candelaría**. Near the latter, try c/Colón (four consecutive possibilities) or c/Montañes (*Hostal Barcelona* at no.10, ☎956/213949, is basic — despite credit-card stickers — but clean and friendly).

The Town

Cádiz is more interesting in its generality — its blind alleys, cafes, and backstreets — than for any particular buildings. But, wandering around, it is certainly worth finding your way to the **Museo de Bellas Artes**, at Pl. de Mina 5, just across from the **Turismo**. This contains a small archaeological display, and a quite exceptional series of saints painted by **Zurbarán**, brought here from the Carthusian monastery at Jerez and one of only three such sets in the country (the others are at Sevilla and Guadalupe) preserved intact or nearly so. With their sharply defined shadows and intense introspective air, Zurbaran's saints are at once powerful and very deeply Spanish — even English figures such as Hugh of Lincoln, or the Carthusian John Houghton, martyred by Henry VIII whom he refused to accept as head of the English Church. Perhaps this is not surprising, for the artist spent much of his life traveling around the Carthusian monasteries of Spain and many of his saints are in fact portraits of the monks whom he met. The museum is open daily except Sunday from 10am to 2pm, and from 5:30 to 8pm; certain sections, including the Zurbarans, have recently been closed for restoration.

Outdoors, it's the **sea fortifications** and waterfront **alamedas** which are most striking and which give most direction to walks around the town. Add to these the huge **Catedral Nueva**, which is sporadically closed for restoration. Even if you don't normally go for High Baroque it's hard to resist the attraction of this building, decorated entirely in stone, with no gold or white in sight, and absolutely perfect proportions. In the crypt, often visitable despite the barricades at the front of the building, is buried Manuel de Falla, the Spanish composer who graces the now-rare 100-peseta note. Opening times are generally from 9:30am to 1pm and from 6 to 8pm (small charge).

Over on the seaward side of the mammoth complex, the "Old" Cathedral, **Santa Cruz**, is also worth a look, its interior liberally studded with coin-in-the-slot votive candles. And, lastly, there are two churches of note for the paintings they contain. Foremost of these is the chapel of the **Hospital de Mujeres** (daily 9am-6pm: ask the porter for admission) which has a brilliant

El Greco of *St. Francis in Ecstasy*. The other, an oval, eighteenth-century chapel, **Santa Cueva** (open daily except Sun. 10am–1pm and 4–6pm; entered by ringing at c/San Francisco 11) has three frescoes on eucharistic themes by Goya.

Ships from Cádiz

Before the decline of passenger **ships** it was possible to sail to London or South America from Cádiz. Today you can go only as far as the Canary Islands of Tenerife (36 hr.) and Las Palmas (43 hr.). A ship makes this round trip every two days in season and every five out; tickets, which cost about the same as for flights, can be obtained from the *Ancona* office, near the port at Avda. Ramón de Carranza 26.

More locally — and for nominal charge — you can get a boat to **Puerto de Santa María**, a twenty-minute ride across the bay; departures are four times a day from the quay by the railroad station.

The Cádiz Coast

Cádiz has a beach of its own — the **Playa de la Victoria**, to the left of the promontory approaching the town — but for clearer waters it's best to cross the bay.

PUERTO DE SANTA MARÍA (the ferry noted above is quicker and cheaper than the bus) is the obvious choice, a traditional family resort for both *Gaditanos* and *Sevillanos* — many of whom have built villas and chalets along the fine **Playa Puntillo**. This strand is a little way out from the town (10-15 min. walk or a local bus), a pleasant place to while away an afternoon; there's a friendly beach bar where for ridiculously little you can nurse a liter of sangría (bring your own food). In the town itself the principal attraction is a series of **sherry bodegas** — long, whitewashed warehouses flanking the streets and the banks of the river. Until the railroad was extended to Cádiz, all shipments of sherry from Jerez came through Santa Maria, and its port is still used to some extent. Most of the firms offer free tours and tastings to visitors (Tues.–Sat., from around 10am–noon), though this is not a regular process and you need to phone in advance. Choose from *Osborne y Cia* (☎956/861600), *Luis Caballero* (☎956/861300) or, in a beautiful, converted, seventeenth-century convent, *Fernando A. Terry* (☎956/862700). For more details and appointments ask at the tourist office in Cádiz before setting out.

Farther along the coast, beaches are more or less continuous, with two of the best flanking the resorts of Rota and Chipiona. These are both popular weekend retreats from Cádiz, and during July and August pretty much packed out. Whether you want to visit **ROTA**, anyway, any time, however, is debatable. Outside the town is one of the three major U.S. bases in Spain — installed in the 1950s by terms of a deal in which Franco hocked strips of Spanish sovereign territory in return for economic aid and international "respectability." The town, dotted with pancake houses and pizza parlors, is warped in the way you'd expect, and some fairly nasty long-standing resentments between locals and U.S. marines flare up from time to time. Recently, the base was the focus of a protest march by thousands, who formed a human chain around its walls demanding that all bases leased to the U.S. be dismantled. Traveling in this part of Andalucía you will frequently see posters of the same persuasion, with the legend *USA Nos Usa* (The USA Uses Us).

CHIPIONA, at the edge of the next point, is simpler: a small, straightahead seaside resort crammed with family *pensiones*. Older tourists come here for the spa waters, channeled into a fountain at the church of Nuestra Señora de Regla, but for most it's the **beaches** that are the lure. South of the town and lighthouse is the long **Playa de Regla**, where it's easy enough to leave the crowds behind; northeast, towards Sanlucar, are sandbars and rocks. If you're planning on staying in the town the **hostales** along the beach are the most attractive in mid-season you'll need help getting a room from the women who meet new arrivals at the bus station.

Sanlucar de Barrameda

Like Puerto Santa María, SANLUCAR DE BARRAMEDA also has its sherry connections. Set at the mouth of the Guadalquivir, it is the main depot for **Manzanilla** wine, a pale, dry variety much in evidence in the bars (or visit *Bodega Hijos de A. Perez Mejia*, at C. Farina 56; Tues.–Sat. 11am–1pm). It's also the setting for some exciting **horseraces** along the beach in the last two weeks of August, the best time to be here. Otherwise, the town as a whole seems drab and in decline; certainly it belies its history, for from Sanlucar Magellan set out to circumnavigate the globe, and Pizarro to conquer Peru. The few buildings of interest — the **ducal palaces** of Montpensier and Medina Sidonia (the former with wild Gothic decoration), and parts of a Moorish castle — are perched above the main part of town on the Cuesta de Belén.

The best thing, though, is the town's shell-encrusted **river beach**, and warm waters, a couple of kilometers' walk from "downtown" and usually quite deserted. This is flanked, on the opposite shore, by the beginnings of the *Coto Doñana National Park*, whose vast marshy expanses with their strictly regulated access signal the end of the coast road to the west. In order to visit the park (see overpage) you'll need to detour via Sevilla or Huelva to MATALASCAÑAS.

Jerez de la Frontera

JEREZ DE LA FRONTERA, inland towards Sevilla, is the home and heartland of sherry (itself an English corruption of the town's Moorish name — Xerez) and also (less known but equally important) of Spanish brandy. It seems a tempting place to stop, arrayed as it is around the scores of wine *bodegas*. But you're unlikely to want to make more than a quick visit (and tasting) between buses; the town itself is hardly distinctive unless you happen to roll in during one of the two big **festivals** — the May Horse Fair (perhaps the most refined of Andalucian ferias), or the celebration of the vintage towards the end of September.

The **tours of the sherry and brandy processes**, however, can be interesting — almost as much as the sampling that follows — and provided you don't arrive in August (when the industry closes down) there are a great many firms and *bodegas* to choose from. The most central, next to the large but derelict ruins of a Moorish *alcázar*, are **Gonzalez Byass**. Tours are given here, as with most other firms, from Monday to Saturday, 9am to 1pm, and are conducted in English — very much the second language in Jerez's sherry fraternities. Many of the firms were in fact founded by British Catholic refugees, barred from careers at home by the sixteenth-century Supremacy Act, and even now they form a kind of Anglo-Andalusian aristocracy (on display, most conspicuously, at the Horse Fair). The Gonzalez cellars — the *soleras* — are perhaps the oldest in Jerez, and though it's no longer used, preserve an old circular chamber designed by none other than Eiffel (he of the tower).

If you feel you need comparisons, most of the other *bodegas* are on the outskirts of town; pick up a **plan** of them and the town from any local travel agent in the center. For **accommodation**, try *Pension Los Amarillos* (c/ Melina 39) has the cheapest beds. The **train** and **bus stations** are more or less next door to each other, eight blocks east of the *alcázar*/Gonzalez *bodega* and the central Plaza de los Reyes Católicos. The most attractive of the town's buildings, including a small archaeological museum in the Ayuntamiento, are just above this in the **Plaza Asunción**.

Huelva Province: the Coast and Coto Doñana National Park

The **province of Huelva** stretches between Sevilla and Portugal but aside from its section of the Sierra Morena (see preceding section) it's a pretty dull part of Andalucía, laced with large areas of swamp — the *marismas* — and notorious for mosquitoes. This dismal habitat is, however, particularly suited to numerous varieties of birds and wildlife, and over 60,000 acres (the largest roadless area in western Europe) have been fenced off to form the **nature reserve of the Coto Doñana**. Here, amid sand dunes, pine woods, marshes and freshwater lagoons, live scores of flamingos, along with rare buzzards, lynx, mongoose, and a startling variety of migratory birds.

The Doñana Reserve and El Rocío

The seasonal pattern which gives **COTO DOÑANA** its special interest is that of its delta waters, which flood in winter and then drop in the spring, leaving rich deposits of silt, raised sandbanks, and islands. Conditions are perfect in winter for ducks and geese, but spring is most exciting when the exposed mud draws hundreds of flocks of breeding birds. In the marshes and amid the cork oak forests behind you've a good chance of seeing squacco heron, black-winged stilt, whiskered tern, pratincole, sand grouse, as well as flamingos, egrets, and vultures. There are, too, occasional sightings of the Spanish imperial eagle, now reduced to fourteen breeding pairs. In late summer and early autumn, the *marismas* dry out and then support far less bird life. The park is also home to some 25 pairs of lynx.

Matalascañas and Doñana Details

To visit the Doñana involves a certain amount of frustration since at present it's open only to brief, organized **tours** by Land Rover — four hours at a time along one of five charted, seventy-kilometer routes. The starting point for these, and the only place to book them, is **MATALASCAÑAS** (or TORRE DE HIGUERA as it used to be known), a fast-growing beach resort just outside the reserve. For details of the four-hour tours (daily in spring/summer at 8:30am and 5pm; around 1600ptas a seat) call in at the *Centro de Recepción del Acebuche* (☎955/245092 or 430432) on the Matalascañas–Almonte road, about 4km from Matalascañas (*Empresa Damas* bus from c/Segura, near the Plaza de Armas, in Sevilla); reserve places in advance. The tours are quite tourist-orientated, and point out only spectacular species like flamingo, imperial eagle, deer and wild boar. If you're a serious ornithologist and are equally interested in variations on little brown birds, the tour isn't for you. Instead, inquire here — or at the Sevilla office at Avda. de la Constitución 21 (☎954/221440) — about the Doñana **blinds** adjacent to the *Centro* (some readers have found them disappointing, but there's a chance you might see the extremely rare Audouin's gull). You'll need to bring your own binoculars. The natural history exhibition at the *Centro* is in itself worth a visit.

Birds and other wildlife apart, Matalascañas is unlikely to excite; with five large hotel complexes and a concrete shopping center, it looks like it's only just been built (as it has), and it would be difficult to imagine a more complete lack of character. In summer, too, the few **hostal rooms** are generally booked solid and unless you plan in advance (any Sevilla travel agent will try to reserve you a room) you'll probably end up **camping** — either unofficially at the resort itself, or at the vast *Camping Doñana Playa*, 18km down the road towards Huelva. This latter site is a little inconvenient without your own transport if you're planning to take regular trips into the Doñana; if you just want a beach, though, it's not a bad option. PLAYA DOÑANA and its continuation PLAYA MAZAGÓN (with another campground) stretch the whole distance to Huelva, and with hardly another foreign tourist in sight. This route is covered at present by just one daily bus.

El Rocío

The other and more usual approach to Matalascañas is via ALMONTE, a small, unmemorable town, and **EL ROCÍO**, a tiny village of white cottages and a church stockade where perhaps the most famous pilgrimage-fair of the south takes place, annually at Pentecost. This, the **Romería del Rocío**, is an extraordinary spectacle, with whole village communities and local "brotherhoods" from Huelva, Sevilla, and even Málaga, converging on horseback and in lavishly decorated ox carts. Throughout the procession, which climaxes on the Saturday evening, there is dancing and partying, while by the time the carts arrive at El Rocío they've been joined by dozens of busloads of pilgrims. What they have all come for — apart from the fair itself — is the commemoration of the miracle of *Nuestra Señora del Rocío*, (Our Lady of the Dew), a statue found, so it is said, on this spot and resistant to all attempts to move it elsewhere. The image, credited with all kinds of magic and fertility powers, is paraded before the faithful early on the Sunday morning.

El Rocío is a nice place to stay in: wide, sandy streets, and a frontier-like feeling. There are two good **hostales**; the *Hostal Velez* is cheap and comfortable. In the spring, as far as **bird-watching** goes, it's probably the best base in the area. The *marismas* and pinewoods adjacent to the town are crammed with birds, and following tracks east and south east of El Rocío, along the edge of the reserve, you'll see many species (up to a hundred if you're lucky).

Huelva and the Coast Down to Portugal

Large, sprawling, and industrialized, **HUELVA** is perhaps the least attractive and least interesting city of Andalucía. It has claims towards being a *"flamenco* capital" but unless you're really devoted it's unlikely you'll want to stop long enough to check this out. By day — and in the evening as well — the only vaguely enticing thing to do is to take the hourly ferry across the bay to **Punta Umbria**, the local resort. This is hardly an inspiring place either, but it does at least have some life, a fair beach, numerous *hostales*, and a campground.

Really, though, by the time you've reached Huelva it's best either to press on inland to the Sierra Morena or straight **down the coast to Portugal**. You're unlikely to attain nirvana anywhere along the drab stretch of coastline between Huelva and the frontier town of Ayamonte, but there's a good bus and train service along this route and at **AYAMONTE** — itself of little interest, and a very tricky place to find anywhere to overnight — a half-hourly car-and-passenger ferry plies across the estuary and border to VILA REAL DE SAN ANTONIO. From here, a good first night's target in Portugal is TAVIRA, on the Algarve railroad line. Vila Real itself is a hard place to find a room in summer.

Sevilla to Cordoba: Carmona, Osuna, and Ecija

CARMONA has a fifteenth-century tower built in imitation of the Giralda. It's the first thing you catch sight of and sets a tone for the place — which in fact is about right, for the town shares a similar history to Sevilla, less than 30km distant. It was an important Roman city (from which era it preserves a fascinating subterranean necropolis) and under the Moors was often governed by a brother of the Sevillian ruler. Later, Pedro the Cruel built a palace within its castle, which he used as a "provincial" royal residence.

It is today a small, picturesque, and interesting town. The bus drops you right by the old Moorish **Alcázar de Abajo**, a grand and ruinous fortified gateway to the old town. There are a couple of cheap **fondas** and a *casa de huespedes* beside it, and this is also the best area for eating (very few of the bars in the old town offer *tapas*). Inside the walls narrow streets wind up past Mudejar churches and Renaissance mansions. There's a map of Carmona pinned up in the porch of **San Pedro** (the church with the Giralda-type tower). Get your bearings and head uphill to the **Plaza San Fernando** (or

"Plaza Mayor"), modest in size but dominated by splendid Moorish-style buildings. Behind it there's a fruit and vegetable market bustling away most mornings.

Beyond is **Santa María**, a fine Gothic church built over the former main mosque, whose elegant patio it retains; like many of Carmona's churches it is capped by a Mudejar tower, possibly utilizing part of the old minaret. Dominating the ridge of the town are the massive ruins of **Pedro's palace**, destroyed by an earthquake in 1504 and now sheltering a remarkably tasteful *parador*. To the left, beyond and below, the town comes to an abrupt and romantic halt at the Roman **Puerta de Córdoba**, from where the old Córdoba road (now a dirt track) drops down to a vast and fertile plain.

The **Roman necropolis** (guided tours 10am-2pm, closed Mon.) lies on a low hill at the opposite end of Carmona; walking out of town from San Pedro take c/Enmedio, the middle street (parallel to the main Sevilla road) for about 450m. Here, amid the cypress trees, are over 900 family tombs dating from the second century B.C. to the fourth century A.D. Enclosed in subterranean chambers hewn from the rock, the tombs are often frescoed and contain a series of niches in which many of the funeral urns remain intact. Some of the larger tombs have vestibules with stone benches for funeral banquets, and several retain carved family emblems (one is of an elephant, perhaps symbolic of long life). You are guided unhurriedly around this extraordinary site and shown the various types of tombs. Most spectacular is the *Tumba de Servilia* — a huge colonnaded temple with vaulted side-chambers. Opposite tis a partly-excavated **amphitheater**, though as yet it isn't included in the tour.

Osuna

OSUNA (like Carmona and Ecija) is one of those small Andalucian towns which are great to explore in the early evening: slow in pace and enjoyable in a quiet un-sightseeing sort of way, with elegant streets of tiled and white-washed houses interspersed by fine **Renaissance mansions**.

The best of these are in c/Carrera, running down from the Plaza Mayor, and in c/San Pedro which intersects it (no. 16 has a superb geometric relief around a carving of the Giralda). The Plaza Mayor has a marvelous **casino**, with 1920s Mudejar-style decor and a grandly bizarre ceiling — open to all visitors and an excellent place to drink. Beside it is a double arch, through which at c/Asistento Arjona 35 is a cheap and very friendly **fonda**. The town also has two *hostales* in c/Carrera; one of these, *San Puertao*, is about the only place in town that serves meals.

Two huge stone buildings lurk on the hilltop: the old university (suppressed by reactionary Fernando VII in 1820) and the lavish sixteenth-century **Colegiata**. This latter (daily 10am–1:30pm and 3:30– 6:30pm) contains the gloomy pantheon and chapel of the dukes of Osuna, descendants of the kings of León and once "the Lords of Andalucía." Downhill, opposite its entrance, is the baroque convent of **La Encarnación**, which has a fine plinth of ninth-century Sevillian *azulejos* around its cloister and gallery. Both of these and a small archaeological museum which you pass on the way up are open daily from 10am to 1:30pm and from 4:30 to 7:30pm.

Ecija

Sevilla and Córdoba are reputedly the hottest cities of Spain; ECIJA lies midway between them in a basin of low sandy hills. It is known, with no hint of exaggeration, as *la sartenilla de Andalucía* (the frying pan of Andalucia). In mid-August the only possible strategy is to slink from one tiny shaded plaza to another, or with a burst of energy to make for the riverbank.

Ecija is one of the most distinctive and individual towns of the south, with eleven superb and decaying church towers, each glistening with brilliantly colored tiles. It has a unique domestic architecture, too — a flamboyant style of twisted or florid forms, best displayed in the **Calle de los Caballeros**, a whole streetful of mansions and palaces. This is a block or two south of the Plaza Mayor (where the bus stops), but otherwise directions are pretty pointless . . . just follow the towers. Most interesting of the churches is **Santa Cruz**, the old mosque.

A couple of **hostales** are located near the center (*Hostal Santa Cruz*, by the church, is much recommended). Cheaper ones are to be found on the outskirts, off the Sevilla–Córdoba road.

Córdoba

CÓRDOBA stands beside a loop of the once-navigable river Guadalquivir, about 160km farther inland than Sevilla. It is today a minor provincial capital, prosperous in a modest sort of way. Once, however, it was the largest city of Roman Spain, and for three centuries it formed the heart of the Western Islamic Empire, the great medieval Caliphate of the Moors.

From these pasts Córdoba is now principally famous for a single building, the **Mezquita** — the grandest and most beautiful mosque ever constructed by the Moors. This stands right in the center of the city, surrounded by the old Jewish and Moorish quarters, and is a building of extraordinary mystical and aesthetic power. Head for it on arrival and keep returning as long as you stay; it has that rare beauty which increases the more you get to feel and understand it, as of course is proper, since the mosque was intended for daily and regular visiting.

The Mezquita apart, Córdoba itself is a place of considerable charm. It has few grand squares or mansions, tending instead to introverted architecture, calling your attention to the tremendous and often wildly extravagant **patios**. These have long been acclaimed, and they are actively encouraged and maintained by the local council, who run a "Festival of the Patios" in May. The council, incidentally, is staunchly communist, and led by the immensely popular mayor Julio Anguita, currently leader of the national party.

Arrival and Practicalities

Finding your way around is no problem. From the **train station** the broad Avda. del Gran Capitán leads down to the old quarters and the Mezquita; the **Turismo** is at the Palacio de Congresos y Exposiciones in c/Torrijos along-

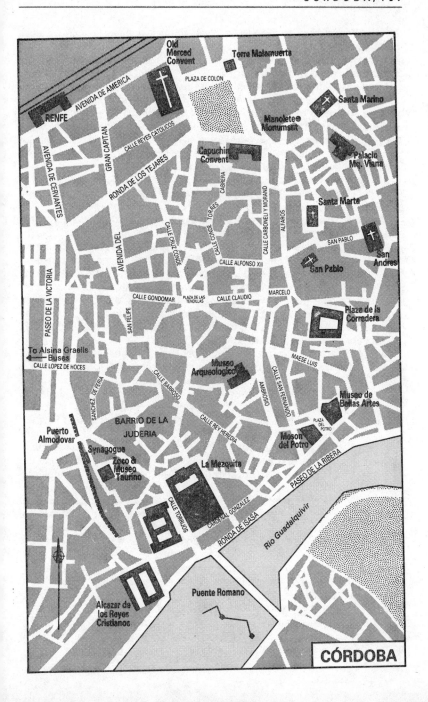

CÓRDOBA

side the Mezquita. There's also a small municipal office in c/Manriquez (mornings only) which gives out an illustrated brochure on places to visit, with a town plan. For information on fringe theatre and music, there's a **cultural center** at Plaza del Potro 10.

Bus terminals are numerous and scattered around the town. The main company, *Alsina Graells*, is at Avda. de Medina Azahara 29, two or three blocks to the west of the Paseo de la Victoria gardens; they run services to and from Sevilla, Granada, and Málaga. For **Sevilla** and **Granada**, you are in fact better off using the trains, which are slightly quicker and cost more or less the same. Going to Granada, however, be sure you take a train via Bobadilla (3 daily; 5 hr.) and *not* via Linares-Baeza (7–11hrs).

The main **Correos** (for *poste restante*) is at c/Cruz Conde 21, parallel to the Avda. del Gran Capitán; **Telefonica** cabins are on Plaza de las Tendillas at the end of this road.

Places to stay are concentrated in the narrow maze of streets above the Mezquita. Try particularly c/Rey Heredia (three *fondas*), c/Romero Barros (the excellent *Fonda Maestre* at no. 16; ☎957/475395), and around. Less obvious, less savory, but likely to have room, are the cheap and very run-down *fondas* in the Plaza de la Corredera. This is a wonderful, ramshackle square, like a decayed version of Madrid's Plaza Mayor, and worth a look whether you stay or not; it hosts a small morning market. Both of the town's **campgrounds** are a little way out. Closest is *Campamento Municipal* (2km to the north on the road to Villaviciosa; regular bus); the other, *Cerca de Largartijo*, is 3km out on the road to Linares.

Bars and **restaurants** are on the whole quite reasonably priced — you need only to avoid the touristy places around the Mezquita, though nearby is a useful self-service with good substantial food (this area is in fact fairly dead in the evenings). There are, however, loads of possibilities in the Judería and in the old quarters off to the right, above the Paseo de la Ribera. One of the best in the former is *El Churrasco* at c/Romero 16 (*not* c/Romero Barros); this has a long-standing reputation for its *churrasco* (a kind of grilled pork dish, served with pepper sauces) and *salmorejo*, a thick Córdoban version of *gazpacho* with hunks of ham and egg; prices to match, sadly. Just around the corner from *El Churrasco*, at the far end of c/Deanes, is a bar full of bullfighting posters which does good cheap food. The *Restaurante La-La-La*, at the junction of c/S. Fernando and the Paseo de la Ribera, has inexpensive set menus. In the middle of the old town on Blanco Belmonte is *El Extremeño*, good for reasonably priced, excellent evening meals, where the enthusiastic owner will guide your choice. There's a good and cheap *vegetarian* restaurant at Plaza del Moreno 3.

For drinking and *tapas*, try *Bar La Mezquita*, a tiny place near the top corner of the mosque. The local barreled **wine** is mainly *Montilla* or *Moriles* — both are magnificent, vaguely resembling mellow dry sherries. The *Solar Plateros* opposite the *Fonda Maestre* specializes in *Montilla*.

Flamenco performances take place at *La Buleria* (c/Pedro López 3, near Plaza de la Corredera) from 9pm on every night; being a cafe-bar there's no entrance fee, but the food and drink are expensive.

Moorish Córdoba and the Mezquita

Córdoba's domination of Moorish Spain began thirty years after the conquest — in 756, when the city was placed under the control of **Abd ar-Rahman I**, the sole survivor of the Umayyad dynasty which had been bloodily expelled from the eastern Caliphate of Damascus. He proved a firm but moderate ruler, and a remarkable military campaigner, establishing control over all but the north of Spain and proclaiming himself *Emir*, a title meaning both "King" and "Son of the Caliph". It was Abd ar-Rahman, also, who commenced the building of the Great Mosque (*La Mezquita*, in Spanish), purchasing from the Christians the site of the Cathedral of St. Vincent (which, divided by a partition wall, had previously served both communities). This original mosque was completed by his son **Hisham** in 796 and comprises about one-fifth of the present building, the first dozen aisles adjacent to the Patio de los Naranjos.

The **Cordoban Emirate**, maintaining independence from the eastern caliphate, soon began to rival Damascus both in power and in the brilliance of its civilization. **Abd ar-Rahman II** (822–52) initiated sophisticated irrigation programs, minted his own coinage, and received embassies from Byzantium. He in turn substantially enlarged the mosque. A focal point within the culture of al-Andalus, this was by now being consciously directed and enriched as an alternative to Mecca; it possessed an original script of the Koran and a bone from the arm of Muhammad, and, for the Spanish Muslim who could not go to Mecca, it became the most sacred place of **pilgrimage**. In the broader Islamic world it ranked third in sanctity after the Kaaba of Mecca and the Al Aksa mosque of Jerusalem.

In the tenth century Córdoba reached its zenith under a new emir — **Abd ar-Rahman III** (912–67), one of the great rulers of Islamic history. He assumed power after a period of internal strife and, according to a contemporary historian, "subdued rebels, built palaces, gave impetus to agriculture, immortalized ancient deeds and monuments, and inflicted great damage on infidels to a point where no opponent or contender remained in al-Andalus. People obeyed en masse and wished to live with him in peace." In 939, with Muslim Spain and part of North Africa firmly under his control, Abd ar-Rahman III adopted the title of "Caliph." It was a supremely confident move and was reflected in the growing splendor of Córdoba, which had become the largest and the most prosperous city of Europe and outshone Byzantium and Baghdad (the new capital of the eastern caliphate) in science, culture, and scholarship. At the turn of the tenth century it had 27 public schools, 50 hospitals (with the first separate clinics for the leprous and insane), 900 public baths, 60,300 noble mansions, 213,077 houses 80,455 shops.

The **development of the Great Mosque** paralleled these new heights of confidence and splendor. Abd ar-Rahman III provided it with a new minaret (which has not survived) 80m high, topped by three pomegranate-shaped spheres, two of silver and one of gold and each weighing one ton. But it was his son **al-Hakam II** (961–76), to whom he passed on a peaceful and stable empire, who was responsible for the most brilliant expansion. He virtually doubled its extent, demolishing the south wall to add fourteen extra rows of columns, and employed Byzantine craftsmen to construct a new *mihrab* or prayer niche; this remains complete and is perhaps the most beautiful example of all Moorish religious architecture.

Al-Hakam had extended the mosque as far to the south as was possible. The final enlargement of the building, under the chamberlain-usurper **al-Mansur** (977–1002), involved adding seven rows of columns to the whole east side. This spoiled the symmetry of the mosque, depriving the *mihrab* of its central position, but Arab historians observed that it meant there were now "as many bays as there are days of the year." They also delighted in describing the rich interior, with its 1293 marble columns, 280 chandeliers and 1445 lamps. Hanging inverted among the lamps were the bells of the pilgrimage cathedral of Santiago de Compostela. Al-Mansur made his Christian captives carry them on their shoulders from Galicia — a process which was to be observed in reverse after Córdoba was captured by Fernando el Santo ("the Saint") in 1236.

The Mezquita

Open daily 8:30am–1:30pm and 3:30–7pm; before 10am entrance free at side doors; prayer niche and cathedral accessible 11am onwards; 250ptas.

As in Moorish times the **Mezquita** is approached through the **Patio de los Naranjos**, a classic Islamic ablutions court which preserves both its orange trees and its fountains for ritual purification before prayer. Originally, when in use for the Friday prayer, all nineteen naves of the mosque were open to this court, allowing the rows of interior columns to appear an extension of the trees. Today, with all but one of the entrance-gates locked and sealed, the image is still there, though subdued and stifled by the loss of those brilliant shafts of sunlight filtering through. The mood of the building has been distorted a little, from the open and vigorous simplicity of the mosque, to the mysterious half-light of a cathedral.

None the less, a first glimpse inside the Mezquita is immensely exciting. "So near the desert in its tentlike forest of supporting pillars," Jan Morris found it, "so faithful to Mahomet's tenets of cleanliness, abstinence, and regularity." The mass of supporting pillars was, in fact, an early and sophisticated innovation to gain height. The original architect had at his disposal columns from the old Visigothic cathedral and from numerous Roman buildings; they could bear great weight but were not tall enough, even when arched, to reach the intended height of the ceiling. His solution (which may have been inspired by Roman aqueduct designs) was to place a second row of square columns on the apex of the lower ones, serving as a base for the semicircular arches that support the roof. For extra strength and stability (and perhaps also to deliberately echo the shape of a date palm, much revered by the early Spanish Arabs) the architect introduced another, horseshoe-shaped arch above the lower pillars. A second and purely aesthetic innovation was to alternate brick and stone in the arches, creating the red and white striped pattern which gives a unity and distinctive character to the whole design.

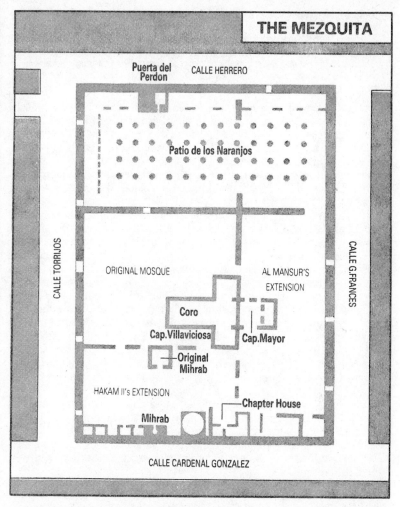

THE MEZQUITA

Puerta del Perdon · CALLE HERRERO

Patio de los Naranjos

CALLE TORRIJOS

ORIGINAL MOSQUE

AL MANSUR'S EXTENSION

CALLE G.FRANCES

Coro

Cap.Villaviciosa

Cap.Mayor

Original Mihrab

HAKAM II's EXTENSION

Mihrab

Chapter House

CALLE CARDENAL GONZALEZ

This uniformity was broken only at the culminating point of the mosque — the domed cluster of pillars surrounding the sacred **Mihrab**, erected under al-Hakam II. The *mihrab* had two functions in Islamic worship: it indicated the direction of Mecca (and hence of prayer) and it amplified the words of the *imam*, or prayer leader. At Córdoba it was also of supreme beauty. As Titus Burckhardt wrote, in *Moorish Art in Spain*:

> *The design of the prayer niche in Córdoba was used as a model for countless prayer niches in Spain and North Africa. The niche is crowned by a horseshoe-shaped arch, enclosed by a rectangular frame. The arch derives a peculiar strength from the fact that its central point shifts up from below. The wedge-shaped arch stones or*

voussoirs fan outwards from a point at the foot of the arch and centres of the inner and outer circumferences of the arch lie one above the other. The entire arch seems to radiate, like the sun or the moon gradually rising over the edge of the horizon. It is not rigid; it breathes as if expanding with a surfeit of inner beatitude, while the rectangular frame enclosing it acts as a counterbalance. The radiating energy and the perfect stillness form an unsurpassable equilibrium. Herein lies the basic formula of Moorish architecture.

Beyond which only details need to be added. The inner vestibule of the niche (which is roped off — forcing you to risk the wrath of the attendants in getting a glimpse) is quite simple in comparison, with a shell-shaped ceiling carved from a single block of marble. The chambers to either side — decorated with exquisite Byzantine mosaics of gold, rust-red, turquoise, and green — constitute the *maksura*, where the caliph and his retinue would pray.

Originally the whole design of the mosque would have directed worshippers naturally towards the *mihrab*. Today, though, you almost stumble upon it, for in the center of the mosque squats a Renaissance **cathedral coro**. This was built in 1523 — nearly three centuries of enlightened restraint after the Christian conquest — and in spite of fierce opposition from the town council. The erection of a *coro* and *capilla mayor*, however, had long been the "Christianizing" dream of the cathedral chapter and at last they had found a monarch — predictably Carlos V — who was willing to sanction the work. Carlos, to his credit, realized the mistake (though it did not stop him from destroying parts of the Alhambra and Sevilla's Alcazar); on seeing the work completed he told the chapter "You have built what you or others might have built anywhere, but you have destroyed something that was unique in the world." To the left of the *coro* stands an earlier and happier Christian addition — the Mudejar **Capilla de Villaviciosa**, built by Moorish craftsmen in 1371 (and now partly sealed up). Beside it are the dome and pillars of the **earlier mihrab**, constructed under Abd ar-Rahman II.

The **belfry**, at the corner of the Patio de los Naranjos, is contemporary with the cathedral addition; rather vertiginously, you can climb it. Close by, the **Puerta del Perdón**, the main entrance to the patio, was rebuilt in Moorish style in 1377. Original "caliphal" decoration (in particular some superb latticework), however, can still be made out in the gates along the east and west sides of the mosque.

The Town

After the Mezquita, Córdoba's other remnants of Moorish — and indeed Christian — rule are not individually very striking. The **river**, though, with its great **Arab waterwheels** and its **bridge** built on Roman foundations, is an attractive area in which to wander. The wheels, and the ruined mills on the riverbank, were in use for several centuries after the fall of the Muslim city, grinding flour and pumping water up to the fountains of the **Alcázar**, or Palace-Fortress. This originally stood beside the Mezquita, on the site now occupied by the **Episcopal Palace**. After the Christian conquest it was rebuilt a little to the west by Fernando and Isabella, hence its name, **"Alcázar** de los Reyes." The buildings (daily 9am–1pm and 5–8pm) are rather drab, having served as the residence of the Inquisition from 1428–1821. They display a few miscellaneous Roman mosaics, unearthed nearby. The gardens, though, are an attractive spot.

Between the Mezquita and the beginning of the Avda. del Gran Capitán lies the **Judería**, Córdoba's old Jewish quarter and a fascinating network of lanes — more atmospheric and less commercialized than that of Sevilla, though souvenir shops are beginning to gain ground. Near the heart of the quarter, at c/Maimonides 18, is a **synagogue**, one of only three in Spain (the other two are in Toledo) that survived the Jewish expulsion of 1492. This one, built in 1316, is minute, particularly in comparison to the great Santa María in Toledo, but it has some fine stucco work elaborating on a Solomon's-seal motif and retains its women's gallery. It is open Tues.–Sun. 9:30am–1pm and 6–8pm, closed Mon; 25ptas.

Nearby is a rather bogus **Zoco** — an Arab *souk* turned into a crafts arcade — and, adjoining this, a small **Museo de Taurino** (Bullfighting Museum; 10am-1pm and 4-7.30pm). The latter is worth a visit, if only for the kitschy nature of its exhibits: row upon row of bulls' heads, two of them given this "honor" for having killed matadors. Beside a copy of the tomb of Manolete — most famous of the city's fighters — is exhibited the hide of his taurine come-uppance, Islero. If bullfighting is your thing, it's possible to go on a guided tour of the city's **bullring** (tours on the hour, 10am–1pm and 4–7pm); complete with distastefully reverential commentary, this includes even the high-tech emergency room. Ask at the *Turismo* for further details.

More interesting, perhaps, and really more rewarding, is the **Archaeological Museum** (open Tues.–Sat. 9am–2pm, 9am–1:30pm Sun., closed Mon.). This is housed in a small Renaissance mansion which, incredibly enough, was found, during the process of its conversion, to incorporate a genuine Roman patio. As a result it is one of the most imaginative and enjoyable small museums in the country, with good local collections from the Iberian, Roman, and Moorish periods. Outstanding is an inlaid tenth-century bronze stag, found at the Moorish palace of Medina Azahara (see below) where it was used as the spout of a fountain.

A couple of blocks below the Archaeological Museum, back towards the river, you'll come upon the **Plaza del Potro**, a fine old square named after the colt (*potro*) which adorns its fountain. This, as local guides proudly point out, is mentioned in *Don Quixote*, and indeed Cervantes himself is reputed to have stayed at the inn opposite, the **Meson del Potro**, which is now used for *artesanía* displays. On the other side of the square is the **Museo de Bellas Artes** (10am–1:30pm and 4–6:30pm) with paintings by Ribera, Valdes Leal, and Zurbaran. Across its courtyard is a small museum (free) devoted to the Córdoban artist **Julio Romero de Torres** (1885–1930), painter of some sublimely dreadful canvasses, most of which depict reclining female nudes with furtive male guitar players.

In the north of town, towards the railroad station, are numerous Renaissance churches — some actually converted from mosques, others owing obvious influence in their minarets — and a handful of convents and palaces. The best of these, still privately owned, is the **Palacio del Marqués de Viana** (Mon, Wed, Sun; guided tours 9am-2pm; ring for entrance).

Medina Azahara

Seven kilometers to the northwest of Córdoba lie the vast and rambling ruins of **MEDINA AZAHARA**, a palace-complex built on a dream-scale by the **Caliph Abd ar-Rahman III**. Naming it after a favorite, az-Zahra (the Radiant), he spent one-third of the annual state budget on its construction each year from 936 until his death in 961. Ten thousand workers and 1,500 mules and camels were employed on the project and the site, almost 2000m long by 900m wide, stretched over three descending terraces. In addition to the palace buildings, it contained a zoo, an aviary, four fishponds, 300 baths, 400 houses, weapons factories, and two barracks for the royal guard. Visitors, so the chronicles record, were stunned by its wealth and brilliance: one conference room was provided with pure crystals, creating a rainbow when lit by the sun; another was built around a huge pool of mercury.

Medina Azahara was a perfect symbol of the western caliphate's extent and greatness, but it was to last for less than a century. **Al-Hakam II**, who succeeded Abd ar-Rahman, lived in the palace, continued to endow it, and enjoyed a stable reign. However, distanced from the city, he delegated more and more authority — particularly to his vizier Ibn Abi Amir, later known as al-Mansur (the Victor). In 976 al-Hakam was succeeded by his eleven-year-old son Hisham II and after a series of sharp moves al-Mansur assumed the full powers of government, keeping Hisham virtually imprisoned at Medina Azahara, even to the extent of blocking up connecting passageways between the palace buildings.

Al-Mansur was equally skillful and manipulative in his wider dealings as a dictator, and Córdoba rose to new heights of prosperity, retaking large tracts of central Spain, and raiding as far afield as Galicia and Catalunya. But with his death in 1002 came swift decline, as his role and function was assumed in turn by his two sons. The first died in 1008; the second, Sanchol, showed open disrespect for the caliphate by forcing Hisham to appoint him as his successor. At this a popular revolt broke out and the caliphate disintegrated into civil war and a series of feudal kingdoms. Medina Azahara was looted by a mob at the outset and in 1010 was plundered and burned by retreating Berber mercenaries.

The Site
Open 10am–1:45pm and 4–5:45pm; closed Mon. and Sun. pm.

For centuries the site continued to be looted as a building quarry; parts, for instance, were used in the Sevilla Alcázar. But in 1944 excavations unearthed the fallen-in materials from a crucial part of the palace — the **Royal House**, where guests were received and meetings of ministers held. It has been meticulously reconstructed, and though still fragmentary, its main hall must rank among the greatest of all Moorish rooms. It has a different kind of stucco work than that at Granada or Sevilla — closer to natural and animal forms in its intricate Syrian *Hom* (Tree of Life) motifs. Unlike the later

Spanish Arab dynasties, the Berber Almoravides and the Almohads of Sevilla, the caliphal Andalucians were little worried by Islamic strictures on the portrayal of nature, animals, or even men — the beautiful hind in the Córdoba museum is a good example — and it may well have been this aspect of the palace that led to such zealous destruction during the civil war.

This reconstruction of the palace gives a scale and focus to the site. Elsewhere you have little more than foundations to fuel your imaginings, amid an awesome area of ruins, hiden beneath bougainvillea and rustling with cicadas. Perhaps the most obvious of the outbuildings yet excavated is the **mosque**, just beyond the Royal House, which sits at an angle to the rest of the buildings in order to face Mecca.

To reach Medina Azahara, follow the Avda. de Medina Azahara out of town, on to the road to VILLARUBIA and POSADAS. About 4km out of town, make a right turn, after which it's another two or three kilometers. Alternatively, a bus from the Calle de la Bodega station will drop you off at the intersection for the final three-kilometer walk. Hitching back into town is easy if you walk back to the turnoff.

EAST: JAÉN, GRANADA, AND ALMERÍA

There is no more convincing proof of the diversity of Andalucía than these eastern provinces: **Jaén**, with its rolling, olive-covered hills; **Granada**, dominated by Spain's highest peaks, the Sierra Nevada; and **Almería**, waterless and in part semidesert.

Granada, a prime target of any Spanish travels, is easily enough reached by train or bus from Sevilla, Córdoba, Ronda, Málaga, or Madrid. And when you've exhausted the city, there are dozens of possibilities, perhaps most enticing being hikes in the **Sierra Nevada** and its lower southern slopes, **Las Alpujarras**. The **Almería beaches**, the least developed of the Spanish Mediterranean, are also within striking distance of Granada and Málaga.

Jaén is slightly isolated from these routes but if you're coming down to Granada from Madrid you might want to consider stopping over in the small towns of **Úbeda** or **Baeza**, served on the main railroad line by their shared station of Linares-Baeza. For a longer stay in the area, a bus from Úbeda takes you to **Cazorla** and its neighboring national park.

Jaén, Baeza, and Úbeda

There are said to be over 150 million olive trees in the **province of Jaén**. They dominate the landscape as infinite rows of green dots against the orange-red earth, occasionally interspersed with stark white farm buildings. It is beautiful is on a grand, sweeping scale, though one concealing a bitter and entrenched economic reality. The majority of the olive groves are owned by a mere handful of families, and for most residents this is a very por area.

Jaen

JAEN, the provincial capital and by far the largest town, is an uneventful sort of place. No particular sights, either, beyond an imposing Renaissance cathedral and the shell of a Moorish castle (now a *parador*). If you stay, there are cheapish places around the Plaza de José Antonio (in the middle of town) and good fish bars one block away in c/Nueva. The **tourist office** (maps), **provincial museum** (extensive but unexceptional archaeological and fine art collections), and **train station** are positioned along the main *avenida*. The bus station stands back a block, halfway down, by the Parque de la Victoria.

Far more appealing are the towns of BAEZA and UBEDA, less than an hour's bus ride from Jaén. Rarely visited, they are elegant and relaxing places to stop over and explore. Each has an extraordinary density of exuberant Renaissance palaces and richly endowed churches, plus fine public squares. Both were captured from the Moors by Fernando el Santo and, repopulated with his knights, stood for two centuries at the frontiers of the Reconquest facing the Moorish kingdom of Granada. The implanted nobles fought constant duels (a favored place of battle being Baeza's Alcázar — until Isabella had it demolished) and strove to outdo each other in the grandeur and extravagant facades of their mansions.

Baeza

BAEZA is tiny, compact, and provincial, with a perpetual-Sunday air about it. At its heart is a combined Plaza Mayor and Paseo, flanked by cafes and very much the hub of the town's limited animation.

The **Plaza de Leones**, an appealing cobbled square enclosed by Renaissance buildings, stands slightly back at the far end. Here, on a rounded balcony, the first mass of the Reconquest is reputed to have been celebrated; the mansion beneath it houses the **Turismo**, who hand out an English-language walking-tour brochure of the town. Finest of Baeza's palaces is that of the **Marqueses de Jabalquinto**, now a seminary, with an elaborate "Isabelline" front (showing marked Moorish influence in its stalactite decoration). Just above it is the sixteenth-century **Cathedral** which, like many of Baeza and Úbeda's churches, has brilliant painted *rejas* (iron screens) by one Maestre Bartolome, a local craftsman. In the cloister part of the old mosque has been uncovered, but the cathedral's real novelty is a huge silver *custodia* — cunningly hidden behind a painting of St. Peter which whirls aside for a 25-peseta coin.

There are some nice **wandering routes** in town: up through the Puerta de Jaén on the Plaza de los Leones and along the Paseo Murallas/Paseo de don Antonio Machado takes you around the edge of Baeza and gives good views over the surrounding plains. While you're in that direction, **El Abuelo**, a house on the Paseo de don Antonio Machado, is worth a glance for its garden sculpture and towering wrought-iron work. It's the first house past the bronze bust of Antonio Machado looking out over the olive groves. You can cut back to the Plaza Mayor via the network of narrow stone-walled alleys — with the occasional arch — that lie behind the cathedral. Going farther afield, near El Abuelo, some tracks lead down to the plain. Take the right-hand fork and after about 45 miutes you'll come to the right-of-way of a former railroad line, now used as a road for farm vehicles. This offers scope for easy walks across country.

Baeza has two cheapish **places to stay**: The *Fonda Adriano* is a gem of a building, an old Renaissance mansion set around a once-open courtyard (now enclosed) with a wood-beamed dining hall. The alternative is the *Hostal Comercio* at c/San Pablo 21, a main road at the end of the central square. Both places serve evening meals — handy as the town has few restaurants. The *Adriano* is at c/Conde Romanones 13, near the Plaza de Leones, but there is no sign above, nor is the street named, and you'll probably need to ask directions.

Úbeda

ÚBEDA, 9km east of Baeza, looks less promising on arrival. It's a larger town, and arrival at the bus station deposits you in the midst of an uninspiring modern suburb. Don't be put off. Follow the signs to the *Zona Monumental* and you'll eventually wind up at the **Plaza de Vázquez de Molina**, a tremendous Renaissance square which immediately overshadows anything in Baeza.

Most of the buildings around this square were the late sixteenth-century work of Andres de Vandaelvira, the architect of Baeza's cathedral, numerous churches in both towns, and the huge Hospital de Santiago that you pass here on your way to the center. At one end of the plaza he built a palace for Felipe II's secretary; it is now the Ayuntamiento and houses a **Turismo**. At the other end Vandaelvira erected the church of **El Salvador**, though this was actually designed by Diego de Siloe (architect of the Málaga and Granada cathedrals). The finest church in Úbeda, its highlight is a gilded, brilliantly animated *retablo* of the Transfiguration; to enter you have to go through the sacristy at the side — ring for the caretaker at the fine doorway in the white wall.

Behind El Salvador, Úbeda comes to a sudden and scenic halt. In the other direction is the Plaza del Generalissimo with a good *raciones* bar and the idiosyncratic church of **San Pablo** — with a thirteenth-century balcony (a popular feature in Úbeda) and various Renaissance additions. The other church worth seeking out is **San Nicolás**, some way to the north, which has an incredibly sinister, "sculpted" chapel whose effect is only partially offset by a life-size, plastic choirboy. Nearby, just behind the market at c/ Trillo 10, is a *casa de huespedes*. Most of the other **accommodation** options are grouped around the main **bus station** in Avda. de Ramón y Cajal, behind the Hospital de Santiago; only the *parador* (in Plaza de Molina) is in the old part of town.

Transportation

The nearest **train station** to both Úbeda and Baeza is LINARES-BAEZA, 13km from Baeza (connecting bus for most trains, except on Sundays). Otherwise, you're dependent on buses. There's a service from Baeza to Úbeda at 8am (15 min.), and from Úbeda to Córdoba (going on to Sevilla) at 9am. If you're coming from Granada, there's a 1pm departure, stopping at Jaén for half an hour, and then arriving in Baeza at 4:15pm.

Cazorla and the National Park

Three buses a day (10am, 1:30pm, and 6:15pm) go from UBEDA to CAZORLA. After a few kilometers the bus turns off the main road to head south, passing through olive country and crossing the Guadalquivir River. The village, at an elevation of 700m, huddles toward the top a valley which runs from the rugged limestone cliffs of the *Peña de los Halcones*. This rocky bluff, with its wheeling buzzards and occasional eagle, marks the southwestern edge of a vast protected area, the **Cazorla National Park**, containing the Sierras of Cazorla and Segura and the headwaters of the Guadalquivir. It's not as lofty as the Sierra Nevada (the highest peaks are 2000m), but outdoes it for beauty, slashed as it is by river gorges, and largly covered in forest. There's practically no public transportation in the park so to explore it well you'll need a car or to be prepared for long hikes; otherwise day trips to the outskirts of the park are possible. Cazorla can also be reached by bus from Jaén, and by daily bus from Granada (currently leaves at 2:30pm, arriving 7:30pm).

Cazorla

During the reconquest of Andalucía **CAZORLA** acted as an outpost for Christian troops. Nowadays, the two castles which dominate the village testify to its turbulent past — both were originally Moorish but later altered and restored by their Christian conquerors.

Arrival is somewhat inauspicious as the main road climbs between concrete apartment buildings, disgorging you into the busy, commercial Plaza de la Constitución (where the privately-run **tourist information center** is located). But look up, and there are staggering vistas to the backdrop of mountains.

A few minutes' walk along the main street (c/de Muñoz) leads to a second square, the Plaza de la Corredera (or *del huevo*, "of the egg," because of its shape). This is traditionally the meeting place for the *señoritos*, the class of landowners and their descendents who, through influence and privilege, still lay claim to the most important jobs and mold local destiny. The seat of the administration, the Ayuntamiento, is here too — a fine Moorish-style palace standing at the far end of the plaza.

Beyond, you reach a labyrinth of narrow twisting streets, and Cazorla's liveliest square, the **Plaza Santa María**. This takes its name from the old cathedral which, having been damaged by floods in the seventeenth century, was later torched by Napoleonic troops. Its ruins, now preserved, and the fine open square form a natural amphitheater for concerts and local events as well as being the popular meeting place. The square is dominated by **La Yedra**, the austere, reconstructed tower of the lower of two castles, which houses the village museum and is well worth a visit. There's a fine view from just above the plaza of the castle perched on its rock.

Practicalities

Cheapest place to stay is the *Pension Taxi*, up the steps opposite the bus and taxi stop; as a resident, you can also eat very inexpensively in their *comedor*. The most pleasant accomodation, also reasonably cheap, is the *Hostal Guadalquivir*, down the steps to the right just as you enter the middle plaza — it's spotlessly clean and very friendly, though disconcertingly close to the municipal slaughterhouse for those with sensitive ears.

Several spit-and-sawdust bars with good *tapas* cluster around the Plaza Santa María, along with the rustic restaurant *Meson la Cueva* which offersau- thentic local food cooked on a wood-fired range but reheated, discreetly, in a microwave. Other places where you can eat well and cheaply are the two *mesones* on Plaza de la Corredera; the one next to the church is excellent value and the other prepares exquisite fish — both serve *raciones*, not meals as such. The only other restaurant in town — avoid the one attached to the *Hotel Cazorla* — is the expensive *La Sarga*, opposite the market. There are two discos (weekends only) and several "pubs" with loud music. At Easter there's the fiesta de Cristo del Consuelo, with fairgrounds, fireworks, and religious processions; the occasion is more private and less professional than in big cities.

The National Park

Judging from the number of *Capra hispanica* (Spanish mountain goat), deer, wild pig, birds, and butterflies that even the casual visitor is likely to spot, the Cazorla reserve is fulfilling its role handsomely. Ironically, though, much of the best wildlife viewing will be at the periphery, or even outside of the park, since the wildlife is most successfully stalked on foot and walking opportuni- ties within the park itself are surprisingly limited.

There are in fact only three signposted trails, all pitifully short. One leads from the Empalme de Vadillo to the Puente de la Herrera via the Fuente del Oso (2km one-way), another of about 1700m curls around the Cerrada (Narrows) de Utrero near Vadillo-Castril village; the best marked segment, through the lower Barossa gorge (see below), is also a mere 1700m long. Public transportation into the park is sparse, and distances between points are enormous. Such problems are complicated by the fact that most of the *camping libre* (free camping) areas shown on the 1:100,000 tourist map of the region have been closed recently; one still-functioning is to be found beyond El Tranco on the dam. There is more accommodation at Coto Ríos (see below), with three privately-run campgrounds and a succession of *hostales* .

Before heading into the park, stop at the tourist office in Cazorla village to buy either the 1:100,000 map entitled *Parque Natural de las Sierras de Cazorla y Segura*, or the 1:50,000 quad called "Cazorla." The staff is friendly but information given out, especially that pertaining to independent ramblings, should be taken with a grain of salt; the office exists to promote nature tours, jeep excursions, photo safaris, and the like, so they have an interest in getting visitors to sign on for their services.

Day Trips from Cazorla

Wild and relatively unspoiled country, with fine panoramas west over the olive plain of Jaén, begins at the edge of Cazorla village, and if you choose to base yourself there, you can make a number of good **day trips**.

Just over an hour's walk away (head up behind the fountain on Plaza Santa María, then pick up the mule track which skirts the hill topped by the ruined upper castle of *Cinco Esquinas*) is the intriguing sixteenth-century **Monasterio de Monte Sion**. Two of the brothers who worked on its reconstruction remain there, and they will show you proudly around their home. Be prepared to step back into the Middle Ages — as exemplified by the scourges hanging over the bed in the cells used for retreat. Another hours' walk beyond the cloister will bring you to the base of **Gilillo**, highest point in the southwest of the park, with a yawning gorge to the right.

You can follow the main trail over a pass from here to a dilapidated *casa forestal* and then down to **Cañada de las Fuentes**, source of the Guadalquivir, within another two hours. Alternatively — and a more feasible day hike — you might bear left at the saddle onto a trail descending towards Cazorla town thorugh the **canyon of Riogazas**. This path ends in a jumble of tractor tracks after an hour, and then you must pick your way down through the various water works for another hour and a half. This five-hour walking day allows ample time for dawdling, but unfortunately many of the pools in the stream on the descent are either difficult to get to or on private property.

Coto Ríos

Two daily **buses** link Cazorla town with **COTO RÍOS** in the middle of the park: one at 6:30am, the other at 2pm, with the latter returning from Coto at 5:30pm.

Taking the early departure allows you to do the **classic walk along the Río Barrosa** as a day hike. Get off the bus at Torre de Vinagre, where there's a visitors center and where the route begins. Cross the Guadalquivir on a low causeway which is a bridge or a ford, depending on the season; 2km after your pass a trout hatchery, and just beyond this is a parking lot where all private vehicles must be left.

From here follow the jeep track along the northwest (true right) bank of the Barrosa, swift and cold even in summer. Within a few minutes a signposted footpath diverges to the right; this also marks the beginning of the **gorge**. Two or three wooden bridges now take the trail back and forth across the river, which is increasingly confined by sheer rock walls. At the narrowest points the path is routed along planked catwalks which are secured to the limestone cliff. The walk from Torre de Vinagre to the end of the narrows takes about two hours.

There the footpath rejoins the jeep road; after another half hour's walk you'll see a turbine and a long metal pipe bringing water from **two lakes** — one natural, one a small dam — up the mountain. The road crosses one last bridge over the Barrosa and stops at the turbine house. When you get to a gate, beyond which there's a steeply rising gulley, count on another full hour up to the lakes. Cross a footbridge and start the steep climb up a narrow track over the rocks below the cliff (at one point the path passes close to the base of the palisade — beware falling stones). At the top of the path is a cavernous ampitheater, where a cascade falls in winter. The trail ends about half way up the cliff, where an artificial tunnel has been bored through rock walk through it to get to the lake.

Allow three and a half hours' walking time from Torre del Vinagre, slightly less going down. It's a very full day's excursion but you should have plenty of time to catch the afternoon bus back, which passes the visitors' center at 5pm.

Granada

If you see only one town in Spain it should be **GRANADA**. For here, extraordinarily well preserved and in a tremendous natural setting, stands the **Alhambra** — the most exciting, sensual, and romantic of all European monuments. It was the palace-fortress of the Nasrid Sultans, rulers of the last Spanish Moorish kingdom, and in its construction Moorish art reached a spectacular and serene climax. But the building seems to go further than this, revealing something of the whole brilliance and spirit of Moorish life and culture. There's a haunting passage in Jan Morris's book, *Spain*, which the palace almost embodies: ". . . Life itself, which was seen elsewhere in Europe as a kind of probationary preparation for death, was interpreted [by the Moors] as something glorious in itself, to be ennobled by learning and enlivened by every kind of pleasure."

Moorish History

Granada's glory was always precarious. It was established as an **independent kingdom** in 1238 by **Ibn Ahmar**, a prince of the Arab Nasrid tribe which had been driven south from Zaragoza. He proved a just and capable ruler but all over Spain the Christian kingdoms were in the ascendance. The Moors of Granada survived only through paying tribute and allegiance to Fernando III of Castile — whom they were forced to assist in the conquest of Muslim Sevilla — and by the time of Ibn Ahmar's death in 1275 theirs was the only surviving Spanish Muslim kingdom. It had, however, consolidated its territory (stretching from just north of the city down to a coastal strip between Tarifa and Almería) and, stimulated by refugees, developed a flourishing commerce, industry, and culture.

By a series of shrewd manoeuvers Granada maintained her autonomy for two and a half centuries, its rulers turning for protection, in turn as it suited them, to the Christian kingdoms of Aragón and Castile and to the Merinid Muslims of Morocco. The city-state enjoyed a particularly confident and prosperous period under **Yusuf I** (1334–54) and **Mohammed V** (1354–91), the sultans responsible for much of the existing Alhambra palace. But by the mid-fifteenth century a pattern of coups and internal strife became established and a rapid succession of rulers did little to stem Christian inroads. In 1479 the kingdoms of Aragón and Castile were united by the marriage of Fernando and Isabella and within ten years had conquered Ronda, Málaga, and Almería. The city of Granada now stood completely alone, tragically

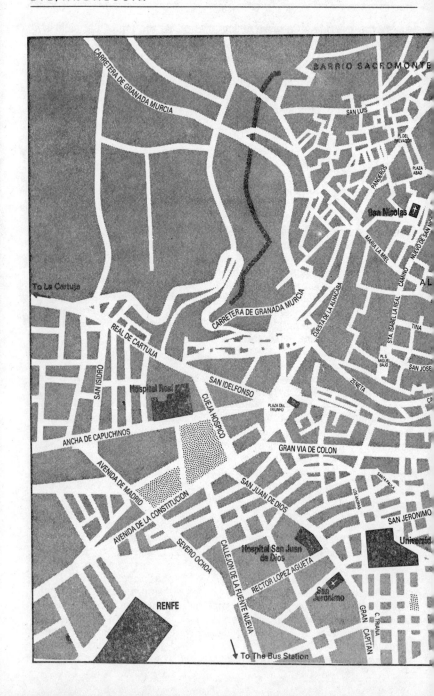

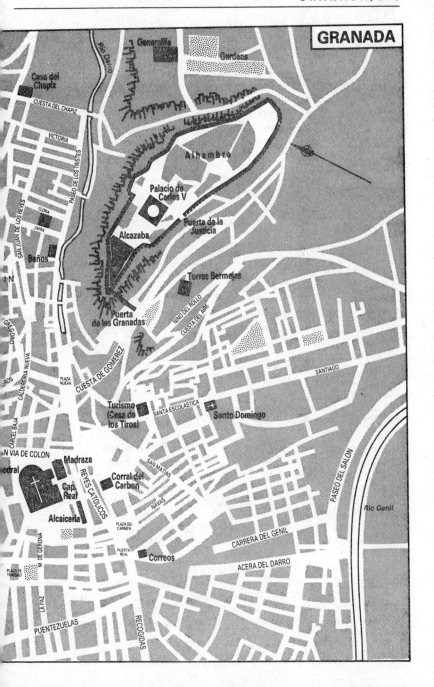

GRANADA

Casa del Chapiz

Generalife

Gardens

Río Darro

CUESTA DEL CHAPIZ

VICTORIA

PASEO DE LOS TRISTES

Alhambra

SAN JUAN DE LOS REYES

GLORIA

ZAFRA

Baños

Palacio de Carlos V

Alcazaba

Puerta de la Justicia

GREGORIO

CALDERERÍA NUEVA

Torres Bermejas

Puerta de las Granadas

NIÑO DEL ROLLO

CUESTA DEL AIRE

CÁRCEL BAJA

PLAZA NUEVA

CUESTA DE GOMEREZ

SANTIAGO

Turismo (Casa de los Tiros)

SANTA ESCOLÁSTICA

Santo Domingo

N VIA DE COLON

Madraza

REYES CATOLICOS

Corral del Carbon

SAN MATIAS

cdral

Cap. Real

Alcaicería

NAVAS

PASEO DEL SALON

Río Genil

Mª DE GERONA

PLAZA DEL CARMEN

CARRERA DEL GENIL

PLAZA DE TRINIDAD

PUERTA REAL

Correos

ACERA DEL DARRO

LA PAZ

PUENTEZUELAS

RECOGIDAS

preoccupied in a **civil war** between supporters of the Sultan's two favorite wives. The *Reyes Católicos* made escalating and finally untenable demands upon it, and in 1490 war broke out. **Boabdil**, the last Moorish king, appealed in vain for help from his fellow Muslims in Morocco, Egypt, and Ottoman Turkey, and in the following year **Fernando and Isabella** marched upon Granada with an army said to total 150,000 troops. For seven months, through the winter of 1491, they laid siege to the city. On January 2, 1492, Boabdil formally surrendered its keys. The Christian Reconquest of Spain was complete.

The Alhambra

There are three distinct groups of buildings on the Alhambra hill: the **Casa Real** (Royal Palace), the palace gardens of the **Generalife**, and the **Alcazaba**. This latter, the fortress of the eleventh-century Ziridian rulers, was all that existed when Ibn Ahmar made Granada his capital, but from its reddish walls the hilltop had already taken its name; *al-Hamra* in Arabic means literally "the red." Ibn Ahmar rebuilt the Alcazaba and added to it the huge circuit of walls and towers which form one's first view of the castle. Within the walls he began a palace, which he supplied with running water by diverting the river Darro nearly five miles to the foot of the hill; water is an integral part of the Alhambra and this engineering feat was Ibn Ahmar's greatest contribution. The Royal Palace was essentially the product of his fourteenth-century successors, particularly Mohammed V, who built and redecorated many of its rooms in celebration of his accession to the throne (in 1354) and conquest of Algeciras (in 1369).

After their conquest of the city **Fernando and Isabella** lived for a while in the Alhambra. They restored some rooms and converted the mosque but left the palace structure unaltered. As at Córdoba and Sevilla, it was their grandson **Emperor Carlos V** who wreaked the most insensitive destruction. He demolished a whole wing of rooms in order to build yet another grandiose Renaissance palace. This and the Alhambra were simply ignored by his successors and by the eighteenth century the Royal Palace was in use as a prison. In 1812 it was taken and occupied by **Napoleon's forces**, who looted and damaged whole sections of the palace, and on their retreat from the city tried to blow up the entire complex. Their attempt was thwarted only by the action of a crippled soldier who remained behind and removed the fuses.

Two decades later the Alhambra's "rediscovery" began, given impetus by the American writer **Washington Irving**, who set up his study in the empty palace rooms and began to write his marvelously romantic *Tales of the Alhambra* (on sale all over Granada — and good reading amid the gardens and courts). Shortly after its publication the Spaniards made the Alhambra a **National Monument** and set aside funds for its restoration. This continues to the present and is now a highly sophisticated project, scientifically removing the accretions of later ages in order to expose and meticulously restore the Moorish creations.

Approaches — and Admission

The standard **approach** to the Alhambra is along the Cuesta de Gomérez, the road which climbs uphill from Granada's central Plaza Nueva. After a few hundred meters you reach the **Puerta de las Granadas**, a massive Renaissance gateway erected by Carlos V. Here two paths diverge to either side of the road: the one on the right climbs up towards a group of fortified towers, the **Torres Bermejas**, which may date from as early as the eighth century. The left-hand path leads through the woods past a huge terrace-fountain (again courtesy of Carlos V) to the main entrance of the Alhambra. This is the **Puerta de la Justicia**, a magnificent tower-gateway which forced three changes of direction, making intruders hopelessly vulnerable. It was built by Yusuf I in 1340 and preserves above its outer arch the Koranic symbol of a key (for Allah the Opener) and an outstretching hand whose five fingers represent the five Islamic precepts: prayer, fasting, alms-giving, pilgrimage to Mecca, and the oneness of God.

Within the citadel stood a complete "government city" of mansions, smaller houses, baths, schools, mosques, barracks and gardens. Of this only the **Alcazaba fortress** and the **Royal Palace** remain; they face each other across a broad terrace (constructed in the sixteenth century over a dividing gully), flanked by the majestic though incongruous **Palace of Carlos V**.

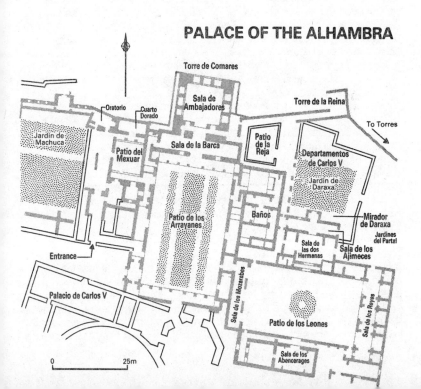

PALACE OF THE ALHAMBRA

Within the walls of the citadel, too, are a fairly expensive buffet **restaurant/bar**, the beautiful **Parador San Francisco** (a converted monastery, where Isabella was originally buried — walk in for a drink), and a three-star **hostal** (the *America*, ☎958/227471; reservations essential). There are a handful of drink stalls around, too, including one, very welcome, in the Portal gardens (towards the Carlos V Palace after you leave the Casa Real). No one, however, seems to mind if you take a bottle of wine into the Generalife and cool it in one of the fountains — and this is perhaps the best way to enjoy and appreciate the luxuriance. See "Practialities" for shops to fix up a picnic.

Admission to the complex (open in summer Mon.–Sat. 9:30am–8:30pm, 9:30am–5:45pm out of season, Sun. 9:30am-5:30pm) costs 425ptas (any discount price is only for Spanish students or those studying in Spain) but is free on Sunday afternoons after 3pm. The tickets have tear-off slips for each part (Alcazaba, Casa Real, Portal and Torres, Generalife) and these you can use over two consecutive days. The two museums in the Palace of Carlos V have separate admission fees of 75ptas. In season the Alhambra is additionally open from 10pm until midnight on Wednesday and Saturday nights (guided tour only and increased price), and there are also occasional concerts held in its courts.

The Alcazaba

The Alhambra palace-complex can get drastically overcrowded in mid-season, with tour buses disgorging their customers at 9:31am on the dot, and the best time to visit the principal rooms is between 2 and 4pm, when most of the tour groups are at lunch. Likewise, 4 to 8pm is not a bad time for visiting, since many coach tours have gone.

Ideally, anyway, it's best to start with the earliest, though most ruined part of the fortress — the Alcazaba — where you can get a grip on the whole site. At its summit is the **Torre de la Vela**, named after a huge bell on its turret which until recent years was rung to mark the irrigation hours for workers on Granada's vast and fertile plain. It was here, at 3pm on January 2, 1492, that the Cross was first displayed above the city, alongside the royal standards of Aragón and Castile and the banner of St. James. Boabdil, leaving Granada for exile in the Alpujarras, turned and wept at the sight, earning from his mother Aisha the famous rebuke: "Do not weep like a woman for what you could not defend like a man".

The **Aljibe**, an underground cistern beneath the area between the Alcazaba and Casa Real, is open for viewing on Monday, Wednesday and Friday from 9:30am to 1:30pm.

The Casa Real (Royal Palace)

It is amazing that the Casa Real has survived, for it stands in utter contrast to the strength of the Alcazaba and the encircling walls and towers. It was built lightly and often crudely from wood, brick, and adobe, and was designed not to last but to be renewed and redecorated by succeeding rulers. Its buildings show a brilliant use of light and space but they are principally a vehicle for ornamental stucco decoration. This, as Titus Burckhardt explains in *Moorish Culture in Spain*, was both an intricate science and a philosophy of abstract art in direct contrast to pictorial representation:

> With its rhythmic repetition, [it] does not seek to capture the eye to lead it into an imagined world, but, on the contrary, liberates it from all pre-occupations of the mind. It does not transmit any specific ideas, but a state of being, which is at once repose and inner rhythm.

Burckhardt adds that the way in which patterns are woven from a single band, or radiate from many identical centers, served as a pure simile for Islamic belief in the oneness of God, manifested at the center of every form and being.

Arabic inscriptions feature prominently in the ornamentation. Some are poetic eulogies of the buildings and builders, others of various sultans (notably Mohammed V). Most, however, are taken from the Koran, and among them the phrase *Wa-la ghaliba illa-Llah* ("There is no Conqueror but God") is tirelessly repeated. It is said that this became the battle cry of the Nasrids upon Ibn Ahmar's return from aiding the Castilian war against Muslim Sevilla; it was his reply to the customary, though bitterly ironic greetings of *Mansur* ("Victor").

Wa-la ghaliba illa-Llah

stylised inscription from the Alhambra

The palace is structured in three parts, each arrayed around an interior court and with a specific function. The sultans used the **Mexuar**, the first series of rooms, for business and judicial purposes. In the **Serallo**, beyond, they received embassies and distinguished guests. The last section, the **Harem**, formed their private living quarters and would have been entered by no one but their family or servants.

The Mexuar

The council chamber, the main **reception hall** of the Mexuar, is the first room you enter. It was completed in 1365 and hailed (perhaps formulaically) by the court poet Ibn Zamrak as a "haven of counsel, mercy, and favor". Here the sultan heard the pleas and petitions of the people and held meetings with his ministers. At the room's far end is a small oratory, one of a number of prayer niches scattered around the palace and immediately identifiable by their distinctive alignment (to face Mecca).

This "public" section of the palace, beyond which few would have penetrated, is completed by the Mudejar **Golden Room** (decorated under Carlos V, whose Plus Ultra motif appears throughout the palace) and the **Patio of the Mexuar**. This has perhaps the grandest facade of the whole palace, for it admits you to the formal splendor of the Serallo.

The Serallo

The Serallo was built largely to the design of Yusuf I, a romantic and enlightened sultan who was stabbed to death by a madman while worshipping in the Alhambra mosque. Its rooms open out from delicate marble-columned arcades at each end of the long **Court of the Arrayanes** (Myrtles).

At the court's north end, occupying two floors of a fortified tower, is the royal throne room, known as the **Hall of the Ambassadors**. As the sultan could only be approached indirectly it stands at an angle to the entrance from the Mexuar. It is the largest room of the palace, perfectly square and completely covered in tile and stucco decoration. Among the web of inscriptions is one that states simply "I am the Heart of the Palace." Here Boabdil signed the terms of his city's surrender to the Catholic kings, whose motifs (the arms of Aragón and Castile) were later worked into the room's stunning wooden dome, a superb example of *lacería*, the rigidly geometric "carpentry of knots." Here too, so it is said, Fernando met with Columbus to discuss his plans for finding a new sea route to India — which led to the discovery of the Americas. The dome itself, in line with the mystical-mathematical pursuit of medieval Moorish architecture, has a complex symbolism representing the seven heavens. Carlos V tore down the rooms at the southern end of the court; from the arcade there is access to the gloomy **Chapel Crypt** of his palace which has a curious "whispering gallery" effect.

The Harem

The **Court of the Lions**, which has become the archetypal image of Granada, constitutes the heart of the harem section of the palace. The stylized and archaic-looking lions beneath its fountain probably date, like the patio itself, from the reign of Mohammed V, Yusuf's successor; a poem inscribed on the bowl tells how much fiercer they would look if they weren't so restrained by respect for the sultan. The court was designed as an interior garden and planted with shrubs and aromatic herbs; it opens on to three of the finest rooms in the palace, each of which looks directly on to the fountain.

At the far end is the **Hall of the Kings**, whose dormitory alcoves preserve a series of unique paintings on leather. These, in defiance of Koranic law, represent human scenes; it's believed that they were painted by a Christian artist in the last decades of Moorish rule. However the most sophisticated rooms, apparently designed to give a sense of the rotary movement of the stars, are the two facing each other across the court. The largest of these, the **Hall of the Abencerrages**, has the most startlingly beautiful ceiling in the Alhambra: sixteen-sided, supported by niches of stalactite vaulting, lit by windows in the dome and reflected in a fountain upon its floor. This light and airy quality stands at odds with its name and history, for here Abu'l-Hasan (Boabdil's father) murdered sixteen princes of the Abencerrage family, whose chief had fallen in love with his favorite, Zoraya; the rust stains in the fountain are popularly supposed to be the indelible traces of their blood.

The **Hall of the Two Sisters**, across the patio, is more mundanely named — from two huge slabs of marble in its floor — but just as spectacularly decorated, with a dome of over 5000 "honeycomb cells." It was the principal room of the sultan's favorite, opening onto an inner apartment and balcony, the

Mirador de Daraxa (Eyes of the Sultana); the romantic garden patio below was added after the Reconquest.

Beyond, you are directed along a circuitous route through **apartments** redecorated by Carlos V (as at Sevilla the northern-reared emperor installed fireplaces) and later used by Washington Irving. Eventually you emerge at the **Peiñador**, or *Queen's Tower*, a pavilion that served as an oratory for the sultanas and as a dressing room for the wife of Carlos V; perfumes were burned beneath its floor and wafted up through a marble slab in one corner.

From there, passing the **Patio de la Reja** (Patio of the Grille) added in the seventeenth century, you reach the **Royal Baths**. These are tremendous, decorated in rich tile mosaics and lit by pierced stars and rosettes once covered by colored glass. The central chamber was used for reclining and retains the balconies where singers and musicians — reputedly blind to keep the royal women from being seen — would entertain the bathers.

Towers and the Palacio Carlos V

Before leaving the palace compound a number of the **towers** are worth a look. Most are richly decorated — particularly the first, the **Torre de las Damas** — which stands in front of its own patio (restored to the original design). The usual exit is through the courtyard of **Carlos V's palace**, where bullfights were once held. The palace itself (begun in 1526 but never finished) seems totally out of place here, but is in fact a distinguished piece of Renaissance design — the only surviving work of Pedro Machuca, a one-time pupil of Michelangelo. On its upper floors is a forgettable *Museo de Bellas Artes*; on the lower, currently closed for repairs but otherwise open from 10:30am to 3pm, is a small collection of *Hispano-Moorish Art*, its highlight the beautiful fifteenth-century "Alhambra vase." These museums are officially closed on Monday, but frequently fail to open on other days.

The Generalife

Paradise is described in the Koran as a shaded, leafy garden refreshed by running water where the "fortunate ones" may take their rest under tall canopies. It is an image which perfectly describes the **GENERALIFE**, the gardens and summer palace of the sultans. Its name means literally "garden of the architect" and the grounds consist of a luxuriantly imaginative series of patios, enclosed gardens, and walkways.

By chance an account of the gardens during Moorish times, written rather poetically by a Moorish historian called Ibn Zamrak, survives. The descriptions that he gives aren't all entirely believable, but they are a wonderful basis for musing as you lie around by the patios and fountains. There were, he wrote, celebrations with horses darting about in the dusk at speeds that made the spectators rub their eyes (a form of festival still indulged in at Moroccan *fantasías*); rockets shot into the air to be attacked by the stars for their audacity; tightrope walkers flying through the air like birds; men bowled along in a great wooden hoop, shaped like an astronomical sphere . . .

Today, devoid of such amusements, the gardens are still evocative — above all, perhaps, the **Patio de los Cipreses**, a dark and secretive walled garden of sculpted junipers where the Sultana Zoraya was suspected of meeting her lover Hamet, chief of the unfortunate Abencerrajes. Nearby, too, is the inspired flight of fantasy of the **Camino de los Cascadas**, a staircase with water flowing down its stone balustrades. This is just above the wonderful little **Summer Palace** itself, with its various decorated belvederes.

From just below the entrance to the Generalife the **Cuesta del Rey Chino** — an alternative route back to the city — winds down towards the river Darro and the old Arab quarter of the Albaicín (see below).

The Albaicín and Around the Town

If you're spending just a couple of days in Granada it is hard to resist using both of them in the Alhambra. It takes a distinct readjustment and effort of will to appreciate the city's later Christian monuments, while the modern parts of town, where you'll arrive by train or bus, are no more interesting than usual. There are, however, a handful of minor Moorish sites and, climbing up from the Darro, the run-down medieval streets of the **Albaicín**, the largest and most characteristic Moorish quarter that survives in Spain.

The Albaicín and other Moorish Remains

The Albaicín stretches across a fist-shaped area bordered by the river, the Sacromonte hill, the old town walls, and the winding Calle de Elvira (parallel to the Gran Vía de Colón, the main avenue which bisects central Granada). The best approach is along the Corredera del Darro, beside the river. At no. 31 in this street are the remains of **Baños Arabes**, marvelous and very little-visited Moorish public baths; for admission, ring for the caretaker who may or may not be there (and will be more cooperative before 2pm). At no. 43 is the **Casa de Castril**, a Renaissance mansion (currently closed for restoration) which houses the town's surprisingly mundane **Archaeological Museum**. Beside the museum a road ascends to the church of San Juan (with an intact, thirteenth-century minaret) and to **San Nicolás**, whose square offers a view of the Alhambra considered to be the best in town.

Outside the Albaicín are the two most interesting Moorish mansions: the **Corral del Carbón**, a fourteenth-century *caravanserai* (an inn where merchants would lodge and, on the upper floors, store their goods), and the **Casa de los Tiros**, actually built just after the Reconquest, and which now houses the tourist office — except (as in recent years) when it's closed for repairs. The Corral del Carbón is a little tricky to find; it's down an alleyway off the c/de los Reyes Catolicos, opposite the **Alcaiceria**, the old Arab silk bazaar, burned down in the nineteenth century and tackily restored to house an arcade of souvenir shops.

Perhaps the most interesting Moorish building in the lower town, though, and oddly one of the least well-known, is the so-called **Palacio Madraza**, a strangely-painted building opposite the Capilla Real. Built in the early fourteenth century, this is a former Islamic college (*medressa* in Arabic) and retains part of its old prayer hall, including a magnificently decorated *mihrab*. It is open somewhat sporadically for exhibitions; you may have to knock for admission.

The Capilla Real, Cathedral, and Churches

The **Capilla Real** (Royal Chapel; daily 11am–1pm and 4–7pm; 100ptas) itself is an impressive building, flamboyant late Gothic in style and built ad hoc in the first decades of Christian rule as a mausoleum for *Los Reyes Católicos*, the city's "liberators." The actual tombs are in fact as simple as could be imagined: Fernando and Isabella, flanked by their daughter, Joana ("the Mad"), and her husband Felipe ("the Handsome"), resting in lead coffins placed in a plain crypt. But above them — the response of their grandson Carlos V to what he found "too small a room for so great a glory" — is a fabulously elaborate monument, with sculpted Renaissance effigies of all four monarchs. In front is an equally magnificent *reja*, the work of Maestre Bartolomeo of Baeza, and an altarpiece which depicts Boabdil surrendering the keys of Granada.

Isabella, in accordance with her will, was originally buried on the Alhambra hill (in the church of San Francisco, now part of the *parador*) but her wealth and power proved no safeguard of her wishes; recently the candle that she asked should perpetually illuminate her tomb was replaced by an electric bulb. In the capilla's **Sacristy** is displayed the sword of Fernando, the crown of Isabella, and an outstanding collection of medieval Flemish paintings — including important works by Memling, Bouts, and Van der Weyden — and various Italian paintings, including works by Botticelli and Pedro Berruguete.

For all its stark Renaissance bulk, Granada's **Cathedral**, adjoining the Capilla Real and entered from the door beside it, is a disappointment. It was begun in 1521, just as the Capilla was finished, but was then left uncompleted well into the eighteenth century.

Nevertheless the city has some fine churches, and with sufficient interest you could quite easily fill a day of visits. North of the cathedral, ten minutes' walk along c/San Jerónimo, is the baroque **San Juan de Dios**, with a spectacular *retablo*, and attached to a majestically portalled hospital (which is still in use). Close by is the elegant Renaissance **Convento de San Jerónimo** (10am–1:30pm and 4–7pm), founded by the Catholic kings though built after their death.

Lastly, on the northern outskirts of town, is the **Cartuja**, perhaps the grandest and most outrageously decorated of all the country's lavish Carthusian monasteries. It was constructed at the height of baroque extravagance — some say to rival the Alhambra — and has a chapel of staggering wealth, surmounted by an altar of twisted and colored marble. Open from 10am to 1pm and from 4 to 7pm, it's a further ten- to fifteen-minute walk beyond San Juan de Dios.

Granada Practicalities

Virtually everything of interest in Granada — including the hills of **Alhambra** (to the east) and **Sacromonte** (to the north) — is within easy walking distance of downtown. The only times you'll need a bus are arriving and leaving, since bus and train stations are both some way out.

The **train station** is a kilometer or so off our map, on the Avda. de Andaluces (continuation of Avda. Calvo Sotelo); to get in or out of town take bus #11 which runs a circular route: inbound on the Gran Vía de Colon and back out via the Puerta Real and Camino de Ronda. The easiest stop is by the cathedral on the Gran Via (take it from across the road heading out). Bus #4 also runs between the train station and Gran Vía. For the **main bus station** — the *Alsina Graells* terminal on the Camino de Ronda — the #11 bus is also your best bet, though you'll be coming around in the other direction so get off or pick it up at the Puerta Real. It stops on the same side of road as the *Alsina Graells* station whether it's coming from, or going to, the center of Granada.

Alsina Graells runs the **bus services** to Jaén, Úbeda, Córdoba, Sevilla, Málaga, Alpujarras (high and low), Motril, Almería and the coast. The three most obvious destinations which require other terminals are: north side of Sierra Nevada (*Empresa Bonal*, Avda. Calvo Sotelo 19), Guadix (*Empresa Autedia*, c/Rector Martín 10, off Avda. Calvo Sotelo) and Valencia/Alicante (*Empresa Bacoma* near the railroad station). Full details — and of much else too — are posted on the walls of the **Turismo**, normally in the *Casa de los Tiros* (c/de Paveneras 19); open Mon-Fri 9.30am-2pm and 5-7.30pm, Sat 9.30am-2pm; temporarily moved to c/Libreros 2, by the Cathedral, off Pl. Bibirramblas).You can buy **maps and guides** for the Sierra Nevada there also, though for a wider selection try the *Librería Dauro* at c/Zacatín 3 (a pedestrian street between the cathedral and c/Reyes Católicos).

Finding a Place to Stay

The **Gran Vía** is the main street of Granada, cutting its way through the middle of town. It forms a 'T' at its end with **c/Reyes Católicos**, which runs left (east) to the **Plaza Nueva** and right (west) to the **Puerta Real**, the city's two main squares.

Finding a **place to stay** in this area is easy, even in season, and prices are no higher than elsewhere in Spain. Try the streets to either side of the Gran Vía, at the back of the Plaza Nueva, around the Puerta Real and Plaza de Carmen (particularly c/de Navas), the Pl. de la Trinidad in the university area, or along the Cuesta de Gomarez, which leads up from the Plaza Nueva towards the Alhambra.

Hostales and **pensiones** are so plentiful around here — and turnaround of guests so regular — that individual places aren't really worth detailing. Two pensiones that are easily missed, however, lie on the far side of the Darro River (across the first bridge after the church on the east end of Pl. Nueva). One is a marked, friendly *casa de husepedes* at the top of the staircase leading from the bridge; the other, unsigned, is at Santa Ana 11 just to the right at the top of the step. Neither is very grand, but they are beautifully situated, and (rare in Granada) quiet. Don't bother trying to find "interesting" accommodation in the Albaicín area — there are no *hostales* there.

The city's **youth hostel**, in the outskirts at Camino de Ronda 171, is open from July through September. If you arrive late, it has some virtue, being only a five-minute walk from the train or bus stations, but it's insititutional and unfriendly. Nearby, alongside the football stadium, is the closest **campground**, *Camping Sierra Nevada*, easiest reached from downtown on the #3 bus. If you want a room near the railroad station, the *Hostal Turin* (Ancha de

Capuchinos 16; ☎958/200311), off the Jardines del Triunfo, is cheap and well-run.

See also the Alhambra, for details of the *hostal* within the citadel.

Drinking and Eating

The star attraction among Granada's bars is undoubtedly the unnamed **bodega** on the corner of c/Elvira and c/Almireceros, near the top of the Gran Vía, opposite the cathedral. It isn't signed outside but is easily recognizable by its windows, painted in nineteenth-century Romantic style with rural drinking scenes. The drink to drink there — and which will get you pointed in the bar's direction at the very drop of its name — is *Kalicasas*, a quite amazing cocktail devised from a little of everything they have. The bar also does excellent *bocadillos* (very cheap) as well as a good variety of barreled wine. When it closes you might feel like moving on to *La Buhardilla* (again no sign; on c/Silleria nearby), about the only bar in the downtown area that stays open **late**, or to one of the places around the university (down towards San Jeronimo). In term time, lots of students hang out in **pubs** near the bus station around the Campo del Principe, a square on the eastern slopes of the Alhambra. The open-air cafes on Plaza Nueva are a nice place to spend the evening and there's a couple of good bars towards the Puerta de Elvira. Or try the bars along Gran Capitán or San Juan de Dios at the other end of town.

For **snacks** on the hoof, the city has numerous possibilities. You can get North African dishes for a moderate sum at *Al-Andaluz*, on Plaza Nueva, and all of Granada seems to get their nocturnal ice cream scoops at *La Perla*, at no. 16 across the square. Pizza by weight, croissants, and pies are sold at *Croissanterie la Petite*, on Plaza del Carmen (corner of c/Salamanca), and for committed cultural imperialists there's a *Cookie Man* stall on Puerta Real. **Hippie-kitsch** enthusiasts might enjoy the North African tea house (joss sticks and all) on c/Caldereria Nueva, just off c/Elvira. Just next door there's a more middle-of-the road place, *Al-Faquara*, serving juices, teas, and crepes to the accompaniment of classical music. Directly across the street, at no. 8, *Panadero Loco* is a **health-food** store stocking such items as whole-grain bread, granola, oriental cooking supplements, etc. In fact the entire lengthy of c/Caldereria Nueva is a bonanza for natural/Moroccan/traditional Spanish groceries, and picnics for Alhambra visits are easily assembled from ingredients here.

For straightforward meals, two of the best **restaurants** downtown — neither especially cheap — are *El Meson* (Plaza Gamboa 2, behind the Ayuntamiento; good for classic Granada food like *habas y jamon*), and *Cunini* (c/Pescaderia 9, off c/Principe behind the Alcaiceria, mainly fish). Several other moderately expensive restaurants are to be found near *El Meson*, around the back of the Ayuntamiento. If you want to splash out, a very good Arab restaurant, *El Amir* at General Narvaez 3, has delicious hummus and falafel, dishes made of rice and ground meat with pine nuts and cinnamon, or meatballs in a spicy sauce. Even more exotic (for Spain, anyway) is the Indian vegetarian restaurant at c/Cruz 2. There's also a vegetarian restaurant, *Raices*, at Pablo Picaso 11, unimaginative for food, though they have wonderful fresh fruit juices.

Other, relatively **inexpensive** food is to be found all over Granada. Most authentic perhaps, on the Plaza San Miguel Bajo in the Albaicín, are two very good *bar/mesones*, plus two adjacent cafes, with a predominantly student clientèle. In the warren of streets between Plaza Nueva and Gran Vía, good value places include the *Nueva Bodega* and *Restaurante León*. Try also the *Gargantua* on Placeta Silleria 7 near Reyes Católicos, or the *Cafeteria-Restaurante La Riviera* on c/Cetti-Meriem in the same neighborhood; the latter features a good *menú economica*, including a vegetarian option. Numerous bars in the same area meet any desire for simpler *tapas* and *raciones*. One last nucleus of cheap eateries is the area around Plaza del Carmen (near the Ayuntamiento) and along c/Navas leading away from it. Just southwest of c/Nava, in the nearby Plaza Mariana Pineda, the cafe-bar *Sampedro* has *tapas* and, next door, the *Bar Gambino* has a *comedor* which serves good roast chicken.

Sacromonte

Like many cities of Andalucía, Granada lays claim to the roots of **flamenco**. Certainly it does have an old and still considerable gypsy population, from whose clans many of Spain's best guitarists, dancers, and singers have emerged.

Traditionally the gypsies inhabit cave homes on the **Sacromonte hill**, and many still do, giving displays of *zambras* to the tourists. These can occasionally be good, though more often they're straight-faced and fabulously shameless rip-offs: you're hauled into a cave, leered at if you're female, and systematically extorted of all the money you've brought along (for dance, the music, the castanets, the watered-down sherry . . .). The simple solution is to take only as much money as you want to part with. Turn up mid-evening; the lines of caves begin off the Camino de Sacramonte, just above the Casa del Chapiz (center top on our map). When the university is in session, the cave dwellings are turned into **discos**, packed with students at weekends. A flamenco venue promoted by the tourist board and to be avoided at all costs is the *Jardin de Neptuno*.

For revelations of a different kind wander up here a little earlier and take a look at the old caves — most of them deserted after severe floods in 1962 — on the far site of the old Moorish wall.

The Sierra Nevada

South from Granada rise the mountains of the **SIERRA NEVADA**, a startling backdrop to the city, snowcapped for much of the year and offering skiing from November until late May. The ski slopes are at **Solynieve**, an unimaginative, developed resort just 28km away (40 min. by bus). Here, except in August, the direct automobile route across the range stops, but from this point you can make the two-to-three-hour hike up to **Veleta** (3470m), the second highest peak of the range — a perfectly feasible day trip from Granada by bus.

The Sierra Nevada is particularly rich in **wildflowers**. Some fifty varieties are unique to these mountains, among them five gentians, including *Gentiana bory*, the pansy *Viola nevadensis*, a shrubby mallow *Lavatera oblongifolia*, and a spectacular honeysuckle, the seven-to-ten-meter-high *Lonicera arborea*. **Wildlife** abounds away from the roads; one of the most exciting sights is the *Cabra hispanica*, a wild horned goat which you'll see standing on pinnacles, silhouetted against the sky. They roam the mountains in herds and jump up the steepest slopes with amazing agility when they catch the scent of the walker on the wind. Birdwatching is also superb, with the colorful hoopoe — a bird with a stark, haunting cry — a common sight.

The best **map** of the Sierra Nevada and of the lower slopes of the Alpujarras (see the section following) is that coproduced by the *Instituto Geográfico Nacional* and the *Federación Española de Montañismo* (1:50,000), generally available in Granada. Marc Dubin's *Spain on Foot* (Mountaineers Books; forthcoming) has detailed route descriptions for both the Sierra Nevada and the Alpujarras.

The Veleta/Mulhacen Ascents and Solynieve

Throughout the year *Autocares Bonal* run a **bus from Granada** to the Solynieve resort and, just above this, to the *Parador de Sierra Nevada*. The bus leaves from the Carrera de Genil (top of Avda. José Antonio, above the Puerta Real) at 9am, returning from the *parador* at 5pm (and passing Solynieve 10 minutes later).

From the *parador* the **Capileira-bound road** actually runs past the **peak of Veleta**; the dirt surface is perfectly hikable even when it's closed to cars. On the way an enterprising roadside vendor dispenses gin and tonic from a bucket of snow. Allow two to three hours up to Veleta from where the bus drops you, two hours down.

If you have a car you can, in summer, drive on over to Capileira (see "Las Alpujarras" following). With a great deal of energy you could conceivably hike the route, though it's a good 25km, there's nothing along the way, and this being the highest motorable pass in Europe, temperatures drop pretty low by late afternoon. An hour beyond Veleta you pass just under **Mulhacen** (the tallest peak at 3481m), two hours of exposed and windy ridge-crawling from the road, and with a sudden, sheer drop on its northwest face, but a gentler slope down to the Siete Lagunas valley to the east.

SOLYNIEVE is a hideous-looking ski-resort — worse than usual — and regarded by serious Alpine skiers as something of a joke. But with snow lingering so late in the year (Granada's *Turismo* should be able to advise on the state of this, or you could contact the *Federacion Andaluz de Esqui*, Paseo de Ronda 78, ☎958/250706), it does have obvious attractions. At least you can have fun. From the middle of the resort an escalator takes you straight up to the main ski lift, which provides access to most of the higher **slopes**, and when the snow is right you can ski a few kilometers back down to the *zona hotelera*. The cheapest **places to stay** are the *Peñonas San Francisco* (just off the main road, ☎958/480122) and, up towards the *parador*, the *Albergue Universitario*; both offer half or full pension.

Ruta de los Tres Mil (High Peaks Traverse)

The classic, full-length, three-to-four day itinerary (the latter figure will apply to most hikers) starts in Jeres del Marquesado on the north side of the Sierra Nevada and finishes in Lanjarón, in the Alpujarras. The longer period entails overnights near Puntal de Vacares; in the Siete Lagunas valley noted above; at the Felix Mendez shelter; and at the Cerro Caballo hut. Slightly shorter, and more practicable, variations involve a start from the Vadillo refuge in the Estrella valley (northwest of Vacares), or from Trévelez in the Alpujarras, and a first overnight at Siete Lagunas.

Whichever way you choose, be aware that the section between Veleta and Elorrieta calls for rope, an ice ax (and crampons before June), and good Class 4 scrambling skills. (There is another difficult section between Peñon Colorado and Cerro de Caballo). If you're not up to this it is possible to detour around the Veleta–Elorrieta section, but you will end up on the ridge flanking the Lanajarón river valley on the *east* rather than on the *west*; here there is a single cement hut (the *Refugio Forestal*) well-placed for the final day's walk to Lanjarón.

The *ruta integral de los tres mil* (complete traverse of all the Sierra's peaks over 3000m high), as the Spanish mountaineers call it, is probably a bit beyond the capabilities of most walkers, but a modified version, starting in Trévelez and ending in Lanjarón (with the detour noted above), is quite feasible though strenuous.

Ascending Mulhacén from Trévelez is a full six hours up one-way, four hours down — assuming that you do not get lost or rest (both unlikely) and that there is no snowpack on Mulhacén's east face (equally unlikely until July). If you decide to try, be prepared for an overnight. Heading out of Trévelez, make sure that you begin on the higher track over the Crestón de Posteros, to link up with *acequias* (irrigation channels) coming down from the top of the Río Culo Perro (Dog's Ass River) valley; if you take the main, tempting trail which goes toward Jeres del Marquesado, and then turn into the mouth of the Río Culo Perro, you face quagmires and thorn-patches that beggar belief. The standard place to camp is in the Siete Lagunas valley below the peak, allowing an early morning ascent to the summit before the mists come up.

Continuing the traverse, you can drop down the west side of Mulhacen (take care on this awkward descent) to the jeep road coming from Veleta. Follow this toward Veleta, and you can turn off the road to make a second overnight at Felix Méndez hut (main area not open until after spring snow-melt, meal service thereafter; the hut's annex with four bunks should always be open). Moving on, to the west, plan on a third night spent at either Cerro Caballo or the *Refugio Forestal*, depending on your capabilities.

For any exploration of the Sierra Nevada, do take a tent, and ample food, in any case. If you cannot reach or find the huts (which are marked correctly on the 1:50,000 map), and the weather turns nasty, you could be in for some unpleasantness.

Las Alpujarras

The road **south from Granada to Motril** climbs steeply after leaving the city, until at 860m above sea level it reaches the **Puerto del Suspiro del Moro** — the Pass of the Sigh of the Moor. Boabdil, last Moorish king of Granada, came this way, having just handed over the keys of his city to the *Reyes Católicos* (see "The Alhambra"). From the pass you catch your last glimpse of the city and the Alhambra. To the east, through a narrow defile, lie the great **valleys of the Alpujarras**, first settled in the twelfth century by Berber refugees from Sevilla, and later the Moors' last stronghold in Spain.

The valleys are bounded on the north by the Sierra Nevada, and on the south by the lesser sierras of Lujar, La Contraviesa, and Gador. The eternal snows of the high sierras keep the valleys and their seventy or so villages well watered all summer long. Rivers have cut deep gorges in the soft mica and shale of the upper mountains, and over the centuries have deposited silt and fertile soil on the lower hills and in the valleys; here the villages have grown, for the soil is rich and easily worked. The intricate terracing that today preserves these deposits was begun perhaps as long as 2000 years ago by Visigoths or Ibero-Celts, whose remains have been found at Capileira. The Moors carried on the tradition, and modified the terracing and irrigation in their inimitable way. They transformed the Alpujarras into an earthly paradise, and there they retired to bewail the loss of their beloved lands in al-Andalus. After the fall of Granada, many of the city's Muslim population settled in the villages, and there resisted a series of royal edicts demanding their forced conversion to Christianity. In 1568 they rose up in a final, short-lived revolt, which led to the expulsion of all Spanish Moors. Even then, however, two Moorish families were required to stay in each village to show the new Christian peasants, who had been marched down from Galicia and Asturias to repopulate the valleys, how to operate the intricate irrigation systems.

Through the following centuries, the valley settled to an impoverished existence, with the land falling into the hands of a few wealthy families, and the general population becoming impoverished laborers. The civil war passed lightly over the Alpujarras; the occasional truckload of Nationalist youth trundled in from Granada, rounded up a few bewildered locals, and shot them for "crimes" of which they were wholly ignorant; Republican youths came up in their trucks from Almería and did the same thing. Under Franco the stranglehold of the landlords increased and there was real hardship and suffering. Today, the population has one of the lowest per capita incomes in Andalucía, with — as a recent report put it — "a level of literacy bordering on that of the Third World, alarming problems of desertification, poor communications, and a high degree of underemployment."

Ironically, the land itself is still very fertile — oranges, chestnuts, bananas, apples, and avacados grow here — while the recent influx of **tourism** is bringing limited wealth to the region. The so-called "High" Alpujarras have become popular with Spanish tourists; Pampaneira, Bubión, and Capileira, all within half an hour's drive from Lanjarón, have been scrubbed and whitewashed. Though a little over-prettified, they're far from spoiled, and have acquired shops, lively bars, good unpretentious restaurants, and small, family-run pensions. Other villages, less picturesque, or less accessible, have little employment, sustained only by farming. Bayacas, for instance, at the bottom of the Río Chico valley above Órjiva, has neither bar nor shop.

Approaches: Lanjarón and Órjiva

The most straightforward **approach to the Alpujarras** is to take the Lanjarón turning off the Granada–Motril road; coming from the south, bear right at Velez Benaudalla, and continue straight to Órjiva, the market town of the region. There are several buses a day from both Granada and Motril to Lanjarón and Órjiva, and one a day from Almería in the east. There's also a bus which goes to Úgijar, in the "Low" Alpujarras, from Granada, via a less scenic route through Lanjarón, Órjiva, Torvizcón, Cadiar, Yegen, and Valor; about four hours to the end of the line. A bus direct to the High Alpujarras leaves the main Granada bus station at 1:30pm daily. It goes via Trévelez as far as Murtas; in the other direction it passes Berchules at 7:15am, Trévelez at 8am, arriving in Granada at noon.

Lanjarón

LANJARÓN has known tourism and the influence of the outside world for longer than anywhere else in the valley, good enough reason perhaps for passing straight through to the higher villages. Its attraction is the curative powers of its waters, sold in bottled form throughout Spain, Between June and October the spa baths are open, and the town fills with the aged and infirm. The place itself is little more than a ribbon of buildings, mostly modern, along the road. Below, marking Lanjarón's medieval status as the gateway to the Alpujarras, is a Moorish castle, now dilapidated and barely visible. A ten-minute stroll reveals its dramatic setting — follow the signs down the hill from the main street and out onto the terraces and meadows below the town.

The countryside and mountains within a day's walk of Lanjarón, however, are beyond compare. Walk up through the back streets behind the town and you'll come across a track that takes you steeply up to the vast spaces of the **Reserva Nacional de la Sierra Nevada.** For a somewhat easier dayhike out of Lanjarón, go to the bridge over the river just east of town and take the sharply climbing cobbled track which parallels the **river.** After two to two and a half hours through small farms, with magnificent views and scenery, a downturn to a small stone bridge permits return to Lanjarón on the opposite bank. Allow a minimum of six hours, including snack-stops and contingencies.

There's no shortage of **hotels and restaurants** in the town. The grand-looking *Hostal España* (☎958/770187) is very good, cheap, and friendly, and the *Bar Galvez* offers inexpensive accommodation and excellent meals. *Bar Suizo* looks like a Swiss tea-room; the fare is excellent. For a quieter spot there's the *Pensión El Mirador* (☎958/770181), a kilometer to the east of town. Midway along the main street is the *Alsina Graells* bus terminal.

Órjiva

Eleven kilometers east from Lanjarón is ÓRJIVA (also spelled Órgiva), the "capital" of the western Alpujarras. It is closer to the heart of the valley but still really a starting point; if the bus goes on to Capileira, you may want to stay on it. If you're **driving** it's worth noting that this is the last stop for gasoline before Cadiar or Ugijar.

Órjiva is a lively enough town, though, with a local produce market on Thursdays, and a number of good **bars and hotels**. Choose from among the *Fonda Simon* and the *Pension Nemesis* facing each other across the road; a *fonda* above the *Bar Ortega*; and a *comidas/camas* next to the *Alsina Graells* office. More luxurious, and not a lot pricier, is the *Hostal Mirasol* (☎958/785159), which also does good *tapas* and reasonable *menus* inside or on their terrace. On the main street is a sixteenth-century Moorish palace which today houses various shops; in its proportions and design it still has a certain beauty. A yoga center, *Cortijo Romero*, just 1km east of Órjiva, often has programs of shiatsu and other activities besides yoga — a sign of the times hereabouts. Órjiva, and surrounding farms and villages, have recently attracted a growing band of expatriate "New Age" Europeans, including the odd English shepherd.

The mountain behind Órjiva is the **Sierra de Lujar**, running into the **Sierra la Contraviesa**. The whole range of hills on the south side of the valley was once densely forested, indeed many years ago the whole of the Alpujarras were well covered with trees, But in 1980 a great forest fire swept for miles along the hillsides, scorching the life from the trees but leaving the wood undamaged; tens of thousands of acres of forest were ruined overnight. It's believed that a pulp paper company paid hoodlums to start the fire — the next day they were buying up the dead trees at a fraction of the real price.

The High (Western) Alpujarras

From Lanjarón, a bus leaves daily at 2:30pm and winds through all the upper Alpujarran villages; hitching, too, is generally good in these rural areas, though cars are few and far between.

Alternatively, if you're inclined to walk — the best way to experience the High Alpujarras — there are a number of paths tbetween Órjiva and Cadiar. Ideally, to avoid getting lost, equipped yourself with the copublished IGN/FEM 1:50,000 map, which covers all the territory from Órjiva up to Berja, and a compass.

Hiking: the Camino Real

A half a century ago the **Camino Real** (Royal Way), a mule track that threaded through all the high villages, was the only access into the Alpujarras. Today what little that's left of it is quiet, used only by the occasional local mule or foreign walker. At their best Alpujarran trails follow mountain streams, penetrate thick woods of oak, chestnut, and poplar, or cross flower-spangled meadows; in their worse moments they deteriorate to incredibly dusty firebreaks, forestry roads, or tractor tracks, or (worse) dead-end in impenetrable thickets of bramble and nettle. Progress is slow, grades are sharp, the heat (between mid-June and September) taxing, and a reasonable knowledge of Spanish is a big help.

For the determined, the most rewarding **sections of trails** include:

Capileira to Bubion: Various sections survive, totalling roughly four hours, but interrupted twice by *acequias* and a new jeep road.

Pitres to Mecina Fondales: Twenty minutes trail, and then a good hour-plus trail from neighboring Ferreirola to Busquistar.

Busquistar toward Trévelez: One hour of trail, and then two-plus hours of road walking.

Portugos toward Trévelez: Two hours' trail, hitting the asphalt a little beyond the end of the Busquistar trail.

Trévelez to Berchules: Four hours trail, but the middle two hours is jeep track.

Trévelez to Juvíles: Three hours trail, including some sections of firebreak.

Cañar, Soportujar, and Carataunas

Walking out from Órjiva, the first settlements you reach, almost directly above the town, are **CAÑAR** and **SOPORTUJAR**. Like many of the High Alpujarran villages, they congregate on the neatly terraced mountainside, planted with poplars and laced with irrigation channels. Both have bars where you can get a **meal and a bed** for the night; both are perched precariously on the steep hillside with a rather somber view of Órjiva in the valley below, and the mountains of Africa over the ranges to the south. Cañar has a sixteenth-century church in a terrible state of disrepair. Just below the two villages, the tiny hamlet of **CARATAUNAS** is particularly pretty, though it has nowhere to stay.

If you have stopped for an amble in these three villages you will by now be familiar with the curious **architecture of the region**. The houses are flat-roofed, low, and built of grey stone; the whitewashing is a recent innovation. Few could afford *cal* (lime) fifty years ago, but now both locals (and tourists) insist on it. The coarse walls are about 750cm thick, for coolness and protection from winter storms. Stout beams of chestnut, or ash in the lower valleys, are laid from wall to wall; on top of these is a mat of canes or split chestnut; upon this flat stones are piled, and on the stones is spread a layer of *launa*, the crumbly grey mica found on the tops of the Sierra Nevada. It must, and this maxim is still observed today, be laid during the waning of the moon for the *launa* to settle and compact properly and thus keep rain out. Gerald Brenan wrote in *South from Granada* of a particularly ferocious storm: "As I peered through the darkness of the stormy night, I could make out a dark figure on every roof in the village, dimly lit by an esparto torch, stamping clay into the holes in the roof."

The Poqueira Gorge and up to Capileira

Shortly after Carataunas the road swings in to the north, and you have your first view of the **Gorge of the Poqueira**, a huge sheer gash into the heights of the Sierra Nevada. Trickling deep in the bed of the cleft is the Poqueira river, which has its source up near the peak of Mulhacén (3482m). The steep walls of the gorge are terraced and well-wooded from top to bottom, and dotted with little stone farmhouses. Much of the country hereabouts looks barren from a distance but close up you'll find that it's rich with flowers, woods, springs, and streams.

A trio of villages — three of the most spectacular and popular in the Alpujarras — teeter on the steep edge of the gorge among their terraces. The first is **PAMPANEIRA**, neat, prosperous, and pretty. Around its main square are a number of **bars, restaurants, and pensiones**; try *Casa Diego* by the fountain. A weaving workshop just down the hill specializes in traditional *Alpujarreño* designs. On the very peak of the western flank of the Poqueira Gorge is the **Tibetan Buddhist Monastery of Al Atalaya**. The Spanish reincarnation of the head lama — one Yeshé — is currently undergoing training under the Dalai Lama in the Himalayas. Lectures on Buddhism are held regularly and facilities exist for those who want to visit the monastery for periods of retreat.

BUBIÓN is next up the hill: there's a *parador*, a bar, and one of the ranches for **horseback riding** in the Alpujarras; trips of from one to five days are offered in groups with a guide (☎958/763135, 763034, or 763038).

CAPILEIRA is the highest of the three villages, with many **bars, hostales and restaurants** — the *Casa Ibero* (aka the *Meson Alpujarreon*) is excellent; the *Meson-Hostal Poqueira* is good value, with one of the best set *menús* in the province. The *Fonda Restaurante El Tilo*, on Plaza Calvario away from the main road, is bound to be the quietest in town. The *Residencia de Artistas* is a house in the village reserved for the use of visiting artists; a part of it is set aside as a **museum** containing various bits and pieces belonging to, or produced by, Pedro Alarcon, the nineteenth-century Spanish writer who visited the Alpujarras and wrote a book about it.

In addition to the direct daily afternoon **bus** from Granada, continuing to Murtas and Berchulas, anything going to Ugíjar and Berja will come very close to Capileira; the bus out to Granada passes by at 9am.

Capileira is a handy base for easy **day hikes** in the Poqueira Gorge. For a not-too-strenuous walk, take the northernmost of of three paths below the village, each with bridges across the river. This sets off from alongside the *Pueblo Alpujarreño* villa complex. The trail winds through the huts and terraced fields of the river valley above Capileira, ending after about an hour and a half at a dirt driveway within sight of a power plant at the head of the valley. You can either retrace your steps or cross the stream over a bridge to follow a jeep track back to the village. In May and June, the fields are tended — laboriously and by hand, as the steep slopes dictate.

Further Along the High Route: Trévelez

PITRES (*Fonda Sierra Nevada* on main square) and **PORTUGOS** (*Hostal Mirador*, ☎958/766014, on the main square; *fonda* at Los Castaños, 1km east), the next two villages on the high route, are not so picturesque as the last three, but more "authentic" and less polished. They also have the advantage that you're likely to find **rooms** during high season, while all around spreads some of the best Alpujarran walking country.

Down below the main road are the three villages of Mecina Fondales, Ferreirola, and Busquistar; along with Pitres, these formed a league of villages known as the *Taha* under the Moors. **FERREIROLA** and **BUSQUISTAR** are especially attractive, as is the path between the two, clinging to the north side of the valley of the Rio Trévelez. You're out of tourist country here and the villages display their genuine characteristics to better effect; there's an unsigned **inn** just uphill from the church in Busquistar but no real restaurant.

The cut into the mountain made by the Río Trévelez is similar to the Poqueira, but on a grander scale and more austere. **TRÉVELEZ**, at the end of the ravine, is purportedly Spain's highest permanent settlement. In traditional Alpujarran style it has upper and lower *barrios*, overlooking a grassy, poplar-lined valley where the river starts its long descent. The village is also well provided with **hostales**, located in both the lower and upper squares, and with *camas* advertised over a few bars. Among **restaurants**, the *Rio Grande*, down near the bridge, has good, solid food; one to avoid is the no-name joint near the upper plaza advertising roast chicken and rabbit — unhappily an absolute rip-off.

Although Capileira is probably the more pleasant base, Trévelez is traditionally the jump-off point for the **high sierra peaks** (to which there is a bona fide path) and for treks across the range (on a lower, more conspicuous trail). The latter is still used, and begins down by the bridge on the eastern side of the village. After skirting the bleak *Horcajo de Trévelez* (3182m), and negotiating the Puerto de Trévelez (2800m), up to which it's a very distinct route, the trail drops gradually down along the north flank of the Sierra Nevada to Jeres del Marquesado. You should count on spending at least one night camping.

East from Trévelez

Heading east from Trevélez, either by vehicle or (preferably) on foot, you come to **JUVÍLES**, an attractive town straddling the road. At its center is an unwhitewashed, peanut-brittle-finish church with a clock that's slighly slow (like most everything else around here . . .). In the evening people promenade in the road, knowing that there will be no traffic, although there's a perfectly good plaza by the church. A single all-in-one *fonda/restaurante/ store* (meals on demand, dour management) is reasonable, with great views east over the valley containing Cadiar from the second floor.

BÉRCHULES, a high village of grassy streams and chestnut woods, lies only 4km beyond Juvíles, but a greater contrast can hardly be imagined. It is a large, abruptly demarcated settlement, three streets wide, on a sharp slope overlooking yet another canyon. The *Fonda/Restaurante Carvol* has decent **rooms**, and next door there's an excellent grocery — a godsend if you're planning on doing any walking out of here, since most village shops in the Alpujarras are primitive.

CADIAR, just below Bérchules and the central town of the Alpujarras, is more attractive than it seems from a distance, and there are a handful of *hostales* and *camas* if you want to stay. Various events are worth keeping in mind, too. There's a colorful **produce market** on the 3rd and 18th of every month, sometimes including livestock. And from October 5 to October 9 a **Wine Fair** takes place, turning the waters of the fountain literally to wine.

Cadiar and Bérchules mark the end of the western Alpujarras, and a striking change in the landscape; the dramatic, severe, but relatively green terrain of the Guadalfeo and Cadiar valleys gives way to an open rolling land that's much more arid.

Eastern Alpujarras

The villages of the eastern Alpujarras display many of the characteristics of those to the west but as a rule they are poorer and much less visited by tourists — and delightful as a result.

Yegen
In **YEGEN**, some 7km northeast of Cadiar, there is a plaque on the house where **Gerald Brenan** lived during his ten or so years of Alpujarran residence. His autobiography of these times, *South from Granada*, is the best account of rural life in Spain between the wars, and describes the visits made here by Virginia Woolf, Bertrand Russell, and the arch-complainer Lytton Strachey. Disillusioned with the strictures of middle-class life in England after World War I, Brenan rented a house in Yegen and shipped out a library of 2000 books, from which he was to spend the next eight years educating himself. He later moved to the hills behind Torremolinos, where he died in 1987, a writer better known and respected in Spain (he made an important study of St. John of the Cross) than in his native England.

Brenan connections aside, Yegen is still one of the most characteristic Alpujarran villages, with its two distinct quarters, cobbled paths, and cold-water springs. It has a **fonda**, just by the main road.

Ugíjar
UGÍJAR, 12km on from Yegen, is the largest community of this eastern part, and an attractive, quiet market town. There are easy and enjoyable walks to the nearest villages, as well as a fairly luxurious, though reasonably priced **hostal** (serving midday meals), and very cheap *camas* opposite the bus stop in the central plaza. Buses run onward to Almería (3 hr.).

The Southern Ranges
The tiny hamlets of the southern Alpujarras have an unrivaled view of the Mediterranean, the convexity of the hills obscuring the awful development and the acres of growers' plastic that mar the coast. There are few villages of any size, as there is less water, but the hills host the principal **wine-growing district** of the Alpujarras. For a taste of the best of its wine, try the *venta* (wine shop) at HAZA DEL LINO (Plain of Linen); the house brew is a full-bodied rosé.

Good, dry red wine, whether from this particular district or not, is in fact available in most of the Alpujarran villages, west or east, and is always worth asking for.

Inland Towards Almería: Guadix

An alternative route from Granada to Almería — covered by the *Empresa Autodia* buses from c/Rector Marín — runs via GUADIX, a crumbling old Moorish town with a vast and extraordinary cave district. This, the Barrio Santiago, still houses some 10,000 people (most of whom, incidentally, are not gypsies), and to take a look around it is the main reason for stopping off.

The quarter extends over a square mile or so in area, just beyond the convincingly ruined Alcazaba (signposted as you come into the old walled part of town and, entered from the adjoining theological school, providing a broad overview). The lower caves, on the outskirts, are really proper cottages with upper stories, electricity, television, and running water. But as you walk deeper into the suburb, the design quickly becomes simpler — just a white-washed front, a door, a tiny window, and a chimney — and the experience increasingly voyeuristic. Penetrating right to the back you'll come on a few caves which are no longer used: too squalid, too unhealthy, their long-unrepainted whitewash a dull brown. Yet right next door there may be a similar, occupied hovel, with a gypsy family sitting outside and other figures following dirt tracks still deeper into the hills.

To reach the Barrio and Alcazaba head into the center of town from the bus station (itself about a 5-min. walk outside the walls), and enter the quarter behind the whitewashed church of Santiago. If you want to stay overnight — and Guadix is a pleasant, modest old place with a grand Plaza Mayor and some good-looking mansions — there is a fonda just inside the walls by a prominent Moorish gateway.

On from Guadix

Heading on from Guadix you can reach the coast at Murcia via the decayed though picturesque towns of BAZA and LORCA.

En route towards Almería you pass through more of the strange, tufa-pocked landscape from which the Guadix caves are hewn, the main landmark a magnificent sixteenth-century castle high above LA CALAHORRA (keys from c/de los Claveles 2 if you stop and it's closed). Guadix–Almería buses normally follow the train line, along the minor N324 over the last section. If you're driving, you might want to keep going straight on the main road, meeting the Almería–Sorbas road at what has become known as LITTLE HOLLYWOOD (see p.238), the old and preserved filmset of *A Fistful of Dollars*.

Almería: Lunar Landscapes and Beaches.

The province of Almería is a strange corner of Spain. Inland it has an almost lunar landscape of desert, sandstone cones, and dried-up river beds. On the coast it is still largely unspoiled; lack of water and roads frustrated development in the 1960s and 1970s and it is only now beginning to take off. A number of good beaches are accessible by bus, and in this hottest province of Spain they're worth considering during what would be the "off-season" elsewhere, since Almería's summers start well before Easter and last into November. In midsummer it's incredibly hot (frequently touching 100°F in the shade), while all year round there's an intense, almost luminous, sunlight. This and the weird scenery have made Almería one of the most popular film locations in Europe — *Lawrence of Arabia* was shot here, along with scores of spaghetti westerns.

Almería: the Capital

ALMERÍA itself is quite a pleasant modern city, spread at the foot of a stark grey mountain. On its summit is a tremendous **Alcazaba**, probably the best surviving example of Moorish military fortification, with three huge walled enclosures, in the second of which are remains of a mosque, converted to a chapel by the *Reyes Católicos*. In the eleventh century, when Almería was an independent kingdom and the wealthiest, most commercially active city of Spain, this citadel contained immense gardens and palaces and housed some 20,000 people. Its grandeur was reputed to rival the court of Granada but comparisons are impossible since little beyond the walls and towers remain, the last remnants of stucco work having been sold off by the locals in the eighteenth century.

From the Alcazaba, however, you do get a good view of Almería's **cave quarter** — the *Barrio de la Chanca* on a low hill to the left — and of the city's strange fortified **Cathedral**, built in the sixteenth century at a time when the southern Mediterranean was terrorized by the raids of Barbarossa and other Turkish and North African pirate forces; its corner towers once held cannons.

Around the cathedral are several **fondas** and **hostales** — much more convenient (and sometimes cheaper) than the **youth hostel** (*Colegio Menor Alejandro Salazar*, July-Aug. only) in the Ciudad Jardín. The **Turismo** here is on c/Hermanos Machado, two blocks towards downtown from the train and bus stations; they have a list of most buses out of Almería in all directions, as well as train schedules. There's a train to Granada very early in the morning, and another in the afternoon. The **bus station** is just a few minutes' walk away from the train station and two buses leave for Granada before the afternoon train.

Almeria **airport** is 8km out of town. Buses make the journey every half hour (the airport stop is by the lone *hostal* on the main road 200m from the terminal), and are much cheaper than the taxis that lurk outside the departure lounge, awaiting unsuspecting visitors. The city also has a **daily boat to Melilla** on the Moroccan coast throughout the summer — an eight-hour journey which can pay dividends in both time and money if you're headed for the east or to Algeria, or if you're driving.

The Beaches and Inland

Almería's best **beaches** lie on its eastern coast; those to the west of the city, particularly AGUADULCE and ROQUETAS DE MAR, have already been exploited and have the dismal air imparted by half-built concrete monsters.

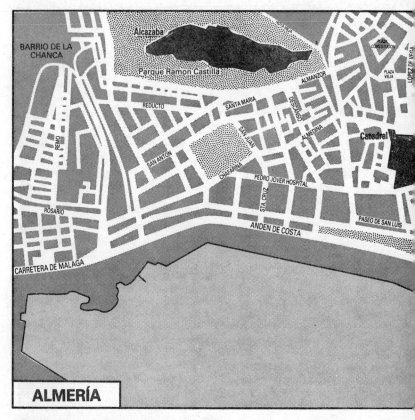

ALMERÍA

El Cabo de Gata and San José

Heading east, the closest appetizing resort is **EL CABO DE GATA**, where there's a lovely expanse of course sand. Five buses a day run between here and Almería, making an intermediate stop at RETAMAR, a retirement resort/vaction-development. Arriving at El Cabo, you pass a lake, the **Laguna de Rosa**, protected by a conservation society and home to flamingos and other waders. In town there are plentiful bars, cafes, and shops, plus a fish market. The two *fondas* above the bars on the beach are both quite expensive; **rooms** at the *Pizzeria Pedro* are cheaper and self-contained. The beach gets windy in the afternoons, and it's a deceptively long walk eastwards to **Las Salinas** (The Salt Pans — exactly that) where you'll find a bar and cafe.

Beyond lies **SAN JOSÉ**, also reached by bus from Almería. The village has a sandy beach in a small cove, with shallow water, and some fine beaches within walking distance. **Rooms** are in fair supply, though prices and standards vary greatly and you'll do well to hunt around; oddly, the *fondas* tend to be pricier than the *hostales*. There are again numerous bars and cafes, and a good supermarket.

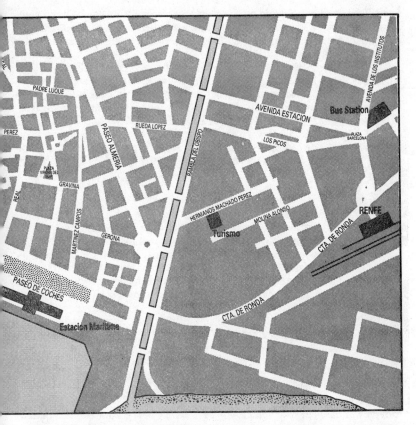

Next along the coast is LOS ESCULLOS, with a good beach but expensive accommodation. LA ISLETA is another fishing town, with a sleepy atmosphere, a sandy beach, and a **hostal** overlooking the harbor; it is reasonably priced and has a good bar for *tapas*, but is often full (or choosy about its customers), and LAS NEGRAS, farther on, has a cove with a pebbly beach and a few bars, but nowhere to stay.

Inland: Movieland

Rather livelier than the eastern resorts is the strip of coast between Carboneras and La Garrucha, centered on the town of Mojacar. This is some way up the coast and to get there you'll have to travel through some of Almería's distinctive desert scenery. There are two possible routes: via Nijar to Carboneras, or via Tabernas and Sorbas to Mojacar.

NIJAR is a neat, white and typically Almerían town, with narrow streets designed to give maximum shade. If you have a car it would make a good base from which to explore the coast around; there are two or three small **hostales**; try *Montes* (☎951/360157; with a *comedor*) on the main road into town. There's also a pizzeria on this road; otherwise eating can be a problem. Níjar's **pottery** is attractive, since traditional patterns and mineral dyes are still in use, giving the ware an archaic quality. Blankets and rugs, made at the local textile mills, are on sale, too.

The most dramatic landscapes, however, lie between **TABERNAS** and **SORBAS**. Both towns have startling appearances, especially Sorbas, whose houses overhang an ashen gorge, but neither are really places to linger — they're basically in the middle of a desert. Just outside Tabernas in a particularly gulch-riven landscape is **LITTLE HOLLYWOOD**, or *YUCCA CITY*, the set of *A Fistful of Dollars* and various other movies. This has been preserved and opened up as a tourist attraction: you can wander into the saloon for a drink, and on Saturday (in season) the fantasy is carried a step further with a mock bank raid.

Mojácar

MOJÁCAR — Almería's main and growing resort — lies a couple of kilometers back from the sea, a striking town of white cubist houses wrapped around a harsh outcrop of rock. In the 1960s, when the main Spanish *costas* were being developed, this was virtually a ghost town, its inhabitants — among them the infant Walt Disney — having taken the only logical step, and emigrated. The town's fortunes suddenly revived, however, when the local mayor, with the popularity of other equally barren spots on the Spanish islands and mainland as an example, offered free land to anyone willing to build within a year. The bid was a modest success, attracting one of the decade's multifarious "artist colonies," and now, twenty years later, they are quickly being joined by package-vacation firms. A ritzy new hotel has just been opened in the town, there's a modern mural in the church, and a general air of burgeoning prosperity — which may, in the long run, work to the disadvantage of Mojácar's charms.

If you want to stay in the town there are a handful of small **hostales**, though without your own vehicle you're probably best off down at **the beach**, where there's a cheap and reasonable **campground**, lots of fine beach bars (currently a little overwhelmed by Spanish heavy-metal), rooms to rent, and several **hostales**. Among the hostales, try either the Puntazo (☎951/478229) or the *Africano*; the latter has a good seafood restaurant. The **beach** itself is excellent and the waters (like all in Almería) warm and brilliantly clear. Bus services, incidentally, reflect Mojacar's popularity with Catalans; you can arrange a ticket to Barcelona, from the beach, at the *Viajes Solar* travel agent at La Gaviota complex.

Carboneras and La Garrucha

West of Mojácar beach are a succession of small, isolated coves, the most accessible of them (and even so, a realistic target only with your own vehicle) reached down a rough coastal track that turns off towards the sea just under 4km down the road to Carboneras. The Mojacar–carboneras road itself switchbacks perilously through the hills some way inland, and as yet offers no real access to the sands. There's no bus either, and you'd need to be pretty committed to escaping the crowds to want to drive this way.

CARBONERAS has an average beach and a couple of **hostales**, marred by the shadow of a massive cement factory around the bay. Beyond, a small road extends to the isolated fishing hamlet of **AGUA AMARGA**, a more attractive spot with a tasteful crop of villas; again, though, getting there will be totally dependent on having a car.

East from Mojacar there's easier access, with occasional buses and reasonably easy hitching to **LA GARRUCHA**, a lively, if distinctly unpretty, town and fishing harbor. This is in the process of development, with villas now thick on the ground and many more in the offing, but it does have a life of its own beside tourism. You probably won't want to stay (there are several **hostales** and a summer-only **youth hostel** if you do), though with a reasonable beach and some fine seafront fish-restaurants it makes a good afternoon's break from Mojácar.

Palomares and Some Bombs

Just for the record (and as a chilling memorial to nuclear madness) it should be recorded that the village of **PALOMARES** lies a few miles to the east around the coast. Here, on January 17, 1966, an American B-52 bomber collided with a tanker aircraft during a mid-air refueling operation. Following the collision three ten-megaton **H-bombs** fell on land and a fourth into the sea, just off the village. Those that fell in the fields were recovered quickly, though one had been damaged, causing radioactive contamination nearby. Fifteen U.S. warships and two submarines searched for many weeks before the fourth bomb was recovered. On 19 March thousands of barrels of plutonium contaminated soil were transported by the USAF for disposal in South Carolina. Nobody has ever convincingly explained how the incident happened. Nor is it known why the bombs didn't explode, for the damaged bomb had actually lost its safety catch.

fiestas

January
1–2 *La Toma* — celebration of the entry of the *Reyes Católicos* into the city — at GRANADA.
6 *Romería de la Virgen del Mar* pilgrimage procession from ALMERÍA.
17 *Romería del Ermita del Santo*. Similar event at GAUDIX.

February
1 *San Cecilio* fiesta in GRANADA'S traditionally gypsy quarter of Sacromonte.
February/March : **Carnival** is an extravagant week-long event (leading up to Lent) in all the Andalucian cities. CÁDIZ, above all, parties, with fancy dress, *flamenco* and camp-comic competitions.

April
Holy Week (*Semana Santa*), too, has its most elaborate and dramatic celebrations in Andalucía. You'll find memorable processions of floats and penitents at SEVILLA (see p.177), MÁLAGA, GRANADA and to a lesser extent in smaller towns like ARCOS, BAEZA and U'BEDA. All culminate on *Good Friday*, with *Easter Day* itself more of a family occasion.

Last week (or 1-2 weeks after Easter) Ten-day *Feria de Abril* at SEVILLA: the largest fair in Spain, a little refined in the way of the city, but an extraordinary event none the less (see p.177). A small April fair — with bull-running — is held in VEJER.

Late April/early May *Festival of the Patios* in CÓRDOBA includes a competition for decorations and numerous events and concerts organized by the local city council.

May
Early May (usually the week after Sevilla's fair) Somewhat aristocratic *Horse Fair* at JEREZ DE LA FRONTERA.

3 "Moors and Christians" carnival at PAMPANEIRA (Alpujarras).

15 *San Isidro Romería* at SENTENIL.

Pentecost (7 weeks after Easter) *Romería del Rocío*, when horse-drawn carriages and processions converge from all over the south on EL ROCÍO (Huelva).

Corpus Christi (variable — Thursday after Trinity). Bullfights and festivities at GRANADA, SEVILLA, RONDA, VEJER, and ZAHARA DE LE SIERRA.

June
Second week *Feria de San Bernabe* at MARBELLA, often spectacular events since this is the richest town in Andalucía.

13 *San Antonio Fiesta* at TRÉVELEZ (Alpujarras) with mock battles between Moors and Christians.

Third week The ALGECIRAS fair and fiesta, another major event of the south.

23–24 *Candelas de San Juan* — bonfires and effigies at VEJER and elsewhere.

30 CONIL feria.

End June/early July *International Festival of Music and Dance*: major dance groups and chamber orchestras perform in GRANADA's Alhambra palace, Generalife, and Carlos V palace.

July
Early July *International Guitar Festival* at

CÓRDOBA: top acts from classical, *flamenco*, and Latin American music.

August
5 TRÉVELEZ observes a midnight *romería* to Mulhacén.

15 (*Ascension of the Virgin*) Fair with *casetas* (dance tents) at VEJER and elsewhere.

27 Grape harvest fiesta at MONTILLA (Córdoba). *Guadlaquivir festival* (**variable**) at SANLÚCAR DE LA BARRAMEDA with bullfights and an important *flamenco* competition. Also the **horseraces** along Sanlucar's beach: the first cycle of races, with heavy official and unofficial betting, takes place around August 17–20; the second tournament takes place exactly a week later.

Late July/early August ALMERÍA's festival generally involves a handful of major jazz and rock concerts in its Plaza Vieja.

September
1–3 Celebration of the *Virgen de la Luz* in TARIFA: street processions and horseback riding.

First/second week *Vendimia* (celebration of the vintage) at JEREZ.

Early in the month RONDA bursts into life with a feria, *flamenco* contests and the *Corrida Goyesca*, bullfights in traditional 18th c. dress.

29–Oct. 2 Feria in Órjiva (Alpujarras).

October
1 *San Miguel* fiesta in GRANADA's Albaicín quarter and dozens of other towns, even at TORREMOLINOS.

travel details

Trains
Málaga–Sevilla 3 daily (3½–4 hr.)
Málaga–Córdoba 10 daily (2½–3½ hr.)
Málaga–Granada 3 daily (3½ hr.)
Málaga–Ronda 3 daily (3 hr.)
(*all the above via Bobadilla*)
Málaga–Madrid 5 daily (8–10 hr.)
Málaga–Fuengirola Half-hourly service in 50 min., via Málaga airport (14 min.) and Torremolinos (28 min.)
Algeciras–Córdoba 4 daily in 5–6 hr., via Ronda (1¾–2 hr.)
Algeciras–Granada 1 daily (5½–6 hr.)
Algeciras–Madrid 3 daily (12½–15 hr.)
(*all Algeciras trains via Bobadilla*)
Sevilla–Ayamonte (and Portuguese Algarve) 3

daily in 3¾ hr., via Huelva (1¾ hr.)
Sevilla–Badajoz 4 daily in 5–7 hr., via Mérida (3½ hr.)
Sevilla–Córdoba 2 daily (1½–2 hr.)
Sevilla–Madrid 6 daily (6½–9½ hr.)
Sevilla–Cádiz 13 daily (1½–2 hr.)
Huelva–Zafra 2 daily (4½ hr.)
Córdoba–Madrid 6 daily in 7–11 hr., via Linares-Baeza (2½–3 hr.)
Jaén–Madrid 5 daily (4½–6 hr.)
Granada–Madrid 3 daily in 6½–10 hr., via Linares-Baeza (3–4 hr.)
Granada–Almería 2 daily in 3¾–4¼ hr., via Guadix (2 hr.)
Granada–Valencia 2 daily in 12 hr., 1 via Linares-Baeza

Buses

From Málaga To Granada (8 daily; 2½ hr.), Ronda (5; 3½ hr.), Algeciras (9; 3½ hr.), Córdoba (2; 4 hr.), Osuna/Sevilla (2; 3 hr./4½ hr.), Torremolinos/Marbella (every half hour; 30 min./ 1½ hr.), Nerja/Motril (6; 1½ hr./2½ hr.), Almería (2; 5 hr.), and Madrid (1; 8 hr.).

From Algeciras To La Línea (for Gibraltar: hourly in 20 min.), Tarifa (9 — last at 7:45pm; ½ hr.), Cádiz (7; 3 hr.), and Sevilla (2; 3½ hr.).

From Ronda To Sevilla (4; 3¼ hr.), San Pedro de Alcántara (6; 2 hr., continuing to Málaga), Setenil/Olvera (1; 15 min./30 min.), Jerez (3 daily, 2½ hr.), Ubrique (2 daily; 45 min.), Cádiz (1 daily, 3½ hr.) and Arcos de la Frontera (3; 1¾ hr.).

From Sevilla To Cádiz (8; 1½–2½ hr.), Aracena (2; 2 hr.), Mérida (3; 3½ hr.), Badajoz (2 via Zafra, 2 via Jerez de los Caballeros; 5 hr.), El Rocío/ Matalascañas (5; 2½ hr./3 hr.), Huelva (7; 2½ hr.), Carmona (10; 45 min.), Ecija/Córdoba (3; 2 hr./3¼ hr.), Madrid (1; 10 hr.), and Ayamonte (access to Portugal's Algarve — 3 daily).

From Cádiz To Conil (6; 1 hr.), Chipiona (9; ½ hr.), and Jerez de la Frontera (8; 45 min.).

From Córdoba To Ecija (4; 1¼ hr.), Badajoz (1; 6½ hr.), Jaén (2; 2 hr.), Granada (3; 4 hr.), and Madrid (1; 8 hr.).

From Jaén To Baeza/Úbeda (7; 1¼ hr./1½ hr.), Granada (7; 2 hr.), and Madrid (3; 6 hr.).

From Granada To Motril (7; 2hr), Guadix (4; 1hr), Alicante/Valencia (3; 5½ hr./7½ hr.), Almería (2; 4 hr.), Sierra Nevada/Alpujarras (4 to Lanjarón and Órjiva in around 2¼ hr.; 1 daily to most of the other villages along most of the routes) and Madrid (1; 8 hr.).

From Huelva To Ayamonte/Portuguese frontier (8 daily).

From Almería To Guadix (2; 2½ hr.), Moá'car (2; 2hr), Granada (2; 4 hr.) and Alicante (2; 7 hr.).

Ferries

From Málaga Daily boat to Melilla (10 hr.)

From Almería Daily (except Sun.) seasonal boat to Melilla (8 hr.)

From Gibraltar Daily seasonal hydrofoil to Tangier (1 hr.)

From Algeciras 3 or 4 ferryboats daily to Tangier (2½ hr.) 6 or 7 to Ceuta (1½ hr.). Daily seasonal hydrofoil to Tangier (1 hr.)

From Tarifa Daily seasonal hydrofoil to Tangier (30 min.); does not run in bad weather.

From Cádiz Ferries to the Canary Islands of Tenerife (36 hr.) and Las Palmas (43 hr.); every two days in season, every five out. Local ferry to Puerto Santa María 4 times daily (20 min.)

CHAPTER FOUR

OLD CASTILE

The foundations of modern Spain were laid in the kingdom of Castile. A land of frontier fortresses — the *castillos* from which it takes its name — it became the most powerful and centralizing force of the Reconquest, extending its domination through military gains and marriage alliances. By the eleventh century it had merged with and swallowed León; through Isabella's marriage to Fernando in 1469 it was to encompass Aragón, Catalunya and eventually the entire peninsula. The monarchs of this triumphant and expansionist age were enthusiastic patrons of the arts, endowing their cities with superlative monuments above which, quite literally, tower the great Gothic cathedrals of **Salamanca**, **León**, and **Burgos**.

Over the past decades these and the other historic cities of Old Castile have grown to dominate the region more than ever. Although its soil is fertile, the harsh extremes of land and climate don't encourage rural settlement, and the vast central plateau — the 700–1000m high *meseta* — is given over almost entirely to grain. Huge areas stretch into the horizon without any landmark to distinguish them, often not even a tree. Surprisingly, however, the River Duero, which has the most extensive basin in Spain, runs right across the province and off into Portugal. And despite being characterized by *meseta* landscape, there are enclaves of varied scenery — in particular the **valley of Las Batuecas** and the lakeland of the **Sierra de Urbión**, where the Duero begins its course.

The sporadic and depopulated villages, bitterly cold in winter, burning hot in summer, are rarely of interest — travel consists of getting as quickly as you can from one grand town to the next. They're all well connected by major roads so that hitching, for once, is relatively easy, and rides tend to be long. The problem with many of the smaller places, and even some of the larger ones, is that they have little appeal beyond their monuments: **Toro**, **Tordesillas**, and **Valladolid**, for example, are important places historically, but their "sights" lack a stimulating setting. The most impressive of the castles are at **Coca**, **Gormaz** and **Berlanga de Duero**. The other architectural feasture of the region is the host of Romanesque churches, a legacy of the **pilgrimage route to Santiago** which cut across the top of the province.

Salamanca and **León** are the two outstanding highlights — ranking in interest and beauty with the greatest cities of Spain, with Toledo, Sevilla, or Santiago. Try and take in some of the lesser towns, too, like **Ciudad Rodrigo**, **El Burgo de Osma**, **Zamora**, or the village of **Covarrubias**. In all of them you'll be struck by a wealth of mansions and churches quite out of proportion to the present, or even imagined past, circumstances and status. In the people too, you may notice something of the classic Castilian *hidalgo* archetype — a certain haughty solemnity of manner and a dignified assumption, however straitened present circumstances, of past nobility.

Salamanca

SALAMANCA is probably the most graceful city in Spain. For four centuries it was the seat of one of the most prestigious universities in the world and although it lost this reputation in the seventeenth century, it has kept the unmistakable atmosphere of a university city. It's still a small place, unmarred by the piles of suburban concrete which blight so many of its contemporaries, and is lent a gorgeous harmony by the golden sandstone from which almost the entire city seems to be constructed. The architectural hoard is endless: two cathedrals, one Gothic, the other Romanesque, vie for attention with Renaissance palaces and gems of Plateresque decoration; the Plaza Mayor is the finest in Spain; and the surviving university buildings are tremendous throughout — all of them distinguished by that same warm stone.

Two great architectural syles were developed, and see their finest expression, in Salamanca. **Churrigueresque** takes its name from José Churriguera (1665–1723), the dominant member of a prodigiously creative family. Best known for their huge, flamboyant altarpieces, they were particularly active around Salamanca. The style is a particularly ornate form of baroque, long frowned on by art historians from a north European, protestant tradition. **Plateresque** came earlier, a decorative technique of shallow relief and intricate detail named for its alleged resemblance to the art of the silversmith (*platero*). Salamanca gave birth to this style, and the native sandstone, soft and easy to carve, played a significant role in its development. Plateresque art cuts across Gothic and Renaissance frontiers — the decorative motifs of the university, for example, are taken from the Italian Renaissance but the facade of the New Cathedral is Gothic in inspiration.

The City

The grand **Plaza Mayor** is the hub of Salamantine life. You get the impression that everyone passes through its cafes and arcaded walks at least ten times a day. Its bare central expanse, in which bullfights were staged as late as 1863, is completely enclosed by one continuous four-story building decorated with iron balconies and medallion portraits. It's the work of Andrea Garcia Quiñones and Alberto Churriguera, younger brother of **José**. Nowhere is the Churrigueras' inspired variation of baroque so refined as here, where the restrained elegance of the designs is heightened by the changing effects caused by the strength and angle of the sun.

From the south side of the Plaza (facing the *Ayuntamiento*), Rua Mayor leads to the vast baroque church of **La Clerecía**, seat of the Pontifical University. At present you can only visit the patio as the church itself has been declared structurally unsafe (Mon.–Fri. 9am–1:30pm and 4:30–8:30pm, Sat. 9am–1pm; closed Sun.). Opposite stands the celebrated **Casa de Las Conchas** (House of Shells), so-called because its facades are decorated with rows of carved scallop shells, symbol of the pilgrimage to Santiago. The early sixteenth-century mansion would be otherwise unremarkable, but it just goes to show what a little decoration can do.

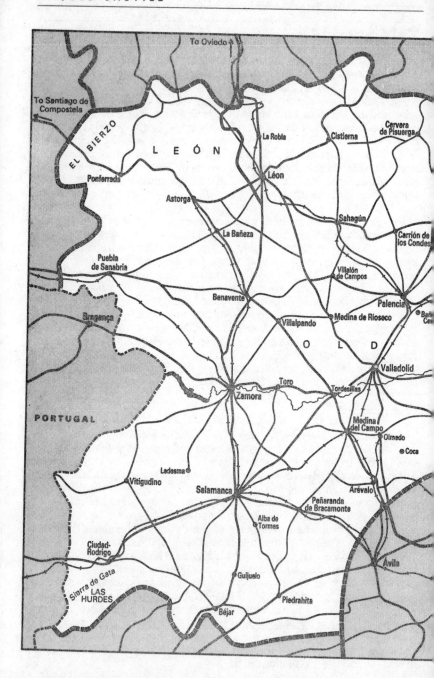

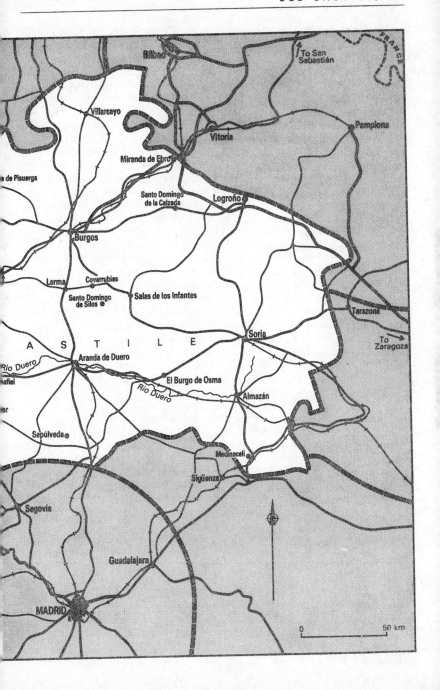

From here c/Libreros leads shortly to the **Patio de las Escuelas** and the Renaissance entrance to the **University** (Mon.–Sat. 9:30am–1:30pm and 4–6:30pm, Sun. 10am–1pm). The ultimate achievement of Plateresque art, this reflects the tremendous reputation of Salamanca in the early sixteenth century. The university was founded by Alfonso IX in the 1220s, and after the union of León and Castile it swallowed up the University of Palencia to become the most important in Spain. Its rise to international stature was phenomenal and within thirty years Pope Alexander IV proclaimed it equal to the greatest universities of the day. As at Oxford, Paris and Bologna, theories argued out here were later accepted as fact throughout Europe. Major contributions to the development of international law were made, and here Columbus sought support for his voyages of discovery from the enlightened faculty of astronomy. The University flourished under the *Reyes Católicos*, even employing a pioneering woman professor, Beatriz de Galindo, who tutored Queen Isabella in Latin. In the sixteenth century it was powerful enough to resist the orthodoxy of Philip II's Inquisition but eventually freedom of thought was stifled by the extreme clericalism of the seventeenth and eighteenth centuries. Books were banned as being dangerous to the Catholic faith and mathematics and medicine disappeared from the curriculum. Decline was hastened during the Peninsular War when the French are said to have demolished 20 of the 25 colleges, and by the end of the nineteenth century there were no more than 300 students. In recent decades numbers have been replenished (present size is about 12,000), though, like so many of Spain's universities, it suffers an intellectual hangover from the appointments and backward operation of Franco's regime. Although socially prestigious, it officially ranks only seventh, well below Madrid, Barcelona, and Sevilla. It does, however, run a highly successful summer language school — nowhere in Spain will you see so many young Americans.

The **facade** of the university is covered with medallions, heraldic emblems, and a profusion of floral decoration (amid which lurks a hidden frog!). The center is occupied by a portrait of Isabella and Fernando surrounded by a Greek inscription commemorating their devotion to the university; above them is the coat of arms of Carlos V, grandson and successor of Isabella. Inside, the old lecture rooms, surprisingly small for a seat of learning that once boasted over 7000 students, are arranged round a courtyard. The **Sala de Fray Luis de León** preserves the original benches and the pulpit from which this celebrated professor lectured. In 1573 the Inquisition muscled its way into the room and arrested Fray Luis for alleged subversion of the Faith; five years of torture and imprisonment followed, but upon his release he calmly resumed his lecture with the words *"Dicebamus hesterna die . . ."* (*"As we were saying yesterday . . ."*). In similar tradition one of the most spirited confrontations of the civil war took place here when Professor Miguel de Unamuno openly challenged the fascist General Millan Astray who could only retort with his motto "Long Live Death!"

The Patio de las Escuelas is surrounded by other university buildings including the **Escuelas Menores**, which served as a kind of preparatory school for the university proper (same hours and admission as university). Especially worth a look though, is the zodiacal ceiling in one of its rooms;

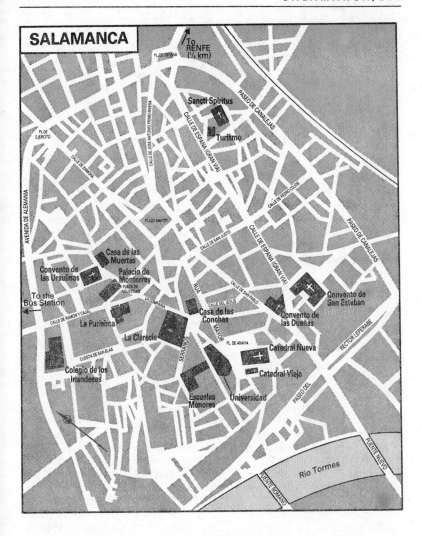

formerly in the chapel, this was moved after two-thirds of it was destroyed by tremors of the 1755 Lisbon Earthquake. Again lecture rooms open off a beautiful Renaissance cloister, whose walls are inscribed with records of academic successes (*vitores*). Adjacent is a mildly interesting **Museo de Bellas Artes** (Tues.–Sun 9am–2pm), installed in the house once occupied by the doctors of Queen Isabella.

As a declaration of Salamanca's prestige, and in a glorious last-minute assertion of Gothic, the **Catedral Nueva** (New Cathedral) was begun in 1512. It was built within a few yards of the university and acted as a buttress for the Old Cathedral which was in danger of collapsing. Both buildings are open from 10am to 2pm and from 4 to 8pm, and entry to the Old Cathedral is via the first chapel on the right in the new one. The main Gothic-Plateresque facade is contemporary with that of the university and equally dazzling in its wealth of ornamental detail. For financial reasons construction spanned two centuries, and thus the building incorporates a range of styles, with some Renaissance and baroque elements and a tower modeled on that of the cathedral at Toledo. Alberto Churriguera and his brother Joaquin both worked here — the former on the choir stalls, the latter on the dome.

The Romanesque **Catedral Vieja** (Old Cathedral) is dwarfed in size and stylistically entirely different. Its most striking feature is the massive fifteenth-century *retablo* by Nicholas Florentino. Fifty-three paintings of the lives of the Virgin and Christ are surmounted by a powerfully apocalyptic portrayal of the Last Judgment; a thirteenth-century fresco on the same theme is hidden away in the **Capilla de San Martín** at the back of the building. The cathedral's distinctive *media naranja* dome, shaped like the segments of an orange, derives from Byzantine models and is similar to those at Zamora and Toro. The exterior is known as the **Torre de Gallo** (Rooster Tower) and can be seen from the Patio Chico next to the New University's south entrance. The chapels opening off the cloisters were used as university lecture rooms until the sixteenth century. One, the **Capilla de Obispo Diego de Anaya**, contains the oldest organ in Europe (mid-14th-c.); the instrument shows Moorish influence and, in the words of Sacheverell Sitwell, "is one of the most romantic, poetical objects imaginable." In the Chapter House there's a small **museum** with a fine collection of works by Fernando Gallego, Salamanca's most famous painter. Active in the late fifteenth century, he was a brilliant and conscious imitator of early northern Renaissance artists such as Roger van der Weyden.

Another faultless example of Plateresque art, the **Convento de San Esteban** (9am–1pm and 4–8pm), is a short walk down c/del Tostado from the large Plaza de Anaya at the side of the New Cathedral. Its golden facade is divided into three horizontal sections and covered in a tapestry of sculpture, the central panel of which (1610) depicts the stoning of its patron saint, St. Stephen. The east end of the church is occupied by a huge baroque *retablo* by José Churriguera, a lavish concoction of columns, statuary, and floral decoration. The monastery's cloisters, through which you enter, are magnificent too, but the most beautiful cloisters in the city stand across the road in the **Convento de Las Dueñas** (10am–1pm and 4–7pm). Built on an irregular pentagonal plan in the Renaissance-Plateresque style of the early sixteenth century, the imaginative upper-story capitals are wildly carved with human heads and skulls. On the opposite side of San Esteban stands the monumental Churrigueresque **Palacio de Calatrava**. The final monument in this quarter worthy of special note is the **Torre del Clavero**. A fifteenth-century turreted octagon, it's at the far end of the Plaza de Colón, behind Las Dueñas.

Most of the remaining buildings of interest are situated in the **western part of the city**. If you follow c/de la Compañía from the Casa de Conchas, you pass the Plaza San Benito, which has some fine houses, and come to the

Plaza Agustinas. In front is the large **Palacio de Monterrey**, a sixteenth-century construction with end towers, unfortunately not seen to best advantage in the narrow street. Across from it is the seventeenth-century Augustinian monastery usually called **La Purísima**, for which Ribera painted several fine altarpieces, including the main *Immaculate Conception*. Behind the Palacio de Monterrey is another interesting convent, **Las Ursulinas** (9:30am–1pm and 4:30–7:30pm). The nuns have assembled a small museum in their *coro*, but the main object of interest, in the church itself, is the marble tomb of Archbishop Alonso Fonseca by Diego de Siloé. Facing the east wall of this church is the impressive facade of the **Casa de las Muertes** (House of the Dead). Diagonally opposite the park from Las Ursulinas, c/de Fonseca, leads to the magnificent Plateresque palace still commonly known as the **Colegio de los Irlandeses**. For centuries this served as the Irish seminary, until it was surrendered in the 1950s, when it was decided to concentrate resources at home. It is a corporate work by many of the leading figures of Spanish architecture in the early sixteenth century, led by Juan de Alava. The patio, now wholly Renaissance, is a particular delight, with beautifully carved portrait medallions, each distinctly characterized. In the chapel there's an altarpiece of which Alonso Berruguete executed both the paintings and the sculptures. Now a teacher training college, the patio and chapel can be visited from 9am to 2pm and from 4 to 7pm.

Finally, for a postcard view of Salamanca, go to the extreme south of the city and cross the oldest surviving monument, the many times restored **Puente Romano** (Roman Bridge), some 1300 feet long and itself worth seeing.

Some Practical Information

Salamanca is connected with Madrid by regular bus and train (via Ávila), and there are onward connections to Portugal, northwards to Zamora, León, and beyond into Galicia or Asturias, and south to Extremadura. The **bus and railroad stations** are on opposite sides of the city, each about fifteen minutes' walk from the center. From the bus station (Avda. de Filiberto Villalobos 73–83) simply turn right and eventually you'll end up in the Plaza Mayor. If you've arrived by train, turn left into Plaza España from where c/ Toro leads to the Plaza Mayor, and c/de España (or the *Gran Vía*) to the main **Turismo** and **Correos** (nos. 25 and 39 respectively). There's also a smaller information office in the Pl. Mayor.

The Plaza Mayor is also the place to go to for **cheap accommodation** — in the small streets surrounding it (especially c/Melendez) you'll find scores of small *fondas* and *hostales*. Out of season you might be able to get a room overlooking the plaza itself (some entrances are in side streets). Even outside this area, there are lots of alternatives (*Gabriel y Galan*, in the plaza of that name, is good), but the cheapest option is a room in a *casa particular*; these are available outside university terms (if you're stopped in the street, try haggling for a bargain). The town is likely to be packed in high season (especially August), when you might have to consider one- or two-star hotels, but these are still reasonable. There are also a couple of **campgrounds** nearby, the best at Sta. Marta, about 5km out but served by regular local buses.

The **cafes** in the Plaza Mayor are nearly twice the usual price but worth every peseta. Close at hand in the Plaza del Mercado (by the **market**, itself a good source of provisions) there's a row of lively *tapas* bars, while the university area offers loads of good value **bars and restaurants** catering to those on student budgets. Look for the town's specialty, *chanfaina*, the nearest Spanish cuisine gets to a curry. A rice-based dish with lamb, black pudding, sausage, etc. cooked in spicy juices, it's on the budget menu at the *Restaurante Roma* on c/Ruiz Aguilera, behind the Pl. Mayor — a street that has other cheapies too. Also off Pl. Mayor, c/del Prado offers the *Bar Marín*, with a reputation for its frogs' legs fried in batter (summer only), and c/Juan del Rey has a good, reasonably-priced restaurant. In the vicinity of the House of Shells, you'll find a couple of cheap and trendy restaurants, and *El Bardo*, in c/Menendez Valdez, has good vegetarian food. Places to look for elsewhere include the restaurant *El Corrillo* (in the plaza of the same name), the bar *La Rayuela* (Rua Mayor) with good music, and two **discos** — *Sergeant Pepper* (c/de San Pablo) and *Titan* (c/Breton).

Ciudad Rodrigo

The unspoiled frontier town of **CIUDAD RODRIGO** — astride the road and railroad to the border post at FUENTES DE OÑORO — is worth a detour even if you don't plan to cross over into Portugal. It's a quiet old place which, despite an orgy of destruction by Wellington in 1810, preserves streets full of **Renaissance mansions**. Walking the circuit of the twelfth-century **town walls** is a thoroughly enjoyable, and satisfying, experience. The route is interrupted only by an austere castle (now a plush *parador*) which overlooks a Roman bridge on the River Agueda and commands an enticing view across into Portugal.

Ciudad Rodrigo also has a **Cathedral**, built in a mixture of styles but originally Transitional. Take a look at the highly unusual eight-part vaults, dome-like in shape, and then root out the sacristan so you can get a view of the building's other most interesting features — the cloisters, half of which are fourteenth-century and half sixteenth-century; the *coro*, with wonderfully grotesque stalls carved by Rodrigo Aleman, who also created those at Toledo and Plasencia; and the narthex, with statues of Apostles. There don't seem to be any regular opening hours but it should be possible to visit late morning or early evening.

The **Turismo**, facing the cathedral at the entrance to the town, will offer you a map and a small information sheet on some of the churches and sixteenth-century palaces, but Ciudad Rodrigo's empty streets are ideal for wandering with no particular purpose. With this in mind, there are two good outdoor **cafes** in the Plaza Mayor. For more substantial food you'll have to head down to the **restaurants** along the main Salamanca-Portugal road. The **rooms** opposite the bus station are cheap and impeccable but if you prefer to stay within the walls of the town there's a *fonda* on c/de los Caceres, the alleyway down the side of the Turismo, and two more on c/del Toro nearby. The **railroad station** is about ten minutes' walk down the road to

Lumbreras. There are five trains a day into Portugal, but two of these are in the dead of night.

La Alberca and the Sierra de la Peña de Francia

East of Ciudad Rodrigo on the borders of Extremadura, some 80km southwest of Salamanca, is the village of **LA ALBERCA**. It has an extraordinary collection of old houses, each seemingly different from the rest, and constructed of diverse materials — wood, small stones, cut stone, rubble, and living rock. Unlike many other places of the picturesque variety, however, nothing has claim to architectural beauty, and there is no main "sight." The whole place has been declared a National Monument and plenty of tidying-up is going on, but the character of a rural community remains; horses still take precedence over cars as the means of transport, donkeys are used by the restorers instead of trucks, and goats, sheep, and poultry often block the streets.

The most elegant houses are in the **Plaza Mayor**, which is dominated by a Calvary; look into the church in the square behind, for its elaborate polychromed pulpit, carved in a popular style. Shops selling 'local crafts' and prominently displaying all the credit cards they accept are the inevitable signs of exploitation, and most of the houses in the Plaza Mayor seem to serve as cafes. Despite this, much of the population seems unaffected and, in the evenings in particular, after the tourists have gone, there is an air of timelessness to the place. Many age-old customs, including ways of dressing, have survived, and the local celebration of the Feast of Assumption on August 15 is considered to be the best in Spain.

The only **buses** are to and from Salamanca, leaving the latter at 5pm, which means you'll have to stay overnight to see the town. Unfortunately a stay here is likely to be relatively expensive, unless you use the campground (only open mid-June to mid-Sept.), which is 5km north. There are a couple of small **pensions**, one on the Pl. Mayor and the other just off it, but these are not always open, and have few rooms. The two-star *Hostal El Castillo* at the far end of the village is the next best bet.

Hiking in the Sierra

Although La Alberca is well worth visiting in itself, it would be a pity not to sample some of the marvelous scenery the area offers. A couple of walks, each lasting about a day, are well worth the effort. The shorter and most obvious is the ascent of the **PEÑA DE FRANCIA**, which provides a spectacular backdrop to the village. A road, following a very circuitous route, goes all the way to the summit; unfortunately there's no short-cut on foot, except at the beginning, where you can save a couple of kilometers by cutting across the campground. Plenty of cars make the ascent, and you might as well hitch a lift one way, as the first half of the climb is not very interesting, the views being generally masked by trees. Further up, you'll be rewarded by fine panoramas not only of the mountain itself (which is disfigured by a television tower serving the whole province and beyond), but also over the wild hills of Las Hurdes to the south and the Sierra de Gredos to the east, as well as the plains below. At the top you can take lunch or rereshments at the *Hospederia* of the monastery, which is occupied during the warmer half of the year by Dominicans from San Esteban in Salamanca.

The second walk — and the more impressive — is southwards to the valley of **LAS BATUECAS**, a National Reserve. This time it's best to bring a picnic, for although fresh water abounds, there isn't a bar, restaurant, or even house in sight until you reach the village of LAS MESTAS, just over the Extremaduran border, some 19km away. After 2km you'll come to the pass of El Portillo, surrounded by solemn, rugged hills. From here on, the road dips and loops spectacularly, offering a different panorama at every turn. You reach the valley floor at the 12km point, and a short road leads to the gate of the **Carmelite Monastery**, founded at the beginning of the seventeenth century for a community of hermits. Only men can enter the precincts (9am–12:50pm and 4:20–6:45pm in summer; 8–11:50am and 3:20–5:45pm in winter) where the simple church and the outsides of the monks' small houses can be seen. One of the first tasks of the monastery was to exorcise the demons and evil spirits which supposedly inhabited the nearby valleys of **Las Hurdes** in Extremadura (see p.120).

In 1933 the great film-maker **Luis Buñuel** stayed in the monastery while shooting his early masterpiece *Land Without Bread* about the extremely primitive lifestyle of the people of these valleys. The film got him into political hot water for allegedly showing Spain in a bad light, but Buñuel fell in love with the region, and with the monastery (then a hotel) whose gardens grew what he claimed were the best vegetables in the world. Three years later he arranged to purchase it, but the outbreak of the civil war sent him into exile, and the place was reoccupied by the Carmelites. Today nine superannuated monks pass their last years in this most beautiful of locations.

To see at least the fringes of the country that Buñuel filmed, it's an easy walk along the rest of the valley, and then up to Las Mestas and Vegas de Coria. However, it's more fun to take the footpath that skirts the outside of the monastery's perimeter wall and follow the course of the river, which forms a gorge with splendid rock formations. There are **caves** with prehistoric rock paintings here, but unfortunately — as so often — the most important ones have been closed off to preserve them from the twin hazards of deterioration and vandalism. After exploring the valley, you have to return the same way. The walk back to La Alberca is a daunting climb; there is little traffic, although the chances of getting a ride from cars that do pass are good.

North to Zamora

Leaving Salamanca to the north, you can be in Zamora within an hour by rail or road. The latter roughly follows the route of the Roman road, the *Vía de la Plata*, that ran down from Astorga in León province to Extremedura. If you're driving, however, you might prefer to take the delightful secondary road to

LEDESMA and head up to Zamora from there. For most of the way this route trails the beautiful River Tormes, where there's excellent fishing (for giant carp), herons and storks in the trees, enormous, delicious mushrooms (*setas*) in autumn, and a variety of meadow flowers in spring. Ledesma itself — little more than a large village these days — retains its ancient walls, the remains of a Roman bridge and baths, and a couple of attractive churches. If you're staying overnight, the *Fonda Mercado* is a good bet. The greenery around here seems untypical of Castile — it's created in large part by the great dam (the *Embalse de Almendra*) almost at the Portuguese border, whose reservoir stretches all the way back to Ledesma.

ZAMORA is the quietest of the great historic cities of the heartland, with a present population of 60,000. In medieval romances it was known as *la bien cercada* (the closed one) on account of its strong fortifications; one siege here lasted seven months. Its old quarters, medieval in appearance, are spread out along the sloping banks of the Río Duero (known as the Douro once it crosses into Portugal) and there are a dozen **Romanesque churches** within ten minutes' walk of the center. Apart from the cathedral with its superlative collection of tapestries, no single church stands out above the others, but their unassumingly beautiful architecture is the city's most distinctive feature. Most of them date from the twelfth century and reflect Old Castile's new-found sense of security after the victorious campaigns against the Moors by Alfonso VI and El Cid — notably the recapture of Toledo in 1085.

The **Cathedral**, enclosed within the ruined citadel at the far end of town, is a fitting climax to this series of ancient churches. Though it was begun in 1151 and overall is Romanesque, the grandiose north entrance is in the classical style of the High Renaissance. A Byzantine-inspired dome, looking quite out of place, is its most striking feature, showing the same turrets and "fish-scale" tiles as the Old Cathedral at Salamanca. The carved choir stalls, which depict lusty carryings-on between monks and nuns, were nailed down for a long time at the orders of a particularly sanctimonious bishop, but are now on view again. The **Cathedral Museum** (11am–2pm and 4–8pm) houses the celebrated and unsurpassed "Black Tapestries." The patrons who commissioned these fifteenth-century Flemish masterpieces clearly demanded their money's worth, since every inch is woven in stunning detail. Traditional Greek and Roman themes were chosen but contemporary dress and weaponry intruded, illustrating how nobles in the Middle Ages liked to see themselves as heroes from the past.

There's an unusual **Museo de la Semana Santa** attached to Santa María la Nueva (turn left opposite the *parador* on your way back to the center); it contains the *pasos* — statues depicting the Passion of Christ — which are paraded through the streets at Easter.

Zamora suffers no more than a trickle of tourism and there's no problem finding **places to stay**. If you arrive by **train** follow Avda. de las Tres Cruces and after about fifteen minutes you'll come to the Pl. Alemania on the edge of the old town; the **bus station** is about two minutes from here, near the Pl. de Toros. Across Pl. Alemania there are some *hostales* on c/San Torcuato and c/Benavente (third left — it leads to the **Turismo** at c/Santa Clara 20), and you'll find a further choice of three cheap **pensions** in the Pl. Mayor at the end of c/San Torcuato. **Leaving**, you can continue north easily enough to León, or take the train north-west into Galicia — to Orense and Santiago. Alternatively, follow the Duero east into the heartlands of Old Castile; if you follow the minor road to Toro (along the south bank of the river) you'll have more opportunities for birdwatching or fishing.

Along the Duero to Toro and Tordesillas

TORO looks dramatic — "an ancient, eroded red-walled town spread along the top of a huge flat boulder," as Laurie Lee described it when he arrived here with a group of German traveling musicians. Its raw red hillside site is best contemplated from the railroad line several hundred feet below the town in the Duero valley. At closer quarters it turns out to be a pleasant, rather ordinary provincial town, embellished with one outstanding Romanesque reminder of its past glory. It did, however, play a role of vital significance in both Spanish and Portuguese history.

The **Battle of Toro** in 1476 effectively ended Portugal's interest in Spanish affairs and laid the basis for the unification of Spain. On the death of Enrique IV in 1474 the Castilian throne was disputed: almost certainly his daughter Juana *La Beltraneja* was the rightful heiress, but rumors of illegitimacy were stirred up and Enrique's sister Isabella seized the throne. Alfonso V of Portugal saw his opportunity and suported Juana. At Toro the armies clashed and the *Reyes Católicos* — Isabella and her husband Fernando — defeated their rivals, to embark upon one of the most glorious periods in Spanish history.

Even before this, Toro had long been a major military stronghold enjoying considerable royal patronage, and the monument that hints most strongly at this former importance is the **Colegiata Santa María la Mayor** (11am–1:45pm and 5:30–7:30pm). It's easy enough to find — simply walk straight through from the main town gate to the far side of Toro, passing two *fondas* near the Plaza de España. The West Portal (ca.1240) is one of the best preserved and most beautiful examples of Romanesque art: seven recessed arches are carved with royal and biblical themes and the tympanum (the central panel above the door) depicts the Virgin Mary. All such portals were originally painted in a variety of colors, and this one is the closest to that pristine decorative state.

TORDESILLAS, too, can boast of an important place in Spain's history. It was here, under the eye of the Borgia Pope Alexander VI, that the **Treaty of Tordesillas** (1494) divided "All Lands Discovered, or Hereafter to be Discovered in the West, towards the Indies or the Ocean Seas" between Spain and Portugal along a line 370 leagues west of the Cape Verde Islands. Brazil, allegedly discovered six years later, went to Portugal — though it was claimed that the Portuguese already knew of its existence but had kept silent to gain better terms. The rest of the New World, including Mexico and Peru, became Spanish.

Further fame was brought by the unfortunate **Juana la Loca** (Joanna the Mad), who spent 46 years in a windowless cell here. She had ruled Castile jointly with her husband Felipe I (the Handsome) from 1504–06 but was devastated by his early death and for three years toured the monasteries of Spain, keeping the coffin perpetually by her side, stopping from time to time to inspect the corpse. In 1509 she wound up in Tordesillas. First Fernando (her father) and later Carlos V (her son) declared Juana insane, imprisoning her for half a century and assuming the throne of Castile for themselves.

Like Toro, the town boasts one outstanding monument: the **Real Monasterio de Santa Clara** overlooking the Duero (Wed.–Sun. 9am–1pm and 3–7pm, Tues. 9am–1pm; guided tour). Known as "The Alhambra of Castile" for its delightful Mudejar architecture, it was built originally as a royal palace by Alfonso el Sabio (the Wise) in 1340. Its prettiest features are the tiny "Arab Patio" with horseshoe arches and Moorish decoration and the superb *artesonado* ceiling of the main chapel, described by Sacheverell Sitwell as "a ceiling of indescribable splendor, as brilliant in effect as if it had panes or slats of mother-of-pearl in it." Also worth seeing are the long medieval bridge over the Duero, the arcaded Plaza Mayor, and the church of San Antolin, now a museum with a surprisingly good collection of sculpture.

If you're staying in Tordesillas be warned that it stands on a major crossroads (of the road from Madrid to Galicia and the direct route from Salamanca to Valladolid) and that the *hostales* on the main road tend to be expensive. You'll find two cheap *fondas* on c/San Antolin just off the Pl. Mayor.

Valladolid

VALLADOLID, at the center of the *meseta*, ought to be exciting. Many of the greatest figures of Spain's Golden Age — Fernando and Isabella, Columbus, Cervantes, Felipe II — lived at some point in the city and for many years it vied with Madrid as the royal capital. In reality its old quarter is today an oppressive labyrinth of dingy streets, and those of its palaces that survive do so in a woeful state of decline. Many of the finest have been swept away on a tide of speculation and official incompetence — to be replaced by a dull sprawl of high-rise concrete. Modern Valladolid may be an expanding industrial city of 400,000, inhabitants but it has lost much that was irreplaceable. Nonetheless, there are a couple of terrific examples of late Gothic architecture, an excellent Oriental museum and — above all — the finest collection of sculpture assembled anywhere in Spain.

The City

At the center of things, as ever, is the **Cathedral**, designed but not completed by Juan de Herrera (architect of El Escorial) and later worked on by Alberto Churriguera; only half of it was ever built, but the model in the museum shows how classically grand the original design was. What stands is a disappointment: the vast dimensions and sweeping arches do have something of Herrera's grandeur but the overall effect is one of plainness and severity. Inside, the *retablo mayor* by Juan de Juni is a typical product actually made for Santa María la Antigua. The **Diocesan Museum** (weekdays 5–8pm; access from the cathedral) is housed in the surviving buildings of a

Collegiate church torn down to make way for the cathedral. Although somewhat overshadowed by the National Museum of Sculpture, this collection contains some worthy religious pieces of the sixteenth and seventeenth centuries. In the large Plaza behind the cathedral stands **Santa María la Antigua**, a Gothic church with modest flying buttresses and a Romanesque bell-tower which culminates in a pyramidal roof. From the corner of the Plaza diagonally opposite the cathedral, c/de las Angustias leads a short distance to Plaza de San Pablo and its unmistakable church.

Although it might not be immediately obvious, the exuberant facade of **San Pablo** is a mixture of styles — the lower part is a product of the lavish form of late Gothic known as Isabelline, whereas the upper part is a Plateresque confection, similar to the New Cathedral and San Esteban at Salamanca. The building is treated purely as a surface for whimsical and highly decorative carvings which bear no relation to the structure that supports it. The facade of the adjacent **Colegio de San Gregorio**, a purer example of the Isabelline style, is adorned with coats of arms, sculpted twigs, naked children clambering in the branches of a tree and several comical long-haired men carrying maces. It's a lot like icing on a cake — Jan Morris, for one, was convinced that the flamboyant facades must be "actually edible."

Behind the gaudy front there's serious business, however, for the Colegio houses the dynamic **Museo Nacional de Escultura Religiosa** (Tues.–Sat. 10am–1:30pm and 4–7pm; Sun. 10am–1.30pm), where the most brilliant works of the Spanish Renaissance are on display. Much the most important figures in this movement were Alonso Berruguete, Diego de Siloé, and Juan de Juni: all three were active in the sixteenth century and spent several years in Florence where they perfected the realistic depiction of anatomy, fell heavily under the influence of Michelangelo, and immersed themselves in the Italian Renaissance. Their genius lies in the adaptation of the classical revival to the religious intensity of the Spanish temperament. The masterpiece of **Alonso Berruguete** (1486–1561) is a massive dismantled altarpiece which occupies the first three rooms of the museum — a remarkable demonstration of Berruguete's skills in painting, relief sculpture and free-standing statuary. **Diego de Siloé** (1495–1565) was even more versatile. He classicized the Gothic cathedral at Granada and was an equally accomplished sculptor — see his *Sagrada Familia* in room 10 and the carved choir stalls in room 11. Works of the Frenchman **Juan de Juni** (1507–77) show an almost theatrical streak and foreshadowed the emotional and naturalistic sculpture of the seventeenth and eighteenth centuries. This later period is best exemplified by the agonizingly realistic work of **Gregorio Fernandez** (rooms 4 and 5, near the ticket desk) and **Alonso de Villabrille** (especially his *Head of San Pablo*, room 27).

While here, you should also take in the beautiful patio with lace-like tracery, and several Moorish-inspired ceilings which have been taken from other buildings in the city. The chapel (entrance is immediately left of the main door, opposite the ticket booth) has many interesting exhibits, including another *retablo* by Alonso Berruguete, this time intact. The chapel is currently undergoing restoration, but the hours are officially the same as the museum.

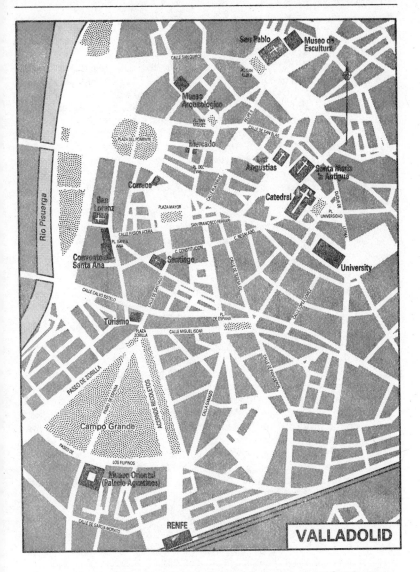

Anyone attracted by the passionate religious sculpture of Valladolid can find further examples in almost any of the historic churches in the city. Santiago houses the only other Berruguete, a large *retablo* with the Adoration of the Magi as the main scene, in a dingy nave chapel; it will be illuminated free of charge if you ask at the sacristy. Another highly regarded piece is Juni's *Virgin of the Knives* in Las Angustias (hours listed outside). Many of these statues (except the ones in museums) feature in Valladolid's

Semana Santa celebrations, which are often claimed to be the best in the country; they are more solemn and far more religious than the internationally famous fiestas in Sevilla, and no less spectacular.

In a surprisingly different vein there's a delightful **Museo Oriental** (weekdays 4–7pm) on the Paseo de Los Filipinos, just off the Campo Grande. This occupies a dozen rooms in the Colegio de Agustinos, which sent missionaries to China and the Philippines for four centuries until their expulsion in 1952. Countless exquisite gems of Chinese art are on show. Among the most striking are some beautiful paintings of nature on rice paper (mainly Sung Dynasty; rooms 1 and 2) and three gorgeous porcelain pieces entitled *The Three Happy Chinamen: Fu, Shou and Lou* (Qing Epoch; room 2). On the way out you can look at the lavishly decorated interior of the church, a good example of the academic style of Ventura Rodriguez, fashionable in the late eighteenth century.

Other museums include the **Museo Arqueológico**, just up from Plaza San Miguel and housed in a Renaissance mansion; it has medieval and prehistoric sections. The **Museo de San Joaquin y Santa Ana** is filled mostly with religious dust-collectors but has a few good statues, plus three Goya paintings in the chapel. (Both open same hours as Museo Nacional de Escultura.)

Valladolid is also a famous academic center. The **University**, just beyond the cathedral, has a portal by Narciso Tome, the man who built the *Transparente* in Toledo Cathedral — one of the very few surviving works by him.

Some Practicalities

Finding your way round Valladolid can be a nightmare — even with our map. Both **bus and railroad stations** are near the Campo Grande, a large triangular park where Napoleon once reviewed his troops; for travel around town and the suburbs, buy a discount *bono bus* ticket. If traveling out of town, avoid Sundays as many buses don't run then. The Turismo is in a corner of the Campo, at Plaza de Zorilla 3 (Mon.–Fri. 9am–2pm and 4–6pm, Sat. 9am–2pm). **Rooms,** while plentiful and reasonably cheap, are spread all over town. You'll find several possibilities near the railroad station, but as in so many Spanish cities the seedy area around the cathedral is the best place to look — there are half a dozen *hostales* in the immediate vicinity. Take c/de Santiago from the *Turismo* and then the fourth street on the right, c/de la Constitución; it's about ten minutes' walk, or two hours if you get lost. For less seedy options, try the market area, particularly c/del Val (*Hostal Greco* on 2nd floor, with another *hostal* underneath).

For **eating**, you're again best off in the central area. There are places around the Pl. de España, others on c/de Santiago near the Pl. Mayor. In c/ Nuñez de Arce, a bar/restaurant of the same name has a good, cheap menu and house specialties, such as rabbit (which can also be eaten as a *tapa racion*) — be warned though, the place fills up quickly. You could also try getting some of your own provisions together at the **market**, on c/de Sandoval.

Valladolid is a major crossroads, and your **onward** options are almost endless; Ávila, Salamanca, León and Burgos are all reasonably close.

Palencia and Around

Heading northeast from Valladolid, **PALENCIA** lies at the heart of a triangle delineated by León, Burgos, and Valladolid itself, but is little affected by tourism. This is no doubt because, despite a rich past, it's not a particularly impressive place now. There are numerous plazas, usually dominated by Romanesque churches built in a rather gaunt white stone; all are pleasant, none outstanding. **Bus and railroad stations** are both situated at the side of the Plaza Calvo Sotelo; at its far corner, the long Calle Mayor opens out, and the **Turismo** is placed inconveniently near the end of it. On the way, you'll pass a couple of cheap but adequate **fondas**; the side streets contain more luxurious accommodation and plenty of reasonably-priced eating places.

The main sight is the **Cathedral**, a noble fourteenth- to fifteenth-century Gothic building whose exterior is relatively plain by Spanish standards, except for the two south portals. Inside, most of the extremely rich decoration is contemporary with, or only slightly later than, the architecture, thanks to the patronage of Bishop Fonseca. Soon after the cathedral was completed, Palencia fell into decline — hence the almost complete absence of baroque trappings. The interior is divided into three compartments: besides the inevitable *coro* and sanctuary, there's also the **Capilla del Sagrario** at the east end. Buy a ticket in the sacristy to see the artistic treasures; one of the staff will take you to the crypt (part Visigothic, part Romanesque) and the museum in the cloisters, which includes a very early *San Sebastián* by El Greco, and Flemish tapestries. In addition, lights are switched on so you can see the various altars, and the chapel doors will be opened — a facility not always available in Spain. The highlight is probably the *retablo mayor*, which contains twelve beautiful little panels, ten of them painted by Juan de Flandes, court painter to Isabella la Catolica — it's the best collection of his work anywhere. Not far from the cathedral is the Río Carrión, spanned by a picturesque old bridge known as **Puentecillas**, which contrasts well with the sturdier and later **Puente Mayor**.

Not far from Palencia, the ugly modern town of VENTA DE BAÑOS is an important railroad junction, where you may have to change trains. If so, it's well worth following the signs to the village of **BAÑOS DE CERRATO**, located at the edge of the town. This has one of the best-preserved monuments of the Dark Ages, a seventh-century Visigothic basilica dedicated to **San Juan**. Its exterior is rather plain; the interior, originally marble-lined, incorporates materials reused from Roman buildings, and horseshoe arches which pre-date the Moors. Ask for the key at the priest's house nearby; you should be able to visit it at any reasonable time, except on Mondays.

The Palencia region has very attractive countryside, and if you follow one of the many rivers in just about any direction you'll find scores of small villages, none exceptional, but all tranquil and charming, usually with a couple of ancient churches and an old stone bridge. The minor road from Palencia to SAHAGÚN — which follows the line of the railroad towards León — is particularly enticing. Just 15km out of Palencia, or fifteen minutes on a local train, is BECERRIL DE CAMPOS, with its delightfully run-down old plaza. **PAREDES DE NAVA**, 10km on, is a rather larger place (even fast trains stop here) with a more specific attraction in the form of the church of Santa Eulalia (11am–2pm and 4–7pm in summer; 11am–2pm and 4–6pm in winter). The great sculptor Alonso Berruguete was born here, as were many of his lesser-known relatives, and the parish church (with a beautifully tiled Romanesque tower) has been turned into a small museum full of their works. The collection is arranged in every available space, and includes works by many of the best-known of Berruguete's contemporaries, gathered from all the churches of this little town. Paredes has three fondas, all with restaurant.

For those interested in pursuing the **pilgrimage route**, FRÓMISTA, on the Santander road, is within easy reach from Palencia (see section below). Otherwise, castle country to the south is an obvious destination.

Three Castles at Coca, Medina del Campo, and Peñafiel

It is said there were once 10,000 castles in Spain. Of those that are left, some 500 are in a reasonable state of repair, and Castile has far more than its fair share of them. The area around Valladolid is especially rich — it's ringed with a series of fortresses, many of them built in the fifteenth century to protect the royal seat.

Less a piece of military architecture than a country house masquerading as one, the **castle of COCA** (one hour by train south from Valladolid, or up from Segovia) is the prettiest fortress imaginable. Constructed from narrow pinkish bricks, encircled by a deep moat, and fantastically decorated with octagonal turrets, merlons, and elaborate castellation, it's an extraordinary design strongly influenced by Moorish architecture. It dates from about 1400, and was the base of the powerful **Fonseca family**, two of whose members became archbishops in Toledo and Sevilla. The interior (Mon.–Fri. 8am–3pm and 3:30–5:30pm, Sat. 9am–2pm) has been completely remodelled and taken over by the Ministry of Agriculture, who own a considerable amount of land around Coca. Their forests near the railroad station (20-min. walk) are excellent for discreet **camping**. The town of Coca itself is totally lifeless, but there are a few bars and if you ask in these you should be able to find a room for the night. While here, try to see the inside of the parish church of **Santa María**, where there are four tombs of the Fonseca family carved in white marble in the Italian Renaissance style. The power of the dynasty is indicated by the fact that they were able to hire the sculptor of the tombs of the *Reyes Católicos* in Granada, Bartolome Ordoñez.

The Moorish design of the brick-built **castle at MEDINA DEL CAMPO** (called *La Mota*) is similar to that at Coca but not quite so exuberant and rather more robust. It was intended as another stronghold for the Fonsecas, but they were thrown out by the townsfolk in 1473. Queen Isabella lived here for several years (and died, in 1504, in a room overlooking the town's Plaza Mayor) after which the castle was reincarnated as a prison, then as a girls' boarding school, and more recently as a cultural center. You can gain admission inside the castle walls any day except Sunday, but there are no rooms to see, and it is the exterior which is more imposing.

In the fifteenth and sixteenth centuries Medina del Campo (City of the Plain) was one of the most important market towns in the whole of Europe, with merchants converging from as far afield as Italy and Germany to attend its fairs. Today the town is more significant as a major railroad junction, but the largest sheep market in Spain is still held here and the beautifully ramshackle Plaza Mayor is still evocative of the days when its bankers determined the value of European currencies. The cheapest **rooms** are offered by a couple of bars on c/de Almirante just off the Plaza.

The elongated **castle at PEÑAFIEL** bears an astonishing resemblance to a huge ship run aground: it is 210m long but only 23m across, with its central tower playing the role of the ship's bridge. Built in 1466 out of the region's distinctive white stone, the castle was planned to adapt to the necessities of the narrow ridge upon which it stands. It's open from about 9 or 10am to 2pm and then from 4 to 7pm, and there should be a caretaker there. From the "prow" of the castle there's a tremendous view of Peñafiel, but you could also venture a horizontal ramble: walking around the hill at the foot of the castle affords good changing views, the best perhaps being from the southwest, in the Plaza del Cosa. This large square is extraordinary in itself; its buildings are wooden, with several tiers of loggias, and it makes the most spectacular bull-ring in Spain when fights are held in August. Nearby is San Pablo, now a college, with a superb brick Gothic-Mudejar apse, to which a Plateresque chapel was later added. If you're **staying**, there are a few **hostales** at the edge of town, near where the buses stop.

The town lies 50km east of Valladolid along the main road to Soria. There's a bus each way to Valladolid in the morning, at lunchtime and in the evening (ignore signs for the railroad station — it was closed to passenger traffic a few years ago). Buses also go to **ARANDA DE DUERO** (same times), from where you can continue to El Burgo de Osma. If you're passing through Aranda de Duero, you should take a look at the south facade of **Santa María**, an ornate Isabelline work in which even the doors are carved. The village itself is quite graceful and picturesque, and has a reputation for delicious roast lamb — *cordero* or *lechazo asado* . Plenty of restaurants vie with each other to tempt you to sample it.

In addition to the castles, this is another area of Old Castile that is rich in **wildlife**. At Peñafiel the Río Duratón flows into the Duero: follow this upstream, to the south, and you'll come to two large man-made reservoirs. The **PANTANO DE BURGOMILLODO** (just to the west of Sepúlveda) is a particularly exciting spot for birdwatchers, surrounded by heaths of wild lavender which are the haunt of Griffon Vultures and other exotic species. From here you can head on towards El Burgo de Osma on the road through **RIAZA**, skirting the foothills of the Sierra de Guadarrama. It's a lovely route, and Riaza itself makes a pleasant place to stop for a while, with several good bars (try *El Museo*) and restaurants, and a couple of places offering rooms. There's also a station here on the main line from Madrid to Burgos.

El Burgo de Osma and Castles of the Duero

EL BURGO DE OSMA, the episcopal center of Soria province, can be reached by bus from Valladolid or, nearer, from Soria to the east. It is a wonderfully picturesque place, with crumbling town walls and ancient colonnaded streets overhung by houses supported on precarious wooden props, and there's a relaxed village atmosphere in the Plaza Mayor.

In this setting the **Cathedral** (10am–1:30pm and 4–7pm), one of the richest in Spain, seems incongruous. Although Gothic in style, it has had many embellishments over the years, notably the superb baroque tower, decorated with pinnacles and gables, which dominates the town. To see many of the cathedral's treasures, you have to buy a ticket. Lights will be switched on for you to see the theatrical *retablo mayor* by Juan de Juni and his pupils, and the dark chapels, one of which contains a powerful Romanesque carving of the Crucifixion. You will also be escorted to the cloisters and the museum, where a number of polyglot bibles are displayed, and an eleventh-century illuminated manuscript of Beatus featuring a bizarre map of the world (probably a fascimile will be on display). Most impressive of all is the tomb of San Pedro de Osma in polychromed limestone, carved with scenes from his life.

You can get some idea of El Burgo's former importance from the fact that it was once the seat of a university. The sixteenth-century building, now a school, is at the edge of town, near where the buses stop. This is also where you'll find all the available **accommodation** — two *hostales*, both two-stars, and a one-star hotel, though they aren't always all open. (*Hostal La Perdiz*, by the garage, is a bit pricey — cheaper, but smaller, is *Hostal Casa Agapito*.) There's also a **campground** (June–Sept.); take the first left off c/Mayor and then turn right along c/Rodrigo Yusto. If you happen to be here in March or April and your sensibilities aren't offended, you could attend the annual *matanza* or slaughter of the pig. It has long been an important country ritual throughout Spain, although it doesn't have the significance it used to when the pig was a main source of food, and it is now promoted as a tourist outing. They usually take place on Sunday afternoons.

Medieval Traces

The hills around the town are excellent for walking, offering a series of changing views. One of them is topped by the ruined **Castillo de Osma**, one of the many fortresses built to defend the nearby Río Duero, which long marked the frontier between Arab and Christian territory. Another castle in a similar condition is at **SAN ESTEBAN DE GORMAZ**, 13km west, a town that also has two Romanesque churches with frontal arcades in the Segovian manner. It also has a larger selection of cheap accommodation than Burgo de Osma.

The most impressive castles, however, are a little further afield, and rather difficult to reach now that the railroad line has been closed down. **GORMAZ**, 15km south of El Burgo, is particularly intriguing since it was originally built in the Caliphate style, and two Moorish doorways dating from the tenth century have survived. Later captured and modified by Christians, it was one of the largest fortified buildings in the West — there are 28 towers in all, ruined but impressive. The inside is a shell, but there are good panoramas from here, and the wonderful views as you approach make the long walk less daunting. **BERLANGA DE DUERO** lies about another 15km south-east, and can also be reached from Soria by daily bus (departure 5pm, return 8am). On a hill above the town stands a fifteenth-century castle with massive cylindrical towers; it's defended by a double curtain wall of an earlier date, reminiscent of Ávila. The best way of going up is via a doorway in a ruined Renaissance palace at the edge of town; entrance is free at all times. The other dominant monument is the Colegiata (usually open), one of the last flowerings of the Gothic style. Its unusually uniform design, in the hall church style, is due to it's having been erected in just four years. Berlanga also has an old-world Plaza Mayor (where markets are held regularly), several fine mansions, arcaded streets, an impressive entrance gateway, and the unique *La Picota* — a pillar of justice to which offenders were tied (it's on an empty lot outside the old town, where the buses stop). Not far from the pillar is the only place to stay that is regularly open, the two-star *Hostal La Hoz*, quite luxurious and a remarkable bargain. It doubles as the town's disco on the weekend, and also has a good restaurant. One of the bars opposite the Colegiata rents rooms at the height of summer.

Eight kilometers south lies the tiny Mozarabic **Ermita de San Baudelio de Berlanga**, the best-preserved and (with San Miguel de Escalada) most important example of this unique style. It was even better before the 1920s when, five years after being declared a National Monument, its marvelous cycle of frescoes was acquired by an international art dealer and exported to the USA. (Similar episodes also occurred in Franco's dictatorship, with his full knowledge and cooperation in arranging huge cover-ups.) After much fuss, the Spanish government got some of them back on indefinite loan, but they are now kept in the Prado. In spite of this loss, the hermitage is worth seeing, not only as a rarity, but also for the beauty of its interior (Tues.–Sat. 10am–2pm and 4–7pm in summer; 10am–2pm and 3:30–5:30pm in winter; Sun. 10am–2pm). Its eight-ribbed vault springs from a central pillar, while much of the space is taken up by the tribune gallery of horseshoe arches. Some original frescoes do remain, including two bulls from the great sequence of animals and hunting scenes of the nave. You can also see the entrance to the cave below, where the original hermit lived.

Thirty kilometers along the main road towards Soria lies **CALATAÑAZOR**, actually situated 1½km down a side road. A severely depopulated medieval village, with walls and the ruins of a castle, it's chiefly remarkable for its houses, with their distinctive red roofs, conical chimneys, decorative coats of arms and wooden balconies. The parish church (10am–1:30pm and 4:30–7:30pm in summer; 10am–1:30pm and 4–6pm in winter) has several valuable works of art. A village guide is based at the *Mesón*, where good, simple meals are served. The only available accommodation is in a two-star *hostal* on the main road where the bus stops, but the place makes an obvious half-day excursion from either El Burgo de Osma or Soria, 30km east.

Soria and Numancia

SORIA is the modest capital of the province of the same name, which consists of the upland valleys of the River Duero. Praised by Spanish Romantic poets of the nineteenth and early twentiety centuries, notably Antonio Machado, who lived here, "martial, mystical Soria" has some of Spain's most impressive castles and what must be regarded as the finest scenery in Castile, along with strong and flourishing folkloric traditions. It seems, nevertheless, to be a place the Spanish have kept largely to themselves. Set between two hills on the banks of the Duero, and dotted with unpretentious medieval mansions and Romanesque churches, Soria is an attractive place despite the encroachments of modern development. For an overall view, climb up to the nearly-vanished castle (take c/Caballeros from Plaza Olivo and follow the signs for the parador).

Just across the Duero, some ten minutes' walk from the center, stands the most freakish medieval monument in the country. The ruined cloisters of **San Juan de Duero** are remarkable for their original and imaginative synthesis of styles. They were built in the thirteenth century by Mudejar masons who playfully combined Moorish interlaced and cusped arches with Christian Romanesque and early Gothic shapes. The cloisters are open from Tues.–Sat. 10am–2pm and 4–7pm, Sun. 10am–2pm — if they're closed, you can get a partial aerial view from a low hill across the road. The church, converted into a museum, is more orthodox in style, but has two unusual little free-standing temples inside. From here, it's interesting to follow Machado's favorite walk along the banks of the river southwards, passing the former Templar church of **San Polo** (now a private home), and coming after 2km to the **Ermita de San Saturio**, a two-tiered complex including an octagonal chapel with thirteenth-century frescoes (May–Sept. Wed.–Mon. 10am–2pm and 4:30–9pm; Oct.–Apr. Wed.–Mon. 10:30am–6:30pm). The landscape here is typical of the province, with its parched, livid, orange earth, and the solemn river lined by poplars.

Returning to the city center, you pass the **co-Catedral de San Pedro**, a rather stolid Plateresque building. Its interior (only open for masses) takes the Spanish penchant for darkness to a ridiculous extreme — its windows admit hardly any light at all. To the side are three bays of a Romanesque cloister which belonged to the cathedral's predecessor — they are really worth seeing and, although there are no fixed opening times, you can generally get in. From here, follow the main road that skirts the old town to reach the convent church of **Santo Domingo**. A twelfth-century building, its beautiful rose-colored facade is decorated symmetrically with sixteen "blind" arches and a wheel window with eight "spokes." The recessed arches of the main portal are excellently preserved and magnificently sculpted with scenes from the life of Christ, including a particularly moving *Massacre of the Innocents*. After this, the dingy interior (normally open except for a couple of short periods of "spiritual exercises" each day) is a tremendous letdown. Also worth a look in the center of town is another fine Romanesque church, **San Juan de Rabanera**, and the massive sixteenth-century **Palacio de los Condes de Gomara**.

The **railroad and bus stations** are both situated on the fringes of the city; the former, which has had its services ruthlessly pruned in the last few years, is at the extreme southwest corner. A new bus station has been built on c/Valladolid in the modern northwest quarters; to walk from one to the other, you can follow the ring road, without having to go into the center. The very helpful **Turismo** is in the Plaza Ramon y Cajal, opposite the entrance to the large Alameda de Cervantes. Around this area there's a wealth of cheap **accommodation** — try Pl. Olivo, c/Ferial (the welcoming *Fonda Ferial* is recommended), c/Campo, or Pl. del Salvador. There are plenty of **eating and drinking places** in this area as well, but the most mouth-watering selection of *tapas* are to be found in the Pl. San Clemente, in the pedestrian-only central area; it can be reached either from the main c/Collado, or else by following c/Aduana Vieja from Santo Domingo.

From Soria there's quite a choice of **destinations**: east into Aragón, north to Logroño and the Basque country, or, staying in the province, south to Almazán and Medinaceli.

Numancia and Agreda

Just 8km to the north of Soria, the rather barren site of Roman **NUMANCIA** (Tues.–Sat. 10am–2pm and 4–7pm in summer; 10am–2pm and 3:30–5:30pm in winter; Sun. 10am–2pm) stands on a hill above the village of GARRAY. The Celto-Iberian town which originally occupied this site resisted Scipio and his legions for over a year, and when finally defeated, the inhabitants destroyed the town rather than surrender it. What survives are some excavated remains of the Roman city that replaced it, with the outline of the streets clearly visible. They're not terribly exciting unless you're an archeology fan. If you do come, you can also visit the Romanesque **Ermita de los Martires** halfway down the hill. Several buses pass this way, but at very irregular intervals; there are a couple of cheap restaurants in Garray in which to kill some time.

About 50km east of Soria, and 20km from Tarazona in Aragón, lies **AGREDA**, a small town which Turismo in Soria is anxious to promote as being of exceptional interest. It does preserve an Arab gateway and the remains of medieval fortifications but, to save you from wasting your time, it should be said that it is essentially a scruffy and unmemorable place.

Sorian Scenery — the Río Lobos Canyon and the Urbión Lakes

About 20km north of El Burgo de Osma lies the entrance to the newly-created **Parque Natural del Canyon del Río Lobos**. Unfortunately there's no bus along this road, but you can approach from the other end, from SAN LEONARDO DE YAGUE, which is on one of the main bus routes between Soria and Burgos. This might be the better base for exploring the park (there are two good *hostales* to choose from); alternatively, you can camp in the officially designated areas around the entrance. From a belvedere on the San Leonardo road there's a superb panoramic view; to the west you have an aerial perspective of the park, while to the south is another of the Sorian castle-crowned villages, UCERO. If you have a car, you can drive along a stony road inside the park for 2km; after that, you'll have to walk. The whole area is impressive, with rocks on both sides of the canyon thrown into fantastic shapes, but the most interesting part lies 1km on from the car park — as well as some of the prettiest rock formations, there's a Romanesque chapel founded by the Templars (kept locked) and, behind this, a beautiful natural cave. From here, the trail continues onwards through fairly similar scenery. At times, the Río Lobos is a mere trickle; its tributaries have dried up completely, providing ready-made walking tracks. For this, or more adventurous treks into the high ground, you really need proper hiking boots, but any shoes will do on the main paths. The park will appeal to bird-watchers; eagles and vultures are often seen, even though they are not protected here.

Vinuesa

Another area of wild beauty is the lake district of the **Sierra de Urbión** in the north of the province. The most obvious base is **VINUESA**, situated just north of the enormous man-made reservoir, *Pantano de la Cuerda del Pozo*. It's on the alternative bus route between Burgos and Soria, and is a spaciously laid-out village with many fine old houses. There's a choice of a two-star *hostal,* or a cheaper *fonda* at the far western end. Nineteen kilometers north lies the most famous of the lakes, the beautiful **Laguna Negra**. There's no public transportation to it, but a good road leads through thickly wooded country, before climbing steeply up the green mountainside. For the last couple of kilometers, by the side of a ravine, the road is much rougher; finally a path leads to the lagoon, which is surprisingly different from what has gone before. Ice-age in origin, set in an amphitheater of mountains from which great boulders have fallen, it presents a primeval picture — Machado was inspired to write some of his most purple verse here. It's of no great size, though, and you can wander nearly all the way round it. The area remains delightfully unspoiled, and the bar and picnic area (the former open June–Sept.) are out of sight, 3km down the mountain. Serious hikers can make the tortuous ascent from the Laguna Negra to the **Laguna de Urbión**, just over the border in Logroño province — a route that takes in a couple of other tiny glacially-formed lakes. A less taxing version of the same excursion, however, is to take the long way round, from the village of DURUELO DE LA SIERRA, some 20km west of Vinuesa.

Another **lakeland region** lies just west of Neila, officially in Burgos province — again near the Burgos-Soria bus route The best base is QUINTANAR DE LA SIERRA, with plenty of cheap accommodation. The star attraction is another *Laguna Negra*, although it doesn't compare with Soria's.

Almazán, Medinaceli, and the Monastery of Santa María de Huerta

Some 35km due south of Soria lies **ALMAZÁN**, which despite a lot of ugly modern development still possesses complete medieval walls, pierced by three gateways. On the Plaza Mayor stands the fine Renaissance palace of Hurtado de Mendoza, with a Gothic loggia at the rear, which can be seen from the road around the walls. The church of **San Miguel**, across from the palace, is worth a visit for its interior — apart from Romanesque and early Gothic features, it has a remarkable dome in the Cordoban style, while the altar has a relief of the martyrdom of St. Thomas à Becket. Services are rarely held, so to gain access you have to find a priest, or try the parish offices in the adjacent square of Santa María, opposite the church of the same name. There's only one *hostal* in town, and a shortage of restaurants — try *Mateo's*, across the river on the extreme northern side, or *Restaurante Toma*, c/ Manuel Cartel 11. However, you are not likely to want to stay for very long, and there are plenty of buses and trains to Soria.

MEDINACELI, perched in an exhilarating breezy position above the Río Jalón 76km down from Almazán, is something of a ghost town — steeped in history and highly evocative of its former glory as a Roman and Moorish stronghold. There's a two-star **hostal** in the village and plenty of cheaper accommodation near the **railroad station** (on the main Madrid–Barcelona line) in the valley. From here a twisting road climbs 3km to the village, but it's quicker and more fun to head straight up the hillside to the **Roman Arch**. This worn but impressive triple archway is unique in Spain, and its presence is something of a mystery: such monuments were usually built to commemorate military triumphs but the cause of celebration at Medinaceli is unknown. Nearby stands the dilapidated Moorish **castle**, now a mere facade sheltering a Christian cemetery. The empty streets all around are full of ancient mansions with proud coats of arms, but the most atmospheric monument must be the **Palacio de los Duques de Medinaceli**. It faces the dusty and desolate Plaza Mayor and is surrounded by rickety old buildings — the whole scene looking like some disused film set. This town was the seat of the rightful heirs to the Spanish throne until, in 1275, Fernando, eldest son of Alfonso el Sabio, died before he could assume his inheritance. His two sons were dispossessed by Fernando's brother Sancho el Valiente (the Brave) and their descendants, the Dukes of Medinaceli, long continued to lay claim to the throne of Castile. Today Medinaceli is a declining village with no more than 1200 inhabitants but its Duquesa remains the most betitled woman in Spain.

Right on the Aragonese border, just half an hour by train or bus from Medinaceli, lies the tiny community of **SANTA MARÍA DE HUERTA**. It is dominated by a fascinating Cistercian **monastery** (9am–1pm and 3:30–7pm), whose story is one of royal and noble patronage brought to a sudden end by the First Carlist War in 1835. The buildings were repopulated in 1930, and the main church has recently been restored. The highlight of the monastic complex is the unsurpassed Gothic refectory (1215–23), whose superb sexpartite vaulting and narrow pointed windows, worthy of the best church let alone a dining-room, were inspired by French architecture. Adjacent stands the kitchen with a mammoth chimney which protrudes above the Plateresque upper cloisters. There's just one place to stay in Santa María de Huerta — an expensive three-star hotel on the main road heading towards Zaragoza.

In the other direction from Medinaceli, Siguenza (p.106) is just 20km away across the borders of New Castile. It's a couple of stops on any train bound for Madrid.

FROM LOGROÑO TO LEÓN: THE PILGRIMAGE ROUTE

The *Camino de Santiago*, the great **pilgrimage route** to the shrine of Santiago at Compostela, cut across the top half of what is now Old Castile. The most usual point of entry into Spain was the Pass of Roncesvalles in the Pyrenees, and the route struck down through Navarra to reach **Logroño**, the first Castilian stage of the journey. **Santo Domingo de la Calzada** was the next important stop, heading on to **Burgos** and through smaller towns on to **León**. Burgos and León are definite musts for any traveler in the region, but it should be said that many of the smaller towns are not worth visiting unless you're particularly interested in tracing the route or have a special interest in Romanesque architecture and sculpture. Most of the route can be followed on public transportation with the odd detour on foot (e.g., to Villalcázar de Sirga), and occasional diversions (e.g., to Frómista, which lies on a different transportation line now).

The route also goes through the region of **La Rioja**, which produces the best wines in Spain, and is situated on the western slope of the Ebro valley. It is an extraordinarily rewarding part of Spain to explore, the river and its tributaries bringing great color to the region, especially in spring and autumn. To the south, the landscape of the region's **sierra** is harsh and beautiful and there are any number of excursions to be made into the hills.

La Rioja: Logroño and the Ebro

LOGROÑO is a modern, prosperous city, lacking in great monuments but pleasant enough with its broad, elegant streets and open squares. It has a lively old section, too, stretching down towards the river Ebro from the twin-towered **Catedral de Santa María la Redonda**. Here the city becomes more than just an extended parade of shop-lined avenues and modern parks, and the narrow streets bustle with an unexpected energy.

Whether you stay or not, you're likely to pass through Logroño at some point since it lies on the borders of Old Castile, the Basque provinces, and

Navarra, a position that has stimulated considerable commerce and light industry. Most importantly, however, this is the very heart of the **Rioja region** where much the finest wines in Spain are produced. As far as tasting the wines and watching the production goes, however, Haro (see below) is a considerably better bet.

Before the wine trade and industry brought prosperity to Logroño, it owed its importance for some six centuries to the **Camino de Santiago**. In almost every town on the route you can still find a church dedicated to the saint; in Logroño it stands close to the iron bridge over the Ebro — the lofty sixteenth-century Gothic structure of **Santiago el Real**. High on its north side, above the main entrance, is a magnificent eighteenth-century baroque equestrian statue of the saint, mounted in full glory in his role of *Matamoros* (Moorslayer), on a stallion which Edward Mullins, in his fascinating book *The Pilgrimage to Santiago*, describes as "equipped with the most heroic genitals in all Spain, a sight to make any surviving Moor feel inadequate and run for cover." Other churches include **San Bartolome**, which has an unrefined but richly carved Gothic portal; and **Santa María la Redonda**. The latter, now the cathedral, was originally a late Gothic hall church with a lovely sweeping elevation, which was extended at both ends in the eighteenth century — the twin-towered facade is a fine example of the Churrigueresque style. It is open in the mornings until 11am, and again from 6 to 8pm.

The heart of Logroño, the gardens of the wide **Paseo del Espolon**, are only a few minutes' walk from the **bus station** (straight up c/del General Vara del Rey, crossing the Gran Vía) or from the **railroad station** (up the Avda. de España, then right at the bus station). The lower (south) side of the Paseo is bordered by c/M. Villanueva, where you'll find the **Turismo** (no. 10). The opposite side of the Paseo, down towards the river, marks the start of the old quarter and has the liveliest **bars and restaurants** and the cheapest **accommodation**. The best place to stay is the *Casa de Huespedes* right on the Pl. del Mercado, the cathedral square; ask at the *Bar La Parra* across the square. There's a **campground** 1km out of town by the river, signposted from the Paseo.

Haro and Rioja Wine

One of the most active centers of Rioja production, **HARO** is an attractive working town and a good, if quiet, place to sample some of the best wines in the region. The Rioja area takes its name from the Río Oja, which flows into the Tirón and thence into the Ebro to the northwest of Logroño. Effectively, though, it is the Ebro that waters the vines, which are cultivated on both banks. Many of the best vineyards are on the north bank in the Basque province of Alava — an area known as the *Rioja Alavesa*. Look out above all for wines described as *Reserva* or *Gran Reserva*, and for the great vintages of '68, '69 and '70 — though many say that with controls getting stricter every year the younger wines are the better ones.

In direct contrast with its ugly neighbor MIRANDA DE EBRO (which, oddly enough, has a **youth hostel** open July to mid-August), Haro retains some lovely reminders of its more imposing past, notably the Renaissance church of **San Tomás**. An imposing sight from just about anywhere outside town, with its wedding cake tower, it's *the* attraction of Haro's old quarter — the Plateresque portal is particularly magnificent. The whole quarter, though, is attractive in a low-key, faded kind of way, its lower margins marked by the **Plaza de la Paz**, a glass-balconied square whose mansions overlook an archaic bandstand. Not much goes on outside the bars and bodegas of this part of town and there are few foreign visitors around — so few that there's no tourist office in Haro, although you might be able to get some information in English from the *Ayuntamiento* at the top of the square.

The excellent local wine is an added bonus to all this. Most of the **Rioja bodegas** are close to the railroad station, and several of them can be visited (although most are closed in August and the first half of September; mornings are best). **Tours** are on an ad hoc basis, the bodegas seeking a healthy audience before they open their doors. Unless you're with a group, ask at the campground (see below) about getting one together; or simply hang around the gates looking interested (but not too thirsty). A good first try is *Bodegas Bilbainas* (right opposite the station) where they make sparkling *Cava* wines as well as red and white Riojas.

There's little cheap **accommodation** in Haro: a couple of *hostales* on the main road running from the bottom left — looking downhill — off the Plaza de la Paz, and a *Casa de Huespedes* off a side street to the right. You're much better off if you camp, as there's an excellent, cheap **campground** (☎941/312737) down by the river below town, with a bar and swimming (in the river or pool) nearby. The **railroad station** — as ever — is some distance out of town; from it, walk down the hill to the main road, turn right and when you reach the bridge (campground off to the right), cross it and head straight uphill. **Buses** (7 daily to Logroño) stop at the Plaza de la Paz. If you had no joy at the bodegas, even the humblest *menú del día* in town is transformed by a bottle of the right stuff. You'll get more — and very cheaply — in the many good **bars** that lie between the *Ayuntamiento* and the church of San Tomás.

Out From Logroño

For a taste of La Rioja's rugged **sierra**, different lands again from the river valleys, head towards ORTIGOSA and into the mountains. One bus a day (currently 5pm from Logroño's bus station) makes the trip, passing through the village of EL RASILLO, itself a quiet place to spend the night with **rooms** available and walks to the nearby lake. The return bus to Logroño is at 8:15am.

CALAHORRA (on the rail line southeast from Logroño; 5 daily buses from Logroño) is an ancient episcopal center. From the train it looks picturesque but first appearances mask the decrepitude of the place — the only building of note is its largely Plateresque **Cathedral**, at the very edge of the town, and that has been largely neglected. If you're here on a Thursday you'll catch the weekly **market** which bustles around the dominant and weatherbeaten church of Santiago. Best place to lunch is the excellent and popular *Casa Mateo* restaurant. **Arriving by train**, it's a twenty-minute walk into the center; turn right at the road and keep straight on up the hill until you reach the green Paseo del Mercadal. At the end of this, to the left, c/Grande leads uphill to the old quarter, where you'll also find a couple of **fondas** — the *Fonda López*, on c/de la Estrella, is good (follow the signs for the Iglesia de San Andrés).

Continuing along the same line you come to ALFARO, once a significant frontier town on the border between Castile and Navarra, but now fallen into a dusty and uninteresting obscurity. Trains on to Zaragoza or Logroño are so infrequent that a stop in Alfaro is hardly worth the wait. However, 4km south lies CASTEJÓN, a major rail junction, so if you're hanging around for connections, Alfaro is handy enough. Castejón's transportation status also means that there are **rooms** (including a two-star *hostal* in the railroad station) and an abundance of banks.

Santo Domingo de la Calzada

From Logroño the pilgrimage route headed due west, passing **NAJERA**. It's dramatically situated below a pink rock formation, but the view from the river is spoiled by ugly modern buildings. There is just one monument of interest here, the late Gothic monastery of **Santa María la Real** (10am–1pm and 4–7pm), which contains a royal pantheon of ancient monarchs of Castile, León, and Navarra — a host of sarcophagi and statues, some of which seem to have been made long after the death of the sitter. Best of all is the cloister of rose-colored stone and elaborate tracery, closer to the Manueline style of Portugal than anything else in Spain. There are several cheap restaurants in town and even a few **places to stay**, but you may want to continue on.

SANTO DOMINGO DE LA CALZADA, 46km west of Logroño, is a perfect example of a town that owes its very existence to the pilgrimage. It takes its name from a saint who settled here in the eleventh century and devoted his life to assisting travelers by paving roads, tending the sick, and engineering bridges (hence *Calzada*, or causeway). Now that it's lost its *raison d'etre*, it's a dull, fairly unattractive place for the most part.

The town does, however, maintain one curiosity — a pair of caged chickens in the cathedral. These peck around in celebration of the local version of a legend popular throughout Spain and Portugal. A young German pilgrim is said to have resisted the advances of an innkeeper's daughter who "wolde have had hym to medyll with her carnally." She retaliated by falsely accusing him of theft, for which offense he was summarily strung up on the gallows. There he was kept alive by the miraculous intervention of Santo Domingo, to the disbelief of the local judge who was busily munching on a roast. "He's as dead as those chickens," claimed the judge, whereupon the birds crowed their disagreement and flew off the table.

The saint's causeway, with a much-modernized bridge, is at the very end of town, on the road to Burgos. His tomb lies in the crypt of the Transitional-style **Cathedral** (officially 8am–2pm and 4–8pm, but sometimes open all day) which looms above everything from the center of town. Santo Domingo was once a fortified town (fragments of the walls can still be seen) and the cathedral's massive west porch used to serve as a fortress. The interior of the cathedral is strongly evocative of what a medieval cathedral must have looked like, with a *coro*, tombs, and *rejas* (and chickens!)— but the *retablo mayor*, the last work of Damien Forment, is a purely Renaissance piece, which makes heavy use of Italian secular motifs (unusually for Spanish religious art). Beside the cathedral stands a pilgrim hospice, now converted to a *parador*, and a handful of fine Renaissance mansions.

You probably won't want to stay, but if you do, you'll discover that **accommodation** is over-priced. Beyond Santo Domingo de la Calzada, the route stretched out across northern Castile, a long straight trek to Burgos, León, and Astorga, before heading over the mountains into Galicia. **Buses** go in the Burgos direction four times a day — it's this route that is followed later in this chapter. It is also possible to trace the trail east, into Navarra, or to head north for the Basque provinces and the coast.

Burgos

BURGOS — to a Spaniard — means the military. An immense army garrison has been stationed here virtually since the civil war when Franco temporarily installed his fascist government in the city. Such associations linger. In 1964 it became one of the centers of the "Industrial Development Plan," part of Franco's strategy to sap the economic strength of the Basques and Catalans and shift the country's wealth to his power base in the Castilian heartlands. Still greater notoriety was earned in 1970 with the so-called *Burgos Trials* in which six Basque nationalists were sentenced to death without proper hearing — Franco, on this occasion misjudging the scale of international outcry, was pressured into commuting the sentences.

There's a curiously apt historical backdrop to all this. For some five centuries of the Middle Ages the city was the capital of Old Castile: in the eleventh century it was the home of El Cid, in the thirteenth century of Fernando el Santo (Fernando III), reconqueror of Murcia, Córdoba, and Sevilla. It was Fernando also who began the city's famous Gothic cathedral, beyond doubt one of the greatest in all Spain, though it too seems somehow to share in the forceful solemnity and severity of Burgos' history. Don't, however, be put off — it is certainly worth seeing and stands in an atmospheric, compact old quarter of impressive gray stone buildings. Additionally, within walking distance of the city are two superb monasteries.

Arrival

Orientation in Burgos could not be simpler, since wherever you are the Cathedral makes its presence felt. The Río Arlanzón bisects the city and neatly delimits the old quarters. The main pedestrian bridge is the **Puente de Santa María**, nearest the cathedral and facing the gateway of the same name. On the "new side" of the river this bridge opens out into Plaza de Vega and c/de Madrid. This is the main area for cheap **bars, restaurants,** and **hostales** — try the Plaza itself and any road off to the left as far as c/de San Pablo. In the *Cafe-bar Luz* (Pl. de Vega 3) you can sample *chocolate con bizcochos*, light sponge fingers with hot chocolate, an alternative to *churros*. There's also a **youth hostel** (☎947/220362) at c/Gen. Vigón, open July to

September. The local **campground**, *Camping Fuentes Blancas*, is out by the *Cartuja* (see end of section for directions), 45 minutes' walk or a bus ride from the center (buses once an hour between 11am and 9pm, leaving from the Cid statue) — it's a very good site with excellent facilities, including free hot showers.

The **bus station** is right in the center of the city at c/ Mirandor 4; the **railroad station** a short walk away at the bottom of Avda. Conde Guadalhorre. You'll find a small information center opposite the west facade of the cathedral but the main **Turismo** (8am–3pm) is at Pl. de Alonso Martinez 7, around the side of the cathedral and up c/Lain Calvo.

Heading in across the Puente de Santa María you are confronted with the great white bulk of the **Arco de Santa María**. Originally this gateway formed part of the town walls; its facade was castellated with towers and

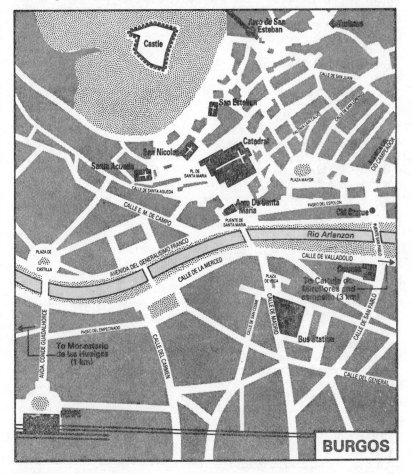

turrets and embellished with statues in 1534–36 in order to appease the wrath of Carlos V after Burgos's involvement in the Revolt of the Comuneros (a reaction of Spanish noblemen to their new Belgian-born King). Carlos' statue is glorified here in the context of the greatest Burgalese heroes: Diego Porcelos, founder of the city in the late ninth century; Nuño Rasura and Lain Calvo, two early magistrates; Fernan González, founder of the Countship of Castile in 932; and **El Cid Campeador**, who was surpassed only by *Santiago Matamoros* in his exploits against the Moors. El Cid was born Rodrigo Diaz in the village of Vivar, just north of Burgos, though his most significant military exploits took place around Valencia; *Cid*, incidentally, derives from the Arabic *sidi* (lord), and *Campeador* means supreme in valor. There's a splendid **equestrian statue** of him — with flying cloak, flowing beard, and raised sword — lording over the **Puente de San Pablo**, the main road-bridge to the old town. The statue, one of the city's principal landmarks, stands at the end of the **Paseo del Espolon**, a fashionable tree-lined promenade around which most of the evening life takes place. Actual **nightlife** is fairly nonexistent, though, surprisingly, there are a few heavy-metal bars in the street around the foot of the castle.

The Cathedral

The old quarters of Burgos are totally dominated by the **Cathedral** whose "wild and slightly mad roof-line" does indeed (as Mullins observed) "seem to hang by invisible threads above the city." Its florid filigree of spires and pinnacles are among the most extraordinary achievements of Gothic art; however, the building is such a large complex of varied and opulent sections that it's difficult to appreciate it as a whole. It is the sheer accumulation of masterpieces — both inside and out — that impresses. Burgos has outstanding individual achievements in ironwork, wood carving, and sculpture, and almost every entrance and chapel seems to be of interest. Oddly enough the most ornate entrance of all, the **Puerta de la Pellejería** at the northeast corner, is in a Renaissance-Plateresque style, quite different from the bulk of the exterior.

Inside the cathedral you're immediately struck by the size and number of side chapels, the greatest of which, the **Capilla del Condestable**, is almost a cathedral in itself. The most curious, though, is the **Capilla del Santo Cristo** (first right) which contains what must be one of the most bizarre and mystical icons in Christendom. This is the *Cristo de Burgos*, a cloyingly realistic image of Christ (ca.1300), endowed with real human hair and nails and covered with the withered hide of a water buffalo, still popularly believed to be human skin. Legend has it that the icon was modelled directly from the Crucifixion and that it requires a shave and a manicure every eighth day. The adjacent **Capilla de la Consolación** has a distinctive early sixteenth-century star-shaped vault — a form adapted from the Moorish "honeycomb" vaults of Granada. Similar influences can also be seen in the cathedral's central dome (1568), highlighted with gold and blue and supported on four thick piers which fan out into remarkably delicate buttresses — a worthy setting for the **tomb of El Cid**, marked by a simple slab in the floor below.

The sumptuous octagonal **Capilla del Condestable**, behind the high altar, contains a third, superb example of star-vaulting. Here the ceiling is designed to form two eight-pointed stars, one within the other. The chapel, with its profusion of stone tracery, was founded in 1482 by Fernandez de Velasco, Constable of Castile, whose marble tomb lies before the altar; the architect was the German Simon de Colonia. Between 1442 and 1458 his father Hans (Hispanicized as Juan) had built the twin openwork spires of the west facade, possibly modelling them on the spires planned for the cathedral in his home city of Cologne. In the third generation Francisco de Colonia built the central dome and the Puerta de la Pellejería. Another father-and-son combination of artists was that of Gil and Diego de Siloé, the former from Flanders but his son born and raised in Spain. Gil worked on the *retablo* in the Capilla de Sta Ana (second left), while Diego's masterpiece, one of the crowning achievements of the cathedral, is the glorious **Escalera Dorada**, a double stairway in the north transept. To get into some of these smaller chapels you'll have to buy a Treasury ticket, which also admits you to the cloisters, the Diocesan museum inside them, and the **Coro** at the heart of the cathedral, which affords the best view into the dome.

Standing like a giant's fashion parade in a gallery beneath the cloisters — and seen from the c/de Paloma outside — are the **Gigantones de Burgos**. (Or rather, they're usually here — they've been temporarily moved to Las Huelgas convent.) These huge carnival dummies are a phenomenon mainly of northern Spain, and although they tend to live in churches and dance through the streets at fiestas (June 27 in Burgos), they are no more religious than Humpty Dumpty, their origins being lost in the haze of folklore and popular history. Here, the crowned giants of Fernando and Isabella represent Spain in an extraordinary international line-up which includes representatives from each of the continents — a turbanned Moor, an African, an Asian, and a Native American. Their little brothers and sisters the *Cabezudos* or "Big-Heads" are a mere eight feet tall with enormous heads. You'll come across such figures at fiestas throughout the north, racing through the streets, brandishing sticks, and terrorizing children.

Overlooking the Plaza in front of the cathedral stands the fifteenth-century church of **San Nicolas**. Unassuming from the outside, it has an altarpiece within by Francisco de Colonia, which is as rich as anything in the city. At the side of San Nicolas, c/Pozo Seco ascends to the early Gothic church of **San Esteban**, which is now being refitted as a museum. Beyond San Esteban lies the ruinous **castle** with a fine view of the city and the surrounding countryside.

The Monasteries

Inevitably the lesser churches of Burgos tend to be eclipsed by the cathedral, but on the outskirts are two monasteries which are by no means overshadowed. The closest, the Cistercian **Monasterio de Las Huelgas**, is remarkable for its wealth of Mudejar craftsmanship. (It lies on the "new side" of the river about 20 minutes' walk from the city center: cross Puente de Santa María, turn right, and follow the signs along the riverbank.) Founded in 1187 as the future mausoleum of Alfonso VIII and Eleanor of Aquitaine, daughter of Henry II of England, it became one of the most high-brow and powerful convents in Spain. It was popularly observed that "if the Pope were to marry, only the Abbess of Las Huelgas would be eligible!'" The main **church**, with its typically excessive Churrigueresque *retablo*, contains the tombs of no less than sixteen Castilian monarchs and nobles. That of the Infanta Blanca (d. 1325), daughter of Afonso III of Portugal, is vigorously carved with heraldic insignia surrounded by Moorish borders. Priceless embroidery, jewelry and weaponry of a suitably regal spendor were discovered inside the tombs, and are exhibited in a small museum. The convent is open from 11am to 2pm and from 4 to 6pm (11am–2pm on Sun.); there's an interesting guided tour in Spanish, from which noone is allowed to stray.

The highlight of the convent is its Mudejar-Gothic **cloister**. Here again are the familiar eight-pointed stars, along with rare peacock designs — a bird holy to the Moors. The **Capilla de Santiago**, an obvious reminder that Las Huelgas stood on the pilgrim route, also has a fine Mudejar ceiling and pointed horseshoe archway. Its cult statue of St. James has an articulated right arm, which enabled him to dub Knights of the Order of Santiago (motto: "The Sword is Red with the Blood of Islam") and on occasion even to crown kings! At the other end of the pilgrim scale the convent was responsible for the nearby *Hospital del Rey* where food and shelter were provided free for two nights. It is presently in a very bad state of neglect, although the portals merit a visit.

The **Cartuja de Miraflores** (Mon.–Sat. 10:15am–3pm and 4–6pm; Sun 11:15am–12:30pm, 1–3pm and 4–6pm) is famous for three dazzling masterpieces by Gil de Siloé. The buildings are still in use as a monastery and most are closed — you can, however, visit the **church**, built between 1454 and 1488 by Juan and Simon de Colonia. In accordance with Carthusian practice, it is divided into three sections for the public, the lay-brothers, and the monks. In front of the high altar lies the star-shaped joint tomb of Juan II and Isabel of Portugal, of such perfection in design and execution that it forced Felipe II and Juan de Herrera to admit "we did not achieve very much with our Escorial." Isabella la Catolica, a great patron of the arts, commissioned it from Gil de Siloé in 1489 as a memorial to her parents. The same sculptor carved the magnificent altarpiece, which was plated with the first gold shipped back from America. His third masterpiece is the tomb of the Infante Alfonso, through whose untimely death in 1468 Isabella had succeeded to the throne of Castile.

Miraflores lies in a secluded spot near the *Camping Fuentes Blancas*, about 45 minutes' walk from the center. (A bus goes on Sundays but returns straight after the well-attended mass; there's a bus to the campground.) This time turn left from the Puente de Santa María; the *Cartuja* is well signposted along c/de Valladolid. There's a good restaurant in the nearby park. To avoid the walk back, you'll have to catch the San Pedro de Cardeña bus, which passes only once a day.

South from Burgos: Santo Domingo de Silos and Around

Southeast of Burgos is another of Spain's greatest Christian monuments, the Benedictine abbey of **SANTO DOMINGO DE SILOS**. There's only one way to reach it — by the bus that leaves Burgos at 5pm or 5:30pm, depending on the season. It heads south to LERMA, whose dukes were once among the most powerful nobles in Spain, but which is now decayed and not of great interest, and then through a series of unspoiled small agricultural communities, before arriving at the monastery, itself located in one of these villages. By the time the bus arrives, it is too late to enter, except to hear Vespers in the church, and as the return to Burgos is at 8am or 8:30am you'll probably have to stay two nights. Men can stay in the monastery itself, if they contact the Guest Master (*Padre Hospederia*) in advance (☎947/380768); he prefers people to stay a few days. This is a wonderful bargain, with comfortable single rooms and good food at a ridiculously low cost. Alternatively, you can stay at the bar in the village and there's also a one-star **hostal** at the foot of the hill to the south.

The main feature of the monastery is the large two-story eleventh-century **Romanesque cloister**, whose beautiful sculptural decoration is in many ways unique. It can be visited from 10am to 1:30pm and from 3:30 to 6:30pm, but if you stay with the monks you have free access at any time. There are eight remarkable, almost life-sized **reliefs** on the corner pillars. Six of them, represen the Passion — *Christ on the Road to Emmaus* is dressed as a pilgrim to Santiago (complete with scallop shell), a detail that shows that pilgrims made a detour from the route to see the tomb of Santo Domingo, the eleventh-century abbot after whom the monastery is named. The same sculptor was responsible for about half of the **capitals.** Besides a famous bestiary, these include many Moorish motifs, which has given rise to speculation that he many even have been a Moor. Whatever the case, it is an early example of the effective mix of Arab and Christian cultures, which was continued in the fourteenth century with the painted Mudejar vault, showing scenes of everyday pastimes. A quite different sculptor carved many of the remaining capitals, including the two that ingeniously tell the stories of the Nativity and the Passion in a very restricted space. A third master was responsible for the pillar with the Annunciation and Tree of Jesse, which is almost Gothic in spirit. You can also see the complete eighteenth-century **pharmacy**, which has been reconstructed in a room off the cloister, and the **museum**, which houses the tympanum from the destroyed Romanesque church.

The **church** itself is an anti-climax, a rather nondescript construction designed by the eighteenth-century academic architect Ventura Rodríguez. Its Romanesque predecessor was too dark for the taste of the times; fortunately, the cloister's size and spaciousness saved it from a similar fate. The monks are famous for their **Gregorian chants**, in which they are considered one of the two or three best choirs in the world. It's particularly worth attending the morning mass (9am) or even better, Vespers at 7:30pm.

Covarrubias and Quintanilla

If you're stuck in Silos all day, don't despair of having nothing to do, as the scenery is far more varied than much of Castile. You could climb the hill for a bird's-eye view of the village and the surrounding countryside. It is also a short walk to the **gorges of Yecla**; take the road to Burgos and turn left at the village; you've then got only a couple of kilometers to go.

The more adventurous can walk to **COVARRUBIAS**, about 18km away, a superbly preserved small town. There's no bus service between Silos and Covarrubias, other than the short distance covered by the Burgos service. It is just possible to see Silos and Covarrubias in a day on foot; the alternative is to approach the village from Burgos — a daily bus service runs between the two. If staying there, bear in mind that apart from the expensive *parador*, there is just one small *fonda* in town. The main sight is the town itself: many of its white houses are half-timbered, with shady arcades, and remnants of the fortifications are still standing, including a tenth-century tower. The **Colegiata** looks plain from outside, but a visit to the interior is a must; to do so, call at the priests' houses left of the entrance. Four adults are needed for a tour group, which shouldn't present a problem in summer, but be insistent if necessary. Inside you'll find a late Gothic hall church crammed with tombs, giving an idea of the grandeur of the town in earlier times. The organ is an amazing seventeenth-century instrument still in good working order; you'll probably have to be content with hearing a recording. There are several good paintings in the museum, but the chief attraction is a triptych whose central section, a polychromed carving of the Adoration of the Magi, is attributed to Gil de Siloé.

An equally important monument, this time a rare Visigothic survival, is to be found at **QUINTANILLA DE LAS VIÑAS**, which lies 4km north of MAZANRIEGOS on the main Burgos to Soria road, about 40km from Burgos. Signs labelled Turismo lead to a house where the caretaker of the **Ermita de Santa María** lives; if he isn't there, he'll probably be at the hermitage itself, a further 1km north. It's a simple building, of which only the transept and the chancel survive. Dating from about 700, it's remarkable for its unique series of sculptures: the outside bears delicately carved friezes, and inside there's a triumphal arch with capitals representing the Sun and Moon, and a block which is believed to be the earliest representation of Christ in Spanish art.

West from Burgos: Frómista and Beyond

FRÓMISTA was the next important pilgrimage stop after Burgos, to which it is connected by a daily bus (although it's reached more easily from Palencia since it lies on the railroad line from there to Santander). The present-day town is much decayed, with a fraction of the population it once had. There's only one sight of any note — the extremely beautiful church of **San Martín**, originally part of an abbey which no longer exists, and is now deconsecrated (Wed.–Fri. 10am–2pm and 5–8pm; weekends 10am–2pm and 4–8pm; Tues. 10am–2pm; admission charge.) The church was built in 1066 in a

Romanesque style unusually pure for Spain, with no traces of later additions. In fact, what you can see now is a result of a turn-of-the-century restoration which was perhaps rather too thorough, although it is pleasing to the eye. The other church associated with the pilgrimage, **Santa María**, is near the railroad station, but it is also redundant and kept locked.

Thirteen kilometers from Frómista lies **VILLALCÁZAR DE SIRGA**, notable for the **church** which the Knights Templar built here — from a distance it seems to crush the little village by its sheer mass, and originally its fortified aspect was even more marked. The Gothic style here begins to assert itself over the Romanesque, as witnessed by the figure sculpture on the two portals and the elegant pointed arches inside. The **Capilla de Santiago** has three polychromed tombs, among the finest of their kind and contemporary with the building. If the church is closed, as it usually is, take the street to the left in front of it and turn left at the corner; the sacristan's house is the first brick building on the right. There are a few quaint old houses in the square, one of which has been converted into a restaurant. There's no public transportation but the next stop, **CARRIÓN DE LOS CONDES**, is only 5km away, and linked by bus to Burgos and Palencia.

Carrión de los Condes

Carrión is dusty and quiet, a mood which belies its sensational past. It's reputed to be the place where, before the Reconquest, Christians had to surrender one hundred virgins annually to the Moorish overlords — a scene depicted on the portal of **Santa María**, situated at the edge of the town, where the buses stop. For fine sculpture, however, look at the doorway of **Santiago**'s own church in the center of town, overlooking the Plaza Mayor. Time has not treated this kindly — burned out during the last century, the church was rebuilt but now stands disused and neglected. The upper frieze reveals a debt to classical art, but finer are the extraordinarily delicate covings above the door, which depict the trades and professions of the Middle Ages. The town's third main monument is the Plateresque cloister of **San Zoilo**, located over the sixteenth-century bridge; a side room off the cloister contains the tombs of the Counts of Carrión, from whom the town's name comes. The nuns of **Santa Clara** have recently opened a small **museum** (Tues.–Sun. 10:30am–12:30pm and 5–7pm in summer; 10:30am–12:30pm and 4–6pm in winter) with a moderately interesting collection, including one of Spain's oldest organs. Their main work of art, however, the theatrical *Pieta* by Gregorio Fernandez, is kept in the church, which is only open for the early morning mass.

Carrión boasts an excellent cheap **restaurant**, *El Resbalon*, situated between Santa María and Santiago; instead of the normal long menu, there is a short blackboard selection of dishes which are freshly prepared in the traditional Castilian style. The same establishment also has a floor of spotless, inexpensive rooms; otherwise there are three other **pensions** to choose from in the main street behind. There's plenty of room for unofficial **camping** down by the river; or, more officially, in the good campground back from the main road.

Sahagún and San Miguel de Escalada

From Carrión you can continue by bus to the next main stop, SAHAGÚN, which also lies on the main railroad line between Palencia and León. No other town so clearly illustrates the effect of the decline from the heyday of the Pilgrimage. Once the seat of the most powerful monastery in all Spain, it's now a largely modern town, above which the towers of the remaining old buildings rear up like dinosaurs in a zoo.

Sahagún is generally thought to be the birthplace of the brick churches built by the Moorish craftsmen who stayed on to work for the Christians after the Reconquest. Unfortunately, the great monastery these days is little more than a memory, and its main surviving sections — the gateway and belfry — date from a period of re-construction in the seventeenth century. However, the twelfth-century parish churches of San Tirso and San Lorenzo remain, each with a noble tower. The town's guide is based at the former, where work has begun on the long-term project of removing the white-wash and returning the place to its original form (Tues.–Sat. 10:30am–2pm and 5–8pm in summer, 10:30am–2pm and 4–7pm in winter; Sun. 10am–3pm). The guide will also show you La Peregrina, a thirteenth-century monastery built by Mudejars — it's in a shocking state of disrepair, but a beautiful little chapel with stuccowork has been restored. San Lorenzo has the most imposing exterior, but the inside has been completely transformed, and is only open for masses on the weekend. Finally, you should see the little museum in the Monasterio Santa Cruz (10:30am–1pm and 4–6:30pm; closed Fri. and Sat.); the nuns here have inherited the great *custodia* made by Enrique de Arfe, founder of a dynasty of silversmiths. Its big sister is the famous one at Toledo; like that one, the only airing it gets is during the Corpus Christi celebrations.

Sahagún has plentiful cheap accommodation. There are three fondas just outside the railroad station; the proprietors of *La Bilbaina* are particularly friendly, and speak English. Otherwise, there are several more around the exit of the road to Carrión, and one in the center of town near San Tirso. Buses leave from the Pl. Mayor; you can follow the Burgos–Frómista–Carrión–Sahagún route by public transportation, but buses are very infrequent (about one a day).

LEÓN is just a short train ride away, but the medieval pilgrim would probably first have made a slight detour to see the monastery of SAN MIGUEL DE ESCALADA, a precious Mozarabic survival from the tenth century. Founded by refugee monks from Córdoba, it's a touching little building, with a simple interior of horseshoe arches, and a later portico, again Moorish in style. At the moment it's the subject of a heavy restoration program, and you can't go inside; best check the current situation with the tourist office in León before setting out. Getting there by public transportation also presents a problem; although there are two buses a day to and from León, one turns back thirty minutes after it arrives, while the other requires spending the night — and there's nowhere to stay.

León

Even if they stood alone, the stained glass in the cathedral of LEÓN and the Romanesque wall-paintings in its Royal Pantheon would merit a very considerable journey, but there's very much more to the city than this. For León is as attractive — and enjoyable — in its modern quarters as it is in those parts preserved from its heyday.

In 914, as the Reconquest edged its way south from Asturias, Ordoño II transferred the Christian capital from Oviedo to León. Despite being sacked by the dreaded Al-Mansur in 996, the new capital rapidly eclipsed the old — a scenario that was to repeat itself as the Reconquest unfolded. As more and more territory came under the control of León it was divided into new administrative groupings: in 1035 the county of Castile matured into a fully fledged kingdom, with its capital at Burgos. For the next two centuries León and Castile jointly spearheaded the war against the Moors — as often as not under joint rule — until by the thirteenth century Castile had come finally to dominate her mother kingdom. These two centuries were nevertheless the period of León's greatest power, from which date most of her finest monuments.

Orientation and Practicalities

León's prosperous modern sectors have been imaginatively laid out with wide, straight streets radiating like spokes from three focal plazas. The first of these is the **Glorieta Guzman El Bueno** near the river and the **railroad station**. From here one can see straight down the Avda. de Ordoño II and across the **Plaza de Santo Domingo** to the towers of the cathedral. Just off the Plaza de Santo Domingo stands the **Casa de Botines**, an uncharacteristically restrained work by Antoni Gaudí (for whom see Astorga, below, and Barcelona). The third key square is the **Plaza de Calvo Sotelo**, connected to the Glorieta by the Avda. de Roma where you'll find a couple of *hostales* and a **fonda**. However, cheap accommodation is scattered all over the city; there's no particular concentration and you don't have to leave the main streets. Handiest for the station are three places just before the bridge in front of it, but probably the prettiest spot to stay is on the Plaza Mayor, where there are a couple of *hostales*, though you might have to share a room. There's a fruit and veg market here several mornings a week. The main **bus station** is just off here on c/de Cardenal Lorenzana; the bus to Zamora, though, leaves from an unmarked bus yard on c/Alcalde Miguel Castado (100m down on the left coming from the Jardin San Francisco). There are a few more cheap places to stay along Avda. de Ordoño II and a good **youth hostel** (July and August only) at no. 4 c/de la Corredera, a continuation of the Avda. de Independencia, which originates in Pl. de Sto. Domingo.

Head straight up from Pl. Sto. Domingo to the cathedral and you'll arrive in the Plaza Regia; here, directly opposite the cathedral's great west facade, stand the main **Turismo** and the **Post Office**. To the right of the cathedral c/de Plegarias cuts down beside the seventeenth-century former town hall, past the church of San Martin and into the plaza of the same name. In this small square and the dark, narrow streets surrounding it you'll discover a wide selection of cheap bars and restaurants, with a good evening atmosphere.

The Cathedral

León's Gothic Cathedral dates from the final years of her period of greatness. Its stained glass windows (13th c. and onwards) are equal to any masterpiece in any European cathedral — a stunning kaleidoscope of light streaming in through walls of multi-colored glass.

It is not simply that León Cathedral has the best stained glass in Spain — which it does: to enter the chill, twilit interior of this place and look around in the gloom until, by chance, the sun chooses that moment to come out is, I felt, to comprehend something of the hold which the Christian faith has been able to retain over so many people and for so long. In general, Spanish churches are exceptionally dark, and in my view exceptionally oppressive; and León is no exception — until the sun comes out. Then, more than any building I have ever set eyes on, it seems to burst into fire.

(Edwin Mullins)

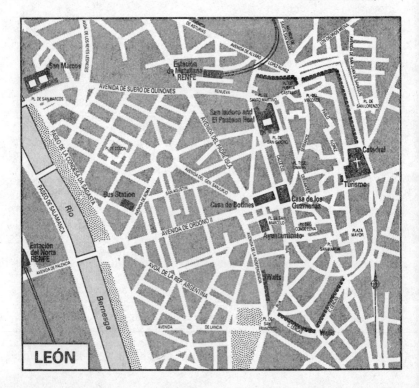

LEÓN

This is one of the most magical and harmonious sights in Spain, and while such extensive use of glass is purely French in inspiration, the colors used here — reds, golds, and yellows — are strictly Spanish. Other elements which take the cathedral further away from its French model are the cloister and the later addition of the *coro*, whose glass screen (added this century to give a clear view up to the altar) enhances the sensation of light with its bewildering refractions.

Outside, the magnificent **west facade**, dominated by a massive rose window, comprises two towers and a detached nave supported by flying buttresses — a pattern repeated at the south angle. The inscription *locus appelationis* on the main porch indicates that the royal court of appeal was held here, and amid the statuary a king ponders his verdict, seated on a throne of lions. Above the **central doorway** a more sublime trial — the Last Judgment — is in full swing: angels weigh souls in the balance, the damned are cast into the fire, and the righteous sing God's praises. The sculpture on this triple portal of the facade is some of the finest on the pilgrim route, although later in date than most. The doorways of the south transept and the polychromed door to the north transept (shielded from the elements by the cloister) are other attractions. The cloister now houses the rather eclectic **Diocesan Museum** (Mon.-Sat. 9:30am–1pm and 4–7pm; Sun. 9:30am–1pm). The cathedral itself is shut between 1:30 and 4pm.

The Pantheon and San Marcos

From the Pl. de Sto. Domingo, Avda. de Ramon y Cajal leads to the church of **San Isidoro** (open all day) and the Royal Pantheon of the early kings of León and Castile. Fernando I, who united the two kingdoms in 1037, commissioned the complex as a shrine for the bones of San Isidoro and a mausoleum for himself and his successors. The church dates mainly from the mid-twelfth century and shows Moorish influence in the horseshoe arch at the west end of the nave and the fanciful arches in the transepts. The bones of the patron saint lie in a reliquary on the high altar.

The **Pantheon**, comprising two surprisingly small crypt-like chambers, was constructed between 1054 and 1063 as a narthex or portico preceding the west facade of the church. It's one of the earliest Romanesque buildings in Spain, and the carvings on the portal which links the Pantheon and church herald the introduction of figure sculpture into the peninsula. In contrast, the capitals of the side piers and the two squat columns in the middle of the Pantheon are carved with thick foliage which is still rooted in Visigothic tradition. Towards the end of the twelfth century the vaults were vividly covered in some of the most significant, imaginative, and impressive paintings of Romanesque art. They are extraordinarily well preserved and their biblical and everyday themes are perfectly adapted to the architecture of the vaults. The central dome is occupied by Christ Pantocrator surrounded by the four Evangelists depicted with animal heads — allegorical portraits which stem from the apocalyptic visions in the Bible's Book of Revelation. One of the arches bordering the dome is decorated with quaint rustic scenes which represent the months of the year. Eleven kings and twelve queens were laid to rest here but the chapel was desecrated during the Peninsular War and the remaining tombs command little attention in such a marvelous setting. Visiting hours of the Pantheon are Tues.–Sat. 10am to 1:30pm and 4 to 6:30pm, Sun. 10am–1:30pm; the guided tour is a bit of a whirlwind affair. With a guide you can also visit the Treasury and Library (same hours as before)— the former contains magnificent reliquaries, caskets, and chalices from the early Middle Ages, but only reproductions of the manuscripts are on view.

If the Pantheon is a perfect illustration of the way Romanesque art worked its way into Spain along the pilgrimage route from France, the opulent **Monasterio de San Marcos** (reached from the Plaza de Calvo Sotelo via Avda. de Primo Rivera) stands as a more direct reminder that León was a station on this route. Here, on presentation of the relevant documents, pilgrims were allowed to regain their strength before the gruelling Bierzo mountains west of León. The original monastery was built in 1168 for the Knights of Santiago, one of several chivalric orders founded in the twelfth century to protect pilgrims and lead the Reconquest. Eventually these power-ful, ambitious and semi-autonomous Knights posed a political threat to the authority of the Spanish throne, until in 1493 Isabella la Catolica subtly tack-led the problem by "suggesting" that her husband Fernando be "elected" Grand Master. Thus the wealth and power of the Order was assimilated to that of the throne.

In time, the Order degenerated to little more than a men's club — Velázquez, for instance, depicts himself in its robes in *Las Meninas* — and in the sixteenth-century the monastery was rebuilt as a kind of palatial head-quarters. Its massive facade is lavishly embellished with Plateresque appliqué designs: over the main entrance Santiago is once again depicted in his battling role of *Matamoros*; more pertinently, protruding above the ornate balustrade of the roofline, are the arms of Carlos V, who inherited the Grand Mastership from Fernando in 1516. The monastery is now a Government-owned 5-star hotel (which has been described as the best in the world), and its wealth and luxury look daunting. You can, however, just ask to look around without having to pay. While inside, ask specifically to see the *coro alto* of the church (access only from the hotel), which has a fine set of stalls by Juan de Juni.

Adjacent to the main facade stands the **Iglesia San Marcos**, vigorously studded with the scallop shell motif of the Pilgrimage. Its sacristy houses a small **museum** (Tues.–Fri. 10am–2pm and 4–7:30pm, Sat. 10am–2pm), whose most beautiful and priceless exhibits are grouped together in a room separated from the lobby of the hotel by an oddly symbolic thick pane of glass. Foremost among them are a thirteenth-century processional cross made of rock crystal, and an eleventh-century ivory crucifix — a tiny piece of Romanesque sculpture, primitive and strangely proportioned, but with the peculiar mark of faith about it.

West to Astorga and Beyond

For the fittest of the pilgrims it was one day's walk of 29 miles from León to the next major stop at Astorga. On the way — at PUENTE DE OBRIGO — you pass the most ancient of the bridges along the route (probably the oldest in all Spain), now by-passed by the new road and offering a delightful and popular spot for a riverside stroll or picnic. ASTORGA itself resembles many of the smaller cities along the way: sacked by the Moors in the eleventh century it was rebuilt and endowed with the usual hospices and monasteries, but as the Pilgrimage lost popularity in the late Middle Ages the place fell into decline. Many of its buildings were ravaged during the Peninsular War and today it seems to be crumbling gently into a peaceful old age.

Not without the odd flurry, though, for the bizarre **Palacio Episcopal** — commissioned by a Catalan bishop from his countryman Antoni Gaudí — injects some real vitality. Its appearance will not surprise anyone who has seen Gaudí's work in Barcelona. Surrounded by a moat and built of light gray granite, it resembles some horror-movie Gothic castle from the mountains of Transylvania, with an interior which, while equally striking, is remarkably spacious. For half a century it stood empty and was considered a scandalous and expensive white elephant, but nowadays it houses the unique and excellent **Museo de los Caminos** (Museum of the Pilgrim Routes; daily 10am–2pm and 4–8pm; inclusive ticket with Diocesan Museum, below). A host of knick-knacks throw interesting sidelights on the story of the Pilgrimage. Hanging on the wall are examples of the documents issued at Santiago to certify that pilgrims had "traveled, confessed, and obtained absolution," and there are photographs of the myriad villages and buildings along the way, and charts to show the precise roads taken through the towns.

Nearby — though stylistically worlds apart — stands the **Cathedral**. Built between 1471 and 1693, it combines numerous architectural styles, but sadly doesn't manage to combine them with any notable success. The **Diocesan Museum** (10am–noon and 4–8pm; entrance to the left of the main facade) is interesting, however, especially for its beautiful twelfth-century wooden tomb painted with scenes from the lives of Christ and the Apostles.

Astorga is the traditional market town of the **Maragatos**, a mysterious race of people, possibly descended from the Berbers of North Africa, who crossed into Spain with the first Moorish incursions of the early eighth century. Marrying only among themselves, they maintained their traditions and individuality well into recent decades. For several centuries almost the entire carrying trade of Spain was in their hands, but muleteers no longer have a role in modern Spain. Nowadays you're unlikely to come across them unless you're plodding through the fields along the pilgrimage route, and their only obvious legacy to the town is a pair of colorful clockwork figures, dressed in Maragato costume, who jerk into action to strike the hour on the town hall clock in Plaza de España. Inside the town hall there's a small **Turismo** , and you'll find some excellent **restaurants** and two cheap **fondas** on c/Sr. Ovalle just off the Plaza. If these are closed, try the *hostales* on the main road; they look grotty but aren't. The *Restaurante La Peseta*, behind the town hall, might also rent you a room. Incidentally, if you're traveling by **train** from Astorga in the direction of Salamanca the relevant platform is cunningly hidden about 100m down the track. If you're coming from Santiago, there's an *Intercar* **bus** at 10:30am that is cheaper than most of the trains.

Ponferrada

Astorga lies on the very edge of the **Bierzo mountains**, the ultimate endurance test for the pilgrims. The region is now dotted with bleak mining communities and the large town of PONFERRADA is dominated by a huge slag heap. But there is an extraordinary contrast between the grim industrial part of town and its picturesque, unspoiled old quarter. The two are separated by a river blackened by coal-mining and spanned by the iron bridge that has given Ponferrada its name.

Above the sharp valley rises the fancy twelfth-century **Castillo de los Templarios** (9am–1pm and 3–7pm, Sat. 9am–1pm; closed Tues). Its turrets and battlements may look like gingerbread but they were built to protect pilgrims against the very real threat of the Moors, and the arcaded streets and overhanging houses of the old quarter grew up in their protective shadow. A quaint *Puerta del Reloj* (Clock Gateway) leads into the **Plaza Mayor**, with a late seventeenth-century *Ayuntamiento*, similar in design to its contemporary counterpart at Astorga. There are several churches in the town but the most important is a short walk away in the outskirts: **Santo Tomás de las Ollas**, a small Mozarabic church, dating from the tenth century, with nine round Moorish horseshoe arches and Visigothic elements. The only place that seems to offer **accommodation** in the old town is the two-star *Hostal Lisboa* at c/Jardines 5, just to the left of the *Ayuntamiento*, but there's no shortage of cheap places in the new quarters.

Leaving Ponferrada you may be tempted to stay on the pilgrim route all the way to its conclusion at Santiago, but it has to be said that the Galician stage (with the supreme exception of Santiago itself) is of less interest than what's gone before, and that the traditional route — through SARRIA and PUERTOMARÍN — is slow and difficult to follow on public transport. It's far easier, and perhaps more interesting, to head for Santiago via either Lugo or Orense.

fiestas

January

30 Processions in BURGOS to Honor *San Lesmes*.

February

3 *Romería* to CIUDAD RODRIGO (Salamanca).
Carnival (the week before Lent) is also particularly lively in CIUDAD RODRIGO (Salamanca).

March/April

Holy Week is if anything even more fanatically

observed than in most areas — processions in all the big cities, particularly VALLADOLID, LEÓN, SALAMANCA, and ZAMORA. The one at MEDINA DE RIOSECO (Valladolid) is also worth aiming for. The Good Friday observance in BERCANOS DE ALISTE (Zamora) is almost chillingly solemn, participants dressed in white gowns, which will later become their shrouds. The week **after Easter** is marked by the *Fiesta del Angel* in ARANDA DE DUERO (Burgos) and PEÑAFIEL (Valladolid).

May

12 *Día de Santo Domingo* celebrated with a traditional fiesta in SANTO DOMINGO DE LA CALZADA (Rioja).

Pentecost (variable) is marked by the week-long *Feria Chica* in PALENCIA and with more religious celebrations in MIRANDA DE EBRO (Burgos).

Corpus Christi (variable) sees celebrations in PALENCIA and VALLADOLID; in BENAVENTE (Zamora) the *Toro Enmaromado* runs through the streets in the evening, endangering the lives of everyone. The following day sees the festival of *el curpillos* in BURGOS.

June

11 LOGROÑO's *Fiestas Bernabeas* run around this date.

12 *Día de San Juan de Sahagún* celebrated in SALAMANCA (of which he is patron) and his birthplace, SAHAGÚN (Leon).

24 *Día de San Juan* sees a secular fiesta with bullfights and dance in LEÓN, more religious observances in PALENCIA. The following week sees a big fiesta in SORIA.

23-26 *Fiesta de San Juan* at SAN PEDRO DE MANRIQUE (Soria) — the first night opens with the famous barefoot firewalking of the *Paseo del Fuego*, described in Norman Lewis's *Voices of the Old Sea*.

29 *Día de San Pedro*. In BURGOS the start of a 2-week-long *feria;* lesser events in LEÓN, and in HARO (Rioja) there's the drunken *Batalla del Vino* celebrating local wine production.

July

22 In ANGUIANO (Rioja) performance of the famous stilt dance — *danza de los zancos*.

August

15 Colorful festivals for the Assumption in LA ALBERCA (Salamanca), COCA (Segovia), and PEÑAFIEL (Valladolid).

16 *Día de San Roque* fiesta in EL BURGO DE OSMA (Soria)

Last week — Festival of *San Agustín* in TORO (Zamora), with the "fountain of wine" and *encierros*, and in MEDINACELI (Soria) musical evenings with Medieval and Renaissance music.

September

8 A big day everywhere — the first day of SALAMANCA's major fiesta, beginning the evening before and lasting two weeks, and a famous bull-running in TORDESILLAS (Valladolid).

21 *Día de San Mateo*. Major *ferias* in VALLADOLID and especially LOGROÑO, where the Rioja harvest is celebrated.

October

1st Sunday *Fiesta de las Cantaderas* in LEÓN. VALLADOLID'S *International Film Week* also falls in October.

November

13 The *Toro Jubilo* runs through the streets of MEDINACELI on the night of the nearest Saturday, suffering agonies best not described here.

travel details

Buses

From Salamanca to Madrid (13 daily, 11 on Sun; 2½-3½ hr.), Tordesillas/Valladolid (4; 1¼/1¾ hr.), León (4; 2½-4 hr.), Alba de Tormes (11; ½ hr.), La Alberca (1; 1½ hr.), Ciudad Rodrigo (7; 1 1½hr.), Ávila (2; 1½ hr.), Zamora (13; 1¼ hr.), Toro (3; 1½ hr.), Peñafiel/El Burgo de Osma/Soria (1; 2½/4/5 hr.), Plasencia/Cáceres (4; 2/3½ hr.), Badajoz (2; 4½ hr.), Mérida/Sevilla (3; 4/7 hr.), Santander (1; 5½ hr.), Ledesma (2; ¾ hr.).

From Ciudad Rodrigo to Fuentes de Oñoro (1 daily except Sun; 35 min.).

From Zamora to Toro/Valladolid (4; ½hr./1½ hr.).

From Valladolid to Burgos (2; 3 hr.), León (4; 2¼ hr.), El Burgo de Osma/Soria (1; ¾ hr.), Peñafiel (3; 1 hr.), and Segovia (3; 2½ hr.).

From Soria to Madrid (4; 3-4 hr.), Almazán (4; ½ hr.), Vinuesa (3; ¾ hr.), Berlanga de Duero (1; 1½ hr.), El Burgo de Osma (3; 1¼ hr.), Aranda/Valladolid (2; 2/3½ hr.), Logroño (3; 2 hr.), Agreda/Tarazona/Zaragoza (4; 1½/2/3¼ hr.), Pamplona (3; 3½ hr.), Guadalajara (2; 3 hr.).

From Logroño to Santo Domingo de la Calzada/ Burgos (2; ½/¼ hr.), Pamplona (4; 2 hr.), Vitoria (8; 1 hr.) and Zaragoza (3; 3 hr.).

From Burgos to Madrid (4; 4 hr.), Soria (2 on each route via San Leonardo or via Vinuesa; 3/

3½ hr.), Carrión de los Condes/Sahagún/León (2; 1½/2½/3½ hr.), Frómista (1; 1 hr.), Santo Domingo de Silos (1; 1½ hr.), Covarrubias (1; 1 hr.), Aranda (6; 1¼ hr.), Santo Domingo de la Calzada (4; 1½ hr.), Logroño (7; 2/2½ hr.), Palencia (4; 1¼ hr.), Valladolid (2; 1¾ hr.), Salamanca (1; 3½ hr.), Bilbao (2; 3 hr.), San Sebastián (2; 3½ hr.), Santander (2; 3 hr.).

From León to Madrid (2; 5 hr.), Astorga/Ponferrada (2; ½/2¼ hr.), San Miguel de Escalada (2; 1¼ hr.), Santander (1; 3 hr.), Oviedo (4; 2 hr.), and Lugo (1; 4½ hr.).

From Palencia to Carrión de los Condes (3; 1 hr.) and Valladolid (2; 1 hr.).

Trains

Salamanca–Madrid 3 daily in 3 hr., via Ávila (1¾ hr.).

Salamanca–Guarda (Portugal) 5 daily (3 hr.) via Ciudad Rodrigo (1½hr.) and Fuentes de Oñoro (2 hr.), with onward connections to Coimbra and Lisbon.

Salamanca–Valladolid 7 daily (2 hr.).

Salamanca–Medina del Campo 8 daily (1 hr.).

Salamanca–Vila Formosa (Portuguese frontier) 4 daily (2 hr.) via Ciudad Rodrigo (1½ hr.).

Medina del Campo–Madrid 9 daily (2½–3 hr.) via Ávila (1 hr.), 2 in 4 hr. via Coca (½ hr.) and Segovia (1¼ hr.).

Medina del Campo–Burgos 5 daily (2½ hr.) via Valladolid (1 hr.).

Medina del Campo–León 6 daily (1½–3 hr.) via Valladolid (1¾ hr.) and Palencia (1¼ hr.).

Medina del Campo–Zamora 3 daily (1¼ hr.) via Toro (1 hr.).

Medina del Campo–Segovia 3 daily (2¼ hr.) via Coca (1 hr.).

Logroño–Zaragoza 5 daily (2–3 hr.).

Logroño–Bilbao 5 daily (3–3½ hr.).

Burgos–Bilbao 6 daily (3–3½ hr.).

Burgos–Irún 10 daily (3½–4 hr.) via Vitoria (1½–2 hr.) and San Sebastián (3–4 hr.).

León–Ponferrada 6 daily (2 hr.) via Astorga (40 min.).

León–Madrid 9 daily (4–6 hr.); to **Sahagún** 9 (½–¾ hr.); to **Paredes de Nava** 7 (1–1¼ hr.); to **Becerril** 3 (1½ hr.); to **Palencia** 17 (1–1¾ hr.); to **Valladolid** 13 (1½–2½ hr.); to **Burgos** 5 (2–3 hr.); to **Medina del Campo** 10 (2–3 hr.); **Oviedo** 9 (2 hr.); **Ponferrada** 10 (2 hr.) via **Astorga** (¾ hr.); **Orense** 6 (4½ hr.); **Lugo** 3 (5 hr.).

Ponferrada–Lugo 4 daily (3½ hr.).

Soria–Madrid 5 (4 hr.) via Almazán (½ hr.).

Soria–Logroño 1 (2½ hr.).

Soria–Zaragoza 1 (3½ hr.).

All **other lines** are now closed.

CHAPTER FIVE

EUSKADI:
THE BASQUE PROVINCES
AND NAVARRA

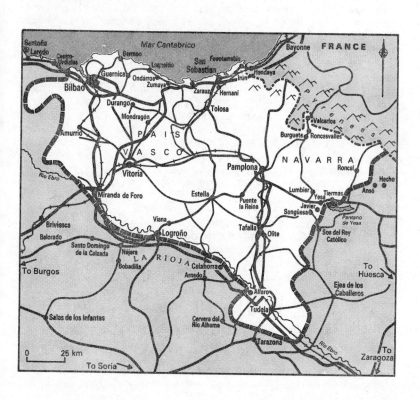

Euskadi is the name the Basque people give to their own land, an area that covers the three Basque provinces, **Guipuzcoa, Vizcaya,** and **Alava,** much of **Navarra,** and part of southwestern France. It's an immensely beautiful region — mountainous, green, and thickly forested. It rains often, and much of the time the countryside is shrouded in a fine mist. But the summers, if you can stand the occasional shower, are a glorious escape from the unrelenting heat of the south.

Despite the heaviest industrialization on the peninsula, Euskadi is remarkably unspoiled — neat and quiet inland, rugged and enclosed along the coast — and transportation everywhere is easy and efficient. **San Sebastián** is the big draw on the coast, a major resort with superb but crowded beaches, but there are any number of lesser-known, equally attractive villages along the coast all the way to **Bilbao,** and beyond into Asturias and Galicia. Inland, there's the exuberant **Fiesta of San Fermín** in **Pamplona,** as well as many other destinations with charms of their own, from the drama of the **Pyrenees** to the quiet elegance of **Vitoria.**

Basque cuisine is accepted as Spain's finest, and the people here are compulsive eaters: try *bacalao* (cod) *a la Vizcaina, merluza* (hake) *a la Vasca, chipirones en su tinta* (squid cooked in its ink) or *Txangarro* (spider crab), which you'll find in very reasonably priced at roadside *caserios* (*baserri* in Basque), on the outskirts of towns throughout the region. You'll also come across traditional Basque food as *tapas* in virtually every bar, freshly cooked and always excellent. The **Basque sport** of *jai-alai,* or *pelota,* is played all over Spain, but others — tree-trunk chopping or dragging giant stones — have yet to catch on. All form an important part of the many local fiestas. There are just two drawbacks to traveling in the region: prices (apart from food) are higher than in much of the country, particularly transportation costs, and accommodation is often hard to find in the smaller towns. One positive advantage, though, is that inland (with the sole exception of Pamplona) there are considerably fewer tourists.

The Basques

No one knows much about the origin of **the Basques.** They are, however, a quite distinct people, generally with a different build from the French and Spanish and often different blood group distribution than the rest of Europe. Certainly their language, the horrendously complex *Euskara,* is one of the most ancient spoken in Europe, predating the migrations from the east which brought the Indo-European languages some 3000 years ago. Some think that the Basques are the last surviving representatives of Europe's aboriginal population, a theory borne out by archeological finds earlier this century; indeed, over the centuries they have had very little contact with the peoples who originally migrated into Europe.

Basque nationalism, though highlighted recently by the horrors of Franco's attempted suppression and the counter-activities of ETA (*Euskadi ta Azkatasuna* — Freedom for the Basques), is no new phenomenon. Richard Ford wrote in the nineteenth century that "these highlanders, bred on metal-pregnant mountains, and nursed amid storms in a cradle indomitable as themselves, have always known how to forge their iron into arms, and to wield them in defence of their own independence." And they have wielded them throughout history: the Visigoth King Recared, unable to subdue the region, used to send his troops out here regularly just to keep them in shape.

For almost the entire history of modern Spain, the Basques have jealously defended their *fueros* — the ancient rights under which they ruled themselves almost as an independent republic — against constant pressure from Madrid and have guarded the wealth brought by their seafaring skills, mineral riches, and industrial enterprise. Only in this century has Basque nationalism become associated with the political left, and that is mostly in reaction to the terrors of Franco's regime. Cut off from their Republican allies by Navarra, which sided with the Nationalists, the Basque provinces were conquered in a vicious campaign that included the infamous German bombing of the civilian population of **Guernica**. Franco's vengeful boot went in hard, and as many as 21,000 people died in his attempts to tame the Basques after the war. Public use of the language was forbidden, and central control was asserted with the gun. But the state violence signally failed, succeeding only in nurturing a new resistance based on **ETA**, whose violent activities included many bombings, and whose most spectacular success was the assassination, in Madrid, of Franco's right-hand man and probable successor, Admiral Carrero Blanco. Even now the military and the *Guardia Civil* are regarded — and behave — as an army of occupation, and a large number of Basques support ETA's aims, if not their methods.

Since the **return to democracy**, however, and at an increasing pace since the election of the Socialists, things *have* changed. The Basque parliament has been granted a fair degree of autonomy in its own affairs (it's the only autonomous community allowed to collect its own taxes), there's a Basque police force (distinguished by their red berets) much in evidence in the streets, the Basque language is flourishing again (and taught in at least half of all primary schools in the region), and the Basque flag (the *Ikurriña*) flies everywhere. Since gaining home rule, it has, like Catalunya and Galicia, been ruled by the right. The government has offered an amnesty to activists who publicly renounce ETA's methods, and is engaged in secret negotiations with ETA leaders to end the violence. But the govenment continues to wield a big stick while granting these concessions: a highly unpopular new army division has been quartered in the area, and, most significantly, an extradition treaty with the French has denied gunmen their former safe refuges across the border. None of this has put an end to ETA activity, but it has marginalized it. Their political wing, *Herri Batasuna* (Popular Unity), has little influence (just over 10 percent voted for them in the last election), in a Basque parliament dominated by the *PNV* (centrist nationalists) and the Socialists, and polls show that while wanting increased autonomy, the majority of Basques oppose forming a breakaway state. The economic recession no doubt has much to do with this — the *País Vasco*'s former industrial glories are now reduced to rusty, out-dated factories and closed-down steel foundries and shipyards. Terrorism keeps away new investment and unemployment is extremely high. In January 1988 a historic anti-terrorism pact was signed by all the Basque parties except *Herri Batasuna*, so condemning ETA's tactics while upholding their goals. There's little doubt that a substantial portion of the Basque population now feels that more will be achieved through the new channels than by the old ETA methods.

An incidental note concerning **language**: almost everywhere, street and road signs are in both Basque and Castilian, the latter usually more prominent. We've stuck with Castilian for simplicity's sake — and because all the tourist brochures and information are still in Castilian — but have given the alternative Basque town and place names where popularly used.

Irún and San Sebastián

Like most border towns, **IRÚN**'s chief concern is how to make a quick buck from passing travelers, and the main point in its favor is the ease with which you can leave; there are trains to HENDAYE in France and to San Sebastián throughout the day, and regular long-distance and international connections. If you can't manage this, it's not such a bad place to spend a night; prices are much lower than in France, and San Sebastián is no place to arrive late at night with nowhere to stay. Irún train station is surrounded by small **hostales**, none of them expensive, and **bodegas and restaurants** specializing in surprisingly good "typical" Spanish food.

San Sebastián

The undisputed best of the Basque resorts, **SAN SEBASTIÁN** (DONOSTIA), just half an hour down the coast from Irún, or linked by regular bus with FUENTERRABÍA, is a picturesque — though expensive — resort with good beaches. Along with Santander, it has always been the most fashionable place to escape the heat of the southern summers, and in July and August it's always packed. Though it tries hard to be chic, San Sebastián is still too much of a family resort to compete in those terms with the South of France, which is all to its good. Set around the deep, still bay of La Concha and enclosed by rolling low hills, it's beautifully situated; the old town sits on the eastern promontory, its back to the wooded slopes of Monte Urgull, while newer development has spread inland along the banks of the Urumea and around the edge of the bay to the foot of Monte Igueldo.

The **old quarter** is the center of interest — it's to these cramped and noisy streets that the crowds retire in the evenings to wander among the many small bars and shops or sample the shellfish from the street traders down by the fishing harbor. Prices tend to reflect the popularity of the area, especially in the waterfront restaurants, but it's no hardship to survive on the delicious *tapas* which are laid out in all but the fanciest bars (check prices first). Here too are the town's chief sights: the gaudy baroque facade of the church of **Santa María**, and the more elegantly restrained sixteenth-century **San Vicente**. Just behind the latter, the excellent **Museo de San Telmo** (Tues.–Sat., 10:30am–2pm and 3:30–6pm, Sun. 10:30am–2pm) is a jumble of Basque folklore and assorted artworks, best of which are the modern paintings by local artists and a series of frescoes by José Sert. Behind this, **Monte Urgull** is criss-crossed by winding footpaths. From the mammoth figure of Christ on

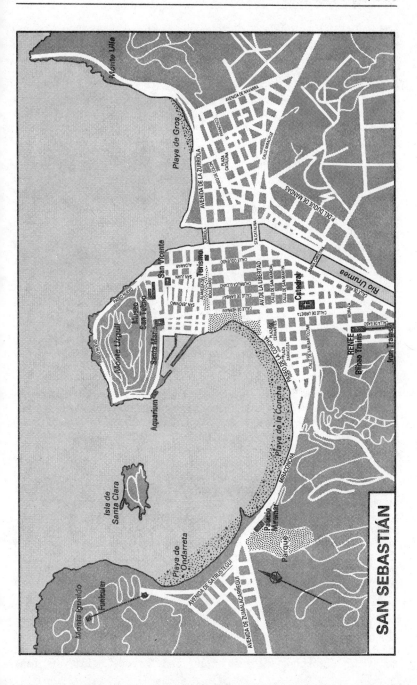

its summit there are great views out to sea and back across the bay to the town; up here too are the dilapidated remains of the castle and a few relics of forgotten sieges on display in what calls itself a military museum (Tues.–Sat. 10am–1pm and 3:30–5:30pm, Mon. 3:30–5:30pm). On the way down you can stop at the **Aquarium** (daily 10am–2pm and 3:30–8pm) on the harbor — not many fish but an extensive history of Basque navigation. Still better views across the bay can be had from the top of **Monte Igueldo**: take the bus (*Igueldo*), or walk around the bay to its base, from where a funicular will carry you to the summit.

There are three **beaches** in San Sebastián: the Playa de la Concha, Ondaretta, and the Playa de Gros. **La Concha** is the most central and the most celebrated, a wide crescent of yellow sand stretching round the bay from the town. Despite the almost impenetrable mass of flesh here during most of the summer, this is the best of the beaches, enlivened by vendors of peeled prawns and cold Cokes and with great swimming out to the sand bars and boats moored in the bay. Out in La Concha bay is a small island, **Isla de Santa Clara**, which makes a good spot for picnics; a boat leaves from the port every half-hour (daily, until 8:30pm). **Ondaretta** is a continuation of the same strand beyond the rocky outcrop which supports the **Palacio Miramar**, once a summer home of Spain's royal family. The atmosphere is rather more staid — it's known as *La Diplomática* for the number of Madrid's "best" families who vacation here. Though it's far less crowded, I wouldn't recommend the aptly named **Playa de Gros.** Outside the shelter of the bay it's very exposed, and it's the repository for all the filth that comes floating down the none-too-clean river.

Some Practical Details

The local **Turismo**, at Andia 13, on the corner of the Plaza de Cervantes overlooking the beach, is very helpful; there's also a national tourist office on c/ Reina Regente, beside the Puente Kursaal. **Accommodation**, though plentiful, is not cheap and can be very hard to come by in season — if you arrive in July or August you'll have to start looking early in the day. The places in the old town are pricey even by local standards, though you will find a wide range of possibilities, many of them on the Alameda Calvo Sotelo. One of the cheapest is a nameless *fonda* by the church of San Vicente. There's better value on the fringes of the neighborhood: try the area around the cathedral, especially calles Loyola, San Bartolomé, and Urdaneta, or on the other side of the river behind the Plaza de Cataluña, where you'll also find a collection of excellent **tapas bars** (ask around in these bars as there seem to be many unoffical residences). San Sebastián's **campground** is excellent, but it's a long way from the center on the landward side of Monte Igueldo and the bus service is poor; there's also an international **youth hostel** (☎943/452970) in the *Ciudad Deportiva Anoeta*, a new development on the outskirts well served by bus #7.

In the evenings you'll find no shortage of action, with **clubs** and **bars** wherever the tourists congregate. The fanciest are along the promenade by the beach, Paseo de la Concha, squeezed between the big hotels; cheaper places are mostly in the old town — the area around the cathedral is popular with local youth. Throughout the summer, too, there are constant **festivals**, many involving Basque sports including the annual rowing races between the villages along the coast. The *International Jazz Festival*, at different locations throughout the town for ten days of July, invariably attracts top performers as well as hordes of people on their way home from the fiesta in Pamplona.

Most **buses** leave from the Plaza Pio XII, the rest from the Plaza de Guipuzcoa: some destinations have services from both places so check with the *Turismo*. The mainline **train station** is across the river Urumea on the Paseo de Francia, although local lines to Hendaye and Bilbao (which do not accept Eurail passes) have their terminus on c/Easo.

The Costa Vasca

There's not much between San Sebastián and Zarauz, but from then on it's a glorious coastline — rocky and wild, with the road hugging the edge of the cliffs — all the way to Bilbao. There are buses that take the highway along this route, but even if you're not planning to stop (and there are plenty of picturesque villages and great beaches to tempt you to do so) it's worth taking the old road for the scenery. The farther you go, the less developed the resorts.

Zaraúz to Bilbao

ZARAÚZ is certainly not the most attractive spot along the coast. Developed as a fashionable overspill of San Sebastián, the old village has been swamped by a line of hotels and pricey cafes sandwiched between the busy road and the busier beach. On the other hand it does have two **campgrounds**, one of them (*Talai Mendi*) very reasonably priced and only a short walk from the beach. Five kilometers on is **GUETARIA**, a tiny fishing port sheltered by the humpbacked islet of **El Ratón** (the mouse). It's a historic little place, one of the earliest towns on the coast, preserving a magnificent fourteenth-century church with the altar raised theatrically above the heads of the congregation. Here too the first man to sail around the world was born, Juan Sebastián Elcano, whose ship was the only one of Magellan's fleet actually to make it back. A huge monument to him gazes out over the harbor.

The coast only really improves when you get to **ZUMAYA** — an industrial-looking place at first sight, but with a center that's refreshingly down-to-earth and unspoiled. There is an excellent **hostal** in the main square and two very different **beaches**. One of these, over the hill behind the town, is a large splash of gray sand enclosed by extraordinary sheer cliffs of layered slate-like rock which channel the waves in to produce some of the best surfing on the coast. There are spectacular rugged walks along the cliff tops to the west. The other, across the river from the port, is yellow and flat, sheltered by a little pine forest. On the road behind this you'll find the **Villa Zuloaga** (closed Thurs.), a small art museum in the former home of the Basque painter Ignacio Zuloaga. Zumaya's local **fiesta** in the first days of July is one of the zestiest around here, with Basque sports, dancing, and steers let loose on the beach to test the mettle of the local youth.

Beyond DEVA, itself an unprepossessing place, the main road veers inland and the coastal route becomes still wilder as it enters the province of Vizcaya. The road is narrow and slow, but there are a fair number of buses along it, and hitching is surprisingly easy. MOTRICO, a plain enough place, would hardly merit a mention were it not for the fact that it boasts no less than five **campgrounds** around its several small beaches and lies at the heart of an area that produces a powerful local wine, *Txacoli*. Admiral Churruca, the "Hero of Trafalgar" to locals, was born here; his imposing statue faces an incongruous neoclassical church, built along the lines of a Greek temple. LEQUEITO is a good bet along this stretch. Still an active fishing port, it has two fine beaches — one beside the harbor, another, much better, across the river to the east of the town. There's little accommodation (one *hostal*, booked in summer, and a few private rooms), but you could always sleep on the beach, where there are showers and, in season at least, a couple of restaurants.

Guernica

Immortalized by Picasso's nightmare picture (finally brought home to Spain after the fall of Franco, and now housed in the Prado, Madrid) GUERNICA, inland and west, is the traditional heart of Basque nationalism. It was here that the Basque parliament used to meet, and here, under the Tree of Guernica (the *Guernikako Arbola*), that their rights were reconfirmed by successive rulers. Sadly it was also Guernica's fate to be chosen for the first-ever mass-bombing raid on a civilian center, in an attempt to blast the soul out of Basque resistance in the civil war. In only four hours more than 1600 people were killed and the town center destroyed. The parliament building (the *Casa de las Juntas*), the elegant church of Santa Mariá, and the tree went miraculously unscathed, but the rest of the town was rebuilt and is, frankly, of little interest. For a Basque, at least, a visit here is more pilgrimage than tourist trip.

The river Mundaca flows from Guernica into a narrow estuary fringed by hilly pine woods and dotted with islets. There is a succession of sandy coves to swim in, but the best spots, made more easily accessible by the local rail line, are at PEDERNALES and especially MUNDACA, where there's a campground perched high above the water with steps leading down to a rocky beach. A passenger ferry plies across the bay to an excellent stretch of sand on the far side, with another campground and a group of holiday villas. Beyond, the train continues to BERMEO, whose fishing fleet is the largest remaining in these waters, a riot of red, green, and blue boats in the harbor. The beach isn't the best, but try some of the fish in the restaurants around the port — the local standards *merluza* (hake) and *bacalao* (cod) are particularly good.

That's about it for the coast as far as Bilbao — the villages beyond are little more than suburbs these days, crowded with the villas of the wealthy. Near to BAQUIO, the road passes LEMONIZ, infamous for the government's attempt to build a nuclear power station and the Basques' fierce resistance to it. The half-finished project has been shelved after two of its directors were assassinated by ETA.

Bilbao

Stretching for some nine miles along the narrow valley of the Nervion, **BILBAO** (BILBO) is a large city but it rarely feels like one, its urban sprawl having gradually engulfed a series of once-separate communities. Even downtown you can always see the green slopes of the surrounding mountains looming beyond the high-rise buildings. A prosperous, modern city, animated in its busy center and surrounded by grim graffiti-covered slums and smoke-belching factories, Bilbao isn't a city of grand sights or glamorous tourism. But it has an unmistakable feel to it, incredibly friendly inhabitants, and some of the best places to eat and drink cheaply in the whole of Euskadi.

Although the city suffered severely from flooding at the end of 1983, there has been little permanent damage and many of the older areas have been dazzlingly refurbished. The main point of interest is the **Casco Viejo**, the old quarter on the east bank of the river — it's here that you'll find the best bars and restaurants among the thronged narrow streets and antiquated shops. Here too are the sights that Bilbao does have to offer: the elegantly arcaded Plaza Nueva (or "de los Martires"), the Gothic Catedral de Santiago and an interesting Historical Museum (Tues.–Sat. 10:30am–1:30pm and 4–7pm). The one sight not here is the **Museo de Bellas Artes** (Tues.–Sat. 10:30am–2pm and 4:30–8pm, Sun. 10:30am–2pm, Mon. 4:30–8pm), in the park off the end of the Gran Vía (see below). This is considered one of Spain's most important collections, and it's a shame that the handful of fine canvases it does have (including works by El Greco, Zurburán and Goya) are swamped by a host of mediocre ones.

Bilbao Practicalities

There are **Turismos** in the Alameda de Mazarredo, and in the Gran Vía which leads from the bridge through the heart of the modern city to the huge stadium of **San Mames** — the "cathedral of Spanish football," as the Basques would have it. Along the Gran Vía are concentrated all the major banks, public buildings, and expensive shops.

The best **places to stay** are the many *hostales* in the *Casco Viejo* itself (especially along c/Bidebarrieta) and the cheaper but less pleasant *fondas* and *huéspedes* on the west bank, above all in c/San Francisco, right across the tracks from the main train station. The nearest **campgrounds** are at PLENCIA on the coast to the east (bus or train to Plencia) or west at the beach of SOMORROSTRA (bus there or train to San Julian de Musques). The latter is just behind a huge oil refinery, but the **beach** isn't bad, and for day-trips you should go either there or to SOPELLANA — both of them very popular with the city's youth. On your **drinking** tours of the city, a couple of places to look out for are the *Herri Taberna* (c/La Ronda 20), which has a strong Basque nationalist atmosphere, and the marvelously atmospheric *Bar Iruña*, in Colon de Larreategui opposite the Jardines de Berastegui. There are two **gay bars** — *Bataclan* at c/Cantera 2 and *Totolo* at c/Barrencalle 8.

There is no central **bus station** in Bilbao, and no two buses seem to leave from the same place, but try to get hold of the *Datos Informativos* leaflet from the **Turismo**; it has complete timetables of all bus routes from the city and tells you where to catch them. Most **trains** leave from the complex of stations by the Puente de la Victoria, but a few local services (to Durango and Guernica, for example) use the Achurri Station to the south of *Casco Viejo*. To get to Bilbao **airport** take the red bus #23 from the stop opposite the church of San Nicolás, just into the *Casco Viejo* before an avenue of market stalls. You can also pick up the bus on its way through the town, either on the Plaza de España or on the left of the river bridge by the museum. The bus goes on beyond the airport, which is quite easy to miss — keep your eyes open.

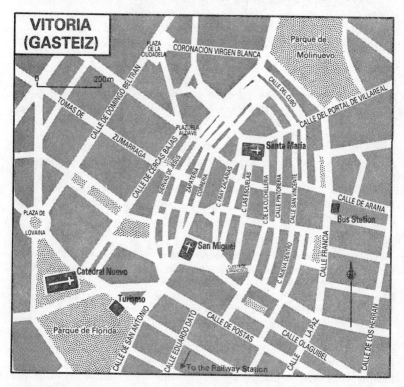

Inland: Vitoria

VITORIA (GASTEIZ), the capital of Alava, crowns a slight rise in the heart of a fertile plain. Founded by Sancho el Sabio, King of Navarra, it was already a prosperous place by the time of its capture by the Castilian Alfonso VIII in 1200. Later, as the center of a wealthy wool and iron trade, Vitoria became seriously rich, and the town still boasts an unusual concentration of Renaissance palaces and fine churches. It's off the tourist circuit but is by no means dull. The university here — or, rather, its students — have made Vitoria one of northern Spain's hippest cities, and the old town is choc-a-bloc with rowdy bars and *tavernas,* not to mention an abundance of excellent, cheap Basque eateries, making it as pleasant a place to while away a few days off the tourist track as you'll find.

The streets of the Gothic old town spread out like a spider's web down the sides of the hill, surrounded on level ground by a neater grid of later development. You'll get the feel of the town simply by wandering through this old quarter — a harmonious place, the graceful mansions and churches all built from the same grayish-gold stone. The porticoed **Plaza de España**, especially, is a gem, a popular location for early evening strolling and drinking. Take time to visit the church of **San Miguel**, just above the Plaza de España and marking the southern end of the old town. Outside its door stands the fourteenth-century stone image of the Virgen Blanca, revered patron of the city. The streets below hold any number of interesting buildings, one of the finest being the **Escoriaza-Esquibel Palace** with its sixteenth-century Plateresque portal, at the opposite end of town on c/Fray Zacarias. A little closer, the old Gothic cathedral of **Santa María** (daily 9am–1pm and 4–6pm) has a superb west doorway, intricately and lovingly carved, whilst inside a delicate stone gallery runs around most of the higher sections of the naves. Behind the cathedral, down the hill on the left, the **Portalón** is the most impressive of the surviving trading houses of Renaissance Vitoria, its dusty red brick and wooden beams and balconies in marked contrast to the golden stone of the rest of the town. Over the road you'll find the province's **Museo Arqueológico** (Tues.-Sat. 11am–2pm and 5–7pm, Sun. 11am–2pm).

Vitoria Practicalities

There's a useful **Turismo** (Mon.-Sat. 8am–2:30pm and 4–7pm) close to the train station, with lots of colorful brochures and a good, free map. Turn left out of the station, take the second right, and it's on c/Ramón y Cajal (in the corner of the park). The **bus station** is across town on c/Francia, a two-minute walk (over the road and straight uphill) from the old town. There are several cheap **places to stay** near the railway station, around the junction of c/de los Fueros and Ortiz de Zarate. For somewhere very cheap, walk from the railway station down c/Dato, the main pedestrians-only shopping street, and left onto c/Florida, where there's an unnamed pensión that's clean and friendly, if a bit unkempt. There are also places near the bus station: two *CH*s on c/de Francia and three more on the first main road on the right which leads to San Miguel. It's nicest to stay, however, in the old quarter, near the action: hike straight up the cobbled Cantón de San Francisco Javier Colegio, across the road from the bus station — there's a *fonda* at c/Nuevo Dentro 36 (third left), another, the *Economica*, at c/Pintorería 72 (fourth left) and, the best of the bunch, *habitaciones* on c/Cuchillería. Ask about these at the *Bar La Riojana* (☎945/268795) at the corner of San Francisco Javier and Cuchillería; they'll take your money and give you a key to the *CH* down the road. The only time you might have trouble locating a room is during Vitoria's annual **jazz festival** held in the third week of July.

The streets of the old town — in particular c/Cuchillería, Pintorería, Hurrería, and Zapatería — are lined with **bars, tavernas,** and **bodegas** differentiated only by the music they play, each spilling out onto the narrow pavements at night. At c/Zapatería 36, just off Virgen Blanca, bar/restaurant *Nestor* has a good *comedor; Ballarín 8*, on the next street over (Calle Herrería) at no. 8, is popular with the locals; and for solid Basque cooking, try *Ambota Oleagarena* at c/Cachilleria 29. For drinks in fancier, and quieter, surroundings, Plaza de España has a nice outdoor cafe, and the lower new town is full of elegant pedestrian thoroughfares and cafes.

Around Vitoria

Attractive though the town is, a significant part of Vitoria's charm is the beauty of the surrounding countryside. Almost every hamlet of mountainous Euskadi has something of interest: an old stone mansion proudly displaying the family coats-of-arms, a richly decorated church or a farmhouse raised Swiss-style on stilts. It doesn't really matter where you go, and it would be limiting to select just one area; to the south lies the wine-growing district of Rioja Alavesa, to the north and west the red hills of the iron ore mines, to the east the mountainous approaches to Navarra. The **Turismo** in Vitoria has piles of glossy leaflets on any number of excursions, not just confined to those with their own transportation (though this is a distinct advantage). There are numerous buses from Vitoria bus station into the locality; the *Turismo*, again, can advise on the various possibilities.

Into Navarra: Pamplona

PAMPLONA (IRUÑA) has been the capital of Navarra since the ninth century, and long before that was a powerful fortress town defending the northern approaches to Spain at the foothills of the Pyrenees. Even now it has something of the appearance of a garrison city, with its hefty walls and elaborate pentagonal citadel. The **Plaza del Castillo** is the center of activity, a great tree-lined square, ringed with fashionable cafes, which according to local legend was the site of a public burning of 10,000 Jews "to honor the marriage of the Conde de Champagne." Before the persecutions and expulsions there was a large Jewish community here, but little trace remains except the narrow streets of the former *Judería* between the plaza and the walls by the cathedral. From the opposite side of the square the c/San Nicolás runs down towards the citadel and the more modern area of the city. It's here, and in its continuation c/San Gregorio, that you'll find most of the cheap *hostales* and *fondas,* a number of excellent small restaurants and loads of raucous little bars. Although Pamplona is a sizable city (as anyone who's tried to walk from the train station can tell you), its center is remarkably compact — nothing you're likely to want to see is more than five minutes from the Plaza del Castillo.

The **Cathedral** is basically Gothic, built over a period of 130 years from the late fourteenth century to the early sixteenth century but with an unattractive facade added in the eighteenth century. It doesn't look promising, but the interior is fine, and the cloister is magnificent. Notice especially the tomb of Carlos III and Eleanor in the center of the nave and the ancient Virgen de Los

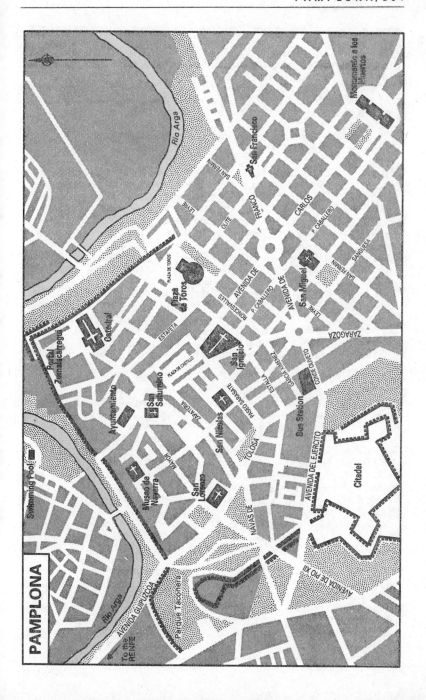

San Fermín: The Facts

Don't expect to find a room in a *hostal* during the fiesta — the town is packed to the gills. However, the **Turismo** opposite the bullring fills with old women willing to rent **rooms** for the night at reasonable prices. If you have no luck, accept that you're going to sleep on the ramparts, in the park or plaza (along with hundreds of others), and check your **valuables** and knapsack at the bus station on c/Conde Oliveto — it's inexpensive, and you can have daily access (this too fills early in the week — hang around and be insistent). There are also free cold showers here.

There is a **campground**, *Ezcaba*, 7km out of town on the road to France, but you have to be there a couple of days before the fiesta to get a place. Facilities include good toilets and showers but they can't really handle the numbers during San Fermín — be prepared for long lines or for going "primitive." Bear in mind that the shop is only really well stocked in the drinks department. The main bonus is that security is tight — admission is by pass only and there's a guard who patrols all night. For the period of the fiesta there are also two **free campgrounds**, one by the river just below *Ezcaba*, and another nearer the center of town along the France road — turn off near the *Restaurante Ezcabarte*. Security at these is doubtful, however. The bus service, which goes to all the campgrounds, is poor (about five a day, first one at 9am, last at 10pm), but it's easy to hitch or, more expensively, get a ride with one of the tour buses that stay at the official campground (they leave in time to see the *encierro*). Wherever you sleep, keep an eye on everything you have with you — there's a very high rate of **petty crime** during the festival; vans are broken into with alarming frequency. Several banks and a post office are open during the festival, so changing **traveler's checks** is no problem.

To watch the *encierro* it's essential to arrive early (about 6am) — crowds have already formed an hour before it starts. The best vantage points are near the starting point around the Plaza Santo Domingo or on the wall leading to the bullring (don't sit on the barriers since the police will make you move). The event divides into two parts: there's the actual running of the bulls, when the object is to run with the bull or whack it with a rolled-up newspaper. It's difficult to see the bulls amid all the runners and they often jump the wooden safety barriers surrounding the ring; down on the ground, you'll sense sheer terror and excitement. Then there's a separate event after the bulls have been through the streets, when steers with padded horns are let loose on the crowd in the bullring. If you watch the actual running, you won't be able to get into the bullring (too many people), so go on two separate mornings to see both things. For the bullring you have to arrive at about 6am to get the free lower seats. If you want to pay for a seat higher up buy from the ticket office outside, not from the hawkers inside, who will rip you off.

We advise against it, but if you do decide to **run**, remember that although it's probably less dangerous than it looks, at least one person gets seriously injured (sometimes killed) every year. Find someone who knows the ropes to guide you through the first time, and don't try any heroics; bulls are weighed in tons and have very sharp horns. Don't get trapped hiding in a doorway and don't get between a scared bull and the rest of the pack. Traditionally women don't take part, though more and more are doing so; if you do, it's probably best to avoid any officials, who may try to remove you. A glass of *Pacharrán*, the powerful local liqueur, is ideal for a dose of courage. Of course, the atmosphere can sometimes get the better of people's judgment: many people have fun hurling themselves from the fountain in the center of town and from surrounding buildings (notably the mussel bar), hoping their friends will catch them below. Needless to say, several people each year are not caught by their drunken pals.

Other events include music from local bands nightly from midnight in the Plaza de Castillo, continuing until abou⁺ 4am in the fairground on the Avda. de Bayona, which is where local political groupings and other organizations have their stands. There are fireworks every evening in the citadel (about 9pm), and a funfair on the open ground beside it. Competing bands stagger through the streets all day playing to anyone who'll listen. If things calm down a bit you can sunbathe, take a shower, catch up on sleep, and even swim at the public **swimming pool** outside the walls below the Portal de Zumalacarregui. **Bullfights** take place daily at 6:30pm, with the bulls that ran that morning. Tickets are expensive (about $15), and if you have no choice but to buy from the hawkers, wait until the bullfight has begun, when you can insist on paying less (the price drops with each successive killing). At the end of the week (midnight, July 14) there's a mournful candlelit procession, the **Pobre de**, at which the festivities are officially wound up for another year. If you're hooked on danger or if you've missed Pamplona, many **other Basque towns** have fiestas which involve some form of *encierro*. Among the best are Tudela (July 24–28), Estella (last week of July and one of the few which has no official ban on women participants), Tafalla (mid-Aug.), and Ampuero in Santander province (Sept. 7–8).

Reyes above the high altar. A *coro* that once filled the body of the church has been demolished in restoration work. Between May and September the **Museo Diocesano** (daily 9am–2pm) can be entered via the cloisters, housed in two superb buildings, the refectory and the kitchen — both are well worth seeing in their own right. Don't miss the many sculpted doorways in the cloister, particularly the *Puerta de la Preciosa* and the chapel with a lovely star vault, built by a fourteenth-century bishop to house his own tomb. Behind the cathedral is the best section of the remaining **walls** with, around to the left, the Reducto de Redín and gate of Zumalcarregui looking down over a loop of the river Arga. Continue in this direction and you'll come to the **Museo de Navarra** in the old hospital building (Tues.–Sun. 10am–1pm and 3–6pm), which displays material on the archeology and history of the old kingdom, along with an art collection that includes a portrait of the Marques de San Adrian by Goya. From here you can walk back to the Plaza via the **market** and the baroque **Ayuntamiento**.

There's more to Pamplona than this — enticing churches, a beautiful park, the massive citadel — and it's an enjoyable place to be throughout the year. But for anyone who has been here during the thrilling week of the **Fiesta of San Fermín**, a visit at any other time can only be a monumental anticlimax. From midday on July 6 until midnight on July 14 the city gives itself up entirely to riotous non-stop celebration. The center of the festivities is the **encierro**, or the running of the bulls, which draws tourists from all over the world, but this has become just one aspect of a massive fair along with bands, parades, and dancing in the streets 24 hours a day. You could have a great time here for a week without ever seeing a bull, and even if you are violently opposed to bullfighting, the *encierro* — in which the animals decisively have the upper hand — is a spectacle not to miss.

Six bulls are released each morning at eight (traditionally it was an hour earlier, so that the festival started on the seventh hour of the seventh day of the seventh month) to run from their corral near the Plaza San Domingo to the bullring. In front, around, and occasionally under them run the hundreds of locals and tourists who are foolish or drunk enough to test their daring against the horns. It was Hemingway's *The Sun Also Rises* that really put "Las San Fermines" on the map and the area in front of the Plaza de Toros has been renamed Plaza Hemingway by a grateful council. His description of it as "a damned fine show" still attracts Americans by the thousand. No amount of outsiders, though, could outdo the locals in their determination to have a good time, and it's an indescribably exhilarating event to take part in.

Other Pamplona Practicalities

The **train station** is some way out of Pamplona, but bus #9 runs every ten minutes right to the citadel end of the Paseo de Sarasate, a few minutes' walk from the Plaza del Castillo. (There is a handy downtown RENFE ticket office at Castilla 8). The **bus station** is more central, on c/Conde Oliveto just in front of the citadel: schedules are confusing, given the number of companies operating from here — see *travel details* at the end of this chapter and the timetable posted at the station. The **Turismo** (daily 9am–9pm) is at c/Duque de Ahumada 3, just off Plaza del Castillo. There's a **laundromat** (just in case if your clothes have borne the brunt of the festivities) at c/de Descalzos (a couple of minutes' walk from the Plaza de San Francisco).

Most of the cheap **fondas and hostales** are in c/S. Nicolás and c/S. Gregorio, off the Plaza del Castillo. However, even outside San Fermín rooms fill up quickly in summer and it might be easier to accept that you'll have to pay a little more to avoid the hassle of trudging around: *Hostal Bearan*, c/S. Nicolás 25, usually has rooms. If you want to continue looking, the streets around the cathedral, over the Plaza del Castillo, yield other possibilities — try c/Navarrareia and c/Estafeta. The best and rowdiest **bars** are on and around the c/S. Nicolás but there's not much in the way of particularly cheap food, except for *Baserri* at no. 32 across from the Bearan. Try instead the streets around c/Major; there are several good *tapas* bars, some basic *comedores,* and cheap restaurants on c/S. Lorenzo and c/Jarauta.

Southern Navarra

South of Pamplona the country changes rapidly; the mountains are left behind and the monotonous plain so characteristic of central Spain begins to open out. The people are different, too — more akin to their southern neighbors than to the Basques of the north.

There is regular bus and train service south to TUDELA (see below), passing through Tafalla and Olite, once known as the "Flowers of Navarra," though little remains of their former glory. **TAFALLA**, particularly, is a shabby provincial town apparently left behind by modern Spain. If you find yourself there, it's worth going to the parish church of **Santa María**, where there is a huge *retablo,* one of the finest in Spain. It was carved by Juan de Ancheta, among the most recognized of the Basque country's artists. **OLITE**, also somewhat forgotten, is more attractive. Now hardly more than a village, it boasts a magnificent castle (daily 9am–2pm and 6–8pm summer) which was once the residence of the kings of Navarra. An amazing ramshackle ramble of turrets, keeps, and dungeons, it is slowly being restored, and part of the building already houses a *parador* which is a pity in a way. There are also two gorgeous old churches, Romanesque **San Pedro** and Gothic **Santa María**, the latter with a superb carved *retablo*. You'll find just one **hostal** here, two-star and frequently full in summer.

The route south continues to **TUDELA** on the banks of the Ebro, Navarra's second city. As you get off the bus or train it seems as ugly a town as you could ever come across, but don't despair — a short walk down the main street takes you into the old town and an entirely different atmosphere. Around the richly decorated **Plaza de los Fueros** are a jumble of narrow lanes little changed since the Moorish occupation of the city was ended by Alfonso I of Aragon in 1114. The twelfth-century **Colegiata de Santa Ana** is a fine strong Gothic construction. It has a rose window above the intricately carved alabaster west doorway which portrays a chilling vision of the Last Judgment. Inside there's an unusual *retablo* and some beautiful old tombs, while the Romanesque cloister has some deft primitive carvings, many badly damaged. The bizarre thirteenth-century **bridge** over the Ebro looks as if it could never have carried the weight of an ox-cart, let alone seven centuries of traffic on the main road to Zaragoza. There are a couple of pricey **hostales** in the main street, through the new part of town, or try the *CH* at c/de Carniceras 13, above the *Restaurante La Estrella*. You'll find many other places to **eat and drink** around the Plaza de los Fueros.

The Pilgrim Route

The ancient **pilgrim route** to Santiago passed through Aragón and into Navarra just before LEYRE, traveling through the province via Sangüesa and Logroño. A modern curiosity worth mentioning before Leyre is **TIERMAS**, overlooking the artificial *Embalse de Yesa*. Now virtually a ghost town, the ruined houses and abandoned main square and roofless church were abandoned in 1960, after which it served for a time as a hippie community. Most of the hippies are long gone, but there's still a steadfast population of four. There's a lakeside **campground** too, below the village, just off the main road.

Traveling south, the **Monasterio de San Salvador de Leyre** stands amid mountainous country 4km from YESA, which is on the main road between Pamplona and Huesca/Jaca and is connected with both places by a daily bus in either direction. Yesa has several **hostales** and a **Turismo** (summer Wed.–Sun. only), and from the village a good road leads up to Leyre, arriving at the east end of the monastery. The guest house there is now run as a two-star hotel (for both sexes), and although far more expensive than staying in Yesa, it is still a remarkable bargain. Theoretically, men should be able to stay at the monastery itself for a nominal fee, but anyone wanting to do this should write or phone ahead.

Although the convent buildings are sixteenth- to eighteenth-century, the church is largely Romanesque, its tall, severe apses particularly impressive. After laying in ruins for over a century, it was restored and reoccupied by the Benedictines in the 1950s and now looks to be in immaculate condition. The leaflet that is available in English at the porter's lodge is useful to shed light on the complicated sculptured facade of the church. Inside, the crypt, with its sturdy little columns, can be illuminated by putting a coin in the slot. Try, also, to catch a service if you can; the Benedictines here employ the Gregorian chant in their masses and are well worth hearing.

From Yesa it's only a few kilometers south to **JAVIER** (one bus daily), birthplace of San Francisco Xavier and home to a fine **castle** (daily 10am–1pm and 4–7pm). Javier had nothing to do with the pilgrim route, but it is something of a place of pilgrimage in its own right, with a museum of the saint's life in the restored keep. The elderly guide takes great glee in describing the horrors that the castle has seen, and particularly a set of extraordinary demonic murals — recently discovered — depicting the dance of death. It's a popular picnic spot and there's a **hostal** in the grounds alongside two churches dedicated to the saint.

The Pilgrim Route proper stopped next at **SANGÜESA**, a delightful small town preserving many outstanding monuments in the south facade of the church of **Santa Maria Real** (at the far end of town beside the river), which has an incredibly richly carved doorway and even sculpted buttresses. Sangüesa is a good town for wandering around in. Many of its streets have changed little in centuries and there are some handsome mansions, the remains of a royal palace and a medieval hospital — the last two currently under restoration. Unfortunately, there is a lack of **accommodation**: the *Pensión las Navas*, opposite the main bus stop, is the only obvious place to stay. There are three **buses** daily to and from Pamplona and one (leaving Sangüesa very early) to the Aragonese town of SOS DEL REY CATOLICO, 12km away.

Puente La Reina

Perhaps no town is more highly evocative of the days of the pilgrimage than **PUENTE LA REINA**. This was the meeting place of the two main Spanish routes: the Navarrase trail, via Roncesvalles and Pamplona, and the Aragonese one, via Jaca, Leyre, and Sangüesa. From here onward, all the pilgrims followed the same path to Santiago, but for slight detours. On the eastern edge of town, the **Iglesia del Crucifijo** was originally a twelfth-century foundation by the Knights Templars, its porch decorated with scallop shells. To one side is the former pilgrim's hospice, later in date, but still one of the oldest extant. In town, c/Mayor has tall buildings, many displaying coats of arms, and another pilgrim church, that of Santiago, whose fine portal is sadly worn. But it's the **bridge** at the end of the street that gives the town its name. The finest medieval bridge in Spain, it was built at the end of the eleventh century by royal command and is still used by pedestrians and animals only — an ugly modern bridge has been constructed for vehicular traffic. There are several places to stay and to eat, most near the main road, which, thankfully, skirts the town — the *Bar la Puente* is clean and fairly cheap.

Buses continue from Puente la Reina to **ESTELLA**, a town rich in monuments and high in interest. During the nineteenth century this was the headquarters of the Carlists in the civil wars, and each May there is still a pilgrimage up a nearby mountain to honor the dead. From the bus station, follow the c/San Andres and you come to Plaza de los Fueros in the center of town. At the corner is the one-star *Hostal San Andrés* and on the streets around are several cheaper *fondas*. There are plenty of bars in this area too, many serving good *platos combinados*; the restaurants, on the other hand (except those attached to the *fondas)*, are expensive.

Most of the more interesting buildings are on the opposite side of the river in the *Barrio San Pedro de la Rua*. Immediately after crossing the bridge, the twelfth-century **Palacio de los Reyes de Navarra** is a rare example of large-scale Romanesque civil architecture. Sadly, you can't go in (the interior has been modernized into various offices) but you can visit the main fortified pilgrimage church of **San Pedro de la Rúa**, whose main doorway shows an unmistakable Moorish influence. From the former Ayuntamiento, an elegant sixteenth-century building opposite the *palacio,* follow c/de la Rúa, which boasts many old merchants' mansions. Farther on, past a stud farm, the abandoned church of Santo Sepulcro has a carved fourteenth-century Gothic doorway. Cross the hump-backed bridge, take the first left, then right uphill, and you come to the church of **San Miguel**: not a terribly inspiring building in itself but with a north doorway that is one of the gems of the pilgrim route. Its delicate capitals are marvelous, as are the modeled reliefs of the *Three Marys at the Sepulcher* and *St. Michael Fighting the Dragon*. The dingy interior is a letdown after this — don't be too disappointed if it's closed.

From Estella, the pilgrim route followed the main road to Logroño. There's a Cistercian monastery at **IRACHE**, near the village of AYEGUI, which is currently being restored (Tues.–Sun. 10am–1pm and 4–7pm): inside it boasts an ornate Plateresque cloister. Seventeen kilometers farther is **LOS ARCOS**, whose handsome church has a Gothic cloister. Of more direct interest is **TORRES DEL RÍO**, 7km farther. This unpretentious village is built around the church of the **Holy Sepulcher**, a little octagonal building whose function is uncertain — it may have been a Templars foundation or a funeral chapel. Local women take turns looking after the monument and someone will probably direct you to one of the houses for the key (access at any reasonable time, for a small charge). Inside it's a surprise to find that the dome is of Moorish inspiration. **VIANA**, where Cesare Borgia died, is worth a short stop, and from there it's only 10km to LOGROÑO and Castile.

The Pyrenees

The mountains of Navarra may not be as high as their neighbors to the east, but they're every bit as dramatic and far less developed, with not — as yet — a single ski-lift in the province. The historic pass of **Roncesvalles** is the major route through the mountains from Pamplona, and always has been — celebrated in the *Song of Roland* and more recently, when Jan Morris called it "one of the classic passes of Europe and a properly sombre gateway into

Spain." It was the route taken by countless pilgrims throughout the Middle Ages; Charlemagne's retreating army was decimated here by Basque guerillas avenging the sacking of Pamplona; Napoleon's defeated armies fought a running battle along the pass as they fled Spain; and thousands of refugees from the civil war made their escape into France along this narrow way.

Roncesvalles and Burguete

There's virtually no habitation along the road as it switchbacks its way up from Pamplona until it reaches the neighboring villages of BURGUETE and RONCESVALLES itself. The Colegiata is the main sight here, with a beautiful Gothic cloister and, in a side chapel, a prostrate statue of Sancho VII el Fuerte (the strong), measuring 2.25m long and supposedly life-size. They also have the chains that Sancho broke in 1212 at the battle of Navas de Tolosa against the Moors — a symbol that subsequently found its way into the Navarrese coat of arms.

Both Roncesvalles and Burguete have hostales, and there are rooms available in private houses as well. If you're a walker or cyclist following the pilgrim route, you might be able to stay in a dormitory at the monastery. They will also give you a booklet to get stamped on the way; ask for Father Javier Navarro. The surrounding country is superb for walking, or simply to sit back and admire. If you're going on all the way into France, you'll come to the border village, VALCARLOS, 18km on. There's no bus between the two but hitching is easy. There's also a helpful Turismo there that will direct you to houses with rooms for rent.

If you are really serious about exploring the mountains, we recommend the remote Valley of Roncal. Just one bus a day heads this way from Pamplona, returning the following day. It passes north of Sangüesa, and briefly into Aragón by the huge Embalse de Yesa (see Tiermas, above) before heading north up the valley of the Esca and back into Navarra. It's a lovely route, crisscrossing the river all the way up through BURQUI and RONCAL to ISABA. There's a *hostal* in Roncal, and, a couple of kilometers to the south, the turn-off to the east for ANSÓ, over the border in Aragón. If you want to stay around here, though, you're much better off continuing to Isaba, where there are any number of rooms available in private houses as well as a small luxury hotel; beyond the village you can camp freely along the banks of the river. For the best walking and magnificent views, hitch up the valley (no public transportation) to the *Refugio de Belagua*, a mountain refuge almost on the border, high among the peaks in a landscape of extraordinary beauty. In the refuge itself Spanish shepherds sit chatting with their French counterparts in their common language, *Euskara*, while the herds graze outside. There's a restaurant and bar, and if you bring a sleeping bag you can rent a basic bed for the night — bring your own food if you plan to stay long. A delicious cheese, *Roncal*, is produced in the valley.

fiestas

January
19–20 *Tamborrada* — march with pipes and drums — in SAN SEBASTIÁN, with more festive action in the evenings.

March
4–12 A series of pilgrimages to the castle at JAVIER, birthplace of San Francisco Javier.

June
21 *Fiesta de la Magdalena* in BERMEO, with torch-lit processions of fishing boats and the usual races and Basque sports. Similar events at the **end of the month** in LEQUEITO, spilling over into early July.

July
First week sees the great fiesta at ZUMAYA, with dancing, Basque sports, and an *encierro* on the beach.
7–14 *Fiestas de San Fermín* in PAMPLONA.
22 Basque sports and boat races all along the coast, especially at BERMEO and MOTRICO.
Third week Jazz festival in VITORIA.
24–29 *Fiesta de Santa Ana* in TUDELA, with bands, marches, and *encierros*.
Last ten days The *International Jazz Festival* in SAN SEBASTIÁN — one ticket covers all the gigs.

August
First weekend Patron saint's celebrations in ESTELLA.

First week *Fiesta de la Virgen Blanca* in VITORIA, with bullfights, fireworks, and *gigantes*.
15 The middle of the month witnesses an explosion of celebration notably in BILBAO, with Basque games and races; ZARAUZ, with rowing regattas; GUERNICA and TAFALLA, with an *encierro;* and above all SAN SEBASTIÁN, where the highlight is an International Fireworks Competition.
31 *Dia de San Ignacio Loyola* is big everywhere, above all in his birthplace, LOYOLA.

September
First week *Euskal Jaiak* (Basque Feasts) in SAN SEBASTIÁN, and the *Fiesta de San Antolin* in LEQUEITO where the local youth attempt to knock the head off a goose — a sort of living Piñata.
8 Fiestas at VITORIA, BERMEO, VIANA, EIBAR, and FUENTERRABÍA among others.
9 In ZARAUZ the start of a week-long Basque festival.
12 SANGÜESA holds its own *encierros*.
14 Patron saint's day in OLITE, with more bulls.
The SAN SEBASTIÁN film festival is also held around the **middle of September**.

December
Christmas Celebrations are particularly exuberant in PAMPLONA. At midnight on Christmas Eve there's an open-air mass by firelight in LABASTIDA (Alava).

travel details

Buses
From Irún to San Sebastián (constantly; ½ hr.); Pamplona (3 daily; 2 hr.)
From San Sebastián to Bilbao (6 daily; 2 hr.); Pamplona (3; 3 hr.); Vitoria (5; 2½ hr.); Zumaya (4; 1 hr.)
From Bilbao to Burgos (4 daily; 2 hr.); Guernica (9; 1 hr.); Lequeito (4; 1½ hr.); Logroño (1; 2¼ hr.); Pamplona (3; 4 hr.); Santander (5; 2½ hr.); Vitoria (8; 1½ hr.); Zaragoza (3; 5 hr.)
From Vitoria to Durango (4 daily; 1 hr.); Logroño (8; 1 hr.) Santander via Castro Urdiales (3 a day 2hr.)
From Pamplona to Estella (10 daily; 1 hr.); Jaca (2, except Sun.; 2 hr.); Logroño (4; 2 hr.); Tudela (4; 1½ hr.); Vitoria (9, fewer Sun.; 1½ hr.); Zaragoza (2–3; 4 hr.); Bilbao (6); Madrid (2); Roncal (1, at 5pm); Puenta de la Reina (hourly); San Sebastián (3–4); Irún (2–3)

Trains
From Irún to Hendaye, France (half-hourly 7am–10pm; 5 min.); San Sebastián (half-hourly 5am–11pm; 30 min.); Paris (2 daily; 8 hr.)
From San Sebastián to Bilbao (9 daily; 1½ hr.); Burgos/Madrid (15 daily; 4½/8 hr.); Pamplona (4 daily; 3½ hr.); Salamanca (2 daily; 9 hr.); Valencia (2 daily; 11 hr.); Vitoria (11 daily; 2 hr.); Zaragoza (2 daily; 5 hr.)
From Bilbao to Guernica (7 daily; 1½ hr.); Logroño (5 daily; 3 hr.); Madrid (3 daily; 8 hr.); Santander (5 daily; 2 hr.)
From Pamplona to Madrid (1 daily; 6 hr.); Zaragoza (7 daily; 2½ hr.)

CHAPTER SIX

ASTURIAS AND CANTABRIA

Barred to the south by the grand mountains of the Picos de Europa, **Asturias** was the one part of Spain never to be conquered by the Moors. It remains today a principality — the heir to the Spanish throne is officially known as the *Príncipe de* Asturias — and an idiosyncratic, slightly separate part of the nation. Its high, remote valleys are mining country, providing the raw materials for the heavy industry of the three cities, **Gijón, Avilés** and **Oviedo**, and a proud radical tradition, born of harsh economic realities, has survived in this rugged terrain. Asturian miners have long been renowned as a maverick and fiercely independent force; legendary for their use of tossed sticks of dynamite as basic weapons, they staged a wildcat rebellion against the Republic itself in 1934, but when civil war came they were its staunchest defenders against Franco.

If European comparisons were to be made, then Wales, with which Asturias shares a Celtic past, would be the obvious candidate. In Spain, the principality has aspects in common with Galicia, to the west, though the differences are equally clear. The wide, rolling meadows that lead down to the coast support a pastoral agriculture impossible on the terraces and tiny Gallego fields, providing food without the same dependence on the sea, and the presence of industry means that there is no equivalent history of poverty and emigration. Traveling along the coast, it might seem that tourism as a business barely exists; if you steer clear of the steelmills of Avilés and the factories of Gijón, you can choose from a succession of old-fashioned and very enjoyable **seaside towns**. Small places such as **Ribadesella, La Isla,** and **Luarca** have a lot to offer.

Inland, everything is dominated by the **Picos de Europa,** perhaps the most stunning of all Spain's mountain ranges and one of the best for hikers, whatever your level of experience. The spectacular scenery and wildlife, and the hospitality of the ancient inns in the hamlets, should be enough to attract even the most reluctant casual walker. And for hiking aficionados there is strong appeal in the region's still embryonic development — a world apart from the organized hiking areas of the Alps, for example.

The Picos can be approached from Asturias, from León to the south, or from the tiny province of **Cantabria,** centered on the city of Santander. This is politically a part of Old Castile, and a conservative bastion amid the separat-

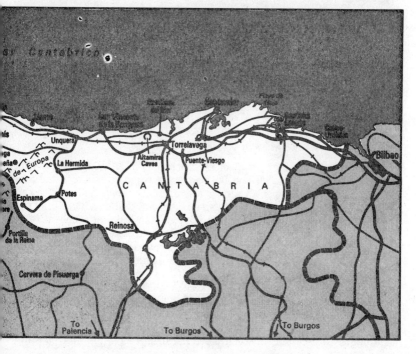

ist leanings of its coastal neighbors. **Santander** itself is an elegant, if highly conventional resort. More attractive and low-key alternatives lie to either side, crowded in the Spanish and French holiday season — August above all — but generally enjoyable. Perhaps the best are **Castro Urdiales**, to the east, and **Comillas** and San Vicente to the west.

Elsewhere in the province there are curiosities in a series of **prehistoric caves**. Several can be seen at **Puente Viesgo**, near Santander, though the most famous, **Altamira**, cannot now be visited — a fact compensated in part by its neighboring village, medieval **Santillana**, whose mansions and rural character, though overvisited, should still be seen.

A quiet pleasure of both Cantabria and Asturias are the wealth of Romanesque — and earlier — churches, scattered about on the hillsides. These reflect the history of independence from the Moors, which began in the Asturian mountain fastness of **Covadonga**, and was slowly to spread south with the Reconquest. The churches are often at their best when least expected, rounding a corner in the countryside, miles from the nearest village. One, however, that is worth a special effort to see is **Santa María del Naranco**, just outside Oviedo.

Transportation

Communications in this region are generally slow, with the one decent road in Asturias following the coast through the foothills to the north of the Picos. If you're in no great hurry, you may want to make use of the **FEVE rail line**, unmarked on many maps and independent of the main *RENFE* system. The railroad begins at Bilbao in the Basque country and follows the length of the Cantabrian coast, with an inland branch to Oviedo, all the way to El Ferrol in Galicia. It is at present undergoing major repairs — with services drastically reduced and occasionally replaced by buses — but despite this (and some evidently wobbly sections) it is a terrific journey, skirting beaches, crossing *rías*, and threading a succession of limestone gorges.

Santander and Around

Long a favorite summer resort of Madrileños, **SANTANDER** has a somewhat French feel — an elegant but somewhat reserved resort in the same vein as Biarritz, or of Spanish San Sebastián. Some people find it a clean and restful base for a short stay, for others it is dull and snobbish. On a brief visit, the balance is probably tipped in its favor by its variety of excellent (if not altogether unpolluted) beaches, and the sheer style of its setting. The narrow **Bahía de Santander** is dramatic, with the city and port on one side in clear view of open countryside and high mountains on the other.

Practicalities

Arriving by train or bus brings you to within a couple of minutes' walk of the port (with its passenger service to Plymouth, England) and the town center. The **RENFE** and **FEVE** train stations are side by side, just off the waterfront and under an escarpment which hides the main roads; the **bus station** is immediately below them on c/Federico Vial. The few buses which don't use that include the eastern coastal connections with Laredo and Castro Urdiales, and long-distance arrivals from Logroño and Santiago — these stop at the Bar Machichaco, a block north of the train stations on c/Calderón de la Barca.

Santander was severely damaged by fire in 1941, losing most of its former pretensions along with its medieval buildings. What's left of the city divides into two separate parts: the **town and port**, which are still quite a tangle, having been reconstructed on the old grid around the cathedral; and the beach suburb of **El Sardinero**, a twenty-minute walk (or bus # 1) direct from downtown, more if you follow the coast around by the wooded headland of **La Magdalena**.

Most of the year rooms are easy to come by, but in July and August, when the city hosts a *Jazz and International Music festival* and an international university, there can be problems. So long as you arrive in normal hours, make first for the **Turismo**, in the arcades of the main square, the Plaza de Velarde. They can supply full lists and a useful events pamphlet, the weekly *Guía Informativa*, and are open Mon.–Fri. 9am–1:30pm and 4–7pm, Sat. 9am–noon. (If you're planning to go on to the Picos, there's a large-scale and superbly detailed relief model of the mountains in the office to help you decide your route).

Good places to start looking for **accommodation** are the c/de Rodríguez (in front of the station; try the *Fonda Maria Luisa*, ☎942/210881, at no. 9), c/de Hernan Cortés and c/de Burgos (right and then left from the main square). All have a number of reasonable *fondas*, *pensiones*, and *hostales*. Alternatively, if you want to be **by the beach**, there are some very popular cheapish places on the Avda. de los Castros at Sardinero, including the *Hostal-Residencial Luisito* at no. 11 (☎942/271971), and a **campground** (*Bellavista*, ☎942/274873) a short walk farther around the coast. *TIVE*, the Spanish student travel agency, can also help locate **rooms in private houses** (*casas particulares*), and, if you're here in winter, they arrange packages to the **ski** resort of Alto Campo (near Reinosa); their office is just off the Plaza de Velarde at c/Canarias 2 (Mon.– Fri. 8am–3pm, Sat. 9am–1pm).

As far as **food** is concerned, try the streets detailed for accommodation above for bars and *comedores*, along with c/San Simón and c/Río de la Pila, above and to the right of Plaza de Velarde. If you're after seafood, wander down (or catch bus # 4) to the **Barrio Pesquero**, the fishing port, to the east (away from the open sea) of the ferry port and stations. There's no shortage of places along the c/ Marqués de la Ensanada — just keep an eye on prices before ordering.

The Beaches and Town

The chief pleasures of Santander are its **beaches**. The first of these, **Playa de la Magdalena**, begins on the near side of the headland. The beautiful yellow strand, sheltered by cliffs and flanked by a summer windsurfing school, is justly popular, as is **El Sardinero** itself. Here, beyond the peninsula, you'll find the 1920s dollhouse palace built by shrewd public subscription for King Alfonso XIII, to whose residence Santander owed its initial fashionable success. If you find both beaches too crowded for your taste, there are long stretches of dunes across the bay at **Somo** (which has a summer **campground**) and **Pedreña**; to get to them, jump on the cheap taxi-ferry which leaves every half hour from the central *Muelle de Ferrys*.

There are any number of possible excursions from Santander — the best of them covered in the following two sections — but few real sights in the city itself. The **Cathedral**, with its Gothic crypt, is of passing interest. So too are the exhibitions of local artists in the **Museo Municipal**, though the free **Museo Maritimo** near the port hosts exhibits ranging from pickled two-headed sardines to entire whale skeletons. There's also a small zoo in the gardens of the Magdalena Palace, which is free and open all day. Worth a little more time, if you're planning to visit the caves at Puente Viesgo (see below), is the **Museo Provincial de Prehistoria** (c/Juan de la Costa 1; Mon.–Sat. 10am–1pm). This is well arranged, displaying and reconstructing finds from the province's numerous prehistorically inhabited caves.

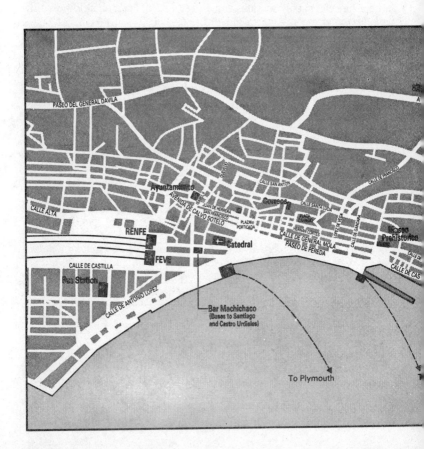

East Around the Coast: Laredo and Castro Urdiales

The coast immediately east of Santander has been heavily developed, with vacation villas and apartment complexes swamping most of the coves. Thus a village such as NOJA, until recently remarkable only for the strange-shaped rocks along its shore, now has seven campgrounds and can barely cope with the tourist invasion. Laredo, similarly, has become an established resort. Things look up, however, as you move east towards the Basque Country.

Laredo and Islares

LAREDO, has a summer profusion of pubs, clubs, and discos almost rivaling Torremolinos. Perhaps because most of its visitors are French, however, it retains the saving grace of style.

In part it's an attractive place, still. In the last century it used to be the provincial capital, and the village-like core of the old town, **El Rastrillar**, rambles back from the harbor, with here and there traces of its former walls

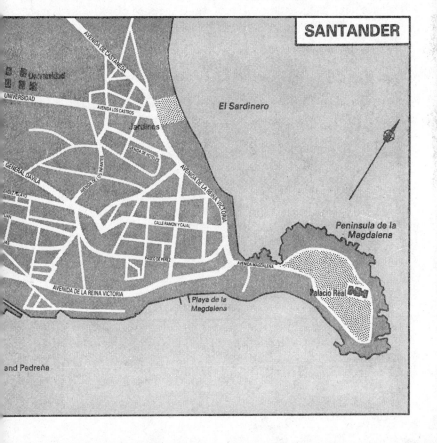

and gates, climbing up towards a splendid thirteenth-century parish church. Beyond the church you can quickly climb out of town to the cliffs and to grand open countryside, while below lies the best beach this side of San Sebastián, a gently shelving crescent of sand well protected from the wind. Nearby are two (June–Sept.) **campgrounds**, *Laredo* (☎942/605035) and *Costa Esmeralda* (☎942/603250).

If you're looking for somewhere less frenetic, the village of **ISLARES**, beyond the next headland, is as yet scarcely developed. There's a beach a short walk past the houses, well sheltered by cliffs, a very modest-sized **campground**, a hostal (the *Arenillas*; ☎942/860766), and hardly anything else except for a few bars.

Castro Urdiales

CASTRO URDIALES is a congenial resort, less developed than Laredo, though with rooms, and space on the beach, at a premium in high season. As well as its tourist functions, the town retains a considerable fishing fleet, gathered around a fine natural harbor. Above this looms a massively buttressed Gothic church and a lighthouse, built within the shell of a Knights Templar castle. The old town itself is relatively unspoiled, with its arcaded streets and tall glass-balconied houses.

The best places to stay, if you can **find a room**, are three *fondas* on the waterfront (the *Bristol*, *La Marina*, and an unnamed place above *Pizzeria Pergola*), or the *Hostal El Cordobes* one block inland at c/Ardigales 21 (☎942/860089). Some excellent fish/seafood bars cluster around the castle end of the harbor on c/El Carrerias, but the best **eating and drinking** is to be done on c/Ardigales, where at no. 7 the *Bar Agora* is a Basque-run establishment with outdoor tables; it's immensely popular and very reasonable for a light lunch. For supper switch across the street to *Restaurante Baracaldo*, which features huge all-seafood *menús* for under 700ptas.

Unfortunately eating and bar-hopping can prove more rewarding than the small **Brazomar beach**, hemmed in by a cement esplanade and overshadowed by two large hotels and a recent spate of high-rises. The popularity of the beach is due mainly to its easy access from Santander and Bilbao (each under an hour away by bus). The Brazomar crowds can be left behind by walking a little east to more secluded coves.

The outbound **bus station**, shared by the companies *Turytrans* and *La Burundesa*, is inside the *Bar Cerámica*, c/Victorina Gainza, about five blocks in from the front. There are through services for all points betwen Irún and Gijón.

West: Santillana and Prehistoric Caves

SANTILLANA DEL MAR, half an hour by bus to the west of Santander, is outrageously picturesque. Jean-Paul Sartre (in *Nausea*) makes mention of it as *"le plus joli village d'Espagne"* — an unlikely source, but arguably an accurate plaudit.

The village preserves virtually intact its medieval appearance — all ocher-colored stone houses, mansions, and farms — and despite much daytrip tourism (and a certain amount of prettification), it retains a disarming charm. It is also full of peculiarities. Despite the name — *del Mar* — Santillana stands some three or four kilometers back from the sea, and while its fine houses flaunt their aristocratic origins the village itself is completely rural. Its single street, with one loop and two plazas, saunters back from the access road towards the wonderful Romanesque church and then stops abruptly amidst farms and fields. The fifteenth-to-eighteenth-century **mansions**, vying with each other in the extravagance of their coats of arms, are splendidly anomalous. One of the best is the **Casa de los Hombrones**, named after two moustachioed figures flanking its grandly sculpted escutcheon. Another, the **Casa de Bustamentes**, established its credentials with a simple motto: "The Bustamentes marry their daughters to kings."

The main church of **La Colegiata** is dedicated to Santa Juliana, an early martyr whose tomb it contains; she is legendarily supposed to have captured the devil and is depicted with him in tow in various scenes around the building. The most outstanding feature, however, is the twelfth-century Romanesque cloister, one of the best-preserved in the whole country, with its squat paired columns and lively capitals carved with animals and hunting scenes. Also eminently worth visiting is the seventeenth-century **Convent of Regina Coeli** (open 10am–1:30pm and 3–6pm), across the main road near the entrance to the village, which houses an exceptional museum of painted wooden figures and other religious art. The pieces, brilliantly restored by the nuns, are displayed with great imagination to show the stylistic development of certain images, particularly of San Roque, a healing saint always depicted with his companion, a dog who licks the wound in his thigh.

Santillana would be a frustrating place just to look around. It is best to **stay the night**, as once the bus tours have dispersed the village seems relatively unaffected — it is still basically a farming community. (Although many of the mansions still belong to the original families, it is very rare for their noble owners even to visit). There are a few **rooms** to let next to the post office in the Plaza de Ramón Pelayo (opposite the *parador*), a few more up a track behind that, and also some by the Ayuntamiento. If these are full try the **hostales** on the main road just outside the village, or, a kilometer or so down towards Altamira and Comillas, the *Fonda-Restaurante San Andres*. Just before the *fonda*, to the right of the road and overlooking the town, there is also the *Santillana* **campground** (☎942/818250), large and a bit soulless, but with a pool and other facilities.

There are several direct buses daily to Santillana from Santander, either from *Bar Machichaco* (including one at 11:30am) or (run by *SA Continental*) from the main station. You can also get to the village by regular buses from TORRELAVEGA, which is on the *FEVE* railroad line, and itself served by buses from *Bar Machichaco*.

Altamira

The prehistoric **CAVES OF ALTAMIRA** lie just 2km off the main road, west of Santillana. They date from around 12,000 B.C., and consist of an extraordinary series of caverns, covered in paintings of bulls, bison, boars, and other animals — all etched in red and black, and delineated in a few confident and impressionistic strokes. When discovered in the 1870s they were in near-perfect condition, with striking and vigorous colors, but in the last few years, sadly, the state of the murals has seriously deteriorated, and the paintings are now **closed** to all but twenty visitors a day, a limit intended to prevent the buildup of surplus moisture (from breathing) in the cavern's atmosphere.

Unless you can prove that you're researching cave-paintings, and write months in advance to the *Centro de Investigación de Altamira* (Santillana, Santander), you stand little chance of getting inside. You can, however, look around a couple of lesser grottoes at the site and a small **museum**, introduced to humor the still considerable flow of tourists (daily except Sun. afternoon 9am–1pm and 4-6pm). Alternatively, content yourself with the herd of sorry bison at the nearby zoo.

Puente Viesgo

More rewarding for casual visitors are the caves at **PUENTE VIESGO**, 29km out of Santander on the road to Logroño (*SA Continental* bus from the main station in Santander). Around the village, set amid magnificent rolling green countryside, are four separate **caves**, the most important of which are **Las Monedas** and **Castillo**. Castillo, in particular, is the one to choose, its paintings clear precursors of the later developments at Altamira. (Tues.–Sun. 10am–1pm and 3–7pm, except Sun. pm).

If you decide to stay, the *San Cristobal* **hostal** on c/Agosto 1 (☎942/751486) is good value.

Toward Asturias: The Coast from Comillas to Gijón

The **coastline west of Santillana** — followed along most of its course by the *FEVE* railroad — is dotted with a succession of enticing resorts. Few are greatly developed and, amid the villages and river valleys, there are strands which see no more than the occasional weekender from Santander. The countryside, with a massed backdrop of hills rolling away towards the Picos, is invariably magnificent.

Cantabria: Comillas and San Vicente

The first resort beyond Santillana, **COMILLAS**, is skirted by the *FEVE* line, though it has good bus connections with both Santillana and (to the west) San Vicente. A curious little town, with cobbled streets and unwieldy mansions, it is set just back from the sea and two superb beaches.

Playa de Comillas, closest of these, is popular, with a little anchorage for pleasure boats and makeshift beach cafes; for greater seclusion walk east, towards the cape, to the longer **Playa de Oyambre**. Both have **campgrounds**, with the *Comillas* (open July–Aug., ☎942/720074) significantly better than *El Rodero* at Oyambre (open June–Oct.). In the town, ten minutes' walk or an infrequent bus ride away, accommodation is limited and in growing demand in summer. The half dozen *hostales* are easily found. Try *Esmeralda* (☎942/720097) or *Fuente Real* at the lower end of the scale; cheaper, and perhaps more likely to have vacancies, are the rooms above the *Mesón el Torron* (☎942/720738) in Plaza de los Tres Caños.

While at Comillas, or even if you're only passing through, you can hardly fail to notice the vast neo-Gothic **Seminario Pontificia**, one of a bizarre group of nineteenth-century buildings above the town. The seminary was built on the commission of the first Marques de Comillas (an industrialist friend of Alfonso XII) by the Barcelona architect Domenech y Montaner. Below it the Marques constructed his own **palace** and chapel, this time designed by Juan Martorell, who was a *modernista* contemporary of Montaner and a friend of Antoni Gaudí, who was responsible for some of the furniture in the chapel. **Gaudí** (see Barcelona) also added his own work to the ensemble: the small Moorish-influenced villa on the slope below. Known as **El Capricho**, the villa, with its ciruclar gestures and optical tricks, and a dome half-suspended in air, has been locked and deserted for some twenty years, though the house opposite has a key to its garden. To reach it, follow the road out of the upper town, towards Santillana, and look out for the sign by a lane to the right.

San Vicente de la Barquera

The approach to **SAN VICENTE DE LA BARQUERA** is dramatic, with the town, marooned on both sides by the sea, entered across a long causeway. From the hill above, an impressive **ducal palace** and Romanesque-Gothic **church** (the latter with restored, gilded altarpieces) looks on.

There's a good sweep of sand on the near side of the causeway (opposite the town), flanked by a small forest and a **campground**. The town itself, a thriving fishing port with a string of locally famed but expensive seafood restaurants, has had its old core encroached upon, and is split by the main coast road with its thundering trucks, but it still makes a good overnight stop. The *Hostal la Paz* (☎942/710180) is clean and spacious. Climbing the stairs which lead from the back of the main square, you will find a good cheap seafood *mesón* halfway up, and the **fonda** *Liebana* (☎942/710211) at the top. Aside from these two establishments, numerous apartments and shops advertise *camas* in their windows.

SAN VICENTE is best left or approached by bus (several connections daily with Santander via Comillas); its own *FEVE* station, as its site dictates, is about 4km south at LA ALCEBASA.

Into Asturias: Ribadesella, Gijón, and Avilés

Asturias officially begins 9km west of San Vicente, at **UNQUERA**. Here buses for the Picos turn up towards POTES, and here too the *FEVE* railroad comes into its own after the inland stretch from Santander. Unquera itself is a pretty dire place to hang around; the restaurant *Riomar* and the *Restaurante/ Bar Granja*, across from the *FEVE* station and also the bus stop, are its two bright spots.

Making for the sea there are a whole series of beautiful coves as soon as you're past **LLANES**, though if you're looking for a base with genuine character and verve, Llanes itself belies its slightly drab outskirts. There is also another popular beach 2km walk east of the town; you can camp on the cliffs above it, and there's spring water down on the sand. Another good beach can be reached from the station, and tiny settlement, of **VILLAHORMES**, though you need to walk a couple of kilometers across the fields. At the station there is just a cafe-bar, *La Peña*, with a grime-caked plane tree and a few dusty tables outside. A thirty-minute walk, or five minutes more on the train, will get you to another diminutive town, **NUEVA**, tucked into a fold of the hills 3km from the sea. Again there does not seem to be any regular accomodation in the village or down by the beach on the other side of the highway.

If you are looking for a room, it probably makes more sense to press on to **RIBADESELLA.**. This is an unaffected little port, sprawled at the mouth of the Sella river, and with dozens of excellent little bars and *comedores* on the streets parallel to the fishing harbor. The *Rompeolas*, three streets back, is a classic cheap *marisquería*, with a long wooden counter and piles of seafood on its wooden tables. Freshly-caught fish are still unloaded most nights (after midnight) at the *lonja*, so it's fun to hang out until then in the bars. Incidentally, all the men in Ribadesella have stunning **haircuts**; assuming that the *peluquería* next to the *Rompeolas* is responsible, it's not to be missed.

Hostales are a bit more expensive than usual, although the impecunious may be able to find *camas*, and there is a **youth hostel** in a beautiful old house right on the beach, ten minutes' walk Among the cheaper *hostal* and *fonda* options, try the *Fonda/Bar Platanito* , *Hostal El Pilar* (☎985/860446), or the *Hostal Apollo* (☎985/860442) near the beach. Although the sands here are now fronted by a luxury hotel and lined with a newly-built promenade, the planners of Ribadasella have restricted development to this part of town, leaving the old quarter still within a minute's walk of green hills of grazing sheep.

The one local tourist attraction is the **Cueva Tito Bustillo**, an Altamira-style cave more impressive for its stalactites than its paintings.

On to the Picos or Gijón

Beyond Ribadasella the railroad again heads inland, and you might just as well follow it, or take an Oviedo-bound bus toward Cangas (change at Arriondas for the last leg — tight timing) in the foothills of the Picos.

Following the coast there are attractive small resorts at both **LA ISLA** and **COLUNGA** (both noted for their seafood and cider), and an atmospheric old town in **VILLAVICIOSA**; but by now you're beginning to move too close for comfort to **GIJÓN**, the main industrial port of Asturias. Enclosed within a grid of smoking factory chimneys, the city — a traditional socialist stronghold — was completely rebuilt after its destruction in the civil war. In August 1936, miners armed with sticks of dynamite stormed the barracks of the Nationalist army; the beleaguered colonel asked ships from his own side anchored offshore to bombard and kill his men rather than let them be captured. Today Gijón's main appeal is a summer **film festival** (late June/early July).

AVILÉS, inland, is also a major industrial center, with a concentration of Asturian steel mills. If you need to change transportation here, it's worth wandering into the center, a tightly-packed old district strewn with four-teenth- and fifteenth-century churches and palaces. Staying in the city, however, is tricky, with the few reasonably-priced hostales invariably full with business clientèle.

The Picos de Europa

The PICOS DE EUROPA, although not the highest mountains in Spain, are for many walkers the most memorable. They are a miniature masterpiece, with a lot crammed into a small area, and they block the horizon as a threat-ening and almost impassable barrier just 25km in from the coast. The whole range is a mere 40km across in either direction, shoehorned in between three great river gorges, and straddles the meeting point of the provinces of Asturias, León and Cantabria. Asturians see the mountains as a symbol of national identity, and Covadonga as the birthplace of Christian Spain.

The region has long been on the map for Spanish hikers and excursionists, and over the last few years has seen a growing influx of northern Europeans, including two or three organised tour groups. The chief attraction is the variety of hikes, which include a spectacular route along the twelve-kilometer Cares Gorge and dozens of other trails, from easy morning rambles in the river valleys and woodlands to major cross-country treks and climbs. It should be stressed that walking here is hard work, with intense summer heat and humidity, and it's wise to stick to the established tracks — the reason they're obvious is that they go somewhere. The slowly undulating plateaus you appreciate from a distance can too easily turn out to be a series of chasms and gorges that entail backtracking, dropping down, winding round and scrambling up to points you never wished to be at.

Up From the Coast: Unquera to Potes

If you're heading for the Picos from Santander, take a look at the excellent relief model of the mountains in the Santander tourist office. That should make your route obvious; the road which follows the twisting course of the Río Deva, leaving the coast at UNQUERA, 12km beyond San Vicente, is the most common approach. There are a couple of buses each day which go all the way to Potes from Santander: one at around 5pm, the other (July to mid-September only) at 9:30am; these pass Unquera about an hour later.

The road forks at PANES, around a gas pump in the middle where an acci-dent is just waiting to happen, and the C6312 skirts away along the Río Gargantas to Arenas de Cabrales and Cangas (2 buses a day along that route — 8am and 5:30pm — starting from Colombres, a village 2km east of Unquera).

Following the inland route, and continuing towards Potes, you enter the eerily impressive gorge of the Deva, the Desfiladero de La Hermida, its sheer sides so high that they deny the village of LA HERMIDA any sunlight

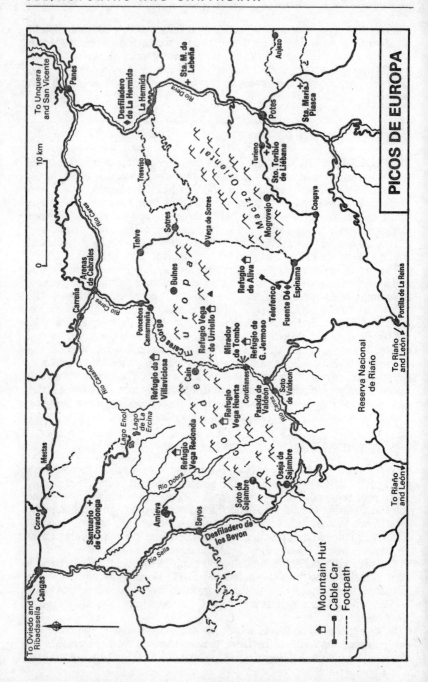

PICES DE EUROPA

HIKING IN THE PICOS

CLIMATE The high altitudes dictate a spring-summer walking season, from early May through September, though there good days even in the depths of winter for walking below the snowline. At all times of year clouds can build up very fast, and rain is cold and heavy; alternatively, or in tandem, sudden mists are always liable to blot out visibility. Accordingly, rain gear and a compass are virutally mandatory. But year-round, reliable **water sources** are sporadic along the trails and it's always worth carrying a bottle.

EQUIPMENT Hiking in summer you don't necessarily need any experience or special equipment, at least on the routes described in this guide; all of these hikes are practicable so long as you're reasonably fit. Wander off the trails, or attempt any actual climbing, and proper equipment and experience are essential — otherwise you may quickly find yourself in difficulties. What with the abundance of sharp, loose stones, and stiff grades, **walking boots** are a distinct plus, and **sunglasses** are useful to combat the glare. If you don't speak Spanish carry a phrasebook as few people speak any English.

BANKS Beware: banks are few and far between, located only at Potes, Arenas de Cabrales, Riaño, and Cangas de Onis. It's easy to go hungry with a whole stash of travelers' checks.

MAPS AND GUIDES Best are those printed by the *Federación Española de Montañismo* (entitled "Los Tres Macizos," single sheet at 1:50,000), and in cooperation with the *IGN* ("Macizo del Cornión"). *Editorial Alpina* covers the western and central massifs in two 1:25,000 sheets. All these maps are old but still fairly accurate, despite recent road-building, and most are available in the Picos at Cangas de Onis, Potes, Sotres, Bulnes, or Arenas de Cabrales. Marc Dubin's *Spain on Foot* (The Mountaineers, $10.95, in press) has extensive coverage of the Picos.

ROOMS/CAMPING You should have few problems, except from the end of July to the end of August when rooms will be chock-full. There are *fondas* in most of the larger villages, half a dozen campgrounds, and a number of alpine *refugios*. The latter vary from organized hostels like the one at Aliva to free, unstaffed huts where you'll need to bring your own food and sleeping bag. Discreet "free-lance" camping is accepted; if the village inns are full, ask permission to pitch your tent on fallow land. *Refugios* are popular and oversubscribed — camping next to them is the norm.

WILDLIFE Birds and mammals are a major attraction, even if for non-enthusiasts. In the Cares gorge you're likely to see griffon vultures, kestrels, black redstarts, rock thrushes, and, most exciting of all for the initiated, wallcreepers. Wild and domestic goats abound, with some unbelievably inaccessible high mountain pastures. Take care, though: passing herds of sheep and goats are left under the sole control of large and ferocious dogs, which tend to be very protective of their territory. Wolves are easy to imagine in the grey boulders of the passes, but despite local mutterings, and their picturesque appearances on the tourist board maps, bears are not a likely sight. An inbred population of about sixty specimens of *Ursus ibericus* remains in the eastern mountains, most of them equipped with radio transmitters.

APPROACHES There are four main approaches to the Picos: from Santander/San Vicente/Unquera to Potes/Espinama/Fuente Dé; from León to Valdeón and Sajambre (via Riaño); from Llanes or Panes to Arenas de Cabrales; and from Cangas De Onis to Los Lagos de Covadonga.

from November until April. From nearby Urdón, it's possible to walk up to Sotres to the west; there are one or two places to stay in La Hermida if it's getting late. The road itself barely appears to climb; instead the mountains seem to swell around you.

Taking the early bus, and picking up the later one, allows you to stop midway at the village of LEBEÑA. Its church, **Santa María**, was built in the early tenth century by "Arabized" Christian craftsmen and is considered the supreme example of Mozarabic architecture. It's worth seeing, with its thoroughly Islamic geometric motifs and repetition of abstract forms, and set in beautiful countryside, the Hermida gorge having by now opened out as sheltered vineyards and orchards.

Potes and Environs

POTES is the main base on the east side of the Picos, still not all that high above sea level (ca. 500m) but with the feel of a sort of frontier post. It's no longer the quaint old town that the tourist board makes it out to be, with tourism very much in the acendance, bu pleasant nonetheless. On Monday mornings, its open-air **street market** is a welcome return to its country roots, with everything on offer from a cow to a mysterious colored sawdust said to cure acne and failed marriages. Potes is also a useful place to **change money** (last banks before the mountains) and, if you haven't already done so, to buy **hiking maps**. The latter are available either from the tourist office or *Fotos Bustamente*, both in the central plaza, or from a couple of kiosks in the same area. If you want a **room** there are numerous *hostales*, especially between *Bustamente* and the bridge, and two *fondas* in the cobbled streets away from the main road, including the *Casa Cuba* (☎942/730064) and *Casa Cayo*. The *Casa de Huéspedes Gomez* (☎942/730218) is a little way out of town, next to the lower Santander/Unquera bus stop.

At **TURIENO** (about 3km along the road to Espinama), an orchard conceals a well-equipped **campground**, *La Isla* (open Apr.–Oct., ☎942/730896), which can arrange pony-trekking; if they're full the *San Pelayao* campground (Apr.–Oct., ☎942/730097) farther on is every bit as good. In sight of some tall peaks, both campgrounds are well-sited for acclimatizing to the mountains, with lots of short walks along narrow mule tracks to villages where the locals don't see many tourists and may well open up the bar just for you. The walk through a profusion of wild flowers and butterflies up to the higgledy-piggledy and timeless hamlets of LON and BREZ is recommended.

Closer to Potes there are also two interesting and easily accessible churches. Three kilometers west along the road is the **Monasterio de Santo Toribio de Liebana**, one of the earliest (8th c.) and most influential of medieval Spain. It is a much reconstructed building, but preserves fine Romanesque and Gothic parts, the largest claimed piece of the True Cross, and some extraordinary Mozarabic paintings (now replaced by reproductions) of the Visions of the Apocalypse. Architecturally more important is the **church at Piasca**, 6km south of Potes. This is pure Romanesque in style, beautifully proportioned, and with some terrific exterior sculpture. Like Santo Toribio it was once a Cluniac monastery, and is flanked by the ruins of monastic and conventual buildings.

Another possible base for exploring the eastern or central groups of the Picos is **COSGAYA**, roughly halfway to Espinama. It's become a little too cute, with modern Swiss-style chalets and the two-star *Hotel de Oso* set in neat paddocks beside a tidy stream, but would still make a good place to stay if the snow stops you from climbing any higher, or you just prefer your walking to be light. The *Mesón de Cosgaya* is good for food, while an excellent **hostal**, *La Casona* (converted from a seventeenth-century farmhouse and not too expensive), is hidden away in the woods to the side of the road.

Espinama and Fuente Dé

From Potes's central plaza there are three buses daily (8am, 1pm, and 8pm, July 1–Sept. 18) to ESPINAMA (20km) and FUENTE DÉ (24km).

ESPINAMA, unspoiled and very ancient, is a great village to spend a night. Deep in the heart of the mountains, a stream bubbles its way between sagging farmhouses, crossed by unsteady wooden footbridges, while stray animals wander the pathways and past the locked, tumbledown church (slowly being restored). The **fonda** *Vicente Campo* (to the left at the end of town towards Fuente Dé) has the feel of a wayfarers' inn, serving decent food (in winter beside a crackling fire); the *Remoña* is more modern, with dry, well-heated rooms. Fallbacks include a *hostal-residencia* run by the *Vicente Campo* to take the overflow from the *fonda*, the *Fonda/Mesón Maximo*, at the Potes end of town, and the *Hostal Nevandi*, both serving meals, while a grocery store provides for picnics and hiking snacks.

The paved road comes to a halt 4km past Espinama, in a steep-sided cul-de-sac of solid rock. This is the source of the Río Deva; debate as to whether its name should be Fuente de Deva or Fuente de Eva has left it called simply FUENTE DÉ. The usual way onward is upward, by **cable car** (*teleférico*), which lurches alarmingly up 900m of sheer cliff. It's an extremely popular excursion throughout the year and in summer you may have to wait a while to ascend. Up top is an extraordinary moonscape, with Spanish daytrippers wandering around in bathing suits, but within a few minutes' walk there is hardly a soul.

From the top of the *teleférico* you can follow a bulldozer track 4km to the **Refugio de Aliva** (open from June 15 to September 30, with its own *fiesta* on July 10) which has *hostal*-like rooms and prices, and a restaurant. From there, you can wind your way back down to Espinama on another jeep track. It is also possible to arrange a ride in a jeep from the top of the *teleférico*, either to Aliva or to Sotres (see below).

Fuente Dé itself is not a settlement but merely a parador (open April to October), a cafe near the cable car ticket office, and a campground, though most people prefer to camp unofficially near Pido hamlet, 1½km above Espinama.

Espinama to Sotres

The hike to Sotres is the most obvious outing from Espinama: a five hour walk, though almost entirely on a jeep track; the jeeps which pass you and coat you with dust might best be put to use by thumbing a ride. If you do walk, set out north from the *Bodega Peña Vieja* in Espinama, under an arching balcony, and onto the dusty (if not muddy) and twisting track behind. This, climbing stiffly, winds initially past hand-cut hay fields and through groups of barns, until tall cliffs on either side rise to form a kind of natural gateway. Through this you enter a different landscape of barren rolling summer pasture, streams running through rocky beds and close-cropped grass nibbled by horses, cows, and flocks of sheep. Over the divide the scenery changes again, into a mass of crumbling limestone; the downhill stretch of track here is slippery and treacherous to all but goats (and maybe jeeps). Vegas de Sotres, at the bottom of the hill, has a seasonal bar selling drinks; from there you need to climb again slightly to reach Sotres.

SOTRES, when it appears, has a grim, almost fortified feel, hanging on to a cliff edge above a stark green valley. There are **rooms** here, best at the *Pensión Cipriano*, which also has a *comedor*; an unmarked *fonda* next door has dormitory bunks (*literas*) but is often taken up by school groups. A third-*pensión* across the way is relatively expensive and won't bargain. *Casa Gallega*, the one store and will do good meals with an hour or two's notice; they also sell cured sheep and sheep/cow cheese, as well as the five-month-fermented *cabrales*, a local specialty similar to roquefort.

Beyond Sotres

Sotres, although it has no bus service, is actually a better base for walking than Espinama. One of the best is the (partly jeep, partly donkey) track to TRESVISO and beyond to URDÓN on the Panes–Potes road, with the final stretch being a spectacularly switchbacked downhill trail.

Most people, though, head west **toward Bulnes**. Road-building has diminished some of the attractiveness of this route but much of the steep cobbled path toward Bulnes still survives (you'll have to persevere to find it from Invernales de Cabao, just below Sotres). After an hour and a half or so you emerge on the broad, windy pass of Pandébano, tufted with heather, rocks, and the unexpected *Bar de los Picos*.

As of 1989 the dirt road up from Invernales ends here but a big battle is shaping up over the area's future. The cheesemakers of Bulnes have agitated for a road to get their products out, preferably via Poncebos (see below), and the government wants to install another *teleférico* from Bulnes up to Amuesa cirque. It looks only a matter of time before a road of some kind is completed — and sadly it will be very close to the sugarloaf peak of *Naranjo de Bulnes*, one of the "sights" of the Picos.

BULNES — actually a double village, CASTILLOS and LA VILLA — is well worth a visit. All facilities are in La Villa; there is a decent mountaineer's *albergue* and a restaurant next door, while camping is straightforward, too. Electric power arrived in 1989, and the *Bar Guillermina* sells t-shirts proclaiming the village a "friend to all mountaineers." The great excursion on from Bulnes — and the reason for this burgeoning commercialization — is the walk along the Cares Gorge (see below).

The Hike up to Naranjo de Bulnes (and Beyond)

From either the pass at Pandébano or Bulnes village there are well-used trails up to the **Vega de Urriello**, the high pasture at the base of the *Naranjo de*

Bulnes. The approach from Pandébano is much easier, along a newly regraded trail, around 2½ hours at average speed. The path up from Bulnes is one of the most drastic in Spain, a good hour longer, and with a slippery scree surface to match. Once up on the plateau you'll find a *refugio*, scheduled to be rebuilt in 1989 or 1990, and (a rarity in the Picos) a permanent spring, as well as large numbers of campers and rock-climbers.

Walkers equipped for an overnight can continue across the central massif to the top of the Fuente Dé funicular, through a roller-coaster landscape unforgiving of mistakes — go in a group and with proper gear. Finding your way, though, so long as you've a reasonable map, is not hard, and descending you can bypass Fuente Dé and instead make a slow lap around the highest peaks. This involves a night's camp at **Vega de Liordes** and a descent down the ravine of **Asotín**, ending at Cordiñanes, within striking distance of the top of the Cares gorge.

From the South: Portilla, Sajambre, and Valdeón

Traveling in Asturias, you often see posters with the slogan "Don't let them destroy our Picos." The threat to the mountains is real; it was a small range to begin with, and every year the despoliation of previously pristine areas seems to increase. The Asturians are doing what they can, but if you enter the Picos from the south, from León through Riaño you will see the worst.

In 1966 the Franco regime claimed right of eminent domain over the entire valley of **RIAÑO**, prior to turning it into a reservoir. Compensation of sorts was paid at that time, and then plans stalled. But in the 1980s the project was revived by the PSOE "socialist" government. The inhabitants of Riaño, most of them children of those who had accepted the "settlement" in the 1960s, were forcibly evicted, with no further compensation offered. The newer generation erected a tent village overlooking their destroyed homes, but that too was bulldozed, after demonstrations broken up by riot police in which men, women, and children were indiscriminately clubbed.

The dam was suddenly sealed, and flooding commenced, during a storm on the afternoon of December 31, 1987. The authorities claimed that conditions were optimal, though it might better be seen as a vain attempt to meet a self-imposed deadline of New Year's 1988, and a convenient way to forestall any more demonstrations. Assuming that the winter of 1988–89 had normal rainfall, flooding will have been completed by spring 1989 — despite the fact that the valley floor allegedly was never cleared of certain toxic agricultural wastes. Massive new viaducts and overpasses have been constructed to reroute submerged highways; in a particularly ironic gesture, the central pylon of the first bridge encountered is rooted exactly in the middle of the former plaza of the old village.

Those who have remained try to make the best of it, even using the bridge for their afternoon promenade. But most of the older inhabitants have long since emigrated. Some individuals — the former bar owners, for example — haven't suffered too much, owning bright new bars in the new town. But most of the investment came from outside corporations, and that's where the profits will go. The water from the reservoir will benefit no one locally; it's all destined to irrigate the plains of León and Palencia to the south. New Riaño meanwhile is becoming equipped with luxury hotels, and anticipates a future as a winter- and water-sports resort, beside what may well be a "beautiful mountain lake." Of course, it's all just a question of persuading people to forget the half-dozen villages, and farmland, drowned below the water.

The Sajambres

From New Riaño twice-weekly (Thur. and Sat.) buses run north along the C637 towards CANGAS. With your own vehicle, you can turn right just before the top of the Puerto Del Pontón (almost continually fogged in since the dam was built), to get to Posada and the Cares Gorge (see below).

The main road heads on to **OSEJA DE SAJAMBRE**, a very pretty village in the southwest foothills of the Picos, high on the steep slope of a broad and twisting valley, and an infinitely nicer place to stay than Riaño. Cheap and traditional **beds and meals** are available at *Viajeros La Fonseya* and *Casa Huéspedes La Rua*, in the center of town near the single grocery store and one other restaurant, or at the *Hostal de Pontón*.

Six kilometers beyond Oseja is **SOTO DE SAJAMBRE**, an excellent base for walkers, with a single hostal (Peña Santa). It's one of the trailheads for the south-to-north traverse of the western Picos massif to the Lakes of Covadonga, as well as a starting point for rambles in the valley of the Río Dobra.

The road to Cangas continues on beside the Río Sella through the **Desfiladero de los Beyos**, which a florid monument claims as the narrowest motorable gorge in Europe, a feat of engineering far surpassing anything in the Alps. There are daily buses (*EASA* lines) in each direction along this entire stretch, but as stated only two services to Riaño.

To reach the central massif of the Picos above Posada de Valdeón, you might take a bus from León up via **PORTILLA DE LA REINA**. Portilla is a peculiar place, in the middle of nowhere at the bottom of a lichen-covered chasm of limestone, and looking as if it's been dropped from a great height by some vexed mountain god. There's nothing for a tourist to see or do; but if you go there you'll remember it a long time. The bus from Portilla gives out at SANTA MARINA DE VALDEÓN, transferring its passengers to a Land-Rover for the final three-kilometer ride on the narrow lane leading down to Posada. Campers would be well advised to halt at the **campground** adjacent to Santa Marina, rather than staying overnight in Posada. **SANTA MARINA DE VALDEÓN** has no indoor accommodation, but is extremely picturesque and has a bar. (It can also be reached on foot from Fuente Dé in about four hours, over a mixed system of jeep tracks and footpaths).

POSADA DE VALDEÓN is a fine mountain village, though steadily losing its identity under the onslaught of the developers; there are building sites everywhere. Three good **fondas** endure, however, the best of them being the *Begoña*, a real old inn in the best tradition, and there is still the grand old *Bar Picos de Europa*, with its stuffed boar. Nothing, either, can detract from the scenic appeal of the place: you can sit outside and admire the huge mountains that hem in the valley and shorten the days. If you are hiking north, Posada has the last stores before Arenas — there is nothing in Cordiñanes, Caín, or Camarmeña, so take heed.

The Cares Gorge

The **Cares Gorge**, the classic walk in the Picos, is remarkable in just about every respect. It's a massive cleft, more than 1000m deep and some 12km long, and separates the central massif from the western one of Cornión. The main section **between Caín and Poncebos** bores through awesome terrain along an amazing footpath hacked out of the cliff face. You need a head for heights, but it's otherwise perfectly safe, and with reasonable energy you can walk it in well under a day.

The usual approach is from Valdeón and Caín to the south, but there is good access from the north, and the walk can be combined with the route up to Bulnes. From Poncebos, at the northern end, for instance, you can get a Land-Rover bus to Arenas de Cabrales and from there a regular bus to Cangas de Onis, Llanes, or Panes.

To the Trailhead: Caín

The gorge proper begins 10km north of Posada, just beyond Caín, and if you're pushed for time (or energy) there is a **Land-Rover** service to the trailhead — 3000ptas per carload.

Most people will prefer to walk the distance, and some of the asphalt can be bypassed by adopting a dirt track leading from the lower end of Posada to the **Mirador del Tombo**, just past the village of Cordiñanes. From the Mirador to Caín it's around 6km, following the upper reaches of the Río Cares along a downhill road. Walking surface aside, the countryside is a delightful foretaste of what lies ahead, with occasional shade from the woods and meadows sprawled at the base of the cliffs.

CAÍN has only recently been connected by road with the outside world, but in summer its streets are now crammed with ramblers and their cars. For the moment, it remains a strange little village, suspicious of its burgeoning tourist trade. Two **fondas**, both low-key, have opened to join its handful of bars. Alternatively, you can camp in the meadow nearby for the princely sum of 200ptas (no amenities whatsoever).

Into the Gorge

Just beyond Caín the valley briefly opens out, then, following the river downstream, suddenly seems to disappear as a solid mountain wall blocks all but a thin vertical cleft. This is where **the gorge** really begins, the path along its course dramatically tunneled within the rock in the early stages before emerging on to a broad, well-constructed, and well-maintained catwalk.

The path owes its existence to a long-established hydroelectric scheme, for which an invisible canal was constructed (often buried inside the mountain) all the way from Caín to Poncebos, and into which the river can be diverted in varying quantities. The footpath is still used for maintenance and each morning a power plant worker walks the entire length, checking water volume in the canal and waking up those who have elected to spend a night out in the mountains. If you feel like being among their number, but with more privacy, there is a side valley leading off to the east about a kilometer into the gorge.

The first stretch of the path is more of an engineering spectacle than a country walk; it tends to be thronged with Spanish merrymakers running riot through the Gaudiesque tunnels and walkways. But once you get 4km or so out from Caín, many of the day-trippers have turned back, and the mountains, freed of most waterworks paraphernalia, command your total attention. They rise, pale and jagged, to either side, with griffon vultures and other birds of prey circling the crags. The river drops steeply, some 150m below you at the first bridge but closer to 300m down by the end.

A little over halfway along, the Cares canyon bends to the right (east) and gradually widens along the final **descent** to PONCEBOS. About 9km into the gorge some enterprising individual has cornered the market on refreshments with a makeshift drink-stand, handy as there's a final ascent before the end. From this uphill section another side path leads up to the bar, *hostal* and **mirador** at the cliffside village of **CAMARMEÑA**, famed for its tremendous perspectives on the Naranjo de Bulnes.

However, most people stick to the main route and finish at **PONCEBOS**, with the *Fonda/Bar El Garganta del Cares* and, a bit farther down past the bridge and next to the power plant, the modern, one-star *Hostal Poncebos*. Either of these might be welcome facilities at the end of a long day, but they're both a bit institutional and somewhat gloomy due to blocked sunlight. They are, incidentally, the only buildings at Poncebos — in no sense is the place a village.

If daylight permits it's preferable to make the superb hour-and-a-half hike up the gorge of the Tejo stream to BULNES (see p.000) and overnight there. The trail begins over the photogenic, medieval bridge of Jaya, located just to the right (south) of the end of the marked Cares traverse trail — there's no need to descend farther toward the *fonda*.. If you have the energy, a very steep path on the west side of the river leads up to a bar and **mirador** at CAMARMEÑA, with further grand views across to the Naranjo de Bulnes.

Another Land-Rover service plies between from the hostal in Poncebos to **ARENAS DE CABRALES** (just plain ARENAS on some maps) 6km to the north and the main village on the northern side of the Picos. This has a lot of hikers passing through in summer but remains an excellent place to stay — very friendly and with a good **hostal** (*Naranjo de Bulnes*), three **fondas** and a helpful **Turismo**. The (unsigned) *Mesón Castaneu*, the "middle" of the fondas, has outstanding à la carte food at *menú* prices. In summer you may find all four places full, but there's a campground 1km to the east. The village also has two **banks** and various stores.

North of the Picos: Cangas de Onis and Covadonga

The foothill area to the north of the Picos is known as **Cabrales**, as is the delicious and exceptionally strong fermented sheep's cheese made in a dozen-odd villages. Coming from the Picos there are twice daily bus connections from Arenas and Cangas (no Sunday service), and regular links with

Oviedo. If you're driving, the secondary road D214 between coastal Nueva and inland Corao is a high winding pass through meadowland that makes a good route to or from the Picos, bypassing Cangas.

Cangas de Onis

The two main routes between the mountains and central Asturias meet at **CANGAS DE ONIS**, at the very edge of the Picos, but magnificently positioned in the broad, lush valley of the Río Sella. The distant peaks provide a magnificent backrop to its big sight, a Roman **bridge**, festooned with ivy, which you'll see splashed across the front of many Asturian tourist brochures. The town's other attraction, less photogenic but more curious, is the **Capilla de Santa Cruz**, a fifteenth-century rebuilding of an eighth-century chapel founded over a Celtic dolmen stone. This, like the Liebana monastery at Potes, is among the earliest Christian sites in Spain, and Cangas, as an early residence of the fugitive Asturian-Visigothic kings, lays claim to the title of "First Capital of Christian Spain." As a town, today, however, it belies such history: a functional place, muscled-in upon by new developments, though good for a comfortable night, and a solid meal, after a spell in the mountains.

Most facilities lie within 400m of the **bus station** (next to the *Café Colón*). A couple of *hostales* (try *El Sella*, by the old bridge) and the *Fonda/Bar El Chofer* (just off the main street) are likely to be full in high season, as is anything else more expensive. The very central *Residencia/Albergue "Rey Pelayo"*, soon to be YHA-affiliated, is the institutional fallback and not bad for that, offering eight-bedded rooms or sleeping-bag dorms. **Eating out**, the *Sidreria/Mesón Puente Romano*, by the bridge, has a grand outdoor setting, with good-value *menús*; *Restaurante Río Grande*, across the square from "Rey Pelayo", has arguably the better food.

Covadonga and the Lakes

The Reconquest can properly be said to have started at **COVADONGA**, 11km southeast of Cangas in the mountains. Here in 718 the Visigothic King Pelayo and a small group of followers are said to have repulsed the Moorish armies — at odds, according to Christian chronicles, of 31 to 400,000. In reality the Moors can hardly have been more than an isolated expeditionary force and their sights were already turned to the more lucrative lands beyond the Pyrennees, where in 732 they were defeated at Poitiers by Charles Martel. But the symbolism of the event is at the heart of Asturian, and Spanish, national history, and the defeat probably did allow the Visigoths to regroup, slowly expanding Christian influence over the northern mountains of Spain and Portugal. As a result, many pilgrims still make their way to Covadonga, and above all else it's a religious shrine.

The focus of a visit is the **cave** used as a base by Pelayo, now a chapel containing the hero's sarcophagus. Guides point out other legendary features, though they're all rather swamped by a grandiose nineteenth-century pink basilica. Huge signs in the streets proclaim "Remember — you have come to pray" — all rather intimidating if you're yearning to whoop it up after a hard day in the mountains. There are a few **fondas** and **hostales**.

After Covadonga the road begins to climb sharply, and 12km beyond you reach the **mountain lakes** of **Enol** and **Ercina**. These are connected by daily bus from June 15 to Sep. 15 (passing Cangas at 11:15 am), but it's not difficult to hitch if necessary. The **Mirador de la Reina**, a short way before, gives you an inspiring view of the assembled peaks. The lakes themselves are placid and swimmable, set high in turf; there's a *refugio* and a campground at the southwestcorner of Lago Enol. A word, incidentally, about weather conditions. Even if it is misty at Cangas or Covadonga, you may find that the cloud cover disperses abruptly just before the lakes; conversely, sunny weather down below is no guarantee of the same up top, so come prepared.

The Cornión Massif

From the lakes a good trail leads east-southeast within three hours to the **Vega de Ario**, where there's a newly-refurbished *refugio*, lots of campers on the meadow, and unsurpassed **views** over the Cares Gorge to the highest peaks in the central Picos. Unless you have good mountaineering skills for the steep descent in the Cares, this is something of a dead-end, as to cross the bulk of the western peaks you'll need to backtrack at least to Lago Ercina to resume progress south.

Most walkers, however,hike south from the lakes to the popular refuge at **Vega Redonda**. The route initially follows a jeep track but later becomes a proper trail through a curious landscape of stunted oaks and turf, very similar to that seen on the way to Vega Ario. Vega Redonda, about three hours' walk, overlooks the very last patches of green on the Asturias side of the Cornión massif. Beyond here rambles are in a different category of difficulty altogether. Nerve and skill are required to cross the badlands to **Llago Huerta**, the next feasible overnight spot — and like Redonda popular with cavers who disappear down various chasms in the area. From Llago Huerta it's possible to descend to Cordiñanes but probably wiser to keep to the main route due south to where the meadows of León beckon. Here you can descend southeast to Santa Marina de Valdeón or southwest to Oseja de Sajambre.

Oviedo And The Asturian Churches

The principal reason for visiting **OVIEDO** is to see three small churches. They are perhaps the most remarkable in Spain, built in a style unique to Asturias which emerged in the wake of the Visigoths and before Romanesque had spread south from France. All of them date from the first half of the ninth century, a period of almost total isolation for the Asturian Kingdom, which was then just 65km by 50km in area and the only part of Spain under Christian rule.

Oviedo, the principality's modern capital, became the center of this outpost in 810 with the residence of King Alfonso II, son of the victorious Pelayo. Here he built a chapel, the *Camara Santa*, to house the holy relics rescued from Toledo on its fall to the Moors. Remodeled in the twelfth century, this now forms the inner sanctuary of the **Cathedral**, a fine Gothic structure at the heart of the modern city. It's open daily from 9am to 1pm and again from 3:30 to 6pm; an admission ticket buys entrance to the Camara Santa and to the delicate fourteenth-century cloister. The **Camara Santa** (Holy Chamber) is in fact two chapels. The innermost, with its primitive capitals, is thought to be Alfonso's original building. The antechapel, rebuilt in 1109, is a quiet little triumph of Spanish Romanesque, each of the six columns supporting the vault is sculpted with a pair of superbly humanized apostles.

Around the cathedral, enclosed by scattered sections of the medieval town walls, is what remains of **Old Oviedo**: a compact, attractive quarter in what, it has to be said, is a fairly bleak industrial city. Much of it was destroyed early in the civil war when Republican Asturian miners laid siege to the Nationalist garrison; the defenders were relieved by a Gallego detachment when on the brink of surrender.

Some of the **palaces** — not least the archbishop's, opposite the cathedral — are worth a look, though none are open to visitors. Of interest, too, is the **Archaeological Museum**, housed immediately behind the cathedral in the former convent of San Vicente (Mon.–Sat. 10am–1:30pm and 4:30–6:30pm, Sun. 11am–1pm). This displays various pieces of sculpture from the "Asturian-Visigoth" churches, the nearest of which, **Santullano**, can be seen

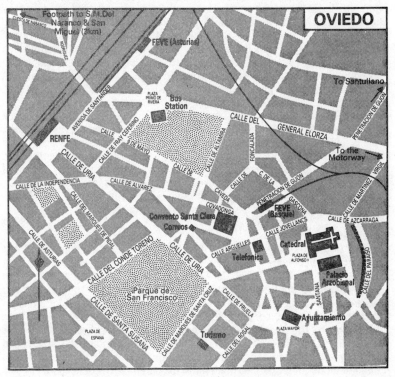

ten minutes' walk to the northeast along the c/de Gijón. By some unfortunate quirk of local city-planning this now stands right next to a divided highway. But if you're cultivating an interest in these buildings it's worth seeing. Built around 830, it's considerably larger and more spacious than the other Asturian churches, with a curious "secret chamber" built into the outer wall. It is kept locked but the keys are available at the priest's house, to the left; there are original frescoes inside, executed in similar style to Roman villas.

Santa María del Naranco

The greatest of the Asturian churches, and the architectural and aesthetic highlight of the principality, is **Santa María de Naranco**, majestically sited on a wooded slope 3km above the city. It's a 45-minute walk from the center, or half an hour from the station; the local tourist office has marked a walking route, starting on one of the pedestrian streets downtown and leading onto a beautiful trail straight to the churches.

Perhaps it is the walk, catching glimpses of the warm stone and simple bold outline of the church through the trees, that makes Santa María such a special, and almost mystical, building. But when you've arrived and gazed upon it from all sides it still seems quite perfect in its harmony of form, decoration, and natural surroundings. "Formidable beyond its scale," to use Jan Morris's phrase. Curiously, it was designed not as a church but as a palace or hunting lodge for Ramiro I (842–52), Alfonso's successor. The present structure was just the main hall of a complex that included baths and stairways, long-gone features which the caretaker may point out. Architecturally, the most interesting features are the open porticos at both ends — an innovation developed much later in Byzantine churches — and the thirty or so decorative medallions which give the appearance of being suspended from the roof. The crypt bears a notable resemblance to the Camara Santa back in town.

A couple of hundred meters beyond Santa María is King Ramiro's palace chapel, **San Miguel de Lillo**, built with soft golden sandstone and red tiles. This is generally assumed to be by the same architect as Santa María, Tiodo (whom some scholars credit also with the Camara Santa and Santullano), though its design, the Byzantine cross-in-square, is quite different. Much of its interior sculpture has been removed to the archaeological museum.

Both churches are open Monday through Saturday in summer from 10am–1pm and 4–7pm, Sunday 10am–1pm; much less reliably out of season.

Oviedo Practicalities

Central Oviedo is easy enough to find your way about. Points of arrival/departure, however, are a little confusing. More or less all **buses** leave from the station in the Plaza Primo de Rivera, although this is underground and easily missed. If you're going somewhere particularly out of the way you might do well to check first with the **Turismo** alongside the **park** (and main *paseo*) of **San Francisco**. For trains, there are two separate **FEVE stations** in addition to the regular **RENFE** one (which serves León). The *FEVE Asturias*, next to the RENFE, is for the line towards Santander; the so-called *FEVE Basque*, oddly enough, serves stations west to El Ferrol. They're a good fifteen minutes apart, so don't try to make too fine a connection.

Accommodation is fairly plentiful, with a smattering of **fondas** north of the cathedral along c/Jovellano (the *Pomar* is friendly), and a range of other options on c/Uria and c/9 de Mayo or c/de Caveda down near the main railroad stations. And lastly, whether you stay or not, don't leave without ordering at least a glass of Asturian *sidra* (**cider**) — if only for bewilderment's sake (onlookers will show you the correct drinking protocol).

Back to the Coast: Cudillero and Luarca

CUDILLERO, accessible by bus from Avilés or (tortuously) from Oviedo, has a harsh, seaward beauty. A small and active fishing port, its arcaded houses rear one upon another over a steep cliffside wedged like a horseshoe around the port. It is justly famed and there are signs that development is on the way: building sites for hotels have appeared along the seafront and an enormous breakwater has been constructed to expand its harbor. But at present, tenuous as this may be, it is quite unspoiled. There are no hotels nor yet even postcards, just have a dozen simple fish tavernas (the local *merluza* is renowned) in the narrow plaza where the high street rolls into the sea. If you want to stay, there are a few **beds** to rent (ask at the last bar on the left of the main street, about 150 meters up from the harbor), or, more officially, a couple of **hostales** two or three kilometers short of town on the road in.

Note that the **campground** that's marked as Cudillero in the *Guía de Campings* is in fact at the fine, sheltered beach of **San Pedro de la Rivera**, some 5km west, near the village of SOTO DE LUIÑA. The campground itself (☎985/348754) is a little regimented, but there are a few good bars in the village.

Luarca

Beyond San Pedro the coast is rocky and the road winds through dark hills before dipping down through thick woods to the port of **LUARCA**. This is one of the most attractive towns along the whole northern coastline, built around an S-shaped cove amid sheer cliffs. Down below, the town is bisected by a small, winding river, knitted together by its many narrow bridges, and giving the place a mellow feel after the ruggedness of Cudillero.

It's a seaside resort in a very modest sort of way, with a slim beach of slightly murky sand, a dozen *hostales* and *pensiones*, and some excellent bars and restaurants around the fishing harbor. Check the good-value menu at *Don Angel*. A few **chigres** (old-fashioned Asturian taverns) survive in the town, where, if you haven't tried it before, you can be initiated into the curious art of *sidra* drinking. The cheapest place to stay is *El Cocinero*, a fine ramshackle old **fonda** in the main square (near the front); other places are to be found in c/del Crucero, a pedestrian street behind the buildings flanking the plaza to the east. The **Turismo** is also on the main square, in the town hall, and has lists of people offering rooms or apartments.

The **beach** itself is actually double, the nearer one narrower but more protected, the other broad one beyond the jetty sometimes subject to seaweed litter. On the clifftop above the beach, a bit of a climb but well-marked from the town center and with facilities to match its superb setting, is *Los Cantiles* **campground** (summer only; ☎985/640938).

Navia and Toward Galicia

The final section of the Asturian coast is marshy and not particularly memorable. The port of **NAVIA** is pleasant but lacks the style and life of Luarca. The best beach along this stretch is by the fishing village of **TAPIA DE CASARIEGO**, popular locally and with three reasonably priced **hostales** plus an entertaining "alternative" *Teatro Popular.*

If you have a car, however, or the patience to fit in with sporadic buses, the **inland routes** from Navia and Tineo to Lugo are said to be fascinating (though without overnight accommodation). At **COAÑA**, 5km from NAVIA, there's a Celtic *citania* (see La Guardia, in Galicia), and beyond that the road winds above the reservoirs of the Navia river before twisting into Galicia and the remote mountainous region around FONSAGRADA.

fiestas

January
22 Saint's day fiesta at SAN VICENTE DE LA BARQUERA

April
Holy Week Celebrations include the *bollo* (cake) festival on Easter Sunday and Monday at AVILÉS.
First Sunday after Easter *La Folia*, torch-lit maritime procession at SAN VICENTE DE LA BARQUERA

June
28 *Coso Blanco* nocturnal parade at CASTRO URDIALES.
29 CUDILLERO enacts *La Amuravela* — an ironic review of the year — and then proceeds to obliterate memories.

July
10 Fiesta at ALIVA.
15 Good solid festival at COMILLAS with greased-pole climbs, goose chases and other such events.
25 Festival of St. James at CANGAS DE ONIS.
Last Sunday *Fiesta de los Vaqueiros* — cowboys at La Brana de Aristebano near LUARCA.
Through July there is a Jazz Festival at SANTANDER, which towards **August** expands into an International Music Festival. This being one of the wealthiest cities of the north, there are usually some prestigious acts.

August
First or second weekend Canoe races on the Río Sella between ARRIONDAS and RIBADESELLA with fairs and festivities at both towns.
First Sunday Asturias Day, celebrated above all at GIJON.
12 Fiesta at LLANES.
17–18 Fiestas have traditionally been held at RIAÑO; whether they now feel they have anything to celebrate is another matter.
31 "Battle of the Flowers" at LAREDO.

September
7–8 Running of the bulls at AMPUERO (Santander).
14 Bull-running by the sea at CARREÑÓN (Oviedo).
16 LLANES folklore festival, strong on dancing.
19 *Americas Day* in Asturias, celebrating the thousands of local emigrants in Latin America; at OVIEDO there are floats, bands and groups representing every Latin American country. The exact date for this can vary.
21 Fiesta of San Mateo at OVIEDO, usually a continuation of the above festival.
22 San Timoteo *romería* at LUARCA.
29 San Miguel *romería* at PUENTE VIESGO.

November
30 Small regatta for San Andrés day at CASTRO URDIALES.

travel details

Buses

From Santander To Laredo/Castro Urdiales (5 daily; 1/1½ hr.), Puente Viesgo (4; 1 hr.), Santillana (6; 45 min.), Comillas (4; 1 hr. — usually change in Torrelavega), San Vicente la Barquera (4;1¼hr..), Potes (2; 3 hr. — possible to pick up in San Vicente or Unquera), Oviedo via Cangas or Llanes — check which (4; 3½ hr.), Bilbao (6; 4 of which continue to French border; 2½ hr.), Vitoria via Castro Urdiales, skips Bilbao (3; 2 hr.), Burgos (2; 4 hr.), Barcelona (1; 11 hr.), Santiago, Vigo, and Portuguese border (2; 10–12 hr.), Madrid (1; 8 hr.)

From Castro Urdiales To Bilbao (7; 1 hr.), Vitoria (3; 75 min.)

From Comillas To Santillana (4; 35 min.) and San Vicente (3; 30 min.)

From San Vicente To Potes (via Unquera; 2 in 1½ hr.) and Ribadesella (3; 2 hr.)

Picos buses Potes–Espinama–Fuente De (3; 1 hr.), Arenas de Cabrales–Cangas de Onis (4; 1½ hr.), Colombres/Panes–Arenas (2; 45/30min.), Cangas de Onis–Covadonga (4, 1 continuing to lakes; 45 min./1½ hr.), Cangas de Onis–Sajambre (1, 2 hr.), León– Posada de Valdeón (1 daily via Riaño and Portilla de la Reina, 4½ hr.). Also **Land-Rover service** between Valdeón and Caín, and Poncebos and Arenas.

From Ribadesella To Villaviciosa/Oviedo (3; 1 hr./2½ hr.), Arriondas (change for Cangas)/Oviedo (5; 20 min./2 hr.)

From Oviedo To Avilés (hourly; 35 min.), Gijón (hourly, 45 min.), Cudillero (1 in 2 hr. — but three

more by changing at Avilés), Luarca/Ribadeo (6; 2½ hr./4½ hr.), Lugo (4; 5 hr.), Betanzos/La Coruña (2; 6/7 hr.), Vigo (2; 10 hr.), León (4, 2 hr.).

Trains

RENFE

Santander–Madrid 3 daily (8–10 hr.), change at PALENCIA for east-west routes.
Oviedo–León 3 daily (2½ hr.)

FEVE

This independent service runs along the north coast between **Bilbao, Santander, and El Ferrol**. The narrow-gauge railroad has a poor record for safety, let alone efficiency, but is at present being modernized, with new cars and extensive right-of-way renovation. Currently only 2 trains per day cover the whole distance in either direction from Santander; shorter journeys vary widely. Main stops in Cantabria and Asturias, from east to west, are: Santander, Torrelavega, Llanes, Ribadesella, Noreña, Oviedo, Gijón, Avilés, Pravia, Cudillero, Luarca, Navia, and, in Galicia, Ribadeo, Foz, Vivero, and El Ferrol. The full journey takes nearly 13 hours, best split over two or more days, with an obligatory change of trains (and stations) at Oviedo.

Ferries

Car/passenger ferry from **Santander** to **Plymouth, England** (twice weekly except from mid-December to mid-January; 24 hr.)

CHAPTER SEVEN

GALICIA

R emote, rural, and battered by the Atlantic, Galicia is a far cry from the popular image of Spain. In appearance it is more like Ireland; indeed the parallels with Ireland are acute, and not just in its climate, culture, and music, or the ever-visible traces of its Celtic past. Above all, despite the green and fertile look of the place, Galicia has a

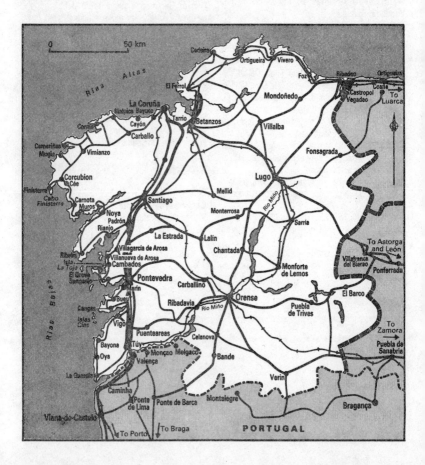

similar history of famine and poverty, with a continuing decline in population owing to forced emigration.

Galicia is lush and heavily wooded, with a landscape dominated by water. The coastline is shaped by fjord-like *rías*, source of the best seafood in Europe and sheltering unspoiled old villages and fine beaches. As you enter Galicia from the east, the rolling meadows of Asturias are replaced by a patchwork of tiny fields, with terraces of vines supported on granite props and allotments full of turnip-tops and cabbages growing on stalks. Archaic inheritance laws have meant a constant division and redivision of the land into little plots too small for machinery and worked with the most primitive agricultural methods; ox carts with solid wooden wheels are still a common sight on the roads. Everywhere you see *horreos*, granaries made here of granite rather than wood, with saints and sculpted air-vents, standing on pillars away from rodents and the damp.

While it is a poor, "backward" part of the country, unlike the south it never seems oppressively so. Food is plentiful, most people being involved in its production, and there's a strength and solidity in the culture, run, uniquely for Spain, by the women. The most common pattern is for women to work the land while the men work at sea, whether that be sailing with fishing boats or as merchant seamen, catching octopus and lobster from rowing boats, minding the *mejilloneiras* (the mussel rafts anchored in the *rías*), or the old standby of smuggling. For centuries men have also sought their fortunes abroad, traditionally in Argentina (there are said to be more Gallegos in Buenos Aires than in Galicia), though more often these days as migrant laborers in Germany and Northern Europe.

With so many men absent, and almost no heavy industry, there is little of the radicalism of Asturias. Galicia has always been deeply conservative; it was the birthplace and first secure foothold of General Franco, and is today dominated by the right-wing Alianza Popular, whose leader Manuel Fraga, another local boy, is currently campaigning to become regional president. And yet there is nonetheless a strong and proud Gallego separatist movement, which may not approach the scale — or political intensity — of the Catalans and the Basques, but has formed links with Brittany and Ireland, and championed the revival of the long-banned local language.

Galego today sounds like a fusion of Castilian and Portuguese, but has existed as long as either (or longer), and is still spoken by an estimated 85% of the population. In the smaller communities few people speak anything else. It is definitely a living language, taught in schools and with literary heroes such as the poet Rosalia de Castro and the essayist and cartoonist Castelao. Road signs and maps these days tend to be in Gallego; we've given Gallego place names in parentheses after the Castilian version, since you may see either form. The most obvious characteristic is the large number of *X*s, which in Castilian might be *G*s *J*s or *S*s; these are pronounced as a soft *sh*.

GALLEGO FOOD

One of the most compelling attractions of Galicia is the local production and provision of food. The quality of the seafood here is said by gourmets to be equaled only in Newfoundland, and with a few exceptions it is not expensive, at least when eaten as *tapas* in bars. Local wonders to look out for include *vieiras* (the scallops whose shells became the symbol of St. James), *mejillones* (the rich orange mussels from the *rías*), *cigallas* (a kind of crayfish usually and inadequately translated as shrimp), *angullas* (little eels from the river Miño), and *choquitos* and *chipirones* (different kinds of small squids best served in their own ink). *Pulpo* (octopus) is so much a part of Gallego eating that there are special *pulperías* which serve it, and it is a mainstay of local country fiestas. In the province of Pontevedra alone, Villanueva de Arosa has its own octopus festival, Arcade one devoted to oysters, and El Grove goes all the way with a generalized seafood fiesta. One word of warning, however; although a wide variety of crabs and lobsters are always on display in the restaurants, make sure to have a price quoted in advance — the cost ot these specialties is often exorbitant, and the demand so great that certain items such as *necoras* (spider crabs) even have to be imported from England to keep up the supply.

Throughout Galicia there are superb **markets**; the coastal towns have their rows of seafront stalls with supremely fresh fish, while cities such as Santiago and Pontevedra have grand old arcaded market halls, piled high with farm produce from the surrounding countryside. Most enjoyable of all are the ports (such as Cambados and Marin), with *lonjas* open to the public, where you can wait for the fishing boats to come home (usually around midnight) and take part in the auctioning of their catch — much of which will have left Galicia well before dawn for the restaurants of Madrid, on the nightly special train.

Another specialty, imported from the second Gallego homeland of Argentina, are the *churrasquerías* (grill houses), often unmarked and needing local assistance to find, where you're served up immense *churrascos*, what we rather limply call "spare ribs" (it's more like a steak with bones in it). The Gallegos don't normally like their food highly spiced, but *churrascos* are traditionally served with a devastating garlic-based *salsa picante*. Other common dishes are *caldo Gallego*, a thick stew of cabbage and potatoes in a meat-based broth, and *lacon con grelos*, ham boiled with turnip greens. The local wines can be great, both the whites and the thick port-like reds (some bars even serve a "black" wine), and are still usually drunk from *tazas*, handleless ceramic cups. Liqueurs tend to be fiery, based on the clear *aguardiente*; one much-loved Gallego custom is the *queimada*, when a large bowl of *aguardiente* with fruit and sugar is set alight and then drunk hot.

When traveling in the province the obvious highlight is **Santiago de Compostela**, the greatest goal for pilgrims in medieval Europe and again emerging as a center for tourists. The cathedral, and the unified architecture of the whole city with its granite colonnades and mossy facades, together make Santiago quite unforgettable. But there are smaller and equally charming old stone towns throughout Galicia, and those that have retained a vibrant sense of life and atmosphere, such as **Pontevedra** and **Betanzos**, can be enjoyable bases for a touring vacation. The coastal countryside is always spectacular, but the best and safest **swimming beaches** are along the **Rías Bajas** towards Portugal, with **El Grove** and **Bayona** the most popular resorts. Far fewer visitors come here than to the Med, and while the sea is never as warm, the pine-fringed coves are delightful. Inland, Galicia can be bleak and empty; the most rewarding route is to follow the Miño (Minho) river upstream from the Portuguese border to towns such as **Ribadavia** and **Celanova**, and then up to the Roman walls of **Lugo**.

THE RÍAS ALTAS AND
SANTIAGO

It's not easy to move around the north coast of Galicia, where the *Rías Altas* (High Estuaries) include both the northernmost and westernmost points of Spain. The roads are poor and barely frequented, and the facilities for visitors are minimal. Although the savagery of the ocean has created a wild and dramatic coastline, even if you have a car it's advisable to choose just a couple of targets. **Vivero** (Viveiro) to the east, and the stretch between **Finisterre** and **Muros** to the west, are good to explore. What's more, apart from Santiago the cities of this area are best avoided; neither El Ferrol nor La Coruña is particularly exciting. On the other hand, no words of praise could be too extravagant for **Santiago**, and if you really want to appreciate this pilgrimage center to the fullest it makes sense to approach it by the ancient Pilgrim Route from Léon. Its one drawback, often exaggerated, is the weather; Santiago must be one of the few cities in the world which actually boasts about its excessive **rainfall**.

The North Coast

The closing stretch of the FEVE railroad, from Luarca to El Ferrol, is perhaps the best, so long as you're in no hurry to arrive. It clings to every nuance of the coastline, looping around a succession of *rías* and rambling through the pine forests and wild looking hills which buffer the villages from the harsh Atlantic. Villages are concentrated at the sides of the estuaries, with the occasional beach tacked beside or below them. By road too it's a slow and painful route; most buses to La Coruña and Ferrol detour inland as far as Lugo rather than tackle the often unsurfaced C642 (at its worst around Ortigueira).

Along the FEVE

RIBADEO, the first Gallego town and *ría*, makes a poor introduction to the region. It does have a certain crumbling charm, and the overgrown main plaza features a few decent bars and a **hostal** or two, but overall, it's drab. The nearest **beach**, the PLAYA DEL CASTRO, is a few kilometers farther west, with **campgrounds** at BENQUERENCIA and REINANTE, but by now you're getting a bit too close to the industrial port of **FOZ**. Beyond that, **CERVO** has little more to boast of than a huge, rust-red aluminium factory, although **MONDOÑEDO**, 20km up the valley of the Río Masma, is an attractive old riverside town.

VIVERO (Viveiro) is something special. Too remote to make its living as a resort, it's an elegant port with a self-confident presence all its own. High glass-fronted houses line the streets, with white wooden frames as delicate as lacework (modeled on those of La Coruña), while the whole ensemble is protected inside an imposing circuit of Renaissance walls and gates. The slope down to the sea is crammed with lively bars full of the local youth (though they seem to go to bed rather early), and the bay shelters several peaceful **beaches**. Just off the PLAYA DE COVAS is a delightful semi-fortified rock, not far from the *Viveiro* **campground** (☎982/560004). In town, several **hostales** and three very cheap **fondas** can be found between the *FEVE* station and the harbor, with the *Serra* (Antonio Bas 2; ☎982/560374) a real bargain. The cafe opposite the station is excellent.

The next two *ría* villages (and FEVE stops) are **EL BARQUERO** (O Barqueiro), a tiny fishing port of slate-roofed houses near Spain's northernmost point, and the larger **ORTIGUEIRA**, set amid a dark mass of pines, with a couple of *hostales*. Public transit being so infrequent, you may rapidly feel stuck if you do decide to visit, and the *Cafe Avenida* in Ortigueira is to be avoided.

El Ferrol

However, a stay in **EL FERROL** is a considerably worse experience than either of these lifeless but innocuous villages. El Ferrol is a massive city which is Spain's principal naval base and dockyard. Dull, depressing, and a little grandiose, it has nothing of interest to see and do. At least they've finally dropped the *del Caudillo* (of the Chief) from the official name, but it still seems an appropriate birthplace for Francisco Franco, the man who did so much to stifle Spanish life and culture.

Getting out shouldn't be too difficult; the **FEVE** and **RENFE** stations are housed in the same building, and the **bus station** is just outside: exit and make two quick lefts, and you'll see it some fifty meters ahead of you. If you need a **bed** for the night, try c/Pardo Bajo, c/del Sol, or c/María, each within a few minutes' walk of the station and the central Plaza de España. You won't have missed anything, though, if you keep going as far as BETANZOS, or farther afield to SANTIAGO, LA CORUÑA, or LUGO.

The Ría de Betanzos

EL FERROL stands more or less opposite LA CORUÑA, only 20km away across the mouth of the **RÍA DE BETANZOS**, but about 70km by road or rail. In fact the coast in between is more appealing than either of the two cities, with the contours of the *ría* speckled with forests and secluded beaches. Heading south from Ferrol, you cross the Río Eume by a vast medieval bridge at **PUENTEDEUME** (Pontedeume), which retains a number of architectural reminders of its former overlords, the counts of Andrade. Just beyond, the *Camping Perbes* (☎981/783104) is sandwiched between woods and water on the PLAYA PERBES near **MIÑO** (Minho).

Betanzos

The town of **BETANZOS** is a really enjoyable place to stay; if you're heading for northern Galicia from Asturias or the south, it serves as an ideal introduction to what's best about the region. The site it's built on is so old, dating back to before the Romans, that what was once a steep seaside hill is now set well back from the coast, at the spot where the rivers Mendo and Mandeo meet. The base of the hill is surrounded by still-discernible medieval walls incorporating many houses, above which rises a mass of twisting and tunneling narrow streets.

A haphazard bar-crawl will unearth a bewildering array of tempting traditional **bars**, as well as take you past a variety of ancient churches and manor houses. (Ask at the *Turismo* for details of an amazing private garden full of decaying pleasure domes and assorted sculpture). Betanzos is short on **accommmodation**, but the **hostal** *Barreiros* (☎981/772259), across the main square from the old town at c/Argentina 6, has cheap and basic rooms, and is run by the same very friendly people who operate the wood-paneled *Mesón dos Arcos* below, which does superb *tapas*.

The countryside around Betanzos is good to explore on foot, either along the rivers or towards the sea. The nearest beaches are those at PERBES, mentioned above, and near **SADA** opposite it, and there are several **campgrounds** in the area. The *Betanzos Ciudad* **RENFE station** is the other side of the river from the town center, but only has frequent connections with Ferrol. The main line from Coruña to Madrid passes instead through *Betanzos Infesta*, at the top of another steep climb; connecting trains run up from *Ciudad*. Bus services are good, except that there's only one per day to Santiago; otherwise you have to go a very roundabout way via La Coruña.

La Coruña

LA CORUÑA (A Cruña) is a surprisingly modern and industrial city, in view of its long history. It was from here that what we have learned to call the "Invincible" Armada sailed in 1588, although its admiral, the seasick landlubber Medina Sidonia, was always convinced the expedition was doomed to failure. Sir Francis Drake not only scattered the Armada, he reached La Coruña in 1589 and burned most of it to the ground. Even its most venerable monument, the much-ballyhooed Roman lighthouse **Torre de Hercules**, was entirely recased in the eighteenth century and there's not a trace of ancient stone to be seen.

You're unlikely to want to spend more than a night in transit amid La Coruña's unsightly sprawl. It's a disappointing place to find on such a good site; like Cádiz it's situated on an outstretched tongue of land washed on each side by the sea, but the town has polluted all the local beaches. If you do stop, the part to head for is the **Ciudad Vieja**, the compact old town above the *Darsena de Marina* harbor: The **train station** is nearby, but from the **bus terminal** you'll need to take city bus #1, which runs to the central square, Puerta Real, at the far end of the Darsena de Marina. There's a **Turismo** on the Darsena where you can get a free map, and **hostales** are quite easy to find in the grid of streets behind. Try c/Estrella (*Centro Gallego*, ☎981/222236); c/San Andrés (*Puenteceso*, ☎981/223744) or c/Los Olmos, or accept one of the offers of a room at the train station.

There's not a great deal to see but there are some pleasant cafes and restaurants, and curious streets entirely faced in glass-covered balconies — a practical innovation against La Coruña's wind and showers. The long curve of the seafront, with the sun reflected from countless panes of glass, is particularly striking. The best churches are Romanesque **Santiago** and **Santa María del Campo**, both a couple of blocks from the Puerta Real. Nearby, overlooking the sea, are the walled **Jardines de San Carlos**, where rests the **tomb of Sir John Moore**, hurriedly buried during the British retreat from the French in the Peninsular Wars of 1809, and immortalized in the jingoistic stanzas of Reverend Charles Wolfe ("Not a drum was heard, not a funeral note . . .") which you will find here inscribed. To reach the **Torre de Hercules**, walk or catch buses #4 or #17a the three kilometers to the end of the isthmus.

Inland To Santiago

The **Pilgrims' Route** to Santiago is the longest-established "tourist" route in Europe, but its final section through Galicia remains as harsh as ever. It's just a minor road now, branching away from the main Ponferrada-to-Lugo highway at the PEDRAFITA DO CEBREIRO pass which marks the Gallego frontier. This is a desolate spot, where hundreds of English soldiers froze and starved to death during Sir John Moore's retreat towards La Coruña in 1809; they cast a great treasure in gold down the ravine to keep it from the pursuing French. The village of CEBREIRO itself is quite appallingly situated to catch the worst of the Gallego wind and snow. Picturesque it may be, a settlement of undulating round thatched stone huts (*pallozas*) surrounding the stark ninth-century church, but there's something nasty about modern Spanish citizens being subsidized by the state to live as "peasants" in antediluvian poverty for the gratification of the occasional idle visitor.

In such a forbidding landscape, however, you can only be impressed by the sheer scale of work that medieval builders put into providing spiritual and material amenities for the pilgrims. Crumbling castles, convents, and humble inns line the road, and it's not hard to imagine what a welcome sight each must have been. If you don't have a car, you won't be able to follow the route on public transportation; some people do still walk it, but it's an arduous business, with little possible accommodation. Many places are now little more than ruins; the MONASTERIO DE SAMOS, famous for its library in the Middle Ages, was devastated by fire in 1951, while of the once-great monastery at **SOBRADO DE LOS MONJES** only a monumental thirteenth-century kitchen and a fine baroque church and cloister remain intact. The whole town of **PORTOMARÍN** was flooded by the damming of the Minho, but its castle of the Knights Templar and church were carried stone by stone to a new site farther up the hillside. **SARRIA**, in its entirety a powerful reminder of the pilgrimage's heyday, is perhaps best worth visiting; it also has a rare **hostal**, the *Londres* (☎982/530689).

Lugo

The *Camino de Santiago* bypassed **LUGO**, although it was a city already ancient even a thousand years ago, and makes a good stop whether you're traveling to Santiago along the north coast or from León. Built on a Celtic site above the Miño (and named after the Celtic sun god Lug), it is the only Spanish town still completely enclosed within superb **Roman walls**. These are ten to fifteen meters high, and have 85 circular towers along a circuit of almost three kilometers; their best feature is that they are broad enough to provide a wide grassy thoroughfare on which you can walk around the whole charming city. The one disappointment is that a busy beltway road makes it impossible to appreciate the walls from any distance, but it does at least keep the traffic out of the center. The **train** and **bus stations** are outside the walls, a fair distance apart but both on the western side of the city. If you enter the town at the **Puerto de Santiago**, the best of its old gates, you can then climb up onto the most impressive stretch, leading past the cathedral.

There's not actually all that much to see in Lugo; it's very much a place to walk around, savoring its granite staircases, narrow arcades, and relaxed gardens. The large mossy **Cathedral**, flanked by three distinctive towers, was, like so many Gallego churches, modeled after the one at Santiago de Compostela, with imitation here perpetuated by the eighteenth-century baroque additions to the facade. Within, it's renowned for a chapel of Our Lady of the *Ojos Grandes*, a Virgin with large and somewhat flirtatious eyes. The **Bishop's Palace** nearby exhibits an unlikely splendor, while the cloisters of the **Provincial Museum** outshadow its collection of archaeological oddments, and in the graceful colonnades of the **Plaza España** you'll find some good cafes and a couple of reasonable restaurants. The Plaza Santo Domingo on the other hand sports a chilling black statue of a Falangist eagle.

Most of the cheaper **hostales** are outside the walls, around the train and bus stations, but it's more fun to be inside. The *Alba* at Calvo Sotelo 16 (☎982/226056), is perfectly adequate, or you could try *La Perla* (☎982/211100) at Catedral 20. For **bars**, explore the very long straight **Rua Nova** leading north. Finally, you can get a good high view of the Miño valley by joining the popular evening promenade in the **Parque Rosalia de Castro**, a little way out of the Puerta de Santiago.

Santiago de Compostela

The great pilgrimage of the Middle Ages, to **SANTIAGO DE COMPOSTELA**, captured the imagination of Christian Europe on an unprecedented scale. At the height of its popularity, in the eleventh and twelfth centuries, the city was receiving over half a million pilgrims each year. People of all classes came to visit the supposed shrine of Saint James the Apostle (Santiago to the Spanish, Saint Jacques to the French), making this the third holiest site in Christendom, after Jerusalem and Rome.

It was in a very real sense the first exercise in mass tourism. For although the shrine was visited by the great — Fernando and Isabella, Carlos V, Francis of Assisi — you didn't have to be rich to undertake the pilgrimage. The various roads through France and Northern Spain which led to the shrine, collectively known as the *El Camino de Santiago* (the Way of St. James or the Pilgrim Route), were lined with monasteries and charitable hospices run for the benefit of pilgrims. Villages were sprung up along the route, and an order of knights was founded for the pilgrims' protection. There was even a guidebook, the world's first — written by a French monk called Aymery Picaud, which recorded, along with water sources and places to stay, such facts as the bizarre sexual habits of the Navarrese Basques (who exposed themselves when excited, and protected their mules from their neighbors with chastity belts). All in all it was an extraordinary phenomenon in an age when most people spent their lives without venturing beyond their own town or village.

Why did they come? Some, like Chaucer's Wife of Bath, who had "been in Galicia at Seynt Jame," had their own private reasons: social fashion, adventure, the opportunities for marriage or even for crime. But for most pilgrims, it was simply a question of faith. They believed in the miraculous power of Saint James, and were told that to make the journey would guarantee them a remission of half their time in purgatory. Not for a moment did they doubt that the tomb beneath the high altar at Compostela Cathedral held the mortal remains of James, son of Zebedee and Salome and first cousin of Jesus Christ. It seems scarcely credible that the whole business was an immense ecclesiastical fraud.

The Life (and Death?) of Saint James

Yet the legend, at each point of its development, bears this out. It begins with the claim, unsubstantiated by the Bible, that Saint James came to Spain, at some point after the Crucifixion, to spread the gospel. He is said, for example, to have had a vision of the Virgin in Zaragoza. He then returned to Jerusalem, where he was indisputably beheaded by Herod Agrippa. His body should, by all rights and reason, be buried somewhere in the Nile Delta. But the legend records that two of James' disciples removed his corpse to Jaffa, where a boat appeared, without sails or crew, and carried them to Padrón, twenty kilometers downriver from Santiago. The voyage took just seven days, at once proving the miracle "since," as Ford wrote in 1845, "the Oriental Steam Company can do nothing like it."

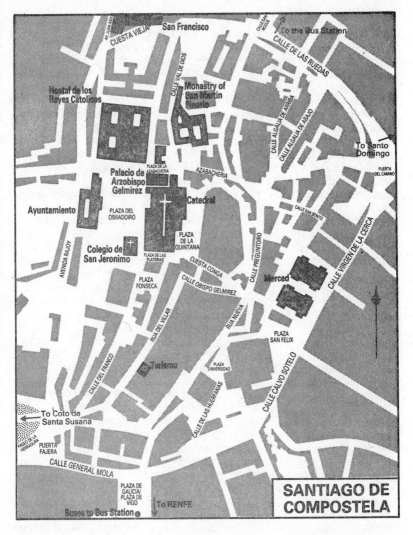

SANTIAGO DE
COMPOSTELA

At this stage the body was buried, lost and forgotten for the next 750 years. It was rediscovered at Compostela in 813, at a time of great significance for the Spanish church. Over the preceding century the Moors had swept across the Iberian peninsula, gaining control over all but the northern mountain kingdom of Asturias, and in their campaigns they had introduced a concept entirely new to the west: *jihad* or holy war. They also drew great strength from the inspiration of their champion, the Prophet Muhammad, whose death (in 632) was still within popular memory and a bone from whose body was preserved in the Great Mosque of Córdoba.

Thus the discovery of the bones of Saint James, under a buried altar on a site traditionally linked with his name, was singularly opportune. It occurred after a hermit was attracted to a particular spot on a hillside by visions of stars, and the hill was known thereafter as Compostela, from the Latin *campus stellae*, meaning "field of stars." Alfonso II, King of Asturias, came to pay his respects, built a chapel, and the saint was adopted as the champion of Christian Spain against the Infidel.

Within decades the saint had appeared on the battlefield. Ramiro I, Alfonso's successor, swore that he had fought alongside him at the Battle of Clavijo (844), and that the saint had personally slaughtered 60,000 Moors. Over the next six centuries *Santiago Matamoros* (Moor-killer) manifested himself at some forty battles, even assisting in the massacre of American Indians in the New World. It may seem an odd role for the fisherman-evangelist, but presented no problems to the Christian propagandists who portrayed him most frequently as a knight on horseback in the act of dispatching whole clutches of swarthy, bearded Arabs with a single thrust of his long sword. (With sublime irony, when Franco brought his crack Moroccan troops to Compostela to dedicate themselves to the overthrow of the Spanish Republic, all such statues were discretely hidden under sheets).

The cult of Santiago was strongest during the age of the First Crusade (1085) and the Reconquest; people wanted to believe, and so it gained a kind of truth. In any case, as Ford acidly observed, "if people can once believe that Santiago ever came to Spain at all, all the rest is plain sailing."

The Setting

After the excesses of the legend it should quickly be stressed that Santiago itself is far more than a historical curiosity. Built in a warm golden granite, it is one of the most beautiful of all Spanish cities, rivaled in the north only by León and Salamanca. The medieval city has been declared in its entirety to be a national monument, and remains a remarkably integrated whole which is all the better for being almost completely pedestrianized. The buildings and the squares, the long stone arcades and the statues, are hewn from the same granite blocks and blend imperceptibly one into the other, often making it impossible to distinguish ground level from raised terrace.

It's a city that's at its best in the rain; in fact it's situated in the wettest fold of the Gallego hills, and its brief but constant showers have earned it the epithet "El Orinal de España" (The Urinal of Spain)! Water glistens on the facades, gushes from the innumerable gargoyles, and flows down the streets. As a result vegetation sprouts everywhere, with the cathedral coated in orange and yellow mosses, and grass poking up from the tiles and cobbles.

The feel of the place is much as it must have been in the days of the pilgrims, with its tourists now as likely to be attracted by Santiago's art and history as by religion. Not that the function of pilgrimage here is dead. It fell into decline with the Reformation — or as the local chronicler Molina reported, "the damned doctrines of the accursed Luther diminished the number of Germans and *wealthy* English (italics ours) — but fortunes have revived of late. Each year on July 25, the Festival of St. James, there is a ceremony dedicating the country and government to the saint at his shrine, and recent pilgrims have included Generals de Gaulle and Franco, and, to put his seal on the myth, Pope John Paul II (in 1982).

The Shrine

All roads to Santiago lead to the **Cathedral**. And this, as Jan Morris asserts, "is still, as it was for those ancient pilgrims, one of the great moments of travel." Traditionally the first member of a party of pilgrims to catch sight of their goal would cry "Mon Joie!" and become "King" of the group; the hill on the eastern side of Santiago thus became known as "Mountjoy." But you first appreciate the sheer grandeur of the cathedral upon venturing into the vast expanse of the Plaza de Obradoiro. Directly ahead stands a fantastic baroque pyramid of granite, flanked by immense bell towers and everywhere adorned with statues of Saint James in his familiar pilgrim guise with staff, broad hat, and scallop-shell badge. This is the famous OBRADOIRO FACADE, built in the mid-eighteenth century by an obscure Santiago-born architect, Fernando Casas y Novoa. No other work of Spanish baroque can compare with it, nor with what Edwin Mullins (in *The Road To Compostela*) sublimely calls its "hat in-the-air exuberance."

The main body of the cathedral is Romanesque, rebuilt in the eleventh and twelfth centuries after a devastating raid by the Muslim vizier of Córdoba, al-Mansur. He failed to find the body of the saint (perhaps not surprisingly), but forced the citizens to carry the bells of the tower to the mosque at Córdoba — a coup which was later dramatically reversed (see "Córdoba" section in *Andalucía*). The building's highlight — indeed one of the great triumphs of medieval art — is the **Portico de Glória**, the original west front, which now stands inside the cathedral behind the Obradoiro. Completed in 1188 under the supervision of one Maestro Mateo, this was both the culmination of all Romanesque sculpture, and a precursor of the new Gothic realism, each of its host of figures being strikingly relaxed and quietly humanized. They were originally painted, and still bear traces of a seventeenth-century renovation.

The real mastery, however, is in the assured marshaling of the ensemble. Above the side doors are representations of Purgatory and the Last Judgement, while over the main door Christ presides in glory, flanked by his *Apostles* (St. John with his eagle, St. Mark with his lion, etc.) and surrounded by the 24 *Elders of the Apocalypse* playing celestial music. *Saint James* sits on the central column, beneath Christ and just above eye level in the classic symbolic position of intercessor, since it was through him that pilgrims could gain assurance of their destiny. The pilgrims would give thanks at journey's end by praying with the fingers of one hand pressed into the roots of the *Tree of Jesse* below the saint. So many millions have performed this act of supplication that there are five deep and shiny holes worn into the solid marble. Finally, for wisdom, they would lower their heads to touch the brow of Maestro Mateo, the humble squatting figure on the other side.

The spiritual climax of the pilgrimage, however, was the approach to the **High Altar**. This remains a peculiar experience. You climb steps behind the altar, embrace the Most Sacred Image of Santiago, kiss his bejeweled cape, and are handed, by way of certification, a document in Latin called a *Compostela*. The altar is a riotous creation of eighteenth-century Churrigueresque, but the statue has stood there for seven centuries and the procedure is quite unchanged. (You also get a God's-eye view from up there, during services, of the priest and congregation). The pilgrims would now make confession and attend a High Mass. You should try to do the latter at least, as a means of understanding Santiago's mystique.

You'll notice an elaborate pulley system in front of the altar. This is for moving the immense incense-burner, "**Botafumeiro**," which, operated by eight priests, is swung in a vast 25-to-30-meter, ceiling-to-ceiling arc across the transept. It is stunning to watch, but takes place only at certain services (Saturday evening mass, around 5pm, is a good possibility; check with the *Turismo*). And be warned that accidents have been known to happen!

The saint's **bones** are kept in a **crypt** beneath the altar. They were lost for a second time in 1700, having been hidden before an English invasion, but were rediscovered during building work in 1879. In fact they found three skeletons, which were naturally held to be those of St. James and his two disciples. The only problem was to identify which one was the Apostle. This was fortuitously resolved. A church in Tuscany possessed a piece of Santiago's skull which exactly fitted a gap in one of those here! Its identity was confirmed in 1884 by Pope Leo XIII, and John Paul II's visit presumably reaffirmed official sanction.

The cathedral is full of collecting boxes; there are two on either side if you wish to kneel before the bones. But to visit the **Treasury, Cloister, Archaeological Museum,** and Mateo's beautiful **Crypt of the Portico**, you need to buy a collective ticket. The late Gothic cloisters in particular are well worth seeing; from the plain, mosque-like courtyard you get a wonderful view of the riotous mixture of the exterior, crawling with pagodas, "pawns," domes, obelisks, battlements, scallop shells, and cornucopias. The museum is behind the balconies overlooking the great cathedral square. These parts of the building — unlike the cathedral itself, which stays open throughout the day — are limited to set hours of 10:30am to 1:30pm and 4 to 7pm.

Around the Cathedral

The **Palace of Archbishop Gelmirez** (10am–1:30pm and 3:30-7pm) occupies the north side of the cathedral, balancing the cloister, with its entrance just to the left of the main stairs. Gelmirez was one of the seminal figures in Santiago's development. He rebuilt the cathedral in the twelfth century, raised the see to an archbishopric, and "discovered" a ninth-century deed which gave annual dues to St. James' shrine of one bushel of corn from each acre of Spain reconquered from the Moors! It was enforced for four centuries, and repealed only in 1834. In his palace, suitably luxuriant, are a vaulted twelfth-century kitchen and some fine Romanesque chambers.

As late as the thirteenth century the cathedral was used to accommodate pilgrims (the *Botafumeiro* was used at least part of the time as a fumigator), but slowly its place was taken by convents founded around the city. Ferdnando and Isabella, in gratitude for their conquest of Granada, added to these facilities by building a hostel for the poor and sick. This, the elegant Renaissance **Hostal de los Reyes Católicos**, fills the northern side of the Plaza de Obradoiro in front of the cathedral. It is now a *parador*, a five-star, state-run hotel, and unless you're staying here do-it-yourself tours are frowned on. Should you get in, there are four superb patios, a chapel with magnificent Gothic stonecarving, and an interesting vaulted crypt-bar (where the bodies of the dead were once stored).

Around the City

The whole city, with its flagstone streets and arcades, is quietly enchanting, and you could spend half an afternoon getting to know the **squares around the cathedral** alone. Each of these is distinct. The largest is the **Plaza de Quintana**, where a flight of broad steps joins the back of the cathedral to the high walls of a convent. It is unreachable by road, and thus takes on the character of a stage, successively peopled by whomever stumbles upon it. Students tend to congregate on the steps between classes, and quiet classical music is broadcast from concealed speakers. The "Puerta Santa" doorway in this square is only opened during those "Holy Years" in which the Feast of Santiago falls on a Sunday. To the south is the Plaza de las Platerías, the silversmiths' square, dominated by an extravagantly ornate fountain, and to the north is the Plaza de la Azabachería, which at one time was the financial center of Spain.

Elsewhere, if you want to add direction to your wanderings, perhaps the best plan is to head for some of the **monasteries and convents**. The enormous Benedictine **San Martín** stands close to the cathedral, the vast altarpiece in its church ("a fricassee of gilt gingerbread" according to Ford) depicting its patron riding alongside Saint James. Nearby is **San Francisco**, reputedly founded by the saint himself during his pilgrimage to Santiago. In the north of the city you'll find two more, baroque **Santa Clara**, with a unique curving facade, and a little beyond it, **Santo Domingo**. This last is perhaps the most interesting of the buildings, featuring a magnificent seventeenth-century triple stairway, each spiral leading to different stories of a single tower, and a fascinating Museum of Gallego Crafts and Traditions (open 10am–1pm and 4–7pm; nominal entrance fee). Many aspects of life displayed haven't yet entirely disappeared, though you're today unlikely to see *corozas*, straw overcoats worn until recent decades by mountain shepherds. You're equally unlikely to completely decipher the exhibit-labeling, which is only in Gallego (and which would seem to be taking regionalism a bit too far).

Outside the main circuit of the city, the one really worthwhile visit is the curious Romanesque church of **Santa María del Sar**. This lies about a kilometer down the c/de Sar, which begins at the Patio de Madre. Due to the subsidence of its foundations Santa María has developed an extraordinary slant of about fifteen degrees, though it remains utterly symmetrical. It also has a wonderfully sculpted cloister, reputedly another work of Maestro Mateo. The church is supposed to stay open all day, but you may have to ask around in the buildings at the back. Finally, to get an overall impression of the whole architectural ensemble of Santiago, take a walk along the promenade of the **Paseo de la Herradura**, in the spacious public gardens just southwest of the old part, at the end of the c/del Franco.

Living: Some Details

Many of the most attractive buildings in old Santiago are still used by the university, and the presence of so many students guarantees that the city has a healthy animation to go with its past. There are excellent bars, with prices rarely above normal; it's the best place in Galicia to hear the local Breton-style music, played on *gaitas* or bagpipes in a tradition known as *"La Tuna"*; and it's also a manageable size — you can wander out for half a dozen blocks and reach wide open countryside. You may well find yourself staying longer than you'd planned. The more modern districts of Santiago, where most of the students actually live, may contain glossier bars and larger shops, but they hold little to appeal to the tourist.

Arriving at the **bus station** you are one kilometer or so north of the town center; bus #10, which everyone climbs onto, will take you in to the Plaza de Galicia (or Plaza de Vigo as it's also known) at the bottom left of our map. Santiago is a major nexus for buses; as well as comprehensive local services, buses run to Portugal, France, Switzerland, and England. The **train station** is a walkable distance from the south, along what is still called the c/del General Franco, which also leads to the Plaza de Galicia. If you're flying, the Labacolla **airport** is some 13km out on the road to Lugo. It's best reached on the main bus between the two towns, although a bus loosely timed to coincide with flights does depart from the *Iberia* offices in town at General Pardiñas 24, going via the train and bus stations. Be warned, if you want to catch an early-morning flight out, that the airport is locked and totally deserted at night, with no place to stay, and the area around patrolled by packs of wild dogs.

Rooms are easy to find and inexpensive, though note that *pensiones* are here often called *hospedajes*. The biggest concentration of places is on the three parallel streets leading down from the cathedral: Rua Nueva, Rua del Villar, and c/del Franco (this last named after the French pilgrims, rather than the late dictator). One particular favorite is the *Hospedaje Lalin* in the c/ Azabachería, which has rooms overlooking the Plaza de Quintana; there's also the *Rajoy* in the Avenida Rajoy just off the Plaza Obradoiro. The cheapest of the bunch, at around 800ptas for a rather basic double, is the *Hospedaje Villa de Cruces* (☎981/580804) at Patio de Madres 16, two blocks above the Plaza de Galicia off c/de Calvo Sotelo. If you have any problems, the **Turismo** at Rua del Villar 43 can provide complete lists. Even for the great **July 25 Festival** (see "Fiestas" at the end of this chapter) there's rarely a problem, with half the bars in the city letting out beds, and landladies dragging you off on arrival; in fact if anything things are more difficult out of season, when much of the cheaper accommodation is rented long-term to students. The closest **campground**, *Camping Santiago* (☎981/888002), is on the north side of town, a short way along the road to Lugo; another, *Camping las Sirenes*, is 8km out on the road to Noya, with a pool and regular buses to the city. Both operate in summer only.

Gallego food — and drink — are at their best in Santiago, with a plethora of good, solid **places to eat**. Among the most famous is *El Asesino* at Plaza Universidad 16, where three sisters serve lunches so cheap and so popular that they don't bother with a sign — just ask to be pointed. Another student haunt is the *Casa Manolo* on c/Benito, while the c/del Franco is full of bars such as *El Bombero* and *Tacita de Oro* with reliable *tazas* and *tapas*. Students and young people also tend to patronize two small bars between Rua Nueva and Rua del Villar, reached by a narrow walkway lead from Cantar Toval. If you've the money to spare, you might also try *Don Gaiceros* in Rua Nueva, perhaps the city's best restaurant. **Bars** change a bit too often, and are in any case too plentiful, for it to be worth offering more than a few suggestions, but on a long night out try and call in at the *Bar Ourense* and *O'Barril* on C/ del Franco, *O Gato Negro* on Rua Nueva, and the unnamed cellar on the Cuesta Conga, indicated by a Portuguese rooster symbol, which has a superbly cosmopolitan jukebox. For a somewhat narrower focus, recorded Celtic music can be heard at *Casa de Crechas* near the Plaza Immaculada.

Other delights hidden in the old streets include the magic shop on c/del Franco, run by a demented old woman with a devastatingly straight face; the lovely formal bookshops of the Rua del Villar, some of which sell novels in English; the shop which specializes in restoring religious statues, on the Plaza Azabachería; and *La Casa de los Quesos* on Rua del Villar, where they sell the traditional breast-shaped cheese, *queso de tetilla*. And if you're shopping for your own food, or if you just like to browse around, don't miss the large covered **market** held daily in the old halls of the Plaza de San Felix. The excellence of the fresh produce does much to explain the shortage of food shops elsewhere in Santiago.

The Costa do Morte

The wild coast to the west of La Coruña and Santiago is often harshly beautiful, its pine forests having scarcely been cut, and villages only occasionally interrupting the line of the shore. The sun setting over the ocean, with mighty Atlantic waves battering the bleak rocky headlands, can be unforgettable. For the medieval pilgrims this was the end of the world, and it remains inaccessible and somewhat forbidding. Irregular buses do run to the larger towns, along slow winding roads, but there are no trains. If you have your own car, it's well worth following the length of the coastal road from La Coruña down to **Finisterre** and around to **Noya** and **Padrón**.

You should be warned, however, that even where the isolated coves do shelter fine beaches, you will rarely find the most minimal resort facilities. While the beaches may look splendid, braving the water is recommended only to the hardiest of swimmers, and the weather is significantly wetter and windier here than it is a mere hundred kilometers farther south. The most exposed and westerly stretch of all, from Camariñas to Finisterre, has long been famed as the **Costa do Morte** (Coast of Death), and Celtic legends, here as at the Breton Finisterre, tell of doomed cities drowned beneath the sea.

The Way to the End of the World

There are few potential stopping points immediately west of La Coruña; you should head first the 35 kilometers to the inland road junction of CARBALLO. From here you are within reach of a succession of tiny seaside harbors, which can barely have expanded since the days of the dolmen-builders, who have left their traces everywhere. **MALPICA**, the closest to Coruña, is a former whaling port with its own beach and an offshore seabird sanctuary, but perhaps the best place to stay is **CORME**. This is a pretty and sheltered fishing village, set back above a deep, round bay, with a minute arcaded plaza (and a fonda nearby). The beach is split by a freshwater stream, and, should you require even greater privacy, deserted sand dunes and forgotten inlets hide within easy walking distance. **LAXE** and **CAMARIÑAS** are similar; the walk out from Camariñas to the lighthouse at **CABO VILÁN** is a worthwhile excursion but bracing to say the least. If you're dependent on public transportation, however, you will probably have to double back as far as Carballo before you can go any farther south.

Finisterre and Around

The town of **FINISTERRE** (FISTERRA in Gallego) still feels as if it's ready to drop off the end of the world, being too remote to get enough visitors to alleviate the abiding poverty. This grey clump of houses wedged into the rocks on the side of a headland away from the open ocean does have a number of cheap **hostales**, such as the *Rivas* (☎981/740027) and the *Cabo Finisterre* (☎981/740000), and better seafood bars include the *Café Tearrón*. The actual tip of the headland is another two-kilometer walk beyond, through a devastated, wind-burned landscape. A lighthouse perches high above the waves; there are no other facilities, and when, as so often, the whole place is shrouded in thick mist and the mournful foghorn wails across the sea, it's an eerie spot. The treacherous "Coast of Death" just north of here has been the scene of innumerable shipwrecks, most recently that of the *Cason* in December 1987, when several towns had to be evacuated to escape the potential explosion of its cargo of dangerous chemicals. Even scavenging for shellfish along the rocks can be lethal; old women have been known to be swept away by the dreaded "seventh wave."

CORCUBIÓN, 14km shy of Finisterre, has the **hostales** *Casa Pachín* (Avda. Marina 4; ☎981/745018), quite cheap but not very welcoming, and *La Sirena* (c/Antonio Porrua, ☎981/745036), but while it may once have been elegant it's now deteriorating fast behind its brave seafront facade. Some of its backstreets are all but abandoned. **CÉE**, by contrast, 2km farther along, is expanding all too rapidly into a major industrial port. That has to be good for the ailing local economy, but it's turning out to be quite an eyesore. The ideal stopover on a car-tour is beside the magnificent white sand beach at **SARDIÑEIRO**, halfway between Finisterre and Corcubión, though there's nothing to do there in the evenings. In a curve of the road nestle the **campground** *Ruta Finisterre* (open June.–Sept., ☎981/745585) and the **hostal** *Playa de Estorde* (open all year, also ☎981/745585), with impressive but relatively safe waves.

Last of the Rías Altas

Around **EZARO**, where the Río Xallas comes to the sea, the scenery is marvelous, more African than European. The rocks of the sheer escarpments above the road are so rich in minerals that they are multi-colored, and glisten beneath the water of innumerable tiny waterfalls. At Ezaro itself a hydroelectric power plant clinging to the bleak hillside manages to look awesomely appropriate, while farther upstream there are warm natural lagoons and more cascades. The *Bar Stop* (☎981/745358) has cheap **rooms**, or you could continue another couple of kilometers to the charming little port of **PINDO**. Beneath a stony but thickly-wooded hill dotted with old houses, there's the *Hospedaje La Morada* to sleep at and the *Marisquería La Revolta* to eat seafood in.

Toward **CARNOTA** the series of short beaches finally join together into a long unbroken line of dunes, swept by the Atlantic winds. The village of Carnota is a kilometer from the shore, but its palm trees and old church are still thoroughly caked in salt. It boasts the longest *horreo* (granite grainstore) in Galicia, and presumably therefore in the world, built for that express purpose in 1966 and Not Interesting in the extreme. However, the **fonda** *Miramar* (☎981/857016) is large, cheap, and comfortable.

The Ría de Muros y Noya

Some of the best traditional Gallego architecture outside Pontevedra can be found in the grand old town of **MUROS**. It rises in tiers of narrow streets from the curve of the seafront to a Romanesque church; everywhere you look are squat granite columns and arches, flights of wide steps, and benches and stone porches built into the housefronts. The old market building in particular is almost a miniature Versailles palace. A sea-facing room in any of the several **hostales** should be a pleasure; *La Muradana* (☎981/826885) is recommended, if the most expensive. Muros shares some of the more enjoyable aspects of the Maine coast on a windy winter's day, with many good *tapas* bars to choose from, and (weather permitting) there's a **campground**, *A Bouga* (☎981/826025) beside the beach 2km out at LOURO. An artificial beach is being prepared in Muros itself, and in some places the prices are already rising in anticipation of a future tourist boom.

The larger town of **NOYA** (Noia), near the head of the first of the RÍAS BAJAS, is according to a legend fanciful even by Gallego standards named after Noah, whose Ark is supposed to have struck land nearby. Scarcely less absurd is Noya's claim to be a "Little Florence," on the strength of a couple of nice churches, and an arcaded street, and if you're coming from Santiago or farther south it makes more sense to pass straight through Noya and head for Muros and beyond. If you do want to halt, you'll be made welcome; the *Tasca Típica* is just what it says, a good old-fashioned bar, and among the **hostales** the *Sol y Mar* (☎981/820900) is the best value.

The southern side of the Ría de Muros y Noya, which is sometimes called the "Cockle Coast," is quite dauntingly exposed, although in good weather the dunes serve as excellent beaches. At **BAROÑA** (Basonas), a rocky outcrop juts from the sand into the sea, and built on top of it you can still see the ruins of an impregnable pre-Roman settlement, with round stone huts enclosed behind a fortified wall. From here you can follow the increasingly bleak coastal road around into the RÍA DE AROUSA, or take a shortcut through the deep lush gorges along the LC301 to PADRÓN.

THE RÍAS BAJAS AND THE MIÑO

Only in the three lowest of the RÍAS BAJAS, the Rías de AROSA, PONTEVEDRA, and VIGO, can Galicia be said to have much of a tourist industry. The summer sun is more dependable and the climate milder, avoiding the worst of the Atlantic storms, which tend just to brush the northwest corner. Each of these narrow inlets is in any case sheltered by islands and sandbanks right offshore. They are deep and calm beneath mountains of dark pines, busy with bright fishing boats and mussel rafts, and fringed with little towns of whitewashed houses and safe bathing beaches. Most of the visitors are Gallego or Portuguese; there is none of the overexploitation of the Mediterranean resorts, and only in the areas around Vigo and Villagarcía is the coastline even built up for any considerable distance. To the south, the slow, wide, mist-filled Río Miño marks the border with Portugal, and can be followed inland in search of unspoiled towns and hilltop monasteries, but the chief pleasures of the region are to be found by the sea. The two most obvious bases are PONTEVEDRA and VIGO, each dominating its own magnificent and spacious *ría*.

Ría de Arosa (Arousa)

Padrón and the North Shore of the Ría

The corpse of Saint James arrived in Galicia by sailing up the Ría de Arosa as far as PADRÓN, where his miraculous voyage ended. The modern town has surprisingly little to show for the years of pilgrimage, save for an imposing seventeenth-century Church of Santiago in which, if you can find the boy in charge of the key, you can see the *padrón* (mooring post) to which the vessel was tied. Padrón is no longer on the sea — the silt of the Río Ulla has stranded it a dozen kilometers inland — and it is not an exciting place to stay, despite having several hostales and a top-quality pulpería (octopus restaurant).

The poet Rosalia de Castro (1837–1885) was born in Padrón, the illegitimate (of course) daughter of a priest. She is still revered as one of the great champions of the Gallego language, and a "Circuit de Rosalia" has been organized to take in the main sites of her life. Chief of these is her former house, which is now a museum. Sorry to say, it's tedious in the extreme, containing little more than a couple of framed 500-peseta banknotes (which feature her portrait), schoolchildren's stick-figure drawings of "Rosalia and her children,"

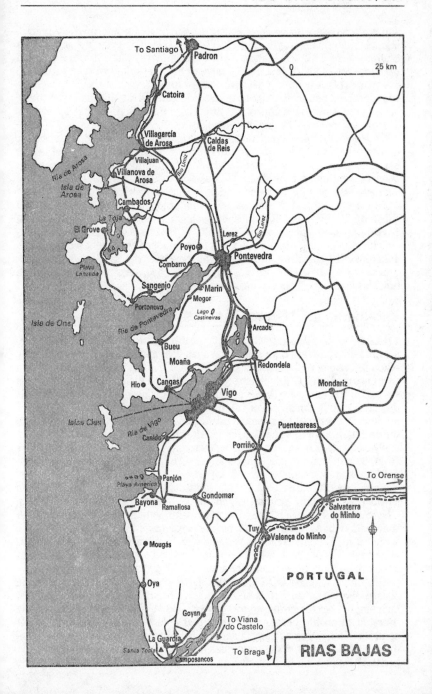

RIAS BAJAS

and a glass case with a pile of cassettes which we are informed are recordings of children singing her poetry. The house itself is ordinary, and is right by the Padrón **RENFE station**, which is a little way out of town; if you had the presence of mind, you could easily see all you wanted without getting off the train. This is a shame, because Rosalia herself was a fascinating woman, who deserves better. Her public image, and cultural significance even today, have brought her the status of an Alfred Lord Tennyson; but her poetry was as fresh and personal as that of Emily Dickinson.

On a slightly more mundane level, Padrón is also renowned in Galicia for its **peppers**, available in the summer months only. What you get in a *tapas* bar under the name of *Pimientos de Padrón* might look like whole green peppers fried in a bit too much oil, but perhaps through the intercession of Santiago they acquire a transcendent sweet flavor.

The north side of the *ría* is quite underpopulated, with only RIANJO (Rianxo), BOIRO, and RIBEIRA being large enough to support **hostales**. **RIBEIRA** (also known as SANTA EUGENIA) is a thriving fishing port, which has good restaurants but also a lot of modern apartment buildings. On either side of the town there are long beaches; the small *Coroso* **campground** (☎981/838002) on the Playa de Coroso, next to the C550 road, provides an escape from staying downtown.

Villagarcía to El Grove: The First Real Resorts

VILLAGARCÍA (Vilagarcía) and its near-neighbor **VILLANUEVA** (Vilanova) to the south are both somewhat shapeless and industrial, but sit in easy reach (by bridge of the wooded **ISLA DE AROSA** out in the *ría*, which has a **campground** and a lot of empty beaches. In Villagarcía itself, which is served on the Santiago–Pontevedra rail line, the cheapest of the **hostales** is the *82* (Pl. de la Constitución 13), or you can try the newer ones nearer the market. The seafront bars remain unaffected by tourism; there's one in which the ancient proprietress nestles behind the counter amid a huge and immaculately clean stack of wartime British newspapers, and the *Bodega de Los Arcos* at no. 68 on the promenade is friendly, lively, and serves good wine, cheese and ham at rock-bottom prices.

On the road towards **VILLAJUÁN** (Vilaxoan) about 1km out of Villagarcía is what is popularly acknowledged to be the best restaurant in Galicia, **Chocolate's**. The walls are festooned with letters of praise from such sources as Juan Perón, *La Oficina del Presidente*, Buenos Aires, and the former P.M. Edward Heath of Westminster, London. The flamboyant owner personally serves clients with two-pound impaled on pitchforks, and the fish is superb — though the prices are around 2500–4000ptas per head.

You enter **CAMBADOS** from the north via a remarkable paved stone square, the **Plaza de Fefiñanes**. There are beautiful buildings on all sides, including a seventeenth-century church and a *bodega*, but it's normally deserted, probably because the road that cuts diagonally across it is not controlled in any way and any pedestrian is therefore at constant risk of imminent death. The rest of the town does not quite live up to the promise of the square. The port is pleasant, with an authentic stench of fish, but the streets generally lack character. Unless you can afford to stay at the **parador** (the *Albariño*, ☎986/542250), there is but one reasonable *hostal*, the *Casa Rosita* (c/Isabel II 11, ☎986/542029).

El Grove

The coast road then curves back on itself to the well-kept town of **EL GROVE** (O GROVE). Apart possibly from Bayona (see below), this is the only town in Galicia whose principal *raison d'être* is the tourist trade, but like Bayona it's none the worse for that. It's full of cheap and small-scale bars, restaurants, and *hostales*, all packed throughout the summer, but there's room for all on the local beaches. The largest of these is *La Lanzada*, which is discussed under the RÍA DE PONTEVEDRA in the next section of this guide, but you can also walk across the sandy causeway to the tiny pine-covered islet of **LA TOJA** (A TOXA). Here, amid the trees, has been built a luxury vacation complex with two five-star hotels, a casino, and sports facilities. Surprisingly, it's not too intrusive, and you're free to wander around and down to any of the scattering of quiet coves. The water is the warmest in Galicia, the sea being so shallow, and there are simple beachside cafes to keep you going. El Grove has literally dozens of **hostales**, mostly along the Avda. González Besada and c/Teniente Domínguez; among the cheapest, and open all year, is the *Encontrada* on Raposeira.

The Inland Route

For the moment there is no sign of the construction of the long-promised (and long-opposed) section of expressway to link Santiago and Pontevedra. If you take the existing inland road (the N550) you come, halfway between Padrón and Pontevedra, to the spa town of **CALDAS DE REIS**. Here there's a Roman fountain, the waters of which, should you be so foolhardy as to drink them, guarantee that you will be married within a year. At the exact point where the road crosses the Río Umia, there's a gorgeous bar/restaurant, **O Muiño**, down under the bridge next to a broad clear weir. The barbecues and the octopus are unbeatable; the one hazard is that a local fly-fisherman may land a trout directly onto your plate!

Ría de Pontevedra

Pontevedra

PONTEVEDRA is the definitive old Gallego town, a maze of cobbled alleyways and colonnaded squares, with granite crosses and squat stone houses with floral balconies. There are some "sights" to see — the museum is good, and there are several interesting churches — but the real joy of visiting Pontevedra is to spend time in an ancient town that is so lively and lived-in. It's perfect for a night out; the traditional local food and drink are both at their best. Pontevedra is very compact, despite being the administrative capital of a province which includes the much larger city of Vigo. The town's growth was curtailed by the silting up of its medieval port (from which one of

Columbus's ships supposedly sailed; there is even a long-standing claim that Columbus was born a Gallego in Pontevedra). There are some slightly dismal industrial suburbs, but the old quarter, the *Zona Monumental*, remains distinct and unchanged, lining the banks of the Río Lérez and cradled in the sweeping crescent of the main boulevards.

Orientation

Both the **bus** and **train stations** are about 1km from downtown, side by side, and served by intermittent city buses which will drop you next to **La Peregrina**. This is a small pilgrim chapel built in the shape of a scallop shell, standing next to a square which has different names on different maps but is known locally as the **Herrería**. This paved *piazza*, lined by arcades on one side and rose trees on the other, is the border between the old and new quarters of Pontevedra. To the east is the town's main church, **San Francisco**; during the annual August festival men on motorbikes have been known to ascend a tightrope from the square to the top of its tower. All around there are fountains, gardens, and open-air cafes, old women playing cards and teenagers courting, and the daily rituals of life going on in a town small enough for everyone to know everyone else.

A selection of narrow lanes lead north from the Herrería into the **Zona Monumental**. Following c/Figueroa, you come to the small and shaded **Plaza de Leña**: *the* postcard image of Pontevedra, a "typical" Gallego square complete with granite columns and a calvary. Two of its mansions have been joined to form an elegant and well-conceived **Museo de Historia** (11am–1pm and 5–8pm), the works of painters such as El Greco and Breughel the Elder finding sympathetic echoes in their setting. Star exhibits include the jet jewelry from Santiago de Compostela, which held a monopoly on the stone throughout the Middle Ages, and the pre-Roman gold. Security is unusually tight; the staff keeps your passport for the duration of your visit.

If you want to buy some of the local earthenware **pottery**, there's a shop selling the standard stuff at reasonable prices on the corner of c/Isabel II and c/Real, or there's a big **open-air market** in the Plaza de Barcelos on the first of each month. Finally, the **Alameda** leading down from the Plaza de España is a grand promenade down to the sea, with a monument to Columbus where the river empties into the Atlantic.

Drinking, Eating, and Staying

All the twisting streets of the *Zona* are packed with tiny **bars**, and jammed late into the night with drinkers and revelers. You'd probably do best to eat in the bars, rather than looking for a restaurant. Platters of fish and jugs of rich white wine are available everywhere, with the c/Isabel II, especially around the junction "Os Cinco Calles," where there's another calvary, being the epicenter of the activity.

Among **bars** to check out during an evening's meandering is *O Salnes* on c/del Puente, near the river, an excellent place to eat, with a wide range of cheap seafood *tapas*. *Tasca O Quente*, high up on the "Campillo," serves *pasa*, a sweet, white, sherry-like wine. You drink it from *porrones*, thin-spouted glass flasks modeled on goatskins, and sit outside on the walls next to the

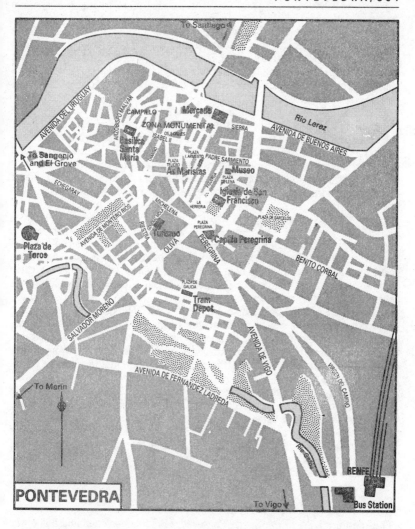

To Santiago

AVENIDA DEL URUGUAY

CAMPILLO

Mercado

ZONA MONUMENTAL

SIERRA

Rio Lerez

AVENIDA DE BUENOS AIRES

ARZOBISPO MALVAR

OS DOLLES
ISABEL II

Basilica
Santa
Maria

To Sangenjo
and El Grove

ECHEGARAY

PLAZA
I. ARMESTO PADRE SARMIENTO

PLAZA
TEUCIDO

As Maristas

Museo

PLAZA
CHLENA

Iglesia de San
Francisco

LA
HERRERIA

PLAZA DE BARCELOS

MICHELENA

RIESTRA

AVENIDA DE MONTERO RIOS

OLIVA

PLAZA
PEREGRINA

Turismo

Capilla Peregrina

PEREGRINA

Plaza de
Toros

BENITO CORBAL

SALVADOR MORENO

PLAZA DE
GALICIA

Tram
Depot

AVENIDA DE VIGO

VIRGEN DE CAMINO

To Marin

AVENIDA DE FERNANDEZ LADREDA

RIO

RENFE

PONTEVEDRA

To Vigo

Bus Station

Basilica de Santa María. At c/Real 14, the elderly Señor Ríos and his wife Alicia run a nameless and unmarked bar in the back of their grocery shop. The two run-down rooms are filled with barrels, wooden tables deeply etched with graffiti, and the dissolute youth of Pontevedra. Here too you drink *pasa* with fresh peanuts.

In *As Maristas*, in the Plaza I. Armesto, wicker baskets of crabs and winkles are propped up on the counter. But the position of this bar in a league of its own is entirely due to its former owner, Paco, now retired, who passed on his recipe for the astonishing liqueur **Tumba Dios**. It's a home-made concoction of *aguardiente* (firewater) and *licor de café*, laced with sundry secret herbs and spices. The alcohol is devastating; the coffee invigorating; and the herbs verge on the hallucinogenic. Paco rationed it out, two small glasses to a customer; if you asked for another he'd say "We're human beings, not animals!", and if you came in drunk he'd deny it even existed. For the morning after, try the *chocolate con churros* at c/Sierra 14, just up from the (very good) covered market.

There is not all that much budget **accommodation** in Pontevedra;the choicest spot in the *Zona* is as usual an expensive *parador*. Two **fondas** are opposite each other on the charming Plaza Teucro (named after the Trojan who allegedly founded the town), a couple more are in the c/Charino, and there are a pair of more or less affordable *hostales* (*Madrid*, Andrés Mellado 11, ☎986/851006; and *Avenida*, Virgen del Camino 70, ☎986/851298). If you can't find a room, consult the lists at the **Turismo** at c/General Mola 3.

North Shore of the Ría

Pontevedra is a good base for expeditions along either shore of its *ría* — such expeditions made necessary by the fact that the town doesn't itself have a beach. To the north, very near, is the **monastery of Poyo**, and farther along the coast the village of **COMBARRO**, justly famed for its waterfront *horreos*, resembling miniature chapels with their granite crosses. Beyond are the towns of **SANGENJO** (Sanxenxo) and **PORTONOVO**, busy and popular resorts whose main selling point seems to be their quite dreadful discos, capable of playing entire *Black Sabbath* live albums twice in succession. Sangenjo is marginally the more attractive, with a market on Monday mornings right by the sea, and has more **hostales**, but neither is very much recommended.

A few kilometers beyond begins the vast **beach** of **La Lanzada**, a favorite of strong swimmers and a mecca for **windsurfers**. In the summer there are temporary enclaves of cafes and restaurants, and **campgrounds** such as *O Revo* (☎986/743160) and *Espiño* (☎986/731248); during the rest of the year it's left to the wild ocean waves. Families looking for safer swimming, or just a nicer place to stay than Portonovo and Sangenjo, are advised to continue to El Grove (see under "Ría de Arosa" preceding).

South Shore of the Ría

The southern bank of the Ría de Pontevedra is less developed and has fewer visitors, although once past Marin it's quite superb. The first stretch, however, is off-putting in the extreme. A very frequent and very slow **tram** service (actually a trolleybus — the original trams were scrapped a decade ago) rattles as far as Marin from the Plaza de Galicia in Pontevedra, and there are faster buses right around the headland from the bus station. Just outside (and upwind from) Pontevedra sits a monstrous paper factory, **La Cellulosa**, where a titanic yellow metal spider spouts mountains of sawdust and excretes a staggering stench; on a bad day you can smell it fifty kilometers away. The factory owners try to make amends for this environmental outrage by sponsoring local youth soccer teams, but as the area's main source of jobs its position is secure, and some people claim that it serves a useful purpose by sparing the district from being over-run with tourists.

Marin

Nearby **MARIN** is not on first impression all that appealing. It's a very busy port, with the seafront cut off from the town by forbidding walls for most of its length, and populated largely by bored cadets from the local naval academy. Even the wooded island in the middle of the *ría* belongs to the Navy, and is inaccessible.

However, Marin does boast the best **churrasquería** in Spain, the *Cantaclara*, which is very cheap and almost impossible to find, being housed in what looks like a deserted blue shed near the harbor, about a mile back towards Pontevedra from the middle of town. The window display has been known to feature two completely skinned dead lambs, one of which is wearing a pair of green plastic sunglasses and has its teeth firmly clamped into the throat of the other. Inside, there's a huge roaring flame from the wooden fire of the barbecue, and the restaurant itself is screened from the bar by stacks of boxes of the Rioja house wine. The charcoal-grilled meat of all kinds is delicious.

The *Cantaclara* is opposite the *lonja*, where the fishing boats come in, and after eating you can wander over to watch them unload and auction the night's catch. That goes on from about 9pm until well after midnight, and just about all night a restaurant called *O Coxo* next to the *churrasquería* cooks the freshly-caught fish for the fishermen. Marin has **rooms** above the *Bar Alameda* in the main square, and the *Hostal del Mar* (☎986/882394) in the Avda. Jaime Janer.

Beyond Marin: Mogor and Bueu

Once past Marin, the scenery rapidly improves, the bay broadening and acquiring a whole series of breathtaking and virtually deserted sandy coves. The coast road itself narrows once past the naval academy outside Marin and leads down toward two little beaches. The second of these, the **Playa de Mogor**, is perfect, with fields of green corn as the backdrop to a crescent of fine, clean sand. A couple of bars overgrown with vines are the only buildings, and the villagers' rowboats are pulled up in the shade of the trees beside a gentle stream. One side is shielded by a thick headland of dark green pines; at the other end you'll find the rocks are deeply carved with religious and fascist symbols and slogans.

In fact rocks all over the surrounding hills were carved by the same man, a shoemaker who spent the afternoons of his declining years glorifying God and Franco with hammer and chisel on every available surface. In the late 1970s, when the carver was in his nineties, a professor found some carvings in Mogor and announced that they were prehistoric. The villagers said no, that's just the old shoemaker. So the professor and the shoemaker spent days combing the area, the shoemaker having to separate his carvings from those which had already been there. Some of the cruder stone spirals were duly authenticated as megalithic remains, and the professor wrote a book and made a TV documentary. The shoemaker died in virtual ignominy.

BUEU (pronounced *bwayo*) is a quiet market town and port about 12km beyond Marin, and offers another stupendous strip of **beach** stretching away from its rambling waterfront. The two **hostales**, *A Centoleira* (☎986/320896) and *Estevez* (☎986/320067), are good value. The main road turns away from the sea here, towards Cangas, but if you make your own way along the coast, towards the village of **ALDAN** and the cape of **HIO**, you'll find an unspoiled expanse of pine trees and empty beaches — an ideal place to go **camping** if you stock up in advance. Hio itself has Galicia's best-known granite *cruceiro* (not a "passenger liner" as the official brochure translates it, but a crucifix), looking down on the spectacular *ría* of Vigo.

Ría de Vigo

The Morrazo Peninsula: South Shore

Following the main road south from Bueu, you cross the steep ridge of the Morrazo peninsula to astonishing views on the far side over the **Ría de Vigo**, one of the most sublime natural harbors in the world. This region was once a hotbed of witchcraft, although Gallegos are careful to distinguish between *brujas* (malevolent witches) and *magas* (wise women herbalists with healing powers). Tradition tells of a local woman who was accused of trafficking with the Devil by the Inquisition in the seventeenth century; she proved her claim to be a *maga*, and received the sentence of having to stand outside Cangas church in her oldest clothes every Sunday for six months. It would seem that she fell afoul of the Holy Inquisition in one of its more lenient moods.

CANGAS, where the road descends, is today a small resort, at its most lively during the Friday **market**, when the seafront gardens are filled with stalls. The town spreads perhaps a kilometer along the coast, though not up the hillside, to reach **Rodeira beach**. The only **rooms** available are at the far end, in the bars *Rodeiramar* (☎986/300011) and *Nova Mar*. The main cluster of **bars and eateries**, however, is around the port. *O Pote* at Avda. Castelao 13, opposite the derelict former fish market, is an inexpensive restaurant specializing in wonderful clams and baby squids, while the *Bar Celta* at c/A. Saralegui, up some steps slightly to the left of the jetty as you face the town, and looking out over the bay, is an excellent old-fashioned *tapas* bar.

A **ferry** (foot passengers only) leaves Cangas for VIGO every half hour, a lovely twenty-minute trip. For a while, two rival companies offered this service, their boats jostling for position on the jetty. A ruthless price-cutting war drove one out of business, and freed the other to charge as much as it wanted — although the 100-peseta fare is far from extortionate. A strike in January 1988 left the operation in the hands of a workers' cooperative. Hourly boats also leave from **MOAÑA**, 5km along the coast, which is similar to Cangas, including a fine long beach, but with fewer facilities. The **hostal** *Elec-Mar* (☎986/311742) is a short steep climb up from the port, or there are rooms at the *Bar Agieiro* on the Cangas road.

Both ferries operate from 6am to 10pm (9am–10:30pm Sun.). The appeal of the Moaña trip is that you sail right alongside the *mejilloneiras* of the *ría*.

These rope-rigged, ramshackle rafts, perched on the sea like water-striders and sometimes topped by little wooden huts, are used for cultivating mussels. On either route, you also see the twin towers of the vast suspension bridge which carries the Vigo–Pontevedra expressway over the *ría*'s narrowest point.

Beyond that is what amounts to a saltwater lake, the inlet of **San Martín**. The road and railroad from Pontevedra run beside it to REDONDELA, separated from the sea by just a thin strip of green fields, and pass close to the tiny San Martín islands which were once a leper colony. The calm waters here are deceptive; somewhere under them lies a fleet of galleons lost in 1702. Seeking shelter from a storm on the open sea, they ironically foundered on hidden sandbanks and went down with the largest single shipment of silver ever sent from the New World.

Vigo

VIGO is a large and superbly situated city, dominating the broad expanse of its *ría*. Seen from a ship entering the harbor, it is magnificent, although once ashore, you may find the views back out to sea to be its most attractive feature. It is so well sheltered from the Atlantic that the wharves and quays which make it Spain's chief fishing port are able to stretch along the shore for nearly five kilometers.

The declining passenger port has kept the prime spot in the middle of this extent. This was where Laurie Lee disembarked "with the whole of Spain to walk through," a journey marvelously recorded in *As I Walked Out One Midsummer's Morning* (see "Books" in *Contexts*). Here too generations of Gallego emigrants have embarked for and returned from South America, and Caribbean immigrants have had their first glimpse of Europe. The Southampton (England)–Vigo service is now suspended, and only the occasional cruise liner docks. Although on most days the only tourists who arrive at the **Estación Marítima de Ría** are those who've come on the ferry from Cangas and Moaña, the steep winding streets of the old city remain crammed with tiny shops and bars catering for the still-plentiful sailors.

Practicalities and Highlights

As you cross the road from the port, you can't miss the **Turismo**, who'll give you a free **map** and mark accommodation on it. You're much better off staying down here in the old streets, such as the Rua Carral, than in the more modern areas where the trains and buses come in, farther up the hill, although there are several to choose from up there as well.

The new **RENFE station** has direct services to Santiago, Barcelona, and Madrid, and down into Portugal. They've yet to build a central bus terminal, however; Vigo is the largest Spanish city not to have one. **Buses** towards Santiago, Orense and Lugo leave from the c/Uruguay, a side street near the train station and ten minutes' walk up from the port. More local buses to Bayona, La Guardia, and Tuy leave from the c/San Amaro, just off the Plaza de España, which is the highest point of the Gran Vía circling the inland side of the city.

Vigo has greatly expanded in the last 100 years without there being anything very much to see. The cobbled streets around the **c/López Puigcerver** (or *Calle Real*; once the main street) remain a focal point for visitors. Along the seafront early in the morning, booths and kiosks revive fishermen with strong coffee, while there and in the nearby **market** their catch is sold; all day long women stand at granite tables rooted in **Real Teofilo Llorente**, with plates of fresh oysters set out for passers-by. On the **Rua Carral** shops sell savage switchblades and exotic marine souvenirs, and in

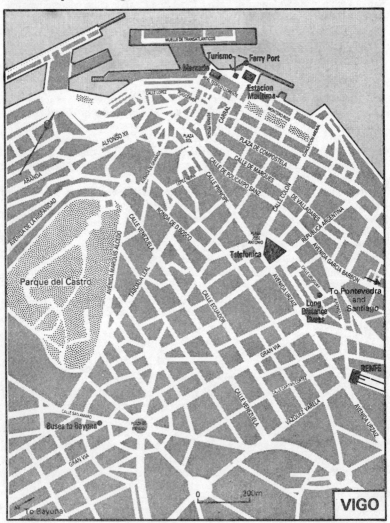

the evening the myriad bars on all the tiny streets come alive. A surprising old-fashioned red-light district still operates on the **Rua Abeleira Menández**, tucked away behind the town hall.

Among the cheaper **restaurants**, *O'Meu Lar* on Rua Fermín Penzal is worth recommending, while the **bars** *Moraña* and *Chevalos* on the c/Real stand out even in what has been called "the best drinking street in Christendom." More expensive tastes will lead you to seek out the local delicacy, *angullas*, the baby eels which arrive in the Río Miño fresh from the Sargasso Sea ready to be eaten. And if you feel the urge to buy a large papier-mâché mod on a papier-mâché scooter, try the *Pitacega* shop on Rua Carral.

The Islas Cíes

There are some reasonable beaches adjacent to Vigo — some, such as the one at **CANIDO**, equipped with campgrounds and *hostales*. However, the most irresistible coves of all must be those on the **ISLAS CÍES**. These are the three islands which protect the entrance to the *ría*, and they can only be reached by boats from the Estación Marítima. One is an off-limits bird sanctuary; the other two are joined by a narrow causeway of sand, which forms a beach open on one side open to the Atlantic and on the other cradling a placid lagoon. A long climb up a winding rocky path leads to a lighthouse with a commanding ocean view, but most visitors stay on the beach, with its sprinkling of bars and a campground in the trees.

This is the only legal accommodation on the islands, so if you want to stay in midseason, phone ahead to make sure there's room (☎986/421622), and take your own food and drink. In the summer there are six boats per day from Vigo (at 9am, 11am, 1pm, 3pm, 5pm and 7pm), the last one back leaving the islands at 8pm, with the round-trip costing around 600ptas. Only a certain number of visitors are allowed to go to the Cíes on any one day; aim for an early boat to guarantee admission. The season lasts only from mid-June to mid-September, and during the rest of the year you can't get out there at all.

Bayona and Around

BAYONA (BAIONA) huddles just short of the open sea at the head of a miniature *ría*, the last and the smallest in Galicia. It is also the region's name resort, though rampant commercialization has barely begun despite its popularity with the Spanish. This small and colorful port was the first place in Europe to hear of the discovery of the New World, when Columbus's *Pinta* appeared on March 1, 1493. Nowadays the harbor contains as many pleasure yachts as fishing boats.

The town is full of reasonably-priced **hostales** such as the *Asturias* (Alférez Barreiro 17, ☎986/355591) and the *Mesón del Burgo* (☎986/355309), and it's a terrific place to stay. The bars in the cobbled alleyway just behind the seafront are excellent; don't miss a fifteen-peseta glass of *pasa* at no. 44, and look for *tapas* at *Jalisco*, *O Buraquiño*, or *O'Breogan* in the road behind. All around the Plaza de Castro, **restaurants** such as *El Tunel* have enticing window displays of live lobsters and assorted shellfish.

The medieval walls which surround the wooded promontory which is Bayona's most prominent feature enclose an idyllic **parador**, partly hidden in a pine forest and with a reputation as Spain's best hotel. It's definitely worth paying the nominal fee to walk around the parapet, with an unobstructed view in every direction, across the *ría* and along the chain of rocky islets leading to the Islas Cíes (which, although near, cannot be reached from Bayona). There's a footpath beneath the walls at sea level, barely used, which gives access to several diminutive beaches. These are not visible from the town proper, which has only a small patch of sand despite its fine esplanade.

There are two good **beaches** next to the road in from Vigo a couple of kilometes before Bayona. The first is the **Playa de América** (take the Vigo–Bayona bus via PANJÓN — Panxon — not Nigran), a superb long curve of clean sand, backed by rows of vacation villas. This has its own **campground** (☎986/365404); the *Baiona Playa Camping* (☎986/350035), however, is nearer the town (and astride both bus routes) on the shorter and scruffier *Playa Ladeira* at Sabaris. Look out for the wonderful Roman stone footbridge at **RAMALLOSA**, between the two, and in Sabaris climb up the hill opposite the beach road for good cheap food at the very welcoming and gregarious *Churrasquería Franky*.

Buses from Bayona run from the c/Carabela la Pinta, near the anonymous new market building, except for the LA GUARDIA buses which barrel straight on around the headland; catch them opposite the *O Moscon* restaurant by the port.

The Coast Route to La Guardia

The road between Bayona and La Guardia, which once threaded through a deserted, windswept wilderness, has recently been improved and is now scattered with *hostales* and hotels; but they're only useful if you have a car. There are no beaches (although the sight of the ocean foaming through the rocks is mightily impressive), or even stores, and only three buses per day. Just outside Bayona on this road is the so-called *Virgen de la Roca*, a massive granite image overlooking the sea; it's possible to climb up inside her and onto the boat she holds in her right hand on appropriately solemn religious occasions. Halfway between Bayona and La Guardia is the town of **OYA** (Oia), no more than a very tight bend in the coast road, beneath which nestles a remarkable baroque **monastery**, with its sheer stone facade surviving the constant battering of the Atlantic.

The scrubby exposed hills around here are home to hundreds of **wild horses**, who sometimes venture down to graze by the sea. In May and June a series of day-long fiestas known as **curros** are held on successive Sundays on the hilltops farther inland. At these absolutely unmissable events the horses are rounded up, counted and branded, and set free again. Wooden corrals are built at clearings in the pine woods, and surrounded by makeshift stalls and bars set up among the trees. The misty dawns see riders swathed in crude, poncho-like blankets scouring the countryside, standing in stirrups like solid wooden wedges as they chase and lassoo the fleeing horses. Penned together the animals are magnificent, all sleek brown bodies and flashing eyes, tossing their unkempt manes and whinnying their disgust at being handled for the first time. It's very much a country festival, hugely enjoyed by the Gallegos you never see in the towns below, feasting on *pulpo* and picnicking in the woods, splashing dark wine from great barrels into chipped white bowls. Those villages currently holding *curros* include LA VALGA, TORROÑA, MOUGAS, and PINZAS. Ask at local tourist offices, or in the bars, for details; they're not organised for tourists, and so may not be advertised.

La Guardia and Celtic Remains

At the mouth of the great Miño river stands the disheveled and slightly disappointing port of **LA GUARDIA**, which is largely the modern creation of emigrants returned from Puerto Rico. In consolation you can **eat seafood** well and inexpensively (sometimes free if it's *tapas*) and search out **rooms**, possibly with a harbor view (*Hostal Martirrey*, José Antonio 8; ☎986/610349; or *Hostal Celta*, ☎986/610911)

Just above the town are the thick woods of **Monte Santa Tecla**, with extensive remains of a Celtic *citania* (pre-Roman fortified hill settlement), common in this part of Galicia, and even more so in northern Portugal. The ruins are about two-thirds of the way up the mountain, about half an hour's climb up a footpath-stairway cut through the forest; the way starts at the edge of La Guardia nearest Tuy.

The **citania** was probably occupied between around 600 and 200 B.C., and abandoned when the Romans established control over the north. It consists of the foundations of well over a hundred circular dwellings, crammed in tight inside an encircling wall. A few of them have been restored as full-size thatched huts; most are excavated to a few feet, though some are still buried. Set in a thick pine grove on the bleak, seaward hillside, the ancient village with its winding stone paths, wells or cisterns, and grand entrance ways, forms a striking contrast to the humdrum roofscape of La Guardia below. On the north slope of the *monte* there is also a large **cromlech**, or stone circle, while continuing upwards you pass along an avenue of much more recent construction, lined with the stations of the cross, and best seen looming out of a mountain mist.

At the top are a church, a small museum of Celtic finds, a relatively inexpensive one-star **hotel** (the *Pazo Santa Tecla*, ☎986/610002), and a cafe/restaurant. This last has a Gallego sign reading "Please don't go; stay and watch the television," but with the view up and down the Portuguese and Spanish coasts and along the Miño, and a good choice of *tapas*, you shouldn't need much persuading to stay.

La Guardia itself has only a small and rather shingly beach, but you can walk around the Monte Santa Tecla and down to the village of **CAMPOSANCOS** (about 3km) where, facing Portugal and a small islet capped by the ruins of a fortified Franciscan monastery, you'll find an adequate stretch of sand along the river bank, and a cafe. The new socialist council in La Guardia, along with promises to improve the look of the place, has pledged to revive a long-defunct ferry service linking the town (or more likely Camposancos) with CAMINHA in Portugal.

Along the Miño

The **RÍO MIÑO** (Minho in Portuguese and Gallego), the border between Spain and Portugal and so wide and beautiful upstream, is surprisingly narrow at its mouth. Only about 100 meters, mostly of sandbank, separate the two countries, and it's barely navigable. No large ships can wend their way inland to Tuy or Valença; Viana is the first port of any size on the Portuguese coast. The miles of dunes that stretch down to Viana in fact make for better beaches than those few around La Guardia on the Spanish side. At present, the first place at which you can cross the river is a few miles upstream at **GOYAN** (Goian), where a very cheap car ferry makes hourly journeys to the delightful walled village of VILA NOVA DA CERVEIRA.

Tuy

TUY (Tui, pronounced *twee*), 30km from La Guardia, is the main Gallego frontier town, staring across to the neat ramparts of Portuguese Valença. It is well connected with both Vigo and La Guardia and worth a visit even if you don't plan to continue across the border. There is, of course, the usual frontier-crossing street of tacky wares, but old Tuy stands back, tiered amid trees and stretches of ancient walls above the fertile riverbank. Sloping lanes, paved with huge slabs of granite, climb to an imposing fortress-like **Cathedral** dedicated to San Telmo, patron saint of fishermen; its military aspect is a distinctive mark of Tuy, scene of sporadic skirmishes with the Portuguese throughout the Middle Ages. There are other churches of interest too, like Romanesque San Bartolomeo, or Gothic Santo Domingo with its ivy-shrouded cloisters. More memorable, though, is the whole rambling pleasure of the place, coupled with a pair of enticing little river beaches. Nobody seems to mind if you camp beside them; otherwise there's a good **fonda** at the end of a small rectangular plaza, just off the main road at the base of the "monumental zone."

It's a twenty-minute walk to the Portuguese border, across an iron bridge designed by Eiffel; the little town of **VALENÇA**, dwarfed behind its mighty ramparts, lies a similar distance beyond. *Don't* do this journey by train or you'll be locked into the carriages for an hour or so while formalities are completed. A ferry, from SALVATERRA DO MINHO farther upstream, crosses to the similarly attractive old Portuguese town of MONÇÃO.

North of Tuy

There is a road from Tuy to GONDOMAR, and from there to BAYONA, which avoids Vigo and makes a spectacular drive through thick virgin forests, but no buses run that way. From **PORRIÑO**, halfway between Tuy and Vigo, the N120 is the most direct route to ORENSE, up very steep bleak mountains with not a habitation in sight. On the way, **PONTEAREAS**, has a **Corpus Christi** festival (in June) when the streets are spread out with gorgeous patterned "carpets" of bright flowers. Nearby, **MONDARIZ** is a pretty spa town with bathing beaches by a secluded river.

Upriver to Ribadavia and Celanova

Whether you follow the main inland highway or the rail line parallel to the Miño, one of the best towns to end up in is **RIBADAVIA**. The trip there by train from Tuy or Vigo is a lovely riverside journey, although the valley of the Miño does tend to fill up with freezing mist until midday or so. The town stands among woods and vineyards above the river, looking far grander than its size would promise, with several fine churches, including the Visigothic **San Ginés**, and a sprawling **Dominican monastery** which was once the residence of the kings of Galicia. Several marvelous **bars** serve the region's excellent, port-like wine, and there are a couple of **hostales**. The *Churrasquería Argentina* at c/Oliviera 8 prepares hearty, foot-long spare ribs, and rents out **rooms**.

The first hydroelectric dam blocks the Miño about 30km below Ribadavia, and it's from then on up that the flooding of the valley makes the river so broad and smooth-flowing, with forests right to the water's edge. The high and winding road along the south bank through **CORTEGADA** to the border at **SÃO GREGORIO** makes a good excursion, and can also be used as part of the route to **CELANOVA**. This is hardly more than a village, dominated by a vast and palatial **Benedictine monastery**. It was here that Felipe V retired into monastic life, having spent much of his reign securing the throne in the War of the Spanish Succession (1701–13). The monastery is now a school, but you can borrow the key to explore its two superb cloisters — one Renaissance, the other baroque — and the cathedral-sized church. Most beautiful of all is the tiny Mozarabic chapel of **San Miguel** in the garden of the monastery. This dates from the tenth century, and is the work of "Arabized" Christian refugees from al-Andalus. Buses also come in from Orense, and the **hotel** *Betanzos* on Castor Elices 12 (☎988/451036) is excellent.

Orense

ORENSE (Ourense) itself, the provincial capital, is worse than disappointing, having lost most of its atmosphere (along with its old buildings) in a straggle of anonymous modern suburbs. There are a few attractive small squares or *plazuelas*, and the approach is deceptively magnificent, across a seven-arched, thirteenth-century bridge. The **Cathedral** is the only building of any special interest, also thirteenth-century and built in imitation of Compostela's, with a painted (but greatly inferior) copy of the Portico de Gloria, and a museum in the cloisters. One startling feature is the police motorcycle depot beneath the steps; a door swings up and they all roar out. There are several **fondas** around the long main drag which leads from downtown to the train station, but Orense has a rather drab, soulless feel — astonishing when you consider that it was the birthplace of Julio Iglesias! (Fidel Castro's family was also from Ourense). It's a half-hour walk out to the **RENFE station**, on the opposite side of the river, so you can't expect to be able to drop in and see anything between trains. You'd do better to stay the night in Ribadavia and just pass through.

Gorges of the Río Sil

The Miño is ever more spectacular the further you go upstream; it arrives at Orense having flowed south from LUGO through the harsh landscape traversed by the *Camino de Santiago*. Twenty kilometers northeast of Orense it meets the Río Sil at **OS PEARES**, a crumbling old village on the main train line. You can walk from there along the **Gorges of the Sil**, with precarious farm terraces tumbling down to a chaos of rocks and foam. High above SAN ESTEBAN is another monastery, the three-cloistered **Monasterio de Ribas do Sil**. On the plain to the north, **MONFORTE DE LEMOS** is a major rail junction. Again, the station is a long way from the town center, but Monforte is a satisfyingly unspoilt and ancient place. Its **Torre de Lemos** looks out across a featureless expanse from the top of a hillful of tumbledown old houses, and there's a strikingly elegant Renaissance **Colegio** lower down.

To the south of the Sil, **MANZANEDA** is the only Gallego ski resort, offering most of the necessary facilities but not always the snow, and on the other side of the mountains is **VERÍN**, where a fine castle above the fortified town, on a site occupied since prehistoric times, is now a *parador*. At Verín you are once more within a dozen kilometers of Portugal, and can take a bus along the TAMEGA river to the rugged Portuguese frontier town of **CHAVES**.

fiestas

January
1 Livestock fair at BETANZOS.
6 Horseback procession of *Los Reyes* (the Three Kings), in BAYONA.
15 *San Mauro* — fireworks at VILLANUEVA DE AROSA.

March
1 CELANOVA's big festival, of *San Rosendo*, at the monastery above town.
28 Wine festival, with partying and music, at RIBADAVIA.
Pre-Lenten *carnivales* throughout the region, along with the *Lazaro* festival, a gathering of both Gallego and Portuguese folk groups, at VERÍN.

April
Palm Sunday Stations of the Cross at Monte San Tecla, LA GUARDIA.
Holy Week Celebrations include a symbolic *descendimento* (descent from the Cross) at VIVERO on Good Friday and a resurrection procession at FINISTERRE.
Second Monday after Easter *San Telmo* festival at TUY.
25 *San Marcos* observance at NOYA.

May
1 *Romería* at PONTEVEDRA.
22 *Santa Rita* at VILLAGARCÍA DE AROSA.

June
Sundays Country fairs and roundups of wild horses, known as *curros*, are held on successive Sundays in the hills above BAYONA and OYA; villages include LA VALGA, TORROÑA, MOUGAS, and PINZAS.
Corpus Christi Flower festival, with flower "carpets" in the streets, in PONTEAREAS.
24–25 Two days of celebration for *San Juan* in many locales, with processions of bigheads and *gigantones* on the 24th and a spectacular parades with fireworks and bands through the following evening.

July
First weekend *Rapa das Bestas* — capture and breaking in of wild mountain horses — at VIVERO and SAN LORENZO (Pontevedra). At the latter the horses are raced before being let loose.
11 *San Benito* fiesta at PONTEVEDRA, with river processions and competitions, and folk groups, and a smaller *romería* at CAMBADOS.

16 *Virgen del Carmen*. Sea processions at MUROS and CORCUBIÓN.

25 Galicia's major fiesta, in honor of St. James, at SANTIAGO DE COMPOSTELA. Among the various ceremonies, it is worth attending mass to see the National Offering to the Shrine (of the country and government) as well as the swinging of the *botafumeiro*. The evening before there's a fireworks display and symbolic burning of a massive cardboard effigy of the mosque at Córdoba. The festival, which is also designated "Galicia Day," has become a considerable nationalist event with traditional separatist demonstrations and an extensive program of political and cultural events happening for about a week in either direction. Lesser events in most other Gallego towns.

29 Octopus fesival at VILLANUEVA DE AROSA.

August

First Sunday Wine festival with tastings of the new Albariño at CAMBADOS; bagpipe festival at RIBADEO; *Virgen de la Roca* observances outside BAYONA.

16 *San Roque* festivals at all churches that bear his name: at BETANZOS there's a "Battle of the Flowers" on the river, at SADA (La Coruña) boat races and feasts.

24 Fiesta (and bullfights) at NOYA.

25 *San Ginés* at SANGENJO.

28 *Romería del Naseiro* outside VIVERO.

Last Sunday *Romería* sets out from SANGENJO to the Playa de La Lanzada.

September

6–10 *Fiestas del Portal* at RIBADAVIA.

8 *San Andreu* at CERVO.

14 Seafood festival at EL GROVE; *romería* with bigheads at VIVERO.

November

11 Fiesta of San Martín at BUEU.

Last Sunday Oyster festival at ARCADE (Pontevedra).

December

Last week Crafts fair "*O Feitoman*" at VIGO.

travel details

Buses

From Santiago de Compostela To La Coruña (hourly; 2 hr.), Betanzos/El Ferrol (4 daily; 1½/2½ hr.), Noya/Muros (10 daily; 1½/2½ hr.), Padrón/Ribeira (12; 1/2½ hr.), Corcubión/Finisterre (4; 3 hr.), Malpica/Camariñas (2; 2/3 hr.), Lalín (1; 1½ hr.), Lugo (6; 3 hr.), Villagarcía/Cambados (5; 1½/2 hr.), Pontevedra (hourly, 1½ hr.), Vigo (10, 2½ hr.), Orense (5, 4 hr.), Madrid (1, 10 hr.), and Oviedo/Santander/Bilbao/Irún (2 daily)

Also **International departures** (☎981/586433) to Oporto/Lisbon, Paris, Amsterdam, London, and Zurich/Geneva

From Pontevedra To Cambados (10; 1 hr.), Villagarcía (12; 1 hr.), Isla de Arosa (6, 1½ hr.), El Grove/La Toja (12; 1 hr.), Bueu/Cangas (16; 45 min./1 hr.), Bandeira (4; 2 hr.), Lalín/Lugo (6; 1½/2 hr.), Vigo (12 by inland expressway, 30 min.; and 12 by the coast, 1 hr.), Orense (4; 2 hr.), Monforte (1; 3½ hr.), Tuy (2; 2 hr.), Mondariz/Arbo (2; 1½/2 hr.), San Clemente/Cuntis (2, 1 hr.), and Andorra (2 weekly; 18 hr.)

From Vigo To Bayona (half-hourly; 45 min.), Tuy/La Guardia (hourly; 1 hr./2 hr.), Bayona/Oya/La Guardia (3 daily; 45 min./1 hr./1 hr. 15 min.), Santiago/Betanzos/El Ferrol (4; 2½/4/4½ hr.), Santiago/La Coruña (5; 2½/4 hr.), Villagarcía (2; 2 hr.), Noya (1; 3 hr.), Orense (8; 2 hr.), Lugo (6; 3 hr.), Carballiño/Chantada (2; 2½/3 hr.), Oviedo (2; 10 hr.), Madrid (2; 9 hr.), and Barcelona (3 weekly; 14 hr.).

From La Coruña To El Ferrol (hourly; 40 min.), Betanzos (12 daily; 45 min.), Lugo (4; 3 hr.), Finisterre (3; 2½ hr.), Corme (2; 1½ hr.), Camariñas (2; 2 hr.), Orense (3; 5 hr.), Vivero (2; 2½ hr.), Ribadeo (2; 4 hr.), Sobrado de los Monjes (1, 2½ hr.), Oviedo/Gijón (1; 7/8 hr.), and Madrid (2; 12 hr.)

From Lugo To Monforte (4; 1½ hr.), Orense (5; 2½ hr.), Foz (1; 2 hr.), Ribadeo (3; 2 hr.), Vivero (2; 2½ hr.), Oviedo (1; 5 hr.), and San Sebastián (1; 10 hr.)

From Orense To Celanova (1; 1½ hr.), Verín/Oporto (1; 1½/8 hr.), A Rua/Ponferrada (2; 2/3 hr.).

Trains

From Santiago To La Coruña (6 daily; 2 hr.), Pontevedra/Vigo (8; 1½/2½ hr.), Orense (3; 4 hr.), and Madrid (2; 8–10 hr.).

From La Coruña To Betanzos (10; 30 min.), El Ferrol (5; 1-11/2 hr.), Lugo/Monforte (2; 2½/3½ hr.), and Madrid (2; 9–11 hr.)

From Vigo To Tuy/Oporto (3; 1½/6 hr.), Orense/ Monforte (5; ¾ hr.), Barcelona (1; 15 hr.); San Sebastián/Irún (2; 12 hr.), and Madrid (2; 8–11 hr.)

From El Ferrol To Lugo/Monforte (2; 2½/3½ hr.)

Also **FEVE** line to Oviedo via Vivero, Ribadeo, and Luarca; 6–7 hr. total run, with only two through trains per day (currently 8am and late afternoon), and some busier stretches.

Local Ferries

From Vigo To Cangas (half-hourly; 20 min.), Moaña (hourly; 20 min.), Islas Cíes (6 daily in summer only; 1 hr.), and Isla de Ons (daily in summer; 2 hr.).

From Goyan To Vilanova do Cerveira, Portugal (hourly, 5 min.)

From Salvaterra do Minho To Monção, Portugal (hourly, 5 min.)

CHAPTER EIGHT

ARAGON

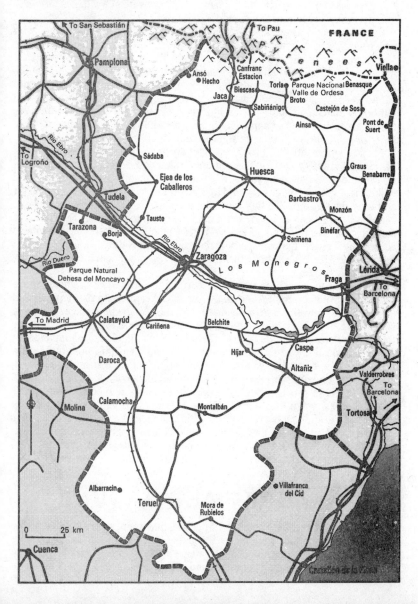

Most people prefer to travel straight through **Aragón**, regarding it as a kind of no-man's-land between Castile and Catalunya (Catalonia). In doing so they miss out on some of the most wonderful scenery in Spain, and some of the county's most attractive hiking. Certainly, coming from Catalunya, you're likely to be struck by Aragón's slower pace. In fact, many of its towns and villages are still untouched by any tourist development.

Politically and historically Aragón has close links with Catalunya, with which it formed a powerful medieval alliance, exerting influence over the Mediterranean as far away as Athens. Locked on all sides by mountains, however, it has always had a separateness, maintaining traditional *fueros* (like the Basques) and an individual kingdom until the end of the fifteenth century. Today, one of the least populated of the Spanish regions, it is well out of the political mainstream; Aragonese "separatists" do exist but they are hardly taken seriously as a movement, and certainly are far overshadowed by those of neighboring Catalunya and Euskadi.

In the south of the province, the isolated mountain villages of **El Maestrazgo** are typical of the region's unhurried aspect. They are little-known and little-visited — you may be an object of some interest to the local children — and the wild surroundings are stamped with severe, dark peaks and long river gorges. To the north, **Jaca** is the site of the first Romanesque cathedral in Spain. Beyond, the Aragonese stretch of the **Pyrenees** is certainly on the hiking and skiing map, but compared to the mountains across the French border, it's still remarkably unspoiled; the major target here, the **Ordesa National Park**, has only recently become accessible by public transportation.

There are, too, obvious but often surprising attractions in the region's distinctive architecture. **Zaragoza**, the provincial capital and the only place of any real size, sets the tone with its remarkable **Aljaferiá Palace**, the most spectacular Moorish monument outside Andalucía. And in a string of smaller towns — **Tarazona, Calatayud, Teruel** — you find the continuation of Moorish styles in **Mudejar** churches, towers, and mansions, built by Muslim workers in the early decades of Christian rule. Aragón also boasts a strong attraction in its local wines, particularly the highly alcoholic reds. Vineyards cover the whole province and it's possible to follow a specific **wine route** south from Zaragoza through **Cariñena** to **Daroca**. If you're visiting any of these "wine towns" such as the Monasterio de Piedra, be warned that for four days around October 12, there is an extended legal holiday for the Fiesta de Nuestra Señora de Pilar, when accommodation is scarce and official institutions are closed (it also coincides with Zaragoza's fiestas).

ZARAGOZA AND AROUND

Throughout Spain the last couple of decades has seen people drift from the villages and mountain regions to the cities, and Aragón is no exception. **Zaragoza** has been a target of this exodus, easily the largest and liveliest city in Aragón, with some excellent bars and restaurants tucked in among some remarkable monuments. It's also a handy transportation center, with good connections up into the Pyrenees and south to the **Mudejar towns** of Tarazona, Calatayud, and Daroca. Between Daroca and Zaragoza itself the "wine route" meanders through the quiet town of **Cariñena**.

Zaragoza

ZARAGOZA (*Saragossa* in its Anglicized form) is the provincial capital of Aragón, with over half the province's one million people and most of its industry. It's an interesting and inviting place, having managed to absorb its suburbs and rapid growth with a rare grace, and reflecting, in its center at least, an air of prosperity in its wide, modern boulevards and stylish shops and bars.

In addition, it preserves a number of very impressive monuments, most spectacularly the Moorish Aljaferia, but also a couple of good museums, some graceful churches, and two cathedrals. The most imposing of these, majestically fronting the river Ebro, is the **Basilica de Nuestra Señora del Pilar** (daily 5:45am–9:30pm), one of Zaragoza's two cathedrals and recently visited by Pope John Paul II. It takes its name from a pillar on which the Virgin is said to have descended from heaven in an apparition before Saint James the Apostle in A.D. 40. The pillar, topped by a diminutive cult image of the Virgin, forms the centerpiece in the Holy Chapel and is the focal point for pilgrims. Around the back of the chapel they line up to touch an exposed (and thoroughly worn) piece of the pillar, encased in a marble surround. As for the rest of the basilica, it was based on the late seventeenth-century plans of Fr. Herrera el Mozo (but altered and largely built by Ventura Rodríguez in the 1750s and 1760s): a monumental structure with four corner towers and a central dome surrounded by ten brightly tiled cupolas. It's quite unlike Spain's famous Romanesque and Gothic cathedrals, and seems almost too big, unsubtle even. But linger a little while for the organ to strike up in the cavernous interior, and it's hard to remain unimpressed. On the high altar, the main treasure of the cathedral, is a magnificent alabaster reredos, a masterpiece of Damien Forment, sculpted in the first decades of the sixteenth century.

Also inside the basilica, off the north aisle, is the **Museo Pilarista** (daily 9am–2pm and 4–6pm), where you can inspect at close quarters the original sketches for the decoration of the domes by Goya, González Velázquez, and Francisco and Ramon Bayeu. The small admission fee also buys entrance to the *Sacristia Mayor*, off the opposite side of the basilica, and to the excellent **Sacristy and Tapestry Museum** (with an art collection on the floor below), connected to the nearby Old Cathedral, at the far end of the pigeon-thronged Plaza del Pilar. Known as **La Seo** (daily 9am–2pm and 4–7pm), this is a Gothic-Mudejar structure with minor baroque and Plateresque additions and a Mudejar wall (to the left of the main entrance) with elaborate geometric patterns. Inside, the five aisles of the nave are impressive, while the superb *retablo mayor* contains some recognizably Teutonic figures executed by the German, Hans of Swabia.

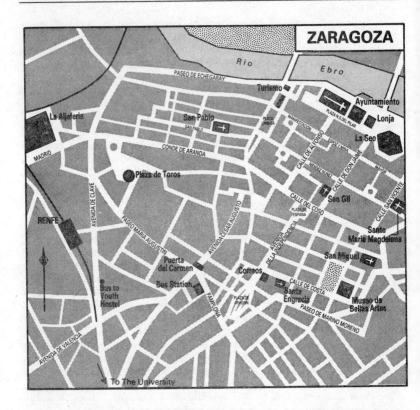

Midway between the two cathedrals stands the sixteenth-century **Lonja**, the old exchange building, with an interior of elegant Ionic columns. Over to the other side of the basilica, and now housing one of the city's tourist offices, is the **Torreón de la Zuda**, part of Zaragoza's medieval fortifications. Adjacent are the remains of **Roman walls**, insignificant ruins but a reminder of the city's Roman past — Zaragoza is a corruption of Caesar Augustus.

South, away from the river, follow the Avda. de la Independencia down to c/de Costa, on which is the church of **Santa Engracia**, with a splendid Plateresque portal and paleo-Christian sarcophagi in the crypt. Farther down, in the Plaza de los Sitios, is the **Museo Provincial de Bellas Artes** (Tues.–Sun. 11am–2pm; students and Sun. free), where numerous exhibits — Iberian, Roman, and Moorish — put both the city and the province of Zaragoza in good historical perspective. The first floor contains an extensive and varied selection of paintings from the fourteenth century to the present day, including a small but valuable collection of portraits by **Francisco de Goya** (1746–1828), the same versatile artist who decorated the basilica. Court painter to Carlos IV, he was a native of Fuendetodos, 45km south of Zaragoza, a village that retains a small and not very significant birthplace-museum. More rewarding if you're seriously interested is the **Cartuja de Aula Dei**, 12km north of Zaragoza, where in 1774 Goya painted a series of eleven murals on the lives of Christ and the Virgin. These unfortunately suffered badly following the Napoleonic suppression, when the buildings were more or less disused, but subsequent repainting and restoration has revealed enough to show the cycle to be one of the artist's early masterpieces. Sadly, only men can gain admission to the church of this strict Carthusian community, and even then on Wednesdays and Saturdays only (10am–1pm and 3–7pm); take the urban bus from *La Zuda* to the terminal at Montañana, from where it's about an hour's walk, straight ahead. Or ask at the tourist office for the times of the country buses that run past the Cartuja itself.

Even if you plan to do no more than change trains or buses in Zaragoza, the city's only surviving legacy from Moorish times is worth a visit. Moorish Spain was never very unified, and from the tenth to the eleventh century Zaragoza was the center of an independent dynasty, the Beni Kasim. Their palace — the **Aljafería** — was built in the heyday of their rule in the mid-eleventh century, and as such predates the Alhambra in Granada and Sevilla's Alcázar. Much, however, was added later, under twelfth- to fifteenth-century Christian rule, when the palace was adapted and used by the *Reconquista* kings of Aragón. From the original design the foremost relic is a tiny, and peculiarly beautiful, mosque, adjacent to the ticket office. Farther on, and currently under restoration, is an original and intricately decorated court, the Patio de Santa Isabella. Crossing from here, the Grand Staircase (added in 1492) leads to a succession of mainly fourteenth-century rooms, remarkable for their carved *artesonado* ceilings. The palace has been closed recently for restoration, but it seems to be nearing completion and may in fact be open. Assuming it is, hours are Mon.–Sat. 10am–2pm and 5–7pm, closed Sun. and Tues. morning and holidays; admission free. Check first at the tourist office. If you're making your way by car, be warned that it's poorly signposted and, with the one-way systems, difficult to find.

If you're interested in chasing the Moorish influence further, four **Mudejar towers** survive in Zaragoza, perhaps the finest of which is the square tower of the church of **Santa María Magdalena**, on the other side of La Seo from N.S. del Pilar, decorated with ceramics. Another is the octagonal tower attached to the church of **San Pablo**, on the way out to the Aljafería from the city center. Inside this church (daily 8–10am and evenings) is a large *retablo* by Damien Forment, this one of painted wood and not as fine as that of N.S. del Pilar. **San Miguel**, a few blocks away from the provincial museum, also has a Mudejar tower and a retable by Forment; the final surviving tower is on the church of **San Gil**, at the head of the El Tubo district.

There are a couple of **museums** worth seeking out too, both housed in impeccably restored palaces. The **Museo Camon Aznar**, Espoz y Mina 23, one block up from N.S. del Pilar (Tues.–Sat. 10am–1:30pm, Sun. 11am–2pm), displays the private collections of José Camon Aznar, one of the most distinguished scholars of Spanish art. It includes a number of minor works by well-known artists and permanently displays most of Goya's prints. The **Museo**

Pablo Gargallo (Mon.–Sat. 10am–1pm and 5–9pm, Sun. 11am–2pm, closed Tues.), on Plaza de San Felipe, is devoted to the works of the eponymous sculptor (1881–1934), an influential local artist during the 1920s.

Some Practicalities

Central Zaragoza is a straightforward grid and getting around presents few problems. Points of arrival, however, are scattered about and rather complicated. From the **railroad station** (*Estación Portillo*), walk down the short c/ General Mayandia, turn right on to Paseo Maria Augustín, take bus #21 right to Plaza del Pilar. Alternatively, it's a not unpleasant 25-minute walk, down to the Puerta del Carmen and then left. There are various **bus terminals**: for Huesca (5 daily) and Valencia/Alicante (1 daily) the main company is *La Oscencia* at Paseo María Augustín 84 (left from the railroad station); for Barcelona (several daily), Daroca (3 daily), and Lleida (Lerida) (Mon.–Sat. 4 daily, Sun. 1 daily), it's *Agreda* at Paseo Maria Augustín 7 (right from the railway station, close to the Puerta del Carmen). For all other destinations check with one of the city's three **Turismos**. There's one in the railway station (daily 9am–7pm) which is fairly useless but can provide a map, a second in the Torreon de la Zuda (Mon.–Fri. 8am–2:30pm/4:30pm–7:30pm, Sat. 9am–2pm), and, most useful, a third across from the Lonja in the Plaza del Pilar (Mon.–Fri. 10am–1:30pm/4:30pm–8pm, Sat. 10am–1:30pm).

There are **rooms** — and several cheap **restaurants** — close to the railway station, down the side streets off Paseo María Augustín. However, more atmosphere, better **accommodation** possibilities, and most of the city's **nightlife** are crowded into an area known as "El Tubo," between the central c/de Alfonso I and c/de Don Jaime I, close to the Plaza del Pilar. There are perhaps twenty *fondas* and *pensiones* here, rarely full, most tucked into wide, airy mansion blocks with deceptively impressive staircases. Try particularly c/Mendez Nunez and the tinier streets off it. Alongside, or often incorporated in, the *fondas* are countless impressive *tapas* bars, some good no-nonsense restaurants, and a few basic *comedores*; glimpse through every half-open door if you can — some of the cheapest are very low-key. Inexplicably, though, "the Tube" closes down early (around 11pm); for **late night** drinking or discos try the fringes of the quarter or the streets around the university, down Herman Cortses from the Puerta del Carmen.

An alternative for accommodation — and open all year except July — is the **youth hostel**, 2km from the center. From the railway station turn right along Avda. Clave, then on to Avda. Valencia; the hostel is at c/Franco y López 4, the fifth road on the right.

If you plan to go **skiing in the Pyrenees** you are probably better off buying a complete package deal from a travel agent in Zaragoza than turning up and going your own way. For the **Astún** resort, for instance, you could buy a weekend or week-long package that includes bed and breakfast in Jaca, bus transportation daily to the slopes, and ski equipment. One of the best agents to try is *Marsans* (Avda. de la Independencia 18), which also runs offbeat excursions to major rock concerts and occasional soccer games. There are other travel agents on Paseo María Augustín, towards the train station.

The Mudejar Trail: Tarazona, Calatayud, and Daroca

One of the most accessible and interesting towns in Aragón, **TARAZONA** lies about halfway along the main road from Zaragoza to Soria. It has the title "Mudejar City" and has even been dubbed "the Aragonese Toledo" — an overstatement, clearly, but if you are in the region it is certainly a worthwhile stop. Coming from the **bus station** the *Hostal Ruiz* — one-star and the most obvious **place to stay** — is a short walk downhill. Beyond, across the bridge, you come to the thirteenth-century church of San Francisco, outside which a rough map of the town shows the principal sights. There is a second, smaller, *hostal* on the road to Soria, across from the swimming pool.

The **Cathedral**, on the same side of the river, was begun in 1152 but dates mainly from the fourteenth and fifteenth centuries. It is a typical example of the decorative use of brick in the Gothic-Mudejar style. Its dome was built to the same design as that of the old cathedral in Zaragoza. The interior is undergoing restoration but with the help of a guide you can visit all parts of the cathedral, including the unusual brick-built cloisters.

It's the older **"upper town,"** though, on the hill overlooking the river, that is of most interest, especially the Plaza de España with its magnificent **Ayuntamiento**: the sixteenth-century Town Hall, with a facade beautifully decorated with coats of arms, sculpted heads, and figures in high relief. A frieze about one foot high, representing the capture of Granada, runs the length of the building. From here you're directed, by way of a *Ruta Turistica*, up to the church of **Santa Magdalena**, whose Mudejar tower dominates the town. Farther uphill lies another church, **La Concepción**, which has another slender brick tower. The *mirador* at Santa Magdalena gives a good view of Tarazona, especially the cathedral and the **Plaza de Toros**, which has been curiously converted into houses but retains the main features of a bullring.

About 15km south of Tarazona lies **Veruela**, one of Spain's great isolated monasteries. It makes an easy excursion, or alternatively a break on the journey to Zaragoza; you should get off the bus at VERA DE MONCAYO — it stops outside the village — and then walk uphill a few kilometers. The monastery, whose perimeter walls give it a strongly fortified appearance, is uninhabited now, but the large church, in the severe twelfth-century transitional style of the Carthusians, is generally kept open. You have to buy a ticket to see the fourteenth-century cloisters and convent buildings (closed for the usual siesta period); be sure to walk around the back for a view of the finely-crafted apses.

Due south of Tarazona (on the railway line from Zaragoza to Madrid) is **CALATAYUD**, a poor and univiting town but one in which you might find yourself if you're changing buses. Founded by the Moors in the eighth century, their influence remained strong throughout the Christian period, and the Moorish character of Calatayud is preserved in a maze of streets and alleys built on hills and a concentration of fourteenth- and fifthteenth-century church towers reminiscent of minarets. Two stunning Mudejar towers stand out, their ornate brickwork worth the wait between buses to see: the earliest of these is attached to the church of **San Andrés**, the largest and more refined to the collegiate church of **Santa María**, which also has a beautifully decorative Plateresque doorway. Ruins of the Moorish castle survive too, on high ground at the opposite end of town from the railway station. The views from here are outstanding, although for a closer view of the towers you'd do better to climb the hill to the hermitage, in the center of the old town. Calatayud's cheapest rooms are in a couple of *fondas* immediately across the square from the railway station at the edge of town, although there is much more accommodation in the center of town.

Calatayud is also the best center for an excursion to the **Monasterio de Piedra** or "Stone Monastery" (bus at 11am daily, returning at 5pm), whose scanty Cistercian ruins boast a beautifully green park in this otherwise harsh, dry landscape. If there are crowds, it will be easy enough to escape them here, though be warned that you're not allowed to take food into the park; if you've brought a picnic you'll have to eat it first. There are two **routes** through the park: blue arrows lead around the cloister and shell of the church to the twelfth-century **Torre del Homenaje**, whose mirador gives a panoramic view over the park; the red arrows take you past a number of romantically-labeled waterfalls, grottos, and lakes.

DAROCA, 40km from Calatayud and connected by both train (2 daily) and bus (better since the railway station is about 2km outside town), is a more pleasant place. A typical Aragonese town, it holds several Romanesque, Gothic, and Mudejar churches, and an impressive run of **walls**, comprising no less than 114 towers and enclosing an area far greater than needed by its present population of 2700. The last major restoration of these was in the fifteenth century, but today, though largely in ruins, they are still magnificent. The town gates are better preserved, notably the stout **Puerta Baja**, with its gallery of arches flanked by two towers and decorated with the coat of arms of Carlos I. For **accommodation** try *Bar Ruejo* on c/Major, which runs right through the town from gate to gate.

The Wine Route: Cariñena

There are vineyards all over Aragón, but some of the best wines — strong, throaty reds and good whites — come from the region to the south of Zaragoza, from the the towns and villages accessible from the train down to Teruel.

MUEL marks the northernmost point of the region and was once a renowned pottery center. Now most of the trains don't bother to stop here and if you want to see the Goya frescoes in its **Hermitage of Our Lady of the Fountain**, it's best to check the bus timetables with the tourist office.

CARIÑENA, too, has seen better days. The town hall clock stands permanently at 4:40 and the sundial on the eighteenth-century baroque church is old and cracked. But trains do stop and the local wine is fine. Out on the main road behind the church, the *Bodega Morte* (open every day) is the most obvious place to taste and buy. There's no tour although there's nothing to stop you from sampling first and then filling your wine bottles ridiculously cheaply from the huge barrels set up for that purpose. If you want to stay — and Cariñena, with its open-air swimming pool, is a quiet alternative to Zaragoza — there are excellent and cheap **rooms** at the *Pension Care* (☎078-820278) and the *Hostal Iliturgis* (both near the church and a 5-min. walk from the railway station). The *Care* has a good *comedor*, and at the *Iliturgis* there's more tasting. I was plied with free champagne and brandy in the restaurant here and then drunkenly embroiled in a singing tournament with fifty or so locals. I lost.

TERUEL AND THE RURAL SOUTH

The main routes of southern Aragón — particularly those connecting up with adjoining provinces — are reasonably well served by buses. **Teruel**, a kind of capital for the region and most distinctive of the "Mudejar towns," is especially well connected, lying on the train route between Zaragoza and Valencia. Off the main routes, though, into the **Maestrazgo** or the still more remote valleys and villages south of Teruel, progress can be slow. Much of this region remains completely untouched by tourism: even surfaced roads are sometimes scarce, and having your own transportation can be a big help (although hitching here is slightly better than in most parts of Spain). The rides are not likely to be long-distance but most people seem willing to stop; and if you can cut through the Aragonese dialects you may be able to arrange a lift for the next morning in some villages.

Teruel

Like Zaragoza, **TERUEL** was an important Moorish city and retained a sizable part of the old community after its Reconquest by Alfonso II in 1171. The Moors' architecture certainly endured, and you'll find here one of the most brilliant towers in the country, **El Salvador**, a sight prominently displayed on all the local tourist brochures. If this fails to excite you, Teruel admittedly doesn't have a lot going for it, but it's a pleasant enough place, and from here you're well located to explore some of the villages of the Maestrazgo, off to the east.

Arriving by train, the **Escalinata**, just outside, leaves you in no doubt as to the town's origins: a flight of steps decorated with bricks, tiles, and turrets is pure civic Mudejar in style. From the top of the steps follow c/El Salvador to the **Torre del Salvador**, first and foremost of the town's four Mudejar towers, covered with intricately patterned and proportioned coloured tiles. The effect is beautiful, one that's echoed closely in its more modest sister tower, **San Martín**, best reached via c/de Los Amantes (third left off c/El Salvador just at the corner of Plaza Carlos Castell). A common feature of all the towers is that they stand separate from the main body of the church, a technique surely influenced by the free-standing minarets of the Muslim world.

The first road to the right off c/El Salvador crosses two streets and leads straight to the **Turismo** at c/Tomás Nogues 1. Slightly uphill and to the left, the church of **San Pedro** (with another tower) has an adjacent chapel (daily 9am–1pm and 3–9pm) containing the alabaster joint tomb of the **Lovers of Teruel**, famous throughout Spain through a thirteenth-century tale of separation and broken hearts. Their bodies were exhumed in 1955 and now lie illuminated for all to see. The tomb is macabrely a kind of pilgrimage-place for newlyweds.

From here c/Hartzembusch leads to the **bus station** (on Ronda 18 de Julio), just beyond which is perhaps the most elegant monument in Teruel: a slender sixteenth-century aqueduct known as **Los Arcos**. In the other direction, towards the center, the **Cathedral** was built originally in the twelfth century (incorporating the last Mudejar tower) but has been gracefully adapted over subsequent centuries. Romanesque windows are incorporated into the brick tower, the lantern combines Renaissance and Mudejar features, while the interior follows the standard Gothic-Mudejar pattern. The carved and painted wooden ceiling of the nave (13th c.) in particular is outstanding.

There's a great deal of **accommodation** in Teruel; try the *Fonda Moderna* and *HR Goya*, on c/Nogues right outside the tourist office; *CH Alcodori*, Temperado 15, next to the San Martín tower; *CH Santa María*, Santa María 4, between the cathedral and the main plaza; and Fonda El Tozal, near the market hall. Be warned that if you're here for the raucous *Vaquilla del Angel* festival at the beginning of July every place in town will be booked solid, and you may have to join everyone else sleeping in the park down by the railway station. The real problem, however, is eating cheaply; there are only three rather expensive two-fork restaurants (one by El Salvador, the other two by the market).

Around Teruel: Albarracín and Ademuz

The extreme south of Aragón — below Teruel — is obscure enough to feature in Spanish magazines as "Undiscovered Spain," an indicator of both the strength of its rural tradition and the speed of change in the rest of the country. Much of the region is hard to get to, and even with your own transportation you'll find *pueblos* a few kilometers from one another not yet connected by proper roads. **ALBARRACÍN**, 37km west of Teruel, is one of the more accessible targets: among the most picturesque towns in Aragón, poised above the Guadalaviar river and retaining, virtually unchanged, its medieval streets and houses. There's a historical curiosity here too, in that from 1165 to 1333 the town formed the center of the small independent state of the Azagras. Over the last few years a small trickle of tourism has begun, and some of the houses have been prettied a bit too much. But its dark enclosed lanes and those buildings that remain *un*restored, with their splendid coats of arms, still make for an intriguing wander — remindergs of lost and now inexplicably prosperous eras. As at Daroca, the **town walls** enclose a far greater area than is needed, and following their circuit you gain a memorable bird's eye view of the town and surrounding countryside. If you want to stay — and you'll have to if you arrive by bus — there are two very

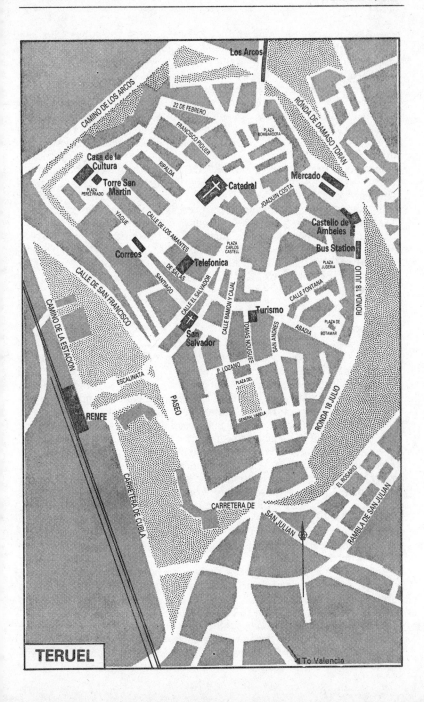

TERUEL

overpriced one-star **hostales** at the foot of the hill near the bus stop, and, oddly enough, a **youth hostel** (☎974/710005), open July to August only, just past the cathedral on c/Santa Maria. For those with transportation, a minor road, not marked on all maps, goes through beautiful country from Albarracín to CUENCA, by way of TRAGACETE.

Considerably more remote, and with a bleak grandeur all its own, **El Rincón de Ademuz**, due south of Teruel, is another strange little region, actually a Valencian province enclosed within Aragonese territory. Tourism here really has yet to make an imprint, and you'll be received everywhere with a marked curiosity. The place to head for — in fact, the only realistic place to get to from Teruel — is **ADEMUZ** itself, without a doubt Spain's tiniest and least significant provincial capital. Strung along a craggy hill at the confluence of two long rivers, Ademuz could make a beautiful base for hiking, though like Albarracín there's a certain fascination in just wandering the streets with their dark stone cottages and occasional baroque towers. If you want to stay, there's a single **hostal**, *Casa Domingo*. For real, energetic **hiking**, TORRE BAJA lies to the north, along the Guadalavia river, the beautiful village of CASTIELFABIB just beyond. The most interesting of these little hamlets, PUEBLO DE SAN MIGUEL, lies to the west, reachable by road only from Valencia.

El Maestrazgo

Albarracín should whet your appetite for a trek into the mountains of the **Upper Maestrazgo**, north east of Teruel. With its severe peaks, deep gorges, and lush fields, it's an area of great variety, and striking, often wild, beauty. Tourism, again, isn't a fact of life here, but you will find at least one simple *fonda* in most of the tiny, scattered villages. The places below are no more than a small selection of villages accessible by bus; armed with a good map and prepared to do some walking you could pick almost anywhere and be satisfied. Inevitably **buses** are infrequent (often their main purpose is to deliver the mail) but most places are connected once a day. If you are traveling by bus, an alarm clock is useful since buses have a nasty habit of leaving before dawn. Main approaches are from either Teruel (1 bus daily to Cantavieja/Villafranca del Cid) or Morella in the province of Castellón.

VILLAFRANCA DEL CID, a village built on and into a hill at the end of the bus route from either Teruel or Morella, gives a typical taste of the region. You'll feel very much a stranger here, but it's not hard to make friends with the local kids, who are likely to follow you around the town gaping. There's a really good *fonda* above a mechanics right by the bus stop, and a bar offering rooms just across the road. Leaving, you'll need to turn in early the night before: the daily bus (which travels on through the villages detailed below, and eventually to Teruel) departs at 5:45am.

It's a rough ride over some rough country, the road at times barely wide enough for the bus, often dwindling to a dusty track, to **L'IGLESUELA DEL CID** — the first stop and also reachable by one bus daily from Morella. The village's name, like Villafranca, bears witness to the exploits of El Cid

Campeador, who came charging through the Maestrazgo in his fight against the Infidel. Its ocher-red dry stone walls, ubiquitous coats of arms, and stream flowing right through the center that is used to irrigate allotments and provide water for the communal washing shed, are striking enough in this remote countryside. But apart from these features it's a shabby sort of place, with little going on and just one *fonda* on the main road. You'd be better moving on.

CANTAVIEJA, 1240m above sea level, is a little livelier, larger than most Maestrazgo villages, though its population is still under a thousand. The whitewashed and porticoed **Plaza Mayor** here is typical of the region, and the escutcheoned Ayuntamiento bears a Latin inscription with suitably lofty sentiments: "This House hates wrongdoing, loves peace, punishes crimes, upholds the laws, and honors the upright." Cantavieja's pair of reasonable **fondas** make it a useful base for exploring the nearby villages: L'Iglesuela del Cid is just 13km away and it's a splendid walk there; **MIRAMBEL**, 15km north east and walkable in about three hours, has a population of a mere 200 and preserves a very ancient atmosphere, with its walls, gateways, and stone houses. The main **bar** offers accommodation (though it has no sign saying so), and if you're lucky your stay will coincide with the Fiesta of Corpus Christi in May, when a communal quail-and-snail paella ("mountain paella") is served in the village.

From Cantavieja there is a choice of two routes back towards more populated parts, both of which are dramatic rides. The first is west to Teruel, twisting a way down across the valleys, following dried-up rivers, and thundering over tight, crumbling stone bridges. On the way you stop at **VILLAROYA**, just beyond the highest point in the Maestrazgo, where there is a bar to restore your shaken nerves. Not long before Teruel the road passes **CEDRILLAS**, with its conspicuous (and ruined) castle high on a hill. But the tortuous road to **ALCORISA** is perhaps even more exhilarating, for some distance following the edge of a precipice and with boulders sometimes blocking the way. It takes the bus nearly four hours to cover the 88km journey, which usually includes a short stop at **EJULVE**, a small village with two *fondas* and a bar decorated with the fearsome head of a boar. It is wild country indeed.

Actually just north of the Maestrazgo, the castle-topped town of **ALCAÑIZ**, about 40km on from Alcorisa, is not as interesting as it looks, but you may well find yourself here; it gives access by bus to VALDERROBRES (see below), and, by bus or rail, east to Zaragoza and west to the coast at TORTOSA or VIÑAROZ via Morella. You probably won't need or want to stay — there are two cheapish **hotels** if you do — but take the time in between bus connections to climb up to the twelfth-century **Castillo**, now ruthlessly modernized as a *parador*. Its heights afford good views over the town and the huge baroque church of **Santa María** which dominates it.

Though pleasant enough, Alcañiz, with a population of over 11,000, doesn't offer the same sense of isolation as the villages to the south. **VALDE-RROBRES**, near the border with Catalunya, on the other hand does, despite being one of the Maestrazgo's most accessible villages. Lying astride the Río Matarrana, whose crystal waters teem with trout, the old town is crowned by a castle-palace once occupied by the kings of Aragón, and a Gothic parish church — **Santa María** — which has a fine rose window. In the Plaza Major, the unassuming seventeenth-century **Ayuntamiento** was considered so characteristic of the region that it was reproduced in Barcelona's *Pueblo Español* in 1929; opposite is a very cheap and hospitable **fonda**.

NORTHERN ARAGÓN: THE PYRENEES

Though less extensive than the Catalan stretch, the Aragonese **Pyrenees** are the most spectacular and enjoyable part of the mountains on the Spanish side. There are a number of possible **routes** into the region. The quickest and most obvious way is direct from **Zaragoza to Huesca** by train. The town itself isn't a very enticing target, but the castle at **Loarre** is worth seeing and there are plenty of buses onwards; trains also run direct to Jaca if you're not in the mood to stop. More scenically, you could travel due east from Zaragoza to **Fraga** and head north from there up to **Barbastro**. Or, with a car, the route up from Zaragoza through the **Cinco Villas**, one of Aragon's most remote (and historic) regions, is a fine one, and leaves you well poised for either the Pyrenees or the mountains of Navarre, farther west.

Once in the mountains, **Jaca** is a central point for walking and/or skiing, and although you no longer need to stop here to reach the best spots, the town remains an attractive diversion, with one monument — its cathedral — the equal of any in Spain. Beyond Jaca, there are several really tempting alternatives for serious hikers, principally the **Parque Nacional de Ordesa** with its canyons and waterfall-dotted valleys, and to the east the **Pico de Aneto**, above the skiing village of **Benasque**. Equally beautiful and remote, the valleys of **Ansó and Hecho**, to the west, offer some less serious but fine rambles amid wonderful mountain scenery. For skiing, you might try the well-organized twin resorts of **Astún-Candanchú**. Sadly, there is no longer any train link through the mountains but you can still make the journey over the Pyrenees into France by bus from **Canfranc**.

Fraga to Barbastro

If you're approaching the Pyrenees from Catalunya, it's possible to skip Zaragoza altogether and follow a little-used minor route from Fraga, just beyond Catalan Lleida. It's not the quickest way into the mountains, of course, and if you're pressed for time you should either head straight for Zaragoza or at least take the bus directly from Lleida to BARBASTRO (5 daily), from where you're within striking distance of Benasque.

Whichever route you decide upon, it's worth taking a morning to visit **FRAGA**, only 25km from Lleida and linked by five buses daily. Its fine brick buildings help maintain the medieval air of the old town, perched high over the Cinco river. The bus will drop you at the bus station, from where you should cross back over the river and strike uphill through the steep and convoluted streets. The tower of the twelfth-century (restored and restyled) church of San Pedro keeps disappearing and reappearing until you reach a tiny square, dominated entirely by the church, with one bar and a *fonda*.

Two very early buses (6am and 7am, not Sun.) run directly on to Huesca from Fraga. Failing that you can either return to Lleida or hitch the minor road north along the eastern banks of the Cinco river to MONZÓN, from where there are buses on to BARBASTRO (the road starts immediately below Fraga's old town, over the bridge from the bus station). This can be hard work; the rides will be few and far between and usually in a variety of farm vehicles, but it's a rewarding route. Great steppes fall away to the west beyond the river while coarse vegetation and red clay cliffs flank the road. There are three or four mean, dusty villages on the way but nothing that tempts a stop until MONZÓN, cut by a dried-up river and topped by a forgotten, half-pint castle growing out of the crumbling rock above. Originally ninth-century, the fortification became a Templar castle in the twelfth century under Ramon Berenguer IV, and has a surviving — and reasonably interesting — single-aisled castle chapel.

There's no other reason to hang around before jumping on the Lleida–Huesca bus to BARBASTRO, 20km down the main road. A historic town of no small importance, it was here that the union of Aragón and Catalunya was officially declared in 1137, sealed by the marriage of the daughter of Ramiro of Aragón to Ramon Berenguer IV, Lord of Barcelona. Barbastro retains an air of importance even now, and what today is little more than a provincial market town is given color by some elegant buildings. The Gothic Cathedral, on a site once occupied by a mosque, has a high altar whose construction was under the authority of Damien Forment: when he died in 1540 only part of the alabaster relief had been completed, and the remainder was finished by his pupils. The Ayuntamiento, a restored fifteenth-century edifice designed by the Moorish chief architect to Fernando el Católico is also worth seeing. And there are some lovely fading mansions in the narrow streets, as well as a central tree-lined *paseo* at the top of the town, below the bus station — home, also, to most of the town's bars. A five-minute walk farther down the hill towards the river gives a choice of several hostales; try c/Argensola, one block back from the crossroads by the river, where *Hostal La Sombra* is cheap and cheerful. The best place to eat is next door in the *Bar Stop Meriendas* — no menu, but with a terrific range of dishes to choose from in the kitchen.

From Barbastro four buses daily leave for Huesca, one each to Benasque and Lleida. Accessible to those with wheels is the small town of ALQUÉZAR, superbly situated to the northwest, with a *colegia* in the cliffs overlooking the town, The *colegia* has a triangular cloister and minor works of art in the restored church upstairs. From Alquezar you can make the fairly spectacular hour-long drive north through the remote Sierra de Guara up to RODELLAR, the road zig-zagging around a series of arid canyons and giving access to some marvelous walks, not least along the Río de Vero.

The Cinco Villas

The **Cinco Villas**, which stretch for some 90km along the border with Navarre, together make up one of northern Aragon's more remote regions: a place of quiet, unexploited towns that tourism has yet to touch. There's one daily bus as far as Sos (see below), but otherwise it's a route best negotiated by car. Even the northernmost of the towns, SOS DEL REY CATÓLICO, falls well short of the Pyrenees proper, although each of them (TAUSTE, EJEA, SABADA, and UNCASTILLO are the others) has a quiet interest and a good feel. "Towns" is in fact a misnomer since none have more than a couple of thousand inhabitants, but they were officially raised to this status by Felipe V for their services in the War of the Succession (1701–13) — hence the grand collective title.

TAUSTE, closest to Zaragoza, has an interesting parish church built in the Mudejar style; nearby **EJEA** retains some elements of Romanesque architecture in its churches. **UNCASTILLO**, as its name suggests, boasts an impressive medieval castle, twelfth-century in origin; so does **SABADA**, this one dating from the thirteenth century, as well as the remains of an early synagogue. But **SOS DEL REY CATÓLICO** is the most interesting town and an excellent place to rest up, especially if you're on your way to or from Javier and Sangüesa in Navarre. The town derives its name from Fernando, "El Rey Católico," born here in 1452 and as powerful a local-boy-made-good as any Aragonese town could hope for. This connection inevitably lends its name to various aspects of the town (the *Fonda Fernandino*, for instance, which with the bar close by provides the only **rooms**) but there's little exploitation and only a token amount of tidying restoration. The narrow cobbled streets, like so many in Aragón, are packed with marvelously grand mansions, including the **Palacio de Sada** where Fernando is reputed to have been born, and there's an unusually early Parish **church**, with a curious crypt dedicated to the Virgen del Pilar. These are the real attractions of the place, but you could wander up too towards the **Castillo de la Peña Fernando** and into the **Ayuntamiento**, which displays — as ever — interesting tidbits of information about local government in a town whose population scarcely tops a thousand.

Huesca and Loarre

Heading for the Pyrenees by bus or rail from Zaragoza, **HUESCA** is the first town you reach. You can miss it entirely, since these days trains continue on to Jaca and Canfranc, and certainly it's one of the least memorable Aragonese towns. The nearby castle at LOARRE, however, is one of Aragón's, indeed Spain's, finest and well worth breaking your journey for.

Huesca itself has a reasonably well preserved "Old Town," and a **Cathedral** with an unusual facade. Its portal (with fine French-style statues of the thirteenth century) is surmounted by a brick Mudejar gallery, covered by a sloping roof, and it has an elegantly pinnacled uppermost section that's Isabelline in style. Next door, the **Museo Diocesano** (daily 11am–1pm and, more variably, 4–6pm) contains a rather mixed collection, though it includes a fine alabaster altarpiece. These aside, though, there's not a lot to occupy you. **Buses** arrive at Plaza Navarra, at the corner of which, on c/Zaragoza, is the cheap *Pensión Chaure*. C/Zaragoza leads down to the **railway station**, from where it leads uphill to a major crossroads, to the left of which the **Cosa Alto** is home to the **Turismo** (at no. 35) and the boundary of the old town. There's another clutch of *pensiones* on Plaza Lizana, just down the hill from the cathedral. If you're here in the evening, the streets off c/San Orencio host the most **action**.

The appeal of Huesca lies more in the many excursions you can make into the surrounding countryside, which is very unspoiled, though remember that buses are scarce and there's often nowhere to stay. Easiest is the trip to **Los Mallos**, a fantastic series of pink "sugarloaf" mountains which can be seen from the Huesca–Jaca train (3 daily in each direction). For a closer look, get off the train at **RIGLOS-CONCILIO** and walk along the road to **RIGLOS** itself, tucked high up underneath the most impressive part of the peaks. Along the way, you'll be rewarded by a series of superb views not only of the Mallos, but also of the valley below. At Riglos there's another station, below the village (unstaffed but the timetable should be posted), up from which you can either catch a train back to Huesca or on to Jaca. There's another good group of Mallos mountains at **AGÜERO**, a completely isolated village about three miles off the main Huesca–Jaca road and easily visible from Riglos. The problem is you can't cross the valley; to get there either walk the seven or so kilometers from Riglos–Concilio station or take a bus (traveling between Huesca and Pamplona) to **MURILLO** and walk the remaining five kilometers from there. The reward is a totally unspoiled village set against the beautiful backdrop of the Mallos, with one formation sticking out like a finger at the end. Ask in the village for the key to the **Iglesia de Santiago**, an unfinished building up a dirt road above the main road. This was loosely associated with the Pilgrim Route (although it lies some way to the south of it) and its doorway carvings are the work of the Master of San Juan de la Peña.

The **Castillo de Loarre** (daily 9am–2pm and 4–8pm), which lies some 40km north west of Huesca, is the best excursion you could make from Huesca, a time-consuming but thoroughly rewarding trip. Depending on when you arrive in Huesca you can get out to it either by **bus** (2 daily to AYERBE via LOARRE village) or **train** (the HUESCA–JACA line runs through AYERBE). Be aware that timetables do their best to conspire against a day trip, and there is nowhere to stay in either Ayerbe or Loarre. Whichever route you take you'll end up doing some walking — the castle is a circuitous six-kilometer haul from the village.

As you approach, the fortress at first seems to blend into the hillside, but gradually it assumes a breathtaking grandeur: a combination of perfect military architecture and stunning views across the plains of Aragón. It was constructed by Sancho Ramírez, King of Navarra (1000–35), as a base for his resistance to the Moorish occupation, and is superbly compact, rising dizzily on a rocky outcrop. A Romanesque church, complete with crypt, is an added delight, with its delicate proportions and no less than 84 individually carved capitals. And, crowning the vertical structure of the castle, two towers — the

Torre de la Reina and the taller Torre del Homenaje — can be climbed by means of iron rungs cemented into the wall. Be careful, though; the rungs, especially those at the top, aren't usually in a good state of repair.

Jaca and the Pilgrim Route

The northernmost town of any size in the Aragonese Pyrenees, **JACA** marked the end of the first stage for pilgrims following the *camino* to Santiago de Compostela (see *Galicia*). The Aragonese route crossed the frontier at CANFRANC via the Somport Pass and headed, eventually, to Jaca. The pilgrims entered the town over one of the finest of the bridges on the Santiago route, the steep, stone **Puente San Miguel**. This is about 2km out of town (follow the main Paseo from below the Ciudadela and then take a sharp right down the rough track) and it commands fine views of the valley in either direction. The main legacy, however, of these years, when Jaca was an early capital of the kingdom of Aragón, is one of Spain's most appealing and architecturally important monuments — the **Cathedral**, dominating as ever the center of town. Built over the first half of the eleventh century, this was the first Romanesque cathedral in Spain, designed as a kind of confirmation of Jaca's role as a Christian capital in what was still almost exclusively a Moorish peninsula. As far as its design goes, the influence of French architecture, carried here along the pilgrim route, predominates, with the introduction of the classic three-aisled basilica, though sadly it has been much adapted over the centuries. It's still impressive, though, and has a powerful added attraction in its **Museo Diocesano** (daily 11:30am–1:30pm and 4:30–6:30pm), installed on the site of the original cloisters (entry from inside the cathedral). This should not be missed, the dark cloisters containing a beautiful collection of twelfth- to fifthteenth-century Aragonese frescoes, gathered from village churches in the area and from higher up in the Pyrenees. If your interest is sparked, there is a comparable — though far more extensive — display of their Catalan equivalents in Barcelona.

Today Jaca is a military town, its milling conscripts attending the local military academy. The military connection is nothing new: the **Ciudadela**, a sixteenth-century fort, still offers good views of the surrounding peaks, and you can visit the interior (daily 11am–noon and 4–5pm) on a free guided tour. It's hardly worth it, though; the outside, with slumbering deer in the grounds, is by far the most interesting part.

There are a few (and only a few) **places to stay** in Jaca, and if you are offered a room at the bus or railway station, you'd be well advised to take it. Otherwise head for the area around the c/Major, where *Pension Vivas*, off c/Major on c/Gil Berges (☎974/ 360531), is worth trying; also cheap is the *Hostal Paris* (☎974/ 361020), very close to the cathedral, and the *habitaciones* in c/Poblacion Morcillo and c/Mayor 53-7. There is a **youth hostel** (☎974/ 360536) on Avda. Perimetral, at the southern end of the town by the skating rink, and two **campgrounds** — closest and cheapest of which is *Camping Victoria* (☎974/360323), 1500m out on C134 (heading west). On the same road, but 4km in the other direction (east to Sabiñánigo) is the plusher

Camping Peña Oroel (☎974/360215). Easily the best place to **eat** in town is *La Fragua*, just across from the *Pension Vivas* on c/Gil Berges, which serves excellent cheap grills done on a range in front of your eyes. *La Cuba*, farther down the road is cheaper still, and c/Gil Berges as a whole is home to some of Jaca's rowdier bars. Try also the *Casa la Abuela* Primera, at c/Poblacion 3 and the *Restaurante Martínez*, on c/Mayor 55.

Arriving by **rail** you'll find yourself a good walk out of town; move quickly and take the local bus which connects with most trains. The **bus station** is on Avda. Jacetania, around the back of the cathedral, and has daily departures to PAMPLONA, (8am), SABIÑÁNIGO (9am), BIESCAS (6pm), ANSÓ/ HECHO, Zaragoza, and Huesca. Note that although the bus timetables don't say so, hardly any buses run on Sundays. If you're making for the mountains the **Turismo**, on Avda. Regimiento Galicia just below the Ciudadela (Mon.–Fri. 9am–2pm and 4–8pm, Sat. 10am–1:30pm and 5–8pm, Sun. 10am–1:30pm), has a whole range of leaflets on hiking and on the local ski resorts, for all of which see below. Really, though, Jaca is a bit of a detour these days. You might come here to stock up on **maps** and the red cartographic **guides** of the region (though these are widely available elsewhere), or, if you've more money to spare than time, to **rent a car**: *Aldecar* on Avda Jacetania is quite reasonable.

Two Monasteries: Santa Cruz de la Seros and San Juan de la Peña

Not far west of Jaca lie two outstanding monasteries of the Pilgrim Route, SANTA CRUZ DE LA SEROS and SAN JUAN DE LA PEÑA. Unfortunately, neither is served by public transportation, although it is possible to walk to both and back in a day, provided you make an early enough start. If that sounds too gruelling, an alternative is to get up early and take the Huesca bus (7:25am) as far as BERNUES, from where it's ten kilometers of steep road to the Upper Monastery of San Juan. Or you could wait for the late afternoon bus to Pamplona and get off at the turning for Santa Cruz. Bear in mind, however, that the only place to stay for the night is the San Juan monastery — and it's a steep climb there for anyone carrying a full pack.

SANTA CRUZ DE LA SEROS is a lovely village situated against the backdrop of the pink mountains of the Sierra of San Juan de la Peña and it feels hauntingly deserted despite the fact there's a fair amount of building work going on here. The truncated but still impressive former **convent church,** Romanesque in style with a fine square tower, dominates the vilage. Someone should appear with the keys to an interior that's surprisingly small. Its most curious feature is a holy water stoup which ingeniously doubles as a column holding up the gallery. There is a **restaurant** across from the convent, specializing in local dishes, but no other shops or places to stay.

From Santa Cruz a road winds its way up the mountain to SAN JUAN DE LA PEÑA — a fairly easy hitch but worth walking for the sake of the views, first over the valley below and then over a vast panorama, with the peaks of the Pyrenees clearly visible to the north, the curiously shaped Peña de Oroel to the east. After 8km you come to the **Lower Monastery of San Juan de la Peña**. At first sight this is rather disappointing; the building is small and partially ruined. But its location, in a hollow under the rocks, is unusual and evocative. It played an early role in the Reconquest and was also where the Latin mass was introduced to the peninsula.

Officially, the monastery is open daily from 10am to 2pm and 4 to 7pm (closed Mon.), but since it is being restored you may be able to enter outside these hours, including Mondays. Inside, the lower church dates back to the ninth century, and has surviving, if fragmentary, wall paintings. Upstairs, there's the Pantheon of the Nobles, with fine Gothic lettering on the wall tombs, and the Romanesque upper church, a simple construction whose three apses are hollowed out of the rock behind. The cloisters beyond are the most beautiful and original part of the building, though sadly only two of the bays are complete, with one other in a fragmentary state. The capitals were excellently carved by an idiosyncratic master who made his mark on a number of churches in the region. He is now known as the "Master of San Juan de la Peña" and his work is easily recognizable by the unnaturally large eyes he gave his figures. To the side of the church, the Pantheon of the Kings was a final addition, remodeled in a cold, neoclassical style in the eighteenth century after the monastery had been abandoned in favor of a new brick baroque building higher up the mountain. This was sacked by Napoleon's troops, after which monastic life never returned to this place.

The **Upper Monastery** can be seen from the outside only, but it is worth climbing up to, if only for the views of the Pyrenees from a nearby mirador. There's a small **hostal** here, installed in the former outbuildings, and a **bar** and **restaurant**.

The Pilgrim Route continued westwards from here, through PUENTE LA REINA, where you'll need to change buses if you're heading to or from Jaca from Huesca or Pamplona. This Aragonese village is of no other interest, unlike the town of the same name in Navarre — for which (and the continuation of the Pilgrim Route).

The Higher Peaks: Hiking and Skiing

There is a wealth of remarkable scenery in Aragón's stretch of the Pyrenees, most of it still largely undeveloped. The peaks and valleys are rapidly acquiring something of a fashionable status among climbers and hikers, who are likely to be your only companions on the approach routes from the south.

As the interest has picked up, more of the area has become accessible through increased **transportation possibilities**. If you're pressed for time, the **Ordesa National Park** is probably as good a taster of the region as any, both for serious and less serious hikers. Buses from Jaca and Huesca serve Sabiñánigo, from where there is a daily minibus to Torla, the best base for the park. Coming by train or bus from Zaragoza, make sure to get a departure before 9am to make the connection.

Benasque, east of the national park, has steeper, sterner hiking and is a top ski resort during the winter. The easiest approach is by the one daily bus from Barbastro. From the north west, there are buses between Sabiñánigo and Ainsa, from where there's a morning connection on to Benasque. Approaching from the Catalan stretch of the Pyrenees, it is possible to hitch from just north of Pont de Suert over the mountains to Castejón, from where it's only 14km to Benasque — though it's worth trying to make it one go.

If none of this suits, **Ansó** and **Hecho** are easily reached by daily bus (not Sun.) from Jaca bus station — gentle resorts, lower than those farther east and with milder walking. Consider, too, the ski centers of **Astún-Candanchú** and **Canfranc**, this last linked by regular train to Zaragoza (and Jaca) and the connecting town for buses across the border into France. Maps and the red *Guía Cartografica* guides are available in Huesca, Jaca, Sabiñánigo, Torla, and Benasque, most of which also boast hiking/skiing shops for any other equipment you might need.

Parque Nacional de Ordesa

One of Spain's first protected national parks, **ORDESA** is also one of the most dramatic, providing — as the tourist leaflet poetically puts it — "a place where all the different elements of nature seem to have agreed that here was the perfect spot to offer an uninterrupted spectacle of enjoyable surprises." The reality is hardly more mundane, with beech and poplar forests, spectacular mountain streams, dozens of spring and early summer waterfalls, and of course a startling backdrop of peaks. Among the fauna of the park, there are golden eagles, lammergeiers, and griffon/egyptian vultures, who nest in the park's palisades. Pyrenean chamois are everywhere, at times in such numbers that hunters are allowed to cull the surplus. There are now very few ibex (*cabra montes*), a species the park was supposed to be protecting. It's a popular destination these days, with easier access than ever by public transportation.

Getting There: Sabañánigo, Biescas, Ainsa

To get to the park **from the west** you need to take the daily 11:30am minibus from **SABIÑÁNIGO** to AINSA, which makes a stop in TORLA. There's not much to Sabiñánigo and you'll probably want to push straight on. The minibus leaves a few meters down the road (to the right) from Sabiñánigo's **bus station**, where the bus from Zaragoza/Huesca will drop you; be warned that it only carries local mail and supplies, and fills quickly. If you can't get on, and you don't want to wait for the following day's bus, the only option is to take a bus as far as **BIESCAS**, 15km away and walk or hitch the remaining 25km to Torla from there. The hitching isn't difficult — until recently this was the way to get to the park — but if you do get stuck, Biescas isn't unpleasant and has a central campground and several bars and restaurants.

Should you decide to stop in Sabiñánigo, there are half a dozen **places to stay** along the main road, the nicest and cheapest the *Fonda Laguarta* (above the *Bar Lara*), just to the left of the bus station. In the evening the same main street is surprisingly lively, the bars spilling out onto the pavements and disgorging a friendly mixture of locals and hikers. The **railway station** is at the far end of the street (right coming out of the bus station) and there are four trains daily to Jaca (20 min.) and Canfranc (1 hr.) although only two of these are practicable for day-trips.

If you're approaching the park from the Catalan Pyrenees, a bus goes from Benasque to Huesca via Barbastro; you must then hitch to **AINSA** from where the Sabiñanigo-based minibus goes to Torla in the afternoon, and from there to Broto, near Torla. Ainsa is a well-preserved town with a fine arcaded square and an exceptional Romanesque church with a dark, primitive interior. Betwen Ainsa and Broto the gorge widens into a broad valley with evidence of large-scale depopulation: medieval villages just off the road are mostly deserted and the fields have gone to seed.

Torla and into the Park

The formerly unspoiled stone village of **TORLA**, 8km from the Ordesa park, is the most obvious approach to the park, and the only feasible base for anyone without their own transportation. A mushrooming of concrete block construction in 1988 has irrevocably sullied the village, but **Accommodation** is easy to come by. There is a reasonable *fonda*, the *Ballarin* (☎486155), owned by the same people who run the two-star *hostal* (☎486172) across the way. You'll see them both signposted high on a building to your left as you enter the village. There's another one-star hotel, with a good bar, in the village, and another, the one-star *Bella Vista*, on the road to Ordesa, as well as two rather posher hotels and rooms above the *Bar Rebeco*. There are two **campgrounds** on this road, too; the *Rio Ara* (by the river, nice and cheap) after about 2km and, a little farther, the *Ordesa*, next to a fancy hotel and pricier, mainly with cars and trailers. There's nothing fancy about the **food** at the *Ballarin's comedor* but it is cheap and filling, and other than one other small restaurant and the more expensive hotels there's nowhere else to eat in Torla. The **bus** back to Sabiñánigo leaves Ainsa at 2pm and runs through Torla at around 4:30pm, stopping just below the *fonda* next to the post office.

You can get to the **PARQUE NACIONAL DE ORDESA Y MONTE PERDIDO** by following the narrow road north out of Torla. It's an attractive route, but it's better with a decent pair of shoes, to take the **footpath** signposted to the right just after *Camping Ordesa* — look for the sign marked *Camino de Turieto* and follow the steep path down over the river via a rather alarming wooden bridge. After that, it's an easy and beautiful two-hour walk to Ordesa, well posted all the way and taking you past some voluminous waterfalls, high above the river. The trail leads right to the **Park Information Office** on the main road, just before the park itself, where you can buy — if you haven't already — a decent **map** of Ordesa: the French 1:50 000 IGN sheet is the clearest, covering Gavarnie in France though not Torla itself. They also sell cheaper maps, perfectly adequate if you're going to stick to a popular, signed path, and can provide information on the free **walking tours** in the park with an experienced mountain guide. These are graded according to difficulty and usually begin from a second information office in Torla (next to the bank).

Once **in the park** there are several possible hikes, though you should know that some of the "paths" marked on the maps are actually climbing routes — don't underestimate their time and difficulty. The most popular and probably the most rewarding hike, not especially difficult, is to the **Circo Soasa** (or *Cola de Caballo* — "horse's tail waterfall"), a five- to eight-hour hike along the path of the Río Arazas and into the upper reaches of a startling valley gorge. This is usually crowded but for a little more peace you could take an upper path which leads to the same spot, marked "Faja de Pelay," a shady route which zigzags gently upwards for about 1½hours. From the top you get an aerial view of the canyon, while above peers a succession of remote peaks and features: Brecha de Rolando (a curious niche, also visible from the French side), Cylindro, and Monte Perdido.

There are shorter and easier hikes than these, to the impressive Cotatuero and Carriata waterfalls, the trailheads for which are at the top of the huge parking lot, a few hundred meters above the information office. Here you'll also find toilets and a restaurant (with a cheapish daily menu), but no other place to buy food. Camping in the park is prohibited but there are quite a number of basic *refugios* (marked on the maps), the nearest — signposted from the parking lot— being the Refugío Goriz, about a four-hour walk. You can camp in its vicinity, and you will have to in mid-summer when it's full for days on end.

One further hike deserves mention, to the French border town of GAVARNIE. This is a fair haul, most easily done from Torla. Follow the road to Ordesa out beyond the campgrounds as far as the bridge (Puente de los Navarros) over the river and then take the left fork (signposted). There's a campground (*Camping Valle Bujaruelo*) after another 4km, and farther up the valley the hamlet of SAN NICOLAS, from where the trail heads over the mountains and down to Gavarnie in six to eight hours. It's possible to reach the same French town from the Ordesa park itself, but it's much harder and takes much longer.

Benasque

The Ordesa park offers the Aragonese Pyrenees the greatest variety of hiking routes, but serious climbers and hikers head farther east to the highest peaks in the range. Pico de Aneto (3404m) and Pico de Poset (3371m) tower above the village of BENASQUE, beautifully situated near the head of a glorious valley carved out by the fast-flowing Río Esera. An old and pretty place, much of Benasque's charm has sadly been lost to the ski trade, which makes its presence felt even in summer. The cheapest room is about 800ptas at one of the two fondas near the bus stop, and the village has seen an influx of sports shops selling designer gear and fancy hotel-restaurants. Still, powerful attractions remain, and a trip here outside the ski season is well worthwhile. The scenery, for one, is truly Alpine, the air bitingly clean and fresh, and there's a delightful thirteenth-century church to take a peek in between hikes. And the ride there from Barbastro by bus, a two-and-a-half-hour journey, is an exciting one, passing unused hydroelectric stations situated on dried-up rivers, and a few isolated villages all built of the same stone. CASTEJÓN DE SOS, about 20km short of Benasque, is the first place that's really Alpine in feel and look, with new Swiss chalet-style hotels and houses. It also has a *fonda* and a campground 4km out of town on the Benasque road.

Hecho and Ansó

The isolation of Aragón's Pyrenean villages is a considerable part of their charm, and some, particularly over to the northwest of Jaca, have a fascination out of proportion to their humble status. Quite apart from the beauty of the surroundings, many preserve unique characteristics. Hecho, for instance, has a dialect known as Cheso, a survival of ancient Aragonese, while at neighboring Ansó the older people still wear traditional dress. Even without these curiosities, both villages are well worth seeing, set in two of the most beautiful valleys in Aragón, full of weird sculpted rocks and enclosed by peaks.

A daily afternoon bus runs from Jaca to HECHO, the largest of the villages, a splendid old place which stood at the heart of the emerging Aragonese kingdom and was birthplace of the "warrior king" Alfonso I. It's very pleasant just to stay here; it offers some excellent walks in the countryside around and an unhurried plaza with tables outside its one bar. It can get crowded, though, especially during July or August, when the village hosts the world-renowned *Symposia de Escultura y Pintura Moderna* — an unlikely and wonderful event that sees the immediate valley turned into an open-air art gallery, with white sculpted blocks strung out along the hillside to the left as you enter the village. There are three *hostales* in Hecho, although all may well be full if you arrive late in the day during summer. The best is right in the Plaza de la Fuente (where the bus stops): if this is full, try asking about private rooms — there are some in the next square down (Plaza Palacio), above the giftshop at the bottom.

A short walk away the beautiful village of SIRESA lies a gentle 2km up the valley, with a ninth-century church standing graceful watch over the hills and a *fonda* above the bar. As a place to stay it isn't especially cheap but the location is great; or there are several excellent camping spots on either side of the village. Continue up the valley to the north of Siresa and you'll eventually reach an official campground (*Camping Oza de Selva*, June–Sept.), surrounded by some tremendous peaks and an excellent starting point for any number of trails and climbs.

Rather than wait for the late afternoon bus, it's a remarkable walk on to ANSÓ from here, 11km west and walkable in around three hours. The road climbs right over the hills into the next valley, Valle de Ansó, from where there are some really fabulous views and, again, some nice places to camp. Two kilometers before Ansó, above the tunnel, are some of the more strangely shaped rocks around, these two known locally as the "Monk and the Nun." Once a prosperous little village, Ansó fell upon hard times with the 1950s and 1960s depopulation of rural Aragón, but today there are signs of a small but definite revival, with a small but regular stream of tourists here to sample the village's restful attractions. The aged church is extraordinarily rich inside and houses an interesting crafts and ethnological museum, and there's even some decent swimming (or at least splashing) down on the small river beach. The valley itself has plenty of hiking potential (buy the *guía cartografica* for the options); or, on a grander scale, you could make for the Valle de Zuriza, 14km to the north, where there is a large campground. There's no bus service, though; you'll have to walk or hitch.

Ansó's growing popularity is reflected in the fact that there are three places to stay, which all fill quickly in summer. If you can, get a room at the new and unusually trendy *Posada Magoria*, a very homey place complete with vegetarian meals eaten communally. Unmarked and easy to miss, it's the next building along from the more conspicuous *Fonda Estanes*, both on the main road that runs through the top of the village. Another choice, though definitely a second one, is the *Hostal Aisi*, down in the plaza above a bar of the same name. There's a restaurant here, and a surprising number of bars for such a small place, most down the cobbled street that leads to the plaza.

From Ansó a minor road continues northwards, eventually joining C137 for nearby RONCAL (see p.308). There's no bus service in this direction. To leave Ansó by public transportation you have to catch the hideously early (6:30am) bus back through Hecho to Jaca, or change at Puente la Reina for Huesca or Pamplona instead. Note that the bus doesn't always call in Siresa on the way back to Jaca — you may have to walk down the hill into Hecho.

Skiing: Astún-Candanchú and Canfranc

There are about half a dozen ski resorts in Aragón's stretch of the Pyrenees and most of them — following the province's hosting of the 1982 University Winter Olympics — are well-equipped. You may find that package deals, bought from any travel agent in northern Spain, work out cheaper than going your own way but there's nothing to prevent you from just turning up. The SNTO publishes a special pamphlet on skiing and there are piles of more detailed information at the tourist offices in Zaragoza, Huesca, and Jaca. It is easy enough to go through these, decide where you feel like going, and phone ahead to check conditions and reserve a room (the latter vital around Christmas or the New Year).

Perhaps the best, and certainly one of the most varied, options is the twin resort of ASTÚN-CANDANCHÚ, directly north from Jaca (with which there are regular bus connections). The resorts — Astún is new, Candanchú established — are just 8km apart, and you can happily alternate between them. Astún is particularly well organized, rarely crowded and has plentiful (generally new) equipment for rent at reasonably modest rates. Other good winter resorts include SALLENT DE GALLEGO to the east (buses from Sabiñánigo via Biescas) and CERLER, very close to Benasque.

South of Candanchú lies CANFRANC, currently the farthest point into the Aragonese Pyrenees that you can reach by train (for the Catalan Pyrenees, see the Catalunya chapter). Ever since the French railways (SNCF) discontinued their part of the trans-Pyrenean line, Canfranc has been saddled with a massive white elephant of a railway station (containing two-star hotel, post office, police station, etc.). The village, such as it is, exists solely to catch the passing tourist trade (mostly French), and sports a few gift shops, hotels, and, everywhere, great mountains looming up overhead. It's just about worth the day's trip from Jaca even if you don't continue into France (see below) as the train ride up the valley is a wild and mysterious trip even in summer. There's also a youth hostel (☎974/378016), open July and August, in VILLANÚA, about 15km north of Jaca on the way up.

Though there's no train, you can still travel on into France by public transportation — by bus, three daily from outside the railway station to OLORON over the border. Currently they depart at 10:45am, 4:18pm and 7:15pm and you will have to pay the fare in French Francs (F38), which means that if you arrive after the banks close, you'll be reduced to bargaining in shops and restaurants to change your pesetas. Buses arrive in Canfranc from Oloron at 9:35am, 12:39pm and 4:18pm, thus allowing for train connections on to Jaca. More information, if you need it, can be had from the Turismo, on the main road back towards Jaca (Mon.–Fri. 9am–2pm and 4–8pm, Sat. 10am–2pm and 4–7pm, Sun. 10am–2pm), who also have plenty of skiing brochures. For food, *Casa Flores* is cheap, excellent, and local; and if you need to stay, there is a one-star *hostal* (the *Marraco*) next door, and a campground (summer only) 5km away on the road towards Candanchú and France.

fiestas

April
8–9 Pilgrimage to the Sanctuario de Nuestra Señora de la Alegria in MONZÓN, the journey made in decorated carriages.

Small-scale but emotional Holy Week celebrations at CATALAYUD and elsewhere. On Maundy Thursday/Good Friday there's the festival of *la Tamborrada* in Calanda, near Alcañiz.

May
1st Friday JACA commemorates the Battle of Vitoria against the Moors with processions and folkloric events.

25 More of the same at JACA for the Fiesta Santa Orosia.

Monday of Pentecost *Romería N.S. de Calentuñana* at SOS.

June
Nearest Sunday to the 19th CANTAVIEJA celebrates the Fiesta de los Mozos: a serious religious event but with dancing and the usual fairground activities.

30 Ball de Benas: small festival at BENASQUE.

July
1st Sunday *Romería del Quililay*, pilgrimage and picnic up the mountain above TARAZONA.

1st–2nd week TERUEL bursts into 10 days of festivities for the Vaquilla del Angel, one of Aragón's major festivals.

Late July/early August International Folklore Festival of the Pyrenees alternates between France and Spain: it's at JACA in odd-numbered years, accompanied by a very full program of traditional music and dance.

July and August Symposium of Modern Art and Sculpture at HECHO sees the hills around the village turned into an open-air sculpture museum.

August
16 Patron saint's festival at BIESCAS — "big heads" and eats.

27 Encierros — crazy local bull-running — at CANTAVIEJA and TARAZONA.

September
Early September TERUEL fair.

4–8 Fiesta at BARBASTRO includes *jota* dancing, bullfights, and sports competitions (e.g., pigeon shooting contests).

8 Virgin's Birthday signals fairs at ALCAÑIZ, HECHO, CATALAYUD, ALACALA DE LA SELVA, and VILLEL.

12 Three days of Patron saint festivities at GRAUS including stylized traditional dances and "dawn songs." *Romería* at L'IGLESUELA DEL CID.

14 Bull-running and general partying at ALBARRACÍN.

October
2nd week Major festival in honor of the Virgen del Pilar at ZARAGOZA with floats, bullfights, and jota dancing.

travel details

Buses

From Zaragoza to Teruel (4 daily; 4 hr.); Huesca (5; 1 hr. 45 min.); Sos (daily at 6:30pm, return at 7am; 2¼ hr.); Lleida (4; 3 hr.); Tarazona (4; 1½ hr.); Barcelona (1 direct; 7 hr.); Valladolid (1; 8 hr.).

From Teruel to Albarracín (daily at 3:30pm, return at 7am; 2 hr.); Cantavieja/L'Iglesuela del Cid/Villafranca del Cid (daily at 3:30pm, return at 5:45am; 2½ hr./3 hr./3½ hr.).

From Alcañiz to Cantavieja (daily at 11:30am, connecting with 1:30pm from Alcorisa; 3½–4½ hr. from Alcorisa) and Valderrobres (3; 1 hr.).

From Huesca to Barbastro/Monzón/Barcelona (2 daily; 50 min./1¼ hr. /4¼ hr.); Sabiñánigo (2 daily, at 10am for connection to Torla, and at 4:45pm; 1½ hr.); Zaragoza (5; 1½ hr.); Fraga (1 daily, for Lleida).

From Jaca to Hecho/Ansó (2 daily except Sun., 1 with change in Puente la Reina at 8am, and at 5pm; 1 hr./1¼ hr.); Biescas (1 at 6pm; 40 min.); Astún/Candanchú (at least daily in season); Sabiñánigo (2 daily, 8am and 1:30pm; 30 min.);Pamplona (2 daily via Puente la Reina); 2hr.; Huesca (2; 1½hr.).

From Barbastro to Benasque (1; 2½ hr.); Huesca (4; 50 min.).

From Sabiñánigo to Torla (1 daily at 11:30am; 1½ hr.); Huesca (2; 1½ hr.); Biescas/Sallent de Gallego (at least 2 daily).

Trains

From Zaragoza Huesca/Jaca/Canfranc (4 daily; 1¾ hr./3½ hr./4½ hr.); Madrid (13 daily; 3½–5½ hr.); Barcelona (16 daily to either Sants or Termino, 6 of them via Tarragona; 4½–6½ hr.); Lleida (9 daily; 1¾–2¾ hr.); Teruel (4 daily, 3 of them continuing on to Valencia; 4 hr.).

CHAPTER NINE

CATALUNYA

With its own language, culture, and, to a degree, government, **Catalunya** (*Cataluña* in Castilian Spanish, traditionally Catalonia in English) is a distinct and sophisticated region. If you want to get to grips with just one part of Spain, it is an excellent choice: easy to get to, very lively, and boasting a broad range of highly individual attractions. For long-term travelers it's a satisfying, and important, counterbalance to the south.

Barcelona, the capital, is very much the main event. One of the most vibrant and exciting cities in Europe, it quite overshadows Madrid in terms of liveliness and interest, and ranks as the sort of place you end up staying far longer than planned. Inland, the **monastery of Montserrat,** Catalunya's main "sight," is perched amid one of the most unusual rock formations in Spain, and there are provincial cities too — **Tarragona, Girona,** and **Lleida** above all — of considerable charm and historic interest. The inland **Pyrenees** hide a cluster of overlooked towns and minor monuments, all far from developed despite the hiking and skiiing opportunites; with the sole exception, that is, of tiny, duty-free **Andorra.** Sadly most of the coastline is a disaster, much of the **Costa Brava** in particular a turgid sprawl of concrete more like the Bronx than the Med. There are parts of the northernmost stretch, from **Cadaqués** to **Port Bou** on the French border, which have managed to retain some attraction (and even some relative isolation from the package-tour hordes) but on the whole if it's beaches you're after you'd do better to keep going south, well out of Catalunya — or take a ferry from Barcelona for the Balearics.

Catalanisme

The **Catalan people** have an individual and deeply felt historical and cultural identity, seen most clearly in the language, which increasingly takes precedence over Castilian on street names and signs. Despite being banned for over thirty years during the Franco dictatorship, Catalan survived behind closed doors and has staged a dramatic comeback since the Generalissimo's death. As in the Basque country, though, regionalism goes back much farther than this. On the expulsion of the Moors in 874, Vilfredo el Peloso (Wilfred the Hairy) established himself as the first independent **Count of Catalunya;** his kingdom flourished and the region became famous for its seafaring, mercantile, and commercial skills, characteristics which to some extent still set the region apart. In the twelfth century came union with Aragón, though the Catalans kept many of their traditional, hard-won rights (*Usatges*) and from then until the fourteenth century marked Catalunya's **Golden Age.** By the end of that time the kingdom ruled the Balearic islands, the city and region of Valencia, Sardinia, Corsica, and much of present-day Greece. In 1359 the Catalan *Generalitat* formed Europe's first parliamentary government.

Eventually, through the marriage of Fernando V (of Aragón) to Isabella I (of Castile), the region was added onto the rest of the emergent Spanish state. Throughout the following centuries the Catalans made repeated attempts to secede and to escape from the stifling grasp of the central bureaucracy, which saw Catalan enterprise as merely another means of filling the state coffers. Early industrialization, which was centered here and in the Basque country, only intensified political disaffection. In the 1920s and 1930s anarchist, communist, and socialist parties all established major power bases in Catalunya. In 1931, after the fall of the dictator Primo de Rivera, a **Catalan Republic** was proclaimed and its autonomous powers guaranteed by the new Republican government. Any incipient separatism collapsed, however, with the outbreak of the civil war, during which Catalunya was a bastion of the Republican cause, Barcelona holding out until January 1939.

In return, Franco pursued a policy of harsh suppression, attempting to wipe away all evidence of the Catalan cultural and economic setup and finally to establish the dominance of Madrid. Amongst his more subtle methods — employed also in Euskadi — was the encouragement of immigration from other parts of Spain in order to dilute regional identity. Even so, Catalunya remained obstinate, the scene of protests and demonstrations throughout the dictatorship. After Franco's death there was massive and immediate pressure — not long in paying dividends — for the reinstatement of a **Catalan government**. This, the semi-autonomous *Generalitat*, enjoys a very high profile, whatever the complaints about its lack of real power. It controls education, health, and social security, with a budget based on tax collected by central government and then returned proportionally. The province's official title is the *Comunitat Autonoma de Catalunya* and it is also known internally as the *Principalitat*. Since autonomy was granted, the state has consistently elected right-wing governments, which may be difficult to understand in view of the recent past but which might be explained by the fact that such regimes are seen to be better able to protect Catalan business interests. The Catalan socialists have recently put forward the idea of creating a federal state, with its own police force and tax collectors, a proposition met with horror by Madrid.

The traveler's main problem throughout the province is likely to be **language** — *Catalá* has more or less taken over from Castilian and you might not realise that *Dilluns Tancat*, for example, is the same as *Cerrado Lunes* (closed Mondays). On paper it looks like a cross between French and Spanish and is generally easy to understand if you know those two, but spoken, it has a very harsh sound and is far harder to come to grips with, especially away from Barcelona where accents are stronger. Few first-time visitors realise how ingrained and widespread Catalan is, and this can lead to some resentment because people won't "speak Spanish" for you. Increasingly, though, Catalan is replacing Castilian rather than cohabiting with it, a phenomenon known as the *venganza* (revenge). Never commit the error of calling it a dialect!

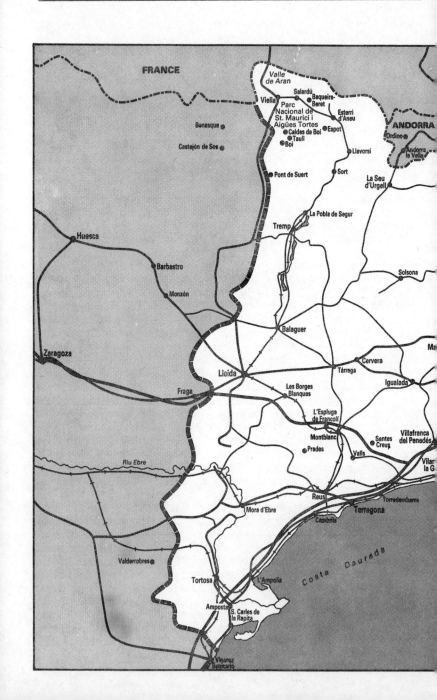

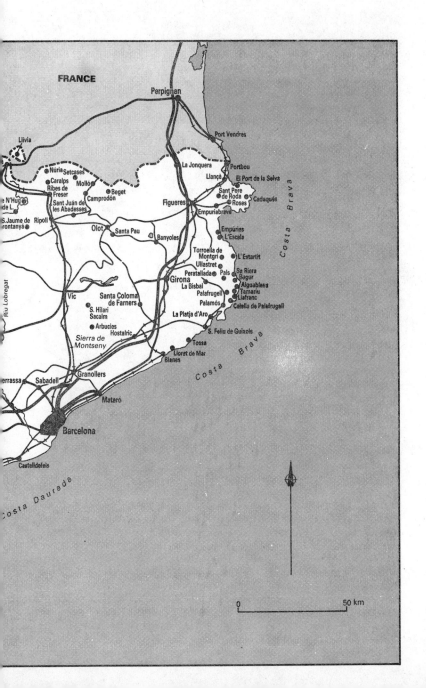

Catalan Glossary

Most **Catalá** words are fairly similar to Castilian, but some are completely unrecognisable. The criteria therefore for the following entries which you might encounter are either that they are very common or that they are very different from Castilian.

One	*un (a)*	Sometimes	*A vegadas*
Two	*dos (dues)*	Never, ever	*Mai*
Three	*tres*	More	*Mes*
Four	*quatre*	Nothing	*Res*
Five	*cinc*	None, some, any,	*Cap*
Six	*sis*	towards	
Seven	*set*	In	*Dins*
Eight	*vuit*	With	*Amb*
Nine	*nou*	Still/yet/even	*Encara*
Ten	*deu*	A lot, very	*Força*
Eleven	*onze*	A little	*Una mica*
Twelve	*dotze*	Near	*(a) Prop*
		Far	*Lluny*
Monday	*Dilluns*	(Six) years ago	*Fa (sis) anys*
Tuesday	*Dimarts*	Self/same	*Mateix*
Wednesday	*Dimecres*	Half/middle	*Mig/mitja*
Thursday	*Dijous*	Stop, enough!	*Prou!*
Friday	*Divendres*	Too much/too many	*Massa*
Saturday	*Dissabte*		
Sunday	*Diumenge*	To work	*Treballar*
		To go	*Anar*
Day before	*Abans d'ahir*	To call, phone	*Trucar*
yesterday		To have dinner	*Sopar*
Yesterday	*Ahir*	(evening)	
Today	*Avui*	To eat	*Menjar*
Tomorrow	*Demá*	Girl	*Una noia*
Day after tomorrow	*Demá passat*	Boy	*Un noi*
		Child/term of affection	*Nen (a)*
Left, Right	*Esquerre (a),*	Dog	*Gosso*
	Dret (a)		
Ladies, Gents (WC)	*Dones, Homes*	Place	*Lloc*
	(Toaleta)	Light	*Llum*
Open, Closed	*Obert (a), Tancat*	Chief, head	*Cap*
		Time, occasion	*Vegada*
Good morning/	*Bon dia,*		
Hello		Drinking glass	*Got*
Good evening,	*Bona nit, Adéu*	Table	*Taula*
Goodbye		Milk	*Llet*
Very well	*Molt bé —*	Egg	*Ou*
Bad	*Malament*	Strawberry	*Maduixa*
Got a light?	*Tens foc?*	Orange	*Taronge*
I like	*M'agrada*	Carrot	*Pastanaga*
Well, then	*Sisplau*	Lettuce	*Enciam*
What do you want?	*Que vols?*	Salad	*Amainda*
Where is?	*On es?*	Apple	*Poma*

When Franco came to power, publishing houses, book shops, and libraries were raided and Catalan books destroyed. While this was followed by a letup in the mid-1940s, the language was still banned from the radio, TV, daily press, and, most importantly, schools, which is why many older people today cannot read or write Catalan (even if they speak it all the time). Conversely, in the capital virtually everyone *can* speak Castilian, even if they don't, while in country areas, many people can only understand, not speak it.

Catalá is spoken in Catalunya proper, part of Aragón, most of Valencia, the Balearic islands, the Principality of Andorra, and in parts of the French Pyrenees, albeit with variations of dialect (it is thus much more widely spoken than several better-known languages such as Danish, Finnish, and Norwegian). It is a Romance language, stemming from Latin and more directly, from medieval Provençal and *lemosi*, the literary French of Occitania. Spaniards in the rest of the country belittle it by saying that to get a Catalan word you just cut a Castilian one in half (which is often true!). In fact, though, the grammar is much more complicated than Castilian and it has eight vowel sounds (three dipthongs). There is a deliberate tendency at present in the media to dig out old words, not used for centuries, which are the least similar to Castilian, even when a more common, Castilian-sounding one exists. In Barcelona, because of the mixture of people, there is much bad Catalan and much bad Castilian spoken, mongrel words being invented unconsciously. In the text we've tried to keep to Catalan names (with Castilian in brackets at least once) — not least because tourist office maps are in Catalan.

BARCELONA

BARCELONA, the self-confident and progressive capital of Catalunya, is a tremendous place to be. Though it boasts outstanding Gothic and Art Nouveau buildings, and some great museums — most notably those dedicated to Picasso and Catalan art — the feel of the city is its most striking and exciting feature. A thriving port and the most prosperous commercial centre in Spain, it has a sophistication and cultural dynamism way ahead of the rest of the country. There is a lot to do in Barcelona, and a multitude of very agreeable ways of not doing it. In part this reflects the city's position, poised beneath France, whose influence is apparent in the elegant boulevards and (not least) in the city's imaginative cooking. But Barcelona has also evolved an individual and eclectic cultural identity, most perfectly and eccentrically expressed in the architecture of **Antonio Gaudí**, reason in itself for visiting the city.

The energy of Barcelona will impress you. It is chanelled into its industry and business, art and music, political protest and merrymaking. It doesn't take long to sense the city's pleasure and pride in being, indisputably, The Best (*Barcelona Mès Que Mai* — Barcelona More Than Ever — as the slogans put it). But there are darker sides to this prosperity and confidence. As more money is poured into the sleek image, poorer areas are left behind, a polarization roughly delineated by *arriba*, the area above Plaça Catalunya, and *abajo*, the lower half of the city. There is a great deal of poverty — people come here from other Spanish cities to beg — and hard drugs are rapidly acquiring a high profile. This means that the **petty crime rate** is high and it's not unusual for tourists to feel threatened in their peregrinations around the seedier areas flanking the Ramblas. If you're *very* unlucky you'll be mugged, so take a few precautions; leave passports and tickets locked up in your hotel, don't be too conspicuous with expensive cameras and, if you are attacked, don't offer any resistance. If you've brought your car, don't leave anything in view, and always remove the tape deck.

With its long tradition of **political activism**, Barcelona continues to be at the forefront of radical Spanish politics. Feminist, gay, peace, and anti-nuclear movements are all highly active, while anarchists remain very much part of the political scene, along with a confusing array of socialist and Catalan nationalist parties. Even on a brief visit you'll probably be aware of this — certainly if you stay during the city's two great fiestas, April 23 or September 24. Though it's now of sparse relevance, George Orwell's *Homage to Catalonia* (describing the worker's uprising of 1936 and the role of Barcelona in the civil war) is still a fascinating book to sit and read in the city's cafes. Although Catalunya is currently under right-wing rule, Barcelona has a socialist council, led by an independent-minded mayor, Pasqual Maragall. He is the main proponent of federalism, though he has garnered little support. There is much antagonism between Maragall and the conservative president of the *Generalitat*, Jordi Pujol; the *Generalitat* recently abolished the individual boroughs that constituted the Metropolitan Corporation, in an attempt to weaken the socialist hold on the city.

Barcelona has also long had the reputation of being the most cosmopolitan city in Spain, above all in design and architecture. In recent years much of the real intellectual impetus has passed to Madrid, and Barcelona, boasting loudly of its European character, is in danger of becoming somewhat self-absorbed and inward-looking, since *Catalanisme* is the staple diet of so much intellectual discussion. Winning the **1992 Olympics**, however, was an important boost, greeted with car-honking euphoria; 70,000 volunteers signed up to help the very next day. There is enormous popular support for sports in Barcelona (especially for soccer, the chief focus of the incessant rivalry with Madrid) and this is partly what gained the nomination. The Olympic Village will be built on the site of former gasworks in Poble Nou, and the stadium over the ruins of the old stadium, built at the foot of Montjuïc for the alternative (anti-Nazi) games to the Berlin Olympics in 1936. Barcelona is being "made beautiful" (another of the slogans) for the occasion and you may find museums and other public buildings closed for restoration. Some are sceptical as to whether it will all be finished in time.

Since Barcelona was chosen as host of the games, it has been the scene of several ETA bombs, a new phenomenon in Catalunya. Although Catalan nationalism itself is generally and historically nonviolent, there has emerged an extremist, very minority group called *Tierra Lliure* which have cooperated with ETA to enable them to operate in Catalan territory.

Orientation

Despite having a population of over 3 million, Barcelona is a surprisingly easy place to find your way around. The **old town** spreads between the harbor and the grid system of the nineteenth-century Eixample (Ensanche). Facing inland, it's bordered on the right (northeast) by the **Parc de la Ciutadella** (*Parque de la Ciudadela*) and on the left (southwest) by the fortress-topped hill of **Montjuïc** (*Montjuich*). In the middle is the **Barri Gòtic** (Barrio Gótico), the medieval nucleus of the city. Bisecting the old town at the edge of the Barri Gòtic, the **Ramblas** — a series of five short streets which combine to form a continuous broad avenue — constitute the main thorough-fare of the city, leading from the harbor to the **Plaça de Catalunya** at the commercial center.

Towards the waterfront to the right (east) of the harbor, below the Parc de la Ciutadella, **Barceloneta** is a former fishing suburb which is still noted for its seafood restaurants. Astride the Ramblas at the port end is the infamous red-light district known as the **Barri Xines** (Barrio Chino), a name which has been borrowed for the equivalent districts in other Spanish towns. Strictly speaking, the Xines is to the southwest, between the harbor and Carrer de l'Hospital, but in practice the streets northeast of the Ramblas are no different. Though highly atmospheric, it can seem — and often be — fairly heavy, certainly late at night.

Inland, the **Eixample**, conceived in the last century as a breathing space for the congested old city and as a symbol of the thrusting commercial expan-sionism of Barcelona's early industrial age, stretches above the Plaça de Catalunya. The simple grid plan of this modern extension is bordered by two huge streets that lead out of the city: the Gran Via de les Corts Catalans and the Avinguda (Avenida) Diagonal. Each block of the Eixample is known as a *manzana* and originally the patio in the center of every one was supposed to contain a garden. Lack of space has meant that most eventually were turned into parking lots and the like; part of the city's current regeneration involves turning many back into open, public spaces.

Beyond the Eixample lie parts of town which were until relatively recently separate villages: **Gràcia**, for example, with its small squares and lively bars; or **Poble Sec** on the slopes of Montjuïc.

Arriving

Most points of arrival are fairly central, with the obvious exception of the **airport**, 12km out of the city. It's linked by a regular and direct train service (every 30 min., 6am–11:30pm, 120ptas) with the main **Estació de Sants**, and once there you can take the metro (Line 3 direct to *Liceu* for the Ramblas, or Line 5 to *Provença* and a change) downtown. If you arrive on a late-night flight you'll have to get a taxi in from the airport for around 1500–2000ptas — at that price you might prefer to sleep in the arrivals lounge until the first train of the morning. Note that services *back to* the airport leave every half hour from Sants (Platform 4), tickets being sold from a special window (marked *Aeropuerto*) in the station.

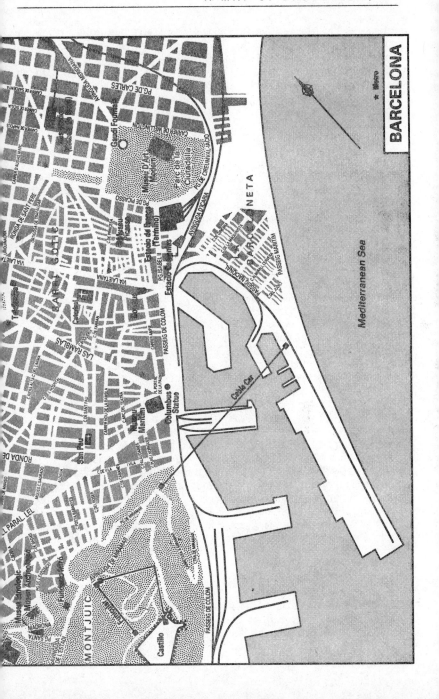

Sants is the busiest train station but if you're coming from France you might end up at the **Estació de França** (also known as the Estació Terminal) next to the Parc de la Ciutadella. From here you can get the metro (Line 4) at Barceloneta or simply walk into the Barri Gòtic. There is no one central **bus terminal** in Barcelona but many buses from elsewhere in Spain arrive at **Estació del Nord** (metro Line 1, *Arc de Triomf*) and the rest will usually drop you at a central point within easy reach of the metro or city buses; see "Directory" below.

It's a good idea to go to a **Turismo** as soon as possible. Any of them will give you a free, large-scale **map** of the city and a public transit map too — invaluable for sorting out the complex bus routes. The main offices are at Gran Via 658 (not far from Plaça Catalunya); Paral.lel 202; the airport; Estació de Sants; Estació de França; and the Monument a Colom (Columbus). There is a **municipal information office** (not really for tourists but invariably helpful) in the *Ajuntament* building in Plaça de Sant Jaume, right in the heart of the Barri Gòtic.

Public Transit

Apart from the medieval Barri Gòtic where you'll want to (and have to) walk, the quickest and cheapest way of getting around Barcelona is by **metro**. There's a flat fare of 50ptas (55ptas Sundays and fiestas) but it's better to buy a *tarja* or T2 which gives you ten journeys at 45% discount and which is also valid on trains (*Ferrocarriles de la Generalitat*) to Sarrià and Tibidabo, on the tramway at Tibidabo, and the funicular railway up to Montjuïc. The metro starts at 5am (6am Sun.) and shuts down at 11pm — just when most people in Barcelona are thinking of going out. It's extended to 1am on Saturday, Sunday, holidays, and the evening before a holiday.

Bus rides cost 50ptas (55ptas Sundays and fiestas) but there's a *tarja* for these too, a T1 costing 330ptas, which can also be used on the metro. Routes, however, are far more complicated than on the underground system; where relevant they are covered in the text. There is a limited number of **night buses** which fill the gap between 11pm and 5am when the daytime services begin again; most of them start in or pass through Plaça Catalunya.

Black-and-yellow **taxis** (with a green roof-light on when available for hire) are cheap and plentiful and well worth utilizing late at night. But they won't take more than four people and charge extra for baggage, or for picking up from Sants. It's easy (if you look like a tourist) to get ripped off, so if you think your *taxista* is not being fair, ask for a *recibo* and the price should then drop. There is now a minimum fare of 200 ptas. To call a cab, try ☎93/3865000, ☎3300804 or ☎3218833.

Finding Somewhere to Stay

The tourist offices in Barcelona dish out lists of **hotels and hostales**, but these are hardly necessary as there is a glut of cheap accommodation (at least until 1992). A hotel information office at the airport (or at Sants station) will book you a place to stay upon arrival, but of course you won't get to see the room beforehand.

Most of the **cheapest accommodation** is to be found in the side streets **off and around the Ramblas**, a convenient and atmospheric area in which to base yourself. Having said that, what may be atmospheric by day can seem plain threatening after dark, and the farther down towards the port you get, the less salubrious, and noisier, the surroundings. As a very general rule, anything above c/Escudellers tends to be all right (though not necessarily clean and/or modern).

Perhaps the best hunting ground is **between the Ramblas and the Plaça de Sant Jaume**, in the area bordered by c/Escudellers and c/ Boqueria. Here there are scores of possibilities from *fondas* to three-star hotels. There are two reasonably cheap *hostales* on the rundown Plaça Reial, dotted with palm trees and arcaded walks; the *Hostal Mayoral* (☎93/3179534) at no. 2 is considerably better than the *Hostal Roma* (☎93/3020366) at no. 11. Note that what is a sunny square by day becomes seedier by night, hash being the very least you'll be offered by the men who lurk at every entrance.

Heading east from the Plaça Reial there are several possibilities down c/de Ferran (but avoid the dirty, noisy *Hostal Lepanto*) and, more expensively, the pleasant *Hostal Rey Don Jaime* (at c/Jaume I, beyond the plaza). Carrer d' Avinyó, a cross street of Ferran, is a good place to hunt, with acceptable *pensiones* at nos. 42 and 58. Other good places nearby (off and around c/ Escudellers) include the *Hostal Cervantes* (☎93/3025168) at c/Cervantes 6 and the nice *Hostal Levante* (☎93/3179565) at Baixada Sant Miguel 2 just off the Plaça Sant Jaume. Carrer de la Princesa, the continuation of c/Jaume I on the far side of Via Laietana, offers several cheaper options, notably the *Pension Princesa*, handy for the Picasso Museum.

On the Ramblas itself you could try *Hostal Maritima* (☎93/3023152) at Ramblas 4, *Hotel Cosmos* (☎93/3171816) overlooking the Ramblas at c/ Escudellers 19, *Quijote* at 70 (☎93/3025599), or the *Hotel Internacional* (☎93/3022566) at Ramblas 78. The farther away from the water you go, the quieter, nicer, and more expensive the places become. There are a couple of good choices on c/Portaferrissa (to the right going inland), the *Hostal Ripalda* (☎93/3181011) at no. 23 and the cheaper, friendly *Pension Fina* (☎93/3179787) at no. 11. With more cash (around 3000–4000ptas double) c/ Sta Anna has three nice two-star hotels with bath and breakfast included.

There are also cheap possibilities on the **west side of the Ramblas**, an area rich in budget restaurants too. Look on c/de Sant Pau and c/Hospital in particular; the *Fonda Mundial* (☎93/2413116) at c/Hospital 123 is exceptionally cheap. C/Junta del Comerç which runs between these two streets, offers the *Hostal Segura* (☎93/3025174) at no. 11, the *Hostal Roma* (☎93/3182099) at no. 21, and the *Hostal Peninsular* (☎93/3018499) at no. 12.

The choice of cheap places outside this immediate area, in the **Eixample** for example, isn't so wide. The *Maria* (☎93/2314110) at c/Consell de Cent 470 and the *Aragon* (☎93/2453949) at c/Aragó 443 are both handy for the Sagrada Familia cathedral, while also very central are the *Hostal Goya* (☎93/ 3022565) at c/Pau Claris 74 and the *Vicenta* (☎93/2151923) at Rambla de Catalunya 84 (metro *Pg. de Gràcia*).

Handier if you've arrived by train at the **Estació de França** (where there is another accommodation office) are the streets immediately around the station, particularly the wide Avda. Marques de l'Argentera (main entrance to the station) and c/General Castaños and c/Ocata (side entrance). Good ones here include the *Hotel Nuevo Colón* (☎93/3195077) at Argentera 11, the *Hotel Oasis II* (☎93/3194396) at Plaça del Palau 17, and the *Hostal Canarias* (☎93/3199003) at c/ Reina Cristina 2. Alternatively, should you arrive by bus at the **Plaça Universitat** there are a number of options between here and the Plaça Catalunya, although pricier on the whole than anything farther down the Ramblas. In particular, on Ronda Universitat, try the *Residencia Australia* or the *hostales Sena* (no. 29, ☎93/3189097) or *Alicante* (no. 4, ☎93/318347).

Youth Hostels and Campgrounds

There are several official and not-so-official **youth hostels** in Barcelona; you'll need a YHA membership card only for official IYHF hostels. Bed and breakfast at any of the hostels listed below costs between 350 and 600ptas a night, and most have kitchens too. The IYHF are responsible for the *Hostal de Joves* (☎93/3003104) at Passeig Pujades 29 (right by the Parc de la Ciutadella and handy for the bus terminal Nord and Estació de França) and the larger *Albergue Verge de Montserrat* (☎93/2138633), miles out at Passeig de Nostra Senyora del Coll 41-51 (Metro *Vallcarca*). The first is friendly, pleasant, and convenient, and they sell block books of metro tickets.

Less official hostels include the *Albergue Pere Tarres* (☎93/2301606) near Sants at c/Numancia 149; the *BCN Youth Hostel* (☎93/3173095) overlooking the Plaça Catalunya at c/Pelai 62; and, at Plaça Reial 17, the eminently avoidable *Kabul Youth Hostel* (☎93/3183190).

As for **campgrounds**, there are hundreds on the coast, but none less than 6km from the city. The nearest is *El Barcino* at Esplugas de Llobregat (open all year, bus from Plaça de Espanya); others are *Prat*, Prat de Llobregat (May to Sept., bus as above) and *Badalona Playa*, Badalona (May to Sept., bus from c/Trafalgar 44, near Arc de Triomf above Parc de la Ciutadella). The **Barcelona Camping Organization** is at c/Diputació 279 (☎93/3174416).

The Old Town

Many of Barcelona's most important monuments remain open throughout the day — from 9am to 8pm — in summer. Tourist offices can supply up-to-date schedules for all of them, and also warn which may be closed for restoration. Scattered as the main sights may be, much the greatest concentration of interest is around the old town (*La Ciutat Vella*). These cramped streets above the harbor are easily manageable, and far more enjoyable, on foot. Start, as everyone else does, with the Ramblas.

Around the Ramblas

It is a telling comment on Barcelona's character that one can recommend a single street — **the Ramblas** — as a highlight. No day in the city seems complete without a stroll down at least part of what, for Lorca, was "the only street in the world which I wish would never end." The tree-lined Ramblas (plural because they are actually several named streets strung head to tail) are the heart of Barcelona's life and self-image. Littered with cafes, shops, restaurants, and newspaper stands (foreign papers a speciality, they usually arrive in the evening), it's a focal point for locals every bit as much as for tourists. In the kiosks under the plane trees you will find pet canaries, rabbits, tropical fish, flowers, plants, postcards, and books (maybe even this *Real Guide!*). You can buy jewelry from a blanket stretched out on the ground, cigarettes from itinerant salespeople, have your palm read and your portrait painted, or just listen to the buskers and watch the pavement artists. The show goes on at night too and if you're there when *Barça* win a match the street erupts with instant and infectious excitement, fans driving up and down with their hands on the horn, cars bedecked with Catalan flags, pedestrians waving champagne bottles.

Heading down from the Plaça de Catalunya you leave the opulent facades of the banks and department stores for a seedier area down towards the port. Not that the Ramblas themselves are ever anything less than respectable (though toting a backpack you'll run the inevitable whispered gauntlet of "Hey!, Hashish?"), but head off into the back streets and the reality of poverty is thoroughly depressing. For all its prosperity, Barcelona has a chronic unemployment problem, and it's worth remembering that petty crime here is some of Spain's worst. The Ramblas cut, too, right through the heart of the notorious red-light district (news kiosks also offer a guide to the brothels) with streets at the harbor end packed with ill-lit clubs, bars, and sex shops. Like any port, Barcelona has a long history of prostitution: Orwell relates how after the 1936 workers' uprising "in the streets were colored posters appealing to prostitutes to stop being prostitutes." Franco, for rather different reasons, was equally keen to clear the streets. Neither succeeded, though measuring by its reputation, the Barri Xines is pretty tame these days (though most won't feel comfortable here after dark).

On and around the Ramblas are a number of buildings which warrant more than a casual glance as you pass. The graceful eighteenth-century baroque **Palau de la Virreina** (no. 99, corner of c/del Carme; Tues–Sat 9am–2pm and 4:30pm–9pm, Sun 9am–2pm) was built by a Peruvian viceroy and named after the wife who survived him. It now houses a fine display of period decorative art, a select collection of European masters, and various miscellaneous, and temporary, exhibitions. More interesting architecturally is the **Hospital de la Santa Creu**, two blocks off to the right down c/Hospital. Built on the site of a tenth-century refuge, it was later transformed into a hospital for pilgrims, the attractive complex of buildings here dating back to the fifteenth-century. Most have been converted to educational use, and you can wander freely among the spacious Gothic cloisters and courtyards. Just inside the entrance are some superb seventeenth-century *azulejos* of various religious scenes; note the figure on the right with the word *Iesus* written in mirror image — a formula signifying death. You can also go into the *Academia de Medicina* whose lecture theater is decked out in red velvet and chandeliers, complete with revolving marble dissection table.

Back on the Ramblas you pass the main food market — the glorious **Mercat Sant Josep** — before reaching the **Liceu** (guided tours Mon.–Fri.

11:30am and 12:15pm), Barcelona's celebrated opera house. A surprisingly modest exterior hides a feast of gilt, glass, and velvet inside. As a result of the *modernista* passion for Wagner, it's an important Wagnerian center; getting a ticket is hard work, but worth it if local soprano Montserrat Caballé (of Freddie Mercury fame) is at home. Advance bookings are made at the office in c/de Sant Pau, and there are sometimes standing-room-only tickets left at the box office on the day. There's a handy metro station here and, more or less opposite, the famous *Café de la Opera*, a wonderful and very fashionable meeting place (every bit as pricey as you'd expect — recent refurbishment has taken away much of its original character). Below the Liceu, c/de Sant Pau leads down to the church of **Sant Pau del Camp** (St. Paul of the Plain), its name a reminder that it once stood in open fields beyond the city walls. The oldest and one of the most interesting churches in Barcelona, Sant Pau was built in the tenth century on a Greek Cross plan. Above the main entrance are curious, primitive thirteenth-century carvings of fish, birds, and faces, while other animal forms adorn the capitals of the twelfth-century cloister.

On the opposite side of the Ramblas, hidden behind an archway and easy to miss, is the elegant nineteenth-century **Plaça Reial**, inspired by Napoleonic town planning. It's decorated with tall palm trees and iron lamps (by the young Gaudí) and these days is the haunt of punks, bikers, Catalan eccentrics, and bemused tourists drinking a coffee at one of the pavement cafes. The heavier nighttime atmosphere is more imagined than real, although there is a genuine "thieves market" in the northeast corner where stolen goods are regularly sold off. Nearby at the **Plaça Boqueria** there's a pavement mosaic by Miró and the fourteenth-century **Iglesia de Santa María del Pi**. Burnt down in 1936, the church was restored in the 1960s and boasts some marvelous stained glass, the best of it in a large rose window. The church is surrounded by three delightful little squares, the middle of which, **Plaça Sant Josep Oriol**, becomes an artists' market at weekends.

Continuing down the Ramblas, Gaudí's magnificent **Palau Güell** stands on Nou de la Rambla (see Gaudí section below) and there's little else until you reach the bottom, except for a poor **Museu de la Cera** (Wax Museum — daily 11am–1:30pm and 4:30–7:30pm) over on the other (northeast) side.

Right at the bottom of the Ramblas, Columbus stands pointing out to sea at the top of a tall grandiose, column: the **Monument a Colom (Columbus)**. You can get inside (Tues.–Sun. 9:30am–1:30pm and 4:30–8:30pm) and risk the elevator to his head (it fell down in 1976) for a fine view of the city. Opposite, in Plaça del Portal de la Pau, are the **Drassanes**, unique medieval shipyards, dating from the thirteenth century. They now house an excellent **Museu Maritim** (Maritime Museum; Tues.–Sat. 10am–2pm and 4–7pm, Sun. 10am–2pm) which includes in its collection a replica of Columbus' flagship, the *Santa María*, moored in the harbor outside. Dwarfed by its modern surroundings, it seems incredible that a ship of this size once carried forty men across the Atlantic.

From here you could take one of the regular **ferries** across the port to the modern docks, but there's little to do once you get there except return. A more dramatic, and expensive, view of the city is offered by the **cable car** (noon–8pm daily) which sweeps right across the harbor from the base of Montjuïc to the middle of the new docks and on to Barceloneta. You may remember Jack Nicholson riding it in Antonioni's *The Passenger*. A new sea-front *paseo*, with benches and trees, has been constructed from the Colom statue to the *Correus* (the post office), making a pleasant place to sit.

Apart from the Palau Guell (see p.424) there is nothing specific to see in the **Barri Xines** (Barrio Chino) and certainly no Chinese; but it is an interesting experience to wander around the triangle of streets directly inland from the Colom statue. During the day, at least, there's a strange mixture of local people going about their ordinary business, drug addicts in various stages of listless decay, police in pairs stopping suspected pushers, sex shops and porno clubs, prostitutes on street corners, and the ubiquitous souvenir shops and tourist hotels. A couple of the more idiosyncratic bars are well worth a visit: the tiny French *Bar Pastis* in c/Santa Monica and the *Bar London*, old haunt of circus artistes, where you can have a go on the trapeze hanging over the bar.

The Barri Gòtic

A remarkable concentration of beautiful medieval Gothic buildings, just a couple of blocks off the Ramblas, the Barri Gòtic forms the very heart of the old city. Once it was entirely enclosed by fourth-century A.D. Roman walls, but what you see now dates principally from the fourteenth and fifteenth centuries, when Barcelona reached the height of her commercial prosperity before being absorbed into the burgeoning kingdom of Castile. Parts of the ancient walls are still visible incorporated into later structures, especially around the Cathedral.

The quarter is centered on the **Plaça de Sant Jaume**, on one side of which stands the restored Town Hall, the **Ajuntament**. Despite appearances you are usually free to wander in and have a look around the fourteenth-century council chamber, the *Salo de Cent*, on the first floor; normally open from 10am to 1pm and 5 to 7pm, it is currently closed to the public except for a tantalizing glimpse into the main courtyard. You can, however, go into the municipal information office on the ground floor and look at its lovely wall paintings, the work of contemporary Catalan artist Albert Rafols Casamada (more of whose work is in the Museum of Modern Art). Across the spacious square rises the **Palau de la Generalitat** (or *Diputació*), present and traditional home of the Catalan government (Sun. only 10am–1pm; you must leave your passport at the entrance while you visit). Restored during the sixteenth century in Renaissance style, it has a beautiful cloister on the first floor with superb coffered ceilings, while opening off this gallery are two fine rooms — the chapel and salon of Sant Jordi (St. George), patron saint of Catalunya — and other chambers of the former law courts.

Just behind this, on a site previously occupied by a Roman temple and Moorish mosque (a familiar pattern), the **Cathedral** (daily 7am–1:30pm and 2–7:30pm) is one of the great Gothic buildings of Spain. Begun in 1298, it was finished in 1448 with one notable exception commented on by Richard Ford in 1845: "The principal façade is unfinished, with a bold front poorly painted in stucco, although the rich chapter have for three centuries received a fee on every marriage for this very purpose of completing it." Perhaps goaded into action, the authorities set to and completed the façade within a ten-year period in the 1880s.

The **interior** used to have a reputation for being gloomy and ponderous, the result of a shortage of windows in the clerestory. Artificial lighting, however, has transformed the place, replacing the dank mystery with a soar-

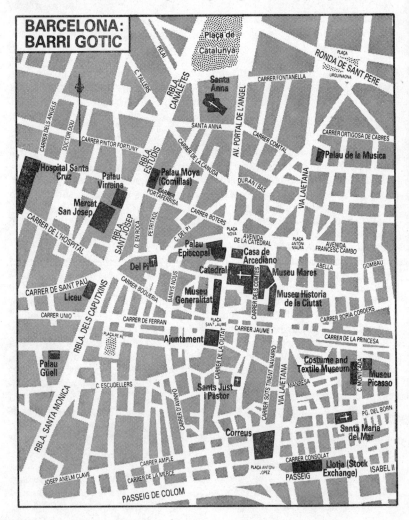

ing airiness to echo the grandeur of the exterior. *La Seu* (as it's known locally) is dedicated to Santa Eulalia, martyred by the Romans for daring to prefer Christianity, and her tomb rests in a crypt beneath the high altar; if you put money in the slot the whole thing lights up to show off its exemplary Catholic kitschiness. See, too, the rich altar-pieces, *rejas*, and carved tombs of the 29 side chapels. Among them is the painted wooden tomb of Ramon Berenguer I, Count of Barcelona from 1018 to 1025, who was responsible for establishing many of the *usatges*, ancient Catalan rights. The colossal Moor's head below the organ is a replacement for one which used to vomit sweets on *el Día de los Inocentes*, the Spanish equivalent of April Fool's Day. Outside, the magnificent **cloisters** look over a lush tropical garden with soaring palm trees and white geese, and open into, among other things, the small **cathedral museum** (Mon.–Fri. 10am–1pm).

Flanking the cathedral are two fifteenth-century buildings closely associated with it: the **Casa de Arcediano** (once the archdeacon's residence, now the city archives) and the **Palau Episcopal**, the bishop's palace. Both have superb courtyards and outdoor stairways (there's a patio at the top of the Palau Episcopal's stairway with Romanesque wall paintings), a frequent feature of the *Barri*. Next to the Palau Episcopal, and at various points in and near Via Laietana, you can see some of the remaining **Roman walls**, and there are well-preserved Roman tombs in the nearby Plaça de la Villa de Madrid.

Barcelona's finest Roman remains, however, were uncovered beneath the former Palace of the Counts of Barcelona (the **Palau Reial**) which now houses the **Museu d'Historia de la Ciutat** (Tues.–Sat. 9am–2pm and 5–8pm, Sun. 9am–2pm). Underground, both Roman and Visigothic remains have been preserved where they were discovered during works in the 1930s. The museum also gives access to the beautiful fourteenth-century **Capilla Reial de Santa Agata** with its tall single nave and unusual stained glass, and to an extension of the royal palace known as the **Saló de Tinell**, a fine spacious example of fourteenth-century secular Gothic architecture. At one time the Inquisition met here, taking full advantage of the popular belief that the walls would move if a lie was spoken; nowadays classical concerts are occasionally held. It was on the steps leading from the Saló de Tinell into the Plaça del Rei (the plaza is in fact the old palace courtyard) that Fernando and Isabella stood to receive Columbus on his triumphant return from America.

The fascinating and extraordinary **Museu Marès** (Tues.–Sat. 9am–2pm and 4–7pm, Sun. 9am–2pm) occupies another wing of the palace, across the plaza. The bulk of this museum consists of an important body of religious sculpture, including a vast number of wooden crucifixes showing the stylistic development of this form from the twelfth to the fifteenth centuries. This is infinitely more interesting than it might sound, but in case boredom should set in, the upper floors house the **Museu Sentimental** of local sculptor Frederico Marès, an incredible retrospective jumble gathered during fifty years of travel, with everything from tarot cards to walking sticks by way of cigarette papers! Don't miss it.

Barcelona's Churches

Walking west from the palace, you'll cross Via Laietana and reach c/ Montcada, down which lies the Picasso Museum (see below). Towards the bottom of this street is the graceful church of **Santa María del Mar**, built on what was the seashore in the fourteenth century. Its soaring lines were the symbol of Catalan supremacy in Mediterranean commerce (much of it sponsored by the church) and it is still much dearer to the heart of the average local than the cathedral. The stained glass, especially, is beautiful. Dating from much the same period is the **Esglesia dels Sants Just i Pastor** behind the Ajuntament (enter from the back, at c/Ciutat), while even older is the **Esglesia de Santa Ana** (in c/Santa Ana, near Plaça Catalunya), built in the twelfth century in the form of a Greek Cross.

For the finest Gothic cloister in Barcelona, however, you have to travel well outside the Barri Gòtic to the **Monastery of Pedralbes** (Tues.–Sun. 10am–1pm) on the western fringes of the city. It's about a half-hour journey by bus (no. 22 from the Passeig de Gràcia, just north of Plaça de Catalunya, to the end of the line) but well worth the effort. Built in the fourteenth century, the church still has some of its original stained glass and the cloisters, on three levels like most of the church, are tranquil and harmonious. You can also visit the rooms where the monks used to live. The monastery is destined to house the Italian religious paintings of the controversial Thyssen-Bornemisza art collection (see "the Prado" in the Madrid chapter) which should make the trip yet more worthwhile.

Even more remote, in a rich suburb, is the Benedictine monastery at **SANT CUGAT DEL VALLÈS** which has a beautiful twelfth-century Romanesque cloister with noteworthy capital carvings of mythical beasts and biblical scenes. They have an unusual homogeneity since they were all done by a single sculptor, Arnau Gatell. Sant Cugat is a fairly quick direct journey on *Ferrocarriles Catalanes* from Plaça Catalunya. Enthusiasts can use the same conveyance to get even farther out to TERRASSA, an otherwise dull place with three pre-Romanesque churches. They are all together some way out of the center of the village; ask for Sant Pere, the biggest, and look closest at Sant Miquel, the most interesting.

Picasso, the Carrer de Montcada, and Other Art

Although born in Málaga, Picasso spent much of his youth — from the age of 14 to 23 — in Barcelona. He maintained close links with Barcelona and his Catalan friends even when he left for Paris in 1904, and is said to have always thought of himself as Catalan rather than Andaluz. The time Picasso spent in Barcelona encompassed most of his "Blue Period" (1901–4) and was the occassion for many of the formative influences on his art. The **Museu Picasso** (Tues.–Sat. 9am–2pm and 4–8:30pm, Sun. 9am–2pm, Mon 4–8:30pm; free Sun.) has one of the most important collections of his work in the world and certainly the only one of any significance (apart from the Prado's *Guernica*) in his native country.

The museum opened in 1963 with a collection based largely on the donations of Jaime Sabartes, friend and former secretary of the artist. On Sabartes's death in 1968 Picasso himself added a large number of works — above all the 44 canvases of the *Meninas* series — and in 1970 he donated a further vast number of water colors, drawings, and paintings. The early periods are the best represented, with works from the "Pink Period" (1904–6) and the Cubist (1907–20) and neoclassical (1920–25) stages predominating, but the museum also boasts a series of minor sketches, drawings, and prints which cover in detail every phase of the artist's work from 1899 to 1972.

The early drawings in which Picasso (still signing his full name, Pablo Ruiz Picasso) attempted to copy the nature paintings in which his father specialized, and the many studies from his art school days, are fascinating. Even at the ages of fifteen and sixteen and he was painting major works: a self-portrait and a portrait of his mother from 1896, copies of paintings in the Prado from the following year. All of this is housed in a strikingly beautiful medieval palace (or, to be more precise, two mansions joined together) converted specifically to house the museum. It's extremely well laid out, following the artist's chronological development, with thorough labeling in Spanish and Catalan.

The Museu Picasso stands on the **Carrer de Montcada**, a street crowded with beautifully restored ancient buildings, many of which are open for visits. One, almost opposite the museum, houses the **Museu Textil i d'Indumentaria** (Tues.–Sat. 9am–2pm and 4:30–7pm, Sun. 9am–2pm), an impressive collection of clothing and tapestries. Continue on down the street (past a lavishly tiled *champanyaria* serving champagne, cider and excellent seafood *tapas*) and you'll come out opposite the great **Basilica of Santa María del Mar** (see "The Barri Gòtic" preceding).

Not too far away, you can still see many of the buildings in which Picasso lived and worked, notably the **Escola de Belles Arts de Llotja** (c/ Consolat del Mar, near Estació de França) where his father taught drawing and where Picasso himself absorbed an academic training. The apartments where the family lived when they first arrived in Barcelona — Passeig d'Isabel II 4 and c/Cristina 3, both opposite the Escola — can also be seen, though only from the outside. More interesting is **Els 4 Gats** (c/Montsió 3, Metro *Catalunya*), the bar opened by Pere Romeu and other *modernista* artists in 1897 as a gathering place for their contemporaries. An imitation of Aristide Bruant's Parisian cabaret *Le Chat Noir*, it was the birthplace of *modernista* magazines, the scene of poetry readings and shadow-puppet theatre and, in 1901, the setting for Picasso's first public exhibition. Today you can have a beer and look at Ramón Casa's wall painting of himself and Pere Romeu on a tandem bicycle, and occasionally there's live jazz in the back room. They've added a modern extension next door, so don't mistake the entrances.

Dedicated Picasso fans might also want to wander up c/Avinyó, heading up from the seafront, looking for the brothel which inspired his seminal cubist work, *Les Demoiselles d'Avignon*; and to seek out an important work of the latter years, the frieze which he designed in 1960 for the College of Architects, on the Plaça Nova opposite the cathedral.

Some Art Galleries

A gallery which was already well-established when Picasso and Miró were young — the **Sala Pares** — can still be seen in all its solid plushness at c/ Petritxol 5 (off Plaça del Pi). It deals exclusively in nineteenth- and twentieth-century Catalan art. Almost opposite there's a plaque on the wall in recognition of the services of another great art dealer, Josep Dalmau. He opened his *Galeries Dalmau* in Via Laietana in 1907 and five years later introduced Cubism — most notably Marcel Duchamp's *Nude Descending Staircase* — to Barcelona. *Galeries Dalmau* are now at c/Consell de Cent 349. Of the smaller private galleries, *Galeria Maeght* (c/Montcada 25) and *Galeria d'Art Joan Prats* (Rambla Catalunya 54) generally have interesting displays, and there are many more. Check the local press for news of anything good.

Bank sponsorship of art is very important in Catalonia and some of the biggest and best temporary exhibitions can be seen at the **Caixa de Pensions'** impressive building at Passeig Sant Joan 108 (Metro *Verdaguer*). They have a good art bookshop there too. Smaller exhibition spaces worth keeping an eye on are the other *Caixa de Pensions* gallery (at c/Montcada 14), the **Sala Caixa de Barcelona** (Passeig de Gràcia 2) and the **Sala Sotcentral** (c/Jaume I) next to the Ajuntament.

Antoni Gaudí and *Modernisme*

Besides modern art, Barcelona offers — through the work of **Antoni Gaudí** (1852–1926) — some of the most fantastic and exciting modern architecture to be found anywhere in the world.

Modernisme, the Catalan offshoot of art nouveau, was the expression of a renewed upsurge in Catalan nationalism in the 1870s. The architect Domenech i Montaner was responsible for giving this a definite direction with his appeal, in 1878, for a national style of architecture, drawing particularly on the rich tradition of Catalan Romanesque and Gothic. It was a time which witnessed expansion in Barcelona. The medieval walls had been demolished and the Eixample grid was giving the city a new look, with a rather French feel to it. By 1874 Gaudí had begun his architectural career, and fourteen years later the young Puig i Cadafalch would be inspired to become an architect as he watched the spectacularly rapid round-the-clock construction of Domenech's *Grand Hotel* on the Passeig de Colom. It was in another building by Domenech (the cafe-restaurant of the Ciutadella) that a craft workshop was set up after the Exhibition of 1888, giving Barcelona's *modernista* architects the opportunity to experiment with traditional crafts like ceramic tiles, ironwork, stained glass, and decorative stone carving.

This combination of traditional crafts with modern technology was to become the hallmark of *modernisme*. Gaudí himself was by training a metal-worker, by inclination a fervent Catalan nationalist. His buildings are the most daring creations of all Art Nouveau, apparently lunatic flights of fantasy but at the same time perfectly functional. Gaudí never wrote a word about the theory of his art, preferring its products to speak for themselves. They demand reaction.

La Sagrada Família

Without doubt Gaudí's most famous creation is the great **Temple Expiatiori de la Sagrada Família** (daily 9am–8pm, 250ptas.; metro Line 5 to *Sagrada Família*), a good ways northeast of the Plaça Catlunya and just north of the Diagonal. In many ways it has become a kind of symbol for the city, and was the only church (aside from the cathedral) left untouched by the orgy of church burning which followed the 1936 revolution.

Begun in 1882 by public subscription (hence its "Expiatory" nature), the Sagrada Familia was conceived originally in an orthodox Neogothic style; Gaudí took charge two years later and was adapting the plans ceaselessly right up to his death. Today the church remains unfinished, though amid great controversy work has restarted based on Gaudí's last known plans. Some maintain that the structure should be left incomplete as a memorial to Gaudí's untimely death,* others that he intended it to be the work of several generations, each continuing in their own style. The current work seems to infringe on the original spirit in either case, but it still ranks as one of the most extraordinary buildings in the world.

The size alone is startling; eight spires rise to over 100 meters. They have been likened to everything from perforated cigars to celestial billiard cues, both of which are good descriptions. For Gaudí they were metaphors for the Twelve Apostles; he planned to build four more above the main facade and to add a 180-meter tower topped with a lamb (representing Jesus) over the transept, itself to be surrounded by four smaller towers symbolizing the Evangelists.

A precise symbolism also pervades the facades, each of which is divided into three porches devoted to Faith, Hope, and Charity. The east facade further represents the Nativity and the Mysteries of Joy; the west (currently the main entrance and nearing completion) depicts the Passion and the Mysteries of Affliction. Gaudí meant the south facade to be the culmination of the *Templo* — the Gloria, designed, he said, to show "the religious realities of present and future life . . . man's origin, his end and the ways he has to follow to achieve it." Everything from the Creation to Heaven and Hell, in short, was to be included in one magnificent ensemble. And if the place looks to you more like a giant building site (as it sometimes can), locally available guides should help to sort out the various elements. Take the elevator which runs up one of the towers, and you can enjoy a dizzy view down over the whole complex and climb still further around the walls and into the towers.

Inside the Temple a small **Gaudí Museum** traces the career of the architect and the history of the building. It is likely to set you on the trail of his earlier work, all of which, astonishingly, dates from before 1911 when he finished the Parc Güell and vowed never to work again on secular art, but to devote himself solely to the Sagrada Familia.

---

*Gaudí was run over by a tram in 1926 and died in the hospital two days later — initially unrecognized, for he had become a virtual recluse rarely leaving the small studio within the church building where he lived and worked. His death was treated as a Catalan national disaster, and all of Barcelona turned out for his funeral procession.

Gaudí's Other Work

Gaudí began his career in Barcelona as an assistant on the **monumental fountain** in the Parc de la Ciutadella (1877–82). The baroque extravagance of its cascade is suggestive of the flamboyant decoration which was to become his trademark but it was from the Mudejar style that he took inspiration for his first major work, the **Casa Vicens** (c/Carolinas 24–26; metro Line 3 to *Fontana*). Its decorative iron railings are a reminder of Gaudí's early training as a metalsmith, and to further prove his versatility (and how art nouveau cuts across art forms), he designed much of the mansion's furniture too.

Much of Gaudí's early career was spent constructing elaborate follies for wealthy patrons. The most important was Don Eusebio Güell, a shipowner and industrialist, who in 1885 commissioned the **Palau Güell**, just off the Ramblas. It's now used as a **theater museum** (Mon.–Sat. 10am–1pm and 5–7pm; Sun. 10am–1pm), so, unusually, you can see the interior; most of the Gaudí houses are still privately owned. Here, Gaudí's feel for different materials is remarkable. At a time when architects sought to conceal the iron supports within buildings, Gaudí turned them to his advantage.

From 1900–1914 Gaudí continued to work for the same patron on the **Parc Güell** (daily 10am–8pm, though the Column Park may be closed for restoration), his most ambitious project apart from the Sagrada Familia. It was commissioned as a private housing estate of sixty dwellings, but only two houses were actually built. The park itself, though, is an almost hallucinatory expression of the imagination, with giant decorative lizards and a vast Hall of Columns, described by Sacheverell Sitwell (in *Spain*) as "at once a fun fair, a petrified forest, and the great temple of Amun at Karnak, itself drunk, and reeling in an eccentric earthquake." The ceramic mosaics were made from "authentic" tiles such as are still found in older Catalan houses. The park contains the house in which Gaudí used to live, now another small **museum** (Sun. only 10am–2pm and 4–6pm) with some of the furniture he designed, a typical mixture of wild originality and brilliant engineering. To get to the park take bus #24 from the Plaça de Catalunya to Travesera de Dalt.

Gaudí's weird apartment block, the **Casa Milà**, at Passeig de Gràcia 92 (metro Line 3 to Pg. de Gràcia) is another building not to be missed. Its structure is said to have been inspired by the mountain of Montserrat, and the flats themselves resemble eroded cave dwellings; hence it is known as *La Pedrera* (the "rock pile" or "stone quarry"). You can visit the courtyard any time and the roof (to see at close quarters the enigmatic chimneys) at 10am, 11am, and noon. Four blocks down on the other side (at no. 43) is the **Casa Battló**, designed to simulate a breaking wave!

The exteriors of three other important Gaudí buildings can also be seen around the city. The **Casa Figueras** (c/Bell Esguard) and the **Colegio Santa Teresa** (c/Ganduxer 87) are both near the *Bonanova* stop on the *Ferrocarriles Catalanes* Peu del Funicular line. The **Finca Parque** is about ten minutes' walk from the Monastery of Pedralbes but you can see no farther than its metal dragon gateway (it's just off the Avda. Pedralbes; metro Line 3 to *Palacio*).

The various tourist offices issue a handy leaflet describing all of Gaudí's works, including a map showing their locations.

Gaudí's Contemporaries

If you've contracted a serious case of *modernista* fever there are several works by Gaudí's contemporaries worth tracking down across the city. Domenech i Montaner designed the **Casa Tomás** (c/Mallorca 291–3), the **Casa Fuster** (Pg. de Gràcia 132), the extraordinary **Hospital de Sant Pau** (a short walk from the Sagrada Familia up the Avda. Gaudí) and, most notably, the **Palau de la Musica** which doesn't seem to have enough breathing space in the tiny c/Sant Pere Mas Alt (off Via Laietana). If you can get a ticket for one of the many fine concerts inside, so much the better, since the building is as fantastic acoustically as it is visually.

For work by Puig i Cadafalch head for the Diagonal. Here you'll find the **Museu de la Musica** at no. 373 and the so-called **Casa de les Punxes** (properly Casa Terrades) at nos. 416–20 (corner of c/Rossello). The **Casa Amatller** stands on the Pg. de Gràcia next to Gaudi's Casa Battló, the two so different in style and feeling that this bit of street is known as the *Block of Discord*. For a rounder, softer style than Puig's, look at Josep Maria Jujol i Gibert's **Casa Planells** at Diagonal 332; he also did much of the mosaic work in the Parc Güell.

Modern Architecture

Barcelona has maintained its reputation for unusual architecture and it looks as if the 1992 Olympics will echo 1888 and 1929 in terms of yet more innovations. Obsessed with being "modern," and feeling that it has a lot of catching up to do after Franco, Barcelona is entering energetically into a phase of making itself first workable and then impressive during the two weeks when the whole world will be watching.

The main architects for the Olympic project are an international bunch, including Japanese, Italian, and Catalan names. The Catalans — among them Oriol Bohigas, Carlos Buxadé, Joan Margarit, Ricardo Bofill, and Federico Correa — have all been leaving their impression upon Barcelona for a number of years. You can see Bohigas's **Habitatges Treballadors Metallurgics**, for example, at c/Pallars 301-319; Correa's **Atalaia de Barcelona** at Avda. Sarrià 71; and Bofill's **Bloc Residencial** at c/Nicaragua 99.

But perhaps the most exciting contemporary buildings of Barcelona are the wonderful "rationalist" works of the late Jose Antonio Coderch, working from the 1950s through the 1970s, and producing such marvels as the curved glass **Trade Towers** at Gran Vía de Carles III, 86–94. Less dramatic but still very pleasing are his blocks of apartments at c/Raset 21–23 and at c/Johann Sebastian Bach 7.

For something of the 1980s, walk around Sants station where Helio Piñon has made a rather comfortless "park" of the Plaça dels Països Catalans. Two minutes' walk away is Luis Peña Ganchegui's **Parc de l'Espanya Industrial**, a line of striped lighthouses at the top of glaring white steps with an incongruously classical Neptune in the water below, seen to best effect at night. If that hasn't cured you, go to Gràcia and see Jaume Bach and Gabriel Mora's work in the **Plaça del Sol**. Farther out there's the pleasant cone-shaped **Plaça de la Palmera** near c/d'Andrade (metro *Besós*) by Richard Serra.

Ciutadella, Montjuïc, Tibidabo, and Their Museums

It's easy enough, even in the middle of Barcelona, to escape for a few hours into greenery and relative peace. The hill of **Montjuïc**, which has a whole string of important museums, is much the largest green area and contains the most of interest; **Tibidabo**, behind the city, has even better views; or, for a quick respite from the center there's the **Parc de la Ciutadella**, easy walking distance from the Barri Gòtic and with definite attractions of its own.

Ciutadella

The **Parc de la Ciutadella** seems to have a peculiar ability to take in far more than would seem possible from its outward dimensions. As well as the lake, Gaudí's monumental fountain, and the city zoo, you'll find here the meeting place of the Catalan parliament and a modern art museum. The last two occupy parts of a fortress-like structure right at the heart of the park, the surviving portion of a **citadel** erected by Felipe V in 1715 to subdue Barcelona after its spirited resistance to the Bourbons in the War of the Spanish Succession. It seems a fitting irony that the main palace structure is once again home to the autonomous Catalan parliament, which first sat here between 1932 and 1939.

The **Museu d'Art Modern** (Tues.-Sat. 9am-7:30pm, Sun. 9am-2pm, Mon. 1-7:30pm) begins with eighteenth-century neoclassical exhibits, but ranges well into the 1980s. It's particularly good on *modernista* and *noucentista* painting and sculpture and there are some fine examples of the work of Casas, Rusiñol, Mir, and Nonell (*modernistas*); and Sunyer, Gargallo, Nognés, and González (*noucentistas*). The genuinely modern collection has also been improved of late, with several rooms now devoted to more recent movements in Catalan art.

The park itself was created for the 1888 Exhibition, which was held within its confines, and many of the *modernista* giants left their mark here. As well as the **monumental fountain**, Gaudí designed the park's gateways. The exhibition's cafe-restaurant, designed by Domenech i Montaner, has now become the **Museu de Zoologia** (Tues.-Sat. 9am-2pm). Don't confuse this with the **zoo** (daily 10am-7pm) on the other side of the park; here the star attraction is Snowflake, a unique (in captivity at least) and much-gawked-at, pure albino gorilla.

Montjuïc

It takes a full day to sample the varied attractions of the **hill of Montjuïc**: five museums, the "Spanish Village," and a castle with grand views of the city. The hill, which takes its name from the Jewish community once settled on its slopes, covers a wide area and if you want to see everything you'll have to plan your time fairly carefully around the various opening times.

The most obvious way **to approach the museums** is to take a bus or the metro to Plaça d'Espanya and walk from there up the imposing Avinguda de la Reina Maria Cristina, past the 1929 International Fair buildings and the rows of fountains, where on Sunday there is a spectacular light and music show (9pm–midnight in summer, 8–11pm in winter). If you'd rather start with the castle, there's the dramatic **cable car** ride from Barceloneta or from near the Colom monument, over the harbor to Jardins de Miramar just below (out of season it runs only at weekends). You can also walk up from Paral.lel; take c/Margarit and the steps which start near Poble Sec's soccer field, and you'll come out at the bottom of the cable car which runs up to the amusement park and the castle. Or there's a **funicular railway** which runs from Paral.lel metro station to the start of the cable car. And lastly there are buses: #61 from Plaça d'Espanya to the amusement park, and #201 from Poble Sec to the same place.

The Museums

If you tackle the stiff climb from the Plaça d'Espanya you'll arrive at the **Palau Nacional**, centerpiece of Barcelona's 1929 International Fair and now home to one of Spain's great museums, the **Museu d'Art de Catalunya** (Tues.–Sun. 9am–2pm; free on Sun.). This has two enormous main sections, one dedicated to Gothic art and the other to Romanesque. The Gothic collection is fascinating, ranging over the whole of Spain and particularly good on Catalunya, Valencia, and Aragón; it's supplemented by a section of sixteenth- to eighteenth-century art including works by El Greco, Zurbarán, and Velázquez. But it's the Romanesque section that is the most remarkable, perhaps the best collection of its kind in the world: 35 rooms of eleventh- and twelfth-century frescoes, meticulously removed from a series of small Pyrenean churches and beautifully displayed. This is really impressive, and while you're unlikely to be familiar with such art (surviving examples are rare and invariably remote) you're equally unlikely not to be converted to its charms. If you get hooked the next biggest collection is in Vic (Catalunya), and there's a similar, smaller collection of Aragonese frescoes in the cathedral museum at Jaca.

More immediately, and also of considerable interest, the **Museu de Ceramica** opens off the main museum (same hours, same ticket) with a comprehensive collection of ceramics going back as far as the twelfth century. In the modern section Picasso, Miró, and the *modernista* Antoni Serra i Fiter are all represented. Also nearby, behind the palace, is the **Museu Etnològic** (Ethnological Museum; Mon. 2–8:30pm, Tues.–Sat. 9am–8:30pm, Sun. 9am–2pm) with extensive collections from Japan, Central and South America, Turkey, and Senegal, all housed in a series of glass hexagons.

Barcelona's important **Museu Arqueològic** (Tues.–Sat. 9:30am–1pm and 4–7pm, Sun. 9:30am–2pm; free on Sun.) stands to the east of the Palau Nacional, lower down the hill and opposite a reproduction of a Greek theater (again built for the 1929 Fair and now used during the summer cultural festival). For the most part the museum is devoted to the Roman period, though there are also Carthaginian relics (especially from the Balearics), Etruscan bits and pieces, and lots of prehistoric objects. The museum is of particular interest if you're planning to visit Empuries, since most of the important finds from that impressive coastal site, and some good maps and photographs, are housed here. Among the more unusual exhibits in the museum is a reconstructed Roman funeral chamber whose walls are divided into small niches for funeral urns; a type of burial known as *columbaria* (literally pigeon-holes) which may be seen in situ at Carmona in Andalucía. The museum recently opened an annex — the "Secret Museum" — to display new acquisitions and pieces previously kept in shortage for lack of space

Also near the Greek theater is the **Fundacio Joan Miró** (Tues.–Sat. 11am–8pm, Sun. 11am–2pm), possibly the most adventurous of Barcelona's museums. Miró was one of the greatest of the Catalan artists, establishing an international reputation while never severing his links with his homeland. He had his first exhibition in 1918 and after that spent his summers in Catalunya (and the rest of the time in France) before moving to Mallorca in 1956, where he died in 1983. His friend, the architect Josep-Luis Sert, designed the beautiful white building that now houses the museum, a permanent collection of paintings, graphics, tapestries, and sculptures donated by Miró himself and covering the period from 1914 to 1978*. The paintings, regarded as one of the chief links between surrealism and abstract art, are instantly recognizable. Excellent temporary exhibitions, which may or may not be to do with aspects of Miró's own work, are a regular feature, and most exciting of all is the recently opened room full of work by other twentieth-century artists in homage to Miró. This includes work by Matisse, Braque, Kandinsky, Giacometti, and Balthus, everything on show greatly enhanced by the beauty of the building itself, set in gardens overlooking the city.

Architecture on the Hill

A short walk over to the other side of the Palau Nacional will bring you to the **Poble Espanyol** or "Spanish Village" (daily 9am–6pm). A complete village consisting of famous or characteristic buildings from all over Spain, this was an inspired concept for the International Fair. As a crash-course introduction to Spanish architecture it's not at all bad — everything is well labeled and at least reasonably accurate — but inevitably the place swarms with tourists. Prices, especially for the produce of the "genuine Spanish workshops" (but even in the bars), are exorbitant. Just down the road next to the Olympic Office, the recent reconstruction of the **Mies van der Rohe Pavilion** (Tues.–Sun. 10am–6pm) is a far greater treat. Part of the German contribution to the 1929 Fair, it's a startlingly beautiful conjunction of hard, straight lines with watery surfaces, its dark green polished onyx alternating with shining glass.

Finally, way above this complex of museums and offering magnificent views across the city, stands the eighteenth-century **Castle** (*Castell de*

---

* For more Miró, go to the **Parc de Joan Miró** (Metro *Tarragona*) and admire the gigantic mosaic sculpture *Dona i Ocell* towering above its small lake. You'll also notice everywhere the starfish logo which Miró designed for the *Caixa de Pensions*; and the España logo on SNTO publications.

Montjuïc), built on seventeenth-century ruins. It has been the scene of much bloodshed — the first president of the Generalitat, Lluís Companys, was executed here by the Franco regime in 1940 — and perhaps appropriately now houses a remarkably good **Military Museum** (Tues.–Sat. 10am–2pm and 4–8pm, Sun. 10am–8pm). Inside are models of the most famous Catalan castles and an excellent collection of Spanish swords and guns, medals, uniforms, maps, and photographs. Real enthusiasts might want to buy the catalogue since labels are poor.

Tibidabo . . . and a Maze

If the views from the Castell de Montjuïc are good, those from the top of **Mount Tibidabo** — which forms the northwestern boundary of the city — are legendary. On one of those mythical clear days you can see across to Montserrat and the Pyrenees, and out to sea even as far as Mallorca. The very name is based on this view, taken from the Temptations of Christ in the wilderness, when Satan led him to a high place and offered him everything which could be seen: *Haec omnia tibi dabo si cadens adoraberis me* (All these things will I give thee, if thou wilt fall down and worship me).

At the summit there's a wonderfully old-fashioned **Parc d'Atracions**, where the amusements include a 1920s *aeroplano* ("Experience the sensation of flying!"), and, from the 1960s, the kind of go-carts The Monkees used to burn around in. In sum, a feast for nostalgists and all would-be kids. Buy a fistful of tickets for rides with your admisssion charge.

All around Tibidado there are pleasant walks through the woods, and there are a couple of bars and a pleasant restuarant close by the tram stop, just below the Parc d'Atracions.

To **get to Tibidabo**, take the *Ferrocarriles Catalanes* light rail line or bus #17 (both from Plaça de Catalunya) to Avda. Tibidabo; from there a tram connects with the funicular railway to the top. On the way up or down you could get off the tram and visit the **Museu de Ciencia** (Tues.–Sun. 10am–8pm) at c/Teodor Roviralta 65, which contains, among other things, a planetarium, and hosts weekend film shows for kids. Opposite the funicular station is another small **museum** (Tues.–Sat. 9am–2pm) with a scientific bent, full of rather touching antecedents of modern technology.

For a different city experience travel right to the end of the #27 bus route where, way up in the fresh air, lies **El Laberint d'Horta**, an eighteenth-century topiary maze which, while in need of major resoration, is a quiet haven on a hot day.

Eating, Drinking, and Other Action

Feeding and amusing yourself in Barcelona is unlikely to be a problem. There are lively restaurants and bars throughout the center and nightlife that, at present, is some of Europe's hippest. It keeps going all night too, the music bars shutting up at 3am, the discos at 5am and (for the seriously dissipated) some semi-legal clubs *opening* between 5am and 9am on weekends.

For **listings** of almost anything you could want in the way of culture and entertainment, buy a copy of the weekly *Guía del Ocio* (60ptas) from any newspaper stall. This has full details of film, theater, and musical events (free and otherwise) as well as extensive sections on bars, restaurants, and nightlife. It's in Spanish but easy enough to decipher. Plusher, at 300ptas, is the monthly *Vivir en Barcelona*. There is a thriving gay scene in Barcelona; *SexTienda*, at c/Rauric 11 (very near Plaça Reial), dishes out a map of gay Barcelona with a list of bars, clubs, and contacts.

Food

There is an ample variety of food available in Barcelona and even low-budget travelers can do well for themselves. The most serious problems that you're likely to encounter are that a lot of places close on Sundays and throughout August, and that at the cheaper end there is often no written menu, the waiter merely reeling off the day's dishes at bewildering speed. Also note that that the *menú del día* (nearly always great value at lunchtime) is rarely available in the evening. Prices in restaurants have gone up quite a bit since Spain's entry into the European Community, especially for wine; watch out, too, for *IVA* (sales tax) on the bill.

Starting with **breakfast**, you can get coffee and bread almost anywhere, but to get into the swing of things head for the Plaça Sant Jaume and the small but popular *Santa Clara*, especially busy with Catalans on Sunday mornings. About 20m away down c/Llibreteria, the tiny *Mesón del Cafe* serves delicious cappuccinos, while in the other direction off c/Ferran you'll find the glossy *El Paraigna* in Plaça Sant Miguel. It's expensive but worth at least one visit, the interior an art nouveau umbrella shop removed from its original location on the Ramblas.

For the food which Barcelona is really proud of — elaborate *zarzuelas* (fish stews), and all kinds of **fish and seafood** — you're best off heading down to the **Barceloneta** district (bus #64 or #17, final stop). In the main street, Passeig Nacional, the seafood restaurants are thick on the ground, one of the best the *Casa Tipa* at no. 6. Avoid, though, the much promoted *El Rey de la Gamba* at nos. 46–48 — the food is poor and overpriced. Although the food *menú del día* exists down here, it can all look intimidatingly expensive until you realise that there's no need to have a full meal. Sitting down for a huge plateful of prawns or mussels and a beer is a popular option. *Bar Ricart*, away from the main drag on c/Almiral Cervera, is new, non-touristy, and one of the better value places here. For fish restaurants right on the beach (in summer, literally) turn on to the tiny c/Judici at the far end of Passeig Nacional; here you can take your pick from the enticing fish on display behind each restaurant. *El Salmonete* at the far end is fashionable at present, but not necessarily the best in quality.

Back in town but still near the harbor, c/Ample and its offshoots — between the Columbus monument and the post office — are famous for their *tapas* bars. Among the best are *La Pulpería* at c/de la Merce 16, *El Tropezón* (c/Regomir 26), and *La Bodega* farther up c/Regomir. The last is a great barn of a place with long wooden benches, delicious food, and one of the most primitive toilets in the city. *Casa Antonio* (c/Correu Vell 4) and *Monteban* (c/D'Ataly 7) are standard cheap places. *Las Siete Puertas* (Passeig Isabel II, under the arcades almost opposite the Correus) is far more expensive, a wood-paneled old standard where Alexander Fleming, among many other famous names, used to eat. The decor has barely changed in 150 years, and while very elegant, it's not exclusive. They do a very good *paella* here, dark in color, but there is a limited number of cheaper dishes. At lunchtime during the week it gets packed with people from the stock exchange across the road — arrive early.

Other good restaurants are easily found all around the Ramblas, particularly in the area around the Plaça Reial and in the Barri Xines. The Ramblas itself is not cheap, but does contain some fine restaurants. *Amaya* (Ramblas 20–24) is so famous for its Basque cuisine that you'll have to fight your way in on a Sunday. At the front it has a very good *tapas* bar. For about the same price you can eat at nearby *Los Caracoles* (c/Escudellers 14), a famous Barcelona landmark whose flamboyant 1940s owner attracted the rich and famous; their signed photos now decorate the walls. The food is no longer that great, but the decor and atmosphere are still worth a visit. *La Parilla* (more prominently labelled *Grill Room*) at no. 8 is a more economic version owned by the same people. The *Cafe Moka*, near the Liceu, is cheaper than its glossy appearance and old-fashioned, formal service would suggest; in 1937 this was occupied by civil guards who were fired on by George Orwell and his POUM colleagues from across the street.

On the west side of the Ramblas things are generally cheaper, though an exception worth seeking out is the *Hotel España* (c/Sant Pau 9–11) where you can eat in *modernista* splendor; the building was designed by Domenech i Montaner, and the *menú del día* is good value at around 900ptas. Close by is the very basic *Romesco* (c/Arc Sant Agustí), famous for its belly-warming *frijoles* (refried beans); and the more stylish *La Morera* (Plaça Sant Agustí) with a cheap and imaginative *menú*. This, as well as the excellent *Egipte*, only 30m away at c/Jerusalem 12, are both listed on the gay map of Barcelona.

In the same general area there are several other good budget options: the *Pollo Rico* (c/Sant Pau 31) does spit roast chicken to eat upstairs or takeaway; whilst *Can Peret* (Plaça de Salvador Seguí, off Sant Pau) is about as cheap as you can get — help yourself to cutlery, wine, and bread. The *Casa Leopoldo* in this area (c/San Rafael 24) is more expensive but has a very good reputation, specializing in seafood. Other possibilities include the *Bar Ideal* on c/de l'Hospital, for good pizzas, and *Bar Lisce* (c/de Tallers near the top of the Ramblas), an inexpensive and hospitable *comedor* with a surprisingly wide range of dishes.

East of the Ramblas, there's not so much choice. *Casa Jose* in the Pl. de Sant Josep Oriol (off c/Boqueria), which has long been listed in many guides as one of the cheapest/best-value places in Barcelona, seems now to be acquiring a reputation as nasty too — although with a 300ptas *menú* you might still feel it's worth a try. Otherwise, try the *Gallo Kirico* (c/Avinyó 19) for Pakistani specalities, or *Sogas* (Avinyó 56), a Catalan cookery in operation since 1890.

Vegetarian restaurants are scattered all over town, the two handiest (and cheapest) are the *Self Naturista* at c/Santa Ana 13, and the *Vegetarian Restaurant* at c/de la Canuda 41, the latter extremely uninspiring. More expensive is the *Vida Sana* at Gran Via 603 (corner Rambla Catalunya), which doubles as a health food store. Close to Sagrada Familia the *Restaurante Vegetariano* (c/Roger de Flor 216, off Diagonal) is cheap but open only from 12:45 to 4:30pm, Monday to Saturday. There's a good macrobiotic shop/restaurant near the bottom of c/Muntaner just below Gran Via. In Gràcia, try the *Illa de Gràcia* in c/Sant Domenec. Two **Indian restaurants** are worth a mention too: the *Govinda* (veggie) at Plaça Villa de Madrid 4 and the *Maharajah* (meaty) at c/Entença 137, near Sants station.

A couple of places worth looking out for if you're up in the **Eixample** are *Mas i Mas*, a modern bar with good, inexpensive *tapas* (c/Córsega 300); *Flash, Flash* (La Granada 25) with over fifty types of *tortilla* and one of the few open Sunday nights; and *Atzavara* (c/Francesc Giner), a slightly more upscale restaurant in Gràcia.

If you want to buy fresh food, of course, or make up your own meals, the covered **market** off the Ramblas (*Mercat Sant Josep*) is the best place to head. There's a good **supermarket**, too, a little farther down on the same side of the road. Catalan **baked items** are wickedly excellent and you'll be tempted by *ensaimadas* (turnovers), pizzas, and cakes at almost any *forn* (bakery) or *patisserie*. In the Barri Gòtic, the excellent *Forn d'Avinyó* sits on the corner of c/Avinyó and c/Ample. To wash things down, *horchata* is a traditional and delicious summer drink, made with *chufa* (tiger nuts) and drunk ice cold. The *Horchatería Fillol* on Plaça de la Universitat (at the corner of Ronda Universitat) serves this as well as enormous milk shakes and other delights; other *horchaterías* and *granjas* are dotted around town.

Drinking and Nightlife

At the time of writing Barcelona has become one of Europe's hippest nightspots. Just why is something of a mystery to everyone except the Catalans, who knew all along. There aren't, in fact, too many places which are *that* good, but gripped by Friday and Saturday night fever it's eminently possible to suspend disbelief.

It's pertinent to stress that clubbing in Barcelona is extremely expensive and that in the most exclusive places even a beer is going to cost you roughly ten times what it costs in the bar next door. Also note that the distinction between a music-bar and a disco is between a closing time of 2 or 3am and 5am — with a corresponding price rise.

"Ordinary" Bars and Cafes

There are hundreds of excellent **bars** and **tapas places** downtown to start your evening. Around the Picasso Museum, on the far side of the Barri Gòtic, is a particularly good area. As well as several places in the c/Montcada itself (including the marvelous blue-tiled champagne/cider bar mentioned earlier) there's *Magic* (Pg. Picasso 40) and a whole range of small and reasonably-priced bars and bistro-restaurants. **Passeig del Born**, the square at the end of c/Montcada behind Santa María del Mar, is crowded with popular bars (including one that specializes in Brazilian cocktails), although the district has been the scene at weekends of a few "tribal clashes." The zone around the Plaça Reial is full of bars, too, haunts of punks and rockers, so check which is which first (from the outside) to avoid a costly faux pas; *Ambos Mundos*, in the square, is fairly tame, with excellent *tapas*. The *Cafe Zurich* (corner of Plaça Catalunya and Ramblas) is a traditional meeting place for trendies and foreigners, and its position makes it *the* place to sit and watch passing crowds, especially from the outdoor terrace, open nearly until midnight. **Gràcia** is full of little squares, the main one Plaça del Sol, bordered by cafe terraces. It's the most studenty area in Barcelona and ideal for low-key, latish drinking. *El Dorado* is rather different, a totally loud, young, bright, bar at Plaça del Sol 4.

Niteries

Moving to the more expensive, trendier places, *bars modernos* are in fashion at the moment, hi-tec places concentrated mainly in the rich kids' stamping ground bordered by c/Ganduxer, Avda. Diagonal and Via Augusta, west of Gràcia. Drinks are expensive and the "in" places change rapidly, with new ones opening up all the time.

Currently two of the hippest of the **"modern"** bars are *Universal* (c/Mariano Cubí 184) and *BCN*, both classics of the genre. *SiSiSi* (Diagonal 442) was one of the first, and still one of the most elegant and laid back; *Soho*, on Diagonal, is another where neon and chrome are taken about as far as they can go. For good, quieter music try the long-established *Zig Zag* (c/Platon 13, a sidestreet near the top of Muntaner). Between 11pm and 2am the *Otto Zutz Disco* (see below) is converted into the *Zutz Bar Cafe*, open to all for drinks and coffee. *Metropol* was another of the first *bars modernos*, opening about seven years ago. It's in a tiny street running parallel between Rambla Catalunya and Passeig de Gràcia, behind the all-night drugstore. It has a cool, elegant interior, excellent music, and a fashion-conscious but fairly mixed clientele, especially at weekends (closes 3am).

One of the most futuristic bars is *Network* (c/Diagonal 616 near *Soho*, easy to miss but on the right as you head west just beyond the Plaça Francesc Macia). The original of this is in New York, and the slick design, worth a peek, is a cross between *Brazil* and *Bladerunner*. Good quality, cheapish fast food is served until late to a mingling of posy TV types. *Nick Havanna*, Rosselló 208, is where the smooth crowd used to come before it became too popular. It's enormous, yet packed to the gills at weekends (until it becomes even more passé in the near future). One whole wall is covered in mini-videos and there are raised steps to sit on for better views of the floor, useful as most people seem to come here to self-consciously watch the rest! The barmen wear very attractive long skirts, and it's open through the small hours.

Velvet, at Balmes 161, is one of the newest modern bars, though in accordance with its name slightly cozier and smoother than the others, with older habitués. The new *Este Bar* (Consell de Cent 257, between Muntaner and Aribau) is far more interesting: "modern" but not severe-looking, with a young, vaguely punky crowd and good music to 3am. Also fairly recent, *Ars*

Studio (c/Atenas 25, with General Mitre) is a large modern bar, with a young, *pijo* (rich kid) clientele. A former movie theater, it still shows old films on Sunday afternoons; nights there's dancing until 3am. Two new places with a rather **different ambience** are the *Yabba Dabba Club* (Avenir 63), the haunt of the spiky-haired crowd, with Gothic decor including candelabras and a sculpted torso protruding from the wall; and *La Fira* (Provença 171), a museum/bar with turn-of-the-century amusement-park rides, some of them operational, plus food and a bar under a circus tent.

Discos

Prince of the **discos** is still *Otto Zutz* (c/Lincoln 15), a three-story warehouse converted into a nocturnal shop window of everything that's for sale or rent in Barcelona. Hairdressers, designers, film directors, and people who wish they were all of the above rub shoulders over $8 whiskeys to the sound of whatever has just come out overseas. The doorman is a status-sensitive gorilla, but with the right rags and face you're in (you may or may not have to pay depending on how impressive you are, day of week, etc.); the disco starts at 2am. One of the chief rivals right now is *City*, c/Beethoven 15, just beyond and above Plaça Francesc Macia, a venue which seems to change name and owner frequently. Same entry criteria apply! *Distrito Distinto* (a long way out at Avda. Meridiana 140 — metro *Clot* or taxi) is a step down but attractive in its way. Mainly gay midweek, on weekends it's a lively sweatbox and in summer has a splendid "urban patio" and very good dance music. *Zeleste* is worth checking out too, a huge former warehouse on whose various levels gigs and lower key events are held, in addition to a disco floor and several bars: it's at c/Almogavers 122, out in Poble Nou.

Alternatives are spread out all over town. *Karma* in the Plaça Reial is a good, studenty place with 1970s sounds, *666* (c/ Llull 145, out in Poble Nou) is home to Goths, or try *Apocalypse* (c/Lepanto 408) for an average no-nonsense disco. In this category you could also try *Studio 54* (Parallel 64), a vast barn of a place with MOR disco music and bad draft beer. Late-night miniature golf (!) features at *Bikini* (Avda Diagonal 571), with the 19th hole a rambling split level disco — recently a good locale for salsa. One of the newest discos is the *Baticano*, c/Borrell, between Provença and Rosselló.

Amongst the **special interest** places is *Ebano* (c/Roger de Flor 114), an Afro-disco where (depending on the night) you're as likely to hear Michael Jackson as Fela Kuti. And there are several old-style **dance halls**, most notably *La Paloma* (c/Tigre 27) with pre-World War II decor and music to match.

Late, Late

Barcelona stays open **very late** on weekends, if you can take it. *KGB* (c/ Alegre de Dalt 55) is the closest thing the city has to a punk club, with live music Wednesday through Saturday and weekend "shift" until 9am. *After Hours* (in *Performance* disco, Provença 43 with Rocafort) opens between 6 and 9 on Friday and Saturday mornings. The latter is not to be confused with *After*, in the *Orfeo* disco (c/Sepulveda 185), in session Friday and Saturday from 5am to 9:30am. Look out also for *Edición Limitado*, who don't make their address too public.

Live Music, Film, Theater, and Other Entertainment

Summer is the worst time for **live music** in Barcelona, but by September things start to liven up. The *Festas de la Merce* at the end of September are an excuse for four days of (free) jazz, classical, and rock concerts all over the city. There is a good **jazz festival** too in November. Many major bands now include Barcelona on their European/world tours at a variety of big venues — keep an eye out for posters. Most of the clubs/discos regularly feature bands (*Zeleste, Otto Zutz, Studio 54* among them) whilst *Bikini* (Avda. Diagonal 571) puts on Spanish groups (Catalan rockabilly is quite something). For jazz you're better off at *La Cova del Drac* (c/Tuset 30) or *L'Auditori* (c/Balmes 245).

If you're curious about homegrown music, a number of **Catalan singer-songwriters** are perennial favorites. Names to look out for include: Serrat, who sings in Castilian, mainly ballads and love songs; Lluís Llach, a hero in Franco's time since he defiantly sang only in Catalan, folky music with political and nationalist content; and Maria del Mar Bonet, who revamps traditional folk songs, be they from Catalunya, Mallorca, or farther afield (but usually in Catalan). See the "Music" section of *Contexts* for further ideas on Catalan music and musicians.

As far as **movies** go, the Generalitat runs an excellent, cheap *Filmoteca* (Travesera de Gràcia 63) showing four different films (often foreign, dubbed, or subtitled) every night except Monday. Other theaters which regularly show good foreign films are *Maldá* (c/del Pi 5), *Verdi* (c/Verdi 32, cheap night Mon.), *Moderno* (c/Girona 175, cheap night Mon.), *Casablanca* (Pg. de Gràcia 115, cheap night Mon.), *Balmes* (c/Balmes 215, cheap night Thur.), and *Arcadia* (c/Tuset 14, cheap night Mon.).

Barcelona has nothing like the **theatrical life** of Madrid but does have some worthy venues and happenings. Ninety-nine percent of it, however, is in Catalan and you'll rarely see a Spanish classic. The *Poliorama* (Ramblas 115) is home of the distinguished Josep Maria Flotats company and puts on Catalan translations of all sorts of material. The *Romea* (c/Hospital 51) was built in 1863 and forced to use Castilian under Franco, but has now come back as the *Centre Dramatic de la Generalitat* with exclusively Catalan productions. The *Teatre Lliure* in c/Montseny (Gràcia) is the home of a progressive company. There are also occasional visiting events at the nineteenth-century *Mercat de les Flors* (c/Lleida 59), worth going to for the architecture alone. Look out, too, for the performance art of *Els Fura del Baus* (Vermin of the Sewer), who aim to shock and lend a new meaning to audience participation, and *Els Comediants*, who work from the Catalan popular theater tradition. The home of commercial theater is down Avda. Paral.lel.

For something more intimate try the *Café Concert Llantiol* (c/Riereta 7) whose Sunday evenings feature curious bits of mime, clowns, and magic (also **children's** theater here on Sunday at 12:30pm). The *Fundació Miró* has children's puppet shows on Sunday mornings, mime, and clowns too at the *Teatre Malic* (c/ Fusina 3).

Tickets for most theaters are available from the kiosk on the corner of c/ Aribau and Gran Via, or from the Centro de Localidades at Rambla Catalunya

2. For the *Mercat de les Flors* productions, you have to go to the Palau de la Virreina (Ramblas 99).

Among other highlights you're likely to come across are the summer events of the Generalitat's **Grec** season: theatrical, music, and dance events at venues including the Greek theater on Montjuïc (info and reservations at the Palau Virreina). **Opera and ballet** are staged at the Liceu, frequently featuring major touring companies. These can be worthwhile for the opulence of the setting alone.

Catalunya's national **folk dance**, the *sardana*, can be seen for free in front of the Cathedral (Sun. 10am–12:30pm, Wed. 7–9pm); in the Plaça Sant Jaume (Sun. 6–8pm) and in the Plaça de Catalunya on Sunday mornings. Mocked in the rest of Spain, the Catalans claim theirs is a very democratic dance; participants (there's no limit on numbers) all hold hands in a circle, each puts something in the middle as a sign of community and sharing, and since it is not overly-energetic (hence the jibes) old and young can join in equally.

Directory

Airlines Almost all are on the Pg. de Gràcia or around the corner on the Gran Via; *Iberia* is on Rambla de Catalunya 18 or on the Plaça de Espanya.

Airport *Prat de Llobregat*, 14km out (☎93/3701011). Regular train connection with Sants.

Anti-Nuclear There's strong anti-nuclear and anti-NATO feeling in Catalunya. *Casal de la Pau* (c/Cervantes 2, 1; ☎93/3183994) is an anti-militarist grouping, while the more broadly based *Comite Antinuclear de Catalunya* (*CANC*) is on c/Gran de Gràcia 126–30 (☎93/2179527).

Balearic ferries Daily services to Palma, Mallorca and several times weekly to Ibiza and Menorca (in July and August they get crowded — book ahead). Times and tickets from *Trasmediterranea* (Via Laietana 2; ☎93/3198212) or from the Estació Maritima at the bottom of the Ramblas.

Banks Main branches are mostly in Plaça de Catalunya and Pg. de Gràcia. *American Express* (Mon.–Fri. 9:30–6pm, Sat. 10am–noon) at Pg. de Gràcia 101, is handy for small amounts (1% commission on cash) and Sat. am. Money can also be changed at the airport, main railway stations, and at *Casas de Cambio* throughout the center. If you want non-Spanish currency when you're leaving the country, try the *Banco Popular*, Pg. de Gràcia 17; most other banks make a fuss unless you've got residence papers.

Beaches The beaches at Barceloneta are cleaner than they used to be, though unbearably crowded in the summer, but the real problem is the polluted water — wisest to use the showers only. You can pay to dip in one of the private *balnearios*, pools lining the front, which are pleasant enough, and there's even a bit of beach fenced off just for women, but it's a bit like sitting in a cage at the zoo. For a day trip, head instead to Sitges, 40km downcoast, or Castelldefels, slightly closer. In the other direction, Caldetas (train from *Cercanias*, Estació de França) has two smallish beaches yards from the station so is very handy. They're a bit crowded, but with locals not tourists. Any beaches nearer Barcelona have scummy water.

Books In English from *Itaca* (Rambla de Catalunya 81), *Come-In* (c/ Provença 203), *Simons and Ko.* (a second-hand store at c/la Granja 13 in Gràcia) and from newspaper stands down the Ramblas. *Llibreria Francesa* at Pg. de Gràcia 91 also has a few. *Leviatan* (c/Santa Ana 21) is a good left-wing bookshop.

Buses The main bus station is the *Estació del Norte* on Avda. Vilanova (for Madrid, Andalucía, Valencia, Costa Dorada, Zaragoza). For the Costa Brava (Lloret/Tossa etc.) go to *Empresa Sarfe* at Pg. de Colom 3 at the bottom of the Ramblas; for Bilbao, Cuenca, and Teruel it's *Ansa-Viacarsa* at c/ Tarragona 169 near Sants. Buses for Lleida, Vall d'Aran, and Andorra leave from *Alsina Graells* at Ronda Universitat 4. And for London (daily in season, 4 weekly out) and the rest of Europe try either *Iberbus* (Avda Paral.lel 116) or *Autocares Julia* (Pl. Universitat 12; ☎393/183895).

Car Rental Agencies include *Atesa* (c/Balmes 141; ☎93/2378140); *Ital* (Traversera de Gràcia 71; ☎93/3215141) *Hertz* (c/Tuset 10; ☎93/2373737), and *Avis* (c/Casanova 209; ☎93/2099533).

Consulates U.S. (Via Laietana 33; ☎93/3199550), Canada (Via Augusta 125; ☎93/2090634).

Cultural Institutes North American (at Vía Augusta 123); and British, at c/ Amigó 83 (☎93/2096388) has English libraries and lists of English-language schools if you're looking for work. Good noticeboards too for Spanish/ Catalan lessons and apartment sharing.

Excursions If you'd like a day or two out of Barcelona, the forest-covered Montseny mountain is the nearest "wild" region. It lies to the northeast and is the highest Spanish mountain so near the sea in the Mediterranean. Public transit doesn't serve the area well, though, and you really need your own vehicle to explore. Arbusies is quite an attractive town and Sant Hilari Sacalm is a good base, with several *hostales*.

Feminism Despite a splintering among Barcelona's feminists there are certain facilities used by all groups. *La Sal* is a feminist bookshop at c/ Valencia 226; *La Nostra Illa* in Gràcia, a women's bar, at c/Reig i Bonet 3 (Metro *Joanic*); and there's a lively women's center, *El Centro*, at c/Rosselló 256, 2 (☎93/2156336). They have a library, hold readings of feminist texts on Thursday evenings and meet for informal drinks/chats on Monday evenings. You can join for just a month, very cheaply.

Fiestas Big event is the *Festa de la Merce* (last week in Sept.); free outdoor concerts, fireworks, human towers, and the parade of giants. Others include Sant Jordi (April 23), San Joan (June 24), and the *Grec* festival in July.

Gay life For gay men, the *Front Alliberament Gai de Catalunya* (c/Villarroel 62, 3°; ☎93/2546398) has a library and holds meetings and video shows. There's a box number to write to for lesbian contacts — *Grup d'Alliberament de la Lesbiana*, Aptat. Correus 2493 Barcelona 080 — but since they take a long time to reply you're probably better off contacting *El Centro* or going to the women's bar on Gràcia (see Feminism). *SexTienda* (c/Rauric 11) publishes and sells a gay map of the city.

Hiking maps *Libreria Quera*, c/Petritxol 2 (off Plaça de Pi) for topographical/general maps and hiking guides.

Hitching For Madrid, Zaragoza, or Tarragona take bus #7 to its terminus on Avda. Diagonal and stand on Diagonal itself at some point beyond. For Girona and France, take the Metro to Glories and stand on the Gran Via; for the south coast (Sitges, etc.) go to Plaça d'Espanya and stand on the Gran Via just beyond the Plaça.

Hospitals Two of the best are *Hospital de la Creu Roja* (c/Dos de Maig 301; ☎93/2359300) and *Hospital Clinic* (c/Casanovas 143; ☎03/3231414). For emergency doctors dial ☎93/2128585; for an ambulance dial ☎93/3000422.

Language Schools By far the cheapest place for Spanish/Catalan classes is the *Escuela Oficial de Idiomas*, Avda. Drassanes (☎93/3293412). First come, first served — big lines at semester opening, followed by lottery system. Or try *International House*, c/Trafalgar 14 (☎93/3188429).

Lost and Found If you have anything stolen or forgotten, try the Ajuntament (*objets perdus*) but you'll be lucky to get it back. Report robberies immediately to the police, who'll give you the certificate that consulates/insurance companies require.

Luggage Storage Lockers at Sants station, open from 7am–11pm, 125ptas a day, and *Alsina Graells* bus terminal.

Markets Junk/flea/antiques (*Els Encants* at c/Dos de Maig; Metro *Glories*; Mon, Wed, Fri, and Sat 9am–8pm); stamps/coins (Plaça Reial, Sun. mornings); books/comics (San Antoni between c/Manso and c/Urgel, left off Ramblas, Sun. mornings); stock market (*Llotja* at c/Consolat del Mar, wear a business suit and they should let you in); food/produce (*Mercat Santa Caterina* at Avda. Francesc Cambó 16, *Mercat de la Boqueria* at Ramblas 101, *Mercat Sant Josep* on the Ramblas); a few stalls with antiques and old clothes, Thurs. only, behind the cathedral.

Monday Many museums close — some just in the mornings, others all day.

Newspapers *El País* (Barcelona edition, Catsilian) is the best, although increasingly criticized for being little more than the mouthpiece of the PSOE; *La Vanguardia* (Barcelona paper, Castilian) is conservative and a big local seller; *El Periodico* (Barcelona paper, Castilian) is a "popular" paper which appeals to both working and middle classes, with big headlines and lots of photos but also extensive coverage of proper news; *Avui* is the chief nationalist paper, printed in Catalan.

Notice boards There are good ones at the cultural institutes (above), plus good ones at the university: go to the main building on Plaça Universitat, take the door on the far left, and, inside, bear left and then right — you'll come to a courtyard with at least two walls full of ride/apartment/class/job offers and requests.

Police Central office at Via Laietana 43. In emergencies dial 091 or 092.

Post office *Correus*, Plaça Antoni Lòpez at the bottom of Via Laietana, open Mon.-Sat. 8:30am–10pm, Sun. 10am–noon; poste restante at Window #17 open Mon.-Fri 9am–9pm, Sat. 9am–2pm.

Ride sharing *Viaje Cómodo* (c/Provença 214; ☎93/2532207) and *Comparco* (c/Ribes 31; ☎93/2466908) both put drivers and riders together for national and international destinations.

Soccer Barcelona (*La Barça*) have had a relatively lean time of it lately, but they still play beautifully, at the mighty (120,000-seat) *Camp Nou* stadium, in the northeast of the city off Avda. Diagonal; bus #54 from Plaça Universitat or Metro *Collblanc*. They have their own *Museo del Futbol* at the stadium (Mon.–Fri., 10am–1pm and 4–6pm, weekends 10am–1pm). The other local team, getting better, is *Espanyol*; in Sarrià, *Ferrocarriles Catalanes* to Bonanova or Maria Cristina, or bus #66 from Plaça Catalunya. Tickets are expensive.

Swimming Pools Municipal pools are often block-reserved by clubs but try the indoor pool at Plaça J. Folch i Torres (Metro *Paral.lel*) Mon.–Sat. 11am–1:30pm; or, in summer, the open-air pool at Montjuïc, near the funicular on Pg. Miramar.

Telephones National and international calls from all kiosks but the latter are really easier to handle from a *Telefónica* office where you pay afterwards. They are at Plaça Catalunya (8am–1pm and 5–9pm daily) and Avda. de Roma 73–91 (24hrs).

Transit routes Dial ☎93/3360000, state destination, and they'll tell you the best combination of public transport (bus, train) to get there. Basically a service for locals, but try English — you might be lucky.

Turismo Main outlet at Gran Via 658 open Mon.–Fri. 9am–7pm, Sat. 9am–2pm. Other branches with slightly longer hours at Estació Sants, Estació França, the airport, and Plaça Portal de la Pau (harbor end of Ramblas).

Train Tickets and information from the *RENFE* office in underground foyer at Pg. de Gràcia, corner c/Aragó.

Travel Agencies Very useful (and not just for students) are the *TIVE* and *ACTEJ* offices at Gran Via 615. Other general travel firms can be found around the Gran Via, Pg. de Gràcia, Via Laietana, and the Ramblas.

Views Terrific city views from the cafe-terrace on top of the *Corte Ingles* store in Plaça de Catalunya.

VD Clinic Free, at Pg. Lluís Companys 7.

Work The best chance of getting work is as an English teacher and the cultural insitutes (see above) will give you a list of schools to try, or look in Yellow Pages under *Academias*. Best time to look is early September when the schools know how many replacement teachers they need. Reputable schools will require at least a one-month intensive teacher training course (supplied by *International House* — see above — among others) and possibly a demonstration lesson. Ask if they provide work permits and *residencias* (or medical insurance if you're not going to be there legally). A word of warning on the legal front: police are cracking down on people without visas and may ask for passport/residence papers on the spot, especially around the Plaça Reial out of tourist season. Be careful with date stamps — you're allowed three months as a tourist.

Around Barcelona: the Mountain and Monastery of Montserrat

The extraordinary **mountain of Montserrat**, with its weirdly shaped crags of rock, its monastery, and its ruined hermitage caves, rises just 40km north-west of Barcelona, off the road to Lleida. It is one of the most spectacular of all Spain's natural sights, a saw-toothed outcrop left exposed to erosion when the inland sea that covered this area around 25 million years ago was drained by progressive uplifts of the earth's crust. Legends hang easily upon it. St. Peter is said to have deposited a carving of the Virgin by St. Luke in one of the mountain caves, fifty years after the birth of Christ. Another tale makes this the spot in which the knight Parsifal discovered the Holy Grail.

Inevitably the monastery and mountain are no longer remote; in fact they're ruthlessly exploited as a tourist trip from the Costa Brava. But don't be put off — the place itself is still magical and you can escape the crowds by striking out into the mountainside, along well-signposted paths to potent and deserted hermitages. The best plan is to stay the night, since the crowds disperse by the early evening. There's a **campground** near the monastery and a couple of **hotels**, the cheapest of which, *Colonia Puig* (☎93/8350268), costs around 1800ptas for a double; alternatively the *Hostal/Residencia El Monasterio* (☎93/8350201) will set you back around 2400ptas; it's best to book in advance. If you're hard up, take your own **food**; it's expensive at the "village" shops and restaurants. Do, however, try the very fresh *mato* (curd cheese) often sold here by stall-holders — it's a very common dessert in Catalunya, usually eaten with honey (*mel i mato*) and sometimes with pine nuts as well.

There are **buses** from Barcelona (leaving the Plaça de la Universitat mid-morning and returning late afternoon — enquire at *Julia Tours* or any travel agent) but the most thrilling approach is by train and cable car. **Trains**, the *Ferrocarriles Catalanes*, leave from beneath the Plaça de Espanya at 9:10am, 11:10am, 3:10pm and 5:10pm, and return at 1:20pm 3:20pm, 5:20pm and 7:40pm. Each train connects with an aerial **cable car** (last ascent at 6:45pm) for what must be the most exhilarating ride in Spain.

The Monastery

It is the **"Black Virgin"** (*La Moreneta*), the icon hidden by St. Peter (and curiously reflecting the style of sixth-century Byzantine carving), which is responsible for the monastery's existence. **The legend** is loosely wrought but it appears the icon was lost in the early eighth century after being hidden during the Moorish invasion. It reappeared in 880, accompanied by the custo-mary visions and celestial music, and, in the first of its miracles, would not budge when the Bishop of Vic attempted to remove it. A chapel was built to house it, which in 976 was superseded by a Benedictine monastery — the predecessor of the present monastic structures, about three-quarters of the way up the mountain at an altitude of nearly 1000m.

Miracles abounded and the Virgin of Montserrat soon became the chief cult-image of Catalunya and a pilgrimage goal second in Spain only to Santiago de Compostela. Over 150 churches were dedicated to her in Italy alone, as were the first chapels of Mexico, Chile, and Peru; even a Caribbean island bears her name. The monastery enjoyed an outrageous prosperity, having its own flag and a form of extraterritorial independence along the lines of the Vatican City. It declined only in the nineteenth century. In 1811 Napoleon's troops devastated the buildings, stole their treasures and "hunted the hermits like chamois along the cliffs." In 1835 it was suppressed for its Carlist sympathies. Monks were allowed to return some nine years later but by 1882 their numbers had fallen to nineteen. But in recent decades Montserrat's popularity has again become established; there are over 300 brothers and, in addition to the tourists, tens of thousands of newly married couples "ascend" on the place to seek *La Moreneta*'s blessing on their union. The main pilgrimages take place on April 27 and September 8, times to be avoided.

The site has become a nationalist symbol as much as a spiritual center. At the beginning of this century Montserrat's Abbot Marcel was a vigorous promoter of the Catalan language, creating a printing press in 1918 which published the Montserrat Bible in Catalan. During Franco's dictatorship books continued to be secretly and illegally printed here, and it was then and afterwards the site of massive Catalan nationalist demonstrations.

The **monastery** itself is of no particular architectural interest, save perhaps in its monstrous bulk. Only the **Basilica** (1560–92) is open to the public. *La Moreneta*, blackened by the smoke of countless candles, stands above the high altar — reached from behind, up a stairway. The approach to this beautiful icon reveals the enormous wealth of the monastery. The time to be here is at the chanting of Ave Maria, around 1pm, when Montserrat's world-famous **boys' choir** sings the *Salve*. They belong to the *Escolania*, a choral school established in the thirteenth century and unchanged in musical style since its foundation. Near the entrance to the basilica is a **museum** (10:30am–1:30pm and 3–5:30pm) containing paintings by Caravaggio and El Greco.

To the Summit

It is the **walks** around the woods and mountainside of Montserrat which are the real attraction. Following the tracks to caves and hermitages you could contemplate what Goethe wrote in 1816: "Nowhere but in his own Montserrat will a man find happiness and peace." Less metaphysically, you can take **funicular railways** to the hermitages of **San Juan** and **San Jeronimo**, near the summit of the mountain at 1300m. Unfortunately fires in the summer of 1986 ravaged the Montserrat hillsides. It's a problem which afflicts the forests of the south of France and Catalunya every summer and is getting worse each year. In part this is because natural debris is no longer cleared as it once was by individuals searching for firewood; the man-made litter left by picnickers, however, is probably the biggest contributary cause. More alarming is the large number of fires started in Catalunya by pyromaniacs and by people who want to build a new house in a tree-covered area but have been refused planning permission.

AROUND CATALUNYA

From Barcelona the whole of Catalunya lies within easy reach, linked by excellent bus and train services. There are two distinct targets: the mountains and the coast. Northwest you can head for the inland **Pyrenees** and in particular for some magnificent and relatively isolated hiking territory around the **Vall d'Aran** and the **Parc Nacional de Aigües Tortes**. To the east, **Andorra** is an anomaly, a combination tax-free hellhole and mountain retreat set amidst quieter, generally neglected border towns, all offering great hiking and, in winter, good skiing. North along the coast there are some beautiful beaches and undeveloped villages in the final stretch of the (otherwise horrific) **Costa Brava**, just below the French border. In **Figueres** there's the added attraction of the extraordinary **Salvador Dalí museum**. Inland, **Girona** is an attractive provincial town. To the south the coast is even less enticing, but here too there are diversions: at least one good beach at **Sitges** and the beautiful coastal town of **Tarragona**. Heading west, the romantic **monastery of Poblet** figures as one approach to the quiet and enjoyable town of **Lleida**.

Throughout the chapter, we've again used Catalan names (with the Castilian in brackets). Most directional and city road signs are now in Catalan but you're unlikely to get confused as the difference is usually only slight; e.g. Girona (Gerona) and Lleida (Lerida).

The Costa Brava: Concrete Nightmares, Classical Ruins, and Salvador Dalí

The **Costa Brava** (Rugged Coast), stretching from **Blanes** to **Port Bou** and the French border, was once the most beautiful part of the Spanish coast with its wooded coves, high cliffs, pretty beaches, and deep blue water. Today, although the natural beauty cannot be entirely disguised, it's an almost total disaster, with a density of concrete holiday high-rises greater even than the Costa del Sol. Properly speaking, however, the worst spot — Lloret — is not on the Costa Brava, which to the locals means the jagged strip beginning farther north. The southern part is fairly horrible, though redeemed in a couple of places. Beyond **Palamos** the main road runs inland and the coastal development is relatively low-key, dominated by apartments and villas rather than big hotels, and still wonderfully scenic. An added attraction here is the ancient Greek site of **Empuries**, within walking distance of **L'Escala**. In the northernmost stretch, picturesque **Cadaqués** is becoming trendier and more expensive by the year; there are quieter, more laid-back coastal villages to the north, right up to the French border — and if you're up there, the dramatically sited monastery and castle at **Sant Pere de Rodes** is a sight not to miss. Near Cadaqués is **Figueres**, birthplace of Salvador Dalí and home to his museum — surreal in itself and infectiously funny. Campers and beach combers should beware the *Tramontana*, a fierce north wind which blows occasionally on this coast.

Buses throughout the region are almost all operated by the *SARFA* company, with an office in every town. Although they are reasonably efficient, it can be a frustrating business either trying to get to some of the smaller coastal villages or simply attempting to stick with the coast. A car or bike solves all your problems; otherwise it's worth considering using Figueres or Girona as a base for lateral trips to the coast — both are big bus terminuses.

There is an expensive daily private **boat service** (*Cruceros*) which runs in the summer from Calella (south of Blanes and not to be confused with the one near Palafrugell) to Palamos, calling chiefly at Blanes, Lloret, Tossa, San Feliu, and Platja d'Aro. Local tourist offices have schedules and prices, but it runs most frequently between Blanes and San Feliu, and the Lloret–Tossa trip, for example, costs 650ptas. It's worth taking at least once, since the rugged coastline makes for an extremely beautiful ride.

Hitching, away from the main tourist-clogged roads, is generally good: if you're trying to head **south** from the French border there's a huge shopping center and truck stop just inside Spain (at LA JONQUERA) where everyone pulls in and which is definitely your best hope for getting a ride.

A point worth mentioning concerns **language**. Obvious on reflection, but easy to forget amid all the rampant tourism in the resorts, is that the Costa Brava is still in Catalunya. Although only the occasional Catalan graffito impinges upon the international flavor, it's handy to remember that on road signs, *platja* is beach; and that when reading time-tables, *feiners* means the same as *laborables* (workdays).

North to Lloret de Mar and Tossa

The first 40km or so of coast outside Barcelona are dominated by the grim industrial towns of BADALONA and MATARÓ, so even for some simple swimming you should stay on the bus or train at least as far as CALELLA (where you can pick up the boat service northwards) or BLANES. This may be pretty dull but it does at least have a sheltered beach, and it's a town rather than just a tourist settlement. There are usually **rooms** here, and it has no fewer than thirteen **campgrounds** as well. The train station is a bit inland, but regular buses go from there to the beach.

Despite the increasingly developed character of the coast as you drive north, nothing on this stretch will prepare you for **LLORET DE MAR**, one of the most extreme resorts in Spain: high-rise concrete prisons, a tawdry mile or so of sand, and alongside it the most prosaic, unimaginative display of cafes, restaurants, and bars you'll ever see. The only life is in the seedy back streets where you can spend your time watching the rip-offs — "flamenco bars," "English pubs" (selling expensive German lager), and "German *konditoreien*" (selling bad Spanish pastries). This is where the cheap *fondas* and *hostales* are, but unless you are a very curious sociologist don't waste your time. Not that it's easy to find a room anyway; virtually everything is block-booked by package tour operators each January. Go anywhere — Girona, Tossa, or Barcelona — that you can reach by bus, rather than stay here.

For an unashamed Costa Brava resort **TOSSA DE MAR** is infinitely preferable and out of season could be quite an attractive place to spend some time. Even in high summer arriving by boat is one of the Costa Brava's high-lights, the medieval walls and turrets pale and shimmering on the hill above the modern town. The walls themselves still surround an **old quarter**, all cobbled streets and flower boxes, offering terrific views over beach and bay. The quarter even houses a **museum** (10am–1pm and 4–8pm) boasting some Chagall paintings. Tossa's best beach is the *Mar Menuda*, around the head-land away from the old town. The main central beach, though pleasant and clean enough, gets crowded even on the gloomiest of days.

If you're going to stay, pick up a free map and accommodation lists from the **Turismo**, in the same building as the **bus station**, and then head straight down the road in front of you and turn right at the traffic circle for "downtown" and beaches. There is cheapish **accommodation** to be had in the warren of tiny streets around the church and below the old city walls; chances of finding a room are better before July and after September, and the more obscure streets away from the front are the ones to check. Even in July, it's possible though, try the *Hostal Muntaner* (c/Sant Antonio 17, ☎972/340084) and other places on and just off this street. There are five **camp-grounds** too, all within a two-to-four-kilometer walk of the centre. **Eating and drinking** is not cheap in Tossa — this is package-tourist land — but there are some good deals around, as well as endless "Full English Breakfast" bargains on the way out to the bus station. There are, incidentally, some excellent seafood restaurants up in the old quarter and just outside the walls, but you'll require big money or a credit card.

To head **north** from Tossa you'll either have to detour by bus to GIRONA (see below), from where numerous buses head back to the coast, or take the boat service which continues up offshore via SAN FELIU to PALAMOS.

Tossa is something of an aberration. The coast immediately to the north is again thoroughly developed and thoroughly spoiled, with another immense concentration of cement in the area around LA PLATJA D'ARO (PLAYA DE ARO). If you've taken the boat, it might be preferable to get off at SAN FELIU DE GUIXOLS — admittedly an out-and-out resort, but at least a reasonably pleasant one with a decent beach as well as a tenth-century monastery. From here buses run directly to Palafrugell without having to detour to Girona. Beyond Platja d'Aro things get worse again. SANT ANTONI DE CALONGE is still being built, the main-road traffic kicking up swirls of concrete dust. Three times daily the Palafrugell bus detours to CALONGE itself, only 2km inland but hardly visited by the beach hordes. It has a closely packed medieval center with a church and castle, but it's really not worth the necessary wait for the next onward bus. Best to stay on board, through PALAMOS (a modern looking place set around a harbor full of yachts), until PALAFRUGELL.

Palafrugell, its Beaches, and Around

PALAFRUGELL, an old town at its liveliest during the morning market, has little to get excited about either. But it has been overlooked by most tourists and hence, even if there's little to see — the only original feature not yet rede-veloped is the desperately dark sixteenth-century church right in the middle

— remains reasonably pleasant. It's also a convenient and considerably cheaper place to base yourself if you're aiming for the delightful coastline a few kilometers away. With no true coastal road, this stretch still retains pine-covered slopes and some quiet little coves with scintillatingly turquoise waters. Beach developments are generally mild, consisting of apartments rather than hotels, and although a fair number of British visitors come here in season, this is where many of the better-off Barcelonans have a villa for weekend and August escapes. All of this makes for one of the nicest (though hardly undiscovered) stretches of the Costa Brava. While you're here try *cremat*, a typical drink of the fishing villages in this region, now most commonly drunk in the waterfront bars of Llafranc and reputedly brought over by sailors from the Antilles. The concoction contains rum, sugar, lemon peel, coffee grounds, and sometimes a cinnamon stick; it will be brought out in an earthenware bowl and you have to set fire to it, occasionally stirring, until (after a few minutes) it's ready to drink.

Accommodation is available at any of the beaches along this stretch, though it is expensive and zealously sought after. Far better to stay in cheaper Palafrugell, only a few kilometers away, and bus in to the beach with everyone else. Of the precious few possibilities in town, the *Pensió Ramirez* (c/Sant Sebastian 29, just off the central square; ☎972/300043) is the cheapest, very clean and attached to an excellent *bar/comedor*. The *Hostal Platja* immediately across the road is more expensive. If the *Ramirez* is full, a better bet is an unnamed *fonda* on c/de les Quatre Cases, a little street very near the church; the rooms are pleasant, and are ranged around a secluded cloistered courtyard. The only other possibility seems to be the *Hostal Anfora* on c/Sagunt — go down c/Sant Sebastian from the main square, cross the plaza, and it's straight ahead.

Such is the popularity of the nearby beaches that a new highway has been built from Palafrugell and, in the summer, a virtual shuttle service runs from the **bus station** to Calella and then on to Llafranc. You might as well get off at Calella, the first stop, since Llafranc is only a twenty-minute walk away and you can get a return bus from there. Other, less frequent services run to Tamariu and to Begur, while all services are drastically reduced before June and after October; see below for full details.

CALELLA is still (just barely) a fishing port. Its gloriously rocky coastline is punctuated by several tiny sand beaches which will be packed to the gills, but the water is inviting and the village's whitewashed villas and narrow streets very attractive. A gentle, hilly walk (20 min.) over some high rocks brings you to **LLAFRANC**, tucked into the next bay, with one goodish stretch of beach and a glittering marina. Llafranc seems a little more upscale, its hillside villas glinting in the sun, its beachside restaurants expensive, but essentially the development in both places remains on an eminently human scale. In Llafranc, there are even a couple of normal **bars** at the marina end of the bay.

TAMARIU, 4km north, is even lovelier, and although it has a smaller beach than either of the other two villages, there are fewer buses to it and consequently fewer people. You could walk through the woods from Llafranc (around 90 min.) although the last part of the winding road, with its speeding traffic, could be rather dangerous with a pack. In any case, walk at least as far as the **lighthouse** above Llafranc, with grand views over the beach villages and Palafrugell set in the plain behind. If you want to stay, there's a **campground** in Tamariu.

For something other than just beaches, and for considerably fewer people, head instead for **BEGUR**, about 8km from Palafrugell and slightly inland. A crumbling hill town, the remnants of its castle command extensive views of the central Costa Brava. The medieval streets harbor a squat church, a couple of empty restaurants, and a *fonda* — and nothing but peace and quiet in the heat of the day. With a little energetic walking, you could reach the beaches of AIGUAFREDA and FORNELLS, or, if you have a car, make for the tranquil coves of SA RIERA and SA TUNA to the north. There is a *hostal* at Sa Tuna, but you'll have to phone ahead in season (☎972/622198). On the way back to Palafrugell, detour to **AIGUABLAVA** where the views are even more scenic than from Begur. There's a *parador* here where it's well worth shelling out for a couple of drinks at the bar just for the sheer luxury of enjoying the pool and getting a look at the marble and mosaic opulence within.

Buses from Palafrugell run to CALELLA and LLAFRANC every thirty minutes from July 1 to September 20 and hourly in June and September 21–30; services to TAMARIU go six times daily in the first period, four times daily in the others; and to BEGUR they go four times a day in the first period only.

Empuries and Around

From Palafrugell you're within striking distance of **EMPURIES** (AMPURIAS), one of the most interesting archeological sites in Spain. Much of its fascination derives from the fact that it was occupied continuously for nearly 1500 years. This was the ancient Greek *Emporion* (literally "Trading Station"), founded in 550 B.C. by Phocian merchants who, for three centuries, conducted a vigorous trade throughout the Mediterranean. Later, in the early third century B.C., it was taken by Scipio and a Roman city — more splendid than the Greek, with an amphitheater, fine villas, and a broad marketplace — grew up above the old Greek town. The Romans were replaced in turn by the Visigoths, who built several basilicas and made it the seat of a bishopric. Emporion only disappeared from the records in the ninth century A.D. when, it is assumed, it was wrecked by either Saracen or Norman pirates.

The **site** (Tues.–Sun. 10am–2pm and 3–7pm; admission 150ptas) lies behind a sandy bay about 2km north of L'Escala (see below). The remains of the original **Greek colony**, which was destroyed by a Frankish raid in the third century A.D. — at which point all moved to the Roman city — occupies the lower part of the site. Among the ruins of several temples, to the left on raised ground, is one dedicated to Asclepius, the Greek healing god whose cult was centered on Epidauros and the island of Kos. The temple is marked by a replica of a fine third-century B.C. statue of the god, the original of which (along with many finds from the site) is in the *Museu Arqueologic* in Barcelona. Nearby stand several large cisterns; Emporion had no aqueduct so water was stored here, to be filtered and purified by means of long pipes (one of which has been reconstructed). Remains of the town gate, *agora* (marketplace, in the center), and several streets can easily be made out, along with a mass of house foundations (some with mosaics in situ) and the ruins of Visigoth basilicas. A small **museum** (entry included in site ticket) stands above, containing helpful models and diagrams of the excavations as well as some of the more minor finds. Beyond this stretches the vast but only partly excavated **Roman town**. Two luxurious villas have been uncovered with halls, porticoed gardens, and magnificent mosaic floors. Some distance farther on are the remains of the forum, amphitheater, and outer walls.

L'ESCALA usually has **rooms** available (try c/de Gracia, running uphill from the central beach towards Empuries, or the *Hostal Riera*, whose restaurant is also the cheapest in town) but it's an expensive and utterly ordinary place with only a crowded piece of central sand to recommend it — apart, that is, from its canning factories, where they package Catalunya's best anchovies. You'd also be a fair hike away from the ruins and the good beaches. You could instead **camp** out on the beaches and in the woods around the archaeological site, where there's little development save one hotel (the one-star *Empuries*) and a few villas. Or, if there's room, stay at the new **youth hostel** (☎972/771200), open all year except mid-December to mid-January, right on the beach by the ruins; cheap meals are available and a **campground** is attached. The wooded shores around here hide a series of lovely cove beaches with shallow water and good sand. At weekends the

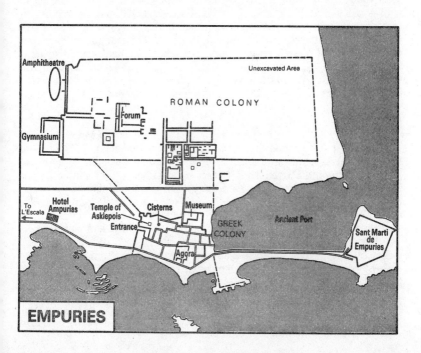

woods are full of picnicking Spanish families, setting up tables, fridges, and camp stoves from the backs of their cars.

A short walk along the shore will bring you to the tiny walled hamlet of **SANT MARTÍ D'EMPURIES**, a lovely decaying place with a couple of shaded bars in its plaza. It's prey to the beachbound tourists at lunchtime but in the evening is peaceful, perfect for a drink amid the light-strung trees. You could even stay here at the *fonda* in the square, an expensive option in high season but quite delightful.

Buses connect L'Escala with either Palafrugell (2–3 daily) or Figueres (2–3 daily), arriving and leaving from the *SARFA* company's office just down the road from **Turismo/Correus** at the top of town. If you're coming from Palafrugell, you might instead like to make your base at **PALS**, a fortified, medieval village long neglected and at last being restored. There are a couple of cheap places to stay right by the bus stop. For traditional Catalan food at moderate prices, go to *Chez Alfred*, c/de la Font.

More realistically, you could stay at **TORROELLA DE MONTGRÍ**, an important medieval port which has been left high and dry by a receding Mediterranean. It now stands 5km inland, beneath the shell of a huge battlemented castle. Nevertheless the place remains distinctly medieval in appearance with its narrow streets, fine mansions, and fourteenth-century parish church. Oddly, only a couple of busloads of tourists a day come to look round, and hardly anyone stays. The *Fonda Mitja*, on c/de Esglesia just off the arcaded Plaça de la Vila, is cheap and excellent should you decide to do so. If you've got transportation, the tiny medieval villages — now rather desolate — of ULLASTRET and **PERATALLADA** are worth a quick visit. At the former there was an Iberian settlement and these ruins can be seen a little way out outside the village. Peratallada is especially beautiful, with a ruined castle, a fortified church and a number of houses embellished by coats of arms and arches. You can get good food there at *Can Nou*, c/d'En Bas, near the towers (closed Wed.). Both villages are inland near LA BISBAL, a ceramics center in an attractive river setting with many cheap **hostales**.

Figueres

The northernmost resorts of the Costa Brava are reached via **FIGUERES** (FIGUERAS), a provincial Catalan town which would pass almost unnoticed were it not for the **Museu Dalí**, (Tues.–Sun. 11:30am–1pm and 3:30–6pm; 250ptas, students 100ptas) installed by the artist in a building as surreal as the exhibits within. You can't miss it, as it's signposted all over town. The most visited museum in Spain after the Prado, the Museu Dalí is a treat, appealing to everyone's innate love of fantasy, absurdity, and participation. You view the face of Mae West through a lens focused on garbage, water plants by putting coins into a Cadillac, walk amidst a complete life-sized orchestra, and gaze fitfully at totem poles of TV sets. Although it does contain paintings and piles of sculpture, the thematically arranged display is not a collection of Dalí's 'greatest hits' — those are scattered far and wide. Nonetheless, the assembly beggars description and is not to be missed. Dalí was born in Figueres and, on January 23, 1989, died there; his embalmed body now lies in a glass case inside the museum, near his famous "taxi" whose dummy-passengers are covered with snails.

Controversy surrounds his final years, with some observers believing that he didn't so much choose to live as a recluse as find himself imprisoned by his three guardians. This situation has also inevitably led to the questioning of the authenticity of some of his later works. The division of his legacy of (genuine or otherwise) paintings will be made yet more complicated by the fact that Dalí, by terms of his last (1982) will, left his entire estate to the Spanish state. Catalan art-boosters are outraged, and promise a battle to keep the canvases from being carted off to the Museo de Arte Moderno in Madrid. Figueres itself tends to be overshadowed by the museum — and neglected by those who have just come to see it and nothing else — but it remains a pleasing town with a lively, central, sloping Rambla and plenty of cheap food and accommodation. After the museum, the main sight is the huge seventeenth-century **castle** to the northeast of town, the last bastion of the Republicans in the civil war when the town became their capital after the fall of Barcelona. It's still in use by the military but the 5km circuit of walls make a good walk.

To reach the middle of town you can simply follow the 'Museu Dalí' signs from the **train station** — walk straight up, across the large square to the right, above and on the right of which is the Rambla. You'll find **rooms** at the top right-hand corner here (two places on c/Pep Ventura) as well as farther down around the Dalí museum, where several bars offer *habitaciones*. There's a good new **youth hostel** (☎972/501213), open all year, at Anicet Pages 2, off the Plaça del Sol (next plaza up from the Rambla), immediately behind the post office; the town **campground** is on the way towards the castle. There is a gaggle of cheap tourist **restaurants** in the narrow streets around the Dalí museum and, more expensively, some nice pavement cafes lining the Rambla which are popular in the evening. For a change, you might want to eat at one of the town's three Chinese restaurants, the cheapest of which (with a good *menú del día*) is down by the railway station. For a food treat, go to the *Hotel Duran* (c/Lausaca 5) where they serve generous regional dishes with a modern touch; it's expensive but has an excellent reputation.

The **Turismo** (Mon.–Fri. 9am–7pm, Sat. 9am–2pm), in front of the post office building, dishes out timetables for all onward transportation. There are **trains** (around 15 daily) to PORT BOU; otherwise the *SARFA* bus company runs **buses** in summer to every other destination: PALAFRUGELL (3 daily), L'ESCALA (2 daily), ROSES (10 daily), and CADAQUÉS (3 daily). The **bus station** is at the top of c/Pompeu Fabra, on the right at the top of the park above the railroad station.

Roses and Cadaqués

ROSES (ROSAS) enjoys a brilliant situation beneath a ruined medieval fortress at the head of a grand, sweeping bay. While nothing can take this away, the town is now a fully blown resort (supermarkets, discos, and English breakfasts) and no longer particularly attractive. Still, the ride in (especially from Cadaqués) is fine: down over the hills, across the plain and to the shore. **Buses** drop you outside the post office, with the town center and restaurants to the left, appalling hotel blocks to the right.

CADAQUÉS is a much better bet. With whitewashed houses lining the narrow, hilly streets, and craggy bays on either side of the village, it's a picturesque place and still something of a working fishing port. Sitting on the sea front, you can watch the fishermen take their live catches straight to the restaurant kitchens. The one minus is the beaches, tiny and all pebbly. In the 1960s Salvador Dalí built a house on the outskirts of town (at Port Lligat) and for some years Cadaqués became a distinctly hip place to be, hosting an interesting floating community. Over the last few years though, it has been "discovered" and is now too trendy for its own good — and too expensive. Still, when all is said and done, Cadaqués remains precious rather than exclusive. There are beautiful people around and more than a few Mercedes, but it all falls far short of, say, a South-of-France snobbery. Out of season Cadaqués could be great but even in midsummer — if you can bear the company and the prices — you'll probably still have fun. Look out for the *Museu Perrot-Moore d'Art Europeu* which has graphics by Dalí.

Finding **rooms** is likely to be a big problem unless you're here outside peak season; try the stepped streets underneath the church and the corresponding area on the other side of the bay. If all else fails, ask around to see which houses rent private rooms. The **campground** (☎972/258126; on the road to Port Lligat, a steep 1km out of town) is outrageously expensive and noisy. There are four **buses** daily to Roses (and on to Figueres) but no bus station; catch them from outside the service station on the way out of town.

In the other direction, halfway back around the Gulf of Roses toward Empuries, one of Spain's newest and most accessible nature reserves can be found just outside Sant Pere Pescador. Here the **Parc Natural dels Aiguamolls de la Empordá** can be entered straight off the beach. Still very much in the throes of being established, and relying heavily on the botany students of Barcelona University and 'green' volunteers, the reserve looks a little raw in places, but attracts a wonderful selection of birds in both the coastal terrain and paddy fields of the area. There are several easy trails laid around the area.

North to the Border

To go any distance north from Cadaqués you need to backtrack to Figueres, the local transportation hub; buses and trains go from there to the French border. The next town to the north, **EL PORT DE LA SELVA**, an intensive fishing port, is easily enough reached by walking or hitching the 13km across the cape, but it isn't a place that'll tempt you to stay. The beaches and campgrounds (one right on the beach) are not particularly enticing, and it's basically a family place with nothing to do in the evenings. It does, however, allow access to Sant Pere de Rodes, the most important monastery in the region; from SELVA DE LA MAR, 2km above the port, a good dirt road takes you right there (another 4km). Alternatively you can approach from VILAJÜIGA where the nearest train station is also located.

The Benedictine monastery of **Sant Pere de Rodes** was one of the many foundations which developed around here after the departure of the Moors. The first written record of it dates from 879 and it quickly rose to glory, accumulating enormous wealth and administering huge territories. From the beginning there were disputes between monks and local feudal lords, since in 934 it became independent, answerable only to Rome, source of innumerable donations and privileges. A goal of pilgrimages in the twelfth and thirteenth centuries, it was gradually fortified and enlarged, its period of splendor lasting 400 years before decadence set in. Many fine treasures were looted when it was finally abandoned in 1789, and the French pillaged it on several occasions; some of the rescued silver can be seen in Girona's Museu d'Art.

Aside from the more recent history of the monastery, a number of historians have suggested that it was built over a pagan temple dedicated to the Pyrenean Venus, Afrodita Pyrene — a theory based on a second- or first-century B.C. Egyptian map, written narratives of the third and fourth centuries A.D., and the discovery of fragments of pagan sculptures and Corinthian capitals in the area. Nearby is the pre-Romanesque church of **Santa Elena**, all that stands of the small rural community which grew up around the monastery. Above the monastery and contemporary with it stands the very ruined **Castillo de Sant Salvador** of which only the walls remain. This provided the perfect lookout site for the invasions (French or Moorish) which normally came from the sea and in the event of which fires were lighted on the hill to warn the whole surrounding area.

Back on the coast, **LLANÇÀ** (LLANSA) makes a handy base for a few days of touring. Once a small fishing town, the road and rail route to France has opened it up to the passing tourist trade, which Llançà is shameless in its attempts to catch. Unlike similar towns, though, it does have other attractions. The beach is a good 2km from the **train station** (buses stop outside), but the old town is much closer, just off to the right. A tiny Plaça Major houses an outsize medieval church (currently under restoration) and the remains of a later defensive tower. Follow the road back down to the port and you pass the restaurants, souvenir shops, and miniature golf courses but it's not yet overwhelming. There is a proper working port at the end of the road, with a coarse sandy beach, all definitely low-key and concrete-free. The *Hostal Miramar* (☎972/380132), right on the harbor front overlooking the beach, usually has singles and doubles available even in high summer, while there are some cheaper *habitaciones* back in the old town. There are two **campgrounds** signposted on the way in from the station.

From Llançà it's possible to pick up trains from Figueres on their way to Port Bou. At several, usually inconvenient, times throughout the day they will also stop at COLERA, only a few kilometers to the north. Much smaller than nearly everywhere on this coast, and much less frequented by passing drivers, there's only fitful development here and it's mostly locals using the very pebbly beach. There's a nice **campground** (*Sant Miguel* ☎972/389018) set well back from the beach, just off the main road, or **rooms** to be had in (and off) the village square.

PORT BOU, 7km farther north, is a fine place to approach by road, over the hill and around the bay. It's worth walking from Colera and suffering the initial steep climb to look down upon the green hills, deep blue water, and small coarse beach. A mere fishing village until the Barcelona–Cérbère railway came into operation, Port Bou is now a stop on the dash in and out of Spain, only 3km from the French border. Not that it's been much affected, as few people bother to get off the train. Walk downhill from the station, past the souvenir stalls, and around the pretty natural harbor and stony beach you'll still see fishermen mending their nets. There are some excellent outdoor **restaurants** lining the quay also, none of them outrageously expensive; you can get an excellent meal here — four courses including fresh mussels and *paella* and wine, say — for around 900ptas. There are a handful of modest-priced *hostales* along the front, and the **Turismo** at the harbor has a list of **rooms** to rent in private houses. Alternatively, stop for lunch and keep going to France or Figueres.

Girona

The ancient walled town of **GIRONA** (GERONA) stands on a fortress-like hill, high above the unusually active Riu Onyar. It's a fine place, full of interest and oddly devoid of tourists considering that the town's airport serves most of the Costa Brava's resorts.

As with so many Spanish towns, much of the pleasure of being in Girona is simply wandering around. The streets are narrow and medieval, the churches (when they're open) are cool and fascinating, while above the river high rows of houses lean precipitously on the banks. Sooner or later you'll hit on the **Cathedral** (daily 10am–6pm), a mighty Gothic building approached by a really magnificent seventeenth-century flight of baroque steps. Inside it is equally awesome, for there are no aisles, just one tremendous single-naved vault with a span of 22m, the largest in the world. This emphasis on width and height is a feature of Catalan Gothic with its "hall churches," of which, unsurprisingly, Girona's is the ultimate example. It was built in the fifteenth century, though there are parts of the cathedral which date back to the eleventh and twelfth centuries, notably the Romanesque cloisters with their exquisite sculpted capitals.

You can visit the cloisters by buying a ticket to the sacristy and **Museu Capitular** (10am–1pm and 4–6pm) which, in this case, is certainly worth doing. The museum has a small but superb collection of religious art, including a perfect *Beatus* illuminated by Mozarabic miniaturists in 974, and the famous *Creation Tapestry* (11th–12th c.), which is the best piece of Romanesque textile in existence. If you find the collection interesting, the **Museu d'Art** (Tues.–Sun. 10am–1pm and 4–7pm) contains further examples; it's housed beside the cathedral in the Episcopal Palace. Among the manuscripts on display here are an eleventh-century copy of Bede and an amazing martyrology from the Monastery of Poblet (no. 103, room 5). From behind the nearby San Domenec convent you can get up onto the former town walls; the other point of access is down by the Plaça Catalunya.

Girona is also remarkable for its **Banys Arabs** (10am–1pm and infrequently 4–7pm, but keys available at San Pere Galligans outside these hours),

GIRONA

built probably by Moorish craftsmen in the thirteenth century, well after the Moors' occupation of Girona (795–1015) had ended. They are the best preserved baths in Spain after those at Granada and show a curious mixture of Arab and Romanesque styles. The layout, a series of rooms for different temperatures, is influenced ultimately by the Romans. The cooling room is the most interesting; niches and a stone bench provide seats for relaxation (after the steam bath), while the room is lighted, most unusually, by a central skylight-vault supported by octagonally arranged columns. To reach the baths, turn right through the Portal de Sobreportas, near the cathedral stairway. Girona also contains the best preserved **Jewish quarter** (thirteenth century) in western Europe; called the *Call*, its main street is formed by c/de la Força, which in turn follows the old Roman road.

From the Plaça de la Catedral another short road leads downhill to the Riu Galligans, a small tributary of the Onyar. The **Museu Provincial Arqueologic** (10am–1pm and 4:30–7pm) stands across the river, to the right, in the former church of San Pedro. It outlines rather methodically the region's history from Paleolithic times. San Pedro's cloisters, however, Romanesque and very close in design to the cathedral's, are worth the walk.

Practicalities

There's plenty of cheap **accommodation** in Girona. One or two *hostales* are near the railroad station; the *Hostal Reymar* (c/Rey Don Martin, near the cathedral; ☎972/200228) is excellent and moderately priced; and the *Hostal Brindis* is worth a try (Avda. Ramon Folch, near the river off the Gran Via de Jaume I; ☎972/203039). You'll also find some *pensiones* near the intersection of c/de la Força and c/Galligans, and a few other possibilities in c/Ciutadans, near the **Turismo** (maps available) in the central Plaça del Vi. There's a second information office at the railroad station where you could pick up a map; the city guides available here also list most of the cheap accommodation. There are several good, reasonably priced **restaurants** on the c/de la Força, near the cathedral. If you're using **Girona airport** (unlikely since most outbound international flights take off from Barcelona) bear in mind that there's no bus service from the town and a taxi will end up being pretty expensive; most charters coming from England are linked directly by bus with the Costa Brava.

Girona's large **bus station** (around the back of the railway station) has frequent services to the Costa Brava, the *SARFA* company running numerous buses to Palafrugell and, twice daily, to Tossa de Mar. There are many other services, which makes Girona a handy base for exploring the nearby coast.

Girona Province: Inland to Banyoles, Besalú, and Ripoll

For an escape into the countryside around Girona you could take a bus to **BANYOLES** (BAÑOLAS). A relaxing, little-developed village, it has a few **hostales** and an excellent, nameless **fonda** for food and beds, plus two **campgrounds**. In town there's the **Monastir San Estaban** and a **Museu Arqueologic** (10am–2pm and 4:30–8pm) housed in the Pia Almonia, a former medieval poorhouse.

Banyoles, though, is most renowned for its particularly beautiful lake, famed for its enormous carp, but presently being contaminated by the droppings of the large numbers of gulls who adorn its surface. The Olympic rowing events will be held here in 1992, after which you can forget about peace and tranquility. Across the water, a thirty-minute walk around the edge, is the tiny hamlet of PORQUERES, with an elegant Romanesque church; you can circle the entire lake in three hours.

BESALÚ (14km to the north; several daily buses on from Banyoles) is probably the most attractive and interesting small town in Catalunya. In appearance it is almost completely medieval, boasting some striking monuments quite out of proportion to its current humble status and it makes a perfect example of the quirky and random twists of Spanish history. At the very beginning of the ninth century Louis, son of Charlemagne, advanced across the Pyrenees and expelled the Moors from this northeast corner of Spain. There arose several independent kingdoms to fill the ensuing vacuum, Besalú among them. Despite a total population of just 800 it prospered, as it had done in a small way since Roman times, and remained a place of some importance well into the thirteenth century.

The most striking reminder of Besalú's past grandeur is a splendid twelfth-century **bridge** over the Riu Fluvià, in the middle of which stands a fortified gatehouse complete with portcullis. More curious, however, is the **Mikvah**, or Jewish bathhouse, on the far side of the bridge (away from the main part of town — turn sharp left back towards the river). Unique in Spain, it was originally attached to a riverbank synagogue in the old Jewish quarter, in the heart of the lower town. The **Plaça Major**, in the middle of Besalú, is entirely enclosed by medieval buildings, including an elegant thirteenth-century **Ajuntament**, now housing the **Turismo**. The majestically porticoed c/ Tallaferro leads off from this square to the ruined shell of **Santa María** (you can't get inside), which for just two years (1018–20) was designated Cathedral of the Bishopric of Besalú; union with Barcelona meant the end of its short-lived episcopal independence. Also worth seeking out are the **Iglesia San Vicente** and the **Monasterio San Pedro**, both excellent examples of Catalan Romanesque. You may find that you can only see inside these churches (and the *mikvah*) as part of a guided tour, running every hour or so from the tourist office. Sadly, there are only two places to stay, and even the less expensive one (*Fonda Sigues*, on the main road) is not exactly cheap. But it's worth staying if you can, since in the daytime Besalú is prey to whirlwind coach parties, but by early evening it settles down to its own infinitely preferable pace of life.

SANTA PAU, between Banyoles and OLOT to the west, has a well-preserved medieval core with an arcaded square and a castle, and parts of the old walls. The area around Olot is volcanic and the rich soils have given rise to lush vegetation, in particular an extensive beech forest. Olot itself (buses from Besalú), modern and sprawling, is an important transportation junction.

Ripoll and Vic

From Olot a road leads northwest to Sant Joan de les Abadesses (see below) or a bus can take you to **RIPOLL**, a modern industrial town set in verdant surroundings. Ripoll has a charming, if small, old quarter and one of the most famous and beautiful monuments of Romanesque art: the Benedictine **Monasterio de Santa María** (9am–1pm and 3–7pm). Founded in 888 by Vilfredo el Peloso, Count of Barcelona, it rose to prominence as a center of learning in the eleventh and twelfth centuries, guided by one Olivia, a cousin of the counts of Besalú. Under Olivia and succeeding abbots the monastery was completely rebuilt, using some of the finest craftsmen of the age.

Much was destroyed by a fire in 1835 but their work may still be seen intact in the **west portal** (now the main entrance to the church) and the cloisters (nominal charge). The delicate columns and arches of the portal contain ornamental designs, zodiacal signs, and an agricultural calendar (e.g. November — slaughter of the pig). These are enclosed by a tremendous sculpted facade of biblical scenes, historical and allegorical, and symbols of the Evangelists. This and the lower gallery of the cloister, with its rhythmic arches and marvelous capitals, both date from the twelfth century, probably the greatest period of Spanish Romanesque. Adjacent to the monastery stands the fourteenth-century church of **San Pedro**, above which has been installed an eclectic **Museu dels Pirineos** (Museum of the Pyrenees; 9am–1pm and 3–7pm), with exhibits ranging from origami to birds' eggs. The **Turismo** stands just to the left, underneath the sundial, and gives out a handy map of town and bus timetables.

You might well want to stay in Ripoll, as the quiet center is refreshingly free of tourists, save the unpredictable busload that descends upon the monastery and then departs. From the **train station** (buses arrive and leave from in front), turn left and you'll see the monastery tower straight ahead. It's a ten-minute walk into town — cross the rail tracks, over the river, then head uphill into the Plaça Ajuntament; the adjacent **Plaça Abat Oliba** contains the monastery, museum and tourist office. The cheapest **places to stay** are in the old streets off this square; best and nearest is the *Fonda Cala Paula* (☎972/700011; just beyond the tourist office, to the left as you look at it). A couple more places are in the Plaça Nova (off Plaça Sant Eudald, halfway down c/Sant Pere): the *Hostal Ripolles* at no. 11 (☎972/700215) and, for connoisseurs of the funky, the *Hotel Payet* at no. 2 (☎972/700250) — reports indicate that it hasn't changed its decor or wiring since the 1940s. The **restaurant** attached to the *Paula* is excellent, with wonderful trout a speciality.

Moving on from Ripoll presents few problems. There are ten daily **trains** south to Barcelona and three or four heading north to PUIGCERDÀ. **Buses** too are legion, provided you can get to Olot (3–4 daily) to the east; from there fairly regular buses take you to GIRONA (via Banyoles/Besalú or Amer), and less regular ones to VIC and FIGUERES. Note that while heading directly east from Ripoll to Figueres looks easy on the map, it isn't; you'll save yourself up to a six-hour wait in Olot for the connecting bus by going instead to Girona and catching one of the frequent trains from there.

If you approach Ripoll from Barcelona or are returning that way (there are frequent trains) you'll pass through VIC (VICH), and it's worth stopping for a look around. Once out of the station, take the road opposite, which leads up to the enormous arcaded square where an important market takes place. (Vic is well known for its excellent *embutidos* — cold sausages — especially *fuet* and *butifarra*). Beyond and to the right of this square lies the old quarter, including some Roman antiquities, a rather dull cathedral (apart from its eleventh-century Romanesque bell-tower) and most interestingly, the **Museu Episcopal** next door. This houses the second most important collection of Romanesque art outside of the Barcelona museum, with a wealth of eleventh- and twelfth-century frescoes and wooden sculptures.

The Romanesque Trail

From Ripoll an important "Romanesque Trail" (pick up the descriptive leaflet from tourist offices) leads northeast into the *Prepirineo* (Pyrenean foothills), but unfortunately many of the sites don't lie on bus routes, so you can only reach all of them if you have your own vehicle or hitch. The first stop is **Sant Joan de les Abadesses**, founded as a Benedictine convent, later a canonical monastery. The austerity of its single-nave, twelfth-century church makes a powerful impression, and it contains a famous wooden sculpture group, the *Santissim Misteri* of 1251, depicting Christ's deposition from the Cross.

The busy town of **CAMPRODON**, to the northeast, with a beautiful medieval bridge at its entrance, is graced by another Romanesque church and makes a good base. It has several cheap *hostales* and is packed with skiers in winter. The countryside around is good for walking and is most scenic in autumn, when the woods are ablaze with the different hues of turning leaves.

Until recently there was no road to the quaint rustic village of **BEGET** (east of Camprodon), but now there's a tortuous one which winds down and down again through terraced slopes. Like most local villages it has suffered crippling depopulation, only coming to life in summer with predominantly Spanish visitors. Its two medieval bridges are impressive, but the jewels are the late twelfth-century church of **Sant Cristofor** (two distinct construction periods can be distinguished in the bell tower) and the *Majestat* it houses. *Majestats* are Romanesque wooden images portraying Christ wrapped in a tunic from head to toe, and more of them were produced in Catalunya than in any other region. Most of the *Majestats*, however, were destroyed in 1936, and this solemn and serene example, dating from the late twelfth or early thirteenth century, is one of the very few that can now be admired in situ. If the church is locked, ask in the souvenir shop opposite. At ROCABRUNA, a short way out of Beget on the main road, there's another small twelfth-century church, plus a couple of good, cheap **restaurants** with simple Catalan fare such as barbecued meats with *alioli*, or *escalibada* (peppers and eggplants baked in the oven, then sprinkled with olive oil).

North from Camprodon, MOLLO and LLANARS have fine Romanesque churches and, to the northwest, SETCASES is another hidden village at the end of a mountain road, famous for its honey.

North from Ripoll to the Border

The region north of Ripoll has been extensively developed as ski terrain, the train providing handy access to most of the resorts. Out of season (i.e. in summer) there's not a great deal of life, which is all to the good if you just want some gentle ambling around. For serious Pyrenean **walking**, the area west of Andorra (see below) offers much more extensive opportunities and a wider range of scenery, flora, and fauna. There are some reasonable targets here, however, and the private rail line up to **Núria** (itself a major ski center) is one of the most stunning trips in Spain. To the northwest of Ripoll, the top half of Berguedà *comarca* (county) constitutes good countryside for gentle cross-country walking. Farther north, by the French border, **Puigcerdà** has the only surviving rail link with France over the Pyrenees, while the odd Spanish enclave of **Llívia** is actually engulfed by France.

If you want to go **skiing** it will almost certainly prove cheaper to visit a Barcelona travel agent and get an inclusive package than to attempt to do it yourself. Of the resorts in this area the best are those around the **La Molina–Super Molina** complex, insomuch as they have more extensive terrain and more challenging runs than most.

Núria

The **private rail line** (*Ferrocarril Cremallera*) to **NÚRIA** is a fabulous introduction to the mountains. After a leisurely start from RIBES DE FRESER
through the lower valley, the tiny two-carriage train lurches up into the
Pyrenees and follows the river between great crags, and then climbs high
above both river and fir forests. Occasionally it stops, the track only inches
from a drop of hundreds of meters into the valley, a sheer rock face soaring
way above you. Once through a final tunnel, the train emerges alongside a
small lake (dry in summer) at the other side of which is the one giant building that constitutes Núria. A severe stone structure, it combines church, tourist office, cafe, hotel, and ski center all in one. The proper title of this place is
Sanctuary of the Mother of God of Núria and came into being when one Sant
Gil found an image of the Virgin here. Said to bestow fertility, the Virgin of
Núria is the patroness of shepherds of the Pyrenees, and baby girls hereabouts are often christened after her.

Should you come across hordes of kids here, it'll probably be a *colonia*
(school camping trip), this being one of their favorite destinations. But solitude is easily found amid the bleak, treeless scenery, and hikers head for
Núria all through the summer. The **hotel** itself is expensive but maintains a
few simple former cells as a kind of cheap hostel. There are also several
bunk-bedded refuges around, though they are often full of Spanish groups.
It's probably easier to camp; you can go just about anywhere you choose, but
the valley beyond is a good spot. You'll need good equipment, even in
summer, since it gets cold at night. A shop in the hotel sells food; fresh bread
arrives by train at noon. You can buy hot snacks or breakfast at the *Bar
Finestrelles* and there's a self-service place for midday or evening meals. The
hotel dining room provides a not too expensive set meal.

Serious climbers can move on from here to the summit of **Puigmal**
(2909m); the 1:25,000 "Puigmal-Núria" *Editorial Alpina* contoured map/
guide is recommended. Most people don't in fact stay at Núria, and a good
option if you're reasonably energetic is to look around for a while (and
perhaps take a boat out on the lake) and then walk back down at least as far
as QUERALPS. This is the best part of the route and more than half the total
distance: one hikes along a beautiful, mostly marked, four-hour trail down in
the river valley below the rail line. From Queralps you can pick up the train
on its way back to Ribes de Freser. The path is not overly ambitious, though
you would do well to leave your pack in Ribes.

The **Núria train** (*InterRail* passes not valid) runs on the hour from 9am to
5pm (except at 2pm) from RIBES-ENLLAÇ, which is a ten-minute walk out of
the center of Ribes de Freser, on the Barcelona road. If you're coming up
from Barcelona on the train towards La Molina and Puigcerdá, you change at
RIBES DE FRESER-RENFE, where the two platforms are right next to each
other. (The station in the town — RIBES VILA — is used only by Núria line
services.) The same number of trains return from Núria each day, the round
trip costing a whopping 1075ptas but worth every cent (one-ways available).
The train journey from Barcelona to Ribes de Freser takes about two hours.

If you want **rooms** in the area there are several places to stay in Ribes de Freser, but it's an unremarkable town. Cheaper and livelier Ripoll is 13km south by train, or stay at the **youth hostel** (☎972/736177) at PLANOLES, the stop after Ribes on the railroad line to Puigcerdà. It's open all year except September and early October and is on Ctra. de Neva, Prat Cap Riu.

La Pobla de Lillet, Castellar de N'Hug and Sant Jaume de Frontanyà

The center of Berguedà *comarca* is **BERGA** (home of the Patum festival) and the area north of it is the most attractive to walkers. (Serious hill-climbers should head northwest to the peak of Pedraforça). Berga is two hours by bus from Barcelona and there is plenty of cheap accommodation — *Fonda Catalunya* (☎93/8210077), for example. A short bus ride beyond here will take you to **LA POBLA DE LILLET**, from where you can branch out on various walks. The village itself is picturesquely situated, an ancient bridge arching a shallow river and the snowy peaks of the Pyrenees framing the whole. Neither of the two **hostales** is particularly cheap (*Hostal Pericas* is the better bet; ☎93/8236162) but camping nearby presents no problems.

It's a steady twelve-kilometer ascent to **CASTELLAR DE N'HUG** and since you can't really leave the road anyway, except for a short section at the beginning and at the end, you miss little by hitching. A little way out of La Pobla de Lillet, on the left, is a disused factory built by the young Gaudí; it looks like a stack of cave-dwellings, eerily empty. Approaching Castellar, you'll come to the **Fonts del Llobregat**, source of the river which divides Catalunya in two, entering the sea at Barcelona. The *fonts* receive many Catalan visitors, who come to it almost as to a site of pilgrimage. Summer droughts frequently beset Catalunya, temporarily drying out many of the rivers, so there's great pride in any durable water source, even if it's a trickle by outsiders' standards. To reach the village from here you can stay with the road or take a steep climb up the back way. Castellar de N'Hug is an old village heaped up the sides of a hill at the base of the Pyrenees. Edelweiss has been found in the region and its rare flowers are sold by licenced gatherers and sellers in the village. A farm beyond the village, on the path going into the mountains, has a couple of horses which it rents out for treks.

Back in La Pobla de Lillet, you could take a steepish hike around the Cingles Vilardell or walk southwards cross-country (about 10km) to **SANT JAUME DE FRONTANYÀ**. If you choose the latter, your route will take you past the tiny circular twelfth-century chapel of Sant Miquel and a few farms to arrive fairy-tale fashion (at the end of a winding road) at a beautiful Romanesque church dating from the eleventh century, in Lombard style with a Latin Cross plan. There's nothing else here except two good cheap restaurants and a hostal. A road goes down to BORREDÀ, where it joins the main road back to Berga.

Puigcerdà

Right on the French border, **PUIGCERDÀ** retains the only rail link over the Pyrenees to France following the closure of the *SNCF* line between Oloron and Canfranc; four trains a day currently leave Puigcerdà for LA TOUR DE CAROL over the border. If France is your immediate aim, it's hardly worth stopping to take in Puigcerdà, a perfectly pleasant place but with no singular attraction. Much of it has been rebuilt in the years after devastating civil war bombardment; one of the few things spared by the bombs was the forty-meter-high bell tower in the Plaça de Santa María. A war memorial stands on the site of the destroyed church. The other end of town seems to have escaped the damage — the church of Sant Domines (on Passeig 10 Abril) is enveloped in an interior gloom which has helped preserve what little is left of some medieval murals. The only other potentially interesting building, the thirteenth-century convent next door, is currently closed for restoration.

For all its paucity of "sights," Puigcerdà, is a likable town, slow and unpretentious. **Accommodation** is plentiful; as well as two *pensiones* on c/Major (which crosses Plaça de Santa Maria) and the pleasant *Hostal Residencia La Muntanya* (✆972/880202) on Plaça de Barcelona (above and to the left of Pl. de Santa Maria), there's the reasonable and wonderfully furnished *Hotel Sala* in c/Alfons I (off the bottom of Pg. 10 Abril; ✆972/880104). Passing French tourists are responsible for bilingual menus and higher prices but the streets around the church and off c/Alfons I hide a selection of more reasonable places to eat.

If you're heading **west** then you might have to spend the night in Puigcerdà anyway as there are only three **buses** a day to LA SEU D'URGELL. Buses leave from in front of the **train station** at the very bottom of town. It's a steep climb up to the center (you'll see the bell tower above you) although if you've arrived by bus it should continue from the station up the hill. There's a **Turismo** to one side of the *Ajuntament* building; walk down c/Major and it's on the right on a terrace overlooking the plain below.

Llívia

An easy six-kilometer detour from Puigcerdà will take you to **LLÍVIA**, a curious Spanish enclave in French territory; hitching shouldn't be a problem, but the walk isn't too strenuous either. You don't need to go through the customs point 1km outside Puigcerdà, just bear left and keep to the main road. There's a second perfunctory checkpoint as you leave Spain and then you are technically in France, with road signs exhorting you not to leave the road unless you are a local permit holder and definitely not to camp anywhere (not that you'd want to).

Once in Llívia, and off the built-up main road, things get positively medieval. The stone streets are tortuous, winding up to a solid fifteenth-century church with an older defensive tower. It's claimed that the **museum** across the road is the site of the oldest pharmacy in Europe; the display features pots, powders, and jars of herbs, plus a reconstruction of the dispensary. In the *Bar Esportiv* below the church the most athletic item in evidence is a rickety pool table, although the one-armed bandit generates a bit of excitement.

Outside, the local sheep and roosters generate the only noise and life, except at weekends and on legal holidays, when the town teems with day-trippers.

The Route To Andorra

The semiautonomous principality of Andorra, now little more than a duty-free parking lot, is not much of an end in itself, and you'll get immeasurably better hiking in the Pyrenees to the west. However, if you're traveling back through France it is a reasonably interesting route, covered regularly by buses from Barcelona's Plaça de Espanya.

Solsona

Around halfway you pass through **SOLSONA**, a smallish, ramshackle town which retains some charm along with its ancient walls and gates. If you want to break the journey this is the best place; there's a good *fonda* (the *Vilanova*) just off the cathedral square, as well as the even cheaper *Pensio Pilar* nearby, with a *comedor* attached. If you arive on a Sunday and these are closed, try the *San Roc*, just off the road to La Seu, opposite the *Bar San Fermin* (which is where most buses stop). The best bars in town are the *Ateixa* (in the old town) and the *Apostrof* (c/Sant Agusti; hidden among new buildings at the top of the old town) — the latter is dedicated to Frank Zappa and serves Guinness! The **Cathedral**, gloomy and mysterious in the best tradition of Catalan Gothic, has some fine stained glass and a diminutive twelfth-century Virgin, reminiscent of the Montserrat icon.

The Routes Onward

Before you reach Solsona there's little of interest in the way of towns or scenery, but once you've left, and the bus has maneuvered its way onto the main road from Lleida, the drama begins. Amid tremendous mountain vistas the road plunges through a great gorge, lined with terraces of rock jutting to over 600m above. Andorra starts to seem an exciting prospect by the time you've reached the final Spanish town, La Seu d'Urgell (see below).

There's a second approach to Andorra, again via La Seu, west along the C1313 from Puigcerdà. This is not a road to hitch on, at least not until the extensive tunneling and road reconstruction program has been completed. Falling rocks, swirling dust, and virtual dirt tracks are the norm from BELLVER DE CERDANYA as far as La Seu; the bus ride can take up to two hours to cover fifty kilometers, with bulldozers clearing the way for convoys of traffic.

La Seu d'Urgell

You'll have to change buses for Andorra in **LA SEU D'URGELL** (SEO DE URGEL), the best base if you don't want to stay in Andorra itself. Named after its imposing twelfth-century cathedral, La Seu is a run-down sort of place, its medieval quarter neglected and atmospheric. The **Cathedral** itself

(Mon.–Sat. 10am–1pm and 4:30–7:30pm, Sun. 10am–1:30pm) has been restored over the years but retains some graceful interior decoration and has an interesting **Museu Diocesano** within its cloisters. The museum contains a tenth-century Mozarabic manuscript with miniatures, the *Beatus*. The old streets around the cathedral are dark and cobbled, with the L-shaped c/ Major running parallel to the town's central thoroughfare (Passeig Joan Brudieu) and then down past the cathedral. This is where all the cheapest places to stay and to eat are: *Fonda Bertran* (c/dels Estudis, off c/Major) is a bit dingy but has an excellent *tapas* bar downstairs, while the *Restaurant Jové* (c/dels Canonges, parallel to c/Major) is very basic and very cheap. There are some fine *tapas* bars around this area too, the *Bar Eugineo* (top of c/Major) being one of the best. One other good place to stay, the *Fonda Bernada* on c/de Sant Ermengol, is on the far side of the Plaça Catalunya (at the top of the green pedestrian walk), across from the old part of town.

If you've got time there are some fine views of the whole valley to be had from the ruins of **Castellciutat**, only a few minutes' walk out of town, along the Lleida road. Either climb the sheer hill to the side of the gas station on the right, or walk another kilometer along the main road and follow the dirt track on the right. A sign here says 'danger' and the scanty remains of the old fortifications are indeed crumbling away, assisted by the quarry below — take care at the edges.

Back in town, the **bus station** is halfway down the wide, tree-lined Passeig Joan Brudieu (on the right), while at the bottom of this pedestrian mall is the **Turismo** (11am–1:30pm and 5–8pm). Buses run south to LLEIDA (2 daily) and east to PUIGCERDÀ (3 daily) as well as to ANDORRA (7 daily Mon.–Sat., 5 on Sun.).

Andorra

The anomalous **Principility of Andorra** gained its semi-autonomy in 1278 when the Bishops of La Seu d'Urgell and the Counts of Foix settled a long-standing quarrel by granting independence under joint sovereignty. To this day the Bishops of La Seu and the French President nominate the judicial officers of Andorra. Here the attractive quaintness stops.

As little as thirty years ago, Andorra — an archaic region which, romantically, happened also to be a separate country — was virtually cut off from the rest of the world. There are still no planes and no trains but today it's basically a drive-in, duty-free supermarket; the main road through the country and into France is clogged with French and Spanish after the (not particularly cheap) hi-fi and electrical gear, the extremely cheap liquor in the hotels and restaurants, and a tankful of discount gasoline (smuggling is a way of life here for the locals too). Andorra has no money of its own, so both pesetas and French francs are accepted.

The road from La Seu d'Urgell to the capital, Andorra la Vella, prepares you for what's ahead. The hills on each side are plastered with billboards advertising liquor and cigarettes, and the first "village," SANTA JULIA, is virtually one huge duty-free emporium, surrounded by parking lots and trailer parks all packed to the gills.

ANDORRA LA VELLA must once have been an attractive little town with its stone church, river, and enclosing hills. Now it's ghastly, a seething mass of souvenir shops, tourist restaurants (six-language menus a speciality), tacky discos, and parked cars. It's consumerism gone mad. The only reason to hang around would be to get something to eat — no shortage of choice and competition fostering low prices — though the tourist office also claims that there are **rooms** available, presumably only taken by drivers who over-did the cheap booze at lunchtime.

It's hard to convince yourself that not all of Andorra is like this (though sadly, much of it is) but with a bit of effort you can effect a partial escape into the magnificent mountain scenery. There are frequent local buses to **ORDINO** (catch them from where the La Seu bus sets you down, near the church), an intriguing and steep eight-kilometer climb from Andorra la Vella, off the main road. Construction work will before long make its small-village existence a thing of the past, but Ordino still retains a handful of old stone buildings and some infinitely quieter surroundings.

From Ordino it's an easy eight-kilometer (2 hr.) walk up the gently undulating valley towards El Serrat. The views get increasingly better and there are several tiny hamlets on the way, mere clusters of houses built over the river. It's all remarkably pleasant given the proximity of the main road but even here the excursion trade is beginning to make itself felt: a suspiciously good restaurant here, a tourist bar there, and everywhere the foundations and works that tell of another nascent hotel or apartment building. At **EL SERRAT** there are some tumbling waterfalls and a couple of hotels offering tea and views from their restaurant terraces. If you wanted to **stay** in Andorra (and these parts are certainly attractive enough) then there's the odd *hostal* on the Ordino–El Serrat road, hotels in both Ordino and El Serrat, and two **campgrounds** — the first and nicest 2km beyond Ordino, the second just before El Serrat.

Buses back to La Seu d'Urgell (for those not continuing to France) leave from Plaça Guillemó in Andorra la Vella, parallel to the main road. Note that the customs check on your way into Andorra is virtually nonexistent. However, on the way out even the local buses are stopped, their contents and passengers prodded. If you're driving but based in La Seu, and it's high season, you might as well leave the car behind and take the bus — the traffic's so bad that a bus isn't much slower, and parking in Andorra is an ordeal as well.

The Catalan Pyrenees

West of Andorra, the Pyrenees become more welcoming in every way. While it's true that the Catalan stretch of the mountains is generally more developed (ski resorts and hydroelectric projects in particular) than its Aragonese counterpart to the west, in the untouched corners it's no less rewarding. Indeed, **Noguera Pallaresa**, the **Vall d'Aran**, and the remoter **Vall Fosca**, one of the gateways to the spectacular **Parc Nacional de Aigües Tortes**, all possess scenery and hiking appeal equal to almost anywhere in the range, on either side of the border. A further lure is the Boí valley, just west of the park, which has the finest concentration of Romanesque churches in the Pyrenees.

Initial access to any of the destinations above is easy enough by bus out of POBLA DE SEGUR, although moving between them is more difficult without your own vehicle, or without a willingness to hike through the mountains.

The Valley of the Noguera Pallaresa

The easterly ride up and into the Vall d'Aran, in the northernmost corner of Catalunya, promises great things. Once a day (at 8am) a bus leaves Barcelona for Pobla de Segur, and except between November and April continues on via the high Port de Bonaigua. Alternatively you can reach Pobla by a spectacular train ride from Lleida; the morning departure arrives in time to connect with the bus. POBLA DE SEGUR straddles the river Segre, just above its confluence with the Pallaresa; trains arrive in the new town, where you must cross the bridge and walk for through the new town for fifteen minutes to the *Alsina Graells* terminal. There are a couple of *fondas* and *hostales* should you need to stay, but food (except in the stores) is expensive and you probably won't want to.

Upon leaving Pobla the bus threads through the spectacular Gorge of Collegats, forged by the Noguera (river) Pallaresa through 300-meter cliffs. As the defile widens you suddenly come upon the rickety village and enchanting twelfth-century Benedictine monastery of GERRI DE LA SAL, linked to each other with an equally ancient bridge. This would be the spot to break a journey up to Aran, especially if you have your own car, though there are only a handful of bars and lodging is doubtful.

The next two towns, SORT and LLAVORSI, have burgeoned in recent years with any number of *hostales* and restaurants, since they've between them become virtually overnight the premier river-running meccas of Europe. After spring snowmelt the area swarms with kayakers and rafters, mostly foreign and encumbered with high-tech gear, but every year in late June all of the communities in the valley, from Sort and Pobla upstream, stage the festival of the *Raiers* (Rafters), reenacting the exploits of the old-time pilots who still put the slick new kayakers to shame.

Beyond Llavorsi you pass the turnoff to ESPOT (see below) before arriving at ESTERRI D'ANEU, the last significant habitation before the pass, and the last stop if the latter is snowed up. It amounts to merely a few huddled houses between the road and the river, an arched bridge, and a slender towered church, but if ever a village deserved the epithet 'graceful', Esterri does. People usually sit out by the roadside, talking and knitting, or frequent the pair of no-nonsense bars. There are several places to stay, the pick of which is the delightful *Fonda Agust* (☎973/626034) in the flagstoned Plaça de l'Església, just behind the church. If Esterri is full up (unlikely), La GUINGUETA D'ANEU, 3km south, has a small roadside line of accommodation (a couple of *fondas* and one hotel) and a nice campground across from the reservoir on the west side of the road.

The road continues ascending, at first through farmland and then through great forests and alpine meadows, before broaching the Port (pass) de Bonaigua. Near the top (2072m) snow patches persist almost year-round, and you've a brief glimpse of half-wild horses grazing and simultaneous panoramas of the valley just left and the Vall d'Aran to come before descending the other side.

The Vall d'Aran

The **Vall d'Aran**, with its majestic Alpine feel, is curiously formed. The Pyrenees comprise two discontinuous chains of mountains and here these overlap for a length of about 50km, creating and completely encircling the valley. Although it has belonged to Spain since the thirteenth century, the valley, with the Garonne River cleaving down the middle, opens to the north and it is easy move between it and France. Like Andorra, it was virtually independent for much of its history, and 'Aran is *not* Catalunya' grafitti is still much in evidence. For centuries it was sealed off from the rest of Spain by snow for eight months of the year, but in 1948 the Viella tunnel was cut to provide a year-round link with the provincial capital of Lleida along the N230 highway.

Among themselves the inhabitants speak Aranés, a language (not a dialect, as a glance at the bizarre road signs will tell you) apparently consisting of elements of Catalan and Gascon with a generous sprinkling of Basque. *Aran*, in this language, means "valley," *Nautaran* "High valley," the most scenic, eastern portion. More surprising, perhaps, is the fact that despite the Baqueira/Beret ski complex and the firm entrenchment of summer tourism, the people have remained overtly friendly, even voluble, to the point of starting conversations unbidden and volunteering information.

On the surface life in the valley seems unchanged; at Unya, spitting distance from the main C142 road, laundry-in-the-fountain-trough is still the rule, and outside of peak season you still have to make "appointments" with the smaller village inn-keepers for evening meals. But the scythe-wielding hay-reapers of summer have as a backdrop vacation chalets for city folk, sprouting at the edge of each and every village. Though rigorously "traditional" in style, they represent an ominous trend.

The biggest engine of change is no doubt BAQUEIRA/BERET, a mammoth and sterile skiing development which is the first thing you encounter coming down from the pass. It's much frequented by the French (thus charging inflated prices), and the surrounding land is virtually all divided into lots waiting to be sold off. No doubt in winter the skiing fraternity have a ball, but in summer — as W.C. Fields said of Philadelphia — Baqueira/Beret is closed.

Salardú and Around

Salardú is the largest of the villages of the *Nautaran*, and is the obvious base for visiting the others, being large enough to offer a range of choice for lodging and eating, but small enough to not be a total zoo (except in August or peak ski season). From bottom to top, you can choose from a **youth hostel** (dirt cheap but YHA card and reservations required); *Fonda Barbara*, on c/ Major, in a popular and often full historic house, but huge meals served to anyone; *Refugi Rosti*, a hiker-oriented establishment on the main square, also in a 300-year old building and with meals; *Bar/Comidas* above the supermarket next to *Barbara*; a *CH* next to *Supermercado Sol y Nieve*; the *CEEC Julio Soler* lodge (dorms or quads priced per bed, institutional but good value); and rooms above *Bar Montaña*, across from *Barbara*. In addition four or five luxury digs publicize themselves around town. Two **banks** are open curious hours: one noon to 2pm, the other 5:30 to 8pm.

Once settled in and fed, it's easy enough to visit the surrounding villages, all centered on beautiful twelfth- and thirteenth-century **Romanesque churches**. **Salardú**'s thirteenth-century church of San Andreu, usually open, is a good start. **Unya**, 700 meters up the hill, boasts a shrine of the same age; the one at **Bagergue** (2.8km uphill, 12th–15th c.) is being restored; **Gessa**'s (1km downhill) has a square, keep-like belfry; and that of **Tredós** (1km upstream) impresses mostly with its massive bulk. Domestic architecture is historically stone masonry and slate roofing, with little deviation even now; foundation plaques on lintels are not of the same vintage as the churches but respectable enough, with dates ranging from the sixteenth to the eighteenth centuries.

In terms of **hiking**, there are no really hard-core walks in the valley except for the eight-hour (round-trip) excursion up to the Liat lakes by the French border, starting out of Bagergue, the most countrified of the *Nautaran* settlements. The trails joining Unya with Gessa and Salardú with Tredós (the latter signposted) are all of fifteen minutes long, but everywhere — even from the asphalt road up to Bagergue — the scenery and views are spectacular. On a clear day, Aneto, highest peak in the Pyrenees at 3404m, looms snowcapped to the west.

Arties and Viella

ARTIES, the next large community, 2½km downvalley, is unfortunately a bit of a letdown; the giant cement plant/strip mine at the outskirts establishes its aesthetics, the *parador* by the main road sets the tone for facilities. Besides the latter there are two or three fancy *hostales*, and three places offering *cambres* (Aranés for "rooms"): the *Portola* and *Ma Jesus* have doubles only, *Montardo* is cheaper but noisy since it's above a bar on the main highway. There are no meals to be had for less than $15, and even the famous thermal baths are shut down. Still it's worth lingering long enough to see the three-naved thirteenth-century cathedral, a worthy national monument; the smaller church of San Joan, across the road from the *Montardo*, is hard to miss.

The bus over the Port de Bonaigua eventually stops at **VIELLA**, around 2:30pm, with the single daily service in the opposite direction at 11am. Most visitors will arrive on the more direct bus run by *La Oscense* from Lleida or El Pont de Suert and upon arrival every superlative has been exhausted. In the final stretch an awesome tunnel (the *Tunel de Viella*), nearly 6km long, brings you right out at the southwest corner of the valley, the road curling down to the town below. This has become intensely developed and smartened up of late, a trend perhaps aggravated by French day-trippers who patronize the numerous supermarkets and gift shops. Yet some old small-holdings still lurk by the side of the Garonne as it runs through town and the church is as decrepit as ever. There's plenty of **accommodation** here, as you might expect, though none of it particularly cheap. Seek out the couple of *pensiones* on an unnamed lane at the bottom right-hand corner of the tree-lined Passeig dera Libertat (left at the river, at the parking sign). Otherwise there's a **campground** 5km away on the road towards France.

Aigües Tortes and Approaches

The most popular target for hikers in the Catalan Pyrenees is the **Parc Nacional de Sant Maurici i Aigües Tortes**, a vast and beautiful mountain-ous area constituting Catalunya's only national park (one of nine in Spain). Covering some 130 square kilometers, it is a rock- and forest-strewn land-scape of harsh beauty, including spectacular snow-spotted peaks of up to 3000m, cirques, and dramatic V-shaped valleys. For the less adventurous, there are any number of middle-altitude rambles to be made through some lovely scenery. The Sant Nicolau valley (in the west) has many glacially-formed lakes and cirques, plus the actual namesake Aigües Tortes (Twisted Waters); the Escrita valley, slightly craggier, contains the Sant Maurici lake.

The most common trees are the fir and the Scotch pine and there's an abundance of flowers in spring and early summer (don't forget that when spring is in the air lower down, winter still has a grip on the higher slopes). As for the fauna, wild boar apparently roam here, and at the very least you should see chamois. In mid-summer many rivers are passable which are otherwise not so, but temperature contrasts between day and night are still very marked and you should always be prepared for foul weather higher up.

Which **approach** to the park you use depends upon which zone you intend to explore, and how strenuous you want you hiking to be. The two main **bases** are BOÍ and ESPOT, at the western and eastern extremities of the park respectively, both set in their own gorgeous valleys. CAPDELLA near the top of the Vall Fosca is ideal if you want to immediately come to grips with the high peaks. Boí is 21km from the the main road at El Pont de Suert, but served by bus; Espot is only 7km off the main Viella–Pobla road, but there's no bus and it's a very steep two-hour climb if the cars won't stop. **Accommodation in the park** is limited to four mountain refuges (with a guardian during the summer — you'll need sleeping bags at a couple), but there are as many more in nearly as impressive alpine areas just outside the park boundaries. There are **campgrounds** close to CALDES DE BOÍ and at Espot (see below). Camping elsewhere in the park is officially forbidden.

Capdella

A bus departs Pobla de Segur for the thirty-kilometer ride to Capdella daily except Sunday at 5:30pm; it's a difficult hitch should it be Sunday. **CAPDELLA**, the highest of a half-dozen villages in the unsung (and rather cramped) Vall Fosca, is split in two: the upper quarter has no facilities, the lower, just under 2km below where the bus stops, is based around the *"Central" (de Energia)*, one of the older power plants in these parts. *Hostal*

Energia, originally built to host the power-company honchos, is very elegant and Old World; *Hostal Monseny*, 800m below, is newer but equally good value; a per-person bill for a double bed and a meal will be well under 1800ptas at both places. There is no store or unattached restaurant in either part of Capdella, so all eating is done table d'hote at your lodging.

From Capdella, it's a half-day trek, past the ugly new Sallente dam, to the wonderful refuge of **Colomina**, an old wooden chalet ceded to mountaineers by the power people. The immediate surroundings have some short outings suitable for any daylight remaining. The more ambitious will the following day trek to Boí via the Estany (Lake) Tort and the Dellui pass. Alternatively, there's the classic (if more difficult) traverse due north into the national park via the Peguera pass. You end up near the base of the Sant Maurici dam, having covered the length of the beautiful Monastero valley, at the refuge of **Mallafre**, poised for further walks as outlined below.

Espot

The approach from Espot is more usual and less strenuous, though purists will object to the possible necessity of road-walking both the seven kilometers up from the turnoff on the Pallaresa road where the bus drops you, and the similar distance beyond to the park entrance. As noted above, the bus begins its run in Barcelona but can easily be intercepted in ARTESA DE SEGRE (also on the Lleida–Seu de Urgell bus route) and LA POBLA DE SEGUR. **ESPOT** itself is still manageable and unspoiled in a way that Benasque, say, isn't. There are about five or six hotels and *hostales* in the predominantly rural village, and the cobbled streets, riverside pastures, and village steps are still reassuringly splattered with goat shit. Most of the old farm buildings below the Roman bridge and around the church are refreshingly unconverted, the only discordant note coming from the rank of Land Rover taxis waiting at the head of the village, all for hire on into the park. There's an **information office** (9am–1pm and 4–8pm) in the school, next to the church, where you can pick up **maps** of the park and other information, and check on conditions if you intend to stay and hike for some time.

Staying in Espot you're going to get ripped off simply because there is nowhere else to go. The only cheap option are the **rooms** advertised next to the *Hotel Roya*, very pleasant and reasonable. If you've more money, the large, rambling *Hotel Saurat* which dominates the center is recommended. Otherwise **camping** is best, with two campgrounds close by: the *Sol i Neu* (open mid-June to mid-Sept.) is excellent and just a few hundred meters from the village, *La Mola* (July-Sept.), 2km farther down the hill, has a swimming pool. As far as **eating** goes, you pay for the views; the cheapest restaurant is right at the entrance to the village.

Encroachment on the integrity of the **park** has been rapid. Two kilometers above Espot, SUPER ESPOT is already developed as a ski resort, albeit a fairly unobjectionable one, and a recent road leads as far in as the **Estany de Sant Maurici**. One of the classic hikes — demanding but not impossibly taxing — is right across the park from east to west, starting at this lake. This is one of the most beautiful spots in the Catalan Pyrenees, beneath the twin peaks of *Els Encantats* (2749m), and the Mallafre refuge noted above is here.

There's another refuge at **Estany Llong**, at the end of three or four walking hours on the wide track, with Caldes de Boí within easy reach. Beware some of the "paths" marked on maps; even where a bona fide trail exists, you may eventually find yourself at the base of steep, snowed-in passes which require special equipment to negotiate. The route from *Refugi d'Estany Llong* across to *Refugi Joan Ventosa*, normally only passable in mid-summer, is a good example. Unless you're a proficient mountaineer, the east–west traverse described is the best idea. Spread it over two or three days and there are some excellent dayhikes to be enjoyed from the huts you'll stay at.

Boí ...

EL PONT DE SUERT, 41 kilometers northwest of Pobla de Segur by bus, is not only a handy jump-off point for the Vall d'Aran but also for the western end of the national park, and it's pleasant enough if you have to spend the night before catching the next day's bus north. There are several accommodation establishments, including **rooms** above a youth-oriented bar on c/ Monasterio Lavaix. The bus service linking Pobla de Segur, Pont de Suert and BOÍ is run by *La Oscense* at 2pm daily; in Pobla the terminal for this line is directly across the street from the tourist office (marked, at the start of the road to Sort). Don't confuse Boí with CALDES DE BOÍ, a spa higher up, above the park entrance which has no cheap accommodation.

In BOÍ there are a few **pensiones** in the village and the *Pension Pascual* by the bridge just below the village (☎973/696014); it's open out of season and has helpful owners and a decent menu. There are also a like number of *hostales* and *pensiones* in nearby BARRUERA (for example the *Ferrer d'Avall*, ☎973/696029). Taxis from the village go into the park, past the artifical Llebreta reservoir, and drop you at the scenic springs of Aigües Tortes. You can either wander around for an hour or so, or forfeit your return ticket and walk back down later (no great hardship). If you walk on into the park, it's relatively level as far as Estany Llong but beyond that point the ascent to the pass overlooking Sant Maurici begins. Should you want to try to hitch a ride into the park, the road entrance is a short way beyond the bridge below Boí.

... and its Churches

The added advantage of approaching (or leaving) the park via Boí is that you will be able to visit the numerous **Romanesque churches** that stud its valley. Only one apse and the bell tower remain of the twelfth-century church of Sant Joan in Boí village, but a short walk on to TAÜLL (a track up on the left takes you away from the road) leads you to the churches of **Sant Climent** and Santa María, both consecrated in 1123. The former is the finer, with an elegant, six-story belfry and highly expressive, richly colored wall frescoes (reproductions — the originals are in Barcelona). The remains of Sant Martí church and Sant Quirze chapel are also here.

Back down in Boí valley, and all within reasonable walking distance of each other, are the churches at ERILL-LA-VALL (12th c., six-story belfry), BARRUERA, DURRO (13th c.), and COLL (12th c.). The best route to Durro is the little-used trail which skirts the hillsides and which you can pick up behind Boí village (ask a local to point it out). If you want to buy an original walking stick, made of boxwood, take a look in the cobbler's shop — some are works of art.

Half of the charm of these various churches is the way they complement, and are complemented by, the natural beauty of the valley, forming an integral part of the landscape. Unfortunately the character of Taull and Boí will probably be changed by the ski resort that is slowly being prepared on the mountains above them, much to the distress of the locals.

The Costa Daurada

The **Costa Daurada** — the coastline from Barcelona to south of Tarragona — is far less exploited than the Costa Brava. Sadly, it is easy enough to see why it has been neglected by the developers. With one or two exceptions (notably **Sitges** and **Tarragona** itself) it seems a rather dull, drab expanse. Beaches can be long but they're often narrow and characterless, while actual towns are sparse and overwhelmed by countless pockets of villas. However, if you just want to rest up by a beach for a while there are perfectly functional possibilities. Most village-resorts have smallish hotels and *hostales* and there are plentiful campgrounds dotted along this entire shore. However they are generally full to the brim with trailers and families and there is a real paucity of small sites. You'll probably meet a few fellow travelers on their way to Zaragoza or the southern coasts, but in general vacationers here are either French or Spanish.

Sitges — and South to Tarragona

Crowded trains from Barcelona-Sants make their frequent way down the coast, stopping first at CASTELLDEFELS where vast numbers alight. The beach here is massive and never gets crowded, but the water is pretty slimy. If you do get off to swim here, make sure it's at CASTELLDEFELS-PLATJA and not at the earlier town stop.

SITGES, 40km from Barcelona, is definitely the highlight as far as the beach towns go. Established in the 1960s as a mecca for the European young whose loose attitudes openly challenged Franco's stiffness, it's now become the great weekend escape for young Barcelonans, who have created a resort very much in their own image. It's also now a major gay summer resort. Sitges is expensive — particularly the bars — and finding **accommodation** can be a problem unless you arrive early in the day. If you're offered a room by someone as you get off the train, take it. Otherwise, the **Turismo**, in Plaça d'Eduard Maristany (in front of the station), should be able to help out. There's a **campground** too, behind the station, a five-minute walk away. It's worth noting that as the town's popularity has increased, petty crime seems to have been exported from Barcelona to Sitges. We've had several reports of robberies (sometimes at knifepoint), so watch your possessions on the beaches, and exercise care at night.

That said, there's a loose, vibrant feel to Sitges with a lot of action, a sophisticated night scene, and crowded but unoppressive **beaches**. There are two strands right in town, divided by a promontory, and dotted with a series of *balnearios* ("bathing stations"), although recent reports suggest that the seawater here has become a bit dubious. Or you can walk a couple of kilometers south, towards Vilanova, where you'll come to the (in)famous **Playas del Muerto**. These are both nude and the second, reached by following the railroad line, is exclusively gay. Back in town, if you've time to fill, there's a small art gallery, the **Museu Cau Ferrat** (Tues.–Sat. 10am–1pm and 5–7pm, Sun. 10am–2pm) on c/de Fonollar — not very distinguished apart from two El Grecos. (The *La Gueltru* museum at VILANOVA, 8km downcoast, has another.) Reasonable **restaurants** are plentiful; try the side streets around the church. The beachfront on the far side of the church is the area for seafood restaurant-bars. International tourism is also beginning to make its mark, with "English breakfasts" now being promoted; the tacky *Dubliner* pub-restaurant deserves some sort of enterprise award for offering two free aspirins with its full breakfast! As a rule the more genteel bars are on the waterfront, while the central thoroughfare is crammed with bars and discos trying to blast each other out.

The **gay scene** is frenetic. The owners of the stylish *Parrots Bar*, at the top of c/Dos de Mayo, run an information service giving free advice about gay hotels, apartments, restaurants, etc.; the service operates from 6 to 8pm (☎93/8940706). Here's a selection of some favored hang-outs. For breakfast (taken late) go to *Elsa's* between the top of c/Dos de Mayo and the parking lot, or the newer *Ivy's* on c/Sant Francisco. Near the gay beach, the *Picnic Bar* is popular for sandwiches, but by early evening everyone's moved on to *Parrots Bar* for cocktails. Popular restaurants are *Olivers* on c/Isla Cuba and *El Trull*. For good value go to *Chez Jeanettes* or *Miami*, both on c/Sant Paulo. The best concentration of bars and discos is in c/Buenaventura; try *Mediterraneo*, *Bourbon's*, and *Reflejos*. Gay women are especially welcomed in the latter two and the *Bar Azul*. On Mondays the place to go is *Atlantica*, set on a cliff top 3km out of town; free buses run throughout the night each way. Wind up any night in *El Retiro*, an all-night cafe-bar.

Carnival here is outrageous, thanks largely to the gay populace. The official program is complemented by a widely recognized but unwritten schedule of events. The climax is Tuesday's late-night parade (left off the official program), in which exquisitely dressed drag queens swan about the streets in high heels, twirling lacy parasols and coyly fanning themselves. Bar doors stand wide open, bands play, and processions and celebrations go on until four in the morning.

Trains to Sitges leave Barcelona's Estació de Sants roughly half-hourly throughout the day (20 min. on the fast train, 40 min. on the normal service). If you intend to stop off again between Sitges and Tarragona make sure you catch a local train and not an express, which will run straight through.

Cunit and Puerta Romana

If Sitges is too crowded and frenetic — a distinct possibility in high season — try CUNIT, about 15km south and probably the best possibility before

Tarragona. It's rather soulless, more a collection of villas than village, but the long beach is handy enough, and rarely full. A rather strange covered **campground** operates (July–Sept.) just behind the beach; otherwise the cheapest place to stay is *Los Almendros* (☎977/675437), on the highway right at the top of the village; it has an outdoor grill and a cheapish menu. The expensive *Hostal La Diligencia*, near the church in the center, has an excellent but appropriately expensive restaurant attached. The cheapest place to eat is *Restaurante Emilio*, c/del Mar 15, a sort of workers' canteen.

About 15km north of Tàrragona, the incredibly ramshackle **PUERTA ROMANA** makes a good swimming and sunbathing spot, with clean sand. It's not on the map or even signposted from the main road, and the nearest train station is TORREDEMBARA, from which you could hitch the 4km north; ask to be put down at *Camping Sirena Daurada* (☎977/801103 or 801303), which is by the main road. This is open throughout the year, changes money, and offers shacks to rent. From there walk straight towards the sea, across the railroad line, and you'll reach Puerta Romana. The nearest village is CREIXELL, a small place on a hill among olive groves (no accommodation). The local eatery is *Restaurant San Miguel*, actually on the main road a few hundred metres from *Sirena Daurada*.

Tarragona

Majestically sited on a rocky bluff rising sheer above the sea, **TARRAGONA** is an ancient place. It was the most elegant and cultured city of Roman Spain, boasting at its peak a quarter of a million inhabitants, and was the base for Scipio's conquest of the peninsula (he wintered here in 281 B.C.). Later, the emperors Hadrian and Augustus both adopted it as a resort, the latter building himself a number of temples around the city. This distinguished past asserts itself throughout the modern city, even before you arrive. Just off the main Barcelona road, 8km north, stands the square, three-storied **Torre de Scipio**, built in the second century A.D. and nearly 10m high. Four kilometers beyond is the triumphal **Arco de Bara**, its contemporary, built over the great Via Maxima. Today Tarragona is the second largest port in Catalunya and its ugly outskirts are home to a huge concentration of chemical industries, oil refineries, and a nuclear power plant.

The **city** divides clearly into two parts and levels: a predominantly medieval, walled upper town, and a prosperous modern extension below. Walking into town from the train station (turn right and straight up the steps) sets you at the very top of the sweeping **Rambla Nova**, a sturdy provincial rival to Barcelona's, lined with fashionable cafes and restaurants. Parallel, and to the east, lies the **Rambla Vella**, marking — as its name suggests — the start of the old town. To either side of the *ramblas* are scattered a profusion of relics from Tarragona's Roman past, including various temples, and parts of the forum, theater, and amphitheater.

The most interesting remains are of the ancient **Necropolis** (Tues.–Sat. 10am–1:30pm and 4:30–8pm, Sun. 10am–2pm, free Tues.), at the end of c/

TARRAGONA

Ramón y Cajal (signposted off the Rambla Nova). Here both pagan and Christian tombs have been uncovered, spanning a period from the third to the sixth centuries A.D. and including rare examples of Visigothic sculpture. Tarragona was enthusiastically Christian; St. Paul preached here (on a site commemorated by the church of San Pablo), and the city became an important Visigothic bishopric.

The Roman forum has survived too. Or rather forums, since Tarragona sustained both a provincial forum (by the cathedral) and a **local forum** (Tues.–Sat. 10am–1pm and 4–7pm), whose viewable remains (signposted) are very near the market hall and square. The site, split by a main road but reconnected by a footbridge, contains a water cistern, house, and sarcophagus, plus a pair of elegant columns.

At the corner of the upper town, on the Plaça de Rei near the cathedral, is an excellent **Museu Arqueologic**, open the same hours as the necropolis and with a joint admission ticket. It displays wide-ranging Roman exhibits and an unusually complete collection of mosaics, exemplifying the stages of development from the plain black-and-white patterns of the first century A.D. to the elaborate polychrome images of the second and third centuries. Right next door there's an excellent new **Museu Historic** (10am–7pm), in the former residence of the Aragonese kings, built over Roman vaults and blessed with unusually good interpretive displays.

From here you can skirt the town walls to reach the **Passeig Arqueologic** (Tues.–Sat. 10am–1:30pm and 4-7pm, Sun. 10am–1:30pm), a promenade running between Roman walls of the third century B.C. and outer fortifications erected by the British in 1707 to secure the city during the War of the Spanish Succession. The megalithic walls of the Iberians are excellently preserved, particularly two awesome gateways; the huge blocks used in their construction are quite distinct from the more refined Roman additions. Among the objects displayed within the Passeig is a fine bronze statue of Augustus, the emperor who finally subdued Celto-Iberian Spain.

The steep and intricate streets of the old town are fascinating, their towering mansions frequently incorporating Roman fragments. The focal point of the quarter is undoubtedly the **Cathedral** (daily 10am–12:30pm and 4–7pm, looser schedule Sun.), which you enter through the cloisters. This magnificent building is the most perfect example in Spain of the transition from Romanesque to Gothic forms. You'll see the change highlighted in the main facade, where a Gothic portal is framed by Romanesque doors, and in the superb cloister with its pointed Gothic arches softened by smaller round divisions. The cloister also has several oddly sculpted capitals, one of which represents a cat's funeral being directed by rats!

The most remarkable (and least visited) of Tarragona's monuments, however, stands 4km outside the city walls. This is the **Roman Aqueduct**, which originally carried water from the Riu Gayo some 32km distant. The most impressive extant section lies in an overgrown valley, off the main road, and in the middle of nowhere; take bus #5, marked *Sant Salvador* (every 20min from stop on c/Cristofor, near Avda. Prat de la Riba 11, second left off c/Ramón y Cajal) and if the driver won't drop you at the site (ask for 'El Aqueducto') get off at Sant Salvador — a ten-minute ride — and walk straight back down the main road towards the highway bridge. The virtually unmarked entrance to the site is on the left below the restaurant. The return bus leaves from back up in the village by the bar. This sounds more complicated than it is, and the trip is undoubtedly worthwhile; the aqueduct's utilitarian beauty is surpassed only by those of similar structures at Segovia and the Pont du Gard, in the South of France. Popularly, it is known as *El Pont del Diable* (Devil's Bridge) due, remarked Richard Ford, to the Spanish habit of "giving all praise to 'the Devil', as Pontifex Maximus."

Practicalities

Cheap accommodation can be tricky to find but it's worth persevering, as Tarragona makes a great stopover with two good **beaches** within easy walking distance. The nicest rooms in town, or at least the rooms in the nicest location, are in the Plaça de la Font, just in the old town off the Rambla Vella — try (in ascending order of price) the *CH Francisco* (☎977/237152; entrance on c/La Palma), the nameless *pension* above the *Bar/Restaurante Turia*, the *Pension El Circ* (Pl. del Font 37, above namesake restaurant), or the more expensive *Hostal Noria*. On the Rambla Vella itself there's the *Pension Planelles* at no. 31, just around the corner from the town hall, and you'll find several places (e.g. *Abella* at no. 26, *Catalonia* at no. 7) on the c/Apocada as well — take any street to the left from the **train** station. If these offer no hope wander down towards the town beach, *Platja Miraclo*, below Rambla Vella, and take Via Augusta for about 2km to *Platja Rabassada*; here there are three **campgrounds** and a number of small hotels. The Tarragona **youth hostel** (☎977/210195; closed Sept.) is some way out, off Avda. President Companys (at the end of Rambla Nova).

Finding somewhere to eat is less fraught with difficulty and there are plenty of possibilities on Plaça de la Font (a good outdoor pizzeria here, or the excellent, cheap *menú* at *Restaurante Turia*) and the streets between it and the Rambla Nova. *Pescado romesco* is the regional speciality and you'll find it on several *menús del día* around town. Romesco sauce has a base of dry pepper, almonds and/or hazelnuts, olive oil, garlic, and a small glass of Priorato wine. Beyond this there are many variations, as cooks tend to add their own secret ingredient. It usually accompanies fish and is only found in this region, since all the ingredients must be local. For **cakes and ice-cream**, Rambla Nova is groaning with pavement cafes all doing a roaring trade, especially at night. For less roaring and more atmosphere, there's an excellent ice cream scoopery on the Plaça del Rei, near the archaeological museum.

South from Tarragona to the Delta de l'Ebre

The coast south from Tarragona is a pretty uninspiring prospect, with the Daurada's nascent Benidorm/Lloret at **SALOU-CAMBRILS**. The actual port of Cambrils is quite neat, and excellent *paellas* are served in the harbor restaurants. There's nowhere else to recommend as a resort until way into the province of CASTELLÓN, for details of which see the following chapter on Valencia and Murcia. Even the beaches —long, thin strips of sand almost universally backed by gargantuan trailer-camping grounds, packed full and miles from anywhere — don't really invite you to stop and swim.

The one town of any size is **TORTOSA**, slightly inland and astride the Riu Ebro. It's hardly an inspirational stop, although it would be a considerably cheaper place to spend the night than any of the resorts to the north. There are a couple of very reasonable *fondas* in the center and an excellent, cheap-ish restaurant right by the bus station. If you fetch up in Tortosa, climb its crumbling castle, which could easily double up as a free and panoramic camp-site. From Tortosa, regular **buses** run to Viñaroz (in Castellón province to the south) and, less regularly, to Alcañiz (in Aragon).

In the bottom corner of Catalunya lies a rather special area, recently desig-nated a natural reserve: the **Delta de l'Ebre** (the Ebro Delta). If the name of the river strikes a chord, it is probably on account of the civil war Battle of the Ebro, which began on July 24, 1938 at Tortosa, lasted four months, and resulted in a massive loss for the Republican cause. In another vein, an old saying has it that Africa begins at the Pyrenees; Catalans have always main-tained, with some fervor, that it begins at the Ebro.

Occupying 320 square kilometers, the sandy delta constitutes the biggest wetlands in Catalunya and one of the most important aquatic habitats in the western Mediterranean. This ecological reserve of brackish lagoons, marshes, dunes, and reedbeds is home to thousands of wintering birds and provides excellent fishing. The area is rather difficult to visit without a car, but if you want tranquility and space, this is the place to head for. The nearest places you can stay are AMPOSTA (*Hostal Baix Ebre*, ☎977/700025) or SANT CARLES DE LA RÁPITA (*Pension Mongar*, ☎977/741168, and *Pension Agusti*, ☎977/740427 are two of many), which supposedly has the best prawns in the Med. Much of the area is a protected zone and hence access is limited, but camping is allowed in certain areas. There are three **campgrounds** at AMPOLLA (north of the delta), one at Amposta, and two at Sant Carles de la Rápita.

Three islands lie between Amposta and the open sea, the biggest being the **Illa de Buda** just by the river mouth. It's covered with rice fields (the main local crop) and you can get to it on the ferry which does trips along the coast and down the river. A ferry also links DELTEBRE with **SANT JAUME D'ENVEJA** on the opposite shore. Wonderful fish dishes are served here, the local speciality being *arros a banda*, similar to *paella* except that the rice is brought before the seafood itself. The road which runs along the right (south) bank of the river leads to the so-called *Eucalyptus* **beach** (sunbathers beware — it's easy to burn in these flat, windy zones); scheduled **ferries** from Sant Jaume, and an excursion boat from Deltebre, also ply downstream. If you're in a group you could hire your own boat for the whole day, heading down from Amposta and going to the river mouth, with a stop for lunch; with costs shared, it's not expensive (contact Jose Sapina, ☎977/702013).

Inland from Tarragona: Poblet, Montblanc, and Lleida

Few ruins are more stirring than the **monastery of POBLET**. It lies in glorious open country, vast and sprawling within massive battlemented walls and towered gateways. Once *the* great monastery of Catalunya, it was more of a complete manorial village, and enjoyed scarcely credible rights, powers and wealth. Founded in 1151 by Ramon Berenguer IV, who united the kingdoms of Catalunya and Aragón, it was planned from the beginning on an immensely grand scale. The kings of Aragón–Catalunya chose to be buried in its chapel and for three centuries diverted huge sums for its endowment, a munificence that was inevitably corrupting. By the late Middle Ages Poblet had become a byword for decadence — there are lewder stories about this than any other Cistercian monastery — and so it continued, hated by the local peasantry, until the Carlist revolution of 1835. Then, in a passionate frenzy of destruction, a mob burned and tore it apart, so remorselessly that Augustus Hare, an English traveler who visited it 36 years later, recorded that "violence and vengeance are written on every stone."

The monastery was repopulated by Italian Cistercians in 1940 and over the past few decades a superb job of restoration has been undertaken. Much remains delightfully ruined, but once inside the main gates you are now proudly escorted around the principal complex of buildings. As so often, the **cloisters**, focus of monastic life, are the most evocative and beautiful part.

Late Romanesque, they open on to a splendid Gothic chapter house, wine cellars, a parlor, kitchen, and refectory. Beyond, you enter the **chapel** in which the twelfth- and thirteeth-century tombs of the kings of Aragón have been meticulously restored by Frederico Marés, the manic collector of Barcelona. You'll also be shown the vast old **dormitory**, to which there's direct access from the chapel choir — a poignant reminder of Cistercian discipline.

There are three **buses** a day to Poblet from Tarragona, leaving from the Plaça Ponent, near the forum. But a more atmospheric approach is to go by **train** (take any going to Lleida) to the ruined station of L'ESPLUGA DE FRANCOLÍ; from here the monastery is a beautiful three-kilometer walk. Unfortunately there is no *consigna* at the dilapidated rail-stop, and there is no place to leave baggage in L'Espluga.

Officially the monastery can only be toured as member of a guided group; unofficially the porter may let you in to walk around alone if it seems that not enough people will collect within a reasonable period of time. Admission is stiff — a few hundred pesetas — and the tours, which take an hour, theoretically depart every fifteen minutes from 10am to noon and again from 3 until 5pm (interior shuts an hour after the times stated).

If you're looking for somewhere **to stay** in the area, there's a *fonda* in L'Espluga de Francolí (Passeig de Canellas), the solitary *Hostal Fonoll* outside the main gate of Poblet, and you'll also find rooms at the walled medieval town of **MONTBLANC**, 8km before the turning to Poblet. This too has a railroad station on the Lleida line, so it's easy to make the link. It is a beautiful, remote place with many fine (albeit minor) Romanesque and Gothic monuments; all are marked on a town plan attached to the town gateway, the *Portal de Boue*, not far from the railroad station. Worth seeking out are the grand Gothic parish church of Santa María and Romanesque Sant Miguel, plus another Museu Marés (accessible weekends only outside of summer). If it's open, there's a very friendly and helpful *Turismo* inside the Ajuntament, as well as some hilarious *gigantón* figures. The friendliest and cheapest place to stay is the *Fonda de los Angeles*, just inside the portal and to the right, although it doesn't appear to stay open during the winter.

If you've got wheels, visit the walled village of PRADES up in the mountains to the southwest. There's another important monastery in the region at SANTES CREUS, northeast of VALLS (back down the rail line toward Tarragona). It's Cistercian again, in a transitional style, with a grand Gothic cloister showing Romanesque traces.

To Lleida

The more circuitous train route from Barcelona to Lleida is via industrial TERRASSA and more pleasant MANRESA. The latter has an important church, but it's in a bad state of repair and you'd need to be fairly dedicated to stop off just for that. LLEIDA (LERIDA), at the heart of a fertile plain near the Aragonese border, has a rich history; first a *municipium* under the Roman Empire and later the capital of a small Arab kingdom, it was reconquered by the Catalans and became the seat of a bishopric in 1149. There's little of those periods extant in today's pleasant city although there is one building of outstanding interest.

The **Old Cathedral** (9am–2pm and 4–8pm) lies enclosed within ruinous castle walls high above the Riu Segre, a twenty-minute climb from the center of town. It's a peculiar fortified building, which in 1707 was deconsecrated and taken over by the military. It remained in military hands until 1940 since, wrote Richard Ford, "in the piping times of peace the steep walk proved too much for the pursy canons, who, abandoning their lofty church, built a new cathedral below in the convenient and Corinthian style!" Enormous damage was inflicted over the years (documented by photos in a side chapel) but the church remains a notable example of the Transitional style, similar in many respects to the cathedral of Tarragona. Once again the Gothic cloisters are masterful, each walk comprising arches different in size and shape but sharing delicate stone tracery. They served the military as a canteen and kitchen. The views from the walls are stupendous, away over the plain, and you can climb back down towards the river by way of the aforementioned **New Cathedral**, a grimy eighteenth-century building only enlivened inside by a series of high, matchbox-sized, stained-glass windows.

Practicalities

If you're staying — and Lleida is well worth a night — there is a cluster of **hostales and habitaciones** on the right as you exit the train station. Continuing straight ahead, the pedestrian streets of Carrer de Carme or Magadalena (there's a Y-fork) blend into Carrer Major; when the name changes you are covered about half the distance between *RENFE* and the bus station. It's possible that you've walked up from the train station on the wide Rambla Ferrán, in which case keep a sharp eye out left for the *Puerta Antigua* (Old Gate), opposite the main bridge over the river. There's a **Turismo** (Mon.–Fri. 10am–2pm and 3:30–7pm) just inside the gate, while beyond it and to the right is the **Plaça Sant Joan** with a few places to stay; *Habitaciones Raco* in the upper left-hand corner (no. 1; ☎973/212194) is cheap, friendly, and quiet (the *plaça* is pedestrianized); the *Sol* close by at no. 9 (☎973/241424) is an acceptable fallback. People with cars would do well to stay at the *Hostal España* (Rambla Ferrán 20; ☎973/236440) since it has a basement garage (extra charge). The **campground** (*Las Balsas*, ☎973/240200) is a couple of kilometers out of town on the Huesca road.

For **eating and drinking**, c/de Cavallers (off c/Major and leading up to the castle) has a string of bars opening onto the street, all serving *tapas* and food. You should be able to get snails the local dish, anywhere along here. If you're on a tight budget try the excellent *Casa Jose*, c/Botera 17 (a block uphill from the pedestrian way; closed Sun.), *Comidas Economicas Demetrio*, c/la Parra 4 (a bit grim), or *Casa Marti*, c/Magdalena 37, where you have the opportunity to eat well, cheaply, and outdoors on the walkway. All of these are just uphill from Plaça Sant Joan or its continuation, c/Magdalena. Be warned that some eating places shut at night — one that doesn't is *Bar Mateo*, just off c/del Carme.

Lleida is a major **bus** terminal — the station is on Avda. de Blondel, (some 600m down the Rambla Ferrán past the *Puerta Antigua*, then right. Buses leave daily for the Pyrenees (La Seu d'Urgell, Viella), Barbastro (for Benasque), Tarragona (3 daily) and Zaragoza (4). There are also five daily buses to the medieval Aragonese town of Fraga, 25km away.

fiestas

January
21–22 Traditional pilgrimage followed by a lively fiesta in TOSSA DE MAR; celebrations too in IGUALADA (Barcelona).

February
3 Dedication of the Basilica at MONTSERRAT accompanied by important services.
Carnival (the week before Lent) sees many events — notably in SOLSONA, BALSARENY and BARCELONA itself. The most outrageous Carnival is in gay SITGES: Saturday sees a children's fancy dress parade, followed by a masked ball; Sunday is family day with an antique car rally in the afternoon; Sunday evening is a kind of dress rehearsal for the Shrove Tuesday climax. **Lent** Passion Plays are performed at ESPARRAGUER (Barcelona).

April
Holy Week (variable) is widely observed; particularly well known are the *Mercat del Ram* in VIC (Barcelona) and the Passion Plays at SANT VICENC, DELS HORTS (Barcelona).
23 *Sant Jordi* (St. George) is an equivalent of Valentine's Day in BARCELONA, with book and flower stalls, and religious celebrations at the Palau de la Generalitat. Traditionally men give a red or yellow rose, women give a book.

May
3 The week-long *Fires i Festes de la Santa Creu* in FIGUERES straddle the 3rd of the month; processions and music.
11 Start of a big week-long fiesta in LLEIDA. On the next Sunday the *Fiesta de la Lana* (wool fair) is held in RIPOLL.
Corpus Christi (variable) sees big processions and streets decorated with flowers in SITGES. In BERGA, *La Patum* is one of the most famous fiestas in Catalunya, when Good combats Evil. Extremely boisterous and noisy, with lots of fireworks thrown around, so wear old clothes. Rooms have to be booked way ahead, or camp in the area and commute.

June
24 *Día de Sant Joan*, celebrated throughout Catalunya, marks the beginning of summer. Nearly every town and village put on the style to some degree. Watch out for things shutting down for a day on either side throughout the region.
29 *Día de Sant Pere* is a further excuse for festivities; many places have events non-stop between the 24th and the 29th — for example:
24–July 22 *Raiers*, festival of the old-time rafters, observed with races down the Noguera Pallaresa at Llavorsi, Sort, Pobla de Segur, and Tremp.

July
10 *San Cristobal* celebrated in OLOT, PREMIA DE MAR and SURIA, all with traditional dances and processions.
11 Special services for *San Benito* at MONTSERRAT.
24 *Festa de Santa Cristina* at LLORET, with dancing and processions in boats.
The *International Music Festival* at CADAQUÉS runs from mid-July through most of August.

August
25 *Festa Major* at TORROELLA DE MONTGRÍ with the usual events.
30 Fiesta at VILAFRANCA DEL PENEDÈS is one of Catalunya's biggest.
The *International Festival of Fantasy and Horror Films* at SITGES falls in August, along with an avant-garde theater season.

September
8 Among others, celebrations in OLOT), CADAQUÉS and MONTSERRAT.
Second week *Encierro* and fiestas at CARDONA — much playing about with bulls.
24 *Virgen de la Merced* celebrated for four or five days leading up to this date in BARCELONA with dances, bullfights and cultural events.

October
Last week *Fires de Sant Narcis* in GIRONA.

December
8 Winter fiesta at CASTELLDEFELS with Catalan dances and processions.

travel details

Buses

From Barcelona To Girona (5 daily; 2½ hr.), Lloret/Tossa de Mar (7; 1½/2 hr.), Palafrugell (6; 4 hr.), Torroella (3; 4½ hr.), Seu d'Urgell/Andorra (2; 5/5½ hr.), the Vall d'Aran (1 at 8am; 7 hr.), Tarragona (8; 2 hr.), Lleida (5; 3 hr.), Valencia (7; 6 hr.), Alicante (5; 9 hr.), Zaragoza/Madrid (4; 5 hr./ 10 hr.), and to Perpignan, France (2; 4 hr.)

From Girona To Banyoles (roughly hourly; 30 min.), Besalú (2–6 daily; 45 min.), L'Escala (3; 1 hr.), and Torroella (2 on weekdays; 1 hr.)

From Figueres To Cadaqués (6; 1 hr.), L'Escala/ Palafrugell (3; 45 min./1½ hr.), Olot (3; 1 hr. 10 min. with 2 daily continuing to Ripoll).

From Tarragona To Montblanc/Lleida (3; 1 hr./2 hr.)

From Lleida To Seu d'Urgell (2; 3 hr.).

Trains

Barcelona–Girona/Figueres 6 daily; 1-2 hr./ 1½ hr.–2½ hr.

Barcelona–Sitges/Tarragona 6 daily; 35 min./ 1½ hr.

Barcelona–Lleida 8 daily; 2–3 hr.
Barcelona–Valencia 7 daily; 4–5 hr.
Barcelona–Zaragoza 13 daily; 4½ hr.–6½ hr.
Barcelona–Madrid 4 daily; 12 hr.
Barcelona–Paris 7 daily; 11–15 hr.
Barcelona–Florence/Rome 2 daily; 18/23 hr.
Barcelona–Venice 2 daily; 18½ hr.

Ferries

Ten boats a week (over seven days) from Barcelona to Palma, **Mallorca** (8 hr.); daily to **Ibiza** (9 hr.) in season, 4 weekly out; 3 to 5 weekly to Mahón, **Menorca**.

Flights

Regular **charters** fly from northern Europe into both Barcelona and Girona, and there's a good chance of picking up tickets in Barcelona for the return leg. Daily **scheduled flights** from Barcelona to both Palma, **Mallorca** and **Ibiza**. Scheduled flights out of Barcelona to international destinations will probably become more numerous as the 1992 Olympics approach.

CHAPTER TEN

VALENCIA AND MURCIA

T he area known as the **Levante** (the East) is a bizarre mixture of ancient and modern, of beauty and beastliness. The rich *huerta* of **Valencia** is said to be the most fertile slab of land in Europe, crowded with orange, lemon, and peach groves and with rice fields still irrigated by systems devised by the Moors. Unsurprisingly, a type of farmhouse is the most characteristic building of the Valencian *huerta,* called a *barraca*, its most striking feature is its steeply-pitched thatched roof. *Valenciano*, a dialect of Catalan, is spoken in some parts of the region; recently revived in schools, it's now being given a higher profile in the capital. There's even an extreme nationalist group who deny the dialect's Catalan origins, but they haven't managed to convince anyone else.

Murcia is officially part of the province of Valencia (the *País Valenciano*), but there could hardly be a more severe contrast with the richness of the *huerta*. In the south the land is desert — southeast Spain, to which Murcia region belongs, is the driest territory in Europe. Fought over for centuries by Phoenicians, Greeks, Carthaginians, and Romans, there survives virtually no physical evidence of their presence or of 500 years of Moorish rule beyond an Arabic feel to some of the small towns and the odd palm tree here and there. And as if the sterility of the land weren't enough, the unfortunate Murcians rank lowest in the popularity stakes in Spain, in a survey taken in the 1970s of where people would prefer their son- or daughter-in-law to come from. The prejudice probably originated in the 1920s when Murcians flooded into Catalunya in search of work and later spread to the entire country.

Much of the region's **coast**, despite some fine beaches, is marred by the highway to the south, the industrial development which has sprouted all around it (with consequent pollution), and of course the heavy overdevelopment of villas and vacation homes. The coves around **Denia** and **Javea** are the prettiest beach areas, but access and accommodation are difficult. The resorts of the **Mar Menor** in Murcia are similarly attractive, but again don't even think of turning up in season if you don't have a reservation. For the "wild" beaches of **southern Murcia**, transportation is the major hurdle, but crowds won't be a problem. **Valencia** and **Alicante** are the major urban centers, and there are several historic small towns and villages a short way inland, such as **Játiva, Orihuela**, and **Lorca**. Throughout the region, trains are usually cheaper than buses on shorter journeys.

There's no shortage of culinary pleasures in this area. Gastronomes tend to agree that the best *paellas* are to be found around (not in) Valencia, the city in which the dish originated. It should be prepared fresh for you, not scooped from some vast, sticky vat; most places will make it for a minimum of two people only. Of the region's other rice-based dishes, the most famous is *Arros*

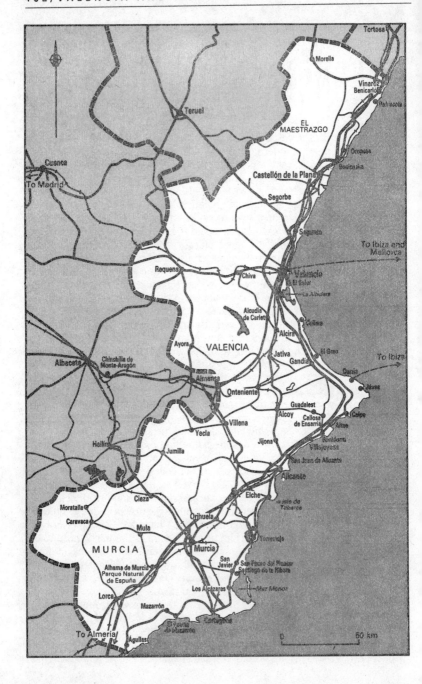

a banda, which is served in two stages: first the rice, then the fish. Another specialty is eels served with piquant *all i pebre* (garlic and pepper) sauce. The sweet-toothed should try *turrón*, made of nuts and honey, it traditionally comes in a soft, flaky variety or very hard like a nougat. (The *turrón* from Jijona is the finest.) You could follow it with a *horchata*, a milky drink made from tiger nuts (*de chufa*) or almonds (*de almendros*).

Morella

MORELLA, 60km inland on the road from Zaragoza to the coast, is the most attractive town in the province of Castellón and one of the most remarkable in this entire area. A medieval fortress town, it rises from the plain around a small hill crowned by a tall, rocky spur and a virtually impregnable castle which dominates the countryside for miles around. A perfectly preserved ring of ancient walls defends its lower reaches. Arriving by bus, you circle the town in one long loop before finally passing through the walls and stopping in front of a shored-up town gate. Chief among the monuments, apart from the castle, is the church of **Santa Mariá la Mayor** (*Iglesia Arciprestal*, open 11am– 2pm and 3:30–6pm), a fourteenth-century Gothic construction with beautifully carved doorways and an unusual raised *coro* reached by a (roped off) marble spiral stairway. A few minutes' walk to the left, at the foot of the castle, is the ruined **Monasterio de San Francisco** (10am–2pm and 3–8pm), currently being rebuilt. Its elegant cloister houses a museum of sorts — a strange collection of curios from the area — and you pass through to spiral up to the **fortress** itself, in ruins but still impressive. It's a tiring climb but there are tremendous views in every direction from the crumbling courtyard at the top — down over the monastery, bullring and town walls to the plains. In the distance are the remains of the weird Gothic **aqueduct** which once supplied the town's water.

Back below the monastery are a couple of small plazas where you can sit at cheap outdoor cafes — especially pleasant in the evening. Nearby (signed) is a private **museum**, nearly all of whose exhibits (painted tiles, fragments of jewelry, broken clocks, fossils, and aged plows) are for sale. In the c/de la Virgen de Villavana is a house where San Vicente Ferrer performed the prodigious miracle of resurrecting a child who had been chopped up and stewed by its mother — she could find nothing else fit for a saint to eat.

The main porticoed street, bisected by steep steps leading down to the lower walls, is an excellent source of bars, bakeries, and cafes. (There's a great *tapas* bar, *El Potrón*, near the above-mentioned plazas too.) Of the several cheap and comfortable **places to stay** in Morella the best is the *Hostal El Cíd* (☎964/160125) right by the bus stop and town gate (Puerta San Mateo) — it has remarkable views of the plain and the distant hills from its balconied rooms. There's also a *fonda*, the *Moreno* (☎964/160105) at c/San Nicolás 12, and nearby is the excellent, if more expensive, *Elias* (☎964/160092). The **Turismo** is a five-minute walk from the bus station, inside the Torres de San Miguel, the main double gate-tower into town; little useful information is on offer, but it does have a small and interesting exhibition of muskets, bullets, and pictures from the Carlist Wars. There's an annual festival of classical music in the last week of August.

Morella is one possible approach to the Maestrazgo region of southern Aragon. Daily **Buses** leave for Alcañiz, (presently at 10am) and Cantavieja/Villafranca del Cid (6:30pm), as well as to Vinaroz (4pm) and Castellón (7:30am).

South to Valencia — The Costa del Azahar

On the coast the first place you come to, from Morella or Catalonia, is **VINAROZ** (*VINAROS* locally) at the mouth of the tiny River Servol. It's one of the better places to stop along this coast, a real town, not developed exclusively for tourists. The beaches here are small but rarely packed and in town there's an elaborate baroque church, with an excellent local produce market nearby. The **Turismo** (9am–1pm and 6–8pm), close to the church, can help you to find cheap rooms. Perhaps the best place to try is the *Fonda Centro* — from the tourist office, bear right over the rotary and it's in the first street on the left. You can eat very cheaply there, too. Anywhere in town the fish is locally caught and excellent; go down to the dockside market in the early evenings to watch the day's catch being auctioned and packed off to restaurants all over the region. *Bar Neus* (which makes excellent iced coffee), opposite the bus terminal, is the main source of information for all timetables or routes from the town; the bus to Morella currently leaves at 4pm. The town's **train station** is a good 2km from the center.

BENICARLÓ, a few kilometers farther south, is very similar, boasting a church with a fine octagonal tower and blue-tiled dome and a small but tranquil beach. Again, there are several cheap places to stay right in the center, plus a **youth hostel** at Avda. de Yecla 4 (☎964/470500) and, like Vinaroz, **campgrounds** on the coast nearby.

PEÑISCOLA, a heavily fortified promontory jutting out into the Mediterranean, is just a little farther down the coast. There was a Phoenician settlement here, and later it saw Greek, Carthaginian, Roman, and Moorish rulers, but the present castle was built by the Knights Templar with alterations by Pedro de la Luna. As Pope Benedict XIII, Pedro ("*Papa Luna*") lived here for six years after he had been deposed from the papacy during the fifteenth-century church schisms. The castle today (where part of *El Cid* was filmed) is heavily restored and largely a museum to Papa Luna, but it's extremely impressive from a distance and the old town that is clustered around its base is extremely picturesque, even if it is heavily commercialized. There are small beaches on either side of the fortress but the best is the town side, even though it's accordingly more crowded. Several reasonably-priced **hostales** can be found near the base of the castle and along the beach road, and lots of restaurants. You'll find the atmosphere rather staid in the evenings. Buses run down the coast from Vinaroz and Benicarló hourly from 8am to 9pm.

There's not much else along this stretch until you hit the grim provincial capital of **CASTELLÓN DE LA PLANA**. Though in itself singularly unattractive, there are a couple of good reasons for stopping here — it's one of the cheapest places to stay along this coast and some surprisingly good beaches are easily reached by local bus. In the town there's really only one thing worth seeing, the **Museo de Bellas Artes** on c/Caballeros (between Plaza Mayor and Plaza Aulas; 10am–2pm and 4–7pm, Sat. 10am–1pm; free admission). It displays ceramics and work by local artists. For cheap **rooms** look on c/Trinidad and c/Navarra near the Puerta Sol. The **youth hostel** is at c/Orfebrer Santalinea 2 (☎964/202300).

The beaches are at GRAO DE CASTELLÓN (*Grao* simply means port) and all along the coast to Benicasim. Buses for both leave regularly from the Plaza Hernan Cortés, heading down to the port and then turning north. If you want total isolation, get off somewhere halfway along; the closer you get to **BENICASIM**, the better and cleaner the beach becomes. The town itself is heavily developed with apartments and villas but there's plenty of cheap **accommodation** — the **Turismo** at Pl. Maria Agustina 5 (9am–2pm and 4–6pm) has a list of *hostales*. Several of the better-value *fondas* are in the old village near the railway station — try *Fonda Baguena*, c/Maestro Cubells 35 (☎964/300089) or *Fonda Chiva*, c/Sto. Tomas (☎964/300905). Slightly more expensive is the *Hostal Montreal*, in the town at c/Barracas 5 (☎964/300681). There's also a year-round **youth hostel** (Avda. de Ferrandiz Salvador, ☎964/300949) and at least seven **campgrounds** in the area.

Beyond Castellón the next worthwhile stop is the fine Roman remains of **SAGUNTO**. This town passed into Spanish legend when, in 219 B.C., it was attacked by Hannibal in one of the first acts of the war waged by Carthage on the Roman Empire. Its citizens withstood a nine-month siege before burning the city and themselves rather than surrendering. When belated help from Rome arrived the city was recaptured, and rebuilding eventually got under way. Chief among the ruins is the **Roman Amphitheater** (2nd c.), the basic shape of which survives intact. The wonderful views from its seats take in a vast span of history — Roman stones all around, a ramshackle Moorish castle on the hill behind, medieval churches in the town below, and, across the plain towards the sea, the black smoke of modern industry.

Further Roman remains are being excavated within the walls of the huge **acropolis-castle**, and numerous smaller finds are on show in the small museum almost next to the theater on the road up to the site. The main road, with frequent buses from Castellón to Valencia, passes below, as do the main Valencia-Barcelona and Valencia-Zaragoza rail lines, with upwards of fifteen trains per day.

Valencia

Valencia, third largest city in Spain, may not come close to having the vitality of Barcelona or the cultural variety of Madrid, but it does at least have a pretty lively night scene, and its clothes and furniture designers are renowned throughout Spain — a Valencian studio has designed the logo for the Barcelona Olympics. It has always been an important city, fought over for the agricultural wealth of the surrounding countryside. After Romans and

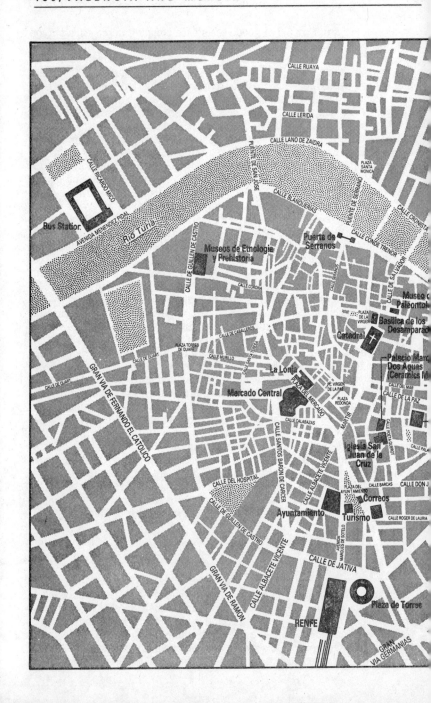

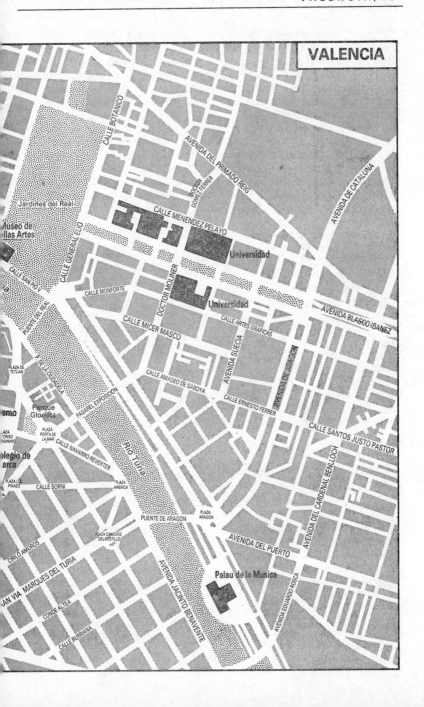

Visigoths, it was occupied by the Moors for over four centuries with only a brief interruption (1094–1101) when El Cíd recaptured it. He died here in 1099 but his body, propped on a horse and led out through the gates, was still enough to cause the Moorish armies — previously encouraged by news of the death — to flee in terror. It wasn't until 1238 that Jaime I of Aragon permanently wrested Valencia back and it has remained one of Spain's largest and richest cities ever since.

Nobody could pretend that this is one of Spain's most attractive townscapes. There are some exquisite corners away from the crowds, a few really fine buildings and a couple of excellent museums, but as a whole the city is sprawling and confused, marred by unthinking modernization. The city walls, which, judging from the two surviving gates must have been magnificent, were pulled down in 1871 to make way for a traffic rotary; and the church of Santo Domingo, said to be the city's most beautiful, has been converted into a barracks — the very barracks from which General Milans del Bosch ordered his tanks onto the streets during the abortive coup of 1981. This fact however isn't representative of the city's political inclination, which has always been to the left — Valencia was the seat of the Republican government during the civil war after it fled Madrid.

Valencia has a generally scruffy appearance and if you're ever here when they're celebrating with fireworks (which is often) you'll see why — the liberal use of gunpowder and the consequent shudderings cause old buildings to shed flaking paint and loose bits of plaster. Probably the most attractive feature of the town is the little plazas which you come upon all the time, usually with some trickling water and often with trees for shade, giving the town a relaxed feel. The most interesting area for wandering round is undoubtedly the maze-like *Barrio del Carmen* (the oldest part of town), roughly between c/de Caballeros and the Rio Turia. In c/de Caballeros, look for the old door knockers placed high up for the convenience of the horseborne gentlemen residents (hence the name of the street).

The City

The distinctive feature of Valencian architecture is its wealth of elaborate baroque facades — you'll see them on almost every old building in town, but none so extraordinary or rich as the **Palacio del Marques de dos Aguas**. Hipolito Rovira, who designed its amazing alabaster doorway, died insane in 1740, which should come as no surprise to anyone who's seen it. Inside is the **Museo Nacional de Cerámica** (Tues.–Sat. 10am–2pm and 4–6pm, Sun. 10am–2pm; free admission to under-21s) with a vast collection of ceramics from all over Spain. Valencia itself was a major ceramics center, largely owing to the size of its *morisco* population. Apart from an impressive display of *azulejos*, the collection contains some stunning plates with gold and copper varnishes (*reflejos*), a trio of evocatively ornate eighteenth-century carriages, and, on the top floor, some fine fifteenth-century furniture. Very much in the same decorative vein as the Palacio is the church of **San Juan de la Cruz** (or San Andres) next door. Nearby, in the Plaza Patriarca, is the neoclassical former university and the beautiful Renaissance **Colegio del Patriarca**, whose small **art museum** (11am–1pm) includes excellent works by El Greco, Morales, and Ribalta. Another Ribalta, *The Last Supper*, hangs above the altar in the college's chapel; in the middle of the Miserere service on Friday mornings it's whisked aside to reveal a series of curtains, behind the last of which, drawn at the moment of climax, is a giant illuminated crucifix. The whole performance is amazingly dramatic, and typical of the aura of miracle and mystery with which the Spanish church still cloaks itself.

It's not far from here, up c/de la Paz, to the **Plaza Zaragoza** (sometimes still known as Plaza de la Reina) and Valencia's **Cathedral**. The plaza is dominated by two octagonal towers, the florid spire of the church of Santa Catalina and the **Miguelete** (14–15th c.), the unfinished tower of the cathedral itself. You can make the long climb up to the roof for a fantastic view over the city with its many blue-domed churches, which will reaffirm your impression that it has no plan. Entrance to the tower, from inside the cathedral, costs 75ptas; hours are not fixed but it's usually open in the morning until about 1pm and again from about 5 to 7pm. The church's attractive and unusual feature is the lantern above the crossing, its windows glazed with sheets of alabaster. The process of removing the many later additions from the original Gothic structure of the main body of the building has been paralyzed by lack of funds. In the **museum** (Mon.–Sat., 1–2pm and 4–6pm except Sun.) is a gold and agate cup (the *Santo Cáliz*) said to be the one used by Christ at the Last Supper — the Holy Grail itself. It's certainly old, and, hidden away throughout the Dark Ages in a monastery in northern Aragón, it really did inspire many of the legends associated with the Grail. Other treasures include a sixteenth-century *retablo* by Fernando de Llanos and Yáñez de la Almedina depicting the life of Christ. Two footbridges allow the clergy to go straight from the cathedral into the Archbishop's Palace and into the tiny chapel of **Nuestra Señora de los Desamparados** where thousands of candles constantly burn in front of the image of the Virgin, patron of Valencia.

(To this day the *Tribunal de las Aguas*, the black-clad regulatory body of the water-users, meets at noon on Thursdays at the Puerta de los Apostoles to judge grievances about the water irrigation system of the *huertas*. Blasco Ibañez (1867–1928) describes their workings in detail in his novel *La Barraca*, which is about peasant life in the Valencian *huerta* amd remains the best guide to the life of that region.)

If you don't much go for baroque excesses, visit the beautifully elegant Gothic **Lonja de la Seda** (the Silk Exchange; Tues.–Fri. 10am–2pm and 4–6pm, weekends 10am–1pm; closed Mon.). On weekdays it still operates as a commercial exchange. Opposite is the enormous **Mercado Central**, a modernist iron girder and glass structure built at the beginning of the century. It's one of the biggest markets in Europe, fitting for *huerta* country, with an amazing variety of local fruit and vegetables, as well as hard-to-find herbs, health foods, dehyde items, etc.

The **Museo de Bellas Artes** (10am–2pm and 4–6pm; not Sun. pm or Mon.) on the far side of the river has one of the best general collections in Spain with works by Bosch, El Greco, Goya, Velazquez, Ribera, and Ribalta as well as quantities of modern Valencian art. Outside is the largest of Valencia's parks — the **Jardines del Real** (also called the Viveros Gardens)

— in the center of which is a small zoo. As you go back into town don't miss the fourteenth-century **Torres Serranos**, an impressive gateway defending the entrance to the town across the Río Turia. (The other remaining gateway is the **Torres de Quart**, a simpler structure but equally awesome in scale.) The river itself is no more than a trickle now, and a huge park is planned to cover the whole of its dried-up course (the main flow was diverted around Valencia after disastrous flooding in the last century). So far only one area has been planted and landscaped, alongside the Avenida Jacinto, in which stands the recently-built **Palau de la Música**, a futuristic glass structure where concerts (mainly classical) are held. To the south of the park they are planning to build a new dormitory city with a "river-garden" in the middle.

Along with the **Museos de Etnología y Prehistoria** (in Avda. de Guillem), another minor museum worth visiting is the **Museo Paleontológico** in c/Almodí. It's in a building called the *Almudí*, a former grain storehouse built in the thirteenth century and rebuilt in the sixteenth century, and now housing an awesome collection of bones and a magnificent collection of shells. Strangely, it's open longer out of season than in summer (Tues.–Fri. 10am–1pm and 4–6:30pm, Sat. and Sun. 10am–1pm; June to mid-Sept. Tues.–Sat. am only; free.)

Practical Details

On Valencia's main square, the extremely tacky **Plaza del Ayuntamiento** (formerly Plaza del País Valenciano), you'll find the post office and the municipal **Turismo**, which gives out a very good map/leaflet (weekdays 9am–1:30pm and 4:30–7pm, Sat. 9:30am– 1:30pm). There's another tourist office in c/de la Paz (weekdays 9am–2pm and 5–7pm, Sat. 9am–1pm), and an information point inside the main **train station**, a few yards down Avenida Marques de Sotelo. At the latter they have a hotel reservation service, but they don't include the cheap *hostales* on their lists. This isn't a problem, though, as most of the cheap **places to stay** are right here, in c/Bailen and c/Pelayo, which run parallel to the tracks off c/Játiva — Pelayo is much quieter. A very friendly and cheap place well away from the noise of the station is the *Hostal Gran Glorieta* at c/Conde Montornes 22, just off Plaza Tetuan, up c/de Colon (☎96/3527885). If it's full (very likely), try no. 16, *Habitaciones Australia*, which is a bit messy but even cheaper. At Avda. del Puerto 69 there's a **youth hostel** (☎96/3590152). The nearest **campground** is 10km south at El Salér (open all year; ☎96/3670411), which also has a youth hostel (☎96/3529506). There's another campground at El Palmar, by the lagoon (open June–Sept.), and more are dotted along the coast.

The **bus station** is some way out and it's worth taking a local bus (#28) into the center (allow 15 min. if you decide to walk). For **bus travel in town** buy a *Bono-Bus* ticket from any *tabaquená*. To get to the **Balearic ferry terminal** from *RENFE*, take the #19 bus; the nearest stop, as you exit the train station, is on the side street to the right (east), though the route starts from a terminus just to the right of the Ayuntamiento as you face it. Starting from the long-distance bus terminal you're better off using the **FEVE** (electric suburban railway). This starts at a station on the Turia directly opposite the Torres Sevranos; you'll have to walk about 700m to your boat on the harbour end of the line.

As for **where to eat**, first of all a few places to avoid. The Plaza del Ayuntamiento is expensive and bad, around the Plaza Zaragoza is not much better, and the same goes for the places on the front at Malvarrosa beach. The food is disappointing to say the least at all the Greek restaurants. At the other end of the scale, for a treat, the best (and most expensive) restaurant in town is *La Hacienda* (c/Navarro Reverter 12, going away from Puerta del Mar towards the Turia; closed Sun.) — its specialty is bull's tail Cordoban style. For regional specialties try the *Gargantua* farther along the street (closed Sun. pm and all Mon.). For bistros and cheap restaurants the best general area is the Barrio del Carmen — c/Roteros, in particular. A traditional place to go for *mejillones* (mussels) is the *Bar Pilar* (on the corner of c/Moza Zeit, just off Pl. del Esparto), where they serve them in a piquant sauce and you throw the shells into buckets under the bar. A couple of good but pricey places are on the corner of Pl. del Carmen and c/Roteros — the *Restaurante la Casa Vella* and *El Méson*, once a famous political bar. In a different part of town, handy if you're staying in c/Conde Montornes, the small and quiet *Restaurante Patos*, (Pl. San Vicente Ferrer) has reasonably priced but quite elaborate dishes. Some mid-range possibilities, between Ayuntamiento and the Turia on the pedestrian walkways, include *Bar Ancoa,* Plaza San Lorenzo at c/Novellos to cheap *platos; Bar Almuoín* on the street of the same name behind the cathedral,for good sea food *raciones*; and two bone fide restaurants, *Clot* and *Rotunda*, on the distinctive round Plaza Rotunda, with moderate menus and unbeatable settings.If you're down to your last pesetas, *Comidas Eliseo*, in c/Conde Montornes, has a very cheap and very greasy menu. A good place for morning coffee or *tapas* is the *Bar Glorieta*, a large old bar on the corner of Pl. Alfonso Magnanimo (closes about 9pm).

You can get **horchata** all over the city but the best traditionally comes from Alboraya, formerly a village in the Valencian suburbs, now absorbed into the city, so keep your eyes open for that name. The oldest *horchateria* in town is the *Santa Catalina* on the bottom corner of Pl. Zaragoza; *El Siglo*, opposite, isn't bad either. The various *heladeriás* (icecream here is wonderful too) and *horchaterías* on Pl. San Lorenzo, just in from the Torres Sevranos are cheap and good.

Nightlife

For what's on and for restaurant addresses, buy the weekly listings guide *Qué y Dónde*, or the similar but slightly less comprehensive *Cartelera Turia*. If you don't know where to go, Valencia can seem dead at night: the action is widely dispersed, with many locations over the Turia. To get there, or go from one zone to another as the Spanish do, you'll either have to do a lot of walking or take taxis (shared, they're not too expensive). The area immediately round the cathedral, where you might expect some movement, is dead at night.

The action also moves around with the season. **In summer** everyone is in the bars lining admittedly polluted Malvarrosa beach — two in particular are the *Genaro* and *Tropical*, large bar/discos on c/Eugenio Vines (the beach road). To get there, take bus #1, #2, or #19 — the last goes from Pl. del Ayuntamiento, the others from the bus station. All go along the Avda. del Puerto and turn into c/Dr. Lluch; get off about halfway along and go down to the beach along c/Virgen del Sufragio — *Genaro* is on your right, *Tropical* is along on the left. The stop for the return bus is one road back from where you got off. You'll probably need a taxi late at night.

The rest of the year there's a great variety of bars to choose from back in town. The youngest and loudest, although a bit out of date now, are again on c/Bailen and c/Pelayo, towards the bottom end. The **Barrio del Carmen** also has dozens of small cafe-bars but the area too is less popular than it used to be. Explore the following streets: c/Serranos, c/de Quart (running into c/de Caballeros), c/Alta and c/Baja, c/Beneficencia, and the four parallel streets of Na Jordana, San Ramon, de Ripalda, and Dr. Chiarri. Other areas to explore for bars are on the other side of the river beyond the Barrio (around c/Ruaya, c/Visitación and c/Orihuela), and behind the Gran Vía de Fernando el Católico (along c/Juan Llorens and c/Calixto).

Most of the **"in" places** are over the Turia in the new university region. The trendiest bars are on Avenida Blasco Ibañez — the *Público* (no. 111), the *Metro* (no. 97), *Hipodromo* and *El Asesino*. The bars of Plaza Xuquer, just off the Blasco Ibañez, are popular meeting-places — *Cuba Litro*, in the corner, serves liter plastic cups of *combinados* (see below), while the *Carajillo* has normal *copas* and the *Pan de Azúcar* serves snack food until late. Wherever you look around here there's a bar worth calling in at — they're particularly thick on the ground in c/Artes Gráficas, c/Rodrígo Poros, c/Alfonso de Córdoba (the town side of the Avenida, down towards the Jardin del Real), and c/Menéndez Pelayo (on the opposite side of the Avenida).

Another fashionable zone is the Pl. Canovas and the side streets off it, full of *pubs* (music bars) where people tend to go to network. The bars along c/Serrano Morales and c/Grabador Esteve are yuppie haunts (the cars outside are a good indicator), but those off the opposite side, down c/Salamanca, c/Altea, and c/Burriana are more mixed. In both cases, each bar has its particular age group and style — there's something for everyone. In many of the bars around Pl. Canovas you can ask the waiters for discount/free entrance cards for discos, but these will only be available early in the evening.

The Valencianos seem to really like *combinados*, or **cocktails**, which don't necessarily have the upscale connotation they have in the States. The *Rincón Latino* (c/Gobernador Viejo 10, off c/Conde Montornes, near Pl. S. Vicente Ferrer) is a smoky cellar where the specialty is cheap Nicaraguan drinks — order a rum and pineapple cocktail and you'll get a tiny glass of each, the idea being to throw back all the rum in one go, quickly followed by the juice. A classic cocktail goes under the name of *Agua de Valencia* and is served by the jug in a series of old bars. The *Cervecería de Madrid* is an old popular haunt where they serve the orthodox *Agua de Valencia* made basically with orange juice, champagne and vodka — it's in c/de la Abadia de San Martín, just below Pl. Zaragoza. The *Café Malvarrosa* (c/Ruiz de Lihoro, off c/de la Paz) has its own *Agua de Malvarrosa*, made with lemon instead of orange. The nearby cafes *Paris* and *Madrid* also have their own versions of the same.

Discos, Jazz, and Fireworks

Most of the discos in town are also in the university area — they include *Distrito 10* (c/Gen. Elio 8, just over the Puente del Real), the yuppified *Jardines del Real* (in the same block) and *Woody* (Menendez y Pelayo 37). Close to the town center for a change is the *Calcatta*, in a converted old house in c/Reloj Viejo, off Pl. Zaragoza — admission is free, the mix of people is good, and the waiters dish out tickets for *Distrito 10*. *Balkiss*, a gay male disco, is at c/Dr. Monserrat 23, very near the Torres de Quart. The rest of the discos are out of town on the main road heading south along the coast: *Spooks Factory* (Carretera El Saler) and *Dreams Village* are near each other, on the Playa de Pinedo, Camino Montañares. Farther down, on the Playa Recati (El Perellonet, below the Albufera), are *Salitre* and *Pomelo* — the former funky, the latter new wave. In Las Palmeras, *La Barraca* is a pop disco and *Chocolate* is pop-rock.

For jazz, the favorite is the *Perdido Club Jazz* at c/Sueca 17; *La Casa Vella*, (see restaurants above) also serves up jazz. Original language films are shown regularly at municipal *Filmoteca*, c/En Blanch 6, and are sometimes also shown at *Albatros Mini-Cines*, Pl. Fray Luis Colomer. Finally a word about Valencia's fiestas, some of the most riotous in Spain. The best is *Las Fallas*, March 12–19, which culminates in a massive bonfire when all the processional floats are burned. In July the city celebrates the feast of St. James with all the usual revelry plus magnificent fireworks.

Outside the City

If the weather's fine, take a half-day trip out to **LA ALBUFERA**, a vast lagoon separated from the sea by a sandbank and surrounded by ricefields. Being one of the largest bodies of freshwater in Spain it constitutes an important wetland, and attracts tens of thousands of migratory birds — a throng composed of 250 species, of which ninety breed here regularly. In the Middle Ages it was ten times its present size but the surrounding paddies have gradually reduced it. Experts, having detected growing contamination by industrial waste, domestic sewage, and insecticide pollution, have recently made it a Natural Park. Whether you're into birdwatching or not, it's a relaxing change from the city — go there to eat a *paella* as the sun goes down in the village of El Palmar (formerly a settlement of fishing huts, now packed with restaurants). Take a bus from El Salér (see "Beaches," below), or the *El Perelló* bus which leaves Valencia from the same bus stop as the Salér bus and at roughly the same times — it stops at El Salér before going on to the lagoon.

Listings

Airlines *Iberia* and *Aviaco*, c/de la Paz 14 (☎96/3520500); *British Airways*, Pl. Rodrigo Botet 6 (☎96/3512284).

Airport Manises, 12km away; ☎96/3709500; bus #15 from bus station (hourly).

Balearic ferries Leave daily for Mallorca (9 hr.) and twice weekly for Ibiza (7 hr.); information and tickets from *Trasmediterranea*, Avda. Manuel Soto 19, but it's a long trip out and you may as well buy tickets from any of the half-dozen travel agents on the Ayuntamiento plaza.

Banks Main branches of most banks are in the area of the Pl. del Ayuntamiento or along c/Játiva. There's a *Barclays* at c/Correos 10, and a *Londres y America Sur* at Pl. Rodrigo Botet 6. Outside banking hours, two branches of the *Caja de Ahorros* are open Mon.–Sat. 9am–8pm: one at c/ Játiva 14, to the left as you come out of the train station, and the other in the *Nuevo Centro*, near the bus station. As savings banks they can only do certain transactions.

Beaches The city beach, Malvarrosa, is polluted. It's best go to El Salér, a long, wide stretch with pine trees and a campground behind it. A bus goes from the Puerta del Mar at the end of Glorieta Park, leaving from just next to the newspaper kiosk (in summer on the hour and half-hour, out of season on the hour). The ride takes twenty minutes and it stops in the village before heading down to the beach and then turning back.

Books English books are available from the *International Bookshop* on c/ Ruzafa, and the *English Book Centre* on c/Pascual y Genis.

Buses Main station at Avda. Menéndez Pidal 13, across the Turia (☎96/ 3497222). Regular services to northern Europe and to London leave from here — offices in the station.

Car rental *Avis* at the airport and at c/Isabel la Católica 17 (☎96/3510734), *Hertz* at the airport and c/Segorbe 7 (☎96/3415036). *Atesa* (often the cheapest) at the airport and Avda. del Cid 64 (☎96/3799108). Many more.

Consulate USA, c/Ribera 3 (☎96/3516973).

Cyclists There are various cycle paths (marked in green) running through the city; watch out for straying pedestrians. For info on the excursions and longer routes organized by the *Consellería de Cultura, Educación y Ciencia de la Generalitat de Valencia*, ask at *ITVA (Institut Turistic Valencia)* c/Gen. Elio 4 (☎96/3625411).

Feminism There's a feminist bar (*La Picola*) at c/Almirante 7 and a women's bookshop (*Librería Dona*) at c/Gravador Estero 34.

Hiking Hikes through various mountain areas in the region are organized year round. You can either join a guided group or, if you want to go it alone, they'll provide route-maps and info. Details from *Per les Nostres Muntanyes* at c/Caballeros 21 near the Pl. del Virgen (6–10pm only, closed weekends), or *ITVA* (see "Cyclists").

Hospitals Provincial on Avda. Cíd, at the Tres Cruces junction (☎96/ 3791600). First Aid station at Pl. America 6 (☎96/3526750).

Luggage Storage Self-store lockers at *RENFE*; 24-hr. access 125ptas a day.

Markets Check out the crowded fleamarket around the Plaza Redonda (off Plaza Zaragoza) and also Pl. San Esteban behind the cathedral. There are also a few stalls alongside the cathedral —best for chewy sugar cane. Every day except Sunday there are stalls selling jewelry, clothes, and knick-knacks along c/de la Paz, spilling over into Plaza Alfonso Magnanimo (near Pl. Porta del Mar).

Police Headquarters — Gran Vía Ramon y Cajal 40 (☎96/3510862). Policiá Municipal, ☎092.

Post Office Main *Correos* at Pl. del Ayuntamiento 1; (Mon.– Sat. 9am–9pm and Sun. am.)

Telephones Pl. del Ayuntamiento 27 (Mon.–Sat. 9am–1pm and 5–9pm).

Tourist Offices Main one at Pl. del Ayuntamiento (☎96/3510417).

Trains *RENFE* on c/Játiva (☎96/3513612). Several each day to Barcelona, Madrid, and Malaga.

Játiva

JÁTIVA (or *Xátiva*) is an ancient town inland from Gandía down the coast, which can be reached from there by bus or from Alicante by train, but it makes a convenient day out from the capital. Probably founded by the Phoenicians and certainly inhabited by the Romans, today it's a scenic, tranquil place to kill a few hours in the relative cool of the hills. Don't let the tourist literature raise your hopes too much — though there's a fine collection of mansions scattered around town, most are private and cannot be entered and most of the churches are in a terrible state and closed. Buses and trains both from Valencia; the train (1 hr.) is half the price and leaves every half-hour.

Coming out of the station, take the first street you see going up (c/Baixada Estacio) until you hit the fairly wide tree-lined Alameda; the **old town** lies above this. On the next street above this and to the left, you'll find the post office, *Ayuntamiento* (or *Casa de la Ciutat*) and farther along, the **Turismo**. They'll give you a leaflet showing a suggested walk (corresponding numbers are marked on street signs themselves) but it's not necessary to follow it slavishly since the place is tiny you're better off discovering things for yourself. It's a fairly long walk up the hill to the **castle** (10:30am–2pm and 4:30– 8pm in summer; closed Mon.) — follow signposts from the Pl. del Espanoleto. On the way, you'll pass the **Ermita de San Feliu** (Tues.–Sun. 10am–1pm and 4–7pm), a hermitage built in transitional Romanesque-Gothic style; ancient pillars, fine capitals and a magnificent Gothic *retablo* are the chief attractions of the interior. The **Museo Municipal** (Tues.–Fri. 10am–1pm and 4–8pm; Sat. and Sun. 10am–1pm) consists of two separate sections, one an archaeological collection, the other an art museum. The latter includes several pictures by Jose Ribera (who was born here in 1591) and engravings by Goya — *Caprichos* and *Los Proverbios*. A portrait of Felipe V is hung upside down in retribution for his having set fire to the city in the War of Succession and his having changed its name.

It doesn't take long to see Játiva, but if you're enjoying the peace and quiet and want to stay, the best place is the *Hostal Margallonero*, Pl. Mercat 42 (☎227/6677) — they also serve cheap food. If you pass a bakery, keep an eye open for *arnadi*, a local specialty — it's a rich (and expensive) sweet made with pumpkin, cinnamon, almonds, eggs, sugar, and pine nuts.

South to Alicante — the Best and Worst of the Coast

South of Valencia stretches a long strip of country with, between Gandía and Benidorm, some of the best beaches on this coast. Much of it, though, suffers from the worst excesses of packaged tourism and in the summer it's hard to get a room anywhere — in August virtually impossible. Campers have it somewhat easier — there are hundreds of campgrounds — but driving can be a nightmare unless you stick to the dull highway.

Gandía

Leaving Valencia, both road and rail pass La Albufera and then the vast Ford plant, one of the Spanish government's earliest successes in persuading multinational companies to invest in the country's cheap labor and favorable tax situation. There's not much else until you get to **GANDÍA**, first of the big resorts. A few kilometers inland from the modern seafront development, the old town is quiet and provincial, with one sight that's well worth seeing, and quite a few cheap rooms. Coming out of the train station, **Turismo** occupies a brown hut, cleverly camouflaged behind some trees opposite — they have some bus timetables and details of the six **pensions** in town. The nearest, which is clean, cheap and spacious, is the *Requena* (c/Tirso de Molino 28, ☎96/2865863) — take the immediate right out of the station, then the second right. If it's full, the road parallel and behind, c/Cardenal Cisneros, has the *Pepita* at no. 8 (☎96/2873488).

Gandía was once important enough to have its own university but the only real testimony to its heyday is the **Palau Ducal de los Borja**, built in the fourteenth century but with Renaissance and baroque additions and modifications. There are regular guided tours throughout the year — in Spanish, but photocopied translations are available at the reception. The lifetime of Duke Francisco de Borja coincided with the golden age of the town (late 15–early 16c) in terms of urban and cultural development, a process in which he played an important part; learned and pious, the Duke opened colleges all over Spain and Europe, and was eventually canonized. The palace contains his paintings, tapestries, and books, but parts of the building itself are of equal interest, such as the *artesonado* ceilings and the pine window shutters so perfectly preserved by prolonged burial in soil and manure that resin still oozes from them when the hot beats down. There are also several beautiful sets of *azulejos*, but these are outshone by the fourteenth-century Arab wall tiles, whose brilliant luster cannot be replicated, as it comes from using pigments from plants that became extinct soon after the Moors left.

Buses run regularly down to the enormous **beach** (10 min.), first winding around the port and then skirting the white sands. Catch it from just alongside the *Turismo* — it's blue and white with "Gandia Playa" on the front. The beach is packed in summer (especially with Spanish families) and lined with high-rise apartments which out of season can be remarkably inexpensive. The beach zone is a good place for good **seafood** and *paellas*. Try *fideua*, a local specialty with a strong seafood flavor, cooked with vermicelli instead of rice. *La Gamba* (Carretera Nazaret-Oliva, a few blocks back from the beach; ☎96/2841310) is excellent but not cheap.

Heading south from Gandía, you have to get a bus — *La Union de Benisa* run regular buses to most places along the coast. To Játiva there are seven buses a day in summer (including Sun. and holidays), and two in winter, run by *Iberbus*. Ask in the *Turismo* for bus company addresses (there's no main bus station).

On to Altea

OLIVA, 8km beyond Gandía, is a much lower-key development. Again the village is set back from the coast and although the main road charges through its center, it's relatively unspoiled and there are a number of **hostales and fondas**. The beach (frequent buses) stretches a long way to the south, almost as far as Denia, so if you're prepared to walk, or better still if you've got transportation, you can escape the crowds altogether. PLAYA DE OLIVA itself has hundreds of villas and apartments (booked up throughout July and Aug.) but is refreshingly free of concrete and tackiness.

DENIA is a far bigger place, a sizable town even without its summer visitors, and less appealing. You might though be tempted to take the daily **boat to Palma**, Mallorca. A rattling narrow-gauge railway (*FEVE*) runs down the coast from here to Alicante, with hourly service throughout the day. Beneath the wooded capes beyond, bypassed by the main road, stretch probably the most beautiful beaches on this coastline — but without your own car you'll find it difficult to get to much of it, and even if you do there's not a cheap room to be found. At the heart of this area is JÁVEA, an attractive village surrounded by hillside villas, and with two smallish beaches hemmed in by hotels. In summer both Denia and Jávea are quite lively in the evenings, especially on the weekend, as they are popular with young people from Valencia.

If you have a car, you could make a detour to the quiet family resort of CALPE and the dramatic rocky outcrop known as the *Peñon de Ifach*. The harbor at its foot is used by a small fleet of fishing vessels. Back on the main road again is ALTEA, set on a small hill overlooking this whole stretch of coastline. Restrained tourist development is centered on the seafront, and being so close to Benidorm it does receive some overspill. In character, however, it's a world apart. The old village up the hill is picturesquely attractive with its white houses, blue-domed church and profuse blossoms. You can eat and drink well here — the main square has a host of bars, pizzerias are lined up along the front, and at the *L'Obrador* (c/Concepcion 8) they serve (at a price) some of the best pasta in the whole area. There are two or three cheap **hostales** at the back of the main square. A sandy beach has recently been artificially created right in front of the town; more pleasant is the stony and windy (but much more spacious) natural beach to the south — it's a twenty-minute walk, or you can take a bus.

Through Benidorm

Beyond Altea there's nothing between you and the crowded beaches at BENIDORM. Only thirty years ago Rose Macaulay could describe Benidorm as a small village "crowded very beautifully round its domed and tiled church on a rocky peninsula." That old part's still there, but so overshadowed by the miles of towering concrete that you'd be hard pressed to find it. If you want hordes of British and Scandinavian sun-seekers, scores of "English" pubs, at least seventy discos, and bacon and eggs for breakfast, this is the place to come. The beach — nearly 6km of it, regularly topped up with imported Moroccan sand — is undeniably impressive, when you can see it through the roasting flesh. Surprisingly, except in August, you can usually find a room in Benidorm, but it takes a lot of walking. The cheaper places are all near the center and away from the sea, but out of season many of the giant hotels and apartment blocks slash their prices drastically. A few of the cheapest places are *Stop* (Pl. de la Cruz 5, ☎965/5852600); *El Trovador* (c/Maren de Comillas 23, ☎965/5860724); and *Tabarca* (c/Ruzafa 9, ☎965/58577080). Addresses of others can be obtained from **Turismo**, at the bottom of c/ Martinez Alejos, near the old village (☎965/853224).

Going on to Alicante, you can get either a bus or train — both are virtually hourly; the bus is slightly more expensive.

Alicante

Don't bother to stop in VILLAJOYOSA, or anywhere else before you reach **ALICANTE**. Locals describe their city as "*la millor terra del mondo*" and while that's a gross exaggeration it is at least a living city, thoroughly Spanish, and a considerable relief after some of the places you've been passing through. There are good beaches nearby, too, most crowded with Spanish vacationers, a lively nightlife in season, and plenty of cheap places to stay and to eat. Wide esplanades such as the Rambla de Méndez Nuñez and Avenida Alfonso El Sabio give the town an elegant air, and around the Plaza de Luceros and along the seafront Paseo you can relax in style at terrace cafes — paying a bit extra for the palm-tree setting, of course. The most interesting area is around the *Ayuntamiento*, where, among the bustle with small-scale commerce, you'll see plenty of evidence of Alicante's large Algerian community — the links with Algeria have always been strong, and boats depart from here for Oran twice a week. And if you're wondering about the auditory traffic signals — Alicante is the headquarters of *La ONCE*, an association for the blind; tickets for their lotteries are on sale all over the town.

Practicalities

The main **train station** is on Avda. Salamanca, but trains on the private *FEVE* line to Benidorm and Denia (no InterRail passes) leave from the small station at the far end of the Playa del Postiguet, and for Santa Pola and Elche from another by the docks. The **bus station** for local and international services is in c/Portugal. There are no longer any **boats** to the Balearics from Alicante, but you can get tickets and information for Denia or Valencia services from any travel agent in the harbor area. The main municipal **Turismo** is in the Pl. del Ayuntamiento (summer 9am–8pm, Sat. 9am–2pm; rest of year 9am–2pm and 5–8pm, Sat. 9am– 1:30pm); another office with

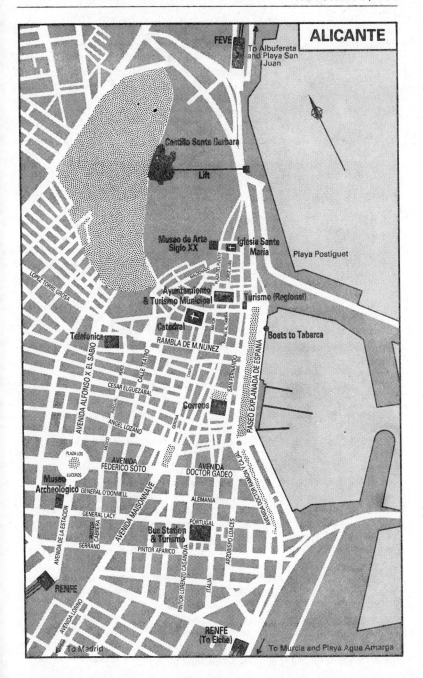

ALICANTE

FEVE

To Albufereta
and Playa San
Juan

Castillo Santa Barbara

Lift

Museo de Arte
Siglo XX

Iglesia Santa
Maria

Playa Postiguet

LOPEZ TORRE GROSA

Ayuntamiento
& Turismo Municipal

Turismo (Regional)

Catedral

Telefonica

RAMBLA DE M.NUÑEZ

Boats to Tabarca

AVENIDA ALFONSO X EL SABIO

CALLE TEATRO

PEREZ

CESAR ELGUEZABAL

POSTIGUET

CHAPI

SAN FERNANDO

PASEO EXPLANADA DE ESPAÑA

ANGEL LOZANO

MEXICO

GERONA

Correos

PLAZA LOS
LUCEROS

AVENIDA
FEDERICO SOTO

AVENIDA
DOCTOR GADEO

Museo
Archeologico

GENERAL O'DONNELL

ALEMANIA

AVENIDA DOCTOR RAMON Y CAJAL

AVENIDA DE LA ESTACION

GENERAL LACY

AVENIDA MAISONNAIVE

PORTUGAL

AVENIDA DOCTOR RAMON Y CAJAL

BERG
CABRERA

SERRANO

Bus Station
& Turismo

PINTOR APARICO

ARZOBISPO LOACES

RENFE

PINTOR LORENZO CASANOVA

ITALIA

AVENIDA LORINO

RENFE
(To Elche)

To Madrid

To Murcia and Playa Agua Amarga

town and regional information is on the seafront *paseo*, and there's a small one for information on the town just next to the bus station. They might try to give you a small map only — ask for their larger leaflet with a map and info included. The **airport** bus stops outside the bus station. *Iberia* offices are at Avda. Federico Soto 9 (☎965/218510) and *British Airways* are at Explanada de España 3 (☎965/200594). Most **banks** are around the Pl. de los Luceros and along the Avda. de la Estacion/Alfonso el Sabio.

Except in August you should have little problem finding a **room**, with the bulk of the possibilities concentrated at the lower end of the old town, above the Explanada de España (a weirdly tiled seafront walk seen on all local postcards) and around the Plaza Gabriél — especially on c/San Fernando, c/San Francisco and c/Castaño. Places to try include the *Olympia* (c/San Francisco, ☎965/5214037), and the *Larensana* (☎965/5207820) and *Paris* (☎965/5207378) at c/San Fernando 10 and 56 respectively. There's a **youth hostel** on Avda. Orihuela 59 (☎965/5281211) and two **campgrounds**, both in the Albufereta to the north; one is open all year, the other summer only.

For the best local **beaches** head for San Juan de Alicante, about 6km out, reached either by bus from the Plaza del Mar (approx. half-hourly) or the *FEVE* Alicante-Denia railway. The town beach — Playa del Postiguet — is crowded and none too clean. There's a *playa libre* just outside town where nudism is allowed, between Playa Agua Amarga and Playa del Saladar/Urbanova take the Line A bus for El Palmeral or the airport bus. For really fabulous beaches, take a day-trip to the **island of Tabarca** to the south — boats leave from the Explanada de España daily in summer, weekly in winter, weather permitting.

The Town and its Nightlife

The rambling **Castillo de Santa Bárbara**, an imposing fortress on the bare rock behind the town beach, is Alicante's only real "sight" — with a tremendous view from the top. It's best approached from the seaward side where a shaft has been cut straight up through the hill to get you to the top. The elevator is directly opposite Meeting Point 5 on the other side of the road from Paya Postiguet (it operates from 9am, last entrance in summer 8:30pm, in winter 7:30pm; Sat. 9am–1:30pm); drivers can reach the castle from the other side. Iberian and Roman remains have been found on the site, but most of the present layout dates from the sixteenth century. Allow yourself about ninety minutes for exploration. The other main attraction is a remarkably good **Museo de Arte Siglo 20** to the back of the *Ayuntamiento*, with works by Picasso, Tapies, Miro, and Dali (May–Sept. 10:30am–1:30pm and 6–9pm; Oct.– Apr. 10am–1pm and 5–8pm; Sun. and holidays open am only; closed Mon.; free admission). The town also has a small **Museo Arqueológico** in the *Palacio de la Diputación* on Avda. de la Estacion.

Cheap **restaurants** are clustered around the *Ayuntamiento*, including a couple of places where you can eat couscous (c/Miquel Saler), and a couple of *churrerrías* (e.g., *La Madrileña* in c/San Jose). Over on the other side of town c/San Francisco, leading off a square near the bottom end of the

Rambla, has a group of cheap restaurant/*tavernas* with seats outside. For *tapas* try the *Taverna Castellana* on c/Loaces, on the other side of Avda. Dr. Gadea — sample their *montaditas* (tiny bread rolls), *croquetas*, and *patatas bravas* (potatoes with spicy sauce). Farther along the road at no. 15 is the *Museo del Jamón* a posher version of the same — the restaurant is expensive but again they have all sorts of *tapas*. On the waterfront Paseo, near the *Turismo*, the *Boutique de Jamón* also specializes in *jamón serrano*. On c/S. Fernando the *Venta del Lobos* does very cheap *carnes a la brasa* (meats cooked barbecue style).

For **drinking** and the best **nightlife**, head into the Barrio Santa Cruz, whose narrow streets lie roughly between the cathedral, Pl. Carmen and Pl. San Cristobal. At night *El Barrio*, as it's called, is avoided by many of the locals, but it's really not too rough, and there are so many bars here that you can easily steer clear of the questionable places. If you enter via the Pl. San Cristóbal or c/Sto. Tomás below it, you'll quickly hit the main area. (The *Cine Astoria*, in the middle of the Barrio, often has **original language films**.) Another area with several popular places on roughly the same level, is on the other side of town, in particular c/Italia and c/Lohaces. *El Lobo Marinero* is a pub-style bar on c/Alemania; *Hollywood* is a more modern music bar on c/ Italia; and on c/S. Fernando, the *Plátano* bar is usually very crowded. In summer the bars along Playa San Juan are always packed.

Fiestas — Alcoy and Villena

In June there is a big **fallas** in Alicante, second only to Valencia's. Another major fiesta in the region, and the most important of its kind (see "Fiestas," below), is the three-day *Fiesta de Moros y Cristianos* in **ALCOY**, about 60km from Alicante. It happens around St. George's Day (*San Jorge* Apr. 23), but the date varies slightly according to when Easter is. Magnificent processions and mock battles for the castle culminate in the decisive intervention of St. George himself — a legend that originated in the Battle of Alcoy (1276) when the town was attacked by a Muslim army. New costumes are made each year and prizes are awarded for the best which then go into a museum (worth checking out). Get there for the action early in the morning. On Day 1 the Christians make their entrance in the morning, the Moors in the afternoon; Day 2 is dedicated to St. George, with several religious processions; Day 3 sees a gunpowder battle, leading to the saint's appearance on the battlements. Access from Alicante is easy, with five buses a day. You may have to commute since there are only two **hostales** in Alcoy: *San Jorge* (c/ San Juan de Ribera 11, ☎543277) and *Savoy* (c/Casablanca 5, ☎542102). The town itself, now heavily industrialized, is not worth visiting apart from on these dates.

After Alcoy's, the *Moros y Cristianos* fiesta in **VILLENA** (beginning of Sept.) is one of the most important. Unlike Alcoy, this small town, is worth a visit at any time, having a well-preserved fifteenth-century hilltop fortress, a richly decorated late Gothic church, a good archaeology museum, and several eighteenth-century mansions. It's on the main road from Alicante, and is connected by bus and train. Another impressive castle, encircled by a double wall, stands 17km away at the village of BIAR.

Inland from Alicante — Elche to Murcia

ELCHE, inland from Alicante to the south, is famed throughout Spain for its exotic palm forest and for the ancient stone bust known as *La Dama de Elche* discovered here in 1897 (and now in the Archaeological Museum, Madrid). The palm trees, originally planted by the Moors, are still the town's chief industry — not only do they attract tourists, but they provide delicious dates (from the female trees), and the fronds (from the male trees) are in demand all over the country for use in Palm Sunday processions and as charms against lightning. You can see the forest, unique of its kind in Europe, almost anywhere around the outskirts of the city but the finest trees of all are those in the specially cultivated **Huerto del Cura** on c/Federico García Sánchiz. Elche is also the home of a remarkable **fiesta** in the first two weeks of August which culminates in a centuries-old mystery play — the celebrations include one of the best examples of the mock battles between Christians and Moors. Over several days the elaborately costumed warriors fight it out before the Moors are eventually driven from the city and the Christian king enters in triumph.

There are buses and trains more or less hourly from Alicante to Elche and outside fiesta time you should have no problem finding somewhere to stay. Elche is also regularly connected with SANTA POLA on the coast — an ugly village but with rooms for rent, good beaches, and ferries to Tabarca, a strange little islet offshore. Inland, the road continues to Orihuela (regular trains and buses).

Orihuela

You wouldn't guess it from the shabby overhanging houses, but **ORIHUELA** had a very aristocratic past — in 1488 *Los Reyes Católicos* held court here. Today many buildings are half-demolished or half-built, with palm trees stranded in the middle of them, and yet at the same time the place has a provincial bustle to it. Though it doesn't take long to see Orihuela's monuments, it's worth spending a whole day (and maybe even a night) to enjoy its pace. Orihuela also has a natural attraction in *El Palmeral*, the second largest palm forest in Spain — walk out beyond Colegio Sto. Domingo or take the Alicante bus (from the center) and ask to be dropped off.

The only **hostal** in town (*Rey Teodomiro*, ☎965/300348) is at the top of the long avenue from the train station — it's cheap, clean, showers are free, and there are scads of rooms. There are two more out by the Palmeral, *Casa Coro* (☎965/302963) and *El Palmeral* (☎965/302500), but they're not very convenient. Cross over the road from the *Rey Teodomiro* and take the first right, and you'll come to the best place to eat — *Méson don Pepe* at c/Valencia 3. It has great *tapas* and a cheap lunch menu during the week — try the *consome al Jerez* (sherry with soup) or the region's specialty, *arroz y costra* (literally "rice with crust," made with rice, eggs, *embutidos*, chicken, and rabbit). From the Glorieta Park, the **Turismo** (8am–3pm and 4–7pm, Sat. am only) is across the river; not all the sights marked on their free map can be visited — many of the seventeenth- and eighteenth-century mansions are closed to the public (though you can roam around the one occupied by the *Turismo)*, and some of the churches are closed for restoration.

Opposite the Turismo is one of the three medieval churches in town, all of which are Catalan Gothic (subsequently altered), a style you won't find any farther south. The oldest part of the **Iglesia de Santiago** (10am–1pm and 5–7pm) is the front portal, the *Puerta de Santiago,* a spectacular example of the late fifteenth-century Isabelline style. Inside, the furniture is baroque but the whole is gloomily somber. Heading back down towards the town center, just past the *Ayuntamiento* (a former palace) you'll see on your right the **Iglesia de Santas Justa y Rufina** — its tower is the oldest construction in the parish and has excellent gargoyle sculptures. Right in the center of the old town is the fascinating **Cathedral** (10:30am–1:30pm and 4–6pm), no bigger than the average parish church, but very unusually and beautifully built with spiralling, twisted pillars and vaulting. A painting by Velázquez, *The Temptation of Saint Thomas,* hangs in a small museum in the nave of the cathedral — and don't overlook the Mudejar-influenced *Puerta de las Cadenas* (14 c.). The **Museo Diocesano de Arte Sacro**, above the cloister, contains an unexpectedly rich collection of art and religious treasures (including a painting by Ribera), many of which are brought out during *Semana Santa,* the town's most important fiesta. There's also a **Museo Semana Santa** (10am–1pm and 5–7pm) not far from the cathedral.

The other main sight in town is the baroque **Colegio de Santo Domingo** (10am–1pm and 6–8pm), out towards the palm forest. It's now in a pretty bad state but has two interior patios and some fine eighteenth-century Valencian tiles in the refectory. For a view of the town and surrounding plains, walk up to the seminary on top of the hill. From Plaza Caturla in the center of town, take the road leading up on the right; not far from the top, there are a couple of steeper short-cuts to the right.

Frequent trains and buses go on to MURCIA. Buses for TORREVIEJA on the coast are run by *Costa Azul* — they leave four times a day from outside *Confetería Bequer* on c/Duque de Tamames, which runs along the bottom of Glorieta Park.

Murcia

MURCIA, according to Augustus Hare (19th c.), would "from the stagnation of its long existence, be the only place Adam would recognize if he returned to Earth." Things have changed slightly — there is industrial development on the outskirts and a movement to spruce up the center, but it remains basically a slow-moving city. It's not really worth going out of your way for, but if you're passing through Murcia, take a look around. The bus station (with an information desk)/is on the edge of town to get to the old part, it's simplest to walk down to the river and follow it to the left till you see cathedral. The train station is on the far side of town on the opposite side of the river. You should have little problem finding a room; the *hostales* are scattered all across the old town. Try *Aitana* (c/San Nicolas), or there are a couple on the other side of the river, just over the *puente viejo.* The **Turismo** is near Pl. de Cetina, behind the cathedral (its black sign barely visible).

The **Cathedral** towers over the mansions and plazas of the center — both literally and in terms of beauty and interest. It's a strange mix of styles, basically Gothic but so covered in later decorative additions that it's hard to tell. The tower, which you can climb, is Renaissance, built in four separate sections by four different architects, while inside the most remarkable aspect is the florid Plateresque decoration of the chapels — particularly the *Capilla de los Velez*. The museum (10am–1pm and 5–8pm) has some fine primitive sculptures and above all a giant processional monstrance — 600 kilos of gold and silver twirling like a musical box on its revolving stand. You should also visit the **Museo Salzillo** (near the bus station; 10am– 1pm and 4–7pm), an extraordinary collection of the figures carried in Murcia's renowned Holy Week procession (which is when they are seen at their best). They were carved in the eighteenth century by Francisco Salzillo and they display all the cloying sentimentality and delight in the "rustic" of that age.

Being a university town, Murcia has a fair nightlife during semesters. The liveliest area is around the university, near the *Museo de Bellas Artes*, in particular the c/de Savedra Fajardo and the side streets off it. There are a few pubs on c/Perez Casas, a small street running between Avda. de la Constitucion and Gran Via Alfonso X, just below the Pl. Circular. Try also a couple of tiny side streets (unnamed on the tourist map) farther down Alfonso X, boxed in by Avda. Jaime I and Alfonso X on the town side of the Archaeological Museum. At lunch time, the whole of the Gran Vía Alfonso X is packed with people drinking aperitifs in outdoor cafes. Very popular at lunch for *tapas* and a drink is the *Bar de las Tapas*, Pl. de las Flores, down towards the river end of Gran Vía Salzillo. If you want to really splurge, a nationally renowned and traditional restaurant is the *Rincón de Pepe* (honored with four forks), at c/Apostoles 34 (between the cathedral and the *Palacio Episcopal*). If you eat at the bar, prices aren't too bad.

There are frequent buses to CARTAGENA (1 per hr.), ÁGUILAS, LORCA and CARAVACA DE LA CRUZ (see below).

The Coast from Torrevieja

The stretch of coast around and below **TORREVIEJA** is just beginning to be exploited — over the last five or six years it has developed at an alarming rate and Torrevieja itself has become a real blot on the landscape. There's plenty of accommodation in the town should you need to stop or use it as a base for traveling elsewhere, and it can be reached by frequent bus service from Alicante or Orihuela. Just to the south is a series of pleasant, small beaches called **las Playas de Orihuela** (as they come within Orihuela's provincial boundary) but since this is being developed as villa/apartment territory there's nowhere to stay. Four soulless *urbanizaciones* spread from Punta Prima to Campo Amor, the latter seeming the most established and most attractive. You can travel to any of them easily from Torrevieja on the Cartagena bus.

The Murcian *Costa Calida* starts at the **Mar Menor** (Lesser Sea), a broad lagoon whose shallow waters (ideal for kids) warm up early in the year, making it a good out-of-season destination. With its high-rise hotels, the "sleeve" (*la Manga*) looks like a diminutive Miami Beach; the ritzy resorts on the land side of the lagoon are more appealing, and they do have a few *hostales*. The main problem is getting a room in season — the area is immensely popular with Spaniards and by April all the cheaper places could be booked up for the summer.

From San Pedro del Pinatar to Cartagena

SAN PEDRO DEL PINATAR, the first resort, is probably your best bet in season as it's not as polished-looking as the others, and is actually more pleasant as a result. The old town is inland a bit, but down on the seafront (a bus ride or 25-min. walk down c/Emilio Castelar) buildings are going up fast. On Monday there's a big market (on the inland side of main road) with food, clothes, and a stand where you can swap, buy, or sell English paperbacks. You can choose from several **hostales**: *Pensión Katherine*, half-way down and a sideroad off c/ Emilio Castelar (☎968/180276); *Alaska*, down by the sea (☎968/181017); *Lucrecia*, on Carretera San Javier-San Pedro (☎968/181982); and *Hostal Mariana*, on the main Avda. Dr. Arturo Guirao (☎968/181013). Also on this road is a really nice place run by a friendly English- and French-speaking couple, the *Pensión Continental* (☎968/183975), where the in-season price includes breakfast and a generous evening meal with wine — it's at no. 57, just along from the **Turismo**. Places to **eat** are in good supply — the *Hogar del Pescador* is a cheap seafood restaurant (c/Lorenzo Morales 2, near the main square); *Restaurante La Pradera* (c/Emilio Castelar) is a ranch-style place, good for barbecued meats; *Mesón La Panocha* (C/Muñoz Delgado, near the seafront) is recommended for *tapas;* and *El Venezuela* is a high-quality if a bit expensive seafood restaurant virtually on the beach.

Much of the town **beach** area, called LO PAGAN, was reconstructed after terrible floods in 1986. Year after year people return to *La Puntica* beach (turn left at the bottom of Emilio Castelar until you reach this side of the "arm") to coat themselves in its **therapeutic mud**, a product of the salt pools behind. It reputedly relieves rheumatism and other such ailments, and is good for the skin. The best beach near here is *Playa de las Llanas*, the other side of the salt-pool area; it's a long way to walk though — from town, go down Emilio Castelar and turn off into Avda. Salinera Española (*puerto* direction).

The next town on the Mar Menor is SANTIAGO DE LA RIBERA, a fancy resort that's popular with *Madrileños*. Felipe, the King's son, is presently based at the *Academia General de Aire* situated here, where future pilots are trained. There's also an important sailing club here, as the calm sea is perfect for novices. The town's **hostales** are only an option out of season. One of the cheapest is *Hostal Muñoz*, quite near the sea (c/Muñoz 5, ☎968/570504); *Hostal don Juan* (Avda. Nuestra Señora de Loreto 2, ☎968/571043), *Hostal K-hito* (c/Maestre 9, ☎968/570002), and *Hostal Trabuco* (Avda. Sandoval ☎968/570051) are close together at the back of the town; or there's *La Obrera Fonda* (c/Zarandona 7, ☎968/570042).

The Cartagena bus stops at San Pedro, Santiago, and Los Alcázares. From San Pedro there's a bus to Cartagena (8 daily, 40 min.), or Murcia (1 hr., 6 daily). There are three **campgrounds** in the area: *Alcázares* (Málaga–Valencia road); *San Javier* (Balsicas road); and *Mar Menor* (Alicante–Cartagena road). From the military airport at San Javier you can get **flights** to Madrid and Barcelona (and in summer there are some *Iberia* flights to London, but they are not cheap charters). The nearest **train station** for this area is BALSICAS (connected with San Pedro and Santiago by bus). A train called the *Costa Cálida* runs direct to here from Barcelona and Madrid in summer.

Continuing down the coast you come to **CARTAGENA**, Murcia's port, which takes its name from the Carthaginians who founded it. Once the most powerful fortress and port in Spain, it's still a major naval base which probably explains why, despite a smattering of interesting ruins and narrow, medieval streets, it's so unpleasant. The one good thing you can say is that there's a lively, if somewhat dangerous, nightlife.

Mazarrón and Águilas

South of Cartagena, just two places on the coast are easily accessible, Mazarrón and Águilas. Very little building has been allowed around the beaches between these two towns, because the area is a breeding ground for tortoises and a species of eagle — for the last decade there have been plans to make it a nature reserve. The few roads that lead down to the better beaches usually end up as tracks. **MAZARRÓN** is really only an option for those with cars, since the resort is ugly and if you stay in the inland village (where there are a few *fondas*) there's no bus to the quieter beaches around. From Cartagena three buses a day make the tortuous 35-minute trip to Mazarrón up and around and down the mountains.

The same bus goes on to **ÁGUILAS**, passing through esparto- covered slopes and fields of tomatoes, one of the few things that can grow in this hot, arid region. Águilas is a better bet all round — though possessing no charm in itself, its beaches are plentiful and reasonably served by public trnaport (see below) Fishing, along with the cultivation of tomatoes, is the mainstay of the economy here, and a fish auction is held at around 5pm every day in the port's large warehouse. **Carnival** is especially wild in Águilas — Franco's prohibition of such festivities was simply ignored here — and for three days and nights the entire population lets its hair down with processions, floats, and general fancy-dress mayhem (see "Fiestas," below).

Hostales tend to be full from mid-July to mid-August. *Hostal Cruz del Sur* is the best to go for, with its seafront position (Levante beach, c/Constitucion 38, ☎968/410171); *Hostal La Aguileña* is in the center at c/Isabel la Catolica 8 (☎968/410303); *Hostal Mar y Sol* is near the station at c/Aire 107 (☎968/410000). These are the cheapest but there are many others in town. There are three **campgrounds**: a new one with a swimming pool, tennis courts, and excellent facilities on Carretera de Cope, at *Urbanizacion "Los Geraneos"*, 4km out of town; one at Calarreona, right on the beach of the same name, 4km out (Carretera Almería); and one at Playa Matalentisco, also on the Almería road, 2km out of town. The **Turismo** has recently moved to Pl. de

Antonio Cortijos, near the port (8:30am–2pm and 6–9pm in summer; 9:30am–1:30pm and 5–7pm rest of year).

The Beaches — and Transportation

It's the **beaches**, essentially, that people come here for. Águilas is now being promoted as a winter resort, as the area's climate gives it better year-round weather than places farther south — it's even different from that of Mazarrón, just up the road. The town itself has two fine beaches but there are about twenty small beaches in the vicinity, with bus service to some. In general, those to the north are rockier and more often backed by low cliffs; to the south they are grittier and more open. The attraction, however, is the lack of development around them — some are totally wild, others have a smattering of villas, others have a bar only. Beaches are cleaned daily from May onwards as a lot of seaweed washes up, and there are plans to make this a year-round operation. **Car rental** is available in Águilas from *Seat* (c/Barcelona 4, ☎968/4101750), for those who want to fully explore all the options.

Heading **north**, get the Calabardina bus (summer only) and ask to be dropped off at *Playa Hornillo*, a nice beach, with a couple of bars nearby. From here it's possible to walk round to *Playa Amarillo*, probably the most secluded and beautiful of the beaches. The same bus can also drop you off for *Playa Arroz*, *La Cola*, or *Calabardina* itself (7km from town) — and if you feel energetic you could walk across Cabo Cope to yet another chain of beaches beginning at Ruinas Torre Cope, but there's really no need to go so far. **South** of Águilas, take the bus marked *Las Lomas*. The beach here is rocky but you can walk to *Playa Matalentisco*, where the shallow areas are ideal for kids. Alternatively, catch the Almería bus (at present 10am, returning 3:30pm) and ask to get off where you want; put your hand out to stop it on the way back anywhere on the main road. The *Las Palomas* beach (known locally as "la Cabana") has the added attraction of a restaurant; beside it is *Calarreona* beach, and then comes *La Higuerica*, 5km from town. Moving south, *Playa Cuatro Calas* has a drinks stand, but no other unnatural presence, and by the time you get to *La Carolina*, on the border of Andalucia, the shore is completely wild.

Trains go from Águilas to Murcia and Lorca, and **buses** run to Almería (daily at 10am), Mazarrón-Cartagena (3 daily), Murcia (7:30am) Lorca (5 daily). One bus a week goes to Madrid and Barcelona. The bus "depot" is the *Bar Peña Aguilena*, Avda. Juan Carlos I, where they also have a selection of good *tapas*. *Cuerva*, by the way, is a local summer drink made of wine, soda, fruit, and rum, a bit like *sangría*.

Inland to Lorca

Many of the historic villages of inland Murcia are accessible only with your own transportation, but one place you can reach easily is **LORCA**, a beautiful former frontier town now slowly being shaken to pieces by the traffic that hammers straight through its center. Yet despite this, and despite its being a busy place, it still has a distinct aura of the past. For a time it was part of the caliphate, but it was retaken by the Christians in 1243, after which Muslim raids were a feature of life until the fall of Granada, the last Muslim strong-hold. Most of the town's notable buildings — churches and ancestral homes - date from the sixteenth century on; many are closed for restoration and some are shut permanently shut.

Around the Town

The place to begin a tour of the town is above c/López Gisbert, at the **Casa de los Guevara**, an example of civic baroque architecture from the end of the seventeenth century and the best mansion in town. The c/Corredera is the main shopping artery; keep an eye out for interesting details on the houses. Near the end on the corner of Pl. San Vicente, and easy to miss, is the **Columna Milinaria**, a Roman column dating from around 10 B.C.: it marked the distance between Lorca and Cartagena on the *Via Heraclea*, the Roman road from the Pyrenees to Cádiz. Go to end of the Corredera and continue in the same general direction until you reach the Gothic **Porche de San Antonio**, the only gate remaining from the old city walls (a **Turismo** leaflet locates the remnants of the walls). Turn back in the direction of the town, go up c/Zapatería, and you'll come out on the Plaza de España, focal point of the town, and seemingly out of proportion with the rest. The impos-ing **Colegio de San Patricio** (10am–1pm and 6–8pm), with its enormous proto-baroque facade, was built between the sixteenth and eighteenth centu-ries — there's a marked contrast between the outside and the sober and refined interior, which is largely Renaissance. Nearby is the *Casa Consistorial*, now the **Ayuntamiento**, with its seventeenth- to eighteenth-century facade, and an equally impressive front is presented by the sixteenth-century **Posito**, down a nearby side street — originally an old grain store-house, it's now the municipal archive.

The **Castle** (13–14th c.) overlooking the town seems an obvious destina-tion but it's a very hot walk and not really worth it, as the two towers of inter-est are open only on November 23. The impoverished *barrio antiguo*, huddled below the castle, can be a little dangerous at night, but it's worth wandering around it in daylight.

Lorca is famed for its **Semana Santa** celebrations which outdo those of Murcia and Cartagena, the next best in the region. There's a distinctly oper-atic splendor about their dramatization of the triumph of Christianity, with characters such as Cleopatra, Julius Caesar, and the royalty of Persia and Babylon attired in embroidered costumes of velvet and silk. The high point is the afternoon and evening of Good Friday.

Practicalities

The **Turismo** is below the Casa de los Guevara on c/López Gisbert (☎968/466157; 9am–2pm and 5:30–8pm in summer; 10am–2pm and 5:30– 8pm in winter). Don't miss the **Centro de Artesanía** next door, displaying work combining traditional crafts with avant-garde design (free admission; 11am–2pm and 5–8pm, Mon. 5–8pm, holidays 11am– 2pm). It really only takes an hour or two to look around Lorca, but it's a good place to stop overnight , with cheap **rooms** all along the highway. Try *del Carmen* (c/Rincón de los

Valientes 3, ☎968/466459), *Casa Juan* (c/Guerra 10, ☎968/468006), *Ciudad del Sol*, (c/Galicia 9, ☎968/467872), or *Genny Regana* (Avda. Fuerzas Armadas 148, ☎968/467033). If you're coming for Holy Week you'll have to reserve at least a month in advance, or stay in Murcia or Águilas. A good place to **eat** is the *Restaurante El Teatro*, Pl. Colon 12 — the square is on same road as the *Turismo*. From Águilas the **train** takes one hour, the **bus** forty minutes. If you're going to Murcia from Lorca, there's both train and bus but the train is cheaper and quicker. Coming to Lorca by train, the station you want is *Lorca Sutullera*.

Caravaca de la Cruz

If for some reason you find yourself stranded in Lorca, a couple of fairly inter-esting towns are not too far away. **CARAVACA DE LA CRUZ**, an important border town, can be reached from Lorca by bus (1 per day, leaving at roughly 2pm) — although it's more easily approached from Murcia (8 buses daily). Again, there is a lot of Renaissance and baroque architecture, several museums, churches, a medieval fortress and, in the castle grounds, an eight-eenth-century temple. Fourteen kilometers on is MORATALLA, spread around the foot of a fortress; its churches are appealing, but the surrounding countryside steals the show.

fiestas

The Valencia area has a particularly power-ful tradition of fiestas and there are a couple of elements that are particular to this part of the country. Above all, throughout the year and more or less wherever you go, there are **mock battles between Moors and Christians**. Recalling the Christian Recon-quest of the country — whether through symbolic processions or recreations of particular battles — they're some of the most elaborate and colorful festivities anywhere. The other recurring feature is the *fallas* (bonfires) in which giant carnival floats and figures are paraded through the streets before being ceremoniously burned.

February

2–5 Moors and Christians battle for the castle in BOCARIENTE (Valencia), with wild firework displays at night.
Carnival (40 days before Easter Week) in ÁGUILAS (Mur.) is one of the wildest in the coun-try after Tenerife and Cádiz.

March

12–19 *The Fallas de San José* in VALENCIA is by far the biggest of the bonfire festivals, and

indeed one of the most important fiestas in all Spain. The whole thing costs as much as 200 million pesetas, most of which goes up in smoke (literally) on the final *Nit de Foc* when the grotesque cardboard and wooden caricatures are burned. These *ninots* may be politicians, movie stars or professional athletes, and anyone else who may be a popular target for satirical treat-ment. Throughout, there are bullfights, music, and stupendous fireworks. The middle of the month, especially around the **19th** (*San José*) also sees smaller *fallas* festivals in JÁTIVA (Val.), in BENIDORM (Alicante), and in DENIA (Alic.).
3rd Sunday of Lent *Fiesta de la Magdalena* in CASTELLÓN DE LA PLANA (Castellón) is marked by major processions and pilgrimages.

April

Holy Week is celebrated everywhere. In ELCHE (Alic.) there are naturally big Palm Sunday cele-brations making use of the local palms, while throughout the week there are also religious processions in CARTAGENA (Mur.), LORCA (Val.), ORIHUELA (Alic.), MONCADA (Val. — with passion plays), and VALENCIA. The **Easter processions** in MURCIA are particularly famous and they continue into the following week with, on the Tuesday, the *Bando de la Huerta*, a huge parade of floats celebrating local agriculture and, on the Saturday evening, the riotous "Burial of the Sardine" which marks the end of these spring festivals.

23 Famous Moors and Christians in ALCOY (Alic.).

25 MORELLA (Cast.) holds the traditional fiesta of *Las Primes*.

May

14 The weekend after this date sees four days of Moors and Christians in PETREL (Alic.).

3rd Sunday Moors and Christians in ALTEA (Alic.).

June

24 *Día de San Juan* Magnificent fallas Festival around this date on the beaches of SAN JUAN DE ALICANTE.

July

Early July *Fiestas de la Santissima Sangre* in DENIA with dancing in the steets, music, and more mock battles.

12–20 Moors and Christians in ORIHUELA (Alic.).

16 In SAN PEDRO DEL PINATAR (Mur.) a maritime *Romeria* in which an image of the Virgin is carried in procession around the Mar Menor.

2nd week *Feria* in VALENCIA with much music and above all fireworks.

25–31 Moors and Christians battle in VILLAJOYOSA (Alic.) by both land and sea.

August

1–15 Local fiesta in SAGUNTO (Val.) and at the same time the great Moors and Christians and a mystery play in ELCHE (Alic.).

15 Local festivities in DENIA (Alic.), JUMILLA (Mur.), and REQUENA (Val.).

September

4–9 Moors and Christians in VILLENA (Alic.).

7–17 *Feria* in ALBACETE.

8 *Mare de Deu de la Salut* — colorful folkloric processions in ALGEMESI (Val.).

10–13 *International Mediterranean Folk Festival* in MURCÍA.

11 Rice festival in SUECA (Val.) includes a national *paella* contest.

22 Fiesta of *Santo Tomás* in BENICASIM (Cast.) with bands and a "blazing bull."

October

Second Sunday BENIDORM celebrates its patron saint's day.

---

travel details

Buses

From Valencia To Alicante (6 daily, 10 in summer; 4 hr.) via Gandía (1¼ hr.), Oliva (1½ hr.), Altea/Benidorm (3 hr./3¼ hr.); Barcelona (7; 6 hr.); Castellón (9; 1½ hr.); Cuenca (3; 4 hr.); Madrid (6; 6 hr.); Murcia (3; 4½ hr.); and Sevilla (1; 12 hr.)

From Alicante To Albacete (2; 2½ hr.); Almería (2; 7 hr.); Barcelona (5; 10 hr.); Cartagena (8; 2 hr.) via Torrevieja (1 hr.) and San Pedro del Pinatar (1¼ hr.); Granada/Malaga (4; 9/12 hr.); Madrid (3; 6 hr.); and Murcia (7; 2 hr.)

From Murcia To Albacete (2; 2½ hr.); and Cartagena (6; 1 hr.)

From Albacete To Madrid (5; 3½ hr.)

Trains

Valencia–Madrid 3 daily in 6–7 hr. via Cuenca (3–4 hr.), 5 in 7 hr. via Albacete (2 hr.).

Valencia–Barcelona 8 daily (5 hr.)

Valencia–Castellón 11 daily (1½ hr.)

Valencia–Zaragoza 3 daily (6 hr.)

Valencia–Alicante 5 daily (2–3 hr.) via Jativa (1 hr.)

Valencia–Játiva 16 daily (1 hr.)

Valencia–Gandía 12 daily (1¼ hr.)

Alicante–Madrid 4 daily (6–10 hr.)

Alicante–Murcia 10 daily ((6–10 hr.)

Murcia–Cartagena 5 daily (1 hr.)

Murcia–Granada 2 daily (8 hr.)

Murcia–Madrid 3 daily (6–8 hr.)

Murcia–Lorca 8 daily (1 hr.)

Murcia–Águilas 4 daily (2 hr.)

Balearic Connections

From Valencia *Trasmediterranea* **sailing**s to Palma, Mallorca (9 hr.) daily except Sunday at 11:30pm; Sunday service in summer; to Ibiza (7 hr.) Tuesday and Thursday at 11:45pm, Saturday and Sunday too in summer. At least 4 **flights** daily to Palma (40 min.), at least 2 to Ibiza (½ hr.)

From Denia *Flebasa/Isnasa* **ferries** to Ibiza Wednesdays and Thursdays at 8am, other days at 4pm (3 hr.; not Tues.). *Ubesa* run connecting buses to/from Valencia and Alicante.

From Alicante At least two **flights** daily to Palma (40 min.) and (summer only) 3 per week to Ibiza (½ hr.)

CHAPTER ELEVEN

THE BALEARIC ISLANDS

The four chief **Balearic islands** — Ibiza, Formentera, Mallorca, and Menorca — maintain a character distinct from the mainland and from each other. **Ibiza**, once again established among Europe's trendiest resorts, is wholly unique, with an intense, outrageous streetlife and a floating summer population that seems to include every club-going Spaniard from Madrid and Barcelona. It can be fun, if this sounds your idea of island activity, and above all if you're gay — Ibiza is a very tolerant place. **Formentera**, small and a little desolate, is something of a beach-annex to Ibiza, though it struggles to present its own alternative image of reclusive artists and "in the know" tourists. **Mallorca**, the largest and best known Balearic, also has battles with its image, popularly reckoned as little more than sun, booze, and beach parties. In reality you'll find all the clichés, most of them crammed into the mega-resorts of the Bay of Palma, but there's certainly much else besides: mountains, lively fishing ports, some beautiful coves, and the Balearics' one real city, **Palma**. This is in fact the one island in the group you might come to for other than beaches and nightlife, with scope to explore, walk, and travel about. And last, to the east, there is windswept **Menorca** — more conservative in its developments, more modest in its clientele and, to be honest, after the others a little dull. Though few people have ever heard of them, there are actually eleven other islets in the group — all uninhabited rocks which can be visited, if at all, only as a daytrip from one of the mainland islands.

Access to the islands is often easiest direct from Britain or northern Europe, with charter **flights** and complete package-deals dropping to absurd prices out of season or with last-minute reservations. From mainland Spain, too, there are charters, though believe it or not these can often cost as much or even more. **Ferries** — from Barcelona, Valencia, Denia (and Marseilles) — are cheaper but still severely overpriced for the distances involved; Denia–Ibiza for example, will set you back some 4000ptas. Likewise, monopolies keep rates high for **inter-island** ferries, and for journeys like Ibiza–Mallorca or even Mallorca–Menorca it can actually be cheaper to fly. The catch here is that, in midseason, flights are often unavailable: the solution is to get up before dawn, head for the airport and get yourself on a waiting list for the first flight of the day — someone always oversleeps. For fuller details on **routes** see the *Travel Details* at the end of this chapter.

Expense and **overdemand** can be crippling in other areas, too. As "holiday islands," each with a buoyant international tourist trade, the Balearics charge considerably above mainland prices for **rooms** — which from mid-June to mid-September are in any case in very short supply. If you go at these times, and you're not into camping, it's good to try and fix up some kind of

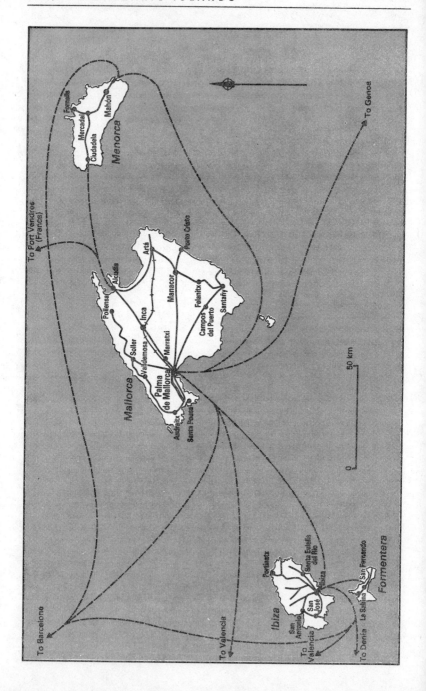

reservation in advance or at least get a bag of small change and phone around before tramping the streets. We've given phone numbers for most of the cheap *hostales* which accept non-agency bookings. Something you may want to do, and which will alleviate accommodation problems to some extent, is to rent transportation: **cars** (also in short supply in season) can be driven off and slept in, **mopeds** will get you and a sleeping bag to some tempting and acceptable spots. Hiring a moped, however, be sure to check your insurance policy: it should definitely include theft (*seguro de robo*) as well as accident. And, in avoiding the latter, dump most of your baggage somewhere before setting out — riding with a pack is both exhausting and dangerous.

As elsewhere, the Balearics have revived their own **dialects** over the last few years. Throughout the islands a dialect of Catalan is spoken, a result of their having been conquered by the Catalan-Aragonese confederation in the thirteenth century. Each of the three main islands have a different sub-dialect, and many inhabitants object to their language being called Catalan at all. On maps especially the dialects can be an enduring source of confusion: Xs are everywhere, TJs replace Ys, SAs LAs. Some words are different entirely. Menorca now calls its capital *Maó* rather than Mahón, while both the island and town of Ibiza are often referred to as *Eivissa*. In speech, though, Castilian Spanish is dominant, and for once in Spain you'll find no shortage of people either with perfect English or French.

IBIZA

IBIZA (*EIVISSA*) is an island of excess. Beautiful, dotted with scores of barely accessible cove beaches that are uncrowded even in high summer, it's nevertheless the islanders and their visitors who make it special. However outrageous you may want to be (and outrageousness is the norm) the locals have seen it all before. By day the thousands of tourists spread themselves, Coppertone-smeared, across the nudist beaches, preparing themselves for the nightly flounce through the bars and clubs.

For years it was *the* European hippie escape, but nowadays the island is as popular with modern youth and sociable gays as it is with its 1960s denizens (who keep coming back). Germans, squeezed into their *lederhosen*, rub bottoms with the trimmest of international designer labels in a remarkably relaxed meeting of the hippie and the hip, and you'll find the latest London, Paris, Madrid, and Milan fashions in the shops here, often before they've been seen at home. There's no need for an excuse to dress up — in fact if you don't it'll be *you* who gets stared at in the evening. **Ibiza town**, in particular, lives glamorously, especially at night; an endless "fashion parade" is watched with benign amusement by the long-inured locals.

This, the capital, is the obvious place to base yourself: only a short bus ride from two great beaches — **Las Salinas** and **Es Cabellet** — and crammed with shops, restaurants, bars, and discos to fill up the nights. Nowhere else can compare, especially the second city, **San Antonio Abad**, which is a highly avoidable package-resort nightmares. **Santa Eulalia**, the only other real town, retains a certain charm in its hilltop church looking down over the

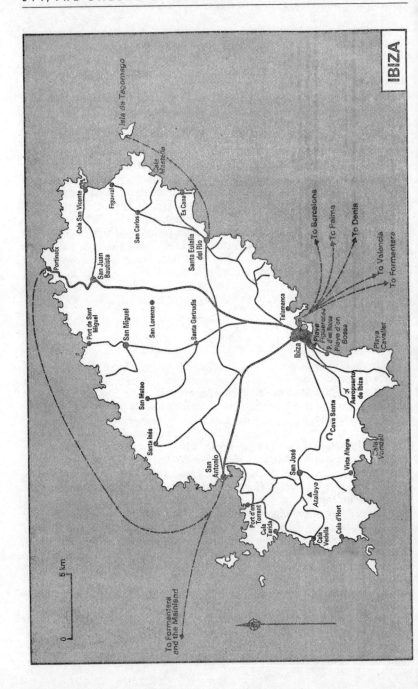

sprawling old town and modern seafront, while close by the persistent can find a number of relatively empty beaches. The same holds true for most of the rest of the coast — plenty of golden sands but a good deal of effort required to reach them. The one major exception is the northern bay of **Portinatx**, connected by a relatively major road and, despite hotel development, with a number of clean, not overly populated beaches. **Inland** there's little of anything — a few villages and vacation homes that are exceedingly pretty to drive through but offer little if you stop. It's a terrain that is alternately productive and scrubland, peppered with small lakes for salt production.

Even before the flower children made Ibiza their vacation home, white powder had put the island on the map. Salt attracted the Greeks and after them the Phoenicians and **Carthaginians** to the island as a regular stop on their Mediterranean cruises; to such an extent, indeed, that Ibiza remains one of the world's most important reliquaries of Punic remains, with hundreds of burials so far uncovered. Under Roman rule it continued to prosper until dropping into the familiar pattern of Spanish history, occupied successively by Goths and Moors before being liberated by the Aragonese early in the thirteenth century. Thereafter decline set in, and despite occasional imperialist ambitions Ibiza was effectively an abandoned and impoverished backwater until the middle of this century,when it began to acquire status as the most chic of the Balearics.

Getting Around the Island

There is good **bus service** between Ibiza Town, San Antonio Abad, Santa Eulalia, Portinatx, and a few of the larger beaches, but renting some form of **vehicle** will widen your options no end (though be warned that the traffic cops delight in using their wheel clamps). It should prove particularly useful on Ibiza for finding **accommodation** — as difficult here as on any of the other islands and even more expensive. You may well be reduced to one of the **campgrounds**. Only one of these (*Camping d'en Bossa* on the road to Playa d'en Bossa, expensive) is at all near the capital; others include three near Santa Eulalia, *Payes*, on Portinatx bay, and among the crowds at *San Antonio* (right in San Antonio Abad) or *Cala Bassa* (on Cala Bassa beach).

Ibiza Town

In physical terms as well as in its atmosphere and adventure, **IBIZA TOWN** is the most attractive place on the island. Most people stay in rented apartments or small pensions which means fewer hotels to ruin the skyline and no package incursions. Approach by sea and you'll get the full frontal effect of the old town's walls rising as if in natural extension of the rocky cliffs which protect the port. Within the walls, the ancient quarter is topped by a sturdy cathedral, whose illuminated clock shines out across the harbor throughout the night.

Daylight hours are usually spent on the beaches at Las Salinas/Es Cabellet or the nearer (but not so nice) Figueretas. At night, before the discos open their doors, the shops stay open until 11pm to provide entertaining window shopping on the way to supper — on c/Mayor you'll find booths six nights a week selling everything from earrings and accessories through naif paintings to the tackiest of souvenirs. Afterwards the groove goes on till dawn, with the last port of call being the *Space* disco, which opens its doors at 6am. As a break from the exhaustive stress of sunbathing and the simple pleasures of wandering the streets, there are two good archaeological museums, and a fancy modern art gallery with prices that will certainly amaze you even if the displays don't.

Arriving and Settling In

The capital is a simple enough place to find your way around. From the **ferry terminal** (*Estación Marítima* — 4 to 7 weekly boats to Barcelona, 6 a week to Denia, 2 to 4 to Valencia, 2 to Palma, Mallorca) the old streets of the *Sa Peña* quarter lead straight ahead towards the walls of the ancient city (*D' Alt Vila*). A waterfront walk will take you from here — past bars and restaurants which at night give front-row viewing for the fashion display — around to the harbor wall from where the entire bay can be surveyed. Continue on past the port and you'll be in the new town, below the old to the west.

If you fly in you'll arrive at the **airport** about 6km out. There's an hourly bus (7am–10:30pm, leaving town on the hour, returning on the half-hour), or you can take a taxi for around 800ptas. In the airport there's an efficient **Turismo** (8am–1pm and 3–8pm) which can provide maps and lists of accommodation as well as details on vehicle rental. Several car rental firms have desks in the lounge, too, and there's a hotel reservation desk (for expensive places) open from 8am to 11pm.

The principal **Turismo**, at Vara de Rey 13 by the *Iberia* office, can offer more extensive lists of **hotels and hostales** for the whole island as well as details of apartments for stays of a week or more — not cheap, but abundant and usually pleasant. If you're confident with Spanish telephones it's obviously easier to phone around, but fortunately the town is small and compact enough to make finding a place on foot perfectly feasible. Most of the cheaper places are in any case in the area around the tourist office (rather than in D' Alt Vila). Even if you stay in Talamanca, though, or on the other side of the port in Figueretas, you're not that far removed from the action. Among the better value options reasonably near the center are: *Hostal Muñoz*, Avda. Bartolomeu Vicente Ramón 3; *Hostal Marina*, c/Virgen; *Hostal Juanita*, c/Juan de Austria 17 (☎971/301910); *Hostal Vara de Rey*, Vara de Rey 7 (☎971/301376); *Hostal Sol Paris*, c/Vicente Cuervo 8 (☎971/301000); and the *Hostal Costa* in Barrio Escandell (☎971/302833). Right at the heart of things on c/Mayor, *Bar Mariano* also has a few rooms for rent.

D' Alt Vila

Traffic enters the walled citadel through the **Portal de las Tablas** and leaves by the **Portal Nou**. The main gate — Tablas — leads into the great space of the **Plaza Desamparados** which is packed with restaurants and bars, as is the length of the path towards the top of the town. The **Museo de Arte**

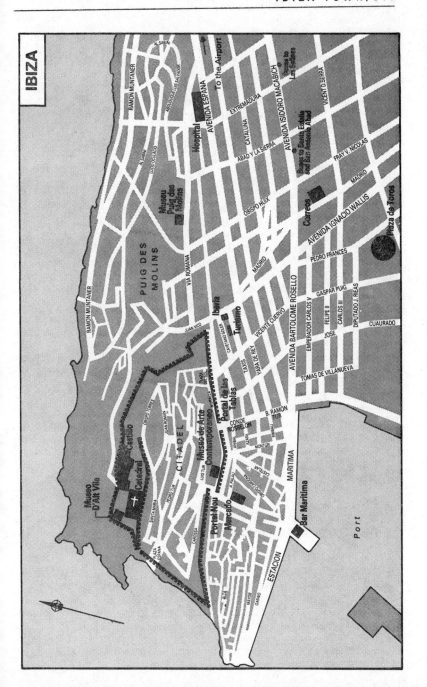

IBIZA

RAMON MUNTANER
AL SABINI
SANTOS LLUIS SALVADOR
To the Airport
AVENIDA ESPANA
Hospital
EXTREMADURA
CATALUÑA
ABAD Y LA SIERRA
AVENIDA ISIDORO MACABICH
Buses to Sant Eulalia and San Antonio Abad
Buses to Las Salinas
VICENT D.SERRA
FRAY V. NICOLAS
MADRID
Museu Puig des Molins
OBISPO HUIX
MADRID
Correos
PUIG DES MOLINS
VIA ROMANA
AVENIDA IGNACIO WALLIS
Plaza de Toros
RAMON MUNTANER
PEDRO FRANCES
JUAN XICO
Ibiza
Turismo
CAETANO SOLER
AVENIDA BARTOLOME ROSELLO
GASPAR PUIG
EMPERADOR CARLOS V
FELIPE II
CARLOS III
DIPUTADO J. RIEAS
CUAURADO
VICENTE CUERVO
YARA DE REY
JOSE
TAXIS
OBISPO TORRES
Portal de les Tablas
CONDE ROSSELLON
B. RAMON FAJRI
TOMAS DE VILLANUEVA
JUAN ROMAN
ANIBAL
CITADEL
Museo de Arte Contemporaneo
AZAR
MONTGRI
Castillo
LUIS TUR
Catedral
SANTA FAZ
Museo D'Alt Vila
MARITIMA
Portal Nou
ESTACION
Bar Maritima
Mercado
CAROSA
Port
PLAZA ESPANA
ALET
MATXE
GARINO
ESTACION

Contemporaneo is here as well, above the arch of the Portal de las Tablas. Open from 10:30am to 1pm and from 6 to 8:30pm (admission 100ptas), it holds bimonthly exhibitions of contemporary artists from around the world. Most of the art is for sale, but prices start at around $80.

Heading upwards along the main street, Sa Carossa (still shown on some maps as the Avenida Generalissimo Franco), you'll find some of the better restaurants, easy access to the top of the walls (*murallas*), and some great views down over the town. In the **Plaza de España**, the sixteenth-century church of San Domingo — with added baroque facade — stands next to its former monastery, converted in 1838 into the *Ayuntamiento*. Across the road a long dark tunnel leads through the walls to a severe cliff walk which eventually takes you to a beachfront bar in the *Molinos* area, while another break in the walls a little higher up will take you towards the cathedral square.

Dedicated to Santa María la Mayor, the **Catedral** is hardly more interesting than any of the other island churches (open 10am–1pm and 4–6:30pm; closed Sat. pm). Its whitewashed interior is picked out in burnt red vertical stripes and there are a few small murals on the walls of the single nave. A plaque commemorates the massacre of churchmen, soldiers, and ordinary Ibizeños at the hands of "marxists" during the civil war. The **museum**, however, is considerably better value than most, especially in its display of luxuriant bishops' regalia: — miters, sandals, gloves, cloaks, and some nifty red-and-white velvet slippers which were obviously of great comfort to ecclesiastical feet on the stone floors. Pictures of past incumbents line the walls, along with a depiction of the Christian reconquest of the island.

Across the square and down some steps is the **Museo D'Alt Vila** (10am–1pm) with a collection of local archeology. The majority of the objects on display are from Phoenician and Carthaginian (Punic) sites, since that's where most of the digs have been concentrated, but there are also some bones from Formentera that date back to 1600 B.C., and various Arab and Roman curiosities. The same ticket covers the **Puig des Molins Museu** (4–7pm) outside the walls, where the many finds from the necropolis are housed. Among the objects discovered in graves are some splendidly decorated terracotta pieces, clay figurines, amphoras, and amulets depicting Egyptian gods. So many funerary sites have been found on Ibiza that for a long time it was assumed that it was some kind of burial island, and although this theory is no longer accepted the finds remain impressive.

One step farther up the hill are the ruins of the thirteenth-century castle, but little remains to be seen apart from the view.

Outside the Walls

Not quite as grand, nor as ancient, the **Sa Peña** quarter snuggles between the harbor and the ramparts, a maze of raked passages and narrow streets, of balconied whitewashed houses virtually constructed on top of one another. Here, especially along the waterfront promenade, the evening *paseo* reaches its peak and everyone — local and visitor alike — gravitates towards the bars and restaurants. Ibizan characters dress up to roam the streets or decorate the clubs and are generally appreciative of enthusiastic support, while the c/ Mayor, above all, is lively until well after midnight. This is where many of the shops are too, occupying almost every doorway that isn't a bar. *The End* is the first stop and the last word in fashion.

For a stroll after supper, head along the waterfront to observe the antics outside the *200* bar and admire the menus and price lists at the flashier restaurants that line the water's edge. *Mariano's* on the corner of c/Mayor may not look like much but its sidewalk seating offers front-row viewing of the parade.

The **new town** is generally of less interest, but there's activity here too, centered on the Paseo Varo del Rey. At dusk the air is filled with birds swooping in and out of the trees which line the pedestrian square, and the *cafe/hostal Montesol* becomes a popular meeting place. The *Bar Maresol* on the opposite corner, towards the waterfront, is another ideal vantage point from which to enjoy the nightly show, but it isn't terribly friendly. Worth seeing, too, if only as a curiosity, is the church of **El Salvador** in Plaza Canalejas: its modern interior boasts a huge pine Christ, looking like Roger Moore in discreet sauna wrap and 1965-vintage haircut.

Nightlife, Eating, and Drinking

Ibiza's bars and discos keep the place alive 24 hours a day; with money and mobility the night is yours, and there's a lot of it. The bulk of the **bars** in which to begin your preparations for a night out are in the aforementioned area around the port and c/Mayor. There are a few **gay bars** here too (*Bobby's, Teatro, JJ's*, and *Movie*) but the most crowded ones are found up by the city walls — *Incognito's* and *Angelo's* are neighbors nestling by the Portal de las Tablas. This is a good area to hang out in any case, with loads of basic stand-up drinking places. Just inside the D'Alt Vila you can watch in rather more style from the patio of *La Muralla*, with tables looking out over the walls.

For the **trendy set** the gathering point is below this, either *Lola's*, Ibiza's first disco in the 1960s but now very much the 1980s pre-club meeting place, or *The Tube*, which has the more colorful crowd. As for **discos**, even if you haven't heard of *Ku, Amnesia*, and *Pacha*, you'll certainly be made aware of them during your wanderings around the port in the evening. Each employs teams of PR artistes who descend on the town in a whirl of enthusiasm to drum up business for their respective establishments. Competition is fierce and you emerge from their assault like a piece of well-spattered fly paper, covered in sticky paper badges promoting the discos. None of them really get going much before midnight, and the dancing goes on until dawn.

Ku — for the moment at least — represents the ultimate. It may not be the most expensive (though 2000ptas admission isn't cheap) but it is the one constantly referred to as epitomizing Ibizan nightlife. The bars and dance floor surround an outdoor swimming pool, there are theme "fiestas" at least twice a week, and a great deal of effort has been put in to create an atmosphere of chic elitism. It's a reputation gained as much for the clientele as for the music, and there are people here whose sole reason for coming to Ibiza seems to be to get to *Ku*. You'll find it 6km out on the road to San Antonio. **Amnesia**, a little closer in the same direction, mixes the best of the *Ku* and

Pacha crowds, and often throws some pretty good parties. This is the one to head for at 3am after a visit to the others and before a final session at *Space* (Playa d'en Bossa). *Pacha* is around the bay near the Casino, and although its publicity rivals that of *Ku*, it is definitely tamer in everything except price (an outrageous 2500ptas). Nearby there's the other possibility, more moderate in every respect, of *Angel's*. There's just one exclusively **gay disco** in town — *Anfora* in the upper part of the D'Alt Vila, a walk away from the popular *Crisco* leather bar.

Before, during, or after all this excitement you're going to need some **food** to sustain you, and the Sa Peña quarter is again the place to head for reasonable prices. One of the best bets for simple dishes of good, fresh food is a nameless, smoky, fluorescent-lit restaurant at c/Cruz 17; along the road on the corner at no. 1, *La Victoria* is another popular and long-established eatery whose *señora* is adept at cursing over-demanding diners through a fixed smile. *Los Pasajeros* is perhaps the trendiest place to dine, with a limited menu and more people-watching than eating going on. It's on the first floor in c/Vicente Soller, an unmarked street connecting c/Mayor with the waterfront — ask for the restaurant by name.

Down by the waterfront, or up in the walled town, you'll be paying a lot more, but there are several extremely classy restaurants in **D'Alt Vila**. *El Portalón* and *D'Alt Vila* both have four-fork ratings (with menus and prices to match) but nearby *El Mesón* also serves very good food for much more realistic prices. *Sam's Hamburger Bar* by the **port** seems popular among the less adventurous (and passing U.S. Marines), while *San Juan* (c/Montgri 8) is cheap but surly.

A couple of good restaurants are to be found just outside town: *Las 2 Lunas* (next door to *Amnesia*), and *Casa Juana* (en route to San José).

You'll find all sorts of other possibilities, and in particular loads of **pizzerias**; unfortunately almost all of these seem to rely heavily on microwave ovens whose timer controls they have yet to master. You can get **early breakfast** in Paseo Vara de Rey, next to *Montesol*, or at the new Estación Maritima, on the west side of the harbor.

If you plan to do it yourself, or want to gather ingredients for a picnic, the covered **market** at the bottom of the ramp into the Portal de las Tablas is not bad, if not quite a match for the market in the new town between Avenidas España and Isidoro Macabich. Be warned, though, that prices are double what they would be in a mainland market and that the selection is not all that great.

Getting Out and About

Although there are buses on Ibiza, things are very much easier and more interesting if you rent your own form of transportation. A **moped** or Vespa is as good a way of seeing the island as any, and considerably cheaper than a car — places which rent them include: *Extra Bikes* (c/Ignacio Wallis and in Figueretas; ☎971/302125); *Moto Rent* (Avda. Bartolome Rosello); *Motos Ribas* (c/Vicente Cuervo 8), and *Motos Valentin* (Avda. Vicente Ramos 19). The tourist office has more extensive lists for both car and bike rental, though some of their information is out of date.

The main **bus routes**, departing from Avda. Isidoro Macabich, are as follows:

San Antonio Abad every half hour;

Santa Eulalia del Rio every half hour;

Portinatx 2 to 5 services daily;

Las Salinas every hour;

San Juan, Cala San Vicente, Playa d'en Bossa, Figueretas and **San Miguel** also have several daily departures each.

Around the Island

South from Ibiza Town: The Beaches

The closest sea and sand to Ibiza town are at **FIGUERETAS**, a built-up continuation of the capital concentrated around a small and rather overexploited bay. Though handy, this and neighboring PLAYA D'EN BOSSA are probably best left to those who end up staying here (e.g., at the expensive *Camping d'en Bossa*). If you're on the move anyway, keep on going to **Las Salinas**. Here, stretching from the airport to the sea, are thousands of acres of **salt flats**. Ibiza's history, and its powerful presence on ancient trade routes, was based on these salt fields (*salinas*), a trade vital, above all, to the ancient Carthaginians. Until comparatively recently it was an important economic resource; the island's only railroad ran from the middle of the marshes to LA CANAL, a dock where an enormous container ship would arrive weekly to be loaded with the bright, white sea salt. Even now, though tourism brings in far more money and the railroad has been torn up, salt production continues.

From where the bus stops you can choose between the beaches of Las Salinas itself and, on the other side of the dunes, **ES CABELLET** (*PLAYA CAVALLET*). Although Es Cabellet is the official nudist beach, full frontal tanning is just as common on **LAS SALINAS**. The atmosphere sums up the attitude of vacationers' Ibiza: there is no tension or ill-feeling at all between the many social groupings, with matronly family gatherings sitting quite happily amid the undressed clones. Both beaches have a couple of *chiringuitos* (beach bars), the farthest of which on Las Salinas offers ultra-modern sounds. At the beginning of Es Cabellet there's even a massage table.

North to Santa Eulalia

Heading north from Ibiza town the roads to Portinatx and the coastal route to Santa Eulalia diverge at the small crossroads of JESÚS. There are a couple of excellent bars here: the *Bar Casablanca* which serves a cheap *menú del día*, and the *Bar Bon Lloch* with a marvelous array of *tapas*. Follow the coast road towards Santa Eulalia and you'll pass an uninspired development area at **CALA LLONGA**. A small sandy beach saddled with package hotels, it's to be avoided unless you're looking for a **campground**; the one here at least is in pleasant surroundings, with a pool, about 500m from the sea. For a swim en route the PLAYA SOL D'EN SERRA, a one-bar cove just before you reach Cala Llonga, is far more attractive.

The town of **SANTA EULALIA DEL RÍO** has at least a modicum of interest — it is situated on the only river in the Balearics and has, nearby, the dwarfed remains of the island's only Roman aqueduct (a tiny wall which takes some finding, by the *Hotel S'Argamassa*). The hilltop church, approached up a slope lined with the Stations of the Cross, is whitewashed and bare except for a garish, glass-encased Christ — typical, in other words. The Museu Barcau by the church seems permanently closed (also typical). Down by the sea you'll find a modern seafront promenade (with information office and *Telefónica*) designed for strolling with no particular purpose, and a clutch of restaurants which are renowned on the island for their abundance and quality. *El Naranjo* (c/San José 31) has a lovely patio full of orange trees; for livelier action you could try the *Harlequin* or *Mozart* bars, or *Studio 64* disco. There's a daily boat from here to FORMENTERA.

Just north of Santa Eulalia the beach at **S'ARGAMASSA** is notorious for its yahoo package tourists, who spend their sober hours waterskiing around the bay or windsurfing — both can be easily arranged. There's a very pleasant **campground** (*Florida*) at PUNTA ARABI, the end of the bay, which also rents cabins — they're quite cheap if you can fill all six beds. **ES CANA**, beyond the point, has a sailing club and boats back to Santa Eulalia or across to Formentera. There's a long-established "hippie market" here, too.

Continuing to the north you'll find another **campground** at PLAYA CALA NOVA: it's slightly more expensive and wins no prizes for beauty, but the amenities are good and it's close to a fine sandy beach. If you've got the wheels, and the patience, CALA LENA, another 2km along the coast, offers a pretty, small, sandy beach with a bar and only private apartments nearby. **CALA MASTELLA**, the next bay, is still more secluded and still harder to get to, but it does offer a bar with food cooked over a wood fire.

Inland, a road heads from Santa Eulalia to Figueral via SAN CARLOS, a one-horse town where Es Cana hippies congregate to socialize. **FIGUERAL** itself consists almost entirely of a vacation complex known as *Club Figueral*, with a supermarket, disco, and phone booth to serve the crowds of apartments. Its beach — just a short walk from this development and the vacation villas — is always busy, with a windsurfing school that runs well-supervised classes. If you want to stay there are a couple of reasonably- priced choices — *Es Alocs* right on the beach or the *Fonda Figueral*. Out in the bay, seen from the road at the top of the cliffs, is the uninhabited island of TAGOMAGO.

Finally in this direction, and around the edge of the same large bay, lies **CALA SAN VICENTE**, which would be exceptionally pretty were it not for gross overcrowding resulting from five large hotels serving the English package-tour market and an ugly hillside *urbanización*. As things stand it's best avoided — the bars and restaurants, despite their quantity, are expensive.

San Miguel and Portinatx

Cutting straight across the island towards its north coast, the road branches about 6km out of Ibiza town, with the right fork heading for Portinatx, the left to San Miguel. Either way you'll pass through some of the island's finest countryside, burnt-red fields of olive, almond, and carob trees, and occasionally a plantation of melons or vines.

On the way to San Miguel the road forks again at SANTA GERTRUDIS; bearing left will take you to San Mateo and eventually around to San Antonio Abad. Santa Gertrudis itself is little more than a village square with a church (of the usual whitewashed variety), a small antique shop and kitchen gardens all around.

At **SAN MIGUEL**, on top of a low hill, there are two artists' studios (worth at least a quick visit) in the square beside the church. There's folk dancing here, too, every Thursday evening at 6pm. The old **port** is a few kilometers beyond — once an attractive small bay, now rather spoilt by the scourges of development. The *Hotel Hacienda* (very de luxe and very expensive) is perched spectacularly above here, up a private road to the west; it's a favorite of holidaying sheiks and honeymooning couples, and has one of the island's best restaurants to boot. There's waterskiing and motorboat rental around the bay, and you can visit the recently opened caves with some spectacular lighting effects and an artifical waterfall cascading over fossil-rich rocks. More adventurous souls might attempt to follow the trail over the hills to **CALA BENIRRAS**, which saves a tedious and even more uncomfortable journey by the signposted road. You'll need to ask the way regularly, but note that the road surface is just beginning to be improved, which no doubt means that the so far magnificently unspoiled cove will soon be overtaken by the tourist juggernaut. At present there are just two bars and a beach where you can rent pedal-boats and other small craft. Catch it while you can.

Portinatx is approached, in a final twisting stretch of road, through a beautiful, fertile valley lined with olive-terraced hills and orderly groves of almond and pine. After rain, in particular, there's a distinctive brightness to the air here and a delightful burgundy glow in the soil. At **CALA XARRACA** you emerge above the sea, with a path leading down to a tiny sandy beach, sparklingly clear water, rocks to dive off, and a lone bar. **CALA XULA**, next along, is in much the same mold, reached by an even steeper track. The **campground** (*Camping Payes*) is less than ten minutes' walk from here or (in the other direction) from Portinatx; you can rent tents, it's cheap and friendly, and it's open all year.

PORTINATX is nowadays purely a vacation resort. Once you've walked the length of its three beaches, tried the harbor sports, and purchased your quota from the souvenir shops there is little left to do. The beaches — Big Beach, Little Beach, and Es Port Beach — have to serve several medium-sized hotels and there's barely room to squeeze a towel in between the sunbeds, all rotated hourly to follow the path of the sun. In the port area you'll usually find a couple of elegant yachts anchored offshore, and climbing up beyond the *Holiday Club* chalets to the old watchtower (one of very few which survive intact and accessible) there's a great view down across the town and its bay and back into the hills. A constant symphony of cicadas buzz their appreciation of the panorama.

If you're looking for a **room**, and the hotels are all agency-booked to capacity (as they probably will be), try the *Hostal Portinatx* (☎971/333064) or the *Hostal Ciguena* (☎971/333105). **Bike rental** is available from *Moto Rent* at the *Bar Mesón Granada* or at the campground.

San Antonio Abad and Around

SAN ANTONIO ABAD is seriously out of place on Ibiza. Its total lack of charm, allure, or style would make it more at home among the worst excesses of Majorca. This is where you'll find the *Club 18-30* patrons practicing their projectile vomiting from fifth-floor balconies and letting it all hang out at beach party orgies. Restaurants along the quay dish up sausage, chips, and beans.

There are several daily **boat journeys** across the bay to the beaches of CALA BASSA and its high-rise hotels; glass-bottomed boat tours of the harbor; and, twice weekly, a complete circuit of the island by boat, calling in at the "hippy market" (now a historical curiosity) at Es Cana. You can also sail round to Portinatx, or across to Formentera or the mainland (6 sailings weekly).

The **Turismo** is at present in the *Ayuntamiento*, though it's shortly to move to new offices down by the harbor; they can provide information on **places to stay**. Probably the best place to look is around c/Soledad and c/Prim, but watch out for tour-company stickers which mean crowds and inflated prices. Reasonable options include *Hostal Tunis* (c/Prim 9), *Hostal Cisne* (Vara de Rey 13, ☎971/340093), *Flores* (Rosello 26, ☎971/341129), and *Horizonte* (Progreso 62, ☎971/340333). **Eating** is no problem, but on the whole food here is either dull or expensive: try *Rías Baixas* in c/Ignacio Riquer, *Grill San Antonio* in c/Obispo Torres, or *Sa Clau* in c/Balanzat, all of which are better than average. **Nightlife** consists of a string of discos with such thrillingly original names as *Playboy, Manhattan, San Francisco*, or the *Idea Club* and music to match. **Bike rental** outlets include *Moto Reco* (c/Ramón y Cajal, ☎971/341355), and on Avda. Dr. Fleming *Moto Rubio* and *Moto Augustín*. If you just want out, **buses** leave for Ibiza town every half hour, four times daily to Santa Eulalia, and frequently along local routes to Cala Conta and Port d'es Turrent.

Heading away from San Antonio you'll find more promising beaches, and fewer people, in just about any direction. Some 4km to the north lies the small beach of CALA SALADA, easily accessible if you've got a vehicle, with fewer crowds, and beach hammocks and windsurfers for rent. Nearby PUNTA GALERA looks promising, but the *urbanización* here is determined to maintain its privacy, and the small beach really doesn't merit the effort of getting past the barricaded gate. Farther north, and inland, the **Chapel of Santa Inés** is the last point of any interest. Much touted by the tourist office, it's a subterranean gallery (Wed. and Sat. only, 10am–1:30pm) in which local Christians worshiped secretly during the Moorish occupation.

Beyond the boat trip destinations to the south there are some excellent beaches, too. CALA BASSA is packed, but it does have a well-equipped **campground**.

Cala d'Hort, Es Cabells, and Cala Yondal

Much more promising is the way to CALA D'HORT, a dull drive in itself, but ending at a lovely quiet beach, one of the island's best seafood restaurants

(*Es Boldano*), and a view of *Es Vedra*, a canine tooth of rock stabbing through the bay just offshore. Ibiza's highest peak, it starred in the film of *South Pacific* as the mysterious island of Bali Hai. The sea looks dirty, but it's natural muck and perfectly safe and pleasant to swim in.

Heading back towards Ibiza town by the southern route, it's possible to cut down from SAN JOSÉ to the coast at ES CABELLS and VISTA ALEGRE. The road that links the two is an engineering marvel, sliced out of the cliff edge, but it's not enough to make the journey worthwhile — there are no beaches to speak of and a couple of remarkably unattractive developments, with further building clearly planned. You're better off heading on towards the capital where the Covas Santa (Holy Caves — 9am–1:30pm and 3–7pm), with some impressive drippy stalactites seventeen meters underground, lie just off the main road. Follow the trail south of the caves and you'll get to CALA YONDAL. Fields of tempting melons and grapes greet your arrival and you can get delicious seafood at the bar, but the beach itself, despite its popularity with the islanders and lizards, is pebbly and uncomfortable. The trip's worth doing once, maybe, but you're unlikely to want to return to disturb the peace.

FORMENTERA

Just three nautical miles south of Ibiza, FORMENTERA is the smallest of the inhabited Balearics (population 4000). The crossing is short, but strong currents ensure that it's slow — over an hour — and rough: keep the seasickness pills handy. Sailing from Ibiza town (round-trip fare is about 1000ptas) you'll get a stupendous view of the citadel astride its cliff and, beyond, you'll pass Isla Ahorcados — "Hanged Men's Island,", once the last stop for Ibiza's criminals — and the sand-fringed Isla Espalmador.

The island's history more or less parallels Ibiza's, though for nearly 300 years — from the early fifteenth century to the end of the seventeenth century — it was left uninhabited for lack of water and fear of Turkish pirate raids. Under the Romans it had been a major agricultural center (its name derives from *frumentaria*, "granary") and when repopulated in 1697 the island was again divided up for cultivation. It never regained its original level of productivity, though, and nowadays is thoroughly barren, the few crops having to be protected, as on Menorca, against the lashing of winter winds. Most of the island is now covered in rosemary, growing wild everywhere, and crawling with thousands of brilliant green lizards.

Modern income is derived from tourism (especially German and British), taking advantage of some of Spain's longest, whitest, and least-crowded beaches. The shortage of fresh water, fortunately, continues to keep away the crowds — there's nowhere for them to stay — and for the most part visitors are seeking escape with little in the way of sophistication. It is however, becoming increasingly popular, and is certainly not the "paradise" it once was. Nude sunbathing is tolerated — indeed the norm — just about everywhere.

La Sabina and San Francisco Javier

Boats from the various Ibiza ports head for the tiny functional harbour of **LA SABINA** where the two waterfront streets are lined with places offering cars, mopeds, or bicycles for rent, interspersed with the odd bar and cafe. This is the place to get yourself mobile, but if possible phone ahead to reserve, certainly if you want a car (try *MotoRent*, ☎971/320278, or *Autos Formentera*, ☎971/320156); mopeds are much cheaper and easier to get. Hemming the town in are two lagoons: the **Estang del Peix**, once used for fish-farming but now devoted to water sports, and the aptly-named **Estang Pudent** (Stinking Pond). Neither offers much incentive to hang around.

The capital, **SAN FRANCISCO JAVIER**, is just a couple of kilometers away, easily reached on foot or by local bus if you're not planning to rent a vehicle. From here, the island's roads and tracks fan out. As well as the white-washed, fortified church — now stripped of its defensive cannon — this metropolis has at least three banks, four bars, a hotel, supermarkets, a pharmacist, a doctor, and a *Telefónica* for international calls. There is also a **Turismo** in the Casa Consistorial, opposite the church, which can supply you with a useless souvenir leaflet about the island, an open-air market adds at least a touch of interest.

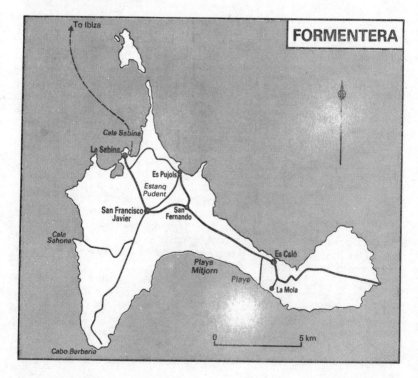

Around the Island

Formentera's main road continues from San Francisco to the island's eastern-most point at La Mola. Along it, or just off it, are concentrated almost all of the island's habitation and most of the beaches. The island's next largest town, SAN FERNANDO — with a bar, a church, and a *hostal* or two — serves the beach of **ES PUJOLS** where Formentera's package-tour industry, such as it is, concentrates (the town itself totally lacks character). Despite relative crowding, it's a beautiful coast with clear water and pure white sand dunes backed by low stands of pine. Windsurfing is taught here in German and Spanish. Northwest, on the **Es Trucadors** peninsula, are the PLAYA DE SES ILLETAS (on the west) and the nudist PLAYA DE LLEVANT (on the east). This is a beautiful spot.

Continuing east, the caves at D'EN XERONI are less than a kilometer outside San Fernando; hang around in the bar by the entrance and there'll be a guided tour as soon as a few people have turned up (the guide doesn't speak English, but the bartender does). The caves were discovered quite by accident in 1975. **PLAYA MITJORN**, on the south side of this narrow stretch of the island, is an enormous stretch of sand broken only by the occasional bar or hotel. Formentera's strict regulations on new building means that this area will remain relatively undeveloped: rather soulless, but definitely the place to head for total isolation, and the main area for nude sunbathing. There are beaches all along, though, and the entire road stretches less than twenty kilometers from one side of the island to the other. At **ES CALO** there are several *hostales*, somewhat incongruously located in a tiny harbor that seems more adapted to its fishing activities, and beyond, the island canti-levers up in a great wedge of rock. At this eastern extremity, and the island's highest point, stands the lighthouse of LA MOLA (which features in Jules Verne's *Journey Round the Solar System*) — with views right across to Mallorca — and in the cool mountain pines around there's about a long-established, and now thoroughly assimilated, settlement of hippies.

To the south of the capital a second track, in thoroughly bad condition, leads towards the lighthouse on CABO BERBERIA. It's an arduous trek and barely merits the effort, but **CALA SAHONA**, a short way down and then off to the right, certainly does. A beautiful cove, among the best on the island, this is a popular place for passing pleasure craft to drop anchor for a while; unfortunately an enormous ugly hotel rather ruins it. There are also a couple of bars, a small restaurant in the sand dunes, and an intriguingly well-guarded private villa not far from the beach.

Practicalities

Most people treat Formentera as a day trip from Ibiza, and if you want to be one of the few who stay you may have difficulty finding anywhere not given over entirely to agency reservations. Among the better possibilities are: *Hostal La Sabina*, just outside La Sabina (☎971/320094); *Casa Rafael*, in San Francisco Javier near the church (☎971/320227); *Hostal Pepe* (☎971/320033) in San Fernando; *Hostal Bar Los Rosales* (☎971/320123) and *Tahiti* (☎971/320122) in Playa Pujols; *Hostal Sol y Mar* (☎971/320180) along Playa Mitjorn, and the *Hotel Sahona* (☎971/320030) in Cala Sahona. Also ask in bars, since most have attached rooms at government prices. If you're looking for a unit with a kitchen, each town has at least one letting agency dealing with apartments and villas, often not badly priced. Although Formentera has no official campground, finding a secluded spot should not prove too difficult. Many **camp** in the pine woods behind Playa Mitjorn, though the police do occasionally swoop down to clear them off. There is a basic bus service from La Sabina but journeys rarely keep to timetables, and they connect only the towns, leaving you long, hot walks to the beaches. **Taxis** are available and cheap, with stands at La Sabina, San Francisco, and Es Pujols; it's best to reserve one the day before you need it. If you're staying on the island, it's wise to buy the 1:25,000-scale map which shows the dirt tracks as well as the asphalt roads.

There aren't many cheap places to eat on the island. All of the *hostales* mentioned above serve **food** — particularly good value at *Casa Rafael* — or you can get your own supplies from the market and supermarket in San Francisco. Es Pujols has the most restaurants, including a Chinese. One of the best is *Capri*, which specializes in fish, and *Cafe de la Opera* is also very popular. For something cheaper, *Pizza Pazza* does the best pizzas and *Bar Escobar* is good in other food. At the western end of Mitjorn is the *Lagartija*, an excellent open-air restaurant run by Belgians serving French cuisine. There is often a singer and the atmosphere is very relaxed. Farther east is the cheap and cheerful *Sol y Luna* which offers good Spanish food at terrific prices.

Generally speaking, beach bars serve better food than the resorts. The *Bar Marie* on the west coast about a mile from the main road is among the best. This is very close to the *Blue Bar*, a beautiful restaurant outside which you can eat, drink, play backgammon, and listen to music; this is one of the trendiest joints on the island, but still relaxed. There are two **discos** in Es Pujols, the *Tipic* and the *Magoo*, the latter the best and staying open until 5am. Both are fairly expensive. At the large complex *Club Hotel de la Mola*, the *Disco Vedra* is open to non-residents. Resident hippies of Es Pujols set up stands and sell jewelry each evening.

MALLORCA

MALLORCA, perhaps more than anywhere in Spain, has a split identity. So much so, in fact, that there's a long-standing joke here about a fifth Balearic island, *Majorca*, a popular sort of place that pulls in an estimated 3 million tourists a year. If this sounds nasty, it is. There are sections of coast where high-rise hotels and shopping centers are continuous, wedged beside and upon one another and broken only by a divided highway down to more of the same. But the spread of this, even after 25 years of development, is surprisingly limited; "Majorca" occupies only the Bay of Palma, a forty-kilometer strip flanking the island capital. Beyond, to the north and east, things are very different. Not only are there good cove beaches (spared the interminal rows

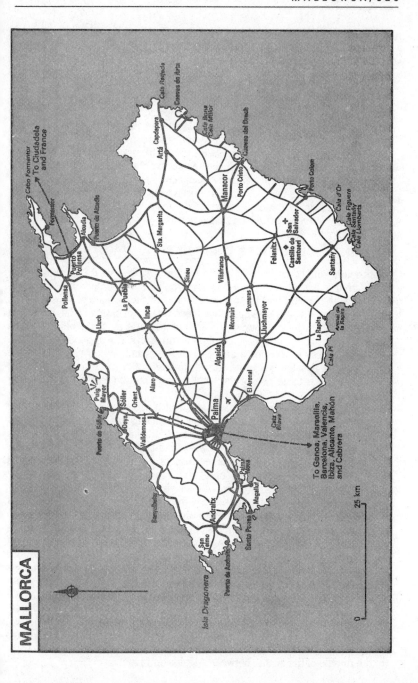

MALLORCA

of plastic sunbathing trays), but there's a really startling variety and physical beauty to the land itself. It's this which drew the original Mallorcan tourists — the nineteenth-century Habsburg archdukes, and later George Sand and Chopin — and it's this which makes the island many people's favorite in the group.

Less known to most people is the **archeological interest** of the island. More than 2000 years ago, along with Menorca, the island suffered a holocaust in which virtually every town, village, and hamlet was burned to the ground; remains of bodies have been found in some of the ruins. Archeologists think it might have been the result of civil disorder or revolution. A few settlements from before the catastrophe can also be seen — the walled third- to first-century village of Capocor Vell, near Lluchmayor (Mon.– Wed. and Fri. 10am–6pm), is still impressive, as is the ancient village of Ses Paisses near Artá. Son Matge, near Valldemossa, is the oldest known site of human occupation on any of the Balaearics.

Arrival: Where to Base Yourself

It's possible you'll arrive by boat from Menorca at **Puerto de Alcudia** in the north of the island, but the odds are you'll find yourself in **Palma de Mallorca**, the capital and the only real "city" in the Balearics. Palma, for all the disasters of its bay, is an attractive place with a considerable life of its own despite the day-tripping tourists — few of whom stay here, being bussed straight from the airport to their out-of-town resorts. It is a good initial base, with easy access to the north and east of the island. When you feel you've exhausted its possibilities move across to **Soller/Deyá**, **Puerto Pollensa**, **Puerto de Alcudia** or one of the small resorts around **Porto Cristo** on the south-east coast.

Accommodation is reasonable at each of these towns, though in July or August it'll be almost impossible to find. **Camping** is an alternative but not particularly provided for — there's only one "official" campround and a scattering of private grounds registered with (and listed by) the Palma *Turismo*. You can, however, survive by discreet use of a tent at many of the island's best beaches: pick a spot near a hotel and, again discreetly, make use of the outside showers they generally provide for guests.

Mallorca's **bus service** is reasonably good and there are even a couple of **train lines** — one, a beautiful ride up through the mountains from Palma to Soller, an attraction in itself. Wheels of your own, though, are again a strong advantage — and if you can manage to **rent a car** you'll have the option of being able to sleep in it. You also allow yourself access to one of the more offbeat forms of island accommodation — staying in any of six **monasteries** that rent cells for the night or week. These are exceptionally cheap (from 2000–12,000ptas for two people, often with two meals included) but, as you'd expect, they're all somewhat remote and often booked up months in advance. If you're interested the most accessible, and most likely to have vacancies, are at *Puig de Maria* (near Pollensa), *Lluch* (also in the northwest), *La Vitoria* (above the bay of Pollensa), *San Salvador* (near Felantix) and *N.S. de Cura* (in the middle of the island, between Algaida and Llucmayor).

Palma airport is 7km east of the city and connected with it (and with most of the Bay of Palma resorts) by a rather frenetic expressway. Cheapest way into town from here is by bus #17 (half-hourly) to the Plaza de España; taxis will set you back about ten times the price. There's a small tourist office at the airport (pick up their lists of *hostales* and car/bike rental outlets) along with various car-rental desks, travel agents, and a seven-day, 24-hour money-exchange booth.

The **passenger port** at Palma is no longer just below the old town, having been moved some 3½km to the west. The connecting bus into town from the ferry terminal is the #1; to catch it, walk 200m out of the terminal to the main road, using the cloverleaf ramp for access, then 200 meters more toward town for the marked stop. Buses run every thirty minutes (fare 75ptas); coming back catch it on the Paseo Borne, but beware of reduced or nonexistent services on Sunday and late at night.

Palma

PALMA is in some ways like a mainland Spanish city — lively, solid, and industrious — though it is immediately marked apart by its insular/Mediterranean aura. The port is by far the largest in the Balearics, the evening *paseo* the most ingrained (if rather tamer than Ibiza's exotic events), and, in the evenings at least, you feel the city has only passing relevance to the tourist enclaves around its bay. Arriving here by sea, it is also beautiful and impressive, with the grand limestone bulk of the cathedral towering above the old town and the remnants of medieval walls. In these are encapsulated much of the city and island's history: Moorish control from the ninth through the thirteenth centuries, reconquest by Jaime I of Aragón, and a meteoric rise to wealth and prominence in the fifteenth century as the main port of call between Europe and Africa.

Orientation and Accommodation

Orientation is fairly straightforward once you're into the center. Around the **cathedral** — *La Sao* — is the **Portela quarter**, "Old" Palma, a cluster of alleyways and lanes that becomes more spacious and ordered as you move towards the zigzag of avenues built beside or in place of the city walls. Cutting up from the sea, beside the cathedral, is **Paseo Borne**, garden promenade as well as boulevard, and way up the hill to the northeast lies the **Plaza Mayor**, mecca for most of the day-tripping tourists.

There are hundreds of *pensiones* and hotels, and your first move in the summer should be to pick up the official lists of these from the **Turismo** at Avda. Rey Jaime III 10, or the city tourist office on the subterranean walkway at the corner of Calles Conquistador and Ventura. Either can also supply various maps, bus schedules, and leaflets (a good one on hiking about the island), and, if you can afford full hotel prices, will try to reserve you a **room**. Best initial areas to look for yourself are around the Plaza Mayor (more expensive), on c/Apuntadores or c/San Felio running west from Paseo Borne (cheaper), and on c/San Jaume at the top of the Paseo Borne (mid-range).

Specific recommendations are probably futile in summer, but out of season the following, all of them cheap and central, are likely to have vacancies:

Hostal Castilla, San Jaime 3 (☎971/724092);

Hostal Terramar, Plaza Mediterraneo 8 (☎971/733961);

Hostal Bahia de Palma, Bosque 14 (☎971/737480);

Pension Brondo, Brondo 1, between San Nicoloás and Borne;

Hostal Pons, General Barceló 8 (☎971/722658);

Hostal Palma, General Barceló 18 (☎971/724417);

Hostal la Paz, Salas 5 (☎971/215010);

Hostal Ritzi, Apuntadores 6 (☎971/714610);

Hostal Tirol, Apuntadores 19 (☎971/711808);

Hostal Goya, Estanco 7 (☎971/726986).

In any event don't bother with the **youth hostel** at El Arenal, way out of town and invariably booked en masse by school groups.

Old Palma

Five hundred years in the making, Palma's **Cathedral** dominates the old city from a hill above the seafront. It's a magnificent building — the equal of almost any on the mainland — and a surprising one, too, with *modernista* interior features designed by Antoni Gaudí. Its original foundation, inevitably, came with the Christian reconquest of the city, and the site taken, in fulfillment of a vow by Jaime I, was that of the Moorish Great Mosque. Essentially Gothic, with massive outer buttresses to take the weight off the pillars within, the church derives its effect through its sheer height, impressive from any angle but startling when glimpsed from the waterfront esplanade. The *Reconquista*-era builders had a point to make, and they didn't hold back.

Entrance is today by the side door, passing the **Treasury Museum**, for which there's an admission charge and regular hours (10am–12:30pm and 4–6:30pm). Inside the nave, you are immersed in a dappled kaleidoscope of light, for once untrapped by the central *coro* (choir) that normally blocks the center of Spanish cathedrals. This innovation, and the fantastic forms of the lighting system above the nave, were Gaudí's work, completed in 1904 under the patronage of an inspired local bishop. At the time these measures were deeply controversial; no *coro* had ever before been removed in Spain, and there was a theoretical/liturgical reform, too, in the adjustments of seating around the altar. The artistic success of the project, though, leaves little doubt, and it was immediately popular. Compared to Gaudí's designs in Barcelona, everything here is simple and restrained but there are touches of his characteristic fantasy. The wrought iron, twisted into forms inspired by Mallorcan window-grilles, seems like some giant tiara, and the lights themselves would do justice to a 1970s rock concert. For those who want to take photos inside, only the altar is properly illuminated, and the lights are switched on automatically for three minutes each quarter-hour, so have the camera ready.

If you can coincide with it, the *Missa solemne* at 10:30am on Sunday is great. Chanting is in Latin, the choir is small but competent, and the curé seems rather enlightened judging by his homily. Also of possible interest are the *Missa cantada* (Sat. 9am) and the Mallorquin mass (Sun. 1pm).

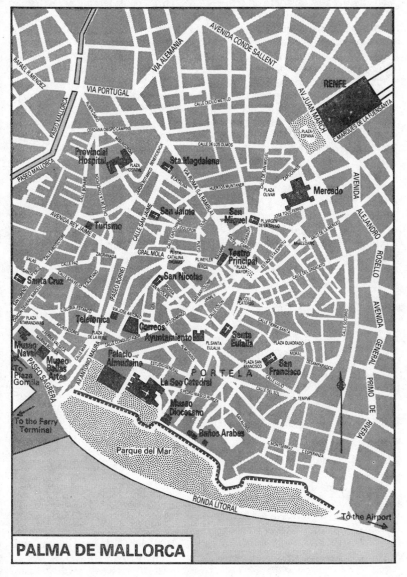

PALMA DE MALLORCA

Opposite the cathedral is the imposing **Palacio Almudaina**, originally the residence of the Moorish *walis* and later of the Mallorcan kings. Visits here are guided, with energetic commentaries repeated in three languages, but for all this it's worth a look (Mon.–Sat. 9:30am–12:30pm and 4–6:30pm, Sun. 9am–2pm). Most of what you see — and there are considerable parts that are cordoned off as the island's official State Apartments — dates from a thirteenth-to-fifteenth-century reconstruction under Christian rule. The Council Room, which is normally on view, is pressed into service once a year when King Juan Carlos convenes Mallorcan assemblies; the small chapel across the court is used by the army's officers for their masses and weddings. The ordinary soldiers, rigged out in toy-town costume to stand guard, are ferociously camera-shy. If none of this sounds too inspiring, there are at least some pleasant gardens attached to the palace and you can climb down through these to the grand fifteenth-century **Lonja**, the city's former stock or commodities exchange. This is now home to frequent and occasionally excellent temporary exhibitions (9am–1pm and 5–9pm). Older maps may also suggest a visit to the Maritime Museum, a few hundred meters farther down the front, but it's now closed, and there is no intention of any reopening. Behind the building, in the Plaza Ataranzanas, most of Palma's *chocolate* and other drug business takes place.

More traditionally rewarding is the *medina*-like maze of streets at the back of the cathedral, and here, at c/Serra 7, you'll come upon a well-preserved *hammam*, or **Baños Arabes** (10am–7pm daily, 75ptas admission). One of the few genuine reminders of the Moorish presence, this is an elegant, horseshoe-arched and domed chamber. But if you've been to the ones in Girona or Granada, these are anticlimactic; the garden outside, with tables where you can snack (on your own food), is perhaps nicer.

Toward the center of town, and occupying, oddly enough, the site of the old Moorish soap factory, the **Convento de San Francisco** is the finest among a host of medieval and worthy churches. A vast building founded towards the end of the thirteenth century, it boasts some majestic tombs and a fine Gothic cloister (daily 8am–1pm, 4–7pm; token entrance fee, priestly escort). Nearby **Santa Eulalia**, the first church to be built after Jaime's arrival, is in a similar vein, airy and high-roofed, and haunted by a history of mass executions of the island's Jews. Just to its west, an elegant, pure example of Renaissance, is the **Ayuntamiento**, with a small municipal museum.

Eating, Nightlife, and Other Practicalities

Eating in Palma is cheaper — or at least *can* be cheaper — than anywhere else in the Balearics. Some of the least expensive places are on or near c/ Apuntadores at the lower end of Paseo Borne. *La Paloma* is quite a good place here, while *Yate Rizz* (on Paseo Borne itself) is cheap in every sense of the word. Elsewhere, there are varied *bocadillos* and cheapish meals at *Bodega Casa Payesa* (c/Molineros — an alley off San Miguel, above Plaza Mayor), cheap *menús* at *S'Antiquari* on the Plaza Santa Catalina Thomas, and a vegetarian restaurant (closed Aug.) in c/Moral. For **breakfast** put it together yourself at *Forn La Pau*, La Paz 14, with excellent whole-grain bread, pizzas, and *ensaimadas* (turnovers). Oddly, just about the only place for an ordinary morning *café con leche* is the ornate (but not expensive) *Granja Royal* at San Felio 2.

Just off c/Apuntadores is one of the world's most unusual **bars**. Called the *Abaco*, this offers an experience other than mere drinking, with an interior like a Busby Berkeley musical: fruits cascading down its stairway, caged birds hidden amid patio foliage, hokey music, and a reputed $500 daily flower bill. Drinks, as you might imagine, are extremely expensive but you're never hurried into buying one. The entrance, easy to miss, is at c/San Juan 1.

Conventional **nightlife** takes place at Terreno along the hotel mile of Avenida Joan Miró. This is not very promising, and can be ludicrously expensive (beware of eating *tapas* in the Plaza Gomilla bars), but if you must there's a fair selection of **discos** — both straight and gay — amid the souvenir shops and *hamburguesa* bars. U.S. Navy personnel provide a rather bizarre leavening to Palman nightlife and two of there favorite haunts (one below the *Hostal Ritzi*, and *Texas Jack's* on San Felio) are best avoided.

Getting out of Palma, **trains** will take you to Soller (see overpage) and Inca/Sa Pobla, **buses** to these and most other destinations. The buses call at various stops around the city, though principal departures are from the Plaza de España by the railroad stations. To rent a car you may have to reserve in advance or else wait around for a couple of days. In ascending order of price, try *Jaybee* (Avda. Joan Miró, Terreno, ☎971/238930), *Arenal* (☎971/263648), *Moto Sud* (☎971/302442) and *BOM* (☎971/266884). For a complete list stop in at the main **Turismo** at Avda. Jaime III 10, or the municipal or provincial offices in, respectively, c/Almudaina and c/de la Constitución. **Banks** are plentiful on and around the Paseo Borne and Avda. Jaime III; for **American Express** services go to *Viajes Iberia* at Paseo Borne 14. The central **Correos** is at c/de la Constitución 6, the **Telefónica** at no. 2, and, last but not least, there's a self-service **laundromat** in Terreno on c/Porras (opposite the *Hotel Aries*, off Avda. Joan Miró; 9am–1:30pm and 4–8pm).

Swimming and Longer Day-Escapes

For a day out from Palma, anywhere in the west or center of the island is accessible, but if you're just after a quick swim you'll probably want to stick to the city's suburbs and its bay. From the Plaza de la Reina and Avda. Antonio Maura there are almost continuous buses shuttling down to the big resorts.

Palmese tend to head east on the #15 bus to the individual *balneario* sections of EL ARENAL. In the same direction, and not too far to walk, is the town beach, just in front of the G.E.S.A. building, but exposed to any southwest wind. You might conceivably be tempted by the Terreno suburb, 4km west of downtown around Plaza Gomilla. This is fairly horrendous, with sand tricky to spot between the rows of plastic and flesh, but at least it's better than the "real" Palma Bay resorts of Palma Nova, Paguera, and Magalluf. It has, too, an attractive **castle** ruin, *Bellver*, set in a large park above the sea and containing an archaeological museum (8am–sunset; closed Sun.).

Unless you're actually booked into a **Palma Bay** hotel — and it can sometimes be as cheap to take a two-week package in Magalluf as to buy a one-way flight to the island from England — you'd be willfully perverse to head that way, for reasons hinted at amply above.

Inland from the bay, though, is a different matter, and once off the expressway it's not hard to forget what you're (only just) missing. From Palma you could certainly find worse ways to spend an afternoon than hopping on a bus to **ANDRAITX**, a small, unaffected town huddled among the hills to the west. From here one of the tourist board's easiest and most enjoyable **hiking excursions** will take you on through the village of S'ARRACO to the ruinous **castle of San Telmo** and to the end of the road, above a rocky stretch of coast looking out towards the equally rocky offshore **Isla Dragonera**.

Northwest from Palma, BANYALBUFAR is a small village clinging to the cliffs over the sea (you need your own vehicle to get there), and an hour's walk down the coast (or tortuous car journey) is a tiny harbor where local fishermen haul in freshly-caught fish.

Heading **east of Palma**, out towards Manacor, **ALGAIDA** also offers an attractive day hike. Taking the minor road leading southeast from the town you can loop round to the village of **RANDA** via a beautifully sited hermitage (*Ermita de la Pau*). At Randa there's a terrific *bodega-restaurant*, and the beginning of a winding track up the **Puig Randa**, the highest mountain in this part of the island. At the top, a fifteen-minute drive or two-hour trek, is the **monastery of Nuestra Señora de Cura**, an active monastery which rents out basic cells, with amazing views.

Western Mallorca

The 38-kilometer journey from **Palma to Sóller** is worthwhile in itself, especially if you do it on the train (*Autocares Llompart* also provides indirect, slightly less scenic bus service 5 times daily). The rail line, constructed on the profits of the nineteenth-century orange and lemon trade, is a delight, dipping and cutting through the mountains and fertile valleys of the Sierra de Tramuntana. Its rolling stock, too, is tremendous: narrow carriages which in the first-class sections seem straight out of Agatha Christie. There are five departures daily, the whole ride taking just under 1½ hours.

Sóller, Town and Puerto

At **SÓLLER** the tracks end, and a tram — another open, wooden thing which looks like it escaped deportation to a Hollywood theme park — takes over for a rumbling, five-kilometer journey down to the port (22 daily each way from 6am–8:30pm, roughly half-hourly). Sóller, the town, is a pretty place, very much in keeping with its transportation, with a small, newly restored **Museo Municipal** and a couple of small **hotels** — *El Guía* (beautiful and 1-star priced, just west of the station; ☎971/630227) and the slightly cheaper *Hostal Nadal* (c/Romaguera, ☎971/631180) — plus the *CH Margartia Trias Vives* (c/Real 3, near *El Guía*; no phone). These are all more likely to have room than anywhere down at the port, though if you're desperate the local *Associao Sollerica* (Social Club) also rents hostel-type beds. Cheapest meals are served at the *Bar Oasis*, below the Plaza Constitución by the tram tracks, though the best **eating** for miles around is again at *El Guía*, even if the conversation (when in English) at adjoining tables tends to outdo Noel Coward or Brideshead Revisited.

PUERTO DE SÓLLER, however, is where most people head for, and its curling postcard-perfect bay must be about the most captured-for-posterity spot on the island after the *Club 18-30* hangouts of Magalluf. However *18-to-30* antics are about the last thing imaginable down here; the place is almost stiflingly staid. There's no point in staying here just for the swimming; while the water is warm and calm, it's surprisingly murky (courtesy of the yachts at anchor), the sand negligible, and privacy nonexistent. If you can, it's better to base yourself in Deyá or Sóller proper and bus it to better beaches.

Outside of peak season there's a chance of a reasonably priced **room** at the *Hostal Miramar*, opposite the tram stop, the *Mare Nostra* or, on the beach, *La Bahía*. In July or August you've hardly a chance. As far as **food and fun** go, the Puerto is slightly upscale, catering rather obviously to the yacht-set. *Bar Pirata* is a nice place, though, producing its own herbal liqueur (*de hierbas*), and the next door *Restaurant Balear* is relatively modest. Such youth as there are down here generally meet at *Bar El Bianco*, before a nightly fling at *St. Germain* — or, for variety, *Patio* or *Alta Mar*.

Biniaraix and Fornalutx

The most obvious excursions from Sóller are to two villages to the east. **BINIARAIX,** 2km, is tiny — virtually a hamlet — but self-contained and large enough to have a small central square, off of which is a Mallorquin rarity: a *taberna*. Here the proprietress squeezes fresh orange juice and sells (factory) ice cream. You can sit at wooden tables watching the sun stream in the windows; no video games, no TV, no hulking *señoritos* smoking at the bar — altogether a nice change.

FORNALUTX, reached from Biniaraix via a narrow back road, is touted as the most attractive village on the island, and unfortunately is beginning to realize it. You'll find an expensive restaurant or two, numerous bars, and as many postcards for sale as in Sóller, but no place to stay — yet. Perhaps this is because almost a quarter of the village's 300-plus houses are foreign-owned, with the new "lords" wishing to preserve its exclusivity. Still it's worth coming this far, just to wander the streets between the honey-colored stone houses, and to watch the fish swimming in the orange-grove irrigation tanks on the way up. Before mid-summer the stream beds are running, as are most of the watercourses in the Sóller valley.

Deyá and Around

Southwest of Sóller, **Route 710** rambles through orchards of fruit, almond, olive, and carob trees, occasionally plummeting down to the sea. Judging from the foreign and Spanish mainland licence plates on the sleek sedans parked in the driveways, it's doubtful that there are any Mallorcan-owned properties left on the road to Deyá. You briefly skim the coast at LLUCH ALCARI and then climb up to the village of DEYÁ (Deia), high in the hills and tucked at the base of formidable cliffs. Famed in every guidebook as the former home of Robert Graves, it was also a focus for British hippie rock-bands of the late 1960s. The village itself is very much the haunt of long-term expatriates, mostly ex-flower children and artistes living on ample trust funds, judging from the sorts of monthly rents charged.

Of the two places catering to overnighters, *Fonda Villa Verde* (☎971/639037) has beautiful premises on the edge of the church-hill cluster, though not cheap at 1600ptas single, over 2000ptas double; *Pensión Miramar*, up the hill on the far side of the road (☎971/639084) falls in the same price range but includes huge suppers in the rate.

Deyá has a beach of sorts, the *Cala de Deyá*, some 200 meters of pebbles and a terrace cafe. It'll do for a swim — the water is clean at least — but it's crowded, and you may have to sit on the boathouse ramps to either side of the cove. The fastest way to get there from Deyá proper is to take the stair-street down from the wash-trough on the main road to the archaeological museum, then follow the road beside the streambed until this ends at a private gate. The well-marked onward path begins just to the right; it's under a half-hour walk down to the water, as opposed to over an hour on the ugly new road.

You may have better luck with rooms and swimming at LLUCH ALCARI, which is in any case the best local beach for Deya. The hotel here, *La Costa d'Or* (☎971/639025), is cheapish by island standards, and the beach is reached through a gate marked 'No Entry' at the bottom of its garden. A bizarre but very wonderful feature of the Lluch Alcari beach is its natural mudbath, formed by a pure mountain stream trickling through the rich red earth. You can coat yourself in this and later wash the sun-dried mud pack in the sea.

Walking in the Tramuntana

Mallorca's best beaches are in the far northeast and southeast of the island; the northwest coast, from Banyalbufar to Cala San Vicente, is mostly sheer, with few anchorages and negligible coves. Conversely the gnarled ridge of the Sierra de Tramuntana provides the best walking on Mallorca, with Sóller (or alternatively Deyá) ideally positioned as overnight bases about midway along. It's little short of a hiker's paradise as long as you don't venture out in midsummer when water is scarce.

If you're interested there's an embarrassment of information for walkers available in various languages, trails are well-marked (though apt to be thorn-bush-clogged), and good maps are readily available from the military authorities in Palma (Via Roma/Ramblas Calso 20, 3°). Useful books available locally include *Twelve Classic Hikes on Mallorca* (sold in the Sóller book-store) and *Guía de Soller* from Turismo.

From Sóller itself, you can accomplish the **Cornadors circuit** by climbing up via the S'Arrom farm to the Cornadors *mirador*, from there down to the

L'Ofre plateau, followed by a descent along wonderful old steps through the Es Barranc canyon. You finish in Biniaraix in just under five hours, with an option to continue to Fornalutx on the signposted *Cami d'es Marroig*.

Leaving Sóller in almost the opposite direction, you can follow the **Camino Viejo to Cala Tuent**. The first leg involves climbing up to C'an Costure, and from there past the Mirador de Ses Barcs (also on Route 710 heading northeast) to the Enchanted Balitx valley. After dropping down to the lowest of three farms there, you toil briefly up to the Coll de Biniamar, where you can detour to Sa Costera villa on a cliff, for spring water and views over the most spectacular portion of the Mallorcan northwest coast. The main route continues parallel to the shore until Cala Tuent, one of the sandiest and quietest of the northern beaches, though also rather dirty. There is a single bar/restaurant, and it's possible to continue another hour to Sa Calobra (see below). It will take four hours to reach Cala Tuent, unless you cheat and take a bus to Mirador de Ses Barcs.

By using the morning bus south to Valldemossa, the famous **Camino del Archiduque** is easily accessible. After an initial ascent to the Mirador de Ses Puntes, you turn right and adopt the ridge above Deyá to follow the *camino*, a gem of nineteenth-century romantic engineering commissioned by an eccentric Austrian aristocrat whose villa at Son Marroig below is now on the bus-tour circuit. His private promenade ends after traversing the rather bleak "roof of the island" on the edge of 400-meter drops, at the detour to Teix peak. The main route dips down into the Cairats valley, past an ICONA hut and the only water since the start, to finish in Valldemossa (5½ hr., including detour up Teix), in time for the afternoon bus back to Sóller.

The descent of the **Torrent de Pareis** is perhaps the most popular "stunt" on Mallorca. From the restaurant at La Escorca, where the bus drops you, you traverse an awesome limestone gorge, emerging at the seaward end on the touristified beach of Sa Calobra. This outing is not practicable in winter or early spring; otherwise high-school groups do it regularly, and its difficulty has been grossly exaggerated in most of the existing literature. Some Class 3 scrambling and a head for boulder-hopping is required, but chocks and pins are installed at the crucial points and there's no problem as long as the rocks are dry. **Sa Calobra**, where you arrive after four-plus hours, is a bit of a letdown (busloads of tourists) but at least you can have a swim while awaiting the boat back to Sóller.

Now that Puig Mayor has a radar station on top and is off-limits, **Puig de Massanella** is the highest peak that can be climbed on Mallorca. On the Pollensa-bound bus from Sóller ask to be set down as close as possible to the gas station before Lluc, from where it's a four-and-a-half hour round-trip, with no complications and a permanent spring near the summit. Northern Mallorca is prone to mists, which may spoil the view, but they usually part at some point in the day. Catch the same bus on its way back to Sóller.

Finally, you can walk **from Sóller to Deyá** in just under three hours by following the rather complicated but accurate instructions in the *Guia de Sóller*. The trail, a real beauty with stunning views over the ocean and intervening farms, winds along a few hundred meters inland from the coast road. The path finally intersects the highway between Lluch Alcari and Deyá, giving you a choice of swimming spots and easy access to buses back to Sóller.

Transportation to Trailheads

Two **buses**, run by different companies, ply Route 710. They are invaluable to hikers, though some of their daily frequencies leave a bit to be desired. *Autocares Llompart* serves the line Sóller–Deyá–Valldemossa four times a day in each direction year-round; in Sóller town the terminal is on the round Plaza America, 600m down the Gran Via from the post office. Another line leaves Sóller daily at 9am (year-round, from beside the tram tracks by the train station) going via the Puerto to the Mirador de Ses Barcs, Escorca, and foot of Puig Massanella, and Lluc monastery before finishing at Pollensa. The same vehicle turns around at 4pm in Puerto Pollensa to retrace its route, arriving in Sóller just after 6pm.

Literary Mallorca: Valldemossa Cartuja

The **CARTUJA DE VALLDEMOSSA** — the island's most famous building after Palma Cathedral — owes its notoriety almost entirely to the novelist George Sand who, with her companion Frederic Chopin, made her home here for four months in 1838–39. Their stay in the monastery is commemorated in Sand's *A Winter in Majorca*, a book that tends to be a little over-played here, being available in just about every European language. By the time the pair arrived the *Cartuja* was in fact monk-abandoned and the cells in which they stayed can hardly have been spartan judging by present standards. Bright, sizable rooms, they all look out onto a private garden and magnificent views, a fact that's been rather cleverly exploited, along with the romantic connotations, in selling various nearby vacation villas. As a mere tourist visitor, though, this is still a beautiful and worthwhile trip. The grounds of the *Cartuja* are peaceful and there's an obvious curiosity in looking round **Sand** and **Chopin's quarters**, with their miscellaneous collections of manuscripts and, of course, Chopin's piano. This took three months of unbelievable complications to arrive, just twenty days before they both left for Paris. Also on display is the old **monastic pharmacy**, decked out in slightly bogus fashion, and a small **municipal museum** with displays on Mallorcan social history.

The *Cartuja* is open daily except Sunday from 9:30am to 1pm and 3 to 6:30pm. The *Hostal Can Mario* in Valldemossa, though rated at one-star, is fairly expensive (bed and breakfast arrangements). There are regular buses (*Autocares Llompart*) up from Palma and Paguera, and you can take these onward, — or hitch, or walk — to DEYÁ (10km), LLUCH ALCARI, and SÓLLER. The closest spot for a swim is Puerto de Valldemossa, but it's a rocky shore and no public transit covers the five kilometers down to the water. Near Valldemossa is the site of SON MATGE, a rock shelter used by Stone Age people around 8,500 years ago. Initially home to a succession of prehistoric families, it later became a cemetery.

Northern Mallorca

Beyond a doubt the most interesting approach to the northern tip of the island — to Pollensa, Lluch, and Alcudia — is the continuation of **Route 710 beyond Soller**, skirting the edge of the Sierra de Tramuntana. If you've a rented vehicle, or if you're taking this in two stages, you'll be able to stop along the way at the Monastery of Lluch (detailed below).

The more direct **central route**, which the railroad follows as far as Inca and Sa Pobla, is rather less memorable. INCA itself is heavily promoted for its distilleries, leather factories, and Thursday market — all called to your attention on a series of billboards along the way. Unless you need to stock up on dish towels or open-toed sandals, both town and market are probably best avoided. Beyond, around SA POBLA, there's a more attractive look to the landscape — arable land liberally scattered with windmills — and at MURO is one of Mallorca's more interesting crafts museums, complete with an original Moorish patio and waterwheel, and comprehensive exhibits from forge and field.

Pollensa, Town and Puerto

Development in this northern corner of Mallorca has focused on the beach of CALA DE SAN VICENTE, once among the best on the island. **Pollensa bay**, across the peninsula (and the last reach of the Tramuntana), is surprisingly unspoiled. Much of its coast is inaccessible — like so much of the north — but by no means all of it. At both PUERTO DE POLLENSA and CABO DE FORMENTOR there are excellent sandy coves.

As a base to capitalize on this, you've a choice between the quiet inland town of **POLLENSA** and its port, 7km distant. The town is dominated by a striking **shrine of Calvary**, atop the Puig de Maria. It's reached by 365 steps which the faithful and penitent climb on their knees past the various stations of the Cross. From the 250-meter high summit there's a tremendous view over the coast, all the way up to both northern capes.

Perhaps better than the view is the **monastery** attached to the shrine, built in 1348 and alternately abandoned and restored by both monks and nuns of various orders. There are **rooms** here for more than sixty guests, and oddly it is busier in winter than in summer; facilities are a bit spartan, with bathing and drinking water drawn from a well in the refectory and carried back to your cell. In compensation the caretaker/cook is friendly and helpful, and the daily per-person rate for bed, breakfast, and supper an absurdly inexpensive 1100 ptas. Even if you custom-order a *paella* feast the bill for the meal will probably not exceed 1500ptas for two.

In Pollensa itself there's little to halt your onward or upward progress, though it's a pleasant enough place to stop off and **eat**. The restaurant by the Torrente San Jordi, still crossed by a Roman bridge, is good and economical; much more expensive, but with well-prepared food and a spectacular herbal liqueur is the *Daus* on the steps to Puig Maria. The one **hotel**, *Juma*, (☎971/

530007), is good value in the unlikely event of its having space. If you're hanging around between buses, or insatiably curious, you could visit the **Museum** dedicated to local artist **Miguel Costa Lloberra,** in the street of the same name.

Over at **PUERTO DE POLLENSA** things are a little more lively, though still pleasantly low-key. The port has a rather split personality: the bad points are the *Pollensa Park Hotel* complex (airport lounge-style), the considerable development going on at the edge of town, and the noisy Alcudia road which runs along the seaside area. Overall, however, the place is very pleasant, especially the now-pedestrianized Avda. Anglada Camarasa, along the waterfront. Once again there's a minor art museum, devoted this time to the Chagallish daubings of the Catalan **Anglada Camarasa** (d. 1959); it's at Paseo Anglada Camarasa 87, open afternoons except Wednesday and Sunday. But the sea and the **coves** are the main and obvious attraction, reached either by walking, rented wheels (mopeds from *Maria's* on c/Juan XXIII, bicycles from *Garage Bernardo Oliver* on c/Formentor), or by one of the regular boat-taxis that ply their way down to Cabo Formentor. On the Formentor road you'll come soon to the *Hotel Formentor*, with a good sandy beach, but crowds of Pollensa-based tourists. Back in town, the beaches are narrow, but not too crowded except near *Pollensa Park*.

Puerto Practicalities

Hotels are slightly expensive but there are two reasonable options: the *Pension Rivoli* (☎971/531207), next to the tourist office by the port, and *Hostal Corro* (☎971/531005), a block in on c/Juan XXIII — or you could camp, unofficially, amid the trees (but see below for note on the Boquer valley).

There are plenty of **eating** places; the best and most expensive restaurant is the *Becfi* on Avda. Anglada Camarasa, apparently visited by both Pete Townsend and King Juan Carlos. The *Pizzeria Llenaire* on the Alcudia road serves good, cheapish pizzas and is better than the *Cafeteria Mestral* on the front.

The night scene is gentle — there's a poor disco at the *Pollensa Park Hotel* and another, the *Chivas*, on Metge Llopis off the main square, which is free (expensive drinks). The best place to hang out, though, is the *Bar Pascalinos* on Avda. Anglada Camarasa: beachfront location, good music, reasonable prices, and a young clientele (many Palmese spend the summer in Puerto Pollensa). The place swings until around 3am. There's an all-night bar next to *Pascalinos*, but it's feeble in comparison.

The Boquer Valley

The road on to the cape is spectacular, passing through a totally uninhabited area with beautiful views. After a kilometer or two keep an eye out for a farm perched above on the left, with a track up to it starting opposite the Avda. Bocharis. An obvious path, beginning from a nearby iron gate, leads through the **Boquer valley**, a favorite of ornithologists and a possible place to camp if Puerto Pollensa is full up. After about 45 minutes you reach a small, shingly beach offering good swimming in clean water (though the shore may be garbage-strewn). For triathlon trainees, there's a grotto, on the right as you face the sea but not visible from the shore, which takes almost half an hour to reach — with swim fins. Look for a black discoloration on the cliffs; close up, the entrance is a mere 4m wide with perhaps a foot of clearance above sea level. Once inside, and accustomed to the unearthly light, you find yourself in a cavern some 7m by 15m, with the ceiling 10m high.

Monastery of Lluch

From Pollensa or its port, the **MONASTERY OF LLUCH** (Lluc) is an easy excursion. The largest monastic complex on the island, its thirteenth-century statue of the Virgin, *La Moreneta*, also makes it Mallorca's principal place of pilgrimage. The big attraction for the nonbeliever is its site — a spectacular outreach of the Tramuntana — and the individualist contributions of **Antoni Gaudí**. Gaudí was responsible here for the monuments marking the stations of the Cross on the route to the shrine, and also made some imaginative adaptations to the baroque interior of the main church. This is open daily from around 10am to 7pm, along with a splendidly eclectic **museum**, mixing displays of Bronze Age pots and artifacts with an episcopal fashion show to rival Fellini's *Roma*.

Accommodation at the monastery is highly organized, featuring self-contained apartment cells with the use of a kitchen and dining room; in summer they're becoming popular so phone ahead if you want to be sure of space (☎971/517025), or settle for the monastic campground. Stay here between mid-September and early June and you'll also catch a **boy's choir** performance, as remorselessly touted as Sand and Chopin are at Valldemossa and constantly piped to greet new arrivals in the car and bus parking lot. Speaking of **bus** service, in addition to the year-round departure from Sóller detailed in preceding sections, there is an April-to-October daily service based in Puerto Pollensa. This leaves at 10am, returning from Sóller at 4:30pm, allowing you ample time at the monastery and its surroundings.

Bahía de Alcudia

The beaches around **Bahía de Alcudia** are longer and more numerous than Pollensa's, and shoreline developments reflect this. Not to any disastrous extent, however, and again both town and port make good bases, are regularly served by buses from Palma.

PUERTO ALCUDIA is inevitably where the action is — a growing resort whose clutch of discos and bars attract crowds from the high-rise hotels and *urbanizaciones* off to its south. Should you want to stay at the port, there's a vague chance of a bed in three reasonable-priced **hostales**: *Calma* (☎971/545343), *Puerto* (☎971/545447), and *Vista Alegre* (☎971/545439). If these are full you could try a kilometer to the east at Alcanada (slightly pricey *hostal* ☎971/545402), up at Alcudia town (see below), or you could **camp** — the island's one official ground is only 8km downcoast at PLATJA BRAVA (on the road, and bus route, to CA'N PICAFORT), although that's also expensive.

The local **Turismo** is a mine of information about just about all possible activities — moped and car rental, windsurfing and waterskiing sessions — all of which vary from one season to the next. The Alcudia beach is pretty good; for a little variety walk round the bay to ALCANADA with its offshore island and abandoned lighthouse, swimmable from the shore. Don't forget, too, that Puerto Alcudia has **ferries** to Ciudadela on Menorca (five weekly at 9am); tickets are best reserved in advance.

Remains of Spain's smallest **Roman theater** can be visited if you turn sharp to the left just before arriving at **ALCUDIA** town, twenty minutes' walk from the port. This apart you're most likely to come here in a quest for **accommodation**. The best and cheapest option is the *Fonda Llabres* (☎971/ 545000), above a pastry shop in the main plaza. An alternative is to make for the **Santuario La Vittoria**, an hour or so's walk off towards Cabo Pinar, with highly monastic cells (no electricity) and a sporadically operating cafe-restaurant.

The Santuario — or *Ermida* as it's also known in Mallorquin — is in any case an enjoyable walk. So are the marshes of **S'Albufera** immediately south of Alcudia, seasonal home to over 200 different species of migratory birds. You need a permit to visit; further information from one of the various tourist offices in Palma (Jaime III 10, Plaza de la Constitución 1; ☎971/729537, 715310, or 723641). Also over in this direction, though easier reached from the holiday complex on Alcudia beach, is the **Cueva de Sant Marti**, an underground chapel used during the years of Moorish rule. Roughly half way along the bay is SON REAL, an Iron Age cemetery dating from about 600 B.C.; dozens of tombs cling to the seashore where part of the site has been swamped by the rising Mediterranean. If you've got wheels, COLONIA DE SAN PEDRO at the southeastern end of the bay is a fishing village situated underneath the Artá mountain range; an hour's walk from here is the hillside hermitage of BETLEM.

Eastern Mallorca

With more easily accessible beaches and an efficient public transit network from Palma, Mallorca's **east coast** is predictably developed. If you're after more than a meter of sand — or a bed for the night — stay away from mid-June until mid-September. On the other hand, if you're lucky enough to be here in spring or late autumn there are a handful of really tempting propositions: **Ratjada** and **Canyamel** in the north, **Porto Colom** and **Porto Petro** in the south. Inland, too, there are attractions in the walled town of **Artá**, the region around **Felanitx**, and the packaged but impressive caves of **Drach**.

Manacor, Artá, and the Upper Coast

Like Inca, **MANACOR** declares its business long before you arrive — vast roadside billboards promote its furniture and artificial pearl factories. On the strength of these the city has risen to become the second urban center of Mallorca, a far smaller place than Palma but sprawling into suburbs on all sides. It's not exactly compelling, but this "life after tourism" does give Manacor an earthiness distinctly lacking elsewhere. If you want to stay and commute to the sea (to Cala Millor, for example) there are three cheapish **accommodations**: *Fonda Pascual Bauza* (c/José López 72 — out towards the Palma road, ☎971/551087), *Hostal Jacinto* (across from the cathedral), and *Hostal Ca'n March* (c/Valencia 7, ☎971/550002). Be warned, though, that others have the same idea.

Following the train line or main highway north brings you to a pair of walled towns: Artá and Capdepera. **ARTÁ**, with an old fortress-hermitage and terraced streets of grandee mansions, is the one to visit. There are a couple of bars here to delay your progress to the coast, (buses leave from outside the *Bar Ca'n Balague*) and an odd little church, San Salvador, unvaulted and shocking pink inside, at the top end of town.

Outside Artá a slightly bewildering choice of roads veer off towards the sea. Following the main road through the village of **CAPDEPERA** — a dusty, impoverished version of Artá, crouched below a fine crenellated castle — you'll come to the **Cabo de Capdepera** and its two cove-developments, **MOL** and **RATJADA**. These are both dominated by German package companies, who here at least seem to have moved in with a little more taste than the British. There's an excellent beach, too, at Ratjada, and diving from the rocks at Mol. What you won't find is a room. Almost every bed is agency-booked from Munich or Bonn, and though the tourist office is happy to give out lists of *hostales* ,even they own their midsummer superfluousness.

The succession of **coves south from here** which dot the coast all the way down to Cala Figuera are all touristified to some degree, though again not necessarily for the worse. Finding a room in season is a problem almost anywhere but if you're willing to **camp** (semi-legally) there are tree-covered hills between the beaches, some of them almost tailor-made for hiding a tent and anchoring guy-lines. The 'coastal route' along this stretch runs for the most part some way inland and even with transport it's a time-consuming business getting from one cove to the next; hitching or relying on buses you'll do best to pick one spot and stick with it.

CALA CANYAMEL is probably as good a choice as any. Like Mol/Ratjada it is a German development, with few and expensive rooms. But the pine-backed beach is one of the best in this half of the island, and if you put up a tent behind it you have easy access to outdoor hotel-run showers. There's also a local sight, the **Cuevas de Artá**: one of the best of numerous eastern Mallorcan caves, high up in the cliffs above the bay and with a majestic Gothic-horror stairway. Groups are guided through from 9:30am to 7pm daily. If you feel like a change of sand, the next bay around, **CALA MILLOR**, is another developed but agreeable resort, this time mixing Dutch and French elements with its Germanic base. You could easily walk between the two, or there are buses to either from Artá and fairly plentiful taxis.

Moving farther downcoast, past vineyards and groves of almonds, various roads converge on **PORTO CRISTO**, once an attractive fishing harbor but now essentially a parking lot for the region's two Big Excursions. These, announced by multicolor and multilingual billboards, are the **Cuevas de Hams** and **Cuevas de Drach**, each of which include underground concerts (more Chopin) in the cost and endurance of a visit. You'd hardly want to see them both; opt for the *Drach* (Dragon) caverns. The lighting here is really very impressive, focused as it is on what the leaflet asserts is "Europe's largest underwater lake," and musicians drift about in boats playing harmoniums. If you've got kids to entertain, Porto Cristo offers two further attractions. Along the same road as the Cuevas de Hams is a **Safari Park**, with a sparse but quite varied collection of wildlife, and in the town is a well-stocked **aquarium**, where the glass tanks magnify such exotic horrors as electric eels, piranhas, and stinging fish. All of these are open from around 9am to 7pm daily.

Felanitx and Around Cabo Salinas

FELANITX, "capital" of the southeastern corner of the island, is an industrious town. It bottles wine, produces ceramics, and manufactures pearls. If you stop — and you may need to change buses here if coming from Palma — sample the local *Ilet*, a wonderful pick-me-up made from milk, sugar and cinnamon, and served in most of the bars. If you're into walking, take the road out towards Porto Colom and turn off along the mountain road to the **Monastery of San Salvador** — another of the Palma Tourist Board's *Twenty Hiking Excursions*. You can rent **rooms** at the monastery — which is thirteenth-century and recognizable from miles around by its massive *Creu* (Cross) *de Picot* and equally vast Monument of Christ — and with a car this could make an interesting base for a few days (☎971/580656 if you want to check on space availability). In any case, it's a magnificent location. You can sometimes get a meal at the hostelry and the monks will point you toward the path, and another good walk, to the **Castillo de Santueri**. From there you can loop back towards Felanitx or down towards the flower-dense village of CA'S CONCOS.

Down on the coast, northeast of Cabo Salinas, are three very appealing resorts: Porto Colom, Porto Petro, and Cala Figuera. **PORTO COLOM,** still an active fishing village, is perhaps the most attractive of all, with a long, easily accessible stretch of sand (*Cala Arenau*) around the bay and a couple of non-agency booked **hostales**: *Porto Colom* (☎971/575223) and *La Pineda* (☎971/575180, with an excellent, not too pricey restaurant). Heading south, past highly exploited CALA FERRERA and CALA D'OR, **PORT PETRO** is like a smaller, quieter version of Porto Colom, its size and natural endowments enough to enrapture even the most hardened Club Med tourist. **Rooms** here, though, are sparse; the only real possibility is the three-star *Hostal Nerida* (☎971/657223).

At **CALA FIGUERA** development is considerably more advanced but the adjoining coves of Llombarts and Santanyi give reasonable escape from the crowds and good access to camping spots. Official **accommodation** is harder to come by, with only the *Hostal Fernando* and expensive *Hostal Oliver* offering non-agency rooms. Inland lie the main vineyards of Felanitx's wine industry, with high stone walls enclosing narrow straight roads, vines and almond trees. The mustard yellow stone quarried round here was used for several Palmese buildings, including the cathedral.

Past Cabo Salinas there is less of promise. The entire southeastern tip of the island is owned by the Spanish banking magnate Joan March, who preserves much of it as a private nature reserve. At **COLONIA DE SANT JORDI**, reached from the inland village of SES SALINES (which is itself owned by March), there's a new and growing *urbanización* — not much fun. **LA RAPITA**, with the best beach on this stretch, **Playa de Trench** (Es Trenc), is mainly holiday villas. So too is **CALA PÍ**, whose chalets are clustered above an inaccessible cove. **SES COVETES**, which has a tiny strip of beach flanked by rocky cliffs, has a semi-organized campground and could be a nice place to rest up. But in summer, at least, it's hardly worth the effort, with tour buses regularly depositing day-trippers from the Palma Bay hotels.

MENORCA

Second largest of the Balearics, **MENORCA** has the greatest number of stone reminders of its prehistoric past (see introduction to Mallorca). These, and the incessant wind, are its most characteristic features. There's not much in the way of excitement, and only a few developed resorts, but if you're looking for peace and for some beautiful, relatively isolated beaches Menorca is probably your best Balearic bet.

Little is known of the island's prehistory, though the physical evidence is there for all to see; the monuments are thought to be linked to those of Sardinia and representative of the second millenium B.C. *Talayot* Culture. **Talayots** are the rock mounds found all over the island — popular belief has it that they functioned as watchtowers, but it's a theory few experts accept. They have no interior stairway, and only a few are found on the coast. Even so, no one has come up with a much more convincing explanation. The best preserved one is found at Torello, near Mahón airport. The megalithic **taulas** — huge stones topped with another to form a T, around four meters high and peculiar to Menorca — are even more puzzling. They have no obvious function, and where they are found, it's almost always alongside a *talayot*. Then there are **navetas** (dating from 1400–800 B.C.), stone slab constructions shaped like an inverted loaf tin. Many have false ceilings, and although you can stand up inside they were clearly not living space — communal pantries, perhaps, or more probably tombs.

In more recent history the deep-water channel of the port of Mahón promoted Menorca to an important place in European affairs. **The British** saw its potential as a naval base during the War of the Spanish Succession and succeeded in having the island handed over to British rule under the Treaty of Utrecht (1713). Spain regained possession in 1782, but with the threat of Napoleon in the Mediterranean, a new British base was established under Admirals Nelson and Collingwood. The British influence is still considerable, especially in architecture: the sash windows so popular in Georgian design are still sometimes referred to as *winderes*; locals often part with a fond *bye-bye*, and there's a substantial expatriate community (with several English-language magazines — *Roqueta* may be of interest). The British also moved the capital from Ciudadela to Mahón (still resented in the former) and

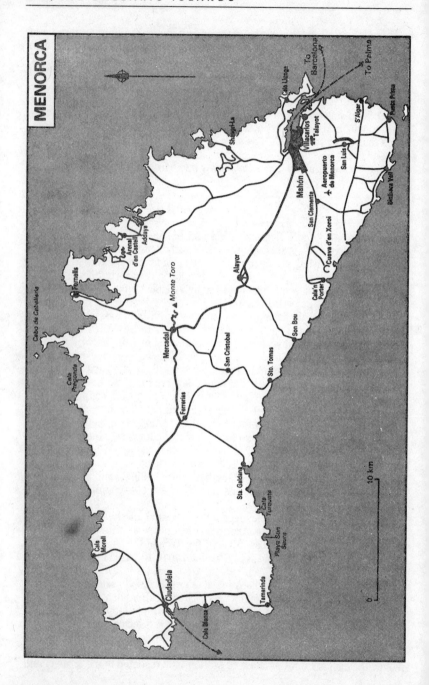

constructed the main island road. More importantly they introduced the art of distilling juniper berries, and Menorcan **gin** (*Xoriguer, Beltran,* or *Nelson*) is renowned.

Before much of it was killed off by tourism, Menorcan **agriculture** had become highly advanced. Every field was protected by a dry-stone wall to prevent the *tramontana* (the vicious north wind) from tearing away the topsoil; even olive trees have their roots individually protected in a little stone well. Nowadays, apart from a few acres of rape and corn, most of the fields are barren, but the walls survive. Any vegetation that dares to emerge above their safety is instantly swept away by the gusts.

Menorcan Practicalities

Menorca is boomerang shaped, stretching from the enormous natural harbor of Mahón in the east to the smaller port of Ciudadela in the west. **Bus routes** are distinctly limited, adhering mostly to the main central road between these two, occasionally branching off to the major coastal towns. You'll need your own vehicle to get to any of the more attractive beaches. There are one or two points to remember, though. To reach any of the emptier sands you'll probably have to drive down a track fit only for four-wheel drive — and the wind, which can be very helpful when its blowing behind you, is distinctly uncomfortable if you're trying to ride into it on a moped. Bear in mind too that gas stations are "strategically placed" (i.e., few and far between) across the island. After 10pm and on Sundays and fiestas the various pumps are open in repertory; take note of the rota posted outside and keep a full tank. It's no fun to be stuck in Mercadal if you're staying in Mahón and the only *gasolinera* open is in Ciudadela.

Accommodation is at an exploited premium, with little of anything outside the bigger coastal towns. Once you find something reasonable, stay there. There's just one **campground**, first category, at Son Bou beach (☎971/371642).

Mahón

MAHÓN (*MAÓ*), the island capital, is likely to be your first port of call. The **airport** (short on amenities and served only by taxi) is just 5km out, and if you arrive by **ferry** from Barcelona or Palma you'll sail into the vast natural harbor here. It is a respectable, almost dull little town, the people restrained and polite. So is the architecture: a strange hybrid of classical Georgian bay-windowed town houses and tall, gloomy Spanish apartment blocks shading the narrow streets. Port it may be, but there's not even a seamy side to Mahón — only one red-light bar, which probably operates at little more than forty watts.

While you'll need transportation to get around the island, Mahón itself is best seen on foot, thanks to its horrendously complicated traffic system. Though walking through the city is an inoffensive, indeed enjoyable, experience, the specific things to see can be covered in a single day. Down towards the docks, four small squares are practically adjacent to each other. The

Plaza España is reached by a twisting flight of steps from the pier and offers great views right across the port and bay; there's a fish market here in the early mornings. Immediately behind is the **Plaza Carmen**, with a simple Carmelite church whose cloisters have been adapted to house the municipal market. Wander on from here up c/Virgen del Carmen and take any of the streets to the left to reach one of the oldest and most atmospheric parts of town, overlooking the port from on high. In the other direction from Plaza España lie the Plaza de la Conquista and the Plaza del Generalissimo Franco.

Plaza de la Conquista has a small **Turismo** and the town's main church, **Santa María**. Founded in 1287 by Alfonso III to celebrate the island's reconquest, its Gothic structure has been much modified — in particular with an unremarkable baroque altarpiece. More interesting is the organ, a monumental piece of woodwork built in Austria in 1810 and lugged across half of Europe at the height of the Napoleonic Wars under the concerned charge of Admiral Collingwood. Its four keyboards and 3000 pipes are quite out of proportion here. There's a *Casa Cultural* in the plaza too, but like so many others it is "temporarily closed" for structural works, and has been since 1976. The **Archeological Museum** which was formerly here has now been moved to the cloister of the Iglesia San Francisco (Mon.–Fri. 10am–1.30pm and 4–7pm). The seventeenth-century Ayuntamiento is around the corner in the **Plaza del Generalissimo Franco** (Mahón is a little slow in bringing its street names into the democratic era), with an attractive arcaded facade, handsome wrought iron balconies, a clock presented by the island's first British governor, and an inscribed stone proclaiming Roman occupation in the first century A.D.

Head down c/Isabel II from here and you get to the church of **San Francisco** — a long, narrow approach which makes it appear as if through a keyhole. There's a fine Romanesque facade, but the confined space never allows it to be appreciated fully. Inside (open Sun. 8–11am, other days after 6pm) are twisted pillars carved by Francisco Herrera, later principal stonemason of Palma Cathedral. Nearby are several former monastic buildings, converted into a school and orphanage despite their ruined appearance — and the aforementioned museum in the cloister.

Mahón's main square is actually the **Plaza Explanada**, some way above all these along c/Hannover and c/Dr. Orfila. There's another tourist office here and it's also home to a bunch of overfed pigeons and a military barracks. Otherwise the only excitement is on Sunday, when the plaza becomes the social hub, with crowds converging on its bars and ice cream parlors, and street entertainers playing to the strolling multitudes. Just off the square, in c/Conde de Cifuentes, is the *Ateneo Científico, Literario y Artístico*, basically a geriatric men's club but also housing a small **museum** which boasts "the most comprehensive collection of dried seaweeds in southern Europe."

The **port area** is considerably more interesting, and you can walk the entire length of the quayside from the *Xoiriguer* gin distillery (free visits and samples during working hours) to the suburb of VILLACARLOS, passing through Cala Figuera and Castelfons. There's a rather sparse **Aquarium** (9:30am–1pm and 4:30–8pm) next to the gin palace. By day this makes a relaxed stroll past any number of small restaurants and bars; at night it's slightly more animated, but not much. Although the whole extent of the port and most of the long bay that leads to it can be seen from the shore, a **boat trip** around the harbor can prove very enjoyable, especially if you take one that includes a visit to the gin factory. They can be booked at most travel agents, or from the aquarium.

At the mouth of the harbor channel — more than 5km from the center of Mahón — is the imposing ISLA DEL REY on which you can see a hospital built during the British occupation. Nowadays its a vacation home for Spanish health workers. **Lanzaretto**, the jutting promontory behind the island, was cut off from the mainland in 1900 by a canal in order to establish an isolated leper colony. On the headland here is the fortress of **La Mola**, still in use and inaccessible, with opposite the site of **Fort San Felipe**, now nothing but ruins and rumors of secret tunnels.

Some Practical Details

The **Turismos** in the Plaza Explanada and Plaza de la Conquista can both provide maps of Mahón, Ciudadela, and the island, and should also have leaflets giving details of accommodation, car rental, banks, beaches, and so on. If possible you should fix up **a room** in advance — certainly in August you'll have difficulty finding anything and prices, thanks to excessive demand, tend to be inflated. On the other hand Mahón *is* your best bet on the island, and those possibilities that exist are all fairly central. The best place to start looking is between the Plaza Franco and Plaza Bastion: try the *CH Minorica* (Iglesia 28, ☎971/362567) on the street linking the two, *Pensión Tito* (☎971/362267) or *Company* on c/Rosario, which crosses this, or *Eric* (☎971/363799) on San Bartolomé just beyond the Plaza Bastion. Other good bets are c/Infanta (*Hostal Orsi*, ☎971/364751; *CH Del Mar*, ☎971/364059) and c/Deya (*Pensión Menorquina*, ☎971/361811), both just off Plaza Reial, and the area above the Plaza Carmen, especially c/Santa Ana and c/Santa Catalina.

Mahón has a place in culinary history as the birthplace of mayonnaise (*mahonesa*), something not much in evidence. You should however have no problem finding **somewhere to eat**. In the Plaza Bastion — beside the only surviving city gate, San Roque — there are two friendly bar/restaurants serving basic fare at reasonable prices. *Alfabrega*, just below here at c/San Jerónimo 31, is also very reasonably priced, as is the place known simply as *Comidas Economicas* at c/Rosario 27 (below the *Pension Company*). The *American Bar* in Plaza Reial is expensive and not too proficient on cocktails, but its outdoor tables overlooking the paved shopping area of c/Goded make it a pleasant place to nurse a coffee. *El Café Charcuteria*, too, on the corner of Rosario and Isabel II, is an elegant hang-out. Other than these, the majority of restaurants are down by the port, where expensive French cuisine, local *tapas* and the standard steak and french fries are all available. There's an excellent *pizzeria* as well.

Other forms of nightlife are fairly limited. There are a couple of reasonably lively **bars** — *Cachita* and *Fragile* — and three **discos** on the road to Villacarlos. These, *Lui*, *Tonic*, and *El Si*, differ only in their decor, with *Lui* winning out as the fanciest.

There are **buses** from Mahón to Ciudadela via Alayor and Ferrerias (7 daily), to San Cristóbal and Santo Tomás (1 a day), to Villacarlos (half-hourly, 8am–9pm), to San Clemente and Cala'n Porter (10 daily), to Punta Prima via San Luis (12 a day), to Son Bou via Alayor (3), and to Fornells via Arenal d'en Castell (3). This sounds like plenty, but to get to the really good beaches you still need your own transportation; there are abundant **car rental** places around the center, but even so it's very hard to get anything in August. It may prove marginally easier to find a **Vespa** or **Mobylette** — try *Gelabert* (the cheapest; c/J. A. Clave 12, ☎971/360614), *Motos Valls* in the Plaza Colón (☎971/362839), or *Nura* on the Muelle Comercial (☎971/366813).

Out and About from Mahón

Menorca's western end is the most accessible part of the island and you can get to most of the places below by bus; emptier nearby beaches, however, will be beyond your reach, and you'll be tied down to the timetable. Given the difficulties with accommodation, all are best treated as day-trips from the capital.

South

VILLACARLOS barely counts as being outside Mahón, since it sits on the bay as a virtual continuation of the city. Nevertheless there's a very different atmosphere. Originally called Georgetown, Villacarlos was built by the British in the 1770s, in a militaristic and very English style; sash windows, doors with glass fanlights, and wrought iron work adorn many of its older houses, while the huge parade ground/plaza is lined with old barrack buildings. A very attractive small hotel (*El Fonduco* or *Hotel Almirante*) was once a private house occupied by Admiral Collingwood after Trafalgar, and its public rooms contain odd mementos of the period. More realistic if you want to stay is the *Fonda Es Castell* on Carrera Gran (☎971/364233), right by where the bus stops, opposite *Rex and Shirley's Pub*. Heading back around the bay takes you through **CASTELFONS** where there are some excellent quayside fish restaurants, and boats across the harbour or back to Mahón.

Farther south you can catch sight of a *talayot* and *taula* at **TREPUCO** on the road to San Luis. There's a certain excitement in this if it is the first you've seen, but it's a pleasure which soon palls — climb to the top of any of these piles of rock anywhere on the island and you'll get much the same view of flattish, bare countryside, broken only by the distant rise of Monte Toro. **SAN LUIS** isn't up to much — a one-square, one-church town with blank windowless houses and a huge sports center — and neither are the places which you can get to on the coast beyond. **PUNTA PRIMA, BINIBECA,** and **CALA ALCAUFAR** all have beaches which primarily serve the local *urbanizaciones*.

By the other road, towards Cala'n Porter, you pass through **SAN CLEMENTE**, with the remains of an early Christian basilica. **CALA'N**

PORTER itself is not of any great interest — a rather shabby little town — but there are some good coves nearby and amazing caves in the cliffs. The **Cova d'en Xoroi** above the bay have had their natural beauty exploited by a local businessman who has installed a bar and disco. The latter opens nightly at 10pm, but loud music thunders out, and you can visit, all day: 200ptas entrance includes a drink under the dripping ceilings. Follow the cliff face around and you'll find more caves around *Cala Coves*, some of them inhabited. They look really impressive (and there are boat trips to see them from Cala'n Porter) but living conditions must be grim.

North

North of Mahón the road to Fonells runs through some of Menorca's finest scenery — the fields are cultivated and protected by great stands of trees, and the land rises as it approaches Monte Toro and skirts around it to the north. There's very little along the way, but at regular intervals you can turn off towards a series of small beachside communities.

CALA MESQUIDA is the first of these, pleasant enough and close to Mahón but somewhat overdeveloped. There's a ruined fortress overlooking the sea. The next fork takes you to **ES GRAU** past the salt marshes of **S'Albufera** (rich in migrant bird life). There's a good beach, an excellent windsurfing school, and offshore the pigeon island of COLOM can be reached by boat. At **Cabo de Favoritx** the lighthouse shines over an extraordinary, almost lunar landscape: slate rocks surround a series of jagged inlets like layers of phyllo dough stubbled with scrubby red and green shrubs. **ADDAIA** is a hilly *urbanización* built about a small port with a poor, unattractive beach, and is probably best left to those who've invested there; this goes for **ARENAL D'EN CASTELL** as well, whose coastline backs on to barren and windswept slopes.

Better than any of these options is to continue all the way to **FONELLS**, a low-rise, classically pretty harbor town arrayed about a broad bay. Though it's been popular with tourists for years, above all for its seafood restaurants, there's been little development. Two fortresses protect the harbor, and the sweeping inlet provides ideal conditions for windsurfers; accordingly there's a residential windsurfing school offering one- or two-week courses in the art. It's pretty good for simple beach lovers too. Such is the renown of local restaurants that King Juan Carlos regularly calls in here on his yacht, and many people phone up days in advance with their orders — prices, though, are regal to match.

For somewhere to stay, and less popular beaches, you can continue round to the north. At **CALA TIRANT** there's a cheap semiofficial campground with a bar and cold showers, more windsurfing, and pedal-boats for hire. Beyond the next point is the Platja of **BINIMEL'LA** — an unofficial nudist beach with deep red sand. There are no trees or shade, and the tortuous track down is appalling, but the surrounding cliffs make for good walks, and a stream running across the beach provides mud which you can plaster all over when you feel the need for protection against the sun.

Across the Island

The road from Mahón to Ciudadela forms the backbone of Menorca, and what little industry the island enjoys — a few shoe factories and producers of the island's famous cheese (*Roque Rico*) and ice cream — is concentrated along it. The last is the main reason for stopping at **ALAYOR**, a market town some 12km out of Mahón. En route you pass two *taulas* and a *talayot* at TALATI DE DALT, and a couple of *navetas* at RAFAL RUBI.

The center of Alayor is a tangle of narrow streets and bright white houses around two churches: imposing Santa Eulalia on a rise behind the main square, and smaller San Diego, pink and gray-marbled. The *La Menorquina* ice cream factory is here, and its magnificent produce can be sampled at the *heladería* (ice cream parlor) on the main street, Carrer Nou. There are at least thirty different flavors, some stuffed with real fruit, as well as sorbets, cakes and exotic combinations. There's also a cheese factory in town (*Quesos Comiga*) producing the open-textured white cheese which is sold throughout Spain.

In the second weekend of August, Alayor lets loose for the **Fiesta de San Lorenzo** — a drunken display of horsemanship and general celebration. As its highlight, with the tiny town square packed, a procession of horses tears through the crowd, bucking and rearing, with their riders clinging on for dear life. Although no one seems to get hurt, you'd probably be best to join the privileged townspeople and witness the spectacle from the safety of an overlooking balcony.

Eight kilometers farther along you arrive at **MERCADAL**, at the very center of the island. Another old market town, it's cramped and rather oppressive, but is the point from which you can set off on the ascent of **Monte Toro**, the island's highest point. This is a steep four-kilometer climb (by road) but there are wonderful vistas from the top: on a good day you can see the entire coastline, on a bad one at least to Cala Fonells in the north. Also at the summit is a convent, its roofline bristling with aerials and radar dishes which make you wonder just to what order these nuns belong. Whatever, the well in its patio provides wonderfully cool fresh water, and there are picnic tables and a cafe. The church contains the remains of an earlier structure, and outside the whole place is dominated by a huge statue of Christ built to commemorate civil war dead.

FERRERIAS is the next town along the route, though there's little to detain you here unless you're interested in the guided tour of the *Rubrica* shoe factory. It's a strange place, little more than a village really, which seems even more insignificant because it's hidden at the bottom of a dip in the road — no sooner do you leave than it has disappeared. One definite plus is the *Vimpi* bar on the plaza at the entrance to town, which serves some of the tastiest *tapas* on the island.

South from here an excellent road will get you down to **CALA SANTA GALDANA**, a truly beautiful cove. The road is new, and along with it has come development; the first thing you see is a twelve-story hotel (*Los Gavilanes*) built right on to the beach. It's becoming a busy resort and there are plans for a campground, but even so the place is not overrun. The beaches are set on two bays divided by a rocky promontory; there's a restaurant built into this and if you climb up behind it you can still enjoy the sensation of being alone.

Getting back, you've no choice but to head through Ferrerias again — a scenic drive through undulating, wooded scenery. The road to SAN CRISTÓBAL and SANTO TOMÁS is equally pretty, but there's little reason to take it. Despite a reputation for folk dancing you won't find much in San Cristóbal, while Santo Tomás, has a sandy beach and good windsurfing, is spoiled by an uninspiring mass of apartments and hotels.

Ciudadela and Around

Like Mahón, **CIUDADELA** (*CIUTADELA* in Menorquin) sits high above its harbor. Here, though, navigation is far more difficult, up a narrow channel which ends in the silted-up estuary of a dry river. If you're driving in, it also suffers from horribly complex one-way traffic flow, the legacy of a particularly crazed traffic engineer.

Until 1722 and the British intervention this was the capital of the island, and its history is considerably richer than Mahón's. Known as *Medina Minurka* under Muslim rule, there are still a few Moorish traces, including parts of the old mosque, now converted to Christian use. In 1558 the city was invaded by the Turks with considerable destruction, especially of old records and documents, and decline was completed by the transferral of the capital to the more strategic setting of Mahón. Nevertheless it remains the seat of Menorca's bishopric, and a thoroughly attractive city. There's far less British influence here; instead, the narrow, cobbled streets lined with vaulted arches have a very Moorish/Andalucian feel to them.

In the center, down by the docks, everything is very compact with the main plazas and points of interest within a few strides of each other. The **Plaza d'es Borne**, looking over the port from the north, is probably the best place to start. This is effectively the main square (formerly *Plaza Generalissimo*), packed with fluttering pigeons and built around an obelisk commemorating the futile defense against the Turks. Flanking the western side is the **Ayuntamiento** (24-hr. **tourist information** run by the municipal police) in the vestibule of which is an extraordinary **museum** of collected chaos. The island seems to use this place as an attic in which to cram anything to do with its earlier days; there are the keys to the ancient walls, nineteenth-century shoes, and bones from the nearby *naveta* of Els Tudons. There are street signs taken down when the first Republic fell, and more recent ones from the Franco era — any amount of junk, in short. The prize possession, though, is the "Red Book," not Mao's, but one of the few documents to survive the Turkish sacking. It contains a record of the grants made by Alfonso III of Aragón after he reconquered the island, and is the pride and joy of the amiable curator.

Many of Ciudadela's churches suffered heavy damage in the civil war and have never been restored; San Francisco, in the south-west corner of the plaza, is an exception. A clean-lined, airy, fourteenth-century Gothic building, it contains some superb carved wood altars and a lovely little domed manger scene as well as the more usual polychromatic saints. There's also an ancient opera house in the square — now reduced to showing reruns of old movies — and three of the city's many "palaces." The Palacio de Torre-Saura, built in the nineteenth century but looking far older, is typical: a frontage proclaiming the family coat of arms is pierced by a giant wooden door through to the patio. Like the Salort residence next door, and most of the others, this one is still owner-occupied, so the impressively luxuriant interior is off bounds. Two which can be seen are the Saura mansions in c/Obispo Vila (now a bank) and in c/del Santissimo, where there are occasional art and antique exhibitions.

There are a couple, too, in the cathedral plaza (Plaza Pio XII): the Bishop's Palace, with a flowery Andalusian-style courtyard, and the Olives residence with a collection of antique furniture. The Cathedral itself was built by Alfonso III on the site of the chief mosque. So soon after the Reconquest, its construction is fortress-like and Gothic, its windows set high and impregnably above the ground. Inside, this gives a beautiful lighting effect, with rays filtering down from the narrow recesses. There's also a wonderfully kitschy pointed altar-arch and a wealth of ornately decorated chapels. Along by its south side the church of Nuestra Señora del Rosario (in which British troops were briefly, and unpopularly, quartered) has a heavy golden facade.

Just beyond in the Plaza España are a block of *voltes* or whitewashed arches, distinctly Moorish in inspiration. The streets leading off this square — Quadrado and Carmen — contain some very attractive period shops and cafes, art deco *farmacias*, and tiled bars. One little street, a narrow, balconied cul-de-sac, is known simply and understandably as *Que no Pasa* (The One that Doesn't Go Through).

In the other direction from the Plaza Borne, Paseo San Nicolás runs dead straight out towards the Castillo San Nicolás and Ciudadela's best hotel, the three-star *Eleycon*. Seen in the aerial view postcards, this broad boulevard looks like some huge tree-lined landing strip. At its end, the octagonal castle stands on unwelcoming rocks looking out towards Mallorca, from whose port of Alcudia there are daily ferries to Ciudadela.

Some Practicalities

The turismo, as already stated, is open 24 hours in the Plaza d'es Borne. They have lists of hostales and casas de huéspedes, but be warned that the choices are extremely limited. Among the more reasonably priced and comfortable are: *Las Persianas* (Pl. Cabrisas 2, ☎971/381445) and *Oasis* (c/San Isidro 33, ☎971/382197), very close to each other and reasonably central; *Pension España* (Calvo Sotelo 13, ☎971/380288) and *Paris* (Carretera Santandria, ☎971/381622), not far from where most buses stop; and *Ibiza* and *Casa Juana* on c/Ibiza, two blocks inland from the Paseo San Nicolas as it runs towards the castle. Restaurants and bars are crowded throughout the center, and there's also a place where you can get excellent roast chicken and other prepared foods to take away.

Buses generally terminate in the Plaza Alfonso III: there is service across the island of course, but also south to the beaches of Santandria and Cala Blanca and the *urbanización* at Tamarinda, and around the bay to Forcat and Los Delfines via Cala n'Bruch and Cala n'Blanes. Car rental is widely available too, or for mopeds try *Motocicletas* (Barcelona 24, ☎971/382282) or *Motos Manolo* (Avda. Conquistador 86, 971/385050).

Around Ciudadela

There are two roads south from Ciudadela. One, which follows the west coast around to TAMARINDA via CALA BLANCA, is well paved — an obvious sign that it leads to new *urbanizaciones* and hotel complexes (and in this case to little else). The other sets off cross-country toward the south coast, branching beyond the HERMITA FATIMA into two tracks which both lead through leafy countryside to unspoiled beaches. If you've rented a moped then be prepared for a bumpy ride and watch out for the dust and muck churned up by passing cars. There's little to choose between their end points — lovely sandy coves at PLAYA SON SAURA, CALA D'ES TALAIER, and CALA TURQUETA. Seven kilometers southeast of Ciudadela are the ruins of SON CATLAR village, including 800m of defensive walls, some buildings, and a religious sanctuary.

Around the bay to the west, the whitewashed modern tourist complex of LOS DELFINES also promises a good route. Although the end of the road peters out in ugly concrete package territory and a rather dull lighthouse at the island's westernmost point, both Los Delfines itself and CALA BLANCA are attractive enough, especially the latter, a small, shallow anchorage with clean soft sand and a good bar.

To the north, if you can find and follow the very limited signs to CALA MORELL, the beach at the end is well worth the effort. Ignore the 'No Entry' signs to what looks like a national park after about 5km, struggle on over rough dirt tracks and sand paths, and you'll emerge in a striking sandy cove squeezed in between pine-clad hills. There are a fair number of local campers here who not only ignore the 'No Entry' signs but are heedless of the fire warnings also; if you're reasonably discreet and don't go around burning down the trees, no one seems to mind your being there. At Cala Morell there are similar **prehistoric tombs** as at Cala Coves, with pillared chambers fashioned out of the cliffs.

fiestas

January

17 *Día de San Antonio Abad* is marked by fiestas in several Mallorcan villages, and in PALMA itself, with bonfires (*foguerones*) in the streets and the blessing of animals. Also celebrated of course, in SAN ANTONIO ABAD (Ibiza) and in CIUDADELA (Menorca) where the Reconquest is commemorated.

19 PALMA (Mallorca) has more bonfires, singing and dancing for *San Sebastián*.

March/April

Holy Weeks *Semana Santa* is as widely observed as everywhere. MAHÓN (Men.) sees a big celebration on **Good Friday**, but the larger ceremonies are all on Mallorca, especially at

PALMA and POLLENSA on Good Friday and the *Romerías* from SA POBLA, LLUBI, and MONTUIRI the **following Tuesday**.

May

Second Sunday *Fiesta de Nuestra Señora de la Victoria* in SOLLER (Mall.) spreads into the following week's *Fiestas de Mayo*, with battles between Moors and Christians.
30 *Fiesta de San Fernando* celebrated in SAN FERNANDO (Form.).

June

23–26 In CIUDADELA (Men.), the major midsummer festival of *San Juan*, with jousting tournaments.

July

9 The *Fiesta Patriotica* in CIUDADELA (Men.) celebrates the resistance to the Turks.
Second Sunday The reconquest of Menorca is celebrated in a fiesta in MERCADAL.
28 The monastery at VALLDEMOSA (Mall.), where Chopin stayed, celebrates *Santa Catalina's* day appropriately enough with a piano concert.

August

2 Moors and Christians battle it out in POLLENSA (Mall.).
5 *Dia de la Virgen de las Nieves* in IBIZA (Ib.); festivities spill over into the next few days.
Second week *Fiesta de San Lorenzo* in ALAYOR (Men.), high jinks on horseback (see text).
23–25 SAN LUIS (Men.) has a similar equine *jaleo* for the festival of *Sant Genis*.
28 FELANITX (Mall.) starts the *Cavallets*, a major week-long festival.
International Festival at POLLENSA: art and sculpture exhibitions, chamber music, etc.

September

8 Fiesta of the Annunciation in MAHÓN (Men.).
Second week *La Diada de Lluc*, traditional and religious festivities in ESCORCA (Men.).

December

3 *Dia de San Francisco* celebrated in SAN FRANCISCO JAVIER (Form.).
Christmas is especially picturesque in PALMA (Mall.) where there are nativity plays in the days leading up to the 25th.

travel details

Note that interisland **flights** can work out cheaper than **ferries**; so too, at times, can some charters between the Spanish mainland and Balearics. Check in an hour early or risk losing your seat. All schedules below are for **summer service** — slightly reduced out of season.

Mainland Ferry Connections

From Barcelona At least daily to Palma (Mall.), 8 hr.; 4 to 7 weekly to Ibiza, 9–10 hr.; 3 to 5 weekly to Mahón (Men.), 9 hr.
From Valencia 6 to 7 weekly to Palma, 9 hr.; Tues. and Thurs. year-round to Ibiza, Sat./Sun. also in summer, 7 hr.; one a week (usually Sat.) to Mahón, via Palma.
Barcelona and Valencia services are operated by Transediterranea, *which has offices in BARCELONA at Via Laietana 2 (☎93/3199612/3198212) and VALENCIA at Avda. Manuel Soto 19 (☎96/3676512) and agents in all the island capitals.*
From Denia Daily except Tues.to Ibiza, 3 hr.
This service is run by Flebasa *(Denia office: ☎965/784011), which also sells combination coach/ferry tickets from Alicante and Valencia.*
From Port-Vendres (France) Weekly ferry to Alcudia (Mall.), 6 hr. A useful — and fairly cheap

— connection, though often overbooked. Details and bookings can be obtained in LONDON through *Zenon Travel* (15 Kentish Town Rd, NW1; ☎01/267-2657); in PALMA through *Hijos de Miguel Estela S.A.* (Paseo de Sangrera 1, ☎971/211526) or at the ports of ALCUDIA or PORT-VENDRES.

Mainland Flights

There are flights to the Balearics on **Iberia** and on both Spanish charter airlines, **Aviaco** and **Spantax**. For details of tickets and special deals stop in at any Spanish travel agent — in summer well in advance.
Charters and reduced Iberia flights are most regularly operated between **Barcelona**, **Valencia**, or **Madrid**, and **Palma** or **Ibiza**.

Interisland Ferries and Flights

Ibiza–Formentera Several daily ferries (1 hr.)
Ibiza–Palma Three ferries a week (4½ hr.); daily flights.
Palma–Mahón One ferry a week (6½ hr.); more or less daily flights.
Alcudia (Mall.)–**Ciudadela** (Men.) Several weekly ferries (2 hr.)

PART THREE

THE
CONTEXTS

THE HISTORICAL FRAMEWORK

EARLY CIVILIZATIONS

The first Spanish peoples arrived on the Iberian peninsula from southern France towards the close of the Paleolithic age. They were cave dwellers and hunter-gatherers and seem to have been heavily concentrated in the north of the country, around the modern province of Santander. Here survive the most remarkable traces of their culture (which peaked around 15,000 B.C.), the deftly stylized cave murals of the animals that they hunted. The finest examples are at Altamira — now closed for general visits, though you can see similar paintings at Puente Viesgo, also near Santander.

Subsequent prehistory is more complex and confused. There does not appear to have been any great development in the cave cultures of the north. Instead the focus shifts south to Almería, which was settled around 5000–4000 B.C. by the "Iberians," **Neolithic** colonists from North Africa. They had already assimilated into their culture many of the changes that had developed in Egypt and the Near East. Settling in villages, they introduced pastoral

and agricultural ways of life and exploited the plentiful supply of copper. Around 1500 B.C., with the onset of the **Bronze Age**, they began to spread outwards into fortified villages on the central *meseta*, the high plateau of modern Castile. At the turn of the millenium they were joined by numerous waves of **Celtic** and **Germanic** peoples. Here, Spain's divisive physical makeup — with its network of mountain ranges — determined its social nature. The incoming tribes formed distinct and isolated groups, conquering and sometimes absorbing each other but only on a very limited and local scale. Hence the Celtic "urnfield people" established themselves in Catalonia, the **Vascones** in the Basque Country, and near them along the Atlantic coast the **Astures**. Pockets of earlier cultures survived, too, particularly in Galicia with its "*citânias*" of beehive huts.

THE FIRST COLONISTS

The Spanish coast meanwhile attracted colonists from different regions of the Mediterranean. The **Phoenicians** founded the port of Gadir (Cádiz) in 1100 B.C. and traded intensively in the metals of the Guadalquivir valley. Their wealth and success gave rise to a Spanish "Atlantis" myth, based around Huelva. Market rivalry also brought the **Greeks**, who established their trading colonies along the eastern coast — the modern Costa Brava — of which there's a fine surviving site at Empuries, near Barcelona.

More significant, however, was the arrival of the **Carthaginians** in the third century B.C.. Expelled from Sicily by the Romans, they saw in Spain a new base for their empire, from which to regain strength and strike back at their rivals. Although making little impact inland, they occupied most of Andalucía and expanded along the Mediterranean seaboard to establish a new capital at Cartagena. Under Hannibal they prepared to invade Italy and in 214 B.C. attacked Saguntum, a strategic outpost of the Roman Empire. It was a disastrous move, precipitating the **Second Punic War**; by 210 B.C. only Cádiz remained in their control and they were forced to accept terms. A new and very different age had begun.

ROMANS AND VISIGOTHS

The **Roman colonization** of the peninsula was far more intense than anything previously experienced and met with great resistance from the Celtiberian tribes of the north and center. It was almost two centuries before the conquest was complete and indeed the Basques, although defeated, were never fully Romanized.

Nonetheless, Spain became the most important center of the Roman Empire after Italy herself, producing no less than four emperors, along with the writers Seneca and Lucan. Again geography dictated an uneven spread of influence, at its strongest in Andalucía, southern Portugal, and on the Catalan coast around Tarragona. In the first two centuries A.D. the Spanish mines and the granaries of Andalucía brought unprecedented wealth and Roman Spain enjoyed a brief "**Golden Age**." The finest monuments were built in the great provincial capitals — Córdoba, Mérida (which boasts the finest remains), and Tarragona — but all across the country more practical structures were undertaken: roads, bridges, and aqueducts. Many were still used well into recent centuries — perhaps the most remarkable being the aqueducts of Segovia and Tarragona — and a few bridges continue in use even today.

Towards the third century, however, the Roman political framework began to show signs of decadence and corruption. Although the actual structure didn't totally collapse until the Muslim invasions of the early eighth century, it became increasingly vulnerable to **barbarian invasions** from northern Europe. The Franks and the Suevi (Swabians) swept across the Pyrenees between 264 and 276, leaving much devastation in their wake. They were followed two centuries later by further waves of Suevi, Alans, and Vandals. Internal strife was heightened by the arrival of the **Visigoths** from Gaul, allies of Rome and already Romanized to a large degree. The triumph of Visigothic strength in the fifth century resulted in a period of spurious unity, based upon an exclusive military rule from their capital at Toledo, but their numbers were never great and their order was often fragmentary and nominal, with the bulk of the subject people kept in a state of disconsolate servility and held ransom for their services in time of war. Above them in the ranks of the military elite there were constant plots and factions — exacerbated by the Visigothic system of elected monarchy and by their adherence to the heretical Arian philosophy. In 589 **King Recared** converted to Catholicism but religious strife was only multiplied: forced conversions, especially within the Jewish enclaves, maintained a constant simmering of discontent.

MOORISH SPAIN

In contrast to the long-drawn-out Roman campaigns, **Moorish conquest** of the peninsula was effected with extraordinary speed. This was a characteristic phenomenon of the spread of Islam — Muhammad left Mecca in 622 and by 705 his followers had established control over all of North Africa. Spain, with its political instability, its wealth, and its fertile climate, was an inevitable extension of their aims. In 711 Tariq, governor of Tangier, led a force of 7000 Berbers across the straits and routed the Visigoth army of King Roderic: two years later the Visigoths made a last, desperate stand at Mérida and within a decade the Moors had conquered all but the wild mountains of the Asturias. The land under their authority was dubbed "**al-Andalus**" a fluid term which expanded and shrunk with the intermittent gains and losses of the Reconquest. According to region, the Moors were to remain in control for the next three to eight centuries.

It was not simply a military conquest. The Moors (a collective term for the numerous waves of Arab and Berber settlers from North Africa) were often content to grant a limited autonomy in exchange for payment of tribute; their administrative system was tolerant and easily absorbed both Jews and Christians, those who retained their religion being known as "Mozarabs." And al-Andalus was a distinctly Spanish state of Islam. Though at first politically subject to the Eastern Caliphate (or empire) of Baghdad, it was soon virtually independent. In the tenth century, at the peak of its power and expansion, Abd ar-Rahman III asserted total independence, proclaiming himself Caliph of a new **Western Islamic Empire**. Its capital was Córdoba — the largest, most prosperous, and most civilized city in Europe. This was the great age of Muslim Spain: its scholarship, philosophy, architecture, and craftsmanship were without rival and there was an unparalleled growth in urban life, in trade, and in agriculture aided by magnificent irrigation projects. These and other engineering feats were not, on the whole, introduced by the Moors who instead took the basic Roman models and adapted them to a new level of sophistication. In **architecture** and the **decorative arts**, however, their contribution was original and unique — as may be seen in the incredible monuments of Sevilla, Córdoba, and Granada.

The Córdoban Caliphate for a while created a remarkable degree of unity. But its rulers were to become decadent and out of touch, prompting the brilliant but dictatorial **al-Mansur** to usurp control. Under this extraordinary ruler Moorish power actually reached new heights, pushing the Christian kingdom of Asturias-León back into the Cantabrian mountains and sacking its most holy shrine, Santiago de Compostela. However, after his death the Caliphate quickly lost its authority and in 1031 disintegrated into a series of small, independent kingdoms, or "*taifas*," the strongest of which was Sevilla.

Internal divisions amongst the *taifas* offered less resistance to the Christian kingdoms which were rallying in the north, and twice North Africa had to be turned to for reinforcement. This resulted in two distinct new waves of Moorish invasion — first by the fanatically Islamic **Almoravides** (1086) and later by the **Almohads** (1147), who restored effective Muslim authority until their defeat at the battle of Las Navas de Tolosa in 1212.

THE CHRISTIAN RECONQUEST

The **reconquest** of land and influence from the Moors was a slow and intermittent process. It began with a symbolic victory by a small force of Christians at Covadonga in the Asturias (727) and was not completed until 1492 with the conquest of Granada by Fernando and Isabella.

Covadonga resulted in the formation of the tiny Christian **Kingdom of the Asturias**. Initially just 40 by 30 miles in area, it had by 914 reclaimed León and most of Galicia and northern Portugal. At this point, progress was temporarily halted by the devastating campaigns of al-Mansur. However, with the fall of the Córdoban Caliphate and the divine aid of Spain's Moor-slaying patron, St. James the Apostle (see Santiago, p346), the Reconquest moved into a new and powerful phase.

The frontier castles built against Arab attack gave name to **Castile**, founded in the tenth century as a county of León-Asturias. Under Fernando I (1037–65) it achieved the status of a kingdom and became the main thrust and focus of the Reconquest. Other kingdoms were being defined in the north at the same time: the Basques founded Navarra (Navarre), while dynastic marriage merged Catalonia with Aragón. In 1085 this period of confident Christian expansion reached its zenith with the capture of the great Moorish city of Toledo. The following year, however, the Almoravides arrived on invitation from Sevilla, and military activity was effectively frozen — except, that is, for the exploits of the legendary **El Cid**, a Castilian nobleman who won considerable lands around Valencia in 1095.

The next concerted phase of the Reconquest really began as a response to the threat imposed by the Almohads. The Kings of León, Castile, Aragón, and Navarra united in a general crusade which resulted in the great victory at **Las Navas de Tolosa** (1212). Thereafter Muslim power was effectively paralyzed and the Christian armies moved on to take most of al-Andalus. Fernando III ("el Santo", the saint) led Castilian soldiers into Córdoba in 1236 and twelve years later into Sevilla. Meanwhile, the Kingdom of Portugal had expanded to more or less its present size, while Jaime I of Aragon was to conquer Valencia, Alicante, Murcia, and the Balearic islands. By the end of the thirteenth century only the Kingdom of Granada remained under Muslim authority and for much of the following two centuries it was forced to pay tribute to the monarchs of Castile.

Two factors should be stressed regarding the Reconquest. First, its unifying religious nature — the **spirit of crusade**, intensified by the religious zeal of the Almoravides and Almohads, and by the wider European climate (which in 1085 gave rise to the First Crusade). This powerful religious motivation is well illustrated by the subsequent canonization of Fernando III, and found solid expression in the part played by the military orders of Christian knights, the most important of which were the **Knights Templar** and the Order of Santiago. At the same time the Reconquest was a movement of **recolonization**. The fact that the country had been in arms for so long meant that the nobility had a major and clearly visible social role, a trend perpetuated by the redistribution of captured land in huge packages, or "*latifundia*." Heirs to this tradition still remain as landlords of the great estates, most conspicuously in Andalucía. Men from the ranks were also awarded land, forming a lower, larger stratum of nobility, the *hidalgos*. It was their particular social code that provided the material for Cervantes in *Don Quixote*.

Any spirit of mutual cooperation that had temporarily united the Christian kingdoms disintegrated during the fourteenth century, and independent lines of development were once again pursued. Attempts to merge **Portugal** with Castile foundered at the battle of Aljubarrota (1385), and Portugese attention turned away from Spain towards the Atlantic. Aragón experienced a similar pull towards the markets of the Mediterranean, although preeminence in this area was soon passed to the Genoese. It was **Castile** that emerged as the strongest over this period: self-sufficiency in agriculture and a flourishing wool trade with the Netherlands enabled the state to build upon the prominent military role played under Fernando III. Politically, Castilian history was a tale of dynastic conflict until the accession of the Catholic kings.

LOS REYES CATOLICOS

Los Reyes Catolicos — **the Catholic Kings** — was the joint title given to **Fernando V of Aragón** and **Isabella I of Castile**, whose marriage in 1479 united the two largest kingdoms in Spain. Unity was in practice more symbolic than real: Castile had underlined its rights in the marriage vows and Aragón retained its old administrative structure. So, in the beginning at least, the growth of any national unity or Spanish — as opposed to local — sentiment was very much dependent

on the head of state. Nevertheless from this time on it begins to be realistic to consider Spain as a single political entity.

At the heart of Fernando and Isabella's popular appeal lay a **religious bigotry** that they shared with most of their Christian subjects. The Inquisition was instituted in Castile in 1480 and in Aragón seven years later. Aiming to establish the purity of the Catholic faith by rooting out heresy, it was directed mainly at Jews — resented for their enterprise in commerce and influence in high places, as well as for their faith. Expression had already been given to these feelings in a pogrom in 1391; it was reinforced by an edict issued in 1492 which forced up to 400,000 Jews to flee the country. A similar spirit was embodied in the reconquest of the **Kingdom of Granada**, also in 1492. As the last stronghold of Muslim authority, the religious rights of its citizens were guaranteed under the treaty of surrender. Within a decade, though, those Muslims under Christian rule had been given the choice between conversion or expulsion.

The year 1492 was symbolic of a fresh start in another way: it was in this year that Columbus discovered America, and the Papal Bull that followed, entrusting Spain with the conversion of the American Indians, further entrenched Spain's sense of a mission to bring the world to the "True Faith." The next ten years saw the systematic conquest, colonization, and exploitation of the **New World** as it was discovered, with new territory stretching from Labrador to Brazil, and new-found wealth pouring into the royal coffers. Important as this was for Fernando and Isabella, and especially for their prestige, priorities remained in Europe and strategic marriage alliances were made with Portugal, England, and the Holy Roman Empire. It was not until the accession of the Habsburg dynasty that Spain could look to the activities of Cortés, Magellan, and Pizarro and claim to be the world's leading power.

HABSBURG SPAIN

Carlos I, a Habsburg, came to the throne in 1516 as a beneficiary of the marriage alliances of the Catholic kings. Five years later, he was elected Emperor of the Holy Roman Empire as

Carlos V (**Charles V**), inheriting not only Castile and Aragón, but Flanders, the Netherlands, Artois, the Franche-Comté, and all the American colonies to boot. With such responsibilities it was inevitable that attention would be diverted from Spain, whose chief function became to sustain the Holy Roman Empire with gold and silver from the Americas. It was only with the accession of **Felipe II** in 1556 that Spanish politics became more centralized. The notion of an absentee king was reversed. Felipe lived in the center of Castile near Madrid, creating a monument to the values of medieval Spain in his palace, *El Escorial*.

Two main themes run throughout his reign: the preservation of his own inheritance, and the revival of the crusade in the name of the Catholic Church. In pursuit of the former, Felipe successfully claimed the Portugese throne (through the marriage of his mother), gaining access to the additional wealth of its empire. Plots were also woven in support of Mary Queen of Scots's claim to the throne of England, and to that end the ill-fated Armada sailed in 1588, its sinking a triumph for English naval strength and for Protestantism.

This was a period of unusual religious intensity: the **Inquisition** was enforced with renewed vigor, and a rising of Moriscos (subject Moors) in the Alpujarras was fiercely suppressed. Felipe III later ordered the expulsion of half the total number of Moriscos in Spain — allowing only two families to remain in each village in order to maintain irrigation techniques. The **exodus** of both Muslim and Jew created a large gulf in the labor force and in the higher echelons of commercial life — and in trying to uphold the Catholic cause, an enormous strain was put upon resources without any clearcut victory.

By the middle of the seventeenth century, Spain was losing international credibility. Domestically, the disparity between the wealth surrounding Crown and Court and the poverty and suffering of the mass of the population was a source of perpetual tension. Discontent fuelled regional revolts in Catalunya and Portugal in 1640, and the latter had finally to be acknowledged as an independent state in 1668.

BOURBONS AND THE PENINSULAR WAR

The **Bourbon dynasty** succeeded to the Spanish throne in the person of Felipe V (1700); with him began the War of Spanish Succession against the rival claim of Archduke Charles of Austria, assisted by British forces. As a result of the Treaty of Utrecht which ended the war (1713), Spain was stripped of all territory in Belgium, Luxembourg, Italy, and Sardinia, but Felipe V was recognized as king. Gibraltar was siezed by the British in the course of the war. For the rest of the century Spain fell very much under the French sphere of influence, an influence that was given political definition by an alliance with the French Bourbons in 1762.

Contact with France made involvement in the **Napoleonic Wars** inevitable and led eventually to the defeat of the Spanish fleet at Trafalgar in 1805. Popular outrage was such that the powerful prime minister, Godoy, was overthrown and King Carlos IV forced to abdicate (1808). Napoleon siezed the opportunity to install his brother, Joseph, on the throne.

Fierce local resistance was eventually backed by the muscle of a British army, first under Sir John Moore, later under the Duke of Wellington, and the French were at last driven out in the course of the Peninsular War. Meanwhile, however, the **American colonies** had been successfully asserting their independence from a preoccupied center and with them went Spain's last real claim of significance on the world stage. The entire nineteenth century was dominated by the struggle between an often reactionary monarchy and the aspirations of liberal constitutional reformers.

SEEDS OF CIVIL WAR

Between 1810 and 1813 an *ad hoc* Cortes (parliament) had set up a **liberal constitution** with ministers responsible to a democratically elected chamber. The first act of Fernando VII on being returned to the throne was to abolish this, and until his death in 1833 he continued to stamp out the least hint of liberalism. On his death, the right of succession was contested between his brother, Don Carlos, backed by the Church, conservatives, and Basques, and his infant daughter, Isabel, who looked to the Liberals and the army for support. So began the **First Carlist War**, a civil war that divided Spanish emotions for six years. Isabel II was eventually declared of age in 1843, her reign a long record of scandal, political crisis, and constitutional compromise. Liberal army generals under the leadership of General Prim effected a coup in 1868 and the queen was forced to abdicate, but attempts to maintain a Republican government foundered. The Cortes was again dissolved and the throne returned to Isabel's son, Alfonso XII. A new constitution was declared in 1876, limiting the power of the Crown through the institution of bicameral government, but again the progress was halted by the lack of any tradition on which to base the constitutional theory.

The years preceding World War I merely heightened the discontent, which found expression in the growing **political movements** of the working class. The *Socialist Workers Party* was founded in Madrid after the restoration of Alfonso XII, and spawned its own trade union, the *UGT* (1888), successful predominantly in areas of high industrial concentration such as the Basque region and the Asturias. Its anarchist counterpart, the *CNT*, was founded in 1911, gaining substantial support among the peasantry of Andalucía.

The loss of **Cuba** in 1898 emphasized the growing isolation of Spain in international affairs and added to economic problems by the return of soldiers seeking employment where there was none. A call-up for army reserves to fight in **Morocco** in 1909 provoked a general strike and the "Tragic Week" of rioting in Barcelona. Between 1914 and 1918, Spain was outwardly neutral but inwardly turbulent; inflated prices made the postwar recession harder to bear.

The general disillusionment with parliamentary government, together with the fears of employers and businessmen for their own security, gave **General Primo de Rivera** sufficient support for a military coup in 1923. Dictatorship did result in an increase in material prosperity, but the death of the dictator in 1930 revealed the apparent stability as a

facade. New political factions were taking shape: the Liberal Republican Right was founded by Alcalá Zamora, while the Socialist Party was given definition under the lead of Largo Caballero. The victory of anti-monarchist parties in the 1931 municipal elections forced the abdication of the king and the **Second Republic** was declared.

THE SECOND REPUBLIC

Catalunya declared itself a republic independent of the central government and was conceded control of internal affairs by a statute of 1932. **Separatist movements** were powerful too in the Basque provinces and Galicia, each with their own demands for autonomy. Meanwhile the government, set up on a tidal wave of hope, was failing to satisfy even the least of the expectations which it had raised. Hopelessly divided internally and too scared of right-wing reaction to carry out the massive tax and agrarian reforms that the left demanded and that might have provided the resources for thoroughgoing regeneration of the economy, it had neither the will nor the money to provide what it had promised.

The result was the increasing polarization of Spanish politics. **Anarchism**, in particular, was gaining strength among the frustrated middle classes as well as among workers and peasantry. The **Communist Party** and left-wing **Socialists**, driven into alliance by their mutual distrust of the "moderate" Socialists in government, were also forming a growing bloc. There was little real unity of purpose on either left or right, but their fear of each other and their own exaggerated boasts made each seem an imminent threat. On the right the **Falangists**, basically a youth party founded in 1923 by **José Antonio Primo de Rivera** (son of the dictator), made uneasy bedfellows with conservative traditionalists and dissident elements in the army upset by modernizing reforms.

In an atmosphere of growing confusion, the left-wing Popular Front alliance won the general election of **February 1936** by a narrow margin. Normal life, though, became increasingly impossible: the economy was crippled by strikes, peasants took agrarian reform into their own hands, and the government failed to exert its authority over anyone. Finally, on July 17, 1936, the military garrison in Morocco rebelled under **General Franco**'s leadership, to be followed by risings at military garrisons throughout the country. It was the culmination of years of scheming in the army, but in the event far from the overnight success its leaders almost certainly expected. The south and west quickly fell into Nationalist hands, but Madrid and the industrialized north and east remained loyal to the Republican government.

CIVIL WAR

The ensuing **Civil War** was undoubtedly one of the most bitter and bloody the world has seen. Violent reprisals were taken on their enemies by both sides — the Republicans shooting priests and local landowners whole-sale, the Nationalists carrying out mass slaughter on the population of almost every town they took. Contradictions were legion in the way the Spanish populations found themselves divided from each other. Perhaps the greatest irony was that Franco's troops, on their "holy" mission to ensure a Catholic Spain, comprised a core of Moroccan troops from Spain's North African colony.

It was, too, the first modern war — Franco's German allies demonstrated their ability to wipe out entire civilian populations with their bombing raids on Guernica and Durango, and radio proving an important weapon, as Nationalist propagandists offered the starving Republicans "the white bread of Franco."

Despite sporadic help from Russia and thousands of volunteers in the International Brigades, the Republic could never compete with the professional armies and the massive assistance from Fascist Italy and Nazi Germany enjoyed by the Nationalists. In addition, the left was torn by internal divisions which at times led almost to civil war within its own ranks. Nevertheless the Republicans held out in slowly dwindling territories for nearly three years, with **Catalunya** falling in January 1939 and armed resistance in **Madrid** — which never formally surrendered — petering out in the next months. As hundreds of thousands of refugees flooded into France, General Francisco Franco, who had long before proclaimed himself Head of State, took up the reins of power.

FRANCO'S SPAIN

The early reprisals taken by the victors were on a massive and terrifying scale. Executions were commonplace in town and village and upwards of two million people were put in concentration camps until "order" had been established by authoritarian means. Only one party was permitted and censorship was rigidly enforced. By the end of World War II, during which Spain was too weak to be anything but neutral, **Franco** was the only fascist head of state left in Europe, one responsible for sanctioning more deaths than any other in Spanish history. Spain was economically and politically isolated and, bereft of markets, suffered — almost half the population were still tilling the soil for little or no return. When General Eisenhower visited Madrid in 1953 with the offer of huge loans, it came as water to the desert, and the price, the establishment of American nuclear bases, was one Franco was more than willing to pay. However belated, economic development was incredibly rapid, with Spain enjoying a growth rate second only to that of Japan for much of the 1960s, a boom fueled by the tourist industry and the remittances of Spanish workers abroad.

Increased **prosperity**, however, only underlined the bankruptcy of Franco's regime and its inability to cope with popular demands. Higher incomes, the need for better education, and a creeping invasion of western culture made the anachronism of Franco ever clearer. His only reaction was to attempt to withdraw what few signs of increased liberalism had crept through, and his last years mirrored the repression of the postwar period. Basque Nationalists, whose assassination of Admiral Carrero Blanco had effectively destroyed Franco's last hope of a like-minded successor, were singled out for particularly harsh treatment. Hundreds of so-called terrorists were tortured, and the Burgos trials of 1970, together with the executions of August 1975, provoked worldwide protest. Franco finally died in November 1975, nominating **King Juan Carlos** as his successor.

SPAIN IN THE 80s

On October 28, 1982 Felipe González's Socialist Workers' Party — the *PSOE* — was elected with massive support to rule a country that had been firmly in the hands of the right for forty-three years. The Socialists captured the imagination and the votes of nearly ten million Spaniards with the simplest of appeals: "for change". It was a telling comment on just how far Spain had moved since Franco's death, for in the intervening years change seemed the one factor that could still threaten the newfound democracy.

Certainly in the Spain of 1976 the thought of a freely elected left-wing government would have been incredible. **King Juan Carlos** was the hand-picked successor of Franco, groomed for the job and very much in with the army — of which he remains official Commander in Chief. His initial moves were cautious in the extreme, appointing a government dominated by loyal Francoists who had little sympathy for the growing opposition demands for "democracy without adjectives." In the summer of 1976 demonstrations in Madrid ended in violence, with the police upholding the old authoritarian ways.

To his credit, however, Juan Carlos recognized that some real break with the past was now urgent and inevitable, and, accepting the resignation of his prime minister, set in motion the process of **democratization**. His newly appointed prime minister, Adolfo Suárez, steered through a Law of Political Reform, allowing for a two-chamber **Cortes** (Parliament). He also legitimized the Socialist Party and, controversially, the Communists. When elections were held in June 1977 Suárez's own centre-right **UCD** party was rewarded with a 34% share of the vote, the Socialists coming in second with 28%, and the Communists and Francoist *Alianza Popular* both marginalized at 9% and 8%. It was almost certainly a vote for democratic stability rather than for ideology and this was reflected in the course of the parliament, with Suárez governing through "consensus politics," negotiating settlements on all important issues with the major parties. The king, perhaps recognizing that his own future depended on the maintenance of the new democracy, lent it his support — most notably in February 1981 when Civil Guard Colonel Tejero stormed the Cortes and, with other officers loyal to Franco's memory, attempted to institute an army **coup**. The crisis, for a while, was real. Tanks were brought out on to the streets of Valencia, and only three of the army's ten regional commanders remained unreservedly loyal to the government. But as it became clear that the king would not support the plotters, most of the rest affirmed their support.

Tejero's continued role as a figurehead for the extreme right is evidenced by the graffiti proclaiming his name everywhere. But for most Spaniards his attempted coup is now an irrelevant and increasingly distant concern. Spanish democracy — even in army circles — has become institutionalized. And in **Felipe González** (known always as "Felipe") and the PSOE it has found a party of enduring stability, and to the left of exasperating moderation.

CONTEMPORARY POLITICS

Significant "change," even well into González's second term, has yet to be seen. Indeed in most political spheres — and above all in their economic policy — the PSOE are hardly distinguishable from the previous UCD administration, or even from the present conservative governments of Britain or West Germany. Control of inflation has been a more urgent target than employment, for all the manifesto promises. Loss-taking heavy industries — steel and shipbuilding especially — have been ruthlessly overhauled, and industries held or taken over by the state have been speedily reprivatized. **European Community** membership, which became a reality in 1986, has in the government's eyes increased the need to put industrial and economic efficiency above social policies: at the same time the pride which most Spanish people felt at this tangible proof of their acceptance by the rest of Europe bought the Socialists more valuable time. On the issue of NATO (or *Otan* as Spaniards know it), perhaps more than any other, Felipe's personal pragmatism was apparent. During the 1982 election campaign the largest rally he attended was against NATO, and he made the closing speech. When the promised referendum was finally held four years later — and to the surprise of almost everyone turned out marginally in favour of staying in — his was one of the main voices in favor of continued membership.

Autonomy, too, has been a major stumbling block. The system of granting varying degrees of self-rule to the regions has had no consistency and little effect on the separatist movements. In Catalunya and the Basque country elections have consistently been won by nationalist parties, and in the latter sporadic terrorism continues — despite an amnesty, talks with ETA, and an increased military presence.

But for all this — and official unemployment figures of around 20% — Felipe remains by far the most popular figure on the political scene, and to date no convincing **opposition** has appeared. The Socialists lead every poll in all but three provinces: Catalunya, the Basque country, and traditionally conservative Galicia. The UCD collapsed in disarray after their defeat in 1982; the Communist Party seems in perpetual self-destruct mode; and Manuel Fraga's *Alianza Popular*, on the right, is tainted by his own past as Franco's Interior Minister. Only from the last quarter were there signs of life, with Fraga proposing a union between his party and the surviving fragments of the Christian Democrat and Liberal centrists under the name *Partido Popular*, perhaps once more under the leadership of former prime minister Adolfo Suárez.

Unless and until this happens, though, internal opposition within the ranks of the PSOE seems a more immediate threat. In December 1988 a **general strike** was supported by virtually all the unions and the great majority of the workforce. Wage controls, continued unemployment, and lack of social security were their main complaints — and the future for Spain seems likely to include some movement, at last, towards tackling these real problems.

On the **positive side**, Spain has boomed throughout the 80s, consistently placing among the fastest growing economies in western Europe, and top of the list for much of the decade. At a local level there has been a flourishing of cultural activity of every kind, much of it sponsored by enlightened and revitalized local councils — especially in Madrid and Barcelona. On an international level, the British have agreed to discuss the sovereignty of Gibraltar and the border has been re-opened. Most significantly for Spaniards, perhaps, the Spanish government's voice is now one which is taken seriously at an international level, acknowledged as having a role in the Latin American peace process, and in the Councils of Europe.

CHRONOLOGY OF MONUMENTS

25,000 B.C.	Prehistoric settlements, mainly around Santander.	Cave paintings at Altamira and Puente Viesgo; also Las Piletas (near Ronda).
1100 B.C.	**Phoenicians** found Cádiz.	
9th–4thc. B.C.	**Celts** settle in the north.	Celtic dolmens and "*citania*": both can be seen at La Guardia (Galicia).
	Greeks establish trading posts along east coast.	Empuries, near Barcelona (Greek site).
3rdc. B.C.	**Carthaginians** occupy Andalucian and Mediterranean coast.	**Celto-Iberian** culture develops, with Greek influence: busts of "La Dama de Elche" etc. in Museo Nacional Arqueológico, Madrid.
214 B.C.	Second Punic War with Rome.	
210 B.C.	**Roman colonization** begins.	Important **Roman sites** at Mérida, Tarragona, Italica, Carmona, Sagunto, Segovia, etc.
414 A.D.	**Visigoths** arrive.	Sculpture and jewelry (in museums at Madrid and Toledo); also isolated churches.
711	**Moors** from North Africa invade, and conquer peninsula within seven years.	
718	Battle of Covadonga: Christian victory leads to formation of **Asturian kingdom**.	Asturian **pre-Romanesque** churches in and around Oviedo and the Picos de Europa.
756	Abd ar-Rahman I proclaims **Emirate of Cordoba**.	Great Mosque (Mezquita) begun at Córdoba, climax of **early Moorish architecture**.
812	Christians discover body of Santiago (St. James) at Compostela.	**Mozarabic** churches built by Arabized Christians in Andalucía — and in the north a century later.
9thc.	Kingdoms of **Catalunya** and **Navarra** founded.	
939	Abd ar-Rahman III adopts title "Caliph."	Medina Azahara palace and extensions to Mezquita at Córdoba in the **Caliphal style**.
967	**Al Mansur** usurps Caliphal powers, and forces Christians back into the Asturias.	
1013	Caliphate disintegrates into *taifas*, petty kingdoms.	Alcazabas built at Málaga, Granada, Almería, Sevilla, Carmona, Ronda, etc.
1037	Fernando I unites kingdoms of Castile and León-Asturias. Ramon Berenguer I extends and strengthens Catalan kingdom.	**Romanesque architecture** enters Spain along the pilgrim route to Compostela. Superb examples throughout Castile and the north — especially at Salamanca, Segovia, Burgos, Ávila, and Santillana.
1085	Christians capture Toledo.	
1086	**Almoravides** invade Spain.	
1147	**Almohads** restore Muslim authority in Andalucía.	Sevilla becomes new Moorish capital in Spain: **Almohad minarets** include Giralda and Torre del Oro.
1162	Alfonso II unites kingdoms of Aragón and Catalunya.	**Cluniac monasteries** built along pilgrim route to Santiago; **Cistercian abbeys** at Poblet and elsewhere.
1212	Almohad advance halted at Las Navas de Tolosa.	**Mudejar** style emerges through Moorish craftsmen working on Christian buildings: good examples in Aragón at Teruel and Tarazona.

1213	Jaime I "El Conquistador'" becomes king of Aragón. **Christian Reconquest** of Balearics (1229), Valencia (1238), Alicante (1266).	First **Gothic cathedrals** built at Burgos (1221), Toledo (1227), and León (1258). Catalan Gothic also develops in 1220s — best seen in Barcelona's Barri Gòtic and at Girona.
1217	Fernando III "El Santo," king of Castile, retakes Córdoba (1236), Murcia (1241), and Sevilla (1248).	Granada's **Alhambra** palace constructed under Ibn Ahmar (1238–75) and his successors. Craftsmen from Granada also construct Sevilla Alcázar for Pedro the Cruel (1350–69).
1479	Castile and Aragón united under **Isabella and Fernando**.	Sevilla Cathedral (1402–1506). **Isabelline** style of late Gothic Age of castle building: Coca and Segovia are outstanding.
1492	**Fall of Granada**, the last Moorish kingdom. **Discovery of America** by Columbus.	Last Gothic cathedrals built at Salamanca (1512) and Segovia (1522).
1516	**Carlos V** succeeds to throne and (1520) becomes the Holy Roman Emperor. "**Golden Age**."	**Renaissance** reaches Spain. Elaborate early style is known as Plateresque (best represented at Salamanca). Later, key figures include Diego de Siloé (1495–1563; Burgos, Granada, etc.) and Andres de Vandaélvira (d. 1565; Jaén, Ubeda, and Baeza).
1519	Cortés lands in Mexico.	
1532	Pizarro "discovers" Peru.	
1556	**Felipe II** (d. 1598).	Juan de Herrera (1530–97) introduces new austerity in the Escorial.
1588	Sinking of the Armada.	**Painters** include: El Greco (1540–1614; Toledo), Ribalta (1551–1628), Ribera (1591–1652), Zurbarán (1598–1664), Alonso Cano (1601–67) and Velázquez (1599–1660). Best collections of all at Madrid's Prado.
1609	Expulsion of Moriscos, last remaining Spanish Muslims.	
1700	War of Spanish Succession brings Felipe V (1713–46), a Bourbon, to the throne. British seize Gibraltar.	**Baroque** develops in reaction to the severity of High Renaissance and reaches a flamboyant peak in the Churrigueresque style of the 18thc. (Salamanca's Plaza Mayor, and altarpieces throughout Spain, and above all the Obradoiro facade at Santiago). Last great cathedrals built at Valencia, Murcia, and Cádiz.
1808	**French occupy Spain**.	Francisco de Goya (1746–1828). Royal Palaces of Madrid and Aranjuez.
1811	Venezuela declares independence: others follow.	
1835	**First Carlist War**.	**Dissolution of monasteries**.
1874	**Second Carlist War**.	
1898	Loss of Cuba, Spain's last American colony.	Antoni Gaudí (1852–1926) and **Modernisme**, or *Modernista* (Art Nouveau) movement in Barcelona.
1923	Primo de Rivera dictatorship.	Pablo **Picasso** (1883–1973; museum in Barcelona, *Guernica* in Madrid); Joan **Miró** (1893–1982; museum in Barcelona); Salvador **Dalí** (1904–1989; museum at Figueres).
1931	Second Republic.	
1936–9	**Spanish Civil War**.	
1939	**Franco dictatorship** begins.	
1953	U.S. makes economic deal with Franco in return for military bases.	
1975	Death of Franco; **restoration of democracy**.	Antonio Saura and **abstract artists** (Museum of Abstract Art, Cuenca).

ARCHITECTURE

Spain's architectural legacy is a highly distinctive one, made up of a mixture of styles quite unlike anything else in Europe. The country was usually slow to pick up on the main currents of European architecture, and when a new style was adopted it was often in an extreme or stylized form. There are French, Netherlandish, German, and Italian currents, but all were synthesized into something uniquely Spanish. Centuries of Moorish occupation have left an indelible mark too, manifested both in the handful of wonderful buildings which represent the highpoint of Moorish civilization in Andalucía, and in a powerful influence on Christian and secular architecture, including the layout of entire towns.

There has been less of the wanton destruction of old buildings in Spain than in most other countries, and in general the architecture here is astonishingly well preserved. There's perhaps less purity of form than elsewhere in Europe — additions over the years have left many buildings with a medley of different styles — but no other country can boast quite as many old churches, castles, and unspoiled towns and villages.

At the risk of making generalizations, it's possible to identify a number of **trends** in the buildings of Spain. As a rule, there is an emphasis on the longitudinal, and on solidity of construction. A heavy use of surface ornament is often popular, with elaborate doorways and rich decoration. Because of the warm climate there is no interest in large windows, but there is a need for cool and open space, which accounts for the prevalence of patios in civic buildings and cloisters in religious edifices, including those which were not monastic. There is also a tendency to break up long vistas by various means, creating a variety of compartments within a large space.

THE ROMAN PERIOD

Although fragments of earlier civilizations do exist, Spain's architectural history (in terms of surviving buildings) begins in the **Roman** period, from which there remain a number of remarkable structures. These have no particular Spanish flavor, nor were they to prove as influential on subsequent developments as in some other countries, but nonetheless the aqueduct at **Segovia**, the bridge at **Alcántara** (the highest in the Roman world), and the theater and associated remains at **Mérida** belong among the first rank of Roman survivals anywhere. There's another fine group in and around **Tarragona**, with walls, a necropolis, an arena, a forum, and a praetorium in the city itself, and more notably an aqueduct, the Centcelles Mausoleum, the Arco de Bar, and the Torre de Scipio, all within a radius of a few miles.

Other Roman monuments worthy of special note include the walls of Lugo, the amphitheater and castle at Sagunto, and the three-span triumphal arch at Medinaceli. Excavations of complete towns can be seen at Empuries, Italica, Numancia, and Bilbilis.

THE VISIGOTHIC AND ASTURIAN PERIODS

The **Visigothic** period, which succeeded the Roman, bequeathed a small number of buildings of uncertain date. Visigothic buildings have simple exteriors, and were the first in Spain to adopt the horseshoe arch (later to be altered and used widely by the Moors). They also developed elements from Roman buildings, the most refined example of which is at **Quintanilla de las Vinas** in Old Castile, a church whose exterior is enlivened by delicately carved stone friezes set in bands; inside there's a triumphal arch over the apse, carved with the earliest surviving representation of Christ in Spain. Other remnants of the era survive at the modern industrial town of **Tarrasa** in Catalunya, formerly Egara, in the shape of three churches, one of which — the Baptistery of San Miguel — dates from the fifth or sixth century; the other two have apses that are probably of ninth-century construction. Other Visigothic buildings include part of the crypt of Palencia Cathedral, and the nearby basilica of San Juan at Baños de Cerrato, documented as seventh century.

Hard on the heels of the Visigothic epoch was the **Asturian** period, named after the small kingdom on the northern coast, which developed its own style during the ninth century. This retained Visigothic elements alongside technical developments that were to anticipate the general European trends still to come. A little group of buildings centered around **Oviedo** — the Camera Santa, the church of Santulano in the city itself, San Miguel de Lillo, and Sta. Maria de Naranco on the slopes of Monte Naranco nearby — are, unusually in Spanish history, clearly superior to, and more highly developed than any contemporaneous work in Europe. The last represents the pinnacle of the style, a perfectly proportioned little building with barrel vaulting and arches supported on pilasters, as well as delicate decoration using Roman and Byzantine elements. The isolated surrounding countryside holds a few similar buildings from the succeeding century, but the Asturian style was soon to be swallowed up by the new Romanesque movement, which swept across the north of Spain from France and Italy.

THE MOORISH PERIOD

By this time most of Spain was under Muslim domination. It remained so, at least in part, until the final defeat of the Moors in 1492. During this period Moorish architecture did not develop in the way we understand the word, and it is best to consider the different epochs of building separately.

The first real style was the **Caliphate**, centered around Córdoba, whose great surviving monument — the **Mezquita** — was built and added to over a period from the eighth to the tenth centuries. The Caliphate style demonstrates most of the vocabulary used by Moorish builders over the years — horseshoe, cusped, and multifoil arches, the contrasting use of courses of stone and brick, the use of interlacing as a particular feature of design, doors surmounted by blind arcades, stucco work, and the ornamental use of calligraphy along with geometric and plant motifs. Various technical innovations, too, were introduced in the construction of the Mezquita, from the original solution of two-tiered arches to give greater height to the ribbed dome vaults in front of the *mihrab* (prayer-niche).

Another example of the Caliphate style, the (now ruined) palace-city of **Medina Azahara**, just outside Córdoba, was no less splendid than the Mezquita. Many of its buildings were produced according to the descriptions of Solomon's temple. In **Toledo**, El Cristo de la Luz is a small-scale Caliphate mosque, and the old Bisagra Gate was part of the fortifications of that time. As the Reconquest progressed, other fortifications went up. Gormaz was begun in around 965. Only part of the original Moorish building has survived, including two gateways. Calatayud, in the north, holds more fortifications of the period, probably of an even earlier date.

With the fall of the Caliphate at the end of the eleventh century, Moorish Spain was divided into independent kingdoms or **Taifas**, giving rise to the *alcazabas* or castles at Granada, Málaga, Guadix, Almería, Tarifa, and Carmona. The Aljaferia palace in Zaragoza also dates from this period, much altered over the years but preserving its mosque and a tower. The strongest *taifa* was at Sevilla, where later the **Almohad** dynasty created an art of refined brickwork and left behind the Patio de Yeso in the Alcázar, the Torre del Oro, which originally formed part of the city's fortifications, and the Giralda — former minaret of the mosque and arguably the finest tower ever built in the Arab world.

The apotheosis of pure Muslim art came, however, with the **Nasrid** dynasty in Granada, the last city to fall to the Christians. The gorgeously opulent palace of the **Alhambra** went up between the thirteenth and fifteenth centuries. Built on a hill against the romantic backdrop of the Sierra Nevada, this structure provided the necessary partner in the union between art and nature sought by the Moorish architects, especially in the lush gardens of the more modest Generalife section. As for the palace itself, the buildings are actually structurally very poor, with no exterior features of note; yet the interior, around the two great courtyards, is one of the most intoxicating creations in the world, the culminating ideal of Moorish civilization, built when it was already in irreversible decline.

MOZARABIC AND MUDEJAR

The Moorish occupation had an indelible influence on the architecture of Spain, and led directly to two hybrid architectural styles unique to the country — **Mozarabic** and Mudejar. The former was the style of Christians subjugated by the Moors who retained their old religion but built in the Arabic style. Their churches are mostly in isolated situations — San Miguel de Escalada east of León, Sta. María de Lebena near the Picos de Europa, and San Baudelio near Berlanga de Duero in Soria Province are the finest examples.

Mudejar is far more common, the style of the Arabs who stayed on after their homelands had been conquered, or who had migrated to the Christian kingdoms. Often they proved to be both the most skillful builders and the cheapest workforce, and they left their mark on almost all of the country over a period of several centuries. They continued to build predominantly in brick, mainly working on the construction of parish churches, resulting in an odd — though unmistakably Moorish — Christian-Islamic hybrid that some claim is barely a distinct architectural style at all. There are details of Mudejar buildings under the relevant European headings, below, although a number deserve inclusion here as being more firmly within the Arab tradition. Among these are the palaces of Tordesillas and the Alcázar in Sevilla; various secular buildings in Toledo; the Chapel of the Assumption or Santiago at Las Huelgas; and the synagogues of Toledo and Córdoba.

THE ROMANESQUE

Back in the mainstream of European architecture, the **Romanesque** style in Spain is most associated with the churches, bridges, and hospices built along the **pilgrim road** to Santiago de Compostela. None of the hospices have survived, but the Puente la Reina in Navarra is the most famous of a number of Romanesque-era bridges. The churches come in various shapes and forms, but all include beautiful sculpture. The Cathedral of Jaca, the monasteries of Sta. Cruz de la Seros, San Juan de la Pena, and Leyre, and the churches of Sta. María la Real at Sanguesa, San Miguel at Estella, San Martín at Frómista, and San Isidoro at León are the most notable examples, but the climax, of the style as of the pilgrimage, came with the great **Cathedral of Santiago** itself. This is now almost entirely encased by baroque additions, but preserves the original shape of the interior. Begun around 1070, it was built to allow as much space as possible for the pilgrims to circulate — hence the large triforium gallery, and the ambulatory with radiating chapels. Santiago's cathedral also served as a model for many contemporary derivations, particularly the nearby cathedrals of Lugo, Orense, and Tuy.

Elsewhere, the influence of the great Burgundian abbey of Cluny, which so influenced the development of the pilgrimage, can be seen most clearly at **San Vicente** in Ávila. Another building closely related to the pilgrimage churches is the monastery of **Santo Domingo de Silos**, where the architecture and superb bas-reliefs of the cloisters, the only surviving part of the original building, are clearly derived from French models. There's an additional ingredient, too: most of the capitals here show an unmistakable Moorish influence — a very early example of the mix of East and West to be found in Spain.

Other Romanesque buildings tend towards regional variants. In **Catalunya**, whose architectural history so often diverges from that of the rest of Spain, the influence was more from Lombardy than France, with tall square bell towers, prominent apses, blind arcading, and little sculptural detail — although this last was later to become important, for example in the cloisters of the Cathedral and San Pedro in Gerona.

Belfries were a dominant feature in **Segovia**, where the main innovation was the construction of covered arcades in the manner of cloisters built against the sides of the building, making the parish churches of this city among the most distinctive in Spain. **Soria**'s churches, particularly San Domingo, recall those of Poitiers, although the fantastic cloister of San Juan de Duero defies classification in its combination of the round-headed Romanesque, early pointed Gothic, and Moorish horseshoe and intersecting arches in one extraordinarily capricious composition. **Zamora** was unusual in having a Byzantine influence; also its portals tended to lack tympana, but had richly carved archivolts. Finally, the **Mudejars** built a number of churches in the Romanesque style in such places as Toledo, Sahagun, Cuellar, and Arevalo.

Military architecture of this period is dominated by the complete walls of Ávila, the best-preserved in Europe, and by the castle at Loarre, the most spectacular of the early Christian castles built to defend the conquered lands. Survivals of civil buildings are few and far between, but there are precious examples in the form of the palaces of Estella and Huesca.

THE TRANSITIONAL STYLE

With the advent of the Cistercian reforms, the **Transitional** style was introduced to Spain in the middle of the twelfth century, first in a series of monasteries — La Oliva, Veruela, Poblet, Santes Creus, Las Huelgas, and Sta. María la Huerta — that are notable for massiveness of construction combined with the introduction of such Gothic characteristics as the pointed arch and the ribbed vault.

In some ways, **La Oliva** can claim to be the first Gothic building in Spain, although in both its solidity and ground plan it is still Romanesque in spirit. The severe, unadorned style of the Cistercians was to have a great impact at a time when the rest of Europe was moving towards appreciating the structural advantages of Gothic, not quickly realized in Spain. The late twelfth and early thirteenth century saw the construction of a number of

cathedrals in the Transitional style — Siguenza, Ávila, Santo Domingo de la Calzada, Tarragona, and Lleida — all of which had fortress-like features and were indeed at times used for defensive purposes. Similar is the Collegiate church at Tudela, although the sculpture here, in direct contravention of Cistercian rules, is among the richest in Spain.

A few buildings of the same period show clear **Byzantine** influence — the Old Cathedral of Salamanca, Zamora Cathedral, and the Colegiata at Toro — each with a distinctive central dome, although their design otherwise shows normal Transitional elements. Closely related are the Cathedral of Ciudad Rodrigo and the often octagonally-shaped buildings associated with the Knights Templars: La Vera Cruz in Segovia, and two mysterious buildings on the pilgrim route whose exact nature is uncertain — Eunate and Torres de Río.

THE GOTHIC STYLE

Examples of the early **Gothic** style in Spain are few, and those that there are seem to derive from French and English sources. The refectory of Sta. María la Huerta is as pure and elegant as the best in France; Cuenca Cathedral, begun about 1200, seems to derive from a Norman or English model. Later, buildings began to develop a more specifically Spanish style, eschewing any notions of purity of form.

Three great cathedrals, commenced in the 1220s, best exemplify the increasingly Spanish features of the churches of the time. Of these, the overall plans and building of **Burgos** and **Toledo** are obviously indebted to French models, but they are far from the grace and lightness of the great French Gothic cathedrals. The windows are much smaller — partly, perhaps, to cut down on excessive sunlight, partly to preserve a greater sense of mystery than their French equivalents did. Both were also given the rich interior decoration that soon became the norm for Spanish cathedrals, most characteristic of which was the *coro*, an elaborate set of choir stalls often enclosed by a *trascoro* or retrochoir, situated in the nave — a feature that looks odd to those used to the chancel-based choirs of northern Europe. The reasons for this are unclear, but it seems it was associated with the predominance of the choir services of the clergy, which meant that the construction of the *coro* made the best use of the space; it may also have been felt that the chancel should be reserved solely for the Holy Sacrament, and not downgraded for any other purpose.

Equally typical are the giant *retablos*, the most important of which are situated over the high altar, again masking the architecture. Generally these were carved and multicolored, and contained a series of scenes from the life of Christ and of the Virgin, perhaps along with statues of saints. Basically their function was similar to that of stained-glass windows in the cathedrals of France, providing pictorial representation of the Bible to an illiterate population. Smaller *retablos*, either painted or carved, were placed over smaller altars. In addition, tombs of monarchs, aristocratic families, bishops, and saints were often placed in specially-built chapels, and sometimes enclosed by iron gates or grilles (*rejas*)which were often of a highly elaborate workmanship and would enclose the entrances to the *coro* and the chancel too. The overall effect of all this decoration can appear oversumptuous to the modern eye, but it gives a better impression of a medieval cathedral than anything that can be found in Northern Europe, where reformation, revolution, war, and restoration have combined to leave buildings that are architecturally far purer but spiritually far less authentic.

The third great cathedral of the 1200s, **León**, was the only one to adopt the normal French system of triple portal, prominent flying buttresses, and large windows filled with brilliantly colored stained glass. Even here, however, there were Spanish touches, such as the cloister and its dependencies, and the later construction of a *coro*.

All the other cathedrals followed the model of Burgos and Toledo. **El Burgo de Osma** is in a way a miniature version of them, although it's purer Gothic in form. **Palencia**, built in the fourteenth and fifteenth centuries, is unusual in that most of its decoration is roughly contemporary with the architecture, with very few later additions. At **Pamplona** and **Huesca**, the architects built in the knowledge that there would be a *coro* in the nave — though ironically these were removed relatively recently by restorers. Pamplona's cloister, the earliest part

of the building, is perhaps the most beautiful Gothic cloister in Spain. It has several fine doorways and a chapel with an exquisite star vault, a feature that was to be Spain's main contribution to the vocabulary of Gothic architecture, as characteristic as fan vaulting in England, although far more common — and with an obvious debt to Moorish models. There are other, equally grand examples of the national Gothic style: **Murcia** and **Oviedo** are two, **Sevilla** a more spectacular one, its vast size determined by the ground plan of the mosque that preceded it.

REGIONAL STYLES

Regional forms of Gothic are found in Catalunya and Aragón. In **Catalunya**, churches were built with huge arcades, omitting the triforium and including only a small clerestory. Long spans were also common; aisles, if there were any, were very nearly the same height as the nave; buttresses were internalized by the construction of tall, straight-walled chapels built between them, lending a rather sober appearance to the outside. Barcelona's **Cathedral of Sta. María del Mar** is a good example of all these features, as is **Palma Cathedral**, although the most spectacular of the Catalan cathedrals is **Girona** — so daring structurally as to be admired more for its engineering than its aesthetic appeal.

In **Aragón** there was strong Mudejar influence, which extended even to the cathedrals of **Zaragoza**, **Tarazona**, and **Teruel**. The towers of these cities, and of **Calatayud**, tend to be either square in shape and decorated with ceramic tiles that glisten in the sun, or else octagonal and of brick only. Both show a virtuoso skill in decoration with what appear to be very basic and unpromising materials. Each of the cathedrals has a central cupola, while Tarazona has an amazing cloister filled with Mudejar ornament. There's another unusual cloister far away from here in Guadalupe, while more orthodox Mudejar Gothic churches are all over, though there's a fine concentration in **Toledo**.

MILITARY ARCHITECTURE

Turning to **military architecture**, a number of fortified towns from the Gothic period still survive. Toledo has several gateways and two bridges of the era, and there are fine examples of walls at Albarracín, Daroca, Morella, Berlanga de Duero, Madrigal de las Altes Torres, and Montblanch. Spain's castles of this period are without parallel in Europe. However, those that had a genuine function in the Reconquest are as a rule in the poorest condition, while those that look most impressive today often had little if any defensive purpose. It should be remembered that there is no Spanish equivalent at any time to the English or French country house. Where great houses were built by the nobility in Spain, they often resembled castles, even if they were never used for military purposes.

Perhaps the finest fourteenth-century castle is that of **Bellver** near Palma, a circular structure built as a summer residence by the kings of Mallorca. The great fifteenth-century castle at **Olite** is a palace in the pastiche form on a grand scale. For all the monumentality of its towers, many are wholly ornamental and would have been quite useless in time of war. Unfortunately, what you see today gives little hint of the richness of the former interior decoration.

Along the banks of the Duero are castles which were genuinely in action at the time of the Reconquest. **Gormaz** is particularly interesting, showing how an originally Moorish building was adapted by the Christians after its capture. **Peñafiel**'s fifteenth-century castle is actually the successor to the one that was built as protection against the Moors; apart from its own severe beauty, it clearly shows the importance of a strong strategic location. The many brick castles in the **area of Segovia and Valladolid** should be thought of more as expressions of the wealth and power of the nobility than as genuine military constructions of the time. These often incorporated Mudejar features, and their construction was often in reality rather delicate; **Coca** is the best example of this.

CIVIL BUILDINGS AND LATE GOTHIC

The legacy of **Gothic civil architecture** is also impressive. Large numbers of towns preserve their medieval character in layout and design, even if many of the houses are not, strictly speaking, original. Important town mansions survive all over the country, often characterized by the carving of a coat of arms on the facade. **Caceres**, in Extremadura, is probably the richest place for seigneurial houses, although most of the other towns in this province are also notable for vernacular architecture of this, and later dates. Elsewhere, the shipyards of **Barcelona** constitute a unique survival from the Gothic period, as do parts of the Barri Gotic, which contains a number of original municipal buildings. Barcelona also has the earliest *lonja*, or exchange — later and more exotic examples of which can be found in Valencia, Palma, and Zaragoza.

Spanish **late Gothic** architecture is particularly spectacular, the increasing ornamentation partly the result of the mid-fifteenth-century influx of artists from Germany and the Netherlands to Spain. **Burgos** and **Toledo** were the center of the developing style. Juan de Colonia built the superb openwork spires of Burgos Cathedral, modeled on those of his native Cologne — which themselves, ironically, existed only on paper until the nineteenth century. His son, Simon, was responsible for other work on the same building, particularly the Capilla del Condestable at the east end, and worked with his father on the Cartuja de Miraflores. At the same time, Anequin de Egas from Brussels began a series of additions to Toledo Cathedral.

A little later the focus shifted to **Valladolid** and became increasingly florid — the **Isabelline** style — reaching its most extreme in the facades of San Pablo and the Colegio San Gregorio. It's not known who was responsible for these, or for the equally ornate facade of Sta. María in Aranda de Duero, though a variety of people have been suggested, not least Juan Guas, who is known to have built San Juan de los Reyes in Toledo, the gallery of the castle at **Manzanares el Real**, and perhaps the Palacio del Infantado in **Guadalajara**. The Isabelline style, at its best, combined the Moorish penchant for hanging decoration with standard European motifs, and has been seen by some commentators as the one chance Spain had to create its own special, unified architectural style. However, Isabelline had a very short life. The queen after whom it was named before long became more enchanted by the Italians, and encouraged the adoption of the Renaissance in Spain.

There was also a counter-movement towards a purer Gothic form. The New

Cathedral of **Salamanca** and the Cathedral of **Segovia** were both begun in the sixteenth century in what was then a wholly archaic language by Juan Gil de Hontanon, and continued by his son Rodrigo. Juan de Alava also built a number of monuments in this style — San Estebán in Salamanca, part of the cathedral at Plasencia, and the cloisters at Santiago. **Segovia Cathedral**, too — unusually for Spain — displays a remarkable unity of form, using the traditional Gothic elements rejected by earlier builders.

THE RENAISSANCE

Oddly enough, the **Renaissance** was introduced to Spain with the **Collegio Sta. Cruz** in Valladolid, just a few hundred yards from the simultaneous construction of two Isabelline facades. The architect, Lorenzo Vazquez, for all his historical importance, remains a rather shadowy figure. (Later, he was to build an Italian Renaissance palace at La Calahorra in Andalucía.) Enrique de Egas, who built the hospitals at Toledo (Sta. Cruz), Granada, and Santiago, and who also worked in a late Gothic style, as witnessed by his Capilla Real in Granada and his design for the adjoining Cathedral, is much better documented.

Much early Spanish Renaissance architecture is termed **Plateresque**, from the profusion of carving which allegedly resembled the work of silversmiths. The term is now applied rather loosely, but it is most associated with **Salamanca**, which is built of an extremely delicate rose-colored sandstone. The supreme masterpiece of the style is the facade of the **University** here, where instead of the wild and irregular carvings of Valladolid, a generation before, all is order and symmetry while equally ornate. The motifs used in Plateresque carving are wholly Italianate — figures in medallions, *putti*, candelabra, grotesques, garlands of flowers and fruit, scrollwork, and coats of arms. No convincing attribution has been made for the University facade, but one Plateresque architect whose work can be traced is **Alonso de Covarrubias**. He built the Capilla de los Reyes Nuevos in Toledo Cathedral, part of the Alcázar, and probably the Hospital de Tavera in the same city, and worked on Siguenza Cathedral, particularly the amazing sacristy.

The facade of the University of Alcalá de Henares is a more severe Plateresque masterpiece by Rodrigo Gil de Hontanon; other important works are San Marcos in León by Juan de Badajoz, and the Hospital del Rey near Burgos.

The **High Renaissance**, by contrast, centered around **Andalucía**, the part of the country that was most lacking in Christian architecture following its liberation from the Muslim powers. The real masterpiece of the style is the **Palace of Carlos V** in Granada — incongruously located in the Alhambra, but a superbly pure piece of architecture. It is rare in being based on a round courtyard, and is the only surviving building by Pedro Machuca. As for churches, the leading architect of the Andalucian Renaissance in this field was Diego de Siloé, who had begun his career as a sculptor in Burgos under his father, Gil, and had built the marvelous Plateresque *Escalera Dorada* in the cathedral there. Following study in Italy, he worked as an architect, devising an ingenious east end for the cathedral at Granada, and designing Guadix Cathedral and El Savador at Ubeda. The last-named was actually built by his pupil, Andreas de Vandelvira, whose own main work is the monumental Cathedral of Jaén. All these buildings show a strongly classical influence.

The severest, purest, and greatest Spanish Renaissance architect was **Juan de Herrera**, who succeeded Juan Bautista de Toledo as architect of **El Escorial**, to which he devoted much of his working life. To many, this vast building is excessively sober, particularly in a country where ornamentation has so often reigned supreme. However, it does have a unique grandeur, and illustrates the Spanish penchant for taking any style to its extremes. Herrera's other main building is the **Cathedral of Valladolid**, though sadly only half of this was ever built, and some of that well after Herrera. In this truncated form it can appear rather cold and somber, although the model for the complete building shows what a well-proportioned, harmonious, and majestic edifice it might have become.

THE BAROQUE

For a time, Herrera's style was to spawn a number of imitations, and early **Baroque** architecture was remarkably restrained — Madrid's early seventeenth-century **Plaza Mayor** by Juan Gomez de Mora being a case in point. In the east, Neapolitan influence was paramount, and led to the building of a large number of dignified churches.

Before long, however, this early phase gave way to an exuberant, playful, and confident style that is perhaps Spain's most singular contribution to European architecture, the **Churrigeresque** — taken from the name of the family of architects, the Churrigueras, with whom the style was most associated. Ironically, their own work in architecture was far less ornate than that of many of their successors, although they also designed **retablos**, which are as embellished as anything that followed; so large as to seem almost pieces of architecture in themselves These were typically of carved wood, painted and gilded, with twisted columns populated by saints in visionary or ecstatic mood and swirling processions of angels. *Retablos* of this type were soon to be found in churches all over Spain. Often the work of far cruder imitators, they raised the ire of visiting Protestant travelers, who used the term "Churriguresque" to signify all that was basest in art. It's still a pejorative term, although the Churrigueras did actually create a number of masterpieces.

Jose, the eldest brother, created a complete planned town in **Nuevo Baztán**, not far from Madrid. Alberto, the youngest and most talented, laid out the **Plaza Mayor** in Salamanca in collaboration with Andrea Garcia de Quiñones — a superb and harmonious piece of town planning, integrated wonderfully with the town's older buildings, and with the plain sides enlivened by carvings deriving from Plateresque work, and the rhythmic facade of the *Ayuntamiento* providing a central focus on the north side.

The Churrigeras' contemporaries were more profusely ornate, often imitating the form of the retablos in their portals, perhaps the finest example of which is the **Hospicio San Fernando** in Madrid by Pedro de Ribera. Another new architectural feature was the *transparente*, in which a lavish altarpiece is lit from above by a window cut in the vault, giving a highly theatrical effect. The most famous example is that in **Toledo Cathedral** by Narciso Tome, a brilliant piece of illusionism when the sun shines through, though in an utterly incongruous setting.

The Baroque style was also, of course, used when making additions to existing buildings, something you see all over Spain. Sometimes the merging of Baroque and medieval was triumphantly successful, as in the mid-eighteenth-century Obradoiro facade of **Santiago Cathedral** by Fernando Casas y Novoa, the climax of about a century's work, encasing the old Romanesque building in a lively Baroque exterior. While the loss of the Romanesque exterior is regrettable, particularly as some of the Baroque building is mediocre, the facade ranks as one of the most joyous creations in all architecture, and the ultimate triumph of Spanish Baroque. Other notably successful Baroque additions are the towers of the cathedrals of El Burgo de Osma, Santo Domingo de la Calzada, and Murcia, which all harmonize surprisingly well with the existing structure, and give them a dimension they previously lacked. Many other additions, however, were far less fortunate: much of the time Baroque builders paid insufficient attention to the scale, style, and materials of the existing work, and even when each is a competent piece of work in its own right, old and new scream at each other in horror.

Because of the trend towards enlivening old buildings, only one complete Baroque cathedral was built in Spain, at **Cádiz**. Nor are there many notable Baroque monasteries, although a number of charterhouses (*cartujas*) were built, not least at **Granada**, which became more and more extreme as construction progressed, culminating in the outrageous *sagrario* (sacristy) by Francesco Hurtado Izquiero. However, Spanish Baroque never found favor at court, where Italian and French models were preferred, and architects and decorators were imported from these countries, producing the Bourbon palaces of Aranjuez, La Granja de San Ildefonso, and Madrid, which stand apart from Spanish buildings of the period. Filippo Juvara, the famous architect of Turin, was summoned to Spain in the penultimate year of his life to design the garden front of La Granja and the overall plan for Madrid, although both were executed by his pupil, Giovanni Battista Sachetti.

NEOCLASSICISM

In time, the court taste changed to **neoclassical**, enforced by the mid-century establishment of academies, and the presiding architectural style became heavy and monumental in scale. The dominant figure was **Ventura Rodríguez**, a technically competent architect who built a lavish Augustinian church in **Valladolid** and completed **El Pilar Basilica** in Zaragoza — a colossal building with elements drawn from a variety of styles that is more notable for its grandiose outline than for any other feature. But Rodríguez's talents were not put to their best use: his facade for **Pamplona Cathedral** would look fine on a bank but is wholly incongruous for a church, and a serious distraction in what is otherwise a fine building; and his plain, rather nondescript church at **Santo Domingo de Silos** is a similarly poor partner for the great cloister there. Another leading neoclassical architect was **Juan de Villanueva**, who built the **Prado** (actually as a natural history museum) and the two **Casitas** at El Escorial.

Spain's subsequent provincial history is mirrored in the paucity of buildings of much consequence. The slow process of industrial and social change meant that there are few of the self-confident expressions of prosperity found all over Northern Europe. There were a host of imitative styles, but it is really only when they are on the small scale that they give much pleasure. **Neo-Gothic**, also, was nowhere near as vital or as prevalent as elsewhere: the cathedrals built in this style, at **San Sebastián** and **Vitoria**, are not especially notable, and the most satisfying work was probably the completion of **Barcelona Cathedral**, which was actually accomplished according to a fifteenth-century plan.

MODERNISME

Barcelona provides the one bright spot in Spain's otherwise gloomy architectural history of the past two centuries, showing once again how distinctive Catalunya's heritage is. The last quarter of the nineteenth century was a turbulent time there — a fact mirrored in the **Modernisme** (or *Modernista*) movement in architecture, which created a remarkable number of challenging, art nouveau-type buildings until well into the present century.

The dominant genius was **Antoni Gaudí**, one of the most distinctive voices of the age — indeed, of any age. He was interested not merely in architecture but also in sculpture and interior design, including lighting. His main architectural influences were Moorish and Gothic, which he considered the greatest European style. From the former he took towers, tromp l'oeil effects, repeated elements, ceramics, cornices, dragons, and the use of water; all employed, like his Gothic influences, in a free and fantastic way. He was also influenced by the natural world; trees, rocks, embankments, animals, birds, eroded and organic forms. He combined all these elements in an amazing — and distinctive — architectural vocabulary. Some of his projects were almost impossibly ambitious. He worked for over forty years on the **Sagrada Familia**, yet only built a small portion. The **Parc Güell** was another vast project for a complete garden city, which was a commercial failure yet has become a successful public park. Still, many less grandiose plans in a variety of forms were completed in Barcelona, and his work can also be seen in Astorga, León, and Comillas.

Gaudí stands out among his **contemporaries**, but there are a number of other architects of the time worthy of note, such as Lluis Domanech y Montaner, who was responsible for the sumptuous Palau de la Musica in Barcelona and who, with Juan Martorell, built at Comillas. These other architects, though, came nowhere near to developing the personal style of Gaudí and were far less utopian in their thinking.

MODERN

Beyond the Modernisme movement, much of Spain's **modern architecture** is best passed over. The buildings for the abortive "Fair of the Americas" in Sevilla in 1929 do have a certain period charm, but there's not much that's good about the bloated public buildings that went up in Madrid before and after the Civil War. The last thirty years have seen the wholesale destruction of large sections of the coast, particularly the south and east, as Spain led the way in speculative building projects, wiping out old communities in order to develop the country's tourist facilities; in addition, many of the larger cities have been spoiled by ugly and unchecked modern sprawl — Valladolid and Zaragoza are particularly good examples of irretrievably damaged cities.

The most prestigious (if politically obnoxious) building project of recent years was Franco's **Valley of the Fallen** outside Madrid, which commemorates the dead of the civil war, and also houses the Generalissimo's own tomb. It's a typical example of the sort of building favored by dictators — classical in inspiration, overbearing in style.

More exciting is the project to complete Gaudí's **Sagrada Familia**, which is likely to take a century or more. It remains to be seen whether the finishing process will take the form of pastiche of the master or modern innovation. Regrettably, the continuing construction of **Madrid Cathedral** is another opportunity missed. The Neo-Romanesque crypt built at the end of last century has been succeeded by a dull medley of Neo-Gothic and neoclassical, which does not look as if it will produce anything very challenging.

Only in Catalunya was modern architecture kept alive at all, through the work of local architects such as Oriol Bohigas, Ricardo Bofill, and Federico Correa (see p.425). Here too, the first signs of a new style are emerging, in a series of massive projects for the 1992 Olympics. A similar process is taking place in Sevilla in preparation for the World Fair.

Away from the big cities, and to Spain's further credit, most of the smaller towns have been untouched by modern building programs, and remain delightfully unspoiled. There has grown up, since the return to democracy, a genuine concern about the country's heritage, which was pretty much taken for granted in the past, and a good deal of restoration work is now underway. Spain's great monuments remain, but there are still equally potent joys to be found in the country's townscapes, whether they be simple agricultural villages, complete small towns such as Santillana del Mar and Covarrubias, or formerly important cities such as Toledo, Segovia, Salamanca, and Santiago.

Gordon McLachlan

SPANISH PAINTING

From the Middle Ages to the present day, the history of Spanish painting is a checkered one, more a series of high spots — El Greco, Velázquez, Goya, Picasso — than a continuous process of development. Influence from abroad has often been a factor, with somewhat mixed results. Yet at its best Spanish painting can stand comparison with that of any other country, not least in its intensity: the great masterpieces of Spain have a power that has seldom been equalled elsewhere.

BEGINNINGS

Early examples of this strength of expression can be found in the **illuminated manuscripts** and **mural paintings** of the eleventh and twelfth centuries. Dominant among the manuscripts are the many versions of Beatus's Commentaries on the Apocalypse, the original text of which, written by an eighth-century Spanish monk, inspired a whole series of versions illuminating the text with brilliantly colored miniatures. These books have found their way into libraries all over the world, but many still remain in Spain, with those in Girona and El Burgo de Osma particularly worthy of note.

The great decorative plans of village churches are also characteristic of the period, especially in Catalunya, though for the most part these are no longer in situ; many were saved earlier this century, just in time to prevent them from deteriorating irrevocably, and have been removed to museums, of which Barcelona's have by far the finest collection. The most imposing example of this style is by the so-called **Master of Tahull**, whose decoration of the apse of the church of San Clemente combines a Byzantine hierarchical composition with the vibrant colors and strong outlines of the manuscript illuminators. His overall rawness and monumentality seem strangely anticipatory of much of the best modern art.

Amazingly, two other highly talented painters also worked in the village of Tahull in the 1120s: art historians have christened them the **Master of Maderuelo** and the **Master of the Last Judgment**. Another notable artist of the period is the **Master of Pedret**, who incorporated scenes of everyday and natural life into his paintings.

Catalan studios also produced painted wooden altar frontals, often based on a central figure of a saint, surrounded by scenes from his life. In time, this grew in scale into the large retablo over the high altar — a key feature of Spanish churches for centuries. The most remarkable frescoes outside Catalunya are those of the Panteón de los Reyes in San Isidoro in León. These date from the second half of the twelfth century, and show a softer, more courtly style, perhaps influenced by French models.

THE CATALAN SCHOOL

In the Gothic period, Catalunya's predominance continued, rivaled only by Valencia. The leader of the school was **Ferrer Bassa** (ca. 1285–1348), who was court painter to Pedro IV of Aragón and a manuscript illuminator. Unfortunately, the only certain surviving work of his comes from late in his long career — a series of murals in the Convent of Pedralbes in Barcelona. These are charming works, notable for their coloring and descriptive qualities, along with a sense of movement and skilled draftsmanship, and are clearly influenced by the paintings of the Sienese school, though they're freer and less refined. Bassa may also have been influenced by the rounder qualities of Giotto and the Florentine School — Italian currents that are also found in the work of the artist's followers, along with various French trends.

The most notable names of this school were **Jaume Serra** (d. 1395), his brother, **Pere Serra** (d. 1408), **Ramon Destorrents** (1346–91), **Luis Borrassa** (d. 1424), and **Ramon de Mur** (d. 1435). **Bernat Martorell** (d. 1452) is perhaps the most appealing of the group, a notable draftsman who worked very carefully and deliberately, striving to give character to faces in his paintings. **Luis Daimau** (d. 1460) came strongly under the influence of contemporary Flemish painting, in particular that of Jan van Eyck, and no other foreign currents are discernible in his surviving work. **Jaume Huguet** (c.1414–92) blended this new realism to the traditional forms of the Catalan school, and can thus be seen as a representative of the International Gothic style of painting.

THE VALENCIAN SCHOOL

The Valencian school tended towards a more purely Italian influence, although one of its main painters, **Andres Marzal de Sax** (d. 1410), may have been German. Other notable names are **Pedro Nicolau** (d. 1410), **Jaime Baco** ("Jacomart") (d. 1461), **Juan Rexach** (1431–92), and **Rodrigo de Osona** (d. 1510), the last of whom was influenced by the Renaissance. The greatest of all the Spanish Primitives, however, was **Bartolome Bermejo** (d. 1495/8), originally from Córdoba, who worked in both Valencia and Barcelona. He seems to have had a fairly long career but only a few works, of a consistently high quality, survive. His earlier paintings, of which the Prado's *Santo Domingo de Silos* is a good example, are sumptuous; the later works, particularly the *Pieta* in Barcelona Cathedral, are altogether more complex, with a haunting sense of mystery and a Flemish and French influence that marks the introduction of oil painting to Spain.

THE CASTILIAN SCHOOL

In Castile, artists of foreign origin predominated — **Deillo Delli** ("Nicolas Florentino") (d. 1470) in Salamanca, **Nicolas Frances** (1425–68) in León, **Jorge Ingles** (dates unknown) in Valladololid, and **Juan de Flandes** (d. 1514) in Salamanca and Valencia. The last became court painter to Isabella la Catolica and introduced a Renaissance sense of space along with the beautiful modeling and coloring typical of the Flemish School. There was a rustic local school active in Ávila, however, and towards the end of the century native artists came increasingly to the fore. Particularly notable is **Fernando Gallego** (ca. 1440–1507), who worked in Zamora and Extremadura. Superficially, his paintings seem strongly reminiscent of Flemish types, but his exaggerated sense of drama — manifested in distorted expressions, strange postures, and movements frozen in mid-course — is far removed from these models. Nonetheless the garments are correctly drawn, and landscape is often a feature of the backgrounds.

Pedro Berruguete (ca. 1450–1504) was originally trained in the Flemish style, but spent an extended period in Italy at the court of Urbino, where he remained until 1482. His productions from this period are so close to those of the Fleming Justus van Gent that art historians have frequently been unable to distinguish between them. On his return to Spain, Berruguete worked in a hybrid style: although his drawing was precise and he introduced chiaroscuro to Spanish art, he persisted in using the traditional gold backgrounds — an anachronistic mixture that is surprisingly satisfying. Berruguete was never a slavishly imitator of Italian models, as were too many of his successors, and his most impressive works are those with crowd scenes, where the differentiation of types and attitudes is remarkable. **Alonso Berruguete** (1486–1561), his son, also went to Italy, and his paintings are heavily Mannerist in style, with strong drawing and harsh colors. His work as a sculptor is more significant: uneven in quality but sometimes truly inspired, with many powerful and intensely personal images. Certainly, he was the most distinctive and arguably the greatest native Spanish artist of the Renaissance.

THE LATE RENAISSANCE

Too often the quality of Italian art was diluted in Spain: neither nudes nor mythological subjects — both of crucial importance in Italy — had any attraction here, and there is hardly an example of either. Instead, there was a sweetening and sentimentalization of religious models. In Valencia, **Fernando Yañez** (d. 1531) and his collaborator **Fernando de Los Llanos** (dates unknown) adopted this facet of the art of Leonardo da Vinci, while **Juan Vicente Masip** (ca. 1475–1550) and his son of the same name, usually referred to as **Juan de Juanes** (1523–79), drew more from Raphael, becoming ever more saccharine as time went on.

Sevilla also had a school of painters, beginning with **Alejo Fernandez** (d. 1543), but although less slavishly imitative of Italian models than the Valencian, it also failed to produce an artist of the very first rank. The Extremaduran, **Luis Morales** (ca. 1509–86), is more notable: he was revered by the common people, who referred to him as "El Divino," but he never found favor with authority, and much of his work is still found in village churches. He is at his best with such small-scale subjects as *Madonna and Child*, which he repeated many times with slight variations. Strongly Mannerist in outlook, his drawing is rather stiff and his colors often cold, but he has a genuine religious feeling.

Ironically enough, it took a foreigner, Domenico Theotocopoulos (1540–1614), universally known as **El Greco**, to forge a truly great and quintessentially Spanish art in the late Renaissance period. He arrived in Toledo in 1575, having come from his native Crete via Italy. Presumably he hoped to find favor at court, particularly in the decoration of El Escorial, but was soon disappointed, and spent the rest of his life painting portraits of the nobility, along with a host of religious works for the many churches and monasteries of Spain's ecclesiastical capital. Having shown himself adept at both the Byzantine and Venetian styles of painting, he drew from both to create a highly idiosyncratic art that was ideally suited to the mood of Spain at the time. Distinguished features of his style include elongated faces and bodies, together with a sense of spiritual ecstasy that gives a strong feeling for the union of the terrestrial and the celestial. El Greco's gift for portraiture, too, is shown not only in his paintings of real-life sitters, but also in those of historical subjects, most notably in the several series of Apostles he was required to produce. His greatest work, *The Burial of the Count of Orgaz*, in Santo Tome in Toledo, displays all the facets of his genius in a single canvas. Later, El Greco's style became increasingly abstract, with a freeing-up of his brushwork that anticipates many subsequent developments in the history of art. Sadly, although he maintained a flourishing studio which produced many replicas, none of El Greco's followers picked up much on his master's style. Most talented was **Luis Tristan** (1586–1624), whose own output was very uneven.

At court, a school of portraiture was founded by a Dutchman, **Antonio Moro** (1517–76), who emphasized the dignity of his sitters in their facial expressions and by giving prominence to clothes and jewelry — a style that was followed by two native artists, **Alonso Sanchez Coello** (1531–88) and **Juan Pantoja de la Cruz** (1553–1608). At El Escorial, minor Italian Mannerists were imported in preference to native artists. An exception was the deaf-mute **Juan Navarret** (1526–79).

In Valencia, **Francisco Ribalta** (1565–1628) began working in a similar Mannerist style, but soon came under the influence of Caravaggio and introduced naturalism and the sharp contrasts of light associated with "tenebrism" into Spain. He was followed by a yet more significant painter, **Jusepe (Jose) de Ribera** (1591–1652). Ribera spent nearly all his career in Naples under the protection of the Spanish viceroys, who sent many of his works back to his native land. He had two distinctive periods: early on in his career he used heavy chiaroscuro and small, thick brushstrokes; later he brightened his palette considerably. Above all he was interested in the dignity of human beings, and whether he painted ancient philosophers in contemplation, saints in solace, or martyrs resigned to their fate, his art is a concentrated one, with the spotlight very much on the main subject. His subjects at times can appear gruesome, but they are very much of their period in that respect, and the treatment is never mere sensationalism. For a long time out of critical favor, Ribera now appears as one of the most accomplished artists of European Baroque.

THE 17TH CENTURY

In the early seventeenth century, Sevilla and Madrid replaced Valencia and Toledo as the main artistic centers of Spain. **Francisco Pacheco** (1564– 1654) was the father figure of the Sevillan school, although nowadays his work as a theorist is more significant than his paintings. He adopted a naturalistic approach as a reaction against Mannerism, and was followed in this by **Francisco Herrera** (ca. 1590–1656) and his son of the same name (1622–85), who painted in an increasingly bombastic and theatrical manner.

Towering high above these, Pacheco's son-in-law, **Diego Velázquez** (1599–1660), is probably the artist the Spanish people take most pride in. Velázquez was a stunning technician. His genre scenes of Sevillan life, painted while he was still in his teens, have a naturalistic quality that is almost photographic. In contrast to many of his fellow countrymen, Velázquez was a slow and meticulous worker: he probably painted less than 200 works in his entire career,some 120 of which survive, almost half of them in the Prado.

In 1623 Velázquez went to Madrid to work for the court, a position he retained for the rest of his life. As well as the many royal portraits, he portrayed the jesters and dwarfs of the palace, giving them a Spanish sense of dignity. In *The Surrender of Breda* he revolutionized history painting, ridding it of supernatural overtones. His greatest masterpieces, *Las Hilanderas* and *Las Meninas*, date from near the end of his life, and are remarkable for the way they immortalize fleeting moments, as well as for their absolute technical mastery, particularly of aerial perspective.

Juan Bautista del Marzo (ca. 1615–67), son-in-law and assistant to Velázquez, was so adept at imitating his style that it is often difficult to determine which works are the originals and which are copies. His independent work, however, is altogether of inferior quality. **Juan Carreno de Miranda** (1614–85) also followed

Velázquez's portrait style very closely, and was also very active as a painter of religious subjects, a field largely abandoned by Velázquez in his maturity.

In Sevilla, the greatest painter was **Francisco de Zurbarán** (1598–1664), who is best known as an illustrator of monastic life of the times. He painted mainly for the more austere orders, such as Carthusians and Hieronymites, and many of his portraits of saints are modeled on real-life monks, some of them single figures of an almost sculptural quality. Zurbarán's palette was a bright one, his lighting effects are subtle rather than dramatic, and he ranks as one of the supreme masters of still lifes, which have a frequent presence in his larger paintings as well as in a few independent compositions. A complete example of one of his decorative schemes is still extant at Guadalupe, but sadly his later work sometimes shows a fall-off in quality: to pay off his debts he was forced to produce a large number of works for export to religious foundations in Latin America.

Zurbarán also sentimentalized his style in order to meet the competition of his highly successful younger contemporary, **Bartolome Esteban Murillo** (1618–82), who spent his entire career in Sevilla. Murillo's light, airy style was in perfect accord with the mood of the Counter-Reformation, and he was to have an important impact on Catholic imagery. His versions of subjects such as the Immaculate Conception, Madonna and Child, and the Good Shepherd, became the norm in terms of the portrayal of traditional dogma. His genre scenes of street urchins and portraits in the manner of Van Dyck made him popular in Northern Europe too, and for a long time he was considered one of the greatest artists of all time. His reputation slumped considerably in the nineteenth century, and it is only in the last few years that critical opinion has turned again in his favor. Certainly his subject matter can seem cloying to modern tastes, but Murillo nearly always painted beautifully, and he was a marvelous story teller. His later works were particularly successful, employing the *vaporoso* technique of delicate brushwork and diffuse forms, and there's no doubt that he was a substantial influence on much subsequent eighteenth- and nineteenth-century painting in Spain, France, and England.

In complete contrast to Murillo, **Juan Valdés Leal** (1622–90) preferred the violent and macabre side of the Baroque. His work was very uneven in quality; the paintings in the Hospital de la Caridad in Sevilla are the most celebrated. **Alonso Cano** (1601–67) was the leading painter of Granada and also active as an architect and sculptor. He led a rather dissolute life, and changed his working style abruptly several times. Perhaps the most successful of his paintings are the mature, pale-colored religious works, which reveal debts to van Dyck and Velázquez.

A large number of artists can be grouped together under the **Madrid school**. One of the earliest was the Florentine-born **Vicente Carducho** (1576–1638), who painted large-scale works in somber colors for the Carthusians and other orders. **Fra Juan Rizi** (1600–81) illustrated contemporary monastic life in a different and less mystical way than Zurbarán. His brother, **Francisco Rizi** (1614–85), favored full-blown canvases of Baroque pomp. **Fra Juan Bautista Maino** (1578–1649) was more influenced by the classical aspects of seventeenth-century art; he painted some notable religious and historical canvases with strong coloring, but with little interest in lighting effects. **Juan de Arellano** (1614–76) and **Bartolomé Peréz** (1634–93) worked mainly with landscape and historical religious works, while **Jose Antolinez** (1635–75) was particularly renowned for his versions of the Immaculate Conception. **Mateo Cerezo** (1626–66) painted fluid religious canvases under the influence of the works by Titian and Van Dyck in the royal collections. The last major figure was probably also the most accomplished: **Claudio Coello** (1642–93), who was a master of the large-scale decorative style, using techniques of spatial illusion and very complicated arrangements of figures. His work at El Escorial shows his style at its best.

THE 18TH AND 19TH CENTURIES

The late seventeenth century and the first half of the eighteenth century was a very thin time in the history of Spanish painting: even the French and Italian artists imported by the Bourbon court were seldom of great merit. One native artist worthy of mention, however, is **Luis Meléndez** (1716–80), who was a master of still-life subjects. **Anton Raphael Mengs** (1728–79) came to Spain from Bohemia in 1761 as court painter, and in this capacity was a virtual dictator of style for a while, spearheading the adoption of an academic, neoclassical tone, particularly in portraiture. His assistant, **Francisco Bayeu** (1734–95), was a prolific fresco painter for both royal and religious patrons, and was also in charge of the cartoons for the Royal Tapestry Factory. His brother, **Ramon Bayeu** (1746–93), worked on similar projects but was far less accomplished.

It was the Bayeus' brother-in-law, however, **Francisco Goya** (1746–1828), who was the overwhelmingly dominant personality of the period. Goya's output was prolific and his range of subject matter and style so immmense that it is hard to believe one man was responsible for so much. Interestingly, he was no prodigy. In his twenties he became a highly competent painter of religious murals, his work at Zaragoza and Aula Dei already surpassing that of his contemporaries. After moving to Madrid, he worked for many years on tapestry cartoons (preparatory drawings), which in their graceful handling and skilful grouping made the most of their rather frivolous subject matter and gave Goya an entry into court circles, after which he became a fashionable portrait painter. It was in this role that his originality began to show through: his portraits eschew any attempt at flattery, and it's clear that he was less than impressed by his sitters. A serious illness in the early 1790s left him deaf and led to a more bitter and sarcastic art; his increasingly fantastic style may have emerged from his developing interest in witchcraft, which resulted in many paintings and two series of etchings: *Los Caprichos* and, later, *Los Disparates*. The marvelous frescoes in San Antonio de la Florida in Madrid are the exception here, among his most beautiful creations ever and containing a remarkable representation of the various social types of the day. But the Peninsular War further darkened Goya's mood, as shown by *May 2nd* and especially *May 3rd*, and by the engravings *The Disasters of War*. The last paintings are probably his most remarkable, especially those of bullfights, in which he showed an extraordinary visual perception, the exactness of which was proved only with the development of the slow-motion camera. Finally there were the despairing "black paintings" made on the walls of his own house, the Quinta del Sordo, now detached and hung in the Prado.

Of Goya's contemporaries, the most interesting are **Luis Paret y Alcazar** (1746–99), who painted rococo scenes under French and Italian influence, and **Vicente Lopez** (1772–1850), an academic portrait painter in the manner of Mengs whose severe portrait of Goya hangs in the Prado. The nearest artist to Goya in style was **Eugenio Lucas** (1824–70), who followed his interest in bullfighting and Inquisition scenes, but did little of stylistic advance. Indeed, most of the nineteenth century was extremely barren in Spanish art history, a period of imitation, largely of French models, at least twenty years late. The most gifted painter was perhaps **Mariano Fortuny** (1838–74), who specialized in small, very highly finished canvases, often of exotic subjects. Other artists worthy of mention are **Dario de Regoyos y Valdes** (1857–1913), the nearest thing to an Impressionist working in Spain at the time; **Joaquin Sorolla** (1863–1923), who was noted for his beach scenes; and **Ignacio Zuloaga** (1870–1945), who painted portraits against landscape backgrounds.

THE 20TH CENTURY

As with architecture, it was Catalunya that took the lead in painting towards the end of the nineteenth century. **Isidoro Nonell** (1873–1911) was best known as a naturalistic painter of the poor. In contrast, **Jose Maria Sert** (1874–1945) was at his best in large-scale mural decorations, particularly in the powerful sepia and gray frescoes he produced for Vic Cathedral, replacements for two earlier sets.

Although born in Málaga, **Pablo Picasso** (1881–1973), the overwhelmingly dominant figure in twentieth-century art, spent many of his formative years in Barcelona, achieving great technical facility at a very early age, and creating many accomplished works in a representational style before the age of twenty. In 1900 he first visited Paris, where the influence of Toulouse-Lautrec made itself felt in the "blue period" of 1901–4, during which he depicted many of society's victims in Paris and Barcelona, following the lead of Nonell. The "rose period" of 1904–6 was perhaps Picasso's most "Spanish" phase (although by now he was living in Paris). Actors, clowns, and models featured among his subjects, and his interest turned to the work of El Greco and ancient Iberian sculpture. The following "Negro period" of 1907–9 marked the break with traditional forms, as manifested in the key work, *Les Demoiselles d'Avignon*. After this Picasso returned to representational painting only for a short time in the 1920s, and from 1910 onward developed Cubism in association with Frenchman Georges Braque.

The movement's first phase, analytical Cubism, was largely concerned with form, with being able to depict objects as if seen from different angles at the same time. This was followed by synthetic Cubism, which showed a revival of interest in color and handling. For a time in the 1920s and 1930s, Picasso combined Cubism with Surrealism, inventing a new anatomy for the human form, and eventually becoming noted as a painter of protest, most markedly in *Guernica*, a cry of despair about the civil war in his native land (which he had by then left for good). Until his death, Picasso worked in a variety of styles, active in sculpture and ceramics as well. He was prolific to an almost unimaginable degree — in 1969 alone he produced almost as many canvases as Velázquez did in his lifetime, among the most notable of which were variations on well-known paintings such as *Las Meninas*.

One of the most faithful Cubists was **Juan Gris** (1887–1927), who favored stronger colors and softer forms than others in the group. In **Surrealism**, two Catalans were among the leading figures: **Joan Miró** (1893–1983) and **Salvador Dalí** (1904–1989). Miró created the most poetic and whimsical works of the movement, showing a childlike delight in colors and shapes, and developing a highly personal language that was freer in form and more highly decorative than that of the other Surrealists. One of his favorite techniques during the Thirties was to spill paint on the canvas and move his brush around in it. He was also active in a variety of artistic media besides paint and canvas: collage, murals, book illustrations, sculpture, and ceramics. Aside from an early period as a Futurist and Cubist, Dalí was more concerned with creating his own vision of a dream world. He was particularly interested in infantile obsessions and in paranoia, and his works often showed wholly unrelated objects grouped together, the distortion of solid forms, and unrealistic perspectives. He also worked on book illustrations, some of them his own texts, and on films. In later years he looked for other stimuli and painted a number of religious subjects. Few other artists in history have shown such talent for self-publicity. There are few artists, either, who have been so easily forged: in his later years Dali reputedly made millions by signing thousands of blank pieces of paper.

Artists of the same generation include **Oscar Dominguez** (1906–57), who used both the Cubist and Surrealist idioms, at times combining the two in a wholly individualistic way. Another isolated figure of note was **Jose Gutiérrez Solana** (1885-1945), whose impoverished upper-class background led him to seek out his subjects amongst the low-life of Madrid he knew so well, adopting a realist approach with strong use of colour.

THE PRESENT DAY

Among the most important living Spanish artists are the members of the "abstract generation," who run a museum at Cuenca devoted solely to their works. By far the most individual figure of the group is **Antonio Saura** (b.1930),

whose violently expressive canvases, the earlier of which are painted in black and white only, are overtly political in tone, showing Man oppressed but unbowed. He uses religious themes in a deliberately humanist or even blasphemous way in his triptyches of crowd scenes, and transformation of the Crucifixion into a parable of secular oppression. The Catalan **Antoni Tapies** (b.1923) is an abstractionist in the tradition of the *Dada* movement; he began by making collages out of newspaper, cardboard, silver wrapping, string, and wire. For a period he turned to graffiti-type work with deformed letters, before returning to experiments with unusual materials, particularly oil paint mixed with crushed marble.

For those who despair of the theoretical and iconoclastic side of the modern movement, **Antonio Lopez García** (b.1936) comes as a refreshing change. Whilst obviously using modern idioms, he is a representational painter of landscapes, cityscapes, still lifes, and nudes of an immediately appealing effect which clearly have their roots firmly in artistic tradition. **Eduardo Arroyo** (b.1937) is a follower of the Pop Art movement, with its emphasis on large-scale depictions of familiar everyday faces and objects.

Gordon McLachlan

WILDLIFE

Despite its reputation as the land of the package vacation, you can't beat Spain for sheer diversity of landscape and wildlife. When the Pyrenees were squeezed from the earth's crust they created an almost impenetrable barrier stretching from the Bay of Biscay to the Mediterranean Sea. Those animals and plants already present in Spain were cut off from the rest of Europe, and have been evolving independently ever since. In the same way the breach of the land bridge at what are now the Straits of Gibraltar, and the subsequent reflooding of the Mediterranean basin, stranded typical African species on the peninsula. The outcome was an assortment of wildlife originating from two continents, resulting in modern-day Iberia's unique flora and fauna.

Spain is the second most **mountainous** country in Europe after Switzerland. The central plateau — the *Meseta* — averages 600–700 meters in elevation, slopes gently westwards, and is surrounded and traversed by imposing *sierras* and *cordilleras*. To the north, the plateau is divided from the coast by the extensive ranges of the Cordillera Cantabrica, and in the south the towering Sierra Nevada and several lesser ranges such as the Serranía de Ronda run along the Mediterranean shores (where these southern sierras continue across the Mediterranean basin, the unsubmerged peaks are today known as the Balearic Islands). The Pyrenean chain marks the border with

France, and even along Spain's eastern shores the narrow coastal plain soon rises into the foothills of the Sierras of Montseny, Espuña, and los Filabres, among others. The ancient Sierras de Guadarrama and Gredos cross the Meseta just north of Madrid, and the Sierra Morena and the Montes de Toledo rise out of the dusty southern plains. So it is not surprising to find that both flora and fauna of Spain possess a distinctly alpine element, with many species adapted to high levels of ultraviolet light and prolonged winter snow-cover.

The center of Spain lies many kilometers from the coast, and thus the **climate** is almost continental in character. The summers are scorching, the winters bitter, and what rain there is falls only in spring and autumn. Moving eastwards, the Mediterranean Sea has a moderating effect on this weather pattern, favoring the coastal lands with mild winters and summers which become progressively hotter as you move southwards towards Africa. What most people tend to forget, however, is that the northern and western parts of the country are endowed with a climate that, if anything, is even worse than that of Britain! Depressions coming in from the Atlantic Ocean are responsible for almost continual cloud cover, high rainfall, and persistent mists along the appropriately named Costa Verde; when the sun does show its face the high humidity can make life very uncomfortable.

These climatic variations have produced a corresponding diversity in Spanish wildlife. The wet, humid **north** is populated by species common throughout Atlantic Europe, especially Ireland, whilst the **southern** foothills of the Sierra Nevada, situated only a stone's throw from Africa, have an almost sub-tropical vegetation. The continental weather pattern of much of the **interior** has given rise to a community of drought-resistant shrubs, together with annual herbs which flower and set seed in the brief spring and autumn rains, or more long-lived plants which possess underground bulbs or tubers to withstand the prolonged summer drought and winter cold.

LANDSCAPE

The Iberian peninsula was once heavily forested, although it is estimated that today only about ten percent of the original **woodland** remains, mostly in the north. Much of the

Meseta was covered with evergreen oaks and associated shrubs such as laurustinus and strawberry tree, but the clearance of land for arable and pastoral purposes has taken its toll, as have the ravages of war. Today tracts of Mediterranean woodland persist only in the sierras and some parts of Extremadura. When it was realized that much of the plateau was unsuitable for permanent agricultural use, the land was abandoned, and is now covered with low-growing, aromatic scrub vegetation, known as *matorral* (maquis). The southeastern corner of the Meseta is the only part of Spain which probably never supported woodland; here the arid steppe **grasslands** — *calvero* — remain basically untouched by man. In northern Spain, where vast areas are still forested, the typical tree species are more familiar: oaks, beech, ash, and lime on the lower slopes, grading into pines and firs at higher levels.

Much of the Meseta is flat, arid, and predominantly brown. Indeed, in Almería, Europe's only true **desert** is to be found, such is the lack of rainfall. But the presence of subterranean water supplies gives rise to occasional **oases**: flashes of green and blue, teeming with wildlife. The numerous tree-lined **watercourses** of the peninsula also attract birds and animals from the surrounding dusty plains. The great Ebro and Duero rivers of the north, and the Tajo and Guadiana in the south have been dammed at intervals, creating **reservoirs** which attract wildfowl in winter.

The Spanish **coastline** has a little of everything: dune systems, shingle banks, rocky cliffs, salt marshes, and sweeping sandy beaches. In Galicia, submerged river valleys, or *rías*, are reminiscent of the Norwegian fjords, and the offshore islands are home to noisy seabird colonies; the north Atlantic coast is characterized by limestone promontories and tiny, sandy coves; the Mediterranean coast, despite its reputation for wall-to-wall hotels and beach towels, still boasts many undeveloped lagoons and marshes, and west of Gibraltar lies perhaps the greatest of all coastal marshlands: the Coto Doñana.

The Spanish **landscape** has changed little since the early disappearance of the forests. While the rest of Europe strives for agricultural supremacy, in Spain the land is still **farmed** by traditional methods. The olive groves of the south, the extensive livestock-rearing lands of

the north and even the cereal-growing and wine-producing regions of the plains are still havens for the indigenous wildlife of the country. It is only since Spain joined the European Community that artificial pesticides and fertilizers and huge machines have made much impact. Even so, Spain is still essentially a wild country compared to much of Europe. Apart from a few industrial areas around Madrid and in the northeast, the landscape reflects the absence of modern technology, and the low population density means that few demands are made of the wilderness areas that remain.

FLOWERS

With such a broad range of habitats, Spain's **flora** is nothing less than superb. Excluding the Canary Islands, about 8000 species occur on Spanish soil, approximately ten percent of which are endemic; that is, they are found nowhere else in the world. Due to the plethora of high **mountains**, an alpine flora persists in Spain well beyond its normal north European distribution, and because of the relative geographical isolation of the mountain ranges, plants have evolved which are specific to each (there are about 180 plants which occur only in the Pyrenees, and over forty species endemic to the Sierra Nevada).

The **buttercup** family makes a good example. In the Pyrenees, endemic species include the pheasant's-eye *Adonis pyrenaica* and the meadow-rue *Thalictrum macrocarpum*; the Sierra Nevada has *Delphinium nevadense* and the monkshood *Aconitum nevadense*, and of the columbines *Aquilegia nevadensis* occurs here alone. *A. discolor* is endemic to the Picos de Europa, *A. cazorlensis* is found only in the Sierra de Cazorla and *A. pyrenaica* is unique to the Pyrenees. Other handsome montane members of this family include alpine pasque flowers, hepatica, hellebores, clematis, and a host of more obvious buttercups.

The dry Mediterranean grasslands of Spain are excellent hunting grounds for **orchids**. In spring, in the meadows of the Cordillera Cantabrica, early purple, elder-flowered, woodcock, pink butterfly, green-winged, lizard, and tongue orchids are dime-a-dozen, and a little searching will turn up somber bee, sawfly and Provence orchids. Farther into the Mediterranean zone, exotic species to look for include Bertoloni's bee, bumblebee, and mirror orchids. Lax-flowered orchids are common on the Costa Brava and high limestone areas will reveal black vanilla orchids, frog orchids, and summer lady's tresses a bit later in the year.

The Mediterranean **maquis** is a delight to the eye and nose in early summer, as the cistus bushes and heaths come into flower, with wild rosemary, thyme, clary, and French lavender adding to the profusion of color. The *dehesa* grasslands of southwest Spain are carpeted with the flowers of *Dipcadi serotinum* (resembling brown bluebells), pink gladioli, and a score or so of different trefoils in May. In the shade of the ancient evergreen oaks grow birthworts, with their pitcher-shaped flowers, bladder senna, and a species of lupin known locally as "devil's chickpea".

Even a trip across the **northern Meseta**, although apparently through endless cereal fields, is by no means a dull experience; arable weeds such as cornflowers, poppies, corncockle, chicory, and shrubby pimpernel are sometimes more abundant than the crops themselves. Where the coastal **sand dunes** have escaped the ravages of the tourist industry you can find sea daffodils, sea holly, sea bindweed, sea squill, and the large violet flowers of *Romulea clusiana*.

MAMMALS

Spain's mammalian fauna has changed little since the Middle Ages; only the beaver has been lost since that time. Unfortunately that doesn't mean that the remaining creatures are easy to see. Although still quite common in the mountains of the north and west, **wolves** keep out of man's way as much as possible (they're sporadically protected in Spain, but are widely regarded as a threat to livestock; the shepherds complain that wolves seem to know when a man is carrying a rifle and react accordingly). Neither are you likely to come across any of the few remaining brown **bears**. In fact, of Spain's enormous wealth of mammals, only a few species are active during the day, and present in sufficient numbers for regular sightings to be made.

In the **northern mountains** — the Pyrenees and the Cordillera Cantabrica — you should get at least a glimpse of chamois, roe and red deer, and possibly wild boar, which can be seen at dusk during the winter when they conduct nightly raids on village potato patches. Wildcats sometimes cross the road in front of you, and red squirrels are quite common, especially in the pine forests. Ibex, with robust scimitar-shaped horns, are common in the Sierras de Cazorla and Gredos, and marmots can occasionally be seen in the Pyrenees.

The typical mammals of **southern Spain** are seldom seen, but include the pardel lynx (a paler animal than the north European one), the Egyptian mongoose, the Mediterranean, or blind, mole, and fallow deer in the umbrella pine woods of the Coto Doñana. No less than 27 species of **bat** frequent caves and woodlands throughout Spain, including four types of horseshoe bat. Over a score of **whale** and **dolphin** species frequent Spanish waters and the Mediterranean shores are is still home to some of the last remaining Mediterranean **monk seals**.

BIRDS

If you care to spend your vacation with binoculars trained on the sky/trees/marshes, then Spain is the one of the best venues in Europe for **birdwatching**. Most people head for the Coto Doñana National Park if it's birds they're after, but other parts of the country are just as rewarding, even if the list of sightings isn't quite so long at the end of the day.

If you have the patience to search out and identify **birds of prey**, Spain is an ideal destination, especially in **summer**, as about 25 species breed here. Some, such as red kites, goshawks, Bonelli's and golden eagles, griffon vultures, peregrine falcons, and marsh harriers can be seen at all times of year in almost any part of the country. Others are confined to certain parts of the peninsula, where climate, landscape, and vegetation combine to provide the right environment in which to raise their young. You will only see the rare black-shouldered kite, for example, in the southwest, or the majestic lammergeier in the high Pyrenees (and sometimes in the peaks behind the eastern coast), while black vultures (about 240 pairs) and the rare Spanish race of the imperial eagle are restricted to the southern half of the country.

Some of these raptors visit Spain only in the **winter**; these are best seen in late fall or early spring on migration, and include the kestrel-like red-footed falcon and magnificent spotted eagle. By contrast, when these birds are leaving for their African and Asian nesting sites, others, like Montagu's harriers, short-toed and booted eagles, Eleonora's falcons and Egyptian vultures, are coming the other way, having spent the winter in warmer climes, but returning to breed in Spanish territory.

There is no less variety in other types of birds; woodpeckers, for example, are most abundant in the extensive forests of the **northern mountain ranges**. White-backed woodpeckers are confined to the Pyrenees, other such rarities as black and middle-spotted woodpeckers may also be seen in the Cordillera Cantabrica, and the well-camouflaged wryneck breeds in the north and winters in the south of the country. Other typical breeding birds of these northern mountains are the turkey-like capercaillie, tree pipits, wood warblers, pied flycatchers, ring ouzels, alpine accentors, citril and snow finches, ptarmigan in the Pyrenees, and that most sought-after of all montane birds: the wallcreeper.

In the open **grasslands** and cereal fields of the Meseta, larks are particularly common. Look out for the Calandra lark, easily identified by the trailing white edge to the wing, although loads of patience and good binoculars are needed to distinguish between short-toed, lesser short-toed, crested, and Thekla larks. Other small brown birds of the plains are rock sparrows and corn buntings, but more rewarding, and a lot easier to identify, are great and little bustards, majestic at any time of year, but especially the males when they fan out their plumage during the springtime courtship display. Look out also for the exotically patterned pin-tailed sandgrouse, the only European member of a family of **desert dwelling birds**, as well as stone curlews and red-necked nightjars, the latter seen (and heard) mainly at dusk.

If you come across an ancient olive grove, or an area of southern Spain where the evergreen oak **forests** are still standing, then stop!. A colourful assemblage of birds is typical of such oases of natural vegetation: hoopoes, azure-winged magpies, golden orioles, great grey and woodchat shrikes, bee eaters, rollers, greater spotted cuckoos, redstarts, and black-eared wheatears. On a sunny summer's day, these birds are active and easy to spot.

Natural inland bodies of **water**, often have wide marshy borders, owing to the fluctuating water level. In these rushy margins look out for water rail and purple gallinule, as well as the diminutive Baillon's crake, and scrutinize reedbeds carefully for signs of penduline and bearded tits. The airspace above the water is usually occupied by hundreds of swifts and swallows; you should be able to pick out alpine, pallid and white-rumped swifts and red-rumped swallows if you are in the southern half of the country, as well as collared pratincoles. These lakes are also frequented by wintering waterfowl (although Spain has no breeding swans or geese), European cranes, and sometimes by migrating flamingos.

The **coastal wetlands** are certainly a must for any serious birdwatcher, with common summer occupants including black-winged stilts, avocets, and most members of the heron family: cattle and little egrets, purple, squacco and night herons, bitterns, and little bitterns. On the Mediterranean coast, especially in low-growing scrub, keep an eye out for a small quail-like bird called the Andalucian hemipode; strangely enough it is closely related to the graceful cranes. Wintering waders are not outstandingly distinctive, though wherever you go, even on the Atlantic coast, spoonbills are frequently encountered. Grey phalaropes visit the northwest corner, as do whimbrel, godwits, skuas and ruff, taking a break from their northern breeding grounds.

The **Balearic Islands** can provide you with a few more exotic cliff-nesting species, such as Cory's shearwater and storm petrels; and the Islas Cíes, off the Galician coast, provide breeding grounds for shags, the rare Iberian race of guillemot, and the southern-most colony of lesser black-backed gulls in the world.

Hundreds more birds could be listed: with a good field you should find many of them for yourself.

REPTILES AND AMPHIBIANS

As with other types of wildlife, Spain is especially rich in amphibians and reptiles, with about sixty species in total. Some of the easiest to see are **fire salamanders**, which occur throughout Spain, albeit with coloration varying from yellow stripes on a black background to vice versa, depending on the exact locality. The best time to see them is in cool, misty weather in the mountains, or immediately after rain.

Three other species of **salamander** live in Spain. The golden-striped salamander (a slender, rather nondescript beast, despite its name) is endemic to northwest Iberia; the large sharp-ribbed salamander is found only in the southwest of the peninsula; and the Pyrenean brook salamander, is confined to the Pyrenees.

Closely related to the salamanders are the **newts**, of which there are only four species in Spain. If you take a trip into the high mountain pastures of the Cordillera Cantabrica, where water is present in small, peaty ponds all year round, you should see the blackish alpine newt; marbled newts can be seen around the edges of many of Spain's inland lakes, and reservoirs. Midwife **toads** strike up their chorus at dusk, and can often be heard well away from water, sometimes causing confusion with the call of the Scops owl. If you search through tall waterside vegetation you may be rewarded by the sight of a tiny, lurid-green tree-frog: striped in the north and west, but stripeless along the Mediterranean coast.

Two species of **tortoise** occur in Spain; spur-thighed tortoises can still be found along the southern coast and on the Balearic Islands, which are also the only Spanish locality for Hermann's tortoise. European pond terrapins and stripe-necked terrapins are more widely distributed, but only in freshwater habitats.

Perhaps the most exotic reptilian species to occur in Spain is the **chameleon**, although again this swivel-eyed creature is confined to the extreme southern shores. **Lizards** are numerous, with the most handsome species being the ocellated or eyed lizard — green with blue spots along the flank. Some species are very restricted in their range, such as Ibiza, Italian, and Lilford's wall lizards, which live only in the Balearic Islands. Similarly **snakes** are common, although few are venomous, and in any case it's sometimes quite difficult to spot them before they spot you and take evasive action themselves. Asps and western whip snakes occur in the Pyrenees, but you are only likely to see horse-shoe whip snakes and false smooth snakes in the extreme south.

INSECTS

Almost 100,000 insects have been named and described in Europe and an untold number await discovery. In Spain, where there are areas where no one knows for sure how many bears there are, insects have barely begun to be explored.

From early spring to late autumn, as long as the sun is shining, you will see **butterflies**; there are few European species which do not occur in Spain, but by contrast there are many Spanish butterflies which are not found north of the Pyrenees. These seem to be named mostly after obscure entomologists: Lorquin's blue, Carswell's little blue, Forster's furry blue, Oberthur's anomalous blue, Lefébvre's ringlet, Zapater's ringlet, Chapman's ringlet, Zeller's skipper, and many others. You need to be an expert to identify most of these, but the more exciting butterflies are in any case better known ones: the Camberwell beauty, almost black and bordered with gold and blue; swallowtails, yellow and black or striped like zebras, depending on the species, but always with the distinctive "tails;" the lovely two-tailed pasha, which is often seen feeding on the ripe fruit of the strawberry tree; and the apollo (papery white wings with distinctive red and black eyespots), of which there are almost as many varieties as there are mountains in Spain. Other favorites include the small, bejewelled blues, coppers, fritillaries, and hairstreaks that inhabit the hay meadows.

Aside from the butterflies, keep an eye open for the largest **moth** in Europe, the giant peacock, which flies by night but is often attracted to outside lights, or the rare, green-tinted Spanish silk moth, a close relative of tropical silk moths. During the day, take a closer look at that hovering bumble bee, as it may be a hummingbird hawkmoth, or a broad-bordered bee-hawk, flying clumsily from flower to flower. Oleander and elephant hawkmoths (resplendent in their pink and green livery) are often seen around flowering honeysuckle bushes at dusk. Many moths have bizarre caterpillars, as for example the lobster moth, which feeds on beech, or the pussmoth, found on willows and poplars, although the adults may be quite nondescript in appearance.

Grasslands and arid scrub areas are usually good hunting grounds for **grasshoppers and** crickets, which you can locate by following their calls. Mole crickets and field crickets live in burrows they have excavated themselves, but look to the trees for the adult great green bush cricket, about 7 to 8 cm long. French lavender bushes in the maquis are a favourite haunt of the green mantis *Empusa pennata*, identified by a large crest on the back of the head (the nymphs are brown, with a distinctive curled-up abdomen). **Stick insects** are harder to spot, as they tend to sit parallel with the stems of grasses, where they are well-camouflaged.

Members of the *Arachnidae* (**spiders**) to be found include two species of **scorpion** in the dry lands of southern Spain. Look out also for long-legged *Gyas*, the largest harvest-spider in Europe, which can be about 10cm in diameter, although the body is little larger than a pea. Spanish **centipedes** can grow to quite a size too; *Scutigera coleoptera*, for example, often live indoors; they have 15 pairs of incredibly long, striped legs, which create a wonderful rippling effect when they move across walls.

WHERE AND WHEN TO GO

Virtually anywhere in Spain, outside of the cities and most popular tourist resorts, rewards scrutiny in terms of wildlife. Perhaps the best thing about this country is that so much wilderness remains to be discovered on your own, without having to rely on guide books to tell you where to go.

The main drawback, however, is getting anywhere on public transportation, which often doesn't stop between departure point and destination. There is rarely any problem getting off a bus when you feel the urge, but you may have problems stopping the next one, which in any case may not arrive until the following day.

The following suggestions, then, are largely limited to those which are easily accessible by public transport. Inevitably this means that other people will be there too: you'll have to head off into the hills on foot in order to experience the best of Spanish wildlife.

Southern Spain is a good choice for any time of year, since even in the depths of winter the climate is mild and many plants will be in full bloom. If you decide on the **northern mountain ranges**, spring and early summer are best. The weather can be temperamental, but for the combination of snowy peaks and flower-filled meadows, it's worth taking the risk. The **interior** of Spain is freezing in winter and almost too hot to bear in midsummer, so spring or fall — to coincide with the occasional rains and the flowering of the maquis and steppe grasslands — are best. Again, if your real interest is the **coastal bird life** of Spain, visit in spring or fall, not only to catch the phenomenal migrations of birds between Africa and northern Europe, but also because accommodation in the resorts can be incredibly cheap outside the tourist season.

THE PYRENEES

The Moors called these mountains *El Hadjiz* — the barricade — which is effectively what they are, isolating Spain from the rest of Europe. The Spanish flanks of the Pyrenees are somewhat hotter and drier than their northern counterparts, but the high passes are nevertheless snowbound for several months in the winter.

If you avoid the ski resorts there are still many unspoiled valleys to explore, with their colorful alpine meadows studded with Pyrenean hyacinths and horned pansy, and some of the highest forests in Europe, extending up to 2500m in places. The **Vall d'Aran**, close to Pico de Aneto (the highest point of the chain, at 3408m), is a botanical paradise at any time of year. Go in spring and you will find alpine pasque flowers, trumpet gentians and sheets of daffodils, among them pale Lent lilies and pheasant's-eye narcissi. A little later in the year sees the flowering of Turks'-cap lilies, dusky cranesbill, and Pyrenean fritillaries, sheltering among the low-growing shrubs on the hillsides; while in autumn, following the annual hay-making, the denuded meadows shimmer with a pink-purple haze of merendera and autumn crocuses.

Farther west, the **Parque Nacional de Ordesa y Monte Perdido** in the Aragonese Pyrenees shelters valleys clothed in primeval pine, fir, and beech forests which are home to pine martens, wildcats, genets, red squirrels, polecats, and wild boar among the 32 mammal species that live within the Park boundaries. Dominating the forests are sheer cliffs with spectacular waterfalls and towering rock formations, the haunt of the sprightly chamois which thrive here in profusion. Although these antelope-like creatures are easily spotted, you will need to have your sights set firmly on the heavens to see the most renowned occupant of Ordesa: the lammergeier. A vulture of splendid proportions, it is now almost completely confined to the Pyrenees and a few eastern ranges in Spain. Its Spanish name — *quebrantahuesos*, or "bone-breaker" — refers to its habit of dropping animal bones from great heights to smash on the rocks below, exposing the tender marrow.

The second national park in the Spanish Pyrenees is that of **Aigües Tortes,** centered on the glacial hanging valleys and impressive cirques of northern Catalunya. The extensive coniferous forests of Scots pine and common silver fir are populated by capercaillie and black woodpeckers. Just above the timberline, early purple orchids and alpine and southern gentians flourish in the superb alpine meadows, and the rocky screes conceal pale, delicate edelweiss and yellow mountain saxifrage. The fast-flowing mountain rivers are home to otters; and the tiny secretive Pyrenean desman, Pyrenean brook salamanders, and alpine newts live in the clear waters of the glacial lake of San Mauricio. In the airspace above the peaks look out for honey buzzards and golden eagles soaring on the thermals, and if you scrutinize the cliff faces you might be rewarded with the sight of a wallcreeper.

CORDILLERA CANTABRICA

This mountain chain runs more or less parallel to the north coast from the Portuguese border eastwards into the Basque country. It has long formed a barrier between the northern coast and the rest of Spain since there are few crossing points, many of which are impassable during the winter. The vegetation is clearly affected by the rain-laden clouds which constantly sweep in from the Atlantic, as can be seen by the extensive oak and beech forests that shroud the slopes. Extensive beef and dairy farming is the traditional way of life, and the majority of the flower-filled meadows have never been subjected to artificial fertilizers and pesticides. One of the most fascinating aspects is the abundance of meadow flowers now rarely found in northern Europe: lizard orchids, heath lobelia, greater yellow rattle, moon carrot, Cambridge milk-parsley, galingale, and summer lady's-tresses — a delicate, white-flowered orchid.

The high point of the Cordillera Cantabrica is the small limestone mountain range of the **Picos de Europa,** visible from miles offshore in the Bay of Biscay. Over sixty species of mammal have been recorded here, ranging from such typical wilderness creatures as brown bears and wolves to snow voles, tiny denizens of the high peaks. Red squirrels, roe deer and chamois are easy to see, but many of the mammals which haunt these mountains, such as genets, beech martens, and wildcats, are secretive, nocturnal beasts.

One of the most outstanding landscape features of the Picos de Europa is the **Cares gorge**, where the river bed lies almost 2000m below the peaks on either side. The sheltered depths of the gorge are home to a number of shrubs more typical of Mediterranean Spain — figs, strawberry trees, wild jasmine, and barberry — and the sheer rock-faces are home to the exotic wallcreeper, a small ash-grey bird with splashes of crimson under the wings, the sight of which is highly coveted by bird-watchers.

The **Covadonga National Park** covers much of the western massif of the Picos de Europa, its focal point being the glacial lakes of Enol and Ercina. In spring the verdant pastures which surround the lakes are studded with pale yellow hoop-petticoat daffodils and tiny dog's-tooth violets, but a visit later in the year will be amply rewarded by the discovery of hundreds of purple spikes of monkshood and the steel-blue flowers of Pyrenean eryngo. A few hours scrambling across the limestone crags away from the lake should be sufficient for excellent views of griffon and Egyptian vultures, or you don't even have to leave the small cafe in the car-park to see alpine choughs scavenging among the litter-bins.

For those who prefer a more gentle scenery, **Galicia**, with its green rolling hills and constant mists, is hard to beat. Few people live in the countryside, which as a consequence is teeming with wildlife. The oak and beech woods of Ancares provide shelter for deer and wild boar; although no chamois, they were hunted to extinction for food during the civil war. The meadows benefit from the frequent rains and you can find all manner of wet-loving plants, such as large-flowered butterwort, bog pimpernel, globe flowers, marsh helleborines, whorled caraway, and early marsh orchids.

If you believed everything you read you'd be tempted to regard inland Spain as a flat, barren plain covered with mile after mile of bleached cornfields. But the wildlife is there; if you know where to look.

A good place to start is the **central sierras**. Just to the north of Madrid, almost bisecting the vast plain of the Meseta, run several contiguous mountain ranges which are well worth a visit. They may not have the rugged grandeur of the Pyrenees but there is plenty of wildlife to be found on the rocky, scrub-covered slopes. Venture into the extensive pine forests of the **Sierra de Guadarrama** to see Spanish bluebells and an unmistakable toadflax, *Linaria triornithophora*, which has large snapdragon-like flowers each with a long tail, sometimes pink, sometimes white. Birds of prey are abundant, and not too difficult to tell apart; both red and black kites can be seen, easily distinguished from other raptors by their distinctly forked tails (the red kite has clear white patches under its wings). Booted eagles are identified by the black trailing edge to their wings, and the Spanish short-toed eagle, here known as *aguila culebrera*, the "snake eagle," is almost pure white below, with a broad, dark head.

Farther west the granite bulk of the **Sierra de Gredos** boasts some of the highest peaks in Spain after the Sierra Nevada and the Pyrenees. Scots and maritime pines occur in the higher levels, sweet chestnut and Pyrenean and cork oaks on the southern slopes. The springtime flora is superb, including lily-of-the-valley, conspicuous St Bernard's and martagon lilies, and several species of brightly-colored peonies. On some of the drier slopes, where the trees have been cleared, the aromatic gum cistus forms a dense layer up to two meters high. There is no need to fight your way through their sticky branches to discover the delights of the flora here; even the edges of the shepherds' tracks are ablaze with asphodels, French lavender, a strange-looking plant called the tassel hyacinth, and the closely related grape hyacinth. But best of all in the Gredos are the ibex, very common in the pine zones between the cirques of Laguna Grande and Cinco Lagunas. Look out also for Egyptian and griffon vultures, red and black kites, and Bonelli's eagles overhead, crossbills and fire-crests in the coniferous forests; and rock buntings, identified by their striped heads, almost everywhere.

Moving away from the mountains there are still sights to be seen in the plains. *Dehesa* parkland is the best habitat, especially for birds: **Monfragüe Natural Park**, in Extremadura, contains some excellent areas of *dehesa*. Golden orioles, woodchat and great grey shrikes, hoopoes, and bee-eaters are impossible to miss, and you might even see a roller. In winter about 7000 common cranes descend on the Monfragüe grasslands, and the flooded river valleys which are an integral part of this park are good viewing points for red-rumped swallows and collared pratincoles in summer.

Monfragüe is perhaps best known for its breeding population of the endangered Spanish **imperial eagle**, easily identified by the distinct white shoulder markings. The central reserve where this raptor nests is open only to permit holders, but you may see them soaring over the *dehesa*. The same can be said for the rare black vulture; a huge bird which is impossible to miss. Monfragüe has the largest known breeding colony (about 60 pairs). Most people head for the huge rock outcrop known as Peñafalcon, where black storks, now extremely rare as a breeding bird in Spain, can be seen perched up on the cliff face, and the sky is constantly filled with griffon vultures coming and going. And look out for a smallish, light-colored hovering bird — it might be a rare black-shouldered kite, which you certainly won't see elsewhere in Europe.

Heading in the other direction, towards Zaragoza in the northeastern corner of the plains, you might consider visiting the **Laguna de Gallocanta**. This is Spain's largest natural inland lake, and has a lot to recommend it. Look out for birds more typical of the arid plains — pin-tailed sandgrouse and stone curlews — as well as those usually associated with fresh water. Gallocanta is a national stronghold for red-crested pochard.

MEDITERRANEAN COAST

Spain's Mediterranean coast conjures up visions of sandy beaches packed with oiled bodies and a concrete wall of hotels stretching from the French border to Gibraltar. Even in the heart of the Costa Brava, though, there's rich wildlife to be found. The **Parc Natural dels Aiguamolls de L'Empordá** in Catalunya is a salt marsh and wetland reserve sandwiched between the A7 expressway and the hotel developments in the Gulf of Roses. It is the nearest thing in Spain to an American nature reserve, with signposted nature trails, a well-equipped information centre, and several bird blinds. This rather detracts from the wilderness aspect of the site, but it is nevertheless a good place to watch out for the 300 species of birds that have been observed here. Apart from the more typical water birds look out for little bittern, black-winged stilt, bearded tit, and purple heron, all of which breed here. Spring is perhaps the best time, when flamingos, glossy ibis, and spoonbills drop in on migration.

If you can't stand the mosquitos which emanate from the marshes, try the drier, Mediterranean scrub areas nearby, which are ideal for spotting red-footed falcons on migration, breeding lesser grey shrikes (the only Spanish locality), stone curlews, great spotted cuckoos, and moustached and Marmora's warblers in summer. And of course, marsh and Montagu's harriers are always present.

Other promising wildlife locations include the fan-like **Delta de L'Ebre** (Ebro Delta), with up to 100,000 wintering birds and a large colony of purple herons. Again isolated from the mainland by the A7 highway, the lagoons and reed-beds here attract squacco and night herons, avocets, and red-crested pochard, with isolated islands providing nesting areas for the rare Audouin's and slender-billed gulls. Look out, too, for lesser short-toed larks, and a multitude of terns, including gull-billed, whiskered, roseate, and Sandwich.

Further south again lies a smaller coastal wetland known as the **Albufera de Valencia**.

It is so close to the city of Valencia that to learn it supports a breeding colony of the rare ferruginous duck is quite a surprise. Other water birds to look out for are red-crested pochard and, during the winter, the extremely rare crested coot, as well as cattle and little egrets, breeding night, purple, and squacco herons, little bitterns, black-necked grebes, and bearded and penduline tits.

SOUTHERN SPANISH SIERRAS

Stretching for miles behind the coastal metropolises of the Costa del Sol, these lofty mountains are a complete contrast from the sun-and-sea image of southern Spain. Perhaps the best-known is the **Sierra Nevada** at the eastern end of the range, which peaks at Mulhacén (3482m), the highest mountain in mainland Spain. Snow persists for much of the year at the highest levels, but the south-facing foothills are only about 150km from Africa. Environmental conditions thus range from alpine to almost tropical. Not surprisingly there is an incredible range of plant and animal life. If you are equipped to visit the high mountains when the snow is starting to melt you should see such attractive endemic plants as glacier eryngo, looking not unlike its Pyrenean counterpart, and Nevada daffodils, saxifrages and crocuses. Later on in the year there is still plenty to see, including the strange, spiny mountain tragacanth, wild tulips, peonies, pinks, alpine gentians, the Nevada monkshood and columbine, and the white-flowered rockrose *Helianthemeum apenniunum*.

Owing to the extreme altitude of the Sierra Nevada, birds more commonly found further north — crossbills, alpine accentors, and choughs — have a final European outpost here. You should also see many of the smaller birds which favor dry, rocky hillsides. Perhaps the most distinguished of these is the black wheatear, the males identified by their funereal plumage and white rump. Farther north, in the limestone **Sierras de Cazorla y Segura**, raptor-watching will be amply rewarded. Cazorla is the only Spanish locality outside the Pyrenees where lammergeiers regularly breed, and the smaller Egyptian vultures are common here. Small numbers of golden and Bonelli's eagles nest in the peaks and goshawks frequent the extensive forests (black, maritime, and Aleppo pines at high levels and holly, holm, and Lusitanian oaks, with narrow-leaved ash and strawberry trees, on the lower slopes).

These mountain ranges, birthplace of the great Guadalquivir river, are rather unusual in Spain in that they run approximately north–south rather than east–west. They also have a flora of some 1300 unique species including such handsome rock-dwelling plants as the crimson-flowered Cazorla violet (*Viola cazorlensis*), the columbine *Aquilegia cazorlensis*, a relict carnivorous butterwort (*Pinguicula vallisneriifolia*), and several endemic narcissi.

To the west lie some extraordinary Jurassic limestone ranges, eroded over centuries into formations known collectively as *torcales*. One of the more famous of these is at **Grazalema**, renowned for its Spanish fir forest. This tree (*Abies pinsapo*) is now restricted to just a handful of localities in southern Spain, including the **Serranía de Ronda**, and a specialized flora has evolved to cope with the dense shade that the trees cast. You should be able to find the colorful peonies *Paeonia coriacea* and *P. broteri*, as well as paper-white daffodils, and the winter-flowering *Iris planifolia*, with a large, solitary flower on a ridiculously short stem. A whole range of typical Mediterranean shrub species grow here, including laurustinus, grey-leaved and poplar-leaved cistus, Spanish barberry, Etruscan honeysuckle, the nettle tree (*Celtis australis*) and *Acer granatense*, a maple species confined to the mountains of southern Spain. Also in these woods breeds the eagle owl, the largest in Europe, which even preys on roe deer and capercaillie.

As a break from the mountains you might consider a visit to **Fuente de Piedra**, the largest inland lagoon in Andalucía (about 3500 acres). Partly because the water is never more than 1.5m deep (the level being further reduced by intense evaporation in summer) and also due to the lack of pollution, large numbers of flamingos construct their conical mud nests here every year. Fuente de Piedra is thus one of only two regular breeding places for greater flamingos in Europe, and has recently been declared a *Reserva Integral*, the most strictly-protected type of nature reserve in Spain. Altogether about 120 species of bird, 18 mammals and 21 reptiles and amphibians have been recorded here.

SOUTHERN ATLANTIC COAST

The more or less tideless Mediterranean ends at Gibraltar, so the coast stretching westwards up to the Portuguese border is washed by the Atlantic Ocean. Here, the low-lying basin formed by the Río Guadalquivir houses one of Europe's finest wetlands: the **Coto Doñana**, Spain's most famous national park.

Perhaps the most renowned spectacle are the breeding colonies of spoonbills and herons in the cork oaks which border the marshes, but equally impressive are the huge flocks of **waterfowl** which descend on the lagoons during the winter. As for breeding ducks, Doñana is the European stronghold for the marbled teal, a smallish, mottled brown dabbling duck which rarely breeds in Europe outside Spain. Ruddy shelduck — large, goose-like birds, generally confined to the eastern Mediterranean — are also present throughout the year, but breeding has not yet been proved. White-headed ducks definitely nest and rear their young here, although the more renowned nursery for this is at the Lagunas de Córdoba in central Andalucía. One of Europe's rarest birds is the crested coot, distinguished from the common coot only at close range by two small red knobs on its forehead, or in flight by the absence of a white wing-bar. It breeds in Morocco, migrating northwards into southern Spain for the winter; Doñana is the only Spanish locality where this species is resident all year round, although again no-one is quite sure whether it breeds here or not.

Water birds aside, keep an eye out for large flocks of pin-tailed sandgrouse, which perform prodigious aerobatics in perfect time, rather like a shoal of fish; and, at ground level, cattle egrets in the grasslands, usually in the company of some of the renowned black bulls of the region. Cattle egrets are most easily distinguished from other egrets by their pinkish legs (black or yellow in all other species). A smaller bird to watch out for is the Spanish sparrow, which commonly makes its nests in the nether regions of the large, untidy nests of the white stork. Doñana also boasts an impressive roll call of birds of prey, including imperial eagle and black vulture.

Some large **mammals** are relatively easy to see in Doñana; red and fallow deer and wild boar display an inordinate lack of fear when approached by man, despite the fact that this area was a Royal Hunting Reserve until quite recently. The same, unfortunately, cannot be said for Doñana's pardel lynxes, of which there are some 25 pairs, estimated to represent about half the total Spanish population. Egyptian mongooses also frequent the dry, scrubby areas, and genets are occasionally seen by day in the more remote, forested parts of the National Park. If you can drag your eyes from the veritable feast of bird-life you might spot a curious creature known as Bedriaga's skink. Endemic to Iberia, this small lizard has only rudimentary legs; you are most likely to see it burrowing rapidly into the sand in an effort to escape detection.

The nearby **Marismas de Odiel**, which lie within the boundaries of the city of Huelva a little to the west, are also very worthwhile. Apart from the flamingos, which are increasingly preferring these saline coastal marshes as breeding grounds to the nearby Doñana, you will also be rewarded by the sight of large numbers of spoonbills, purple herons, and other typical southern Spanish waterbirds.

THE BALEARIC ISLANDS

Despite the sun-seeker image of the Balearic Islands, there are many remote spots which have escaped the ravages of the tourist industry. Even on the big ones you can escape easily enough, and in total there are fifteen islands (most uninhabited).

One of the wilder regions is the **Sierra de Tramuntana** which runs along the northern coast of Mallorca, dropping abruptly into the sea for much of its length. It is a good place to see the diminutive Eleonora's falcon and enormous black vulture. Around your feet you can feast your eyes on an array of exotic plants such as *Cyclamen balearicum*, an autumn-flowering crocus (*Crocus cambessedesii*), *Helleborus lividus* (a rare member of the buttercup family), the pink-flowered *Senecio rodriguezii*, and many other endemic species of peony, birthwort, and hare's ear. Even in January many plants are in flower, but the best time of year to see the blossoming of the islands is from March to May.

Away from the mountains, other wildlife refuges are the low-lying coastal marshes which have to date defied the hotel trade. On Mallorca that of *S'Albufera* is a birdwatcher's paradise. The maze of tamarisk-lined creeks and lagoons is the summer haunt of water rail, spotted crake, little egrets, and a little careful scrutiny may reveal more secretive denizens: Savi's, Cetti's, Sardinian, moustached, fantailed, and great reed warblers. Also easy to get to are the saltpans known as **C'an Pastilla**, close to the airport at Palma, where black, whiskered, and white-winged black terns, as well as Mediterranean and Audouins's gulls (this latter bird is the rarest breeding gull in Europe), are frequently seen.

The Balearics are also ideal places for watching the endemic races of lizards; they are usually quite undeterred by your presence, and make excellent subjects for portrait photography! If you are keen on marine life, don't forget your flippers and snorkel, as the underwater scenario is superb.

Teresa Farino

ENVIRONMENT AND CONSERVATION

Protecting the environment of a country which encourages well over 40 million tourists to leave their footprints in the sand each year could easily be perceived as a lost cause. But since most of these visitors flock to, and stay on, a comparatively narrow coastal strip, the damage is contained.

The environmental impact of **"costa"** tourism, with its pressures on water supply, sewage disposal, and landscape, is a specialist subject in its own right, and one in which the battles are by no means over. According to the Barcelona-based environment group *DEPANA*, there is cause for worry over the second boom in coastal tourism as foreigners start to buy vacation homes. Meanwhile in inland, rural areas encroachment is fostered by domestic vacation home buyers.

Concerned people in Spain have a common complaint: while there may be lip service paid to environmental matters, actually goading bureaucracy into action is a different matter. The only language understood by all sides is an economic one; the good news being that the value of the environment to tourism is becoming increasingly evident and important in bargaining terms.

PROTECTED AREAS

Protection, then, is the name of a game increasingly played in the political arena, in which environmental benefit becomes almost incidental. Spain is still one of the wilder places of Europe, and wilderness can be found surprisingly close to some of the major urban and touristic centers. There are about a dozen **Parques Nacionales** (national parks) with a total protected area of more than 17,000 square kilometers, or 3.4 per cent of Spain's total land area. This, of course, is chicken feed compared to the level of ecological threat, but protection of the environment isn't yet on the worry list of the average Spaniard, and doesn't attract priority spending.

The stirrings of a movement towards environmental education can be seen in the creation of regionally nominated and managed **Parques Naturales** (more like wildlife reserves). So far the majority of these are in Catalunya, Galicia, and Andalucía, but they now exist in every part of the country, and natural parks, with their fairly comprehensive protection, already cover an area three times larger than national parks.

Even Spain's highest profile national park, though, the **Coto Doñana**, was recently in the headlines for an ecological disaster in which 30,000 birds including coots, spoonbills, pintails, and mallards died as a result of a combination of drought and the toxic run-off cocktail of seven pesticides used illegally in adjacent areas. The **Parque Nacional de Aigües Tortes**, too, has lost international recognition as a national park because of continuing hydro-electric exploitation of its lakes.

WETLANDS

In 1980 Spain had 10,852 square kilometers of wetlands, six times more than France. It has not been so ready as some other nations to condemn wetland out of hand and rush to get it drained. The country was an early signatory of the Ramsar Convention, an international agreement (the only one of its kind) to protect wetland. Three Spanish sites of international importance had been nominated by 1985. None of this, however, has prevented the steady decline of wetland areas, either by pollution or indirect draining.

The **Coto Doñana**, perhaps the most important wetland, is facing chronic drought and is suffering both from chemical run-off pollution (which caused the disaster mentioned above) and from detrimental agricultural practices. Just across the Río Guadalquivir from the Doñana, the last remaining unprotected wetland of the region has been drained and converted into farms.

The **Tablas de Daimiel** in La Mancha, too, are well known in conservationist circles for their deteriorated condition. Once recognized as being one of Europe's most important wetlands, and designated *Reserva Nacional* in 1966, then *Parque Nacional* in 1973, the area has nonetheless suffered terribly. Most blame is put on local viniculture upstream, with its irrigation and resultant heavy demand on artesian water. The Río Guadiana dried up in 1982 and the nearby Cigüela is heavily polluted. In the summer months particularly, the region can hardly support wildlife at all and certainly no longer attracts the once fabulous amounts of waterfowl which earned it world-wide fame.

There is some comfort in knowing that the plight of the Tablas has been officially recognized, with the launch of a project aimed at restoring former water levels. Naturalists are certain that if the water returns so will the birds and ditto the visitors.

La Albufera de Valencia was once one of the largest bodies of freshwater in Spain, but it too is shrinking rapidly and is now ten times smaller than it was in the Middle Ages. On a more positive note, the most accessible wetland of the lot, **Aiguamolls de La Emporda**, just behind the tourist beaches of the Costa Brava, is in the throes of being established as a *Parque Natural.*

HUNTING

The greatest confrontation over environmental issues in Spain involves hunting and farming groups. Many middle-aged and older men in Spain believe a shotgun is an accessory that they shouldn't be seen without in the countryside, and feel personally threatened at the news of the establishment or expansion of protected areas. One of the most emotive subjects is the protection of **wolves**. In areas where they have been protected, in the north especially, numbers have grown rapidly. Over recent years, outraged farmers have taken to increasingly militant demonstrations in an attempt to "protect" their land.

The figures speak for themselves. Although national parks protect more than 300,000 acres, **hunting reserves** (*reservas nacionales de caza*) cover a vastly greater area — almost 4 million acres to date. Largest is *Saja* in Cantabria, which is larger than all the mainland national parks put together. And although more species than ever before are protected and now forbidden to the hunter (ibex, bears, capercaillie, and most of the major birds of prey, for instance) there is no shortage of demand for other hunting trophies such as wild boar, deer, and chamois. Supermarkets stock all hunting gear, including shotgun cartridges during the open season, and walkers have to take care not

to look shootable on weekends in season, when the hills are aloud with the sound of double barrels.

As long ago as 1970 there were well over 1 million hunting licences issued annually, and exceeding quotas or **poaching** is considered virtually normal procedure, especially in areas where shooting and trapping provide an extra source of income for the poor. **Waterfowl** is a popular target, with huge numbers being killed each year. In the Ebro delta near Tortosa on the Mediteranean coast, for example, it is estimated that up to 34,000 ducks are killed each hunting season, though a 1980–81 census showed there were only 53,000 ducks present. Part of the area is now natural park.

The shooting and netting of **common birds** is also a major problem, as it is in much of southern Europe and North Africa. The annual slaughter of migrating birds in the Pyrenees, for a start, contributes substantially to the overall global figure of 900 million bird deaths each year. Latest European estimates for Spain are that about 30 million birds, often accused of being agricultural pests, are caught each year.

ACID RAIN

Spain was among the first countries to sign and ratify the UN's *Convention on Long Range Transboundary Pollution*, which came into effect in 1983, claiming that: "Spain recognizes the need to take the prevention of air pollution into account in overall energy policies." However as the time for accession to the European Community in 1986 drew near, the tone changed. There were strong political hints at this stage that the adoption of environmental policies was going to prove "difficult and costly." Spain's rapid growth as an industrial nation is a further blow to the environment.

In 1983, 58,000 acres of Spanish forests were showing signs of damage from acid rain. But most of this is home-produced: as far as Europe is concerned, Spain is one of the six countries receiving the least acid rain (18 percent of its total) from foreign sources. This compares with the UK's smaller figure of 12 percent or Italy's 22 percent*. Scandinavian countries record much higher "imported"

---

*These figures are provisional: meteorologists stress there is still insufficient data for accuracy.

levels. On the other hand Spain's domestic sulphur pollution accounts for 63 percent of its total. The country is the sixth largest source of sulphur in western Europe. Worst affected by acid deposition are parts of the north coast downwind from major industrial centers such as **Bilbao** and **Avilés**, and around the power stations of **Serchs** (Barcelona), **Andorra**, and **El Serrallo** (Castellon). It is believed that industry in Avilés alone has been generating 24,000 metric tons of SO annually. A technical commission established to study pollution in the forests of **El Maestrazgo** and **El Port de Tortosa-Beseit**, which spread over three provinces, blamed emmissions from Andorran industry for the damage, which seems, on the face of it, like an attempt to whitewash Spain's own problem.

NUCLEAR POWER

In 1985 Spain had eight functioning **nuclear reactors** with a joint electrical power output when on-line of 5,577 MWe. It was predicted that capacity would grow until 1990, with no further growth foreseen. Since then Spain has announced a shelving of plans for five light-water reactors, and is decommissioning three plants.

Spain was a forerunner in **alternative energy**, with the construction in 1980 of two 500-kilowatt solar thermo-electric plants costing $30 million. However, it is now clear these stations have not been an economic success, an experience shared by the French with their Pyrenean installation.

WATER

It is not surprising that domestic and general industrial use of Spain's **water resources** has rocketed in the past 25 years. Having used about 13 billion cubic meters in 1960, the population became three times as demanding by 1985, using about 40 billion cubic meters. As far as **water treatment** facilities are concerned, only 29 percent of the population had access to any form of water treatment process in 1985.

Paul Jenner and Christine Smith

MUSIC

Music in Spain is going through some good times, and has been since the return to democracy. In the past decade homegrown talent has flourished as never before in almost every field, from traditional regional music to experimental rock.

The one problem facing musicians — as everywhere — is a record industry dominated by multinational companies. Reaching a wide audience or getting decent record distribution is virtually impossible for anyone out of the mainstream. The media seems interested only in pop. Artists in other areas, whether folk, jazz, *flamenco*, or traditional, have difficulty getting their records reviewed in the press let alone played on radio or TV.

Nevertheless at a local and live level almost every type of music can be heard, the performers sustained by enthusiastic groups of aficionados. Only in one area has Spanish music noticeably declined of late — the songs of political protest which were so successful in the early 1970s have now all but disappeared.

FLAMENCO

Flamenco is, undoubtedly, the most important musical-cultural phenomenon in Spain, and the most defined in the sense that a racial aspect (gypsy/non-gypsy) plays an important role. Although it's linked fundamentally to Andalucía, the *flamenco* map also covers parts of Madrid, Extremadura, and the Levante. Where *flamenco* came from and how it began is a source of considerable controversy around Sevilla and Cádiz, its center of gravity. But its "laws" were established in the nineteenth century. There is a classical repertoire of more than sixty *flamenco* songs and dances — some solos, some group numbers, some with instrumental accompaniment, others acapella. The prevailing sentiment, with few exceptions, is one of suffering and pain. /

At present there are some good singers and fantastic guitarists around, and although the record industry doesn't take much notice of them, there are albums on the market by both old masters and contemporary artists. The former can be heard on many *flamenco* anthologies, as well as on their own records. Of the latter, the following **guitarists** are worth special mention: Paco de Lucía, universally known (and by some despised) for his flirtations with jazz; Manolo Sanlúcar; the Habichuelas; Tomatito; Paco Cepero; and Gerardo Nuñez. Of the **singers**, the most popular is Cameron de la Isla: look out too for Enrique Morente; El Cabrero; Juan Peña (El Lebrijano); the Sorderas; Fosforito; José Menese; Carmen Linares; and Fernanda and Bernarda de Utrera.

For many years Salvador Tabora and Mario Maya have been (separately) staging **flamenco-based spectacles**, at times to the outrage of purists. In a similar vein, there are a number of joint projects in which *flamenco* artists and Andalucian orchestras from North Africa have worked together. Enrique Morente and El Lebrijano are names to look out for in this field, and also the exciting early results of collaboration between *Ketama*, a young Madrid group, and Toumani Diabate, a *kora* player from Mali.

FOLK

Folk music as it might be understood in the rest of Europe or in North America never had much of a chance to develop in Spain. In the 1970s, when Francoism's end began to look conceivable, political songs were all-important. They didn't leave much room for a movement of folk music to take shape, and only a few groups survive from that era: *Oskorri*, *Al Tall*, and *Nuevo Mester*.

What folk music there is is at its most developed in the northwest of the peninsula, from Galicia to Euskadi. The *Festival del Mundo Celto* at Ortigueira played a leading role in the early 1980s, bringing together musicians from Wales, Ireland, Scotland, and Brittany with those from Galicia and Asturias. It was followed by other festivals in Galicia (Vigo, Moañas, Lugo) and in Asturias (Oviedo), though none of these have yet established themselves as regular events.

The best **Gallego** group is *Milladoiro*, well known in Celtic circles throughout Europe. Their chief rivals include *Doa*, *Na Lua* (who combine saxophone with bagpipe), *Citania* and *Xorima* (both traditional and acoustic), *Palla Mallada* (hyper-traditional), and *Alecrín y Brath* (electronic folk).

The Celtic movement in Asturias centers around two festivals in Oviedo (*Oviedo Folk* and *Noche Celta*). Most Asturian groups are fairly traditional, especially *Ubiña*, with excellent bagpipe-players, and *Lliberdón*. *Beleño* and the young *Llan de Cubel* are slightly more prepared to experiment. Look out, too, for the excellent harpists Herminia Alvarez and Fernando Largo. In Cantabria *Cambrizal* and *Luétaga* are names to watch out for.

In terms of public support, **Euskadi** heads the league, and it shows. *Oskorri*, an excellent electro-accoustic group, has been mentioned above. Two others are *Ganbara* and *Azala*, both really fine. Also impressive is the singer-songwriter Benito Lertxundi, whose energies generally go into traditional Basque music but who has also recently branched off into Celtic. Finally, *Txanbela*, *Izeki*, and *Lauburu* all deserve a mention.

Catalunya generally lags behind where folk is concerned. The only reliable names are *La Murga* and the young and promising *Tradivarius*. Vaguely related, though not strictly folk, are a series of orchestras who play traditional dance music: some closer to salsa like the *Orquesta Platería* and the *Salseta del Poble Sec*, others more traditional like *Tercet Treset* and the *Orquesta Galama*.

In the **Balearics**, despite geographical isolation, several groups have formed: *Musica Nostra*, *Sis Som*, *Calitja* and *Aliorna*, who are traditional, and *Coanegra* and *Siurell Electric*, more progressive. *Calabruix*, is an electro-acoustic duo.

From **Valencia**, *Al Tall* are an interesting band whose last project was a joint effort with *Muluk El Hwa*, a group from Marrakesh; *Alimara* are involved with both music and traditional dance; *Salpicao* experiment with

---

REGIONAL TRADITIONS

Spain has an exceptional wealth of **traditional folk music**, with a variety as broad as the cultural differences between regions. Recovery of these traditions since Franco has been uneven; at times the dictator's unifying policies were sadly successful, with some local styles lost forever. The regime's tactics included censoring lyrics, prohibiting the use of certain instruments like the *txistu* in the Basque country — which they claimed was a nationalist weapon — and banning the celebration of some deeply-rooted popular *fiestas*, including even Carnival in some places.

Nevertheless popular festivals and rituals have always been accompanied by particular songs and dances, and the strength of traditional styles was far too strong to crush entirely. Today they are being revived everywhere. Below is a brief run-through of the those most characteristic of each region.

CASTILE-LEÓN AND EXTREMADURA

Old Castile and León is the land of the *seguidilla* and the *jota*, enlivened by the *dulzaina* (an oboe) or the *gaita charra* (a flute) respectively, and the *tamboril* (small drum). Other dances like *ruedas* or *entradillas* have developed from old rituals.

In New Castile and Extremadura variations of the *jota* are again the most common.

ANDALUCÍA

Andalucía is of course most famous for *flamenco*, but it also has a rich folklore based around **traditional festivals**. In general, Christmas and Easter celebra-

tions are very popular. The half-religious, half-playful celebration of El Rocío stands out in particular. As well as *malagueñas*, *fandangos*, *jotas*, and others, there is one style, **la sevillana**, which has foregone local status and been adopted throughout the rest of the peninsula.

As for instruments, the guitar is queen of Andalucía, but you might also see the comparatively rare *flauta del Alosno* (a type of flute) and the *gaita gastoreña* (a clarinet). Many of the traditions are kept alive by groups known as *verdiales* (literally reciters) and *troveros* (minstrels) in western Andalucía. The *copla* and *tonadilla* (short, popular songs with light-hearted tunes) are among the traditions enjoying a comeback.

EUSKADI

The Basque country, fiercely jealously of its ancient culture, preserves a number of archaic instruments like the *txalaparta* (a log which is tapped) and the *alboka* (a double clarinet made from bulls' horns) are still used. The **trikitixs**, a simple line-up of tambourine and accordion, is especially popular, and competitions are held each year to find the best players.

Also very keen on competition are the **bertsolaris**, native improvising singers who go in for personal, one-to-one challenges.

Of the dances, the *zorticos*, with their complicated rythym, and the *arresku*, or ribbon dance, are perhaps the most striking.

flamenco-based fusions; and *Canem*, the youngest of all, are also promising.

Three folk festivals which have the **Mediterranean** as a reference point, and in which the countries bordering it participate, are held in Spain. The pioneer was the *Trobada de Musica del Mediterranea* in Valencia. This was followed by one in Vilanova i la Geltrú, and by *Cançons de la Mediterrania* in Palma, Mallorca.

Aragón, after years in the wilderness, is beginning to see a bit of a folk revival under the auspices of groups like *Hato de Foces*, *Cornamusa*, and the *Orquestina del Fabriol*. The scene in **Castile** has for many years been dominated by the activity of *Joaquín Díaz*, a phenomenally hard-working and prolific recorder, and by *Nuevo Mester de Juglaría*. *Manuel Luna* and *La Musgaña* are also worth

listening out for, and the singer *María Salgado* deserves a mention too. In Segovia, *Rebolada* is a newly formed group which includes eight *dulzainas* in its line-up.

In **Andalucía** there are just two folk groups of much interest: the very traditional *Almadraba* from Tarifa, and the more revivalist *Lombarda* from Granada. It is also in Tarifa that Andalucía's only well-known festival is held, although there's another interesting one in the Alpujarras for the *trovos*.

Sephardic (medieval Iberian Jewish) music can be included here as a cross between folk and traditional styles. Two female singers — Rosa Zaragoza and Aurora Moreno — are the most interesting in this field; the latter is also involved in Mozarabic *jarchas* (Arabic verse set to music).

CANTABRIA AND ASTURIAS

In Cantabria and Asturias the *rabel* (like a viola) is very important, accompanied usually by **humorous folk songs**. *Pasiegos* and *Asturianadas* (in Asturias), and *vaqueiradas* (in Cantabria), are the songs to listen out for.

Bagpipes, a traditional local instrument, are also coming back into fashion in Asturias.

GALICIA

Galicia is the most Celtic region in Spain, although it also has an appreciable Portuguese component to its heritage. The *muiñeira*, the *pandeirada* and the *fandango* are danced to the sound of a quartet of **bagpipes** joined by drums and percussion. The **zanfona** (hurdy-gurdy) is coming back into popularity in the region, but above all various "schools of bagpipes" have emerged in the 1980s — some of them with more than 30 pipers playing together.

ARAGÓN

The *jota*, a robust and melodic song danced in pairs, is synonymous with Aragón, although it's also common in many other parts of Spain. The music for it is played on string instruments — lute, *bandurria* (similar to a lute), and guitar. Also worth looking out for are the *dances*, a suite of popular dances always performed with much ceremony.

A particularly good Aragonese festival, **La Tamborrada**, is held in Calanda (Buñuel's birthplace, about 20km from Alcañiz), where at midnight on

Maundy Thursday the whole village pours onto the streets bashing drums.

Across the state in the Pyrenees, a very unusual percussion instrument of medieval origin — the *chicotén* or *ton-ton* — is still in use.

CATALUNYA

The national dance of Catalunya is the **sardana**, a circular, collective dance performed with solemnity and dignity. The accompanying instrumental group is called a **cobla** and it includes the *flabiol* (a type of long flute), the *tambori* (drum), and tenor and soprano oboes. Another Catalan oboe is the *gralla*, whose notes orchestrate the raising of a human castle (*castell*).

VALENCIA

Valencia, like the Balearics, conceals traces of Arabic culture in the depths of its own. Wind instruments are important here, and no village can hold its head up if it doesn't have its own decent band. All along the coast of the Levante, *jotas* and *parranadas* are the most characteristic dances, although in Murcia, the *auroros* and *animeros* (a group dance) are of special interest.

THE BALEARICS

Substantial differences exist between the islands. **Ibiza and Formentera** retain ancient folk dances, while those of **Mallorca and Menorca**, *boleros* and *jotas*, are much more modern. Yet another bagpipe, the *xeremies*, is benefitting from the current revival.

ROCK

Even when it comes to **rock and pop** music, it is hard to talk of Spain as a single entity. In the 1970s Madrid was dominated by heavy rock, with a series of groups whose fans lived in the working-class districts of the capital and in the dormitory towns of the outskirts. Meanwhile, in Barcelona, the scene was split between musicians who were producing a very cool jazz-rock and those into a warmer Catalan salsa. On the fringes were the singer-songwriters and the Latin American groups who, despite Franco, managed to tour Spain.

Halfway through the decade, though, the **punk** reaction began to take hold among teenagers just as it did in England and the USA. Some of the older rockers, like *Ramoncín*, attempted to take punk on board; younger bands, like *Kaka de Lux* (phonetically, Luxury Shit), tried to take it to its logical conclusions. The latter were very young and nobody took them seriously — they didn't even know how to hold a guitar. Nevertheless, punk broke up the old order and set the scene for the 1980s.

Today groups are flourishing everywhere. In every Spanish city there are dozens of them, all making demo-tapes and looking for a break. Straightforward pop is the main area of activity, but there have been various phases in which punks, *tecnos*, *garajistas*, *siniestros*, Romantics, and rockabillies and others have succeeded and overlapped one another. All the bands below are reasonably established, have cut records, and are currently active. The list also includes the odd older rocker who still manages to play the part with dignity!

Madrid still has the most bands and the best, covering a wide range of styles and stances. A long-time favorite in the *Real Guide* office is "Alaska" — one-time muse of modernity — and her group *Dinarama*, more about making a sensation than serious music, but brilliant live. There then come a series of bands that have been working successfully for a few years: *Radio Futura*, the intellectuals of Spanish rock; *Nacha Pop*, *Los Secretos* (vaguely country); *Mecano* (pretty-boys who sell records by the truckload); *Aviador Dro* (futuristic); and *Mermelada* (straight-ahead rock 'n roll). A slightly younger generation includes: *Gabinete Caligari* (macho Hispano-pop); *Los Coyotes* (Latin rockabilly); *La Frontera* (cowboy); and *La*

Unión. Also from Madrid, but in a rather separate category, are *Hombres G* and the *Toreros Muertos*, both of whom aim their music at a teenybop audience. The *Toreros* are the more interesting. Of the older survivors, *Casal* (whose last disc was a Tom Jones anthology), *Miguel Ríos*, and *Ramoncín* stick to classic rock while *Rosendo*, *Obus*, and *Barón Rojo* lean towards heavy metal.

In **Barcelona** three very different groups stand out: *El Ultimo de la Fila*, a duo with interesting lyrics and a Mediterranean sound, *Loquillo y Los Trogloditas*, and *Los Rebeldes*, former rockabilly heroes now seeking new directions.

The **Basque Country** scene is divided into two: radical rock is represented by *Korkatu*, *Hertzainak*, *Eskorbuto*, and *La Polla Records*, who use hot rhythms, reggae, ska, etc., as a base for their political message; and *Duncan Dhu* and *La Dama se Esconde*, blander but more universal.

From **Galicia** (especially Vigo) has emerged a surprising number and diversity of bands — *Siniestro Total*, *Os Resentidos*, and *Semen Up* among them — which, though they haven't made great records, have succeeded in livening up the scene. **Asturias** can offer just one reasonably well-known group, *Los Ilegales*, powerful rockers with a strong live set.

From **Andalucía** there's the Malagueño combo *Danza Invisible*, and a Sevillan mafia made up of *Martirio* (who combine pop and traditional songs), *Pata Negra* (interesting mix of blues, flamenco, and rock, marred by the occasional Claptonesque guitar solo), and *Kiko Veneno* (the brains of the bunch).

As for **venues**, most are makeshift and temporary, so look out for posters and publicity, especially around festival times. In the cities, many bars may have a live gig once a week or so. Of the bigger places, *Universal*, *Jacara*, *Astoria*, and the *Rock Club* are all worth checking out in Madrid; in Barcelona, *Zeleste*.

SINGER-SONGWRITERS

There's a long history of **singer-songwriters** in Spain, but few have managed to adapt themselves to the times. In **Catalunya**, where the *Nova Canço* (New Song) until recently had a wide base of appeal, many singers have simply dropped out of sight. Among those still going strong are *Joan Manuel Serrat*, one of the big record sellers in Spain, who sings both in Catalan and Castilian; *Marina Rossell*, searching for "a Mediterranean music without frontiers," and the lyrical Lluis Llach. Also hanging in there are *Quico Pí de la Serra* and, from Valencia, *Raimon*.

In the **Balearics**, *Maria del Mar Bonet* is a singer-songwriter who also dabbles in folk and jazz. She remains firmly at the top. One of the newest names in Catalan singing is the Mallorquin *Tomeu Penya*, while *Joan Bibiloni*, whose instrumental pieces (a cross between jazz and New Age) have been hitting the international circuit, also lives in Mallorca. In **Valencia**, *Miquel Gil*'s joint efforts with *Terminal Sur* have had interesting results.

Euskadi has a similar situation to Catalunya. *Mikel Laboa* is an old name going strong but not producing anything new, while younger artists like *Txomin Artola* and his former companion *Amaia Zubiría* have yet to establish themselves. Other names include *Imanol* (sophisticated), and *Ruper Ordorika* (rocky). In **Galicia**, *Emilio Cao* switches back and forth between traditional folk and more modern singer-songwriting.

Madrid is again the center of the scene, even if few of the performers are native. Names you might see include *Luis Eduardo Aute*, who has a huge following, and *Joaquín Sabina*, an Andalucian who plays a catchy simple rock with lyrics younger musicians can identify with. *Ana Belén*, the Asturian *Victor Manuel*, and *Pablo Guerrero* from Extremadura, are worth seeing too. Also living and singing in Madrid are *Javier Krahe*, *Luis Pastor*, *Hilario Camacho*, *Ricardo Solfa*, and a series of young people like *Javier Batanero*, *Paco Ortega*, *Isabel Montero*, and especially *Javier Bergia*, best and most original of the latest generation.

Andalucía has two good names, the popular *Carlos Cano*, who has revived the traditional Andalucian *copla*, and *Javier Ruibal*.

Chief meeting-place and **venue** of singer-songwriters in Madrid is the pub *Elígeme*. The *Instituto de la Juventud* also organizes an annual show-concert of young singer-songwriting, and another for young folk talent.

Musicians and groups who are **hard to categorize** but just as creative include the *Orquesta de las Nubes*, Juan Alberto Arteche's *Finis Africae*, Luis Delgado's *Ishinohana*, and Luis Paniagua and his various projects, particularly with the *Atrio Musical de Madrid*.

JAZZ

Jazz in Spain always had loyal fans tucked away in small clubs, but since the end of the 1970s it has really taken off. There are many festivals and a good number of established groups. Bop and hard bop predominate, but there are also many experiments with fusion and traditional jazz. On TVE (the national TV channel) there's an established program, *Jazz Entre Amigos* (Jazz Among Friends), and two magazines *Quartica Jazz* and *Solo Blues*, report what is happening in Black music. Jazz schools are also influential, created by or around foreign musicians who have settled in Spain, the most important being that of Abdu Salim in Sevilla .

Three great musicians exemplify the best in **current Spanish jazz**: the Catalan pianist *Tete Montoliu* and the Madrid saxophonists *Pedro Iturralde* and *Jorge Pardo*. All three head their own groups and Jorge is also working on projects with Paco de Lucía. Other combos that stand out are the *Canal Street Band*, which plays traditional jazz every Tuesday in the *Whisky Jazz Club* in Madrid; the *Clamores Band*, also very traditional; the ultramodern *O C O*; *Vlady Bas's* group; and those of *Tomás San Miguel*, *José Antonio Galicia*, and *Gerardo Nuñez*, all of them in Madrid.

The most established **festival** is held at San Sebastián in July. Vitoria celebrates one in the same month, and there are two in Madrid: one in May (*Fiestas de San Isidro*), the other in November. November is jazz month in Spain, when there's also a festival in Barcelona and many smaller events which take the opportunity of featuring some of the artists who are playing in the two major cities. Other worthwhile events are the *Festival de Jazz* in the streets of Murcia, and the *Muestra de Jazz* for young exponents, organized by the *Instituto de la Juventud* in Ibiza.

Clubs worth special mention include, in Madrid, the *Central*, *Clamores*, and the *Colegio Mayor San Juan Evangelista* (in the University); *La Cova del Drac* in Barcelona; *Perdido* in Valencia; and *Georgia* in Almería.

Manuel Dominguez

RECORDS

Records are good value in Spain, and it's easy to build up a colection of classics from the last decade and the present. Whatever else you purchase, don't miss out on the wonderful Paco de Lucía crosssovers. And if the list below exhausts you, there is always Julio Iglesias.

FLAMENCO

Antología del Cante Flamenco (Hispavox; 3 LPs).
El Cante Flamenco, Antología Histórica (Philips; 6 LPs).
Medio Siglo de Cante Flamenco (Ariola; 10 LPs).
Magna Antología del Flamenco (Hispavox; 20 LPs).
Camarón *Viviré* (Philips).
Carmen Linares *Carmen* (Gasa).
Gerardo Nuñez *El Gallo Azul* (Gasa).
Paco de Lucía *Siroco* (Philips).
Paco de Lucía y Paco Peña *Paco Doble* (Philips).
Juan Peña Lebrijano y Orquestra Andalusí de Tanger *Encuentros* (Ariola/Globestyle).

FLAMENCO-JAZZ CROSSOVER

Paco de Lucía *Solo Quiero Caminar* (Philips), *Live . . . One Summer Night* (Phonogram).
Lole . . . y Manuel (Gong Fonomusic).
Ketama *Ketama* (Nuevos Medios/Hannibal).
Triana *Montoya* (CBS).

ROCK

Pata Negra *Blues de la Frontera* (Nuevos Medios/Hannibal).
Danza Invisible *A Tu Alcance* (Twins).
Duncan Dhu *El Grito del Tiempo* (Gasa).
El Ultimo de la Fila *Como la Cabeza al Sombrero* (PDI).
Ilegales *Chicos Palidos para la Máquina* (Hispavox).
Kiko Veneno *La Pequeño Salvaje* (Nuevos Medios).
Kortatu *Kolpez Kolpe* (Ohiuka).
La Frontera *Tren de Medianoche* (Polygram).
Loquillo y los Trogloditas *Morir en Primavera* (Hispavox).
Los Rebeldes *Mas Allá del Bien y del Mal* (CBS).
Martirio *Estoy Mala* (Nuevos Medios).
Nacha Pop *El Momento* (Polygram).
Radio Futura *La Canción de Juan Perro* (Ariola).

FOLK

Al Tal y Muluk el Hwa *Xarq al-Andalus* (RNE).
Aurora Moreno *Aynadamar* (Saga).
Azala *Zaldiko Maldiko* (Elkar).
Benito Lertxundi *Mauleko Bidean* (Elkar).
Gambara *Harat Honat* (Elkar).
Joaquin Diaz *Kantes Djudeo-Espanyoles* (Saga).
La Musgaña *El Diablo Cojuelo* (Sonifolk).
Luis Paniagua *Neptuno* (El Cometa de Madrid).
Lliberdon (Sonifolk).
Manuel Luna *Como Hablan las Sabinas* (RNE).
Milladoiro *Galicia no Pais das Maravillas* (CBS).
Na Lua *A Estrela de Maio* (Edigal).
Oskorri *Hamabost Urte* (Elkar).
Salpicão (RNE).

SINGER SONGWRITERS

Carlos Cano *Quedate con la Copla* (CBS).
Emilio Cao *Amiga Alba e Delgada* (Edigal).
Javier Bergia *La Alegría del Coyote* (Fono-Astur).
Joan Manuel Serrat *Bienaventurados* (Ariola).
Luis Eduardo Aute *Templo* (Ariola).
Lluis Llach *Astres* (CBS).
Marina Rossell *La Barca del Temps* (CBS).
María del Mar Bonet *Gavines y Dragons* (Ariola).
Pablo Guerrero *El Hombre que Vendió el Desierto* (Gasa).

REGIONAL TRADITIONS

Magna Antología del Folklore Musical de España (Hispavox; 17 LPs).
La Voz Antigua (Guimbarda; 3 LPs).

MISCELLANEOUS

Finis Africae *Un Dia en el Parque* (Gasa).
Ishinohano *La Flor de Piedra* (El Cometa de Madrid).
Orquesta de las Nubes *Manual del Usuario* (Gasa)

BOOKS

T R A V E L /
I M P R E S S I O N S

Laurie Lee *As I Walked Out One Midsummer Morning* (Norton, 1985 $22.50; also Penguin, 1971, $6). The account of Lee's walk through Spain — from Vigo to Málaga — and his gradual awareness of the forces moving the country towards civil war. As an autobiographical novel, of living rough and busking his way from the Cotswolds with a violin, it's a delight. As a piece of social observation it remains painfully sharp. In *A Rose For Winter* (Penguin, 1971, $5.50) he describes his return, twenty years later, to Andalucía.

Norman Lewis *Voices of the Old Sea* (Penguin, 1986, $5.95). This belongs to a different region (Catalunya) and a different age (the early 1950s). Again, however, it's an ingenious blend of novel and social record, charting the lives of two remote Catalan villages and the breakdown of the old ways in the face of a new revolution: tourism.

Gerald Brenan *South From Granada* (Hippocrene, 1976, $20.50, or Cambridge Univ. Press, 1980, $14). An enduring classic. Brenan lived in a small village in the Alpujarras in the 1920s, and records this, and the visits of his Bloomsbury contemporaries Virginia Woolf, Lytton Strachey, and Bertrand Russell. See also his *The Face of Spain* (Penguin, 1988, $7.95).

Jan Morris *Spain* (Prentice Hall Press, 1988, $24.95). As an introduction to Spain this is exceptionally good in its sweeping control of place and history — but also quirkily naive. Everything is seen as symbolic, which is fine if fleshing out Philip II, rather less so applied to

the recent past: "the Spanish people seem almost ideal material for dictatorship . . . in Franco's day most Spaniards fell easily enough into its rhythms . . . ." Judge for yourself.

James A. Michener *Iberia* (Fawcett, 1984, $5.95) Hoary old bestseller, first published in 1968, offering a series of exceptionally shallow "insights" into Spain along with the author's personal sub-Hemingway adventures.

Richard Ford *A Handbook for Travellers in Spain and Readers at Home* (Southern Illinois University Press, 3 vols., 1966, $50); *Gatherings from Spain* (Arden Library, 1976, $17.50). The *Handbook* must be the best guide ever written to any country and stayed in print as a *(John) Murray's Handbook* (one of the earliest series of guides) well into this century. Massively opinionated, it is an extremely witty book in its British, nineteenth-century manner, incredibly knowledgeable, and worth flicking through for the proverbs alone. Copies of *Murray's* may be available in second-hand bookshops — the earlier the edition the purer the Ford. The *Gatherings* is a rather timid abridgement of the general pieces.

George Borrow *The Bible in Spain* (1842; reprinted David & Charles 1986, $15.95), *The Zincali* (1843; o/p). Ford's contemporary and friend, Borrow subtitled the first book "Journeys, Adventures and Imprisonments of an Englishman.". Slow in places but with some very amusing stories. *Zincali* is an account of the Spanish gypsies, whom he got to know pretty well.

Washington Irving *Tales of the Alhambra* (Sleepy Hollow Press, 1982, $23.95). If you're going to Granada you'll find this on widespread sale locally, and you'd do well to pick it up. Half the book is oriental stories, set in the Alhambra; the rest are accounts of Irving's own residence there and the local characters of his time — equally compelling.

George Sand *A Winter in Majorca* (Academy Chicago Publications, 1978, $8.95). Sand and Chopin spent their winter at the monastery of Valldemossa. They weren't entirely appreciated by the locals, in which lies much of the book's appeal. Local translations, including one by late Mallorcan resident Robert Graves, are on sale around the island.

Edwin Mullins *The Pilgrimage to Santiago* (Taplinger Publishing, 1974, o/p). Hard to know how or where to classify this. It is by far the best book on the Santiago legend and its fascinating medieval pilgrimage industry. Mullins follows the route, points out the churches along the way, and gives incisive accounts of their social and architectural history.

Rose Macaulay *Fabled Shore* (OUP, 1986, $9.95). The Spanish coast as it was in 1949 (read it and weep), from Catalunya to the Portugese Algarve.

W. Somerset Maugham *Don Fernando* (Ayer, 1977, $28). Reprint of a 1935 edition with Maugham's views on everything from Spanish food to El Greco and Cervantes.

Kate O'Brien *Farewell Spain* (Beacon, 1987, $8.95); **H. V. Morton** *A Stranger in Spain* (Methuen, 1983, $16.95); **V.S. Pritchett** *The Spanish Temper* (Greenwood Press, 1976, o/p); **Sacheverell Sitwell** *Spain* (Hastings House, o/p); **Hans Christian Andersen** *A Visit to Spain 1862* (o/p); **Nikos Kazantzakis** *Spain* (Creative Arts, 1983, $6.95); **Walter Starkie** *Raggle Taggle Gypsy Tales* (E.P. Dutton, 1933, o/p); **Ernest Hemingway** *The Sun Also Rises* (Macmillan, 1987, $4.95), *For Whom the Bell Tolls* (Macmillan, 1988, $5.95). These all have their good points, and of course Hemingway's two Spanish novels have their devotees. Good for long rail journeys, at the very least.

HISTORY AND SOCIETY

MEDIEVAL AND BEYOND

J.H. Elliot *Imperial Spain 1469-1716* (New American Library, 1977, $10.95). Best introduction to "the Golden Age" — both academically respected and extremely readable.

Manuel Fernández Alvarez *Charles V* (Thames & Hudson, 1975, o/p); **Peter Pierson** *Philip II* (Thames & Hudson, 1977, $16.95). Good studies in an illustrated biography series.

John A. Crow *Spain: The Root and the Flower* (University of California, 1985, $12.95). Cultural/social history from Roman Spain to the present.

Joseph F. O'Callaghan *History of Medieval Spain* (Cornell University, 1983, $22.95). Exactly as the title says.

David Howarth *The Voyage of the Armada* (Penguin, 1981, $7.95). An account from the Spanish perspective of the personalities, from king to sailors, involved in the Armada.

THE 20TH CENTURY

Raymond Carr *Modern Spain 1875-1980* (Oxford Univ. Press, 1981, $12.50). Good, middle-of-the-road introduction to the period; see also Carr's more academic *Spain 1808-1975* (OUP, 1982, $26) and *Spain: Dictatorship to Democracy* (George Allen & Unwin, 1981, $14.95), the latter coauthored with Juan Pablo Fusi.

Hugh Thomas *The Spanish Civil War* (Harper & Row, 1977, $40). Massive, classic, exhaustive study.

Ronald Fraser *Blood of Spain* (Pantheon, 1980, $12.95). Subtitled "The Experience of Civil War, 1936-39," this is an equally definitive piece of research, constructed entirely of oral accounts. *In Hiding* (Pantheon, 1972, o/p), by the same author, is a fascinating individual account of a Republican mayor hidden by his family for thirty years until the civil war amnesty of 1969.

Ian Gibson *The Assassination of Federico García Lorca* (Penguin, 1983, $6.95). Brilliant reconstruction of the events, and with it a compelling examination of fascist corruption and of the shaping influences on Lorca, twentieth-century Spain, and the civil war.

Paul Preston (ed.) *Revolution and War in Spain* (Routledge, Chapman & Hall, 1985, $12.95). Selection of essays on the civil war period, most of them from a regional perspective — the Basque country, Catalunya, and the abortive revolt in Asturias in October 1934.

George Orwell *Homage to Catalonia* (Harcourt Brace Jovanovich 1969, reprinted 1980, $4.95). Stirring account of the early exhilaration of revolution in Barcelona, and Orwell's growing disillusionment with the factional fighting among the Republican forces.

Arthur Koestler *Dialogue with Death* (Macmillan, 1952, o/p). Koestler was reporting the war in 1937 when he was captured and imprisoned by Franco's troops — this is essentially his prison diary. In *Darkness at Noon* (Bantam, 1984, $4.50) he fictionalized these and other events into the one exceptional English novel about the civil war.

J. M. Maravall *Dictatorship and Political Dissent* (St. Martin, 1979, $26). One of the most fascinating studies of modern Spanish politics and a book which demands admiration for its subject: the serious and unified resistance of students and trade unionists to Franco.

CONTEMPORARY SPAIN

John Hooper *The Spaniards* (Penguin, 1987, $6.95). Excellent, insightful portrait of post-Franco Spain and the new generation. If you buy no other book on the country, this should be it.

Robert Graham *Spain: A Nation comes of Age* (St. Martin's Press; 1984, $14.95). An examination of Spain's metamorphosis from the Franco regime to democracy.

ART AND ARCHITECTURE

Titus Burckhardt *Moorish Culture in Spain* (McGraw Hill, 1972, o/p). An outstanding book which opens up ways of looking at Spain's Islamic monuments, explaining their patterns and significance and the social environment in which, and for which, they were produced.

José Gudiol *The Arts of Spain* (Thames & Hudson o/p). General summary, from prehistory to Picasso. Not very distinguished.

Sacheverell Sitwell *Spanish Baroque* (Ayer, reprint of 1931 edition, $15). Again interesting only in the absence of anything better.

Numerous **individual studies** of Picasso, Miró, Dalí, and Gaudí as well as the classic Spanish painters are of course also available.

SPANISH LITERATURE

CLASSICS IN TRANSLATION

St. Teresa of Ávila St. Teresa's autobiography is said to be the most widely read Spanish classic after Don Quixote. Takes some wading through, but fascinating in parts. Various translations, but the easiest to find is *The Life of Saint Teresa of Ávila by Herself* (Penguin, 1987, $6.95).

San Juan de la Cruz St. Teresa's spiritual companion was also a poet: you may be able to find a translation of his shorter works by South African poet Roy Campbell (whose meeting with Laurie Lee is described in *As I Walked Out...*).

Miguel de Cervantes *Don Quixote* (New American Library, 1965, $4.95, and Silver Burdett Press, 1985, $4.95). The big one. Graham Greene's *Monsieur Quixote* (Washington Square, 1982, $5.95) is an amus-

ing companion for the original. If you want to try Cervantes, in a more modest way, *Two Spanish Picareque Novels* (Penguin, 1969, $5.95) is a good place to start.

Pedro de Alarcón *The Three-Cornered Hat and Other Stories* (1874, Penguin 1975, o/p). Ironic nineteenth-century tales of the previous century's corruption, bureaucracy, and absolutism.

Leopoldo Alas *La Regenta* (Penguin, 1985, $14.95). A more involved nineteenth-century novel by a rough Spanish equivalent to Thomas Hardy.

Benito Pérez Galdós *Torquemada* (Columbia University, 1986, $24.95). Another nineteenth-century novel by a rediscovered author now reckoned among the greatest of his generation and often described as the "Spanish Balzac"; the story of a Madrid moneylender as vicious as his famous namesake.

MODERN SPANISH WRITERS

Arturo Barea *The Forging of a Rebel* (Viking Press, 1972, o/p). Brilliant autobiographical Trilogy, taking in the Spanish war in Morocco in the 1920s, and Barea's own part in the civil war.

Juan García Hortelano *Summer Storm* (Grove, 1962, o/p). First and possibly finest of the early 1960s "Realist Novels."

Manuel Vázquez Montalban *Murder in the Central Committee* (Academy Chicago Publications, 1985, $13.95). The lights go out during a meeting of the Central Committee of the Spanish Communist Party and the General Secretary is murdered . . . a terrific thriller, set in Barcelona and introducing the great gourmand-detective Pepe Carvalho. Recommended!

Other names to look out for include **Juan Goytisolo**, whose **Marks of Identity** and **Landscapes After the Battle** reflect an uneasy relationship with his homeland, to which he returned after years of exile; **Llorenç Villalonga**, whose lyrical *The Doll's Room* is set in nineteenth-century Mallorca and was originally written in Catalan; and **Michel del Castillo**, especially his gripping civil war novel *The Disinherited*. These are all available in British-published translations. **Luis Buñuel**'s autobiography *My Last Breath* is also worth looking out for.

In **Spanish**, modern novelists worth watching for include **Luis Martín Santos** (*Tiempo de*

Silencio); **Alfonso Grosso** (*Con Flores a María*); **Mariano Antolín** (*Wham!*, *Hombre Arañal* — the Spanish William Burroughs); **Montserrat Roig** (best of contemporary feminist writers); **Rafael Sánchez Ferlosio** (*El Jarama*, *Alfanhuit*); **Mercé Roderada** (*La Plaza del Diamante*); **Pío Baroja** (*El Arbol de la Ciencia*); **Miguel Delibes** (*El Camino*, or any others); **Camillo José Cela**; and of course, the other **Montalban** Pepe Carvalho novels.

PLAYS AND POETRY

Pedro Calderón de la Barca *Plays* (University Press of Kentucky, 1985, $9). Collected works of the great dramatist of Spain's seventeenth-century "Golden Age." You may also find translations of **Lope de Vega**, the nation's first important playwright.

Federico García Lorca *Five Plays: Comedies and Tragicomedies* (New Directions, 1964, $7.95). Preeminent pre-civil war playwright and poet. Arturo Barea's *Lorca: the Poet and His People* is also of interest.

J. M. Cohen (ed.) *The Penguin Book of Spanish Verse* (Penguin, 1988, $8.95). Mainly British poets, including many combatants, record or recall their civil war experiences.

SPECIFIC GUIDES

Marc S. Dubin *Spain on Foot* (The Mountaineers, 1990, $10.95). Best of the hiking guides, covering the entire peninsula and Mallorca. Other useful guides include **Robin Collomb**'s *Picos de Europa*, *Gredos Mountains and Sierra Nevada*, plus others (published in Britain by West Col, sometimes available in Spain), though they are aimed primarily at climbers, and **Kev Reynolds**' *Walks and Climbs in the Pyrenees* (published in Britain by Cicerone Press, again often available locally), more user-friendly, though half devoted to the French side of the frontier.

Valerie Crespi-Green *Landscapes of Mallorca* (Hunter, 1987, $10). One of a good series, with easy walks, car tours, and picnic sites.

Peterson, Mountfort and Hollom *Field Guide to the Birds of Britain and Europe* (Stephen Greene, $22.95). Standard reference book — covers most Spanish birds though you may find yourself confused by the bird-song descriptions.

Heinzel, Fitter, and Parslow *Collins Guide to the Birds of Britain and Europe* (Stephen Greene, 1988, $15.95). Alternative to the above. Also includes North Africa and the Middle East.

Oleg Polunin and Anthony Huxley *Flowers of the Mediterranean* (Salem House, 1987). Useful as a field guide but by no means exhaustive.

ONWARD FROM SPAIN

The most obvious onward travel from Spain is into PORTUGAL — worth the journey if only for a couple of days' contrast, with a gentler, slower pace of life and scenery to match. Costs are much the same, with pensãos taking over from hostales, and on the whole, restaurants from bars. It's an extremely easy move, too, as simple as getting on a train or bus across the border. For full details *The Real Guide to Portugal* would seem an obvious investment, as too, if you're traveling back through FRANCE, would *The Real Guide to France*.

MOROCCO

If you have time, — even just a few days — an exciting possibility is to take in **MOROCCO**. It's only 2½hrs by ferry from Algeciras to Tangier, less by hydrofoil from Tarifa, but things change fast. Morocco looks, sounds, and feels different, and you have to re-adjust to the most everyday aspects of life. For longer trips, get *The Real Guide to Morocco* (forthcoming). Here are some brief notes to get you started:

Arrival: Ferries run both to Tangier, and to Ceuta and Melilla, the two Spanish colonial enclaves on the Moroccan coast. Tangier, unless you've got a car, is the best choice, even if it is a slightly tricky place to get acclimatized. More than anywhere in Morocco — with the possible exception of Tetouan, the first Moroccan town past Ceuta — it is rampant with "guides" and hustlers, all out to exploit your initial innocence. Don't take one. Just make straight for a hotel (turn left along the waterfront for a good selection) or, if you aren't up for the experience, get a train straight out.

Trains: Tangier is the start of the railroad line, with connections to Fes, Meknes, and Marrakesh (the great Imperial Cities), and to Casablanca, Rabat, and the coastal resort of Asilah. Asilah and Rabat are perhaps the easiest places to get used to the country.

Buses: Most main routes have *CTM* buses (run by the state) and there are also more erratic private local lines. Only slightly more expensive is to share a *grand taxi* — big taxis carrying six passengers on a straight fee basis.

Costs: Hotels and basic cafe meals are very inexpensive — and you don't need to bargain. There is always a choice between rooms in the *Medina* (the "old town") and in the *Ville Nouvelle* (usually built during the years of French colonization): the former, though cheap, often lacks such conveniences as running water.

Currency: *Dirhams* are the standard unit, at about seven to the dollar. You may hear them subdivided into *francs* (100 to the dirham).

Highlights: The cities of Fes and Marrakesh, the High Atlas mountains, and the southern "desert routes." All easily accessible by local transportation.

Language: French is very widely spoken, although Moroccan Arabic (very different to "Classical Arabic") is the main language. In the mountains most communities speak one of three Berber dialects.

THE CANARIES

Although way down in the Atlantic, the **CANARY ISLANDS** are firmly Spanish territory. There are flights from most Spanish airports and from Agadir and Layoune in Morocco, or ferries from Cádiz or Agadir. None of these are cheap, however, and you might be better off making an entirely separate trip (charter deals from northern Europe are often better value) or trying for a stopover on the way home.

THE MAGHREB CIRCUIT

Lastly, ambitious travelers might consider the "**Maghreb circuit**" — crossing Morocco, **ALGERIA,** and TUNISIA before catching another ferry up to **ITALY**. This is perfectly feasible if you have the time and energy; the only special requirement is an Algerian visa (from the consulate in the Moroccan border town of Oujda) and the changing of $150–200 (depending on exchange rates) into Algerian currency on entering the country. But for 12km on the Moroccan/Algerian border, this entire route can be covered by train — the cruelly misnamed Trans-Maghreb Express. In Algeria you can also detour by bus into the Sahara — to the immense and beautiful oasis of Biskra, for instance. Tunisia, the easiest and most liberal of the Maghreb nations, has a *Real Guide* forthcoming; so too does Italy.

LANGUAGE

Once you get into it, Spanish is the easiest language there is — and you'll be helped everywhere by people who are eager to try and understand even the most faletring attempt. English is spoken, but only in the main tourist areas to any extent, and wherever you are you'll get a far better reception if you at least try comunicating with Spaniards in their own tongue. Being understood, of course, is only half the problem — and getting the gist of the reply, often rattled out at a furious pace, may prove far more difficult. Nevertheless you'll be getting there.

The rules of **pronunciation** are pretty straightforward and, once you get to know them, strictly observed. Unless there's an accent, words ending in d, l, r, and z are **stressed** on the last syllable, all others on the second last. All **vowels** are pure and short.

A somewhere between the 'A' sound of back and that of father

E as in get

I as in police

O as in hot

U as in rule

C is lisped before E and I, hard otherwise: *cerca* is pronounced "thairka."

G works the same way, a guttural 'H' sound (like the *ch* in loch) before E or I, a hard G elsewhere – *gigante* becomes 'higante'.

H is always silent

J the same sound as a guttural G: *jamon* is pronounced hamon.

LL sounds like an English Y: *tortilla* is pronounced torteeya.

N is as in English unless it has a tilde (accent) over it, when it becomes NY: *mañana* sounds like manyana.

QU is pronounced like an English K.

R is rolled, RR doubly so.

V sounds more like B, *vino* becoming beano.

X has an S sound before consonants, normal X before vowels. More common in Basque, Gallego, or Catalan words where it's *sh* or *zh*.

Z is the same as a soft C, so *cerveza* becomes "thairvaitha."

Below is a list of a few essential words and phrases, though if you're travelling for any length of time a dictionary or phrase book is obviously a worthwhile investment. If you're using a **dictionary**, bear in mind that in Spanish CH, LL, and Ñ count as separate letters and are listed after the Cs, Ls, and Ns respectively.

BASICS

Yes, No, OK	*Si, No, Vale*
Please, Thank you	*Por favor, Gracias*
Where, When	*Donde, Cuando*
What, How much	*Qué, Cuanto*
Here, There	*Aquí, Allí*
This, That	*Este, Eso*
Now, Later	*Ahora, Mas tarde*
Open, Closed	*Abierto/a, Cerrado/a*
With, Without	*Con, Sin*
Good, Bad	*Buen(o)/a, Mal(o)/a*
Big, Small	*Gran(de), Pequeño/a*
More, Less	*Mas, Menos*
Today, Tomorrow	*Hoy, Mañana*
Yesterday	*Ayer*

GREETINGS AND RESPONSES

Hello, Goodbye	*Ola, Adios*
Good morning	*Buenos días*
Good afternoon/ night	*Buenas tardes/noches*
See you later	*Hasta luego*
Sorry	*Lo siento/disculpeme*
Excuse me	*Con permiso/perdón*
How are you?	*¿Como está (usted)?*
Not at all/You're welcome	*De nada*
I (don't) understand	*(No) Entiendo*
Do you speak English?	*¿Habla (usted) Ingles?*
I don't speak Spanish	*No hablo Español*
My name is . . .	*Me llamo . . .*
What's your name?	*¿Como se llama usted?*
I am Canadian American	*Soy Canadiense/a Americano/a.*

NEEDS - HOTELS AND TRANSPORT

I want	*Quiero*
I'd like	*Querría*
Do you know . . . ?	*¿Sabe . . . ?*
I don't know	*No se*
There is (is there)?	*(¿)Hay (?)*
Give me . . .	*Deme . . .*
(one like that)	*(uno así)*
Do you have . . . ?	*¿Tiene . . . ?*
. . . the time	*. . . la hora*
. . . a room	*. . . una habitacion*
. . . with two beds/	*. . . con dos camas/*
double bed	*cama matrimonial*
It's for one person	*Es para una persona*
(two people)	*(dos personas)*
. . . for one night	*. . . para una noche*
(one week)	*(una semana)*
It's fine, how much is it?	*¿Está bien, cuanto es?*
It's too expensive	*Es demasiado caro*
Don't you have anything cheaper?	*¿No tiene algo más barato?*
Can one . . . ?	*¿Se puede . . . ?*
. . . camp (near) here?	*¿ . . . acampar aqui (cerca)?*
Is there a fonda nearby?	*¿Hay una fonda aquí cerca?*
How do I get to . . . ?	*¿Por donde se va a . . . ?*
Left, right, straight ahead	*Izquierda, derecha, derecho*
Where is . . . ?	*¿Donde esta . . . ?*
. . . the bus station	*. . . la estación de autobuses*
. . . the railway station	*. . . la estación de ferrocarriles*
. . . the nearest bank	*. . . el banco mas cercano*
. . . the post office	*. . . el correo (la oficina de correos)*
. . . the toilet	*. . . el baño/sanitario*
Where does the bus to . . . leave from?	*¿De donde sale el autobus para . . . ?*
Is this the train for Mérida?	*¿Es este el tren para Mérida?*
I'd like a (return) ticket to . . .	*Querría un boleto (de ida y vuelta) para . . .*
What time does it leave (arrive in . . .)?	*¿A qué hora sale (llega en . . .)?*
What is there to eat?	*¿Qué hay para comer?*
What's that?	*¿Qué es eso?*
What's this called in Spanish?	*¿Como se llama este en Espanol?*

NUMBERS AND DAYS

1	*un/uno/una*	11	*once*
2	*dos*	12	*doce*
3	*tres*	13	*trece*
4	*cuatro*	14	*catorce*
5	*cinco*	15	*quince*
6	*seis*	16	*diez y seis*
7	*siete*	20	*veinte*
8	*ocho*	21	*veintiuno*
9	*nueve*	30	*treinta*
10	*diez*	40	*cuarenta*

50	*cincuenta*
60	*sesenta*
70	*setenta*
80	*ochenta*
90	*noventa*
100	*cien(to)*
101	*ciento uno*
200	*doscientos*
500	*quinientos*
700	*setecientos*
1000	*mil*
2000	*dos mil*
1989	*mil novocientos ochenta y nueve*

first	*primero/a*
second	*segundo/a*
third	*tercero/a*

Monday	*lunes*
Tuesday	*martes*
Wednesday	*miercoles*
Thursday	*jueves*
Friday	*viernes*
Saturday	*sabado*
Sunday	*domingo.*

Just about any Spanish **phrasebook** or **dictionary** will serve in Spain, but those available in North America are increasingly geared to New World, Latin American usage. More old-fashioned publications may be better for Spain itself. *Langenscheidt, Cassels, Collins,* and *Bantam* all produce useful dictionaries; *Berlitz* and others publish separate Spanish and Latin-American Spanish phrasebooks

SPANISH TERMS: A GLOSSARY

ALAMEDA park or grassy promenade.

ALCAZABA Moorish castle.

ALCÁZAR Moorish fortified palace.

ARTESONADO inlaid wooden ceiling of Moorish origin or inspiration.

AYUNTAMIENTO town hall (also CASA CONSISTORIAL).

AZULEJO glazed ceramic tilework.

BARRIO suburb or quarter.

BODEGA cellar, wine bar, or warehouse.

CALLE street.

CAPILLA MAYOR chapel containing the high altar.

CAPILLA REAL Royal Chapel.

CARTUJA Carthusian monastery.

CASTILLO castle.

CHURRIGUERESQUE extreme form of baroque art named after José Churriguera (1650–1723) and his extended family, its main exponents.

COLEGIATA collegiate (large parish) church.

CONVENTO monastery or convent.

CORO central part of church built for the choir.

CORO ALTO raised choir, often above west door of a church.

CORREOS post office.

CORRIDA DE TOROS bullfight.

CUSTODIA large receptacle for Eucharist wafers.

IGLESIA church.

ISABELLINE ornamental form of late Gothic developed during the reign of Isabella and Fernando.

LONJA stock exchange building.

MERCADO market.

MIHRAB prayer niche of Moorish mosque.

MIRADOR viewing point.

MODERNISME (MODERNISTA) Catalan/Spanish form of Art Nouveau, whose most famous exponent was Antoni Gaudí.

MONASTERIO monastery or convent.

MORISCO Muslim Spaniard subject to medieval Christian rule — and nominally baptized.

MOZARABE Christian subject to medieval Moorish rule; normally allowed freedom of worship, they built churches in an Arab-influenced manner (MOZARABIC).

MUDEJAR Muslim Spaniard subject to medieval Christian rule, but retaining Islamic worship; most commonly a term applied to architecture which includes buildings built by Moorish craftsmen for the Christian rulers and later designs influenced by the Moors. The 1890s–1930s saw a Mudejar revival, blended with art nouveau and art deco forms.

PALACIO aristocratic mansion.

PARADOR luxury hotel, often converted from minor monument.

PASEO promenade; also the evening exercise thereon.

PATIO inner courtyard.

PLATERESQUE elaborately decorative Renaissance style, the 16th c. successor of Isabelline forms. Named for its resemblance to silversmiths' work (*platería*).

PLAZA square.

PLAZA DE TOROS bullring.

POSADA old name for an inn.

PUERTA gateway.

PUERTO port.

REJA iron screen or grille, often fronting a window.

RETABLO altarpiece.

RÍA river estuary in Galicia.

RÍO river.

ROMERÍA religious procession to a rural shrine.

SACRISTIA, SAGRARIO sacristy or sanctuary of church.

SEO, SEU, LA SE ancient/regional names for cathedrals.

SIERRA mountain range.

SILLERIA choir stall.

SOLAR aristocratic town mansion.

TAIFA Small Moorish kingdom, many of which emerged after the disintegration of the Córdoba caliphate.

TELEFÓNICA the phone company; also used for its walk-in offices in any town.

TURISMO tourist office.

POLITICAL PARTIES AND ACRONYMS

AP *Alianza Popular*, right-wing coalition under Manuel Fraga; in throes of changing name (or possibly fragmenting) to *Partido Popular*.

CONVERGENCIA I UNIO conservative party in power in Catalunya.

CNT anarchist trade union.

ETA Basque terrorist organisation. Its political wing is *Herri Batasuna*.

FALANGE Franco's old fascist party; now officially defunct.

FUERZA NUEVA descendants of the above, also on the way out.

MC *Movimiento Comunista* (Communist Movement) small radical offshoot of the PCE.

OTAN NATO.

PCE *Partido Comunista de España* (Spanish Communist Party).

PNV Basque Nationalist Party — in control of the right-wing autonomous government.

PSOE *Partido Socialista Obrero Español*, the Spanish Socialist Workers' Party — currently in power under Prime Minister Felipe González.

UCD *Unión del Centro Democrático* center-right (Social Democrat) party, held power in the last government under Calvo Sotelo.

UGT *Unión General de Trabajadores*, the Spanish AFL-CIO.

INDEX